THE NEW EUROPEAN CRIMINOLOGY

In an age of air travel and electronic information flows, crime can no longer be seen in national terms. This reader gathers together leading criminologists from all over Europe to consider crime and responses to crime within and across borders. For the first time, it allows students to experience at first hand the most exciting work in European criminology and to compare the dominant discourses of crime in different parts of Europe.

The five sections of the book look at:

- the effects of European harmonisation on crime
- criminal justice, law enforcement and penal reform
- different forms of organised crime
- local crime in international contexts
- possible future directions for criminology including the need for environmental criminology and some suggestions for a new criminology of war.

The New European Criminology constitutes the most comprehensive collection available of key debates from key figures in the field. It will be an essential text for students and an essential source of reference for scholars.

Vincenzo Ruggiero is Professor of Sociology at Middlesex University, **Nigel South** is Professor of Sociology at the University of Essex and **Ian Taylor** is Professor of Sociology at the University of Durham and Principal of Van Mildert College.

THE NEW EUROPEAN CRIMINOLOGY

Crime and social order in Europe

Edited by
Vincenzo Ruggiero, Nigel South
and Ian Taylor

London and New York

First published 1998
by Routledge
11 New Fetter Lane, London EC4P 4EE

Simultaneously published in the USA and Canada
by Routledge
29 West 35th Street, New York, NY 10001

Typeset in Baskerville by RefineCatch Limited, Bungay, Suffolk
Printed and bound in Great Britain by
TJ International Ltd, Padstow, Cornwall

British Library Cataloguing in Publication Data
A catalogue record for this book is available from the British Library

Library of Congress Cataloging in Publication Data
The New European Criminology : crime and social order in Europe /
edited by
Vincenzo Ruggiero, Nigel South and Ian Taylor.
p.   cm.
Includes bibliographical references and index.
1. Crime – Europe.   2. Criminology – Europe.   3. Criminal justice,
Administration of – Europe.   I. Ruggiero, Vincenzo.   II. South,
Nigel.   III. Taylor, Ian R.
HV6938.5.E94   1998
364.94 – dc21   97–45101
CIP

ISBN 0–415–16293–9 (hbk)
ISBN 0–415–16294–7 (pbk)

CONTENTS

CONTENTS

CONTENTS

FIGURES

TABLES

CONTRIBUTORS

Malin Åkeström is Associate Professor of Sociology and Director of the Network for Research in Criminology and Deviant Behaviour at the University of Lund in Sweden. She is the author of *Crooks and Squares* (1985) and *Betrayal and Betrayers* (1991), as well as numerous articles on various criminological subjects.

Pino Arlacchi is Professor of Sociology at the University of Sassari and Secretary of the UN International Drug Control Programme. He is also the chair of the Falcone Foundation. He earned international recognition after the publication of *Mafia Business* (1986). Among his most recent books, *Il processo. Giulio Andreotti sotto accusa a Palermo* (1995).

Francis Bailleau is a sociologist working at the Centre National de la Recherche Scientifique in Paris. His current research is concerned with juvenile justice and crime prevention. Among his latest works is the book *Les jeunes face à la justice pénale* (1996).

Nils Christie is Professor of Criminology at the University of Oslo. Among his most recent works, *Crime Control as Industry* (1993).

José Cid is Professor of Criminal Law and Criminology at the Universidad Autónoma of Barcelona. He has been a visiting scholar at the University of Bologna and at the London School of Economics. He is the author of *Pena justa o pena útil?* (1994) and co-editor of *Reduccionismo penal y alternativas a la prisión* (forthcoming).

Philippe Combessie is Doctor in Sociology and Researcher at the Centre National de la Recherche Scientifique. He teaches sociological research methods at the University of Paris 5. He is award winner of the 'Prix Gabriel Tarde 1996' for his book *Prisons des villes et des campagnes* (1996), and co-editor of *Approches de la prison* (1996).

Amedeo Cottino, Ph.D., is Professor of Sociology of Law at the University of Turin. He has published several books and articles on the issues of crime and justice in both traditional and contemporary societies. His present research focuses on the themes of equality before the law and legal ideologies.

Willem de Haan is Professor of Criminology at the universities of Groningen and Utrecht. He has published in many academic journals, and is the author of *The Politics of Redress. Crime, Punishment and Penal Abolition*. He has worked on public safety, street crime, violence and criminal policy. He is editor of 'Tijdschrift voor Criminologie'.

Colin Dunnighan is Lecturer in Criminology at the University of Teesside. He is an ex-police officer with a particular interest in the role of informants. With Dick Hobbs, he is undertaking a study of serious crime networks, a project funded by the British Economic and Social Research Council.

Claude Faugeron is Research Director at the Centre National de la Recherche Scientifique in Paris, and a member of the Groupement de Recherche Psychotropes, Politique, Société. She has lectured at the University of Montreal, at the Ecole des Hautes Etudes en Science Sociale and at the Catholic University of Louvain. She has a wide publication record, including her latest *Approches de la Prison* (1996).

Yakov Gilinskiy is the head of the deviancy section of the Russian Academy of Science based in St. Petersburg. He is involved in research ranging from trends in antisocial behaviour in the Baltic regions to organised crime in Russia.

Evi Girling is Research Fellow in the Department of Criminology at Keele University. She holds a Ph.D. in social anthropology, and has published work on 'language death' amongst Gaelic speakers in the Scottish Highlands. She is currently researching children's conceptions of punishment.

Dick Hobbs is Professor of Sociology at the University of Durham. He has published on deviance, cultures and professional crime. He has an interest in ethnographic research and the role of entrepreneurship in shaping deviance strategies.

Ruth Jamieson is Lecturer in Criminology at Keele University. Her current research and teaching interests are in the area of gender, war, transnationality and crime, notably in exploring the relationship between crime, armed conflict and the state, and the gender-specific nature of social regulation during states of emergency. She was previously a Programme Evaluation Manager in the Canadian Department of Justice.

Vassilis Karydis is Assistant Professor of Criminology and Penology at the Democritus University of Thrace. He is a member of the editorial board of the criminological journal *Chronicle*, and a steering committee member of the European Group for the Study of Deviance and Social Control. He is a former advisor to the Ministry of Justice. His latest book is *Criminality and Migrants in Greece* (1996).

Elena Larrauri is Professor of Criminal Law and Criminology at the

Universidad Autónoma of Barcelona. She has worked on Fulbright scholarships in Santa Barbara (California) and Frankfurt, and as visiting scholar in Hamburg, Jerusalem and Oslo. She is author of *La herencia de la criminologia crítica* (1991), and co-author of *Victimologia: presente y futuro* (1993), and *Violencia doméstica y legítima defensa* (1995).

Roger Lewis is the Director of the Centre for HIV/AIDS and Drugs Studies in Edinburgh. He has been a research ethnographer and has worked both in Britain and in Italy. His books include *Big Deal. The Politics of the Illicit Drugs Business* (co-authored) (1985), and *Droga e criminalità. Il caso di Verona* (co-authored) (1994).

Ian Loader is Lecturer in the Department of Criminology at Keele University. He is a co-author of *Cautionary Tales* (1994) and author of *Youth, Policing and Democracy* (1996). He is currently conducting research on policing and cultural change in post-war England.

Rob Mawby is Professor of Criminology and Criminal Justice at the University of Plymouth. He is the author of numerous books and articles on the criminal justice system, especially policing and victimology, and much of his recent work has a cross-national dimension. Books include *Comparative Policing Issues* (1990), *Critical Victimology* (co-authored, 1994), and *Comparative Policing: Issues for the Twenty-First Century* (editor, 1997). He has recently completed directing a project comparing police response to victims in England, Germany, Poland, the Czech Republic and Hungary.

Dario Melossi is Associate Professor of Criminology at the Law Faculty of the University of Bologna. He is currently working on a comparative study of social control in Italy and other advanced societies, and on immigration and social control in the context of the construction of the European Union.

Rod Morgan is Professor of Criminal Justice at the University of Bristol. His most recent work includes *Sex Offenders: A Framework for the Evaluation of Community-Based Treatment* (with Barker) (1993), *The Politics of Sentencing Reform* (with Clarkson) (1995), *The Future of Policing* (with Newburn) and *The Oxford Handbook of Criminology* (co-edited) (2nd edition, 1997). He regularly acts as an expert advisor to the Council of Europe and to Amnesty International regarding custodial conditions.

Vesna Nikolić-Ristanović is a Senior Researcher at the Institute for Criminological and Sociological Research, and teaches at the Centre for Women's Studies in Belgrade, Serbia. She has written widely on violence against women, women's crime, fear of crime, victimology and criminology of war. She was national co-ordinator for the first International (Crime) Victim Survey in Serbia carried out in 1996.

Letizia Paoli has completed her Ph.D. on the Sicilian mafia at the European

University Institute of Florence. She is currently a visiting academic at the Justus Liebig University of Giessen.

Patricia Rawlinson lectures at the University of Wales at Bangor. Her doctoral thesis was on the relationship between organised crime and the legitimate structures in the former USSR. Other research includes security in the Baltic States and organised crime, and law-enforcement co-operation between East and West Europe.

Vincenzo Ruggiero is Professor of Sociology at Middlesex University in London. He has worked on criminological theory, political corruption, illicit drugs, prison systems, corporate and organised crime. He has published numerous articles, authored seven books and edited fifteen. He is currently researching a book on the European metropolis and social movements.

Fritz Sack is Professor Emeritus of Criminology at the University of Hamburg. He has introduced interactionist and constructionist approaches into German criminology. He has published on a wide range of issues including the ecology of crime, terrorism, police technology, diversion from and privatisation of the penal system. Recently, he has taken an interest in modernisation and crime, particularly with respect to the transitional societies of Central and Eastern Europe.

Sebastian Scheerer is Professor of Criminology at the University of Hamburg. He has authored and edited books on drugs, political violence, and criminological theory. He is presently working on a post-labelling critique of critical criminology, a critique which is not aimed at establishing yet another general theory of crime.

Nigel South is Professor of Sociology at the University of Essex (England), where he is also an associate of the Institute for Environmental Research, and a member of the management committee of the Human Rights Centre. He has published extensively in the areas of criminology and social policy, and has recently begun to work on crime, health and the environment. He is co-editor of a special issue of *Theoretical Criminology* with the theme 'For a Green Criminology'.

Richard Sparks is Professor of Criminology at Keele University. He is author of *Television and the Drama of Crime* (1992) and co-author of *Prisons and the Problem of Order* (1996). He is currently conducting research on risk and penal policy.

Heinz Steinert is Professor of Sociology at the Goethe University in Frankfurt, and director of the Institute für Rechts- und Kriminalsoziologie in Vienna.

Ian Taylor is Professor of Sociology at the University of Durham and Principal of Van Mildert College. He is joint author of *The New Criminology* (1973) and joint editor of *Deviance and Control in Europe* (1973). He has recently held a visiting professorship at the University of Stockholm, and is currently research-ing in the fields of urban change and also criminology. His most recent major publications include the co-authored volume *A Tale of Two Cities: Global Change, Local Feeling and Everyday Life in the North of England* (1996).

Henrik Tham is Professor of Criminology at Stockholm University. He has worked on inequality and social exclusion. His most recent publications con-cern drug policies and criminal policies in relation to the welfare state in Sweden.

Sophie Vidali is a Researcher at the Laboratory of Criminological Sciences, Faculty of Law, Democritus University of Thrace. Her Ph.D. research focused on political terrorism. She has also worked on corruption, young offenders, and the social exclusion of women.

Jock Young is Professor of Sociology at Middlesex University. He was born in Scotland and studied at the London School of Economics. His most recent book is *The New Criminology Revisited* (with P. Walton). He is currently completing a new book entitled *From Inclusive to Exclusive Society*.

INTRODUCTION

Towards a European Criminological Community

Vincenzo Ruggiero, Nigel South and Ian Taylor

Immediately after World War II, Thomas Mann sorrowfully examined the reasons for the barbarity which had just come to a close, combining economic explanations with a cultural excursus into the significance of nationalism. From his intellectual isolation in the USA, he saw nationalism as a *Faustian* infatuation in which the 'pride of the intellect couples with the archaism of the soul' (Mann, 1945). Before him, the author of *Faust* himself had suffered a similar isolation in opposing unhealthy patriotism, a 'demonic scourge' which led to his advocacy of the 'super-national' and the universal, whether through literature or through politics. Both Goethe and Mann were 'exiles', though the former only in spirit, desperately searching for ways in which nationalism could be diluted, even dispersed. Goethe went so far as to suggest the desirability of national diasporas from each European country, a 'pre-post-modern' vision of a world where nationalities constantly mix while national borders slowly crumble. Thomas Mann felt that exile itself was assuming a different meaning: no longer a transition period while awaiting the return home, but a prelude, he thought, to the dissolution of nation states and the eventual unification of the world (world government). It is a reminder of the persisting strength of nationalism, and of the economic and socio-cultural celebrations of national *differences*, that, more than fifty years on, these visions remain, for the most part, dreams.

The conference from which most of the following papers were selected,[1] took place amid growing anxiety over the viability of the grand European dream. The aspirations of ever-closer political and economic union are perhaps more muted, certainly more controversial, in the late 1990s than for some time in the recent past. It is not difficult to identify economic uncertainties and changes in social welfare systems preparatory to further economic harmonisation, as one of the key defining developments underpinning current anxieties. Throughout the 1960s, at the time when the European idea was being most energetically mobilised in different parts of Western Europe, the overall unemployment rate (on

1

official measures) averaged just 1.6 per cent. In the 1970s, this annual average rose to 4.2 per cent; in the 1980s to 9.2 per cent and, by 1993, this figure reached a total of 11 per cent (Judt, 1996: 6). In 1996, in some member-states of the European Union – notably France (12.5 per cent), Ireland (12.4 per cent) and Italy (12.5 per cent) – unemployment rates reached their highest figures since the harmonisation of international measures in 1993 (*Guardian*, 1 August 1996). Yet, simultaneously, some of these European countries experienced high growth rates, especially in the years 1994–6 (Marazzi, 1995; ISTAT, 1996). In this context it is easy to see how 'visions' give way to anxieties, as growth, profit and strong economic management take increasing priority over stability, job security and social provision.

In a modest way, this book itself reflects a 'vision'. However, this particular vision is neither utopian nor dependent on great transformations, for it simply concerns the facilitation of more communication between European scholars studying in fields related to crime, social order and criminology.[2] The conference in Manchester and this collection as one outcome, are contributions to this goal. In this introduction we wish to achieve three things. First, to introduce the reader to the political economy of 'market Europe' in the late twentieth century, and to provide a schematic background against which our essays on 'crime and social order' can be read. Second, to provide a sketch of the criminological context into which the collection falls. We make no attempt to provide a detailed map of 'the state of European criminology': this would be a separate project. Our concern here is to contribute to the development of a sense of a 'European criminological community'. Finally, we shall outline the structure of the collection and the coverage of the chapters.

Whose Europe?

It should be recognised that the moves towards European unification have been varied in their outcomes. Perhaps the classic example of this is found in the case of countries where economic growth has been strong yet accompanied by rising unemployment. It is no coincidence that the dyad of 'exclusion' and 'inclusion' should have recently risen to achieve such prominence on the agendas of European social science and policy debate (Paugam, 1996). It is not only from the point of view of generating or promoting employment as a priority that the European Union has been unsuccessful, it has also produced unwelcome inconsistencies and inequalities. For example, some economic sectors have suffered the consequences of policy decisions which have clearly advantaged other sectors. Notably, manufacturing industry in some countries has been favoured to the detriment of agriculture, a policy which has exacerbated *internal* national inequalities between rural and industrial areas. In a typical case, while the Italian car manufacturers Fiat earned a large grant to build a new 'total quality' plant (Cersosimo, 1994), southern Italy was forced to import agricultural products from abroad (Vinci, 1996). The net result of this policy has been that unemployment in southern Italy has now risen to over 20 per cent. Similar dynamics have been observed in France and Spain. In Britain, while large farming companies have benefited substantially from European aid, smaller farmers have been pushed to the margins of the market.

Such variations go hand in hand with a related ideological process whereby the priorities of free market liberalisation seem to be assuming universal acceptance across the political spectrum. For example, across member-states of the Community, there is inescapable evidence of a general increase in social inequality and in feelings of insecurity, and this is occurring even amongst those in employment (Revelli, 1996). The increase in both inequality and insecurity appears to be as ineluctable as the erosion of welfare rights for various differently-disadvantaged sections of the population. The ideological process through which the attack on the 'welfare-consensus' has been mounted (Samson and South, 1996), and which is undermining the social rights of both the employed and the unemployed, is legitimised by a view of Europe as a 'uniform economic entity' which must be 'fit to compete' if it is to survive in global market competition with 'external economic powers'. Hence, it is only by accepting the deterioration of work conditions and a dramatic reduction in welfare provision that Europe can face up to its North American and Asian competitors.

The attempt to impose such a programme as the 'only way' to produce 'leaner and fitter' economies has had a visible impact on the way in which the European Union is prepared to receive non-European immigrant workers. From the early 1960s onwards, western Europe has been a magnet for immigrants from at least three different sources – obviously from countries which have felt the impact of European colonisation, especially during the nineteenth century; latterly, from the Mediterranean 'fringe' (notably North Africa) and, most recently of all, from Central and Eastern Europe. In 1993, the best estimates suggested that Western Europe as a whole was home to 7.5 million 'foreign' workers (of whom nearly five million reside in France and Germany, comprising about 10 per cent of the labour force) (Judt, 1996: 7). In the mid-1990s – the French government continuing its push against 'illegal immigrants', with the increasing electoral strength in France of Le Pen and the National Front and Haider and his party in Austria, with high levels of anxiety on the question of eastern European and north African immigration in Italy, and with nearly every other major European country revising its rules and regulations in the sphere of immigration and asylum (Bunyan, 1993) – we are obviously witnessing a fundamental shift in the sentiments of European electorates and governments in the direction of support for a tough, pro-exclusionary stance. How this exclusionary momentum may feed into that other major challenge facing the European Union as a whole, namely the question and implications of offering EU membership (and the common benefits involved in such membership) to the countries of the former Soviet bloc, is an inescapable and fraught issue.[3]

Market Europe and social justice

The idea of Europe now being mobilised is a very specific, corporate-liberal model, bound up with a belief in the discipline of the enlarged free market of the European Union (post-Maastricht) and the opportunities which such a market, properly liberalised, are thought to yield. It is a conception of Europe in which, increasingly, the objective of integration is dictated by a specifically *economic* argument, namely that Europe must pursue a growing share of international markets. Other concerns, for example, the creation of a new inter-national *public sphere* for Europe do not seem to be high on the agenda. In other words, the very idea of Europe is increasingly that of 'market Europe', organised around a federal bank and a federal currency, and the daily movements of the financial markets rather than, for example, a Europe of the Parliament or the European Court, or a Europe of civil and political rights. In terms of criminological interests, European harmonisation is producing regulatory and control developments which strongly mirror these economic developments, including facilitation of the surveillance of individuals and their movement, and the creation of a nascent police agency in Europol (Anderson *et al.*, 1995). Ultimately, as elsewhere in the developed world, the emphasis on the market is leaving little space for the development of public and state institutions, and for the consequent production of social cohesion and justice (O'Neill, 1994). This trend is perhaps most damaging in those states of eastern Europe (notably Russia) which have embraced 'market forces' to the detriment of public services and aspects of civic life. (The consequences of this choice are discussed elsewhere in this volume.)

Like all ideological constructions of the 'market', the idea of 'market Europe' – for all that the actual institutions of the market are increasingly dominated by corporations, monopolies and oligarchies – carries with it ideas of 'liberalism', namely freedom of choice, free competition, and the merits and joys of consumerism. However, this is not a liberalism in which there is any given sense of duty or responsibility for others: indeed, in some versions of this liberal vision, such a sense of responsibility for others would be seen as an impediment to the very freedom of the market. The idea of a 'pure' free market, as enshrined in the Maastricht Agreement, is being challenged across Europe by various groups opposing cuts in social provision, calling for the creation of new jobs, and in general fighting the overall deterioration of work conditions. For our purposes, it is important to emphasise that the 'free market' idea and its current implementation have powerfully contributed to the ways in which the 'crime and social order' question has been formulated across western, and now eastern, Europe.

Hidden employment and crime

'Market Europe' entails an increase in unemployment across various European states – West and East – parallel expansion of some specific areas of manufacturing industry and low-paid service sectors. However, the aggregate unemployment figures referred to earlier, do not convey a complete picture of European labour markets. Official rates of 'inactivity', for example, say little about hidden forms of work, and may in some contexts over-represent while in others they under-represent the actual scope and nature of labour activity. In most European countries a varying number of individuals are employed illegally or semi-legally, and in consequence are both underpaid and lack access to legal rights. In some cases the workers' connivance with employers takes the form of the former signing wage receipts nominally indicating a certain wage, while in reality the employer only pays a fraction of the nominal sum. In some countries unemployment figures are an underestimate because they do not include those who fail to register as unemployed, either because of lack of information over their rights to benefits, or because the rules regarding their right to register have been toughened. What we are trying to describe here is a situation in which categories of employment and unemployment defy neat distinctions, as labour markets are becoming increasingly flexible and casual, and as official unemployment and actual economic inactivity do not always coincide.

The processes of 'casualisation' and 'flexibilisation' have made their impact not only on those who inhabit the margins of the labour market, but also upon those who are employed. Implicated here, in various European contexts, are the consequences of the processes of 'downsizing' and decentralisation affecting many enterprises. Such enterprises may continue to employ a number of workers legally, but also indirectly employ other workers illegally. We are thinking here of firms which sub-contract operations to smaller subsidiaries, which may either be independently run or may actually be controlled by the mother industry for which they produce. Examples of the use of illegal labour employed by 'subsidiaries' are found in most European countries in the building, clothing and food industries (Ruggiero, 1997a).

This hidden labour market has numerous points of contact with the criminal market proper, that is to say with the market where clearly illegal goods and services are exchanged. The increasing political emphasis on market forces has promoted a blurring of the distinctions between these markets, such that significant proportions of those employed in them may shift from activity in one sphere to the other, because of the proximity of the hidden and the overtly criminal economies. In other words, those employed legally may be encouraged to find occasional employment in crime, and vice-versa. The different sectors of the illegal economy themselves overlap and cannot be sharply distinguished, sharing common interests and strategies which form the bases of what can be described as 'bad' or 'dirty' economies (Centorrino, 1990; Hobbs, 1995; Ruggiero, 1996a; Ruggiero and South, 1997; Punch, 1996).

Market Europe therefore encourages two types of symmetric crimes. First, it makes illegal labour desirable to legitimate employers, who end up benefiting from illegal migration and from its competitive costs. Indirectly, employers also benefit from the trafficking in human beings, a contemporary form of slave trade which is quickly gathering momentum in Europe. Second, 'market Europe' creates the conditions for the hidden sectors of the economy to intertwine with more conventional crime activities, thus making 'employment in crime' more likely.

Enterprise culture and the priorities of criminal justice

The vision of market Europe that is currently being promoted creates an environment conducive to the creation of new forms of both conventional and corporate crime. Both are inspired by the new 'enterprise culture' which has developed since the 1980s. With respect to conventional crime, forms of illicit entrepreneurship are developing which adopt rational economic strategies and seek constant innovation. The collapse of the Berlin Wall has further stimulated this process, generating criminal innovation, in both a Mertonian and a Schumpeterian sense. Crime, in other words, is arising from the conditions that Schumpeter (1961) associated with economic innovation: the exploitation of new economic opportunities and new commercial networks, the creation of new needs for commodities and services, and/or the re-arrangement of productive processes and labour organisation. Contemporary examples include: the trafficking in drugs from, through and to Russia, the smuggling of cigarettes from France through former East Germany, and the smuggling of human beings from Albania (Ruggiero and South, 1995; Ruggiero, 1997b). This innovatory 'spiral', involving the need to remain one step ahead of enforcement and legislative responses, entails the recruitment of 'criminal labourers' who have no power or means of control over the activities in which they are employed, and who perform the most dangerous tasks of the criminal economy on behalf of entrepreneurs whose identity they either do not know or they wish to remain unaware of! Similarly, the increasing emphasis on the new enterprise culture has led to the creation of *grey* sectors of the economy where licit entrepreneurs continually 'test' the boundaries between acceptable and unacceptable business practice (Taylor, 1992; 1997). The numerous cases of insider dealing, corporate illegalities, political corruption and other forms of institutional crime across Europe (Della Porta and Mény, 1995; Leiken, 1997) suggest that in a de-regulated atmosphere, experimental challenges to the 'rule of the acceptable' are frequently mounted and may, in time, serve to weaken and re-define what is ruled as 'unacceptable'. An important example today and for the future is illegal arms trafficking, where a 'grey' international market is developing in which transactions come to be regarded as neither entirely legal nor entirely illegal (Phythian and Little, 1993; Ruggiero, 1996b). A 'necessary evil', grey markets represent policy in flux, a new political background against which we see the development of new international, commercial and diplomatic links.

While creating new criminal opportunities for all social groups, 'market Europe' does not respond to the different forms of illegality in the same or equal fashion. It is true that in recent years, in both Italy and France, many politicians and entrepreneurs have been prosecuted for civil and criminal offences

(Vogelweith and Vaudano, 1995; Ruggiero, l996c; Palombarini, 1996). However, the priorities of criminal justice prevailing in the new Europe are less concerned with the social damage which may actually result from political and/or corporate criminality, and more concerned to identify, in general terms, those potentially 'dangerous groups' in society, representative of 'Otherness', regardless of their real significance in criminal economies. The particular definitions of prioritised criminality with which the new Europe is operating lead, in the main, to the targeting of vulnerable actors and deviants, and the identification of those 'folk devils' seen as sources of public anxiety and insecurity and who can conveniently be associated with images of crime (Sim *et al.*, 1995). The detention of asylum seekers in Britain and of 'foreigners' whose only crime consists of their presence in French territory are cases in point.

A similar politics of criminal justice and penology appears to be prevailing in the former socialist countries, where the inherited inability of the elites to monitor themselves has generated widespread opportunities for powerful actors to engage in illegal practices. These practices are, in a sense, an aspect of the 'privatisation of politics' which still predominates in central and eastern European transitional democracies (Offe, 1996). The intolerance of such democracies towards 'dangerous groups', and 'others' in general, has grown as a result of rediscovered localisms and rekindled nationalisms. In this respect, even the re-unification of Germany has been cited as the cause of conflicts and intolerance, as policies aimed at strengthening 'national unity' place in jeopardy the living conditions, 'the civil rights and the cultural opportunities of the non-German population' (ibid.: 26; see also Sack in this volume).

While the elites enjoy a high degree of impunity, fear of crime in central and eastern European countries tends to assume the features which prevail in their western counterparts – that is, it tends to focus strongly on conventional illegality (Van Dijk and Van Kesteren, 1996). It is difficult to assess the extent to which the growing fear of crime impacts on the growth of the prison population in these transitional democracies. Nevertheless, in 1994 the imprisonment rates in countries such as Belarus, Estonia, Latvia, Lithuania, Moldova, Russia, Rumania and Ukraine were between four and ten times higher than the average rates observed in western Europe (Walmsley, 1995). Prison overcrowding in these countries involves even greater transgression of the United Nations Standard Minimum Rules for the Treatment of Prisoners than in the West:

> The need to ensure respect for human dignity and the need to sustain health and self-respect ..., the need for decent accommodation arrangements, the need for adequate regime activities and treatment programmes, and the need for opportunities for employment are all crucial requirements that are more difficult to achieve when numbers are high and rising.
>
> (ibid.: 80)

Such difficulties, which are also encountered in western European countries, are compounded by the legacy of prison buildings which are often decrepit and where no efforts were made in the past to refurbish them, because the official 'ideology was that crime would disappear in a socialist society and that prisons would not be needed' (ibid.: 74).

Which Europe?

The developments sketched above are, of course, by no means universally supported or irreversible. Industrial action across Europe has proven that the establishment of 'market Europe' will encounter resistance and obstacles from both traditional work-based trade-union organisations as well as new oppositional movements and groups. The 'Florence manifesto' (*AltrEuropa*, 1996) produced by groups of women and focusing on equality in Europe is one expression of this oppositional tendency. The opposition of women's groups to the establishment of 'market Europe' focuses on the restrictions affecting social services which translate into an increasing burden on women through exploitation of their unpaid social and household labour. Similarly, the 'Paris manifesto' (Accattatis, 1996), arising out of collaboration between many intellectuals across France, Italy and Germany, calls for a 'Europe of the people' as opposed to a 'Europe of the oligarchies'. The Europe posited in such initiatives is one which reflects upon the enormous quantities of wealth produced in the whole of Europe versus the inequalities in the distribution of opportunities and reward across Europe.

These and other initiatives question the character and legitimacy of *market* Europe. They pertain to the social, institutional and penal spheres of European life, in a continuum which, if embryonically, is trying to formulate responses to each of these. Future examples here might include: the efforts of groups of Italian, French and Spanish jurists, magistrates and judges to set up discussion networks in which strategies for the fight against political corruption can be identified (Barca and Trento, 1994); or the networks of drug users and workers exchanging ideas and devising proposals for decriminalisation and the development of care for drug users in prison and those in the community (see for example *Fuori Luogo*, a monthly published by the *Forum Droghe* in Italy). Such efforts face enormous difficulties which, in the main, arise from differences in the political and judicial cultures of European countries. However, to place excessive emphasis on such 'difference' may simply lead to a form of paralysis, excluding even the possibility that discussion of such differences may lead to constructive comparisons and, ultimately, to common understanding of issues and strategies (Ryan, 1996; Nelken, 1994).

Our argument here is that the stress placed by some commentators on cultural and political *localism* as an insurmountable obstacle to progressive European development, tends to border on a form of relativism which ecumenically embraces everything, yet simultaneously ignores socially injurious actions of cross-border significance, in the name of respect for local specificity. Pertinently,

European oligarchies (whether born of corporate interests or state alliances or both) do not allow themselves to be restricted by such cultural relativism and have shown how they can develop powerful common interests despite local and traditional differences. This is not a new phenomenon: an 'inquisitive' traveller like Laurence Sterne, in his sentimental journey through France and Italy in the eighteenth century, found the ruling classes of these countries the least interesting to his investigation, because of their predictability and astonishing similarity (Sterne, 1768). A 'Europe of the people', aimed at the development of a European public sphere, should be led by what is best within the European tradition rather than being dragged downward to the worst expressions of civil life in the name of harmonisation. What we aim to have outlined here is a vision of a Europe in which the experience of 'others' and their 'difference' leads to 'a participative and critical sharing of that difference' (Gadamer, 1989).

For a European criminological community

In 1975, Bianchi *et al.* edited and provided an introduction to a volume of papers from the first conference of the 'European Group for the Study of Deviance and Social Control', held in 1973 in Italy. The tenor and concerns of this introductory essay clearly reflect the critical spirit in which that conference took place. But the essay also reflects a keenness to maintain a momentum towards European criminological exchange. Over twenty years later, the European Group still flourishes but those gathered at its early meetings might perhaps have hoped for more progress towards collaboration and communication than has been achieved to date.

Readers in search of nostalgia or with an interest in the 'archaeology of criminological knowledge' might like to consult the contents page of the Bianchi *et al.* 'time capsule' and, in particular, consider how the reports from individual nations compare with the situation today. One recently provided resource for such comparison has been the series of 'Crime and Social Order in Europe' newsletters produced under the auspices of the British ESRC programme which led to the conference upon which this book draws. The four issues produced between October 1995 and late 1996 provided many national reports from both west and east Europe, as well as providing overviews of work on a more thematic basis.[4]

Such reviews are instructive, for when we begin to consider the breadth of recent and current contributions to projects of communication and comparison throughout European criminology, we can see very encouraging signs of great activity. For example, when the School of Criminology of the Katholieke University of Leuven celebrated its twenty-fifth Anniversary in 1994, it chose to do so not through introspective or retrospective focus on its past achievements, but by accepting an invitation from the International Society of Criminology to host the 49th International Course in Criminology. This event brought together many leading and new scholars in European criminology and reflected a spirit of 'rapprochment between European countries . . . in spite of the many obstacles' (preface to conference volume). The collected papers, presented in several languages and brought together in two volumes, (Fijnaut *et al.*, 1995), convey a determination to ensure that while the 'blurring of borders' in Europe will have 'fundamental repercussions on the criminological field' (Dillemans, 1995), these should be challenges that we respond to as colleagues engaged in a shared and comparative enterprise.[5]

Enthusiasm alone, however, will not help us build such an enterprise. To describe the state of criminology in Europe is no easy task (Shapland, 1991). Nor is it any easier to establish what 'crime' is in Europe, as each country prioritises one form of offending against another (Nelken, 1994). Matters are further complicated by the fact that national responses to crime alone are far from enough to inform us about the most disruptive acts characterising national contexts. Responses to crime in different European countries may be the result of the demand for punishment, rather than the specific reality of crime (Wilkins, 1991). *Penal grammars* evolve within specific cultural traditions and, inevitably, end up shaping national criminologies. Such cultural traditions have, in some national cases, strengthened expertise and developments in comparative analysis of law, in other cases promoted sociological perspectives, and in others encouraged practical engagement with issues such as crime prevention and social order. But of course, like the borders of our states, criminological interests blur and today most of the breadth of criminological concerns are probably represented in some work in most western European nations. This may well not be the case in eastern Europe however, where the field is still opening up – but even here, the field is diversifying.

This volume is an embryonic project aimed to render different European criminological traditions and developments more accessible. In this, as well as in future work, we also aim to help develop a pan-European (east and west), sense of, and means for the development of, a 'European Criminological Community'. We are aware that the development of such a 'community' is bound to experience moments of crisis and periods of disenchantment, when differences will appear to be insurmountable. But are these not also characteristics of the development of political, economic and social European unity in general? With Dahrendorf (1996), we share the opinion that it is important to recognise the emergence of such crises, and that it is crucial to 'use' them wisely, rather than turning them into hurdles to development and mutual understanding. Indeed, the fact that we are able to provoke such crises signals the importance that the development of such a European Criminological Community possesses.

Outline of the book

The chapters in this book represent only an initial attempt to help develop an understanding of trends and concerns in criminological work within Europe. Readers should appreciate the different approaches, and degrees of development, within criminological debate in the European countries covered. However, these differences notwithstanding, this book provides an important sample of some of the most exciting work carried out in a number of countries within the European criminological community. It is also a testimony to the value of, and demand for, the exchange of ideas, dissemination of work and development of common understanding in European criminology.

We have given Part I of the book the title 'European prospects', and have resisted the temptation to add the adjective 'bleak'. This is because the chapters comprising this part, though exuding a degree of pessimism as regards the future of the more vulnerable social groups in Europe, also provide some openings towards possible change. Ian Taylor, for example, describes the relentless pro-liferation of market economic policies across Europe and their impact on cit-izens' anxiety, marginalisation and crime. At the same time, he also stresses that it is urgent to move towards a shared sense of a common European citizenship, and remarks that a dynamic political sphere working in the public interest could (and should) develop in response to 'market Europe' and its outcomes. Similarly, Fritz Sack is critical of the state of criminology in Europe, and includes in his critique the role of the state in shaping the discipline and the social issues which crimin-ology addresses, thereby defining the field of the discipline. But he also advocates the creation of institutional forms of governance capable of genuinely promoting freedom and participation. The chapters by Dario Melossi and Jock Young also underline the difficulties with which we are faced in the development of Euro-pean harmonisation. However, their views with respect to social exclusion brought about by such development sound, as in Young's chapter, like implicit calls for devising new forms of community which are not totally dependent on the whims of the market.

With Part II ('Penality and criminal justice') we address several topical issues confronting criminologists and social reformers alike. Francis Bailleau writes on the inadequacy of the penal system in France in responding to problem youth, while Claude Faugeron describes the changes occurring in the use of imprison-ment, the current way of thinking about the function of punishment, and the evolution of prisoners' rights. Nils Christie critiques the systems of 'pyramidal justice', which are commonly 'unquestioned', as if arising from the rules of Moses engraved in granite. He highlights the expansion of these types of justice systems while describing an opposing tendency whereby more egalitarian systems of justice might slowly establish themselves. With Philippe Combessie's chapter we return to the inadequacy of imprisonment and the exploration of its symbolic power to 'colonise' the social and physical areas surrounding prison institutions. Amedeo Cottino pinpoints how penal systems are embedded in unequal societies and how, therefore, they reproduce inequality in their own working. Pepe Cid and Elena Larrauri perform a similar exercise with respect to penal policies in Spain. Rod Morgan's chapter, in turn, focuses on another aspect of penality and Euro-pean harmonisation, as he describes the activity of the European Committee for the Prevention of Torture. The very existence of such a committee sums up some of the problems with punishment in contemporary Europe. Finally, Rob Mawby discusses the findings of a research study centred on victims' feelings about crime and the police in a number of East and West European countries. His chapter is useful as one way of thinking comparatively about justice in Europe, in relation, that is, to a specific dimension of the justice system – police as 'a service'.

Part III focuses on recent developments in the economic sphere of 'criminal business' in Europe. In the chapters in this section one senses that 'market Europe' not only triggers and shapes fear of crime, anxiety, and street illegality, but also determines the conditions for the growth of organised forms of criminal activity. Pino Arlacchi tackles some definitional issues regarding, and identifies some features of, illegal markets, while Yakov Gilinskiy describes the interface between liberalised markets and organised crime in Russia. Roger Lewis addresses the specific activities surrounding the illicit drugs economy in the Balkans. Patricia Rawlinson argues for a re-definition of Russian organised crime, while Letizia Paoli assesses the importance of the confessions of mafia 'turncoats' for the re-conceptualisation of Italian–American organised crime.

With Part IV the book moves from general conceptualisations and tendencies to the description of specific localities in which the validity of various concepts and trends may be assessed. Dick Hobbs and Colin Dunnighan base their challenge to 'global–transnational–international' studies of organised crime on their findings in localised ethnographic investigation. Evi Girling, Ian Loader and Richard Sparks re-visit the concepts of globalisation and insecurity against a specific local context, the English town of Macclesfield. Malin Åkerström analyses the moral panic surrounding violent crime in Sweden, while Sophia Vidali and Vassilis Karydis conduct a similar analysis, respectively, of problem youth and immigration in Greece. Henrik Tham offers a comparative study of crime and the welfare state in Sweden and the UK, and finally Willem de Haan discusses myths and realities of street robbery in Amsterdam.

We have chosen 'Horizons' as the title for Part V of the book because the chapters contained in it allude to future challenges and oppotunities for criminology in Europe. Heinz Steinert explores the theoretical developments underpinning the very concepts of crime and punishment, and while feeling that such developments have caused an inexplicable retreat on the part of critical criminologists, he stresses that his is not a formulation of a new critical criminology of some sort, but a critique of the very theoretical legitimacy of criminology. Sebastian Scheerer complements this analysis with an 'archaeological' examination of the notion of punishment. Nigel South argues that European criminology should 'think green', and warns that criminologists should consider the future potential for social damage generated by the irresponsible manipulation of the environment by corporate interests and governments. Vesna Nikolić-Ristanović examines the impact on crime of the war in the region around the former Yugoslavia, and raises important issues which, inexplicably, have long been beyond the remit of criminology. Finally, Ruth Jamieson picks up the challenge identified here by arguing for a 'criminology of war' in Europe. The crossover between some key aspects of wartime contingencies and everyday life in 'peacetime', she stresses, should encourage criminologists to make the necessary theoretical, as well as empirical, connections.

Quite contrary to the pessimism and deconstructive/destructive messages of some recent commentators on the state of 'late-modern criminology' (see discussion in South, 1997), the pages in this volume demonstrate the vitality and diversity of criminology in Europe. We hope readers will share with us some of our excitement about the future prospects for European criminology.

Notes

1 'Crime and Social Order in Europe', Manchester, 7–10 September 1996. This book consists primarily of a selection from over seventy papers delivered at that conference. The editors would like to take this opportunity to thank all those who presented papers and the others who took part in the conference. We wish to acknowledge here the very high standard of the papers delivered and emphasise the difficulty of making decisions about which to include or exclude. Our apologies to those authors whom we had to omit.

2 We are conscious here that many such persons in Europe declare – 'I am *not* a criminologist – but I *do* study crime and social order!'.

3 Mirrored by similar questions concerning the eastward expansion of NATO.

4 For example, in issue 3, South (1996) provides a short bibliographical review of some recent texts which prioritise a *European* perspective over parochial, national preoccupations or familiar transatlantic (i.e. Euro-USA) orientations. The 25 books fall, roughly, into 7 areas: policing across borders (public and private); studies of prison systems in Europe; human rights and civil liberties issues; feminist analysis and debate; drugs – use, policy and policing; organisational and economic crime; and 'general' conference volumes.

5 Other recent comparative studies (not mentioned in South, 1996) include: Harding *et al.*, 1995, on criminal justice in the Netherland, and England and Wales (cf. Downes, 1988); and Robert and van Outrive, 1995, on trends in criminological research in Europe.

References

Accattatis, V. (1996), 'Cittadini europei o sudditi delle multinazionali?', *AltrEuropa*, 2 (5): 6–16.

AltrEuropa (1996), 'Manifesto di Firenze per l'eguaglianza dei sessi nell' Unione Europea', October–November, 2 (5): 20.

Anderson, M., den Boer, M., Cullen, P., Gilmore, W., Raab, C. and Walker, N. (1995), *Policing the European Union: Theory, Law and Practice*, Oxford: Clarendon Press.

Barca, L. and Trento, S. (1994), *L'economia della corruzione*, Rome/Bari: Laterza.

Bianchi, H., Simondi, M. and Taylor, I. (eds) (1975), *Deviance and Control in Europe*, London: Wiley.

Bunyan, T. (1993), *Statewatching the New Europe. A Handbook on the European State*, London: Statewatch.

Centorrino, M. (1990), *L'economia 'cattiva' del Mezzogiorno*, Naples: Liguori.

Cersosimo, D. (1994), *Viaggio a Melfi. La Fiat oltre il fordismo*, Rome: Donzelli.

Dahrendorf, R. (1996), *Perché l'Europa? Riflessioni di un europeista scettico*, Rome/Bari: Laterza.

Della Porta, D. and Mény, Y. (1995), *Démocratie et corruption en Europe*, Paris: La Découverte.

Dillemans, R. (1995), 'Opening Address', in Fijnaut *et al.* (eds), op. cit.

Downes, D. (1988), *Contrasts in Tolerance*, Oxford: Clarendon Press.

Fijnaut, C., Goethals, J., Peters, T. and Walgrave, L. (eds) (1995), *Changes in Society. Crime and Criminal Justice in Europe*, The Hague: Kluwer.

Gadamer, H. G. (1989), *Das Erbe Europas*, Frankfurt: Suhrkamp Verlag.

Harding, C., Fennell, P., Jorg, N. and Swart, B. (eds) (1995), *Criminal Justice in Europe: A Comparative Study*, Oxford: Clarendon Press.

Hobbs, D. (1995), *Bad Business*, Oxford: Oxford University Press.

ISTAT (Istituto Nazionale di Statistica) (1996), *Rapporto sull'Italia*, Bologna: Il Mulino.

Judt, T. (1996), 'Europe: The Grand Illusion', *New York Review of Books*, XLIII (12): 6–9.

Leiken, R. (1997), 'Controlling the Global Corruption Epidemic', *Foreign Policy*, 105: 55–76.

Mann, T. (1995 [1945]), *La Germania e i tedeschi*, Rome: Il Manifesto.

Marazzi, C. (1995), *Il posto dei calzini*, Bellinzona: Casagrande.

Nelken, D. (ed.) (1994), *The Futures of Criminology*, London: Sage.

Offe, C. (1996), *Varieties of Transition. The East European and East German Experience*, Cambridge: Polity Press.

O'Neill, J. (1994), *The Missing Child in Liberal Theory*, Toronto: University of Toronto Press.

Palombarini, G. (1996), 'PM in salsa francese', *Micromega*, 4: 162–6.

Paugam, S. (1996), *L'exclusion. L'état des savoirs*, Paris: La Découverte.

Phythian, M. and Little, W. (1993), 'Parliament and Arms Sales: Lessons of the Matrix Churchill Affair', *Parliamentary Affairs*, 46: 293–308.

Punch, M. (1996), *Dirty Business*, London: Sage.

Revelli, M. (1996), *Le due destre. Le derive politiche del postfordismo*, Turin: Bollati Boringhieri.

Robert, P., van Outrive, L., with Jefferson, T. and Shapland, J. (eds) (1995), *Research, Crime and Justice in Europe: An Assessment and Some Recommendations*, Sheffield: Centre for Criminological and Legal Research, University of Sheffield.

Ruggiero, V. (1996a), *Organized and Corporate Crime in Europe. Offers That Can't Be Refused*, Aldershot: Dartmouth.

Ruggiero, V. (1996b), 'War Markets: Corporate and Organized Criminals in Europe', *Social & Legal Studies*, 5 (1): 5–20.

Ruggiero, V. (1996c), 'France: Corruption as Resentment', in Levi, M. and Nelken, D. (eds), *The Corruption of Politics and the Politics of Corruption*, Oxford: Blackwell.

Ruggiero, V. (1997a), 'Trafficking in Human Beings. Slaves in Contemporary Europe', *The International Journal of Sociology of Law*, 25(3): 231–44.

Ruggiero, V. (1997b), 'Criminals and Service Providers. Cross-National Dirty Economies', *Crime, Law and Social Change*, 28(1): 27–38.

Ruggiero, V. and South, N. (1995), *Eurodrugs. Drug Use, Markets and Trafficking in Europe*, London: UCL Press.

Ruggiero, V. and South, N. (1997), 'The Late-Modern City as a Bazaar', *British Journal of Sociology*, 48 (1): 54–70.

Ryan, M. (1996), 'European Penal Systems. Interview with Mick Ryan', *Crime and Social Order in Europe*, ESRC Newsletter, N. 2: 10–11.

Samson, C. and South, N. (1996) 'Social Policy Isn't What It Used to Be', in Samson, C. and South, N. (eds) *The Social Construction of Social Policy*, London: Macmillan.

Schumpeter, J. (1961), *The Theory of Economic Development*, New York: Oxford University Press.

Shapland, J. (1991), 'Criminology in Europe', in Heidensohn, F. and Farrell, H. (eds), *Crime in Europe*, London: Routledge.

Sim, J., Ruggiero, V. and Ryan, H. (1995), 'Punishment in Europe: Perceptions and Commonalities', in Ruggiero, V., Ryan, M. and Sim, J. (eds), *Western European Penal Systems*, London: Sage.

South, N. (1996), 'Eurovisions: Some Recent Europe-Focussed Contributions on Criminology, Crime and Control', *Crime and Social Order in Europe*, ESRC Newsletter 3, June: 4–5.

South, N. (1997), 'Late-Modern Criminology: Late' As in 'Dead' or 'Modern' as in 'New', in Owen, D. (ed.), *Sociology After Postmodernism*, London: Sage.

Sterne, L. (1967 [1768]), *A Sentimental Journey Through France and Italy*, Harmondsworth: Penguin.

Taylor, I. (1992), 'The International Drug Trade and Money Laundering: Border Control and Other Issues', *European Sociological Review*, 8 (1): 181–193.

Taylor, I. (1997), 'Crime and Social Insecurity in Europe', *Criminal Justice Matters*, 27 (Spring): 3–5.

Van Dijk, J. and Van Kesteren, J. (1996), 'The Prevalence and Perceived Seriousness of Victimization by Crime: Some Reflections of the International Crime Victims Survey', *European Journal of Crime, Criminal Law and Criminal Justice*, 4 (1): 48–67.

Vinci, L. (1996), 'La risposta al monetarismo', *AltrEuropa*, 2 (2): 19–28.

Vogelweith, A. and Vaudano, H. (1995), *Mains propres, mains liées. France–Italie: la leçon des affaires*, Paris: Austral.

Walmsley, R. (1995), 'The European Prison Rules in Central and Eastern Europe', *European Journal on Criminal Policy and Research*, 3 (4): 73–90.

Wilkins, L. T. (1991), *Punishment, Crime and Market Forces*, Aldershot: Dartmouth.

Part I

EUROPEAN PROSPECTS

1

CRIME, MARKET-LIBERALISM AND THE EUROPEAN IDEA

Ian Taylor

To the extent to which the resistance in Scandinavia and other places in Europe is directed only against a Europe run by the Brussels bureaucracy, that is against a systematic unification process which does not yet have a shared political life-world to support it, to that extent these impulses could be transformed into a demand for a democratic Europe. The one true hurdle consists of the absence of a common public, of an arena for dealing with issues of common concern. Whether such a forum for communication will arise ironically depends mostly on intellectuals as a group who unceasingly talk about Europe without ever doing anything for it.

(Habermas 1996: 16)

'Market liberalism' and crime across Europe

As we approach the end of the century, the advance of 'economic liberalism' – or of a free market, untramelled (and, indeed, encouraged) by Governments – is observable right across Europe – from Ireland to Russia, from Spain to 'social-democratic' Scandinavia. So also are the far-reaching effects. Not least of these effects, of course, is the increase in unemployment across the European Community itself, which we identified in the introduction of the volume, and also a general economic polarisation of the broader society. This rapid 'marketisation' of Europe now extends as far as the culture and sport traditionally associated with the individual countries on the European continent. The Verona Opera is now marketed by the European tourism industry as much as La Scala in Milan; and on television across Europe the English Premier League is now as widely available as Serie A from Italy. Fashion shows from London are as heavily publicised as those in Paris and Milan, and we can watch rock-diving from Portugal as well as Alpine skiing, and cycling competitions from all over Europe, not just the Tour de France. We have a Europe, in fact, in which many new levels of social and cultural activity have rapidly become commodities for sale on the European (and in many instances the global) market.

The energetic advance of the 'free market' is closely associated with the advance of a set of what we might call 'market liberal' discourses in the public sphere of political and cultural commentary, most notably in the media of Europe. It is, above all, a discourse which identifies the viewer or the listener as a consumer of 'goods', and which glorifies the idea of choice across a range of different market places (unlimited tourist experiences, multiple channel televisions; a range of private health and personal insurance schemes, etc.). The most obvious examples of restless 'market liberal' talk are to be found on satellite and cable television programmes, especially their consumer, audience-participation or talk-show programmes, and in the popular-newspaper and popular-magazine press in Europe, apparently inexhaustible in their journalists' constant search for new styles, new stars and new scandals. But this search for 'new' stories that will attract the attention of a jaded or exhausted audience is observable even in the quality newspapers of old Europe (from *Die Zeit* to the *Guardian*), but is most apparent in the mass-popular journalism of the new Europe (tabloid-style newspapers, the teenage and popular culture press, and voyeuristic magazines dedicated to the provision of 'privileged' glimpses of the lives of the wealthy and/or 'the stars' of media and popular culture). So, for example, Italian television (an extreme example, no doubt, as a result of the continuing influence of Mr Berlusconi and his Finnivest conglomerate) now appears like a seamless flow of the very latest images from the fast-changing market-place of popular culture – a mediascape in which, as Umberto Eco has so brilliantly described, *everything* appears as a part of the 'hyper-reality' of the post-modern world, governed only by ever-more satiated, restless consumer desires (Eco, 1985, 1995). The target of this daily exercise in dissemination of media messages is the individual viewer understood only as *a consumer of and in the image market*. Television in other European countries assumes a different specific shape from Italy, but the general pull in the direction of 'market-liberalism' as a taken-for-granted backdrop to television, radio and newspaper representation of the wider world is unmistakable almost everywhere.[1]

Deeply embedded in this flow of television and media discourses, I would want to argue, is a specific set of market-liberal scripts (or 'discourses') which define the kinds of expectations placed on elected politicians and on different public and private agencies (schools, hospitals, police) responsible for the delivery of specific services in the market society. Absolutely fundamental a feature of this discursive logic is the idea that the citizen is to be thought of as a consumer who is 'entitled' (by virtue of financial power and payment, rather than for any other particular reason, e.g. 'public importance') to receive 'service' (good food, good health, good entertainment, or, indeed, as we shall argue, good policing) from different 'providers' in the market place.[2] So also there is embedded within this television discourse (both in fictional or entertainment programmes and in current-affairs reports) a very particular account of *the problem of crime* in various EC countries. My purpose in this paper is to try and identify some of these assumptions – indeed, to engage in the 'deconstruction' of these hegemonic media scripts. It is *not* my intention here to suggest that Europe's problems with crime can be seen only as a media construction, but it *is* my concern to show that the discursive representation and reportage of such crime is of fundamental importance. I want to deal with five defining aspects of market-liberal discourses on crime in Europe – first, the question of crime and social anxiety; second, the curious couplet of the nation and the market; third, the question of The Other (with its recent descent into the issue of Evil) and the connected issue of 'social exclusion'; fourth, the lionisation of an independent individual life in the market and the associated attack on social care; and, finally, I want to highlight *the hyperbole* – and, indeed the absence of doubt, reflexivity and 'evaluation' – that is a characteristic feature of this market liberalism, apparently across much of Europe.

Crime and social anxiety

Market liberalism has a very particular perspective on the question of anxiety and the connected, highly topical field of risk. Being a discourse of the market society, of course, market liberalism is actively interested in *encouraging* a certain level of anxiety amongst citizens in general – on the one hand, in the case of citizen-workers, a certain level of job- and personal insecurity (as an encouragement to individual 'competitivity') and, on the other, in the case of citizen-consumers – as Vance Packard understood many years ago in his farsighted study of 'built-in obsolescence' (Packard 1961) – a certain productive level of insecurity with respect to the possession, or lack of possession, of the never-ending supply of new consumer goods. The willingness to take risks, especially of a financial kind, might be thought an essential attribute in the character-armour of the market entrepreneur, and certainly was so described in much of the earliest entrepreneurial free-market literature of the 1980s (cf. Keat and Abercrombie 1991). One continuing feature of the culture of the market in the 1990s is the emphasis which is placed on the widening of such risk-taking capacity or interest to a wider section of the population, as for example when taking out insurance, borrowing monies for the purchase of a home or entering directly into dealings in the stock and bond markets.

One of the most difficult problems for market individualists in the 1980s and 1990s has been that of deciding on the optimal acceptable level of regulation of such financial services markets. This is a continuing and unpredetermined issue within free-market societies. Even in the aftermath of a series of money-laundering, long-term frauds, and insider-trading scandals in Britain – the prospect for survival of the Serious Fraud Office, set up in the 1980s specifically to regulate this kind of serious economic fraud, is looking slim, despite the election of the new Labour Government. In Italy, the continuing struggles between Silvio Berlusconi's *Forza Italia* party and the Clean Hands judiciary can also be understood as a (very vigorous) debate about the appropriate parameters of legitimate business and government practice in competitive market environments (della Porta 1996, 1997); and current indications, in June 1997, suggest that many of the trials that were scheduled as a result of judicial investigations in the early 1990s may be about to be shelved.

So we would argue that there *is* a market liberal interest in encouraging a certain level of anxiety in individuals, in the name also of encouraging a vigorous mix of entrepreneurial and competitive culture (and also in the name of discouraging the malign and inert condition of 'state dependency'). But there is a distinction between the kind of restless anxiety thought desirable amongst possessive individuals and a more generalised sense of anxiety about, or amongst, those without such a possessive advantage. In some European societies in the 1990s, the issue being raised is whether the free market in non-legitimate business activities (burglary, car theft, computer thefts, the drug trade, etc.) is beginning actually to threaten the overall sense of peace and order on which regular social exchange (including market exchange) must to some degree depend. There is a particularly intense anxiety in many European societies, for example, about the increases in rates of violent crime (see Table 1.1).

Anxieties about crime were in a sense confined just to the idea of violence 'in the street' or in other public spaces. Across Europe – but again to different degrees – fears about the safety of the private sphere of the household (in many ways, the more privileged or valued site of a consumer market society) were undermined by widely-reported increases in burglary and other kinds of intrusion (see Table 1.2).

Table 1.1 Increases in reported violent crime, 1987–1994

Country	Per cent
France	61
The Netherlands	59
England and Wales	57
West Germany	31
Italy	5

Source: NACRO Criminal Justice Digest 87 (January 1996): 16

Table 1.2 Increases in reported rates of domestic burglary, 1987–1994

Country	Per cent
England and Wales	41
Italy	25
France	18
The Netherlands	14
West Germany	3

Source: NACRO Criminal Justice Digest 87 (January 1996): 16

The high rates of victimisation of citizens of different European countries have been further confirmed by Professor van Dijk's International Victimization Survey of 1992 and by a host of other surveys.[3] Surveys also identify the increasing levels of fear and anxiety experienced by the citizens of these societies, firstly, with respect to the safety of public space in general (especially in the evening hours) and, secondly, of the private sphere of the household. There are some important issues here – not least as to whether the levels of anxiety expressed in such surveys are 'really' about crime and the chances of criminal victimisation, or whether the fears expressed about crime are actually a convenient and socially-approved kind of metaphor through which survey respondents can articulate, in a shorthand fashion, a much more complex sense of restlessness and anxiety – not least the general unease which a full-blown free-market environment produces culturally and psychologically.

The really distinctive characteristic of market liberalism's response to the question of fear of crime and social anxiety is the idea that such matters, like the response of the consumer to other products and services, are in effect a 'challenge to managers' – not least, in this instance, a challenge to managers of the police and legal systems in respect of their communication with 'the public' (the consumers). Both at national and local level, police and crime-prevention partnerships are put under pressure to explain how they are delivering *their product* – in this case, the different identifiable 'outputs' from their ongoing struggles against crime or social anxiety about crime. Writing some years ago about the United States' unending 'war against crime', Jeffrey Reiman argued that it was in the interest of the managers of this struggle (the FBI and other federal agencies, as well as different police forces at the level of individual states) always to be seen *to be losing*, albeit in a noble and determined manner (sustaining what he called a *Pyrrhic* defeat): in this fashion, he argued, the agencies would continue to persuade the American tax-paying public of the seriousness of the criminal threat in America, and continue to vote through the budgetary dollars (Reiman 1979, 1984). In the cost-conscious, tax-cutting 1990s, however, this strategy carries serious risks (witness, for example, the imposition of stringent 'performance measures' and the encouragement given private security companies to respond to the new market demands for the delivery of crime-prevention or anxiety-reduction in competitive market societies). The increasing off-loading of whole sections or agencies of the criminal justice system to the private sector, coupled with the imposition of a variety of performance measures (for example, on police forces), gives a new importance to the language of evaluation and 'payment by results'. In Britain, in the early 1990s, the other discursive strategy of the then Conservative Home Secretary – concerned to offer a demonstration of 'outcome' and 'results' – was to focus on the rapid increase of the prison population, as evidence of the sheer number of 'villains' who had effectively been incapacitated and therefore were not any longer involved in crime. In this sense, Mr Howard actually wanted to run a demonstration project, declaring that 'prison works'.[4] In many European societies at the beginning of 1997, for example, one of the issues being most urgently investigated by many senior managers of European police forces was the recent, much-publicised success of the New York Police Department (NYPD) in producing sharp *drops* in recorded crime in that city. There was much interest in the re-organisation of the system of management that had apparently occurred in the NYPD earlier in the 1990s, and especially the introduction of computerised 'crime pattern analysis' systems and more flexible deployment of officers.[5] There was also an increasing interest, that is, in the idea that the effective and more 'systematic' management of police forces (with the assistance of Close Circuit Television and/or computerised systems of pattern analysis) could produce *a real reduction* in the amount of actually-occurring crime, even in divided and marketised societies.

The nation and the market

One of the most important and definitive features of the crime problem in Europe is the fact of the internationalisation of its aetiology, set against the unremitting national organisation of social and political response. The spread of short-term and long-term unemployment is occurring, albeit unevenly, right across Europe (Judt 1996), as also are the processes of immiseration, and housing shortage, which are institutionalising a set of ghettoes[6] in the inner-city or on the outer edges of Europe's old industrial cities (Wiles 1993). The homeless people and vagrants begging on the streets – the new Gypsies of the late twentieth century – appear to have become a permanent feature of our cities. So these same social processes (with their various expressions in increasing rates of drug abuse, domestic violence, suicide and ill-health) are widespread amongst those millions of European citizens who have been unsuccessful in their struggle for a place in the competitive market society. We shall return to these citizens in our discussion of the phenomena of inclusion and exclusion. Our point for the moment is that the processes that are producing and intensifying, these problems are international, but the responses to them are only being framed *at the level of individual nation-states*, and it is increasingly clear that the national institutions are unable in and by themselves to respond. Generally speaking, the market, and not the nation-state, is *sovereign*.

The cutting-edge of what Edward Luttwak has identified as a new 'turbo-charged' phase in the development of capitalism in the 1990s is located in the tiger economies of south-east Asia, with growth rates now twice as high as those in the West as a whole (Jacques 1995). But we also must note that those particular western economies (like the United States) which have been most successful and adaptive in their responses to world competition, have done so partly on the back of the modernity achieved in the earlier post-war period but also on the basis of the de-regulation of the local labour markets undertaken in more recent times (Luttwak 1995). Over 10 million new jobs have been created in the United States during the time of the first Clinton administration, and although these are over-whelmingly jobs of a low-paid and insecure variety, the overall official rate of unemployment has continued to decline.[7] The response of the 'international community' in Europe to the unfolding of this crisis of unemployment-and-competitivity – for all the best efforts of Jacques Delors in his last months at the Commission attempting to mobilise a flexible new working hours and employment programme – has been muted (cf. The Group of Lisbon 1995). Initiatives have effectively been restricted to strategies of attempted *containment* (or, indeed, 'protection') of the problem of unemployment (and its effects) at the level of individual nation-states. The absence of an international European-wide initiative, to which activist national governments might contribute support and encouragement (in the face of global capitalist turmoil) is a tragic illustration of under-development in what Habermas (1996) calls the 'political life-world' of Europe. In the absence of such a shared political life-world, it is no surprise that the response on the part of the national elites to crime (and, indeed, to most other associated issues of social dislocation) in each European society is led only by those who are given technical or managerial responsibility of managing national or local policing or national penal systems. The 'struggle against crime' narrows down, as we have already suggested, to the struggle over good practice and/or effective management of the social control system, and also, perhaps, the management of the information system through which the citizenry as a whole are kept up to date with the never-ending 'Pyrrhic' struggle.

Crime and 'the Other'

The most obvious and least contentious dimension of the argument in this paper, I suspect, points to the extraordinary energy which is devoted, especially in a competitive market society, to demonising an increasing variety and range of the national population (so de-limiting further the numbers of those who are deemed to be legitimate full members of market society). As many papers in this volume clearly demonstrate, this process – of 'demonisation of Others' – is at work in many different European member-states, notably in the treatment given immigrants and other outsiders who want to be part of the new market Europe (refugees, asylum-seekers and others). This demonisation of Others, of course, works to legitimise the denial or withdrawal of national or European support and services from these 'Others' (on the self-evident grounds of 'desert') and it may also contribute to the ascription of these Others into a specifically criminal, or villainous category, both in media reports and in commonsense descriptions. Ever since the pioneering work of Stan Cohen (1972), students of criminology have been familiar with the ways in which – even in a relatively prosperous period of the high modern mixed economy – young people were routinely cast into the role of 'folk devils' and/or positioned as the subjects of some 'moral panic' about the condition of the social order as a whole. The work of the Birmingham School in Britain in the late 1970s was important for the further development of this perspective, unpacking the more specifically *ideological* and *political* messages which are often built into 'moral panics' and, even more pointedly, during more extended 'Law and Order campaigns' – spelling out, by allusion and suggestion, the uneven relationship, for example, between racial group membership and national identity, or alternatively, describing, once again by allusion and indirect references, the emergent rationale for paramilitary styles of policing in Britain (Hall *et al.*, 1978). In these last years of the twentieth century, as many commentators have noted, the attempted construction of moral panics has increased apace (certainly in the British popular press) – taking in, most notoriously, a series of panics about parasitical and malevolent single-mothers, at the one extreme, and a range of evil and insidious drug-pushers and/or paedophiles, always at work in numbers outside the local school, at the other. The issue for us is not whether these panics do or do not depict actually-occurring social problems specifically in free-market Britain: the stories are usually not outright inventions.

The issue is in part one of causal explanation: whether these problems are presented accurately in terms of their actual prevalence and intensity in lived social experience in Britain and/or whether these problems are present *as the cause of* social dislocation, personal unhappiness or trauma, or the quality of life in particular neighbourhoods, or whether they are best understood as the effects of other social and economic processes. Other than advancing this quite conventional social scientific query, however, it is also obviously important to be alert to the significance of the increasing prevalence and prominence of 'panic' in the popular press in respect not just of the question of the level of crime, with an increasingly unstable empirical reference (violence, drugs, AIDS, serial killers, child sexual abuse and paedophilia), but also to other connected questions (the sphere of sexuality, in particular, and, with that, the question of gender roles).[8] The intensified process of panic and the thrust-to-exclude finds expression in many countries in the treatment of refugees, asylum-seekers and other migrants, but is also observable in some European societies in the response of the political class to the economic polarisation occurring within market societies. In Italy, there is widespread popular anxiety over the sudden new visibility and intrusiveness of street prostitution, by North African and Eastern European girls (and boys) on the main streets of Northern towns, with no earlier experience of such an intrusive form of sex trade (Pavarini, 1995); and it requires little imagination to see how this kind of anxiety can be translated at the level of regional and national politics into repressive exclusionary policies directed against 'foreigners' in general (as also has happened in recent years in southern France). In Moscow, there is now a quite agitated level of public concern about personal safety on the streets, which in February 1997 was reported to have found local expression in a new by-law allowing citizens of that city to carry guns for self-protection – a local expression of American 'concealed-carry' gun law.[9] In Sweden, there is currently a palpable and widespread anxiety about the presence of a larger immigrant population, no matter how closely regulated that population is by state policing and housing agencies. In Norway and Finland, there is marked anxiety over the porousness of the borders which these two Scandinavian societies share with 'market Russia', where 'everything is for sale'. It seems clear that the character of local anxieties about 'crime' are most powerfully to be understood as the short-hand through which the unsettling realities of the new 'market Europe', actively doing business with the larger world (as we all now must do), are given local meaning. This challenge is rendered no easier by the recognition of the ways in which market Europe itself throws up a series of opportunities for graft and fraud on the part even of elected political leaderships themselves (as, for example, was revealed to have happened in Italy during the late 1980s, and in the same period, in France, with politicians on the left, like Bernard Tapie, as well as more right-wing figures, like Jacques Médecin, the long-time Mayor of Nice).

The speedy re-cycling by the European media of an ever increasing range (a market selection, indeed) of folk-devils often assumes a quite fanciful, not to say fantastic, character, and may then in short order be dropped. So, for example, in 1993, according to a reporter for *The European* newspaper, European citizens were about to be confronted by an epidemic of 'syringe bandits' – street muggers armed with syringes containing what they claimed to be HIV-positive material. One instance of this kind of confrontation has been reported in Lisbon the previous week (*The European*, 29 July–1 August 1993). The 'syringe bandit' panic had a particularly short career. But we have also been witness, during the early 1990s, to a succession of nihilistic and voyeuristic cinematic portrayals, not least at the hands of Quentin Tarantino, of 'serial murder' and of 'murder for thrills'. Stratton has recently argued that the issue is not so much whether the 'serial killer' construct corresponds directly to real events specific to the modern world, for example, the eleven murders believed to have been committed by Franscisco Garcia Escalero in Spain in 1987, the Fred and Rosemary West murders in Britain (which went to trial in 1995) or the murders of children by a ring of paedophiles in Belgium (the Dutroux case) (coming to light in August 1996) – all of which were the subject of saturation coverage in the international press. Stratton argues that there have always been instances of such serial killing, and he cites examples from the late medieval period and also from the early industrial-capitalist period (Stratton 1996). The issue is that of explaining the *sudden discursive priority* which is being given to this kind of statistically uncommon event, and the themes of Evil and Possession which are used to 'explain' these events (and, by implication, the kinds of crime which are committed by Others). It seems self-evident that this intense and unending re-invention and vivid characterisation of a range of evil new villains and criminals is intimately related, discursively, with the continuing thrust taking place politically and institutionally towards the exclusion, segregation or incapacitation of a widening range of dangerous Others.

Crime, social dislocation and social care

In a lecture given in London in 1990, the social-democratic American criminologist Elliott Currie noted how the wholesale shift to 'free market society', encouraged by the tax-cutting 'reforms' of the Reagan and Bush administrations, worked to undermine even the minimal framework of welfare support and care provided by the public welfare agencies in that country. At the time of massive de-industrialisation, especially in the old Rust Belt cities and on the west coast, the populations experiencing the greatest loss of income and personal security were also precisely the populations from whom state support was most energetically withdrawn.[10] The retreat from the welfare state is now occurring in most developed western societies, including even the exemplary case of Sweden (Tham, this volume). Apologists for this continuing attack on welfare speak, on the one hand, of the contribution which the welfare state is alleged to have made to the production of 'state dependency', dominated by unhealthy statist bureaucracies, and, on the other, try to insist that these welfare states often worked, unjustly, to the benefit of the middle classes more than they did to the working or under-classes of Europe. What these critics do not discuss, however, is the real prospect which now faces young people, the unemployed, and other identifiable populations (the elderly poor) in market Europe, where employment is scarce, in which there is very little public provision by the state, and in which the overall culture of competitive anxiety, antipathy to the generalised 'Other' and overwhelming regard for oneself has undermined the play of voluntary caring activity. One of the paradoxes of the 1970–2000 period across Europe, indeed, has been the coincidence of the rise of market liberalism, on the one hand, and the continuing articulation, on the other, of a set of rhetorics, derived from the anti-psychiatric movements of the 1960s,[11] focused on the release of mental patients and other hitherto institutionalised populations into 'the community'. The 'community' into which these needy people have been persistently and increasingly released has been a void that is filled by a set of unreliable and unregulated initiatives which, as many recent scandals have revealed, have often been led by individuals with very mixed sets of motivations and concerns. The public territories of many European cities are now home to a set of identifiable casualties of this process of 'de-institutionalisation' and 'care in the community' – from homeless and vagrant young people to elderly 'bag ladies', and a vast range of disoriented and confused others – in a return to what many observers recognise is many ways akin to the circumstances of the feudal period. In California, Mike Davis, Christian Parenti and others have described the rapid colonisation of zones of Los Angeles and San Francisco (the Mission district) by a residual and increasingly desperate population of the new poor (Davis 1990, Parenti 1995). In Canada, a society which, in the aftermath of the North American Free Trade Agreement, is face-to-face with the realities of a down-sizing public sphere, John O'Neill keenly observes the terrifying prospect facing generations of young people whose 'life-chances are pre-determined by the deadly odds in a society that renders health, education and justice scarce commodities' (O'Neill 1994: 11). The prospect facing young people in France is subject to a similar analysis by Bailleau in the volume. One does not have to stray far beyond the routinely-recycled rhetorics of market liberalism, as contained on the airwaves and on television, to hear the more anxious voices of young people themselves, confronting the material realities of life in free market society. The guidance which might be provided for this generation by an earlier generation, attuned to the safety net and the range of public institutions that characterised mixed-economy welfare states – by what O'Neill calls 'the covenant of care' as distinct from a contract with the market – *is* substantially irrelevant. In determining job opportunity, life prospects and general 'quality of life' for individuals, the market once again is now sovereign.

Market liberalism, hyperbole and critical evaluation

One of the defining characteristics of this restless market society, in its global and more local forms, is its unrelenting tendency to hyperbole. Hyperbole is the chosen form of language and 'vision' which is brought, apparently without distinction, to most new consumer products, from new clothing styles, to new pop-music sounds, or to new kinds of alcoholic drink. This constant tendency to hyperbole seems to be closely associated, as well, with a kind of messianic belief in the overall project of the 'market society' as a dynamic and potentially liberating form of life. Individuals are implicitly being promised the possibility of financial success (through entrepreneurial risk-taking or, failing that, in Britain, through the National Lottery) or alternatively the 'liberation' of being reliant on one's own efforts (rather than the benevolence of a single employer, whether in the state or the private sector). In Britain, this unreconstructed and messianic appeal to the liberating possibilities of 'enterprise culture' does not have the same overall popular purchase that it had in the late 1980s (at a time when house-prices and dividends seem to be locked into an unending upward spiral) (Keat and Abercrombie 1991), but there is little doubt that the broad parameters of this messianic version of market liberalism still continue to describe the thinking and sensibilities of those sections of the commercial middle class who have continued to 'do well' in the 1990s.

We have indicated earlier that the preferred response of the market liberal to serious crises of crime, and to other unfolding problems of individual and social dislocations and harm, is to see them as challenges to managers of particular, segmented markets. So the preferred focus of the market liberal in respect of crime and fear of crime is to separate out statistics on the severity of a particular crime problem from their immediate and historical context, and to make the reduction of *that statistic* the object of managerial strategic thinking and action. Similar moves are apparent in Britain in the re-organisation of health and education, with the regular release of different performance measures, in league-table form, into the public sphere.[12] We do have a problem with this approach to social evaluation and assessment – which is, specifically, the way in which 'the statistic' is selected as the object of energetic action, rather than the more complex and much more challenging and difficult configuration of dislocation and disadvantage affecting many areas of market society. There is a strong sense that this market liberalism, with its prioritising of the entrepreneur and risk-taker, shares a messianic and self-believing quality with Stalinism, not least its valorisation of the Stakhanovite-like commitment of the citizen to never-ending working hours. And for all its interest in the audit of internal aspects of the market regime, it is profoundly resistant (like the Soviet system itself) to the critical evaluation of the overall logic of the system (mass unemployment, increasing inequality, increasing acceleration and exhaustion of the employed workforce etc.). So, indeed – if we are to talk statistics – we should always note which particular indices *are* selected, and thereby 'allowed in' to the narrowing universe of public discussion and debate in free market societies, and which are not. In a study of Canadian television news in the mid-1980s, for example, Peter Bruck pointed to the priority that had come routinely to be given in the final segment of the evening news to closing prices in the international stock exchanges, and to the way in which the television audience was invited to identify with upward shift in these indices as a measure of personal or national well-being (Bruck 1987, 1989). Bruck argued for the adoption by the daily press and television media of a set of what he called 'alternative news indices' – daily measures of unemployment statistics, of the loss of jobs in particular areas, of statistics on health and educational attainment in different local institutions, and a range of other measures of social well-being. In our own field, of the analysis of crime and the 'fear of crime', and the study of social control, it would surely be possible to identify a range of different measures of success, quite variously defined. Foremost among these might be some agreed measure of levels of fear and anxiety in particular local areas or national societies, independent of actual levels of reported crime (with all the obvious problems attending to a reliance on such figures as a reliable measure of well-being).[13] But so also should any critical overall evaluation of the achievements of free-market societies be willing to take on board the kinds of statistics which few free-market liberals actively want to allow into public discussion. One of the most obvious sets of such statistics is that which illuminates the intensification in the use of penal measures that has been occurring, after the American example, in most western European societies in very recent years (see Table 1.3).

This set of statistics – very rarely headlined in national news coverage in market-liberal Europe – is clear evidence of a continuing increase in the use of incarceration by national governments and national criminal justice systems across the continent, and therefore of the more extended experience of the 'pains of imprisonment' by several thousands of European citizens. In the eighteen European societies for which we have statistics for 1991 and 1995, there was an increase *in just these four years* of 23.6 per cent in the overall prison population, from a total of 263,389 in 1991 to 325,463 in 1995. This intensification of penal discipline had been continuing from the early 1980s, but was at this period accelerating rapidly, impeded only by the financial limits in public budgets. In some European countries, indeed, the suspicion was that the cost to the public purse of this expansion of penal discipline was quickly approaching if not exceeding the public costs of the Welfare State at its high point in the late 1970s, when such a level of public expenditure was seen as provoking a 'fiscal crisis of

Table 1.3 Prison populations, European member-states (excluding Luxembourg) 1991–1995 [14]

Country	Prison population September 1991	Prison population September 1995	Prisoners per 100,000 population 1995	Per cent change 1991–1995
Spain	36,562	40,157	122.0	9.8
Portugal	8,092	11,829	119.0	46.2
Scotland	4,860	5,657	110.0	21.4
Northern Ireland	1,660	1,740	106.0	0.5
England and Wales	44,336	51,265	99.0	15.6
Austria	6,655	6,180	77.0	6.7
France	48,675	53,178	86.0	9.1
Italy	32,368	49,102	86.0	51.7
Germany	49,658	68,408	84.0	37.8
Belgium	6,035	7,561	76.0	25.3
The Netherlands	6,662	10,329	67.0	55.0
Denmark	3,243	3,421	66.0	0.5
Greece	5,008	5,878	60.0	1.7
Sweden	4,731	5,794	66.0	22.5
Finland	3,130	3,132	61.8	0.06
Ireland	2,114	2,032	60.0	−0.2

Source: Prison Statistics, England and Wales, 1991; *The Prison Population in 1994* (Home Office Statistical Bulletin 8/95); Criminal Statistics, England and Wales, 1995 (Cm. 3421)

the State' and an intolerable burden on the amount of capital available for market investment. We agree with Elliott Currie in a second lecture given in London in 1996, that the determined introduction of these kinds of statistics into public debate – in this case, illustrating the rapidly increasing use of prisons as an expensive system of social warehousing, is one way of encouraging a more open and rational consideration of crime and penal policy than the hyperbole of market-liberal politicians and an event-conscious liberal media wants normally to allow or encourage (Currie 1996). We may also find it useful, however, to examine statistics of this kind as evidence of the unevenness of developments (a 50 per cent increase in the prison population in Italy in two years, on these measures, as against only a 5 per cent increase in France), and therefore as a first move in the analysis and explanation of useful practices and exemplars being followed in different member-states of the Community.

Conclusion

Our primary concern in this paper has been to try and sketch out a position of critique *vis-à-vis* the ideas of market liberalism which are currently so dominant across Europe.[15] The position from which we speak has not been filled out in detail here, except for our insistence on the idea that the international impact of market developments must be met by an equally international response. We do believe there is an urgent need to move towards some shared sense of a common European citizenship and some kind of shared 'political life-world' with which we can all respond to the exigencies of life in a common European market. Market-liberal rhetoric recognises the trans-national character of a selection of crime problems discussed in the public sphere – specifically, trans-national criminal trades in drugs and other illicit substances and the trans-national movement of criminals themselves – but speaks only to trans-national police responses. It also insists (though its preoccupation with 'the statistic') on conceptualising these trans-national problems in isolation from their (inescapable) context of inter-national 'market Europe' itself, as if there could be some clear and agreed dif-ferentiation (in the present turmoil of turbo-charged change) between legitimate and illegitimate activity, or the moral standing of different nation states or differ-ent entrepreneurial classes. The medium-term conception of Europe we want to develop here is that of a modern and dynamic people's Europe, characterised by networks of public as well as market institutions, and working *in the public interest*. In the short term, however, we are aware that the idea of Europe itself, in the form in which it is presently formulated in Brussels (a centralised and essentially unaccountable bureaucracy, and a set of partnership initiatives conducted across the length and breadth of market Europe) is itself threatened by its association with crime. The European Commission is widely credited with being responsible, directly or indirectly, for $7 billion loss of revenue (or some 10 per cent of its annual budget of $66 billion), in the form of a vast range of frauds successfully conducted against or through the Commission or on the part of its own staff and agencies).[16] The scale and range of the frauds and corruptions that have been unearthed in Europe in recent years have given rise to the creation of a whole new specialist field of applied European criminology,[17] but, rather more import-antly, have contributed significantly to the escalating attacks on 'Brussels' and the idea of Europe as such, being mounted by nationalist politicians across Europe. It is in no sense inconceivable that the continuing increases in levels (and types) of crime in different European societies may be used by these same nationalist forces as part of an argument about the impossibility of effective European collabora-tion, on an analogy, perhaps, with problems which 'Europe' has experienced in the sphere of military and foreign policy. It is absolutely vital for a progressive and contemporary criminology, working with a commitment to the future public interest, to argue and demonstrate that the problems of crime in Europe (for example, the trades in drugs, guns and people, and the hidden economy support-ing the circulation of stolen goods, vehicles, high technology and other major items of stolen property) – like the problems of escalating inequality – require collaborative international response (not just at the level of policing and con-tainment of the crime statistic), and, indeed, call for the creation of new public institutions (including a common European politics) above the level of 'the market'.

Notes

1 In the fast-changing transitions currently taking place in Russia, the newspaper that has emerged as the most widely read and influential daily paper in Moscow is the tabloid *Moskovsky Komsolets*, specialising in cartoon representations of leading politicians, on the one hand, and extended 'juicy' crime and sex stories on the other. *Moskovsky Komsolets* is currently the object of an extended, Bahktinian analysis, by my doctoral student, Serge Timoshenko.

2 In Britain, this particular feature of market-liberal ideology has been enshrined in the idea of a Charter, in which every public agency (and some private ones) are required to post a public document outlining the contract commitment which they as a market institution are making to the public as consumers. Prior to full-blown privatisation, for example, British Rail had to make a commitment on arrival times of trains, under-pinned by a guarantee of financial refunds. National Health Service trusts and hospitals have been required to make Charter commitments on times to be spent awaiting operations, as well as on speed of service in emergency and other public wards.

3 For a useful summary of existing European statistics on reported crime, and also a selection of the key statistics from the international victimisation surveys, see Killias 1995.

4 For more detailed discussion of the 'Prison Works' moment in the long struggles against crime of Mr Michael Howard, the British Home Secretary, see Taylor 1993.

5 Rudolph W. Giuliani and William J. Bratton *The Year of Change: Re-engineering the New York City Police Department (A Progress Report on the Crime Control Strategies of the NYPD)* New York City: NYPD January 1995. There are strong grounds for seeing the managerial changes introduced into the New York Police Department, in the name of efficiency and effectiveness, as being at least as effective as the shift towards the policing of 'incivility' offences in reducing overall levels of crime in New York. The New York experience may be an instance of the real benefits that *can* flow from creative manager-ial responses to problems of 'under-resourcing' or scarcity in the public (and private) sector, and which it should be no part of a progressive or modern politics to reject.

6 The use of the term 'ghetto' is intended by Wiles to signify the creation of a residential territory in which a poor population has been consigned, like the Jews in the Second World War, for an undetermined period of time or perhaps *for ever*. These territories are not the 'transitional zones' identified by the Chicago School, as a temporary home for a new migrant population, prior to its upward progress in the local labour and housing markets. It is in that sense (i.e. of speaking of an area of residence from which there is now no natural escape) that we should make sense of the housing estates on the periphery of Paris described in the movie *La Haine* or by Francois Maspero in his own personal odyssey around the Parisian 'suburbs' (Maspero 1990).

7 In May 1997, the official unemployment rate in the United States was registered as 4.8 per cent, the lowest for twenty-four years (*International Herald Tribune* 7–8 June 1997).

8 On the question of 'panic' in the spheres of sexuality and gender roles, see the work of the Canadian Marxist-turned-post modernist Arthur Kroker (Kroker and Kroker, 1987; Kroker *et al.*, 1989).

9 *Channel Four News*, Britain, 12 February 1997.

10 On the first moves taken in this attack on the poor in the United States, see Priven and Cloward 1982.

11 In Britain, the influence of R. D. Laing and David Esterson (along with the widely read

critique of total institutions by the American sociologist Erving Goffman) was pivotal. In Italy, the key figures included Franco Basiglia, a strong supporter of the movement to 'de-institutionalise' the population of Basaglia, his home hospital, and other asylums (cf. Ciacci 1975).

12 In his Aachen lecture of 1996, Václav Havel referred to the prevalence of these strategies, without further enquiry, simply as 'the characteristically modern blind faith in quantitative indices.' (Havel 1996: 38).

13 There is a strongly held view amongst criminologists studying the problem of crime in high-stressed and high-crime urban areas in free-market societies that any reduction in reported crime must first be investigated in terms of a decline in willingness to report victimisation to the police. This unwillingness-to-report may be a function, in turn, of a general reduction in the amount of insurance held by residents of such areas, or alternatively the increasingly widespread phenomenon of witness-intimidation.

14 Close scrutiny of the official figures on the increases in the prison population across Europe in the late 1980s and early 1990s suggests many different lines of enquiry. There is strong evidence, for example, that the greatest levels of increase occurred, in many European member-states, in the two years from 1991 to 1993, and that the increases have now started to level off. The relationship between the increases of 1991–3 and the 'economic cycle' in Europe calls out for further investigation. There is also, more obviously, significant unevenness in the resort to increased use of penal discipline in the different member-states – increases having been greatest, between 1991 and 1995, in the Netherlands (a 55 per cent increase, transforming a country which traditionally has made minimal use of prison into a more 'typical' European regime; Italy (51.7 per cent) and Portugal (46.2 per cent). On these figures, the country making heaviest use of prison (per 100,000 population) is Spain, having taken on this pole position from Northern Ireland and Scotland in the two years from 1993.

15 We should emphasise, at this point, that the critique of free-market society advanced here does not constitute an endorsement of all that went before, in the form of bureaucratic welfare-statism. Nor either does this position involve a rejection of the role of market 'discipline' and/or competition, especially in the economic market place of production and consumption. With Elliott Currie (1990, 1996), however, we do see a distinction between societies in which a principled political decision has been taken to protect key areas of social provision (health, education and welfare) from the market, and societies in which everything has gone to market. The critical position being advanced here, in the tradition of all that is best in social science, is an attempt to grasp the difference between the rhetorics of 'free-market liberals' and lived experience in free-market societies.

16 *European*, 30 September–2 October 1995.

17 Cf. for example, the International Anti-Corruption Conferences, originally established in Hong Kong in 1981, held its fifth conference in Amsterdam. The proceedings of this conference are reported in Punch *et al.* 1993.

References

Bruck, Peter A. (1987) 'The Commodification of Social Relations: Television News and Social Intervention' *Journal of Communication Enquiry* 11 (2): 79–86.

Bruck, Peter A. (1989) 'Stategies for Peace, Strategies for News Research' *Journal of Communication* 39 (1) (Winter): 108–129.

Ciacci, Margherita (1975) 'Psychiatric Control: a report on the Italian situation' in Herman Bianchi, Mario Simondi and Ian Taylor (eds) *Deviance and Control in Europe*, London/New York: John Wiley.

Cohen, Stanley (1972) *Folk Devils and Moral Panics: the making of the Mods and Rockers*, London.

Currie, Elliott (1990) 'Crime and Free Market Society: Lessons from the United States', unpublished lecture given to the International Conference on Crime and Policing, Islington, London.

Currie, Elliott (1996) 'Is America really winning the war against crime and should Britain follow its example?', NACRO 30th Anniversary Lecture, London: National Association for the Care and Resettlement of Offenders.

Davis, Mike (1990) *City of Quartz: Excavating the Future in Los Angeles*, London: Verso.

della Porta, Donatella (1996) 'The System of Corrupt Exchange in Local Government' in Stephen Gundle and Simon Parker (eds) *The New Italian Republic: from the fall of the Berlin Wall to Berlusconi*, London: Routledge.

della Porta, Donatella (1997) 'The Vicious Circle of Corruption in Italy' in Donatella Della Porta and Yves Mény (eds) *Democracy and Corruption in Europe*, London/Washington: Pinter.

Eco, Umberto (1985) *Travels in Hyper-reality* (translated by William Weaver), London: Picador (Secker and Warburg).

Eco, Umberto (1995) *Apocalypse Postponed* (translated by Robert Lumley), London: Flamingo (Harper Collins).

Group of Lisbon (1995) *Limits to Competition*, Cambridge, Mass./London: M.I.T. Press.

Habermas, Jurgen (1996) 'Interview' (by Mikael Carleheden and Rene Gabriels) in *Theory, Culture and Society* 13(3) (August): 1–18.

Hall, Stuart, Clarke, John, Critcher, Charles, Jefferson, Tony and Roberts, Brian (eds) (1978) *Policing the Crisis: Mugging, the State and Law and Order*, London: Macmillan.

Havel, Václav (1996) 'The Hope for Twilight Europe' in *New York Review of Books* Vol. XLIII No. 8 (20 June): 38–41.

Jacques, Martin (1995) 'The Asian Century' in *Demos* 6: 6–8.

Judt, Tony (1996) 'Europe: the Grand Illusion' in *New York Review of Books* Vol. XLIII No.12 (11 July): 6–9.

Keat, Russell, and Abercrombie, Nick (eds) (1991) *Enterprise Culture*, London: Routledge.

Killias, Martin (1995) *European Sourcebook of Crime and Criminal Justice Statistics (Draft Model)*, Strasbourg: Council of Europe.

Kroker, Arthur and Kroker, Marilouise (eds) (1987) *Body Invaders: Panic Sex in America*, Montreal: New World Publishers.

Kroker, Arthur, Kroker, Marilouise and Cook, David (eds) (1989) *The Panic Encyclopedia*, Montreal: New World Publishers.

Luttwak, Edward (1995) 'Turbo-Charged Capitalism and its Consequences' in *London Review of Books* (2 November): 6–8.

Maspero, Francois (1990) *Les Passages de Roissy Express*, Paris: Editions du Seuil (English edition: *Roissy Express: a journey through the Paris Suburbs*, transl. Paul Jones, published by Verso 1994.

O'Neill, John (1994) *The Missing Child in Liberal Theory: towards a covenant theory of family, community, welfare and the civic state*, University of Toronto Press.

Packard, Vance (1961) *The Waste Makers*, London: Verso.

Parenti, Christian (1995) 'Urban Militarism' in *Z Magazine* (June): 47–52.

Pavarini, Massimo (1995) 'Working for Secure Cities in Emilia-Romagna' (interview conducted by Ian Taylor) in *ESRC Crime and Social Order Research Programme, Newsletter No. 1* (October): 3–4.

Piven, Frances Fox and Cloward, Richard (1982) *The New Class War: Reagan's Attack on the Welfare State and its Consequences*, New York: Pantheon

Punch, Maurice, Kolthoff, Emile, Van der Vijver, Kees and Van Vliet, Bram (1993) *Coping with Corruption in a Borderless World: Proceedings of the Fifth International Anti-Corruption Conference*, Deventer/Boston: Kluwer Law and Taxation Publishers.

Reiman, Jeffrey (1979) *The Rich get Rich and the Poor get Prison*, New York: John Wiley (Second edition 1984).

Stratton, Jon (1996) 'Serial Killing and the Transformation of the Social' in *Theory, Culture and Society* 13(1) (February): 77–98.

Taylor, Ian (1993) 'Driving the Vermin off the Streets' in *New Statesman and Society* (8 October): 16–18.

Wiles, Paul (1993) 'Ghettoization in Europe?' in *European Journal on Criminal Policy and Research* 1(1): 52–69.

2

CONFLICTS AND CONVERGENCES IN CRIMINOLOGY: BRINGING POLITICS AND ECONOMY BACK IN

Fritz Sack

Introduction

To recall the vulnerable status of criminology's claim to science is rather like taking owls to Athens. But that is what Jacek Kurczewski did in a presentation to the International Association of Criminology in 1988, commenting on the inadequacy of the concept of crime for dealing with the fundamental changes then occurring in Poland (Kurczewski 1988). I want to follow his example, some years later, in looking at the relationship between 'talk of crime' and the political transformations that have been occurring in my own country, Germany, in the period since 1990.

Before doing so however, let me indicate that we could be using many more examples – Somalia, Yugoslavia, Iraq, Iran, Brazil, South Africa, China, Zaire, Albania – I could continue this list – but where would I stop? As is obvious, I have set fire to all the neighbour's houses but not to my own. This, indeed, seems to me the real litmus test for my point: do we also have to include in this list countries within 'actually existing' capitalism? Isn't there a sense in which one could say that crime and law are no longer appropriate terms to describe and analyze their empirical reality? Isn't there a sense of cynicism when we look at the raw material which we criminologists receive from the penal law, and also when we reflect upon the data that *is not* produced in these societies as well?

Criminology provides partial answers to some of our anxieties about developments in these societies. However, it seldom interprets and theorizes them in a way that could be taken as full answers. Instead of enumerating these studies in any detail, I would prefer to describe two ongoing series of events in my own country that might help us arrive at some answers in a different way.

'Hate crimes': new questions and old answers

The first series of events to which I wish to draw attention are the crimes against foreigners that have occurred during the last four or five years all over the old and the new Germany, and which have received front-page and prime-time coverage in all parts of the world. Better known cities like Lübeck and Rostock, and lesser known places like Hoyerswerda, Mölln and Solingen have become infamous and synonymous with the idea of 'hate crimes'.[1]

The German official term for 'hate crimes' is 'fremdenfeindliche Straftaten' which could be translated as 'crimes against foreigners' and which are also sometimes defined as crimes that are motivated by the denial or contest of the victim's right to live or stay in Germany. As with hate crimes, the defining criterion of 'crimes against foreigners' is purely subjective. The categorization of an act as a 'crime against foreigners' does not depend on the act itself, nor solely on the status of the victim as a foreigner, but on circumstances and contexts that allow attribution of motives to the actor. Hostility against foreigners in this sense may be indicated by personal attacks and assaults committed by young people on unknown and unrelated foreigners, by acts of arson against buildings and shelters for foreigners or asylum seekers, or other self-evident examples. However, there is a wide range of less obvious incidents which leave considerable room for the exercise of discretionary power by the police and the authorities.

One aspect of this definitional process deserves special emphasis. The most important fact to be examined about an actor who has committed a crime against a foreigner, is his or her membership of, or affiliation with, right-wing or fascist movements. This, however, can easily be established only in cases of those tightly organized right-wing movements which have a formal membership, written programmes etc. Such connections become more difficult to identify, the more that acts and crimes of racism and xenophobia have to be considered as situationally-induced behaviour based upon underlying 'subterranean' values, widespread within society, and providing easy 'techniques of neutralization'. It should also be noted that senior politicans have a vested interest in reducing the profile of such crimes, resulting in a 'low record' of crimes against foreigners which follows from a systematic underreporting of these crimes, estimated at between about 25 to 30 per cent.[2]

There was a sudden and dramatic increase in crimes against foreigners very soon after German unification in 1993, but also a sharp reduction in subsequent cases, as shown in Table 2.1.

There is no easy explanation for these developments. Geographical distribution of incidents does not show a higher relative incidence of these crimes in the new Länder, as is sometimes believed, nor does the social profile of 'hate criminals' show a disproportionate implication of lower-class persons. The decrease may partly be attributed to the response of the public to the initial set of figures in 1993 and the high profile incidents then being reported. In several big cities,

Table 2.1 Crimes against foreigners[3]

Types of crime	1992	1993	1994	1995	1996
Homicides	6	6	0	0	0
Attempted homicides	28	18	8	0	11
Bodily injuries	576	727	494	315	307
Arson	596	284	80	37	27
Other crimes	5120	5687	2908	1508	1887
All crimes	6336	6721	3491	2468	2232

such as Hamburg, Munich and Berlin, thousands of persons joined in 'candle chains' to demonstrate against spectacular incidents of racist crime.

On a more general level one might ask what criminology has to offer for the analysis of these incidences of crimes against foreigners. What else except this new name or concept of 'hate crimes' does criminology have at its disposal to deal with these criminal attacks on people who are foreign, strange, weak, handicapped, outsiders? Are we prepared to do more than count the acts; study the perpetrators according to the variables provided by biology, psychology, sociology and – more recently, biogenetics; try to identify among them retrospectively (prospectively would perhaps take us a little too much time), those who resist, desist or persist?[4] Do we have the conceptual tools to deal in scientific terms with the commonsense wisdom that there are 'actors behind' these actors? If we were able to identify such backstage actors we could at least administer to them all the instruments, tools and tests we have developed, to study the frontstage actors. This might sound to some readers a little bit too ironic, but the approach of some criminologists invites such an attitude.

Scepticism about criminology's role is still more appropriate if we look on foreigners not as victims but as perpetrators of crime. Crime committed by foreigners has been a permanent issue of public and political debate since Germany became a kind of 'unrecognized' immigration nation, with more than 5 million foreigners in residence, most of whom are denied most citizens' rights even if they have worked and lived in Germany for many years, and indeed even if they were born in Germany. In relation to this group of people living in Germany, the crime issue is a general and political rather than a criminological problem. The status of a foreign person living in Germany is much more affected by perceptions and realities of their involvement in crimes than that of native Germans. A whole series of empirical criminological studies have been conducted to compare rates of crime of native Germans and foreigners. Some of these have stressed the higher incidence of crime behaviour among foreigners, while others have highlighted the differential treatment and visibility of foreigners within the criminal justice system.

I have raised various questions which I believe point to 'blind spots' on the criminological landscape. Is criminology part and parcel of the mentioned 'actors behind' the actually incriminated actors? I know that I am stretching the concept of 'actor' to a point that the more legally-minded readers may find shocking and hair-raising – but has criminology by adapting itself to the legal concept of crime complied too far with the normative version of action as defined in the penal law? Wouldn't criminology profit more from the conceptual tools of action and agency theory that have been developed in the social sciences in the last decade in the works of authors like Giddens, Bourdieu, Joas, or White (1992), to mention just a few of those who have pushed theoretical and empirical research in this area beyond the limits of Weber and the voluntarism of Parsons?

Crimes of 'transaction': limits of criminology

Let me now turn to the second set of events that Germany is experiencing since the fall of the Berlin wall – socio-political change and crime.

What can be observed in the new parts of Germany with respect to rising crime rates and a growing fear of crime in the population[5] has been 'commonsense' to criminologists since Quetelet, Lassagne and Durkheim; crime is normal and has regularities related to the specific structures of society. My argument, however, is not primarily related to this 'normal' process of the increase in crime according to the iron laws of Quetelet and Durkheim. Nonetheless, some rough ideas about the magnitude of official figures may help the reader to contextualize the whole story of the crime problem in unified Germany. In Table 2.2 I have listed some overall figures for crime in selected years before and after unification that show the tremendous growth of crime in the new Länder.

As can be seen from Table 2.2, the general increase in crime during the last 30 years in the Federal Republic parallels the pattern in all capitalist societies of the West. Of greater interest is the growth rate of crime for the new parts of Germany. For this purpose one needs some kind of crime measure that refers to the former

Table 2.2 Offences known to the police in Germany

Year	Total offences (in 100,000)	Crime rates (offences per 100,000 pop.)
1963	1.68	2.914
1973	2.560	4.131
1983	4.345	7.074
1994	6.538	8.038
1994 (o.L.)	*	7.665
1994 (n.L.)	*	9.784
1995	6.668	8.179
1995 (o.L.)	*	7.774
1995 (n.L.)	*	10.094

* The figures are drawn from 'Polizeiliche Kriminalstatistik Bundesrepublik Deutschland', ed. by the Bundeskriminalamt, Wiesbaden. These generally refer to the Federal Republic, *except for the years 1994 and 1995, where 'o.L.' means 'old Länder' and 'n.L.' designates the 'new Länder'*.

GDR. Though for obvious reasons such a measure is difficult to arrive at, there are safe grounds for the guess that the crime rate in the former GDR was far below 2,000, and that this means that the crime rate in the new Länder has grown within a couple of years by three to five times. To my knowledge there has never been a similar growth-rate of crime in any other country of the world, except, of course, the other ex-socialist countries. What is, however, unique and exceptional for Germany is demonstrated by the comparison of the respective crime rates for the two parts of the country in 1994 and 1995. The overall crime rate in the new Länder exceeds that of the old Länder in 1994 by 27.6 per cent and this gap has been further widened in 1995 (29.8 per cent).

Tempting as it might be to speculate on the implications and consequences of this dramatic change in the level of crime in the new parts of Germany,[6] I shall refrain from doing so and turn to another still more intriguing aspect of the problem. What I want to draw criminologists' attention to is what I would call a certain surplus rate of crime in these regions which will escape the notice of 'book-keeping' criminology.[7] These crimes don't show up in our criminological laboratories, in our survey work or other data, be they cross-sectionally or longitudinally generated. They are not part of the 'narratives' of criminology.

I would suggest calling them transaction crimes, in the double sense of the political and economic meaning of the concept of 'transaction'. An even better term might be 'opportunity' crimes, which fits well with the grammar of both economic and criminology. I refer to crimes that are related to these unprecedented social, political and, above all, economic transformations. These crimes range from daily frauds to abuse of trust, ignorance, fear and uncertainty. These crimes extend upward to the top-level crimes of the soldiers of fortune, gold diggers and – to use a term from Merton's famous anomie theory – robber barons who dominate the process of privatization.[8]

The ugly side of this process of transformation has clear moral implications. In the name of the moral superiority of the capitalist system we produce millions of broken identities and self-concepts, devalue skills, competences and biographies, terminate careers, and destroy the hopes and expectations stimulated in the first place. This process is occurring to an unprecedented extent – as the historical process of political and economic transformation is itself unprecedented. I think everybody would agree on the paradox that inside the morally corrupted world of real socialism there existed thousands of small moral worlds populated with millions of people with untainted moral integrity whose sense of social justice is now hurt again, and to an unprecedented extent.[9]

There is one specific aspect of the destruction of life-worlds in the former GDR that needs special emphasis because of its official and legal nature. The 'Treaty of Unification' that was signed between the West German government and the freely-elected East German government that existed in the months between March and October 1990 contained the very significant principle of restitution before compensation. This principle turned out to be disastrous for more than two million people in the new Länder. It gave to persons who had escaped from the GDR (mainly before the construction of the wall in 1961) the right to retrieve their state-confiscated property from those East Germans who meanwhile had been granted the right to use this abandoned property. According to this law, many East Germans have lost their homes and private houses and many others are still threatened by it, with many conflicting claims still being tested in the courts.

The last Prime Minister of the GDR, a Christian Democrat, has meanwhile called this new law the biggest and most damaging mistake made in the process of German unification. The whole moral, even perverse, dimension of this rule was revealed when one realizes that people who were glad to have crossed the Iron Curtain to participate in the West German 'economic miracle', could now represent themselves as 'victims', whereas the East Germans who had used the property in good faith and arranged their own and their families' lives around it were removed and 'expelled' from *their* own life-world.[10]

How could one translate these effects and consequences of the transformation process into a criminological 'grammar'? Though I have talked about 'transaction' or 'opportunity' 'crimes', there will be contradictions and oppositions to this suggestion, at least by those readers who stick to a positivistic and legalistic position. One could ask, in order to stay in the realm of criminology, whether this massive process of victimization could be treated as a case for criminology's latest offspring, i.e. for victimology?

Or do we have to leave the arena of criminology altogether? Before taking some steps in that direction in my last section, I would like to introduce an idea that I have taken from Charles Tilly's extensive studies and publications on modern West European history during the last two centuries, especially on the mechanisms and processes of nation-building and state formation.

Tilly distinguishes two opposite models for the birth period and circumstances of state building which deserve being quoted to a criminological public, not least because they are cast in the words of our discipline:

> If protection rackets represent organized crime at its smoothest, then . . . state making – quintessential protection rackets with the advantage of legitimacy – qualify as *our largest examples of organized crime*. At least for the European experience of the last few centuries, a portrait . . . of state makers as coercive and self-seeking entrepreneurs bears a far greater resemblance to the facts than do its chief alternatives: the idea of a social contract, the idea of an open market in which operators of . . . states offer services to willing consumers, the idea of a society whose shared norms and expectations call forth a certain kind of government (emphasis added).
>
> (Tilly 1985: p. 169)

Misleading and risky, sometimes even irresponsible as analogies and comparisons always are, and despite the fact that history never repeats itself (except, as

Marx once observed with respect to French history, as a farce): don't we have to transcend the limits of criminology in trying to analyse the forms of 'socio-political change' that produce state-market relationships akin to organized crime?

The question is rhetorical, of course. But it has considerable consequences for criminology as a scientific enterprise. The tools and the competence of criminology are restricted to and imprisoned within the narrow walls of normal, peaceful and consensual times and societies – rare instances, indeed. Anthropologists examining this state of affairs within criminology would probably identify a condition of scientific ethnocentrism. Such a criticism would explain very well why criminology shows so much reluctance to engage with, and has so many difficulties in analysing, the terrain of social reality on which crime meets politics and vice versa.

Criminology meets economics, or 'from P.C. to E.C.'

Or should I say: where crime meets economics? I think it important to remark on a theoretical issue that I consider one of the most trenchant though least discussed and still less resolved, analytical problems in and for criminology.

To begin with a widely accepted truism: it is increasingly the case that economic reason wins over political reason, and that regulation by the market increasingly replaces regulation by the state. This phenomenon is evident in all areas of politics and state activity. It is this evolution of late 'real capitalist' societies which was alluded to in an article in the *New York Times* of 12 January 1993 under the title 'From P.C. to E.C. – from political to economic correctness' (Warde 1995).

The field that criminology deals with is by no means excluded from the influence of economic and market forces, as has recently been shown by Nils Christie (1993). Most visibly and significantly, this is true in those parts of the criminal justice system where the principles of the rule of law are at their most weak, i.e., in its entrance and in its exit institutions, in the police and in prison. This is evidenced by the massive development of market structures and services in these two areas in recent years.

How can we interpret and theorize this development? What does the growing intrusion of economic and market rationality into all kinds of areas of social and moral life mean for the type of society in which we are living or to which we are heading to? I would like to argue *against* a widespread (often more implicit than explicit) view that fails to make a decisive distinction between the market and the state. By this I mean that there is a growing tendency to conceive of the market and the state simply as two different – more or less exchangeable – systems or principles of social regulation or social control. In terms of functional structuralism they are considered and conceived of as functional alternatives. The choice between these two modes of regulation should be grounded on nothing other than considerations of expediency, efficiency or cost-benefit-relations.

In my view, this perspective ignores a distinction between the two modes of regulation that is of vital theoretical importance. The state and the law as the main single mechanism of government is fundamental to all our conceptions, convictions and traditions of a moral enterprise.[11] However, as scholars as various as Smith, Bentham, Marx, Durkheim, Weber and many others have shown, whatever characteristics the market has, 'moral enterprise' is not significant among them. Substituting 'market costs' for the state and law is equivalent to weakening and dropping the moral mode of social regulation. Imposing an economic perspective on social relations means undermining and eroding the vigour and force of moral obligations.

To return to the case of Germany's contemporary crime problems: the outcry among the people of the new parts of Germany might, therefore, be explained by a fatal and even tragic misunderstanding. A well-known dissident from former East Germany, Bärbel Bohley, made the embittered and depressing statement: 'What we wanted was justice, what we received was the state rule of law', thereby capturing a sentiment widely shared among East Germans

With her statement, Bohley gave expression to her deep disappointment about the inadequacy of the new law with respect to injustice and the harm the GDR had done to its people. The people of the GDR had hoped for a new moral and political order, but instead have received a new economic order which has an institutionalized indifference towards moral issues.

What does this all mean for criminology? Isn't this development accompanied by a kind of feeling that the term 'crime' has lost its emphatic moral sense, that it is an odd and old-fashioned term that no longer fits with the type of social relations and collective existence we are both subjected to, and reproduce, in our daily praxis and routines?

I am trying here to state, in different terms, what other colleagues (e.g. Sessar 1993), have highlighted as a growing discrepancy between the penal law model of adequate reaction to crime and the victim's and general public's model of reaction. Isn't criminology faced in any case with a growing disregard for its scientific output by those it addresses – policy makers, victims, perpetrators, the public? Doesn't this represent a situation that requires different reactions (other than the ritualized admission that there are still many blind spots and gaps to be cleared up and closed in our criminological knowledge)? This admission is all too hastily and equally ritualistically accompanied by the assurance that criminology is still on the 'right path' and merely needs more money and more resources for essentially doing more of the same? Can we not find answers other than these self-referential reactions that in the long run may simply produce a situation of ever more 'knowledge' for ever fewer listeners and users? A situation that might well ultimately transcend any sense of scientific discourse and require us to take refuge in the language of poetry, fiction, comedy or tragedy or a mixture of all of these?

To some, these questions might sound as if they arise out of those discourses which have come together under the umbrella of postmodernism. It is certainly true that post-modern thought has arrived at last at the shores of criminology, although this is not yet very evident in the average literature and textbooks of criminology.[12] It is most evident in the proliferating area of feminist studies in criminology.

Criminology should have a vital interest in learning from the attempts by scholars in different disciplines to grasp a new understanding of social developments that are changing the type of society we live in. Sociologists have moved – perhaps too early and too submissively – beyond concepts like class, status and stratification and talk all too exclusively about risk and new dimensions and levels of individualism that reshape the macro-structures of society as well as the micro-structures of our lives.

However, criminology need not only be the receiving partner in such a discussion about these pervasive changes in modern societies which surely have to do in the first place with the penetration of economic thinking and rationality in society. The contributions it has to offer are tremendous. It seems worth reminding ourselves that the penal law and crime played a paradigmatic role for sociological theory, notably for functional structuralism in the version from Durkheim to Parsons (though the emphasis placed on economic reasoning and structures by Durkheim was significantly lost in the work of Parsons).[13] The importance of the dimension of economics is currently finding renewed recognition (Christie 1993; Cohen 1985; Garland 1990).

If one contrasts this view and the implications of the role of economics with respect to the social order of modern societies, with the view that one traditionally finds in criminology, there are differences that are hard to reconcile. There is no need to recapitulate the key role that economic factors have played in the history of criminology – first and foremost as an 'independent variable' for the explanation of crime. Taylor (1994) has recently recaptured the essential aspects of this criminological tradition and convincingly underscored the need for its revitalization.

I would argue that during the last two decades there has been a sort of subversive invasion of economic reasoning in criminology and in criminal policy that has not attracted the recognition that it requires until very recently. This invasion takes the form of the resurrection of the classical utilitarian model of 'economic-man' and the renewal of imperialistic claims of an all-embracing nature, to explain human behaviour for the purposes of regulation and governing. This development is variously called neo-utilitarianism, new political economy or in its most de-politicized and theoretically pretentious version presents itself as 'rational choice theory'.

We can briefly identify just some of the ways in which this is happening. First of all, criminal behaviour and criminal policy are among the favourite areas of human behaviour to which rational choice theory has been applied. The seminal paper of Gary S. Becker on 'Crime and Punishment: An Economic Approach' (1968), which released and triggered a host of empirical and theoretical studies, set the tone and paved the way in this direction. Becker explicitly claims – as do all the later authors who use this approach – to be in a position to supersede all other criminological theorizing,[14] from Sutherland to Merton to Howard S. Becker to Gottfredson and Hirschi, and so on.

The same holds true – and this leads me to an author who has interfered in criminological thinking even more and with greater influence – for the political scientist James Q. Wilson whose famous distinction between the search for root causes of crime and those approaches that are politically and pragmatically feasible, aims at debunking criminological *theories* of all kinds.[15] The rationale for this approach was developed most clearly in a collection of articles more than twenty years ago (J. Q. Wilson 1975) and has been still more explicitly elaborated and emphasized in Wilson and Herrnstein's bestseller *Crime and Human Nature* (1985), which represents (on the basis of an eclectically collected mass of empirical criminological results), a kind of theoretical reasoning which ultimately falls within an essentially rational choice perspective.

The main impact, however, that the *The Reasoning Criminal* (Clarke and Cornish 1986) – has had in criminological thinking, concerns applied criminology, in the field of criminal policy, the 'hidden and real curriculum' of the discipline. The return and resurrection of classical thinking in penal policy, known, and criticized – among others and most vividly perhaps by Christie's *Limits to Pain* (1980) – as neo-classicism, was in theoretical terms an offspring and a reinforcement of rational choice thinking. It was the basis for the huge body of deterrence research in criminology during the 1970s and the 1980s.

Since deterrence theory (despite its political attraction and convenience) had to struggle against its own self-evident failure, criminal policy has moved on to a new comprehensive strategy – accompanied and again encouraged by the behavioural model of 'homo-economicus' and the rational actor. The glamorous new term and policy in the area is, as is well known, 'prevention'[16] which, for the most part, boils down to increasing the costs of crime by 'target hardening', safety devices for the protection of property, environmental and architectural design, creating 'defensible spaces' and establishing all kinds of other forms of situational measures of prevention.

In my view, criminology should certainly confront rational choice theory. It should insist that a 'political economy of crime and crime control' cannot be constructed simply by reiterating what is known about the relationship between economic factors and indicators of crime or crime control. This has its uses, but it would be far more worthwhile and cost-effective if we also emphasized the need to study the connections between wealth and crime, rather than the relationship between poverty and crime, which has been the favourite issue for criminologists interested in the impact of economic factors on crime. I would also argue that we have to go beyond Bonger's and van Kan's economic analyses of crime at the beginning of the century, albeit their studies were based on a far more complex and culturally sensitive model of interrelationships between the worlds of economy and crime than those studies which break the relationships down to links between systems of variables.

The theoretical and empirical efforts which have been and must yet be made, toward the establishment of a 'political economy of crime and crime control' have to build on this legacy, but they also have to transcend it. A first necessary step in this direction would have to be to 'deconstruct' the abstractions of the concepts and categories of economic discourse and translate them into the grammar of social relations and interactions. This would provide a closer and clearer examination of the compatibility of the 'logic' of economic or market relations with the relational logic that exists in the life domains beyond the economy.

In conclusion, let me add two further general remarks concerning my criticism of the way criminology deals with the vital relationship between crime and economics. The dividing lines between the various discourses that exist in criminology (or indeed, other social sciences) can no longer be cast in socialist or bourgeois terms. The ultimate reference point – and the base line for my arguments – is the still unfinished road to political and individual freedom. This must go beyond the freedom to invest, to allocate economic resources and capital, and to consume.

If there is any lesson which has to be retained from the global failure and collapse of communist socialism, it is surely the conviction that the state has to be excluded from being the first and foremost agency for achieving this freedom. The achievement of freedom has never followed a line from the top to the bottom, but always from the bottom to the top. Freedom is still a sharply and decisively divided good – between and within societies. To extend freedom and render it accessible to larger parts of any society and to encourage it in a greater number of societies, would require us to introduce democratic and participatory measures and rules into economic institutions and decisions.

Admittedly, there is nothing new in this idea. Any sense of over-familiarity which it conveys to the reader might be due to its seemingly utopian character. However, what invites some optimism is this. The principle that was at the heart of the driving forces which have changed our world in the last 200 years was an economic one. There is no doubt that this principle continues to operate at an ever-accelerating rate and that it lies behind the deep transformations we are experiencing in our societies today. There is, therefore, reason to believe and to hope that our capitalist economic structures and institutions will eventually be subject to the same processes of dissolution, destruction, and transformation that they have so successfully released, organized and achieved in the first 200 years of their influence.

I am aware that some readers might have preferred more 'sound' facts and data and welcomed more answers and fewer questions in this paper. In response, I would like to conclude with a quotation from a scholar who works in a similarly fact-based discipline. In his inaugural lecture at the illustrious Collège de France, the holder of the chair for ancient history, Paul Veyne, described his conception 'doing history' in the following way:

> one cannot resist the idea ... that in historiography the questions that
> are sociological are more important than the answers that are empirical.

... In other words, it is more important to have ideas than to know truths; ... It amounts to setting an end to naivety and to realize that what is existing does not need to exist (transl. by the author).

(Veyne 1988: 42)

Could this not also be good advice for 'doing criminology' in the future?

Notes

1 'Hate crime', or as it is also described, 'bias crime', is a category in penal law rather than a criminology concept. Though a rather ambiguous and easily mishandled term, it is used as an aggravating motivational qualification in respect of certain crimes against members of minority groups 'motivated entirely or in part by the victims difference' (McDevitt 1993: 356)

2 The figures about the degree of underreporting are based on a private communication from the special branch of the Bundeskriminalamt.

3 The figures have been made available by the special branch of the Bundeskriminalamt. They are published as Parliamentary Documents (Bundestagsdrucksache) only. Another source that gives some different figures because of a different reporting system is the annual report of the Federal Office for the Protection of the Constitution (Bundesverfassungsschutzamt).

4 These terms, as is well known, belong to the conceptual and political gains that have been produced by the most recent and methodologically most sophisticated offspring of positivist and penal law oriented criminology which is, of course, the booming and money-raising research area of cohort analysis and longitudinal studies. Apparently the worldwide increase of violence has delivered criminologists a new password for releasing large amounts of funding to follow this theoretically unsound route for criminological research, as can be gathered from a recent review symposium in *Contemporary Sociology* on a US government sponsored report of high-ranking criminologists and other scientific experts on 'Understanding and Preventing Violence' which is additionally upgraded by its publication under the auspices of the National Academy of Sciences (Kornblum *et al.* 1993).

5 Though there has been an increase in the crime rates during the last years of the former GDR there is a growth rate of crime in these new parts of Germany, as, of course, in the other ex-socialist countries, since the fall of the wall that unsurprisingly is beyond the limits we are accustomed to in all western democracies. This development is also reflected in the inflationary rise of fear of crime in the new parts of Germany. Since details cannot be displayed here, the interested reader might at least be referred to some relevant sources. F. v.d. Heide and E. Lautsch (1991) give an interesting view on the development of the crime rates during the last five years of the former GDR. The change in crime rates since the unification is treated by K. Sessar (1993), G. Kaiser (1994) and K. Boers (1996). For reasons of considerable discrepancies between fear-of-crime rates between persons from the new Länder and those from the old Länder as well as between victimization risks and fear-of-crime rates there has been a special research interest and emphasis on the fear-of-crime issue. S. Babl (1993), K.-H. Reuband (1993) and W. Bilsky (1996) concentrate on this, while K. Boers *et al.* (1994) and G. Kaiser and J.-M. Jehle (1995) present the overall results of some victimization studies.

6 The most frequently given answer to the rise of crime in the ex-socialist countries is taken from modernization theory. As I have argued elsewhere (Sack 1997), the reference to this body of sociological thinking does not so much qualify as explanatory but has to be understood as highly political in the sense of diverting criticism from the (capitalist) present by making the (socialist) past responsible.

7 To do empirical research on these social facts would require criminology to leave behind and transcend the categories, methodological devices and empirical procedures we are taught to use in representing the world(s) of crime and criminals. Notably criminology would have to take seriously 'crime' as perceived and applied in everyday behaviour and interaction.

8 A chapter of any full-length text on the criminological aspects of this process of privatization, if it is ever written, would have to center around the transactions initiated and arranged by probably the biggest holding company that ever existed in human history. The 'Treuhandanstalt' which was established – and dominated – by the West German government soon after the collapse of the GDR was charged with the transformation of all state-owned property of the former GDR into private property rights. The 'Treuhandanstalt' has now finished its main job and has been formally dissolved though there still exist regional successor institutions. Its most significant net result consists in the fact that around 90 per cent of the created new property rights belong to persons and companies coming from the West. What comes to one's mind when trying to find an analogous process of historical scope and range, including its criminological implications, is (in a reversed and adapted sense), Marx's famous analysis of the 'so-called original accumulation of capital', *Capital* (vol. 1, chapter 24).

9 Criminology, and probably social science in general, may lack the conceptual and linguistic tools adequately analyzing and representing these social facts and products. It seems as if one has to look for a different generic type of texts to grasp the sense and the structure of these phenomena. An excellent case in point is an essay in the newsmagazine *Der Spiegel* that is written by a former dissident of the GDR, now a member of the federal parliament (Weiss 1993).

10 The East German writer, Daniela Dahn (1994) has provided details of the magnitude of the problem and the destructive effects restitution cases have had on the lives of individual persons, families and whole communities. She also points to the cynical fact that West Germans may claim back their former property whereas East Germans who have lived, for instance, as Jews in the GDR are now, for procedural reasons, refused any right to lay claim on their property thought to have been 'aryanized' by the Nazis.

11 To be sure, this does not hold true for radical constructionist positions, such as systems theory in the version of Niklas Luhmann, who would take and interpret the grammar of morality in functionalist terms and would not assign to it any ontological or essentialist sense. Notably in his many publications on the sociology of law he insists on the separation of law and morality, on the indifference of law towards moral criteria going so far as to assume that law even 'produces' and engenders immoral effects and results (Luhman 1995).

12 Suffice it to mention the following: Nelken (1994), who has brought a fine collection of articles that are heavily inspired by post-modern thought; Morrison (1995), who deserves mention for his textbook in criminology that takes post-modern thinking as a vantage point to discuss the analytical structure and the history of criminology.

13 Durkheim's concept of anomie was virtually based on the threat of economic primacy in modern societies. It was reformulated by Merton in his famous anomie theory in a

way in which the economic dimension almost disappeared – as I have tried to show elsewhere (Sack 1997).

14 Posner (1995: 3–4), one of the most influential proponents of the Chicagoan economic imperialism in the social sciences, bullishly claims that: 'A fatalistic mood has overcome the discipline of criminology, which has failed to come up with solutions or even melioratives to the problem of crime', after having discarded as futile for 'lowering the US crime rate' the 'rehabilitative approach' as well as the attempt 'to eliminate the fundamental causes of crime'.

15 It seems worth noting and remembering that Wilson's attack on criminological wisdom appeared as early as 1975 when he first published his *Thinking About Crime* which, incidentally, was really directed more against the policy proposals of the legendary 'President's Commission on Law Enforcement and Administration of Justice' than against criminology itself. I discussed this work two decades ago (Sack 1978).

16 Of course, this is no new concept. On the contrary, for penal law and criminology, prevention has been the leading idea of modern criminal law since Beccaria and the Enlightenment. Yet there is something decisively new about the way prevention is used and defined during the last two decades in western societies. Prevention has taken on a more pro-active, offensive and intrusive quality which for the realm of penal law can best be observed with respect to the changing and proliferating role the police have been granted in all democratic societies. Though there exists a vast amount of litera-ture on this process, criminology and penal policy have not yet really come to grips with it. I have tried elsewhere to spell out some reflections on this development (Sack 1993).

References

Babel, Susanne, 'Mehr Unzufriedenheit mit der öffentlichen Sicherheit im vereinten Deutschland. Ein Zusammenstellung objektiver und subjektiver Indikatoren zur Kriminalität'. In: *Gewalt in der Gesellschaft. Eine Dokumentation zum Stand der Sozialwis-senschaftlichen Forschung seit 1985*, Bonn 1993, pp. 61–73.

Becker, Gary S. 'Crime and Punishment: An Economic Approach'. In *Journal of Political Economy* 76, 1968, p. 169–217.

Bilsky, Werner, 'Die Bedeutung von Furcht vor Kriminalität in Ost und West'. In: Monatsschrift für Kriminologie und Strafrechtsreform 79, l996, pp. 357–371.

Boers, Klaus, 'Sozialer Umbruch und Kriminalität in Deutschland'. In: *Monatsschrift für Kriminologie un Strafrechsreform* 79, 1996, pp. 314–337.

Boers, Klaus, Uwe Ewald, Hans-Jürgen Kerner, Erwin Lautsch and Klaus Sessar, eds, *Sozialer Umbruch und Kriminalität*. Vol. 2: *Ergebnisse einer Kriminalitätsbefragung in den neuen Bundesländern*. Bonn 1994.

Christie, Nils, *Limits to Pain*, Oslo 1980.

Christie, Nils, *Crime Control As Industry. Towards GULAGS, Western Style?*, Oslo 1993.

Clarke, Ronald, and Derek Cornish, *The Reasoning Criminal*, Berlin – New York 1986.

Cohen, Stanley, *Visions of Social Control. Crime, Punishment and Classification*, Oxford and Cambridge l985.

Dahn, Daniela, *Westwärts und nicht vergessen Vom Unbehagen in der Einheit*, Berlin 1996.

Forrester, Viviane, *L'horreur économique*, Paris (Fayard) 1996.

Garland, David, *Punishment and Modern Society. A Study in Social Theory*, Oxford 1990.

v.d. Heide, Frank, and Erwin Lautsch, 'Entwicklung der Straftaten und der Aufklärung-squote in der DDR von 1985 bis 1989'. In: *Neue Justiz* 1991, pp. 11–15.

Kaiser, Günter, 'Entwicklung der Kriminalität in Deutschland seit dem Zusammenbruch des realen Sozialismus'. In *Zeitschrift für die gesamte Strafrechtswissenschaft* 106, 1994, pp. 469–501.

Kaiser, Günter, and Jörg-Martin Jehle, eds, *Kriminologische Opferforschung. Neue Perspektiven und Erkenntnisse. Teilband 2: Verbrechensfurcht und Opferwerdung.* Heidelberg 1995.

Kornblum, William, Ruth Horowitz and Travis Hirschi, Review symposium on: 'Understanding and Preventing Violence', ed. by Albert J. Reiss, Jr., and Jeffrey A. Roth, Washington, D.C., 1993, in: *Contemporary Sociology* 22, 1993, pp. 344–350.

Kurczewski, Jacek, *Crime and Abuse of Power*, unpubl. paper, September 1988.

Luhmann, Niklas, 'Jenseits von Barbarei' In: N Luhmann, *Gesellschaftsstruktur und Semantik. Studien zur Wissenssoziologie der modernen Gesellschaft*, vol 4, Frankfurt 1995, pp. 138–150.

Marx, Karl, *Der 18te Brumaire des Louis Napoleon, Marx Engels Werke*, Bd. 8, Berlin 1960 (zuerst 1852).

McDevitt, Jack, Review of: Gregory M Herek and Kevin T Berrill, 'Hate Crimes: Confronting Violence against Lesbians and Gay Men', Newbury Park, CA, 1992. In: *Contemporary Sociology* 22, 1993, p. 356ff.

Morrison, W. (1995) *Theoretical Criminology: from Modernity to Post-Modernism*, London: Cavendish.

Nelken, D. (1994) *The Futures of Criminology*, London: Sage.

Posner, Richard A., 'The most punitive nation. A few modest proposals for lowering the US crime rate'. In: *The Times Literary Supplement*, 1 Sept. 1995.

Reuband, Karl-Heinz, 'Steigt in der Bundesrepublik die Verbrechensfurcht? Widersprüchliche Ergebnisse aus der neuen Umfrageforschung', In: Eva Kampmeyer and Jürgen Neumeyer, ed., *Innere Unsicherheit*, München 1993, S. 41–50.

Sack, Fritz, 'Probleme der Kriminalsoziologie'. In: René König, ed., *Handbuch der empirischen Sozialforschung*, vol. 12, 2nd enl. ed., Stuttgart 1978, pp. 192–492, 252ff.

Sack, Fritz, 'Strafrechtliche Kontrolle und Sozialdisziplinierung', in: D. Frehsee *et al.*, eds, *Strafrecht, soziale Kontrolle, soziale Disziplinierung, Jahrbuch für Rechtssoziologie und Rechtstheorie*, Bd. 15, 1993, pp. 16–45.

Sack, Fritz, 'Umbruch und Kriminalität – Umbruch als Kriminalität'. In: Klaus Sessar and Martin Holler, eds, *Kriminalität und die Umbruchsprozesse in Mittel- und Osteuropa. Eine Tagung*, Pfaffenweiler (Centaurus) 1997 (in press).

Sessar, Klaus, 'Crime Rate Trends Before and After the End of the German Democratic Republic'. In: Bilsky/Pfeiffer/Wetzels, eds, *Fear of Crime and Victimisation*, Stuttgart 1993, pp. 231–244.

Taylor, Ian. 'The Political Economy of Crime'. In: Mike Maguire, Rod Morgan and Robert Reiner, eds, *The Oxford Handbook of Criminology*, Oxford 1994, pp. 469–510.

Tilly, Charles, 'War Making and State Making as Organized Crime', in: Peter B. Evans, Dietrich Rueschemeyer and Theda Skocpol, eds, *Bringing the State Back In*, Cambridge University Press 1985, pp. 169–191.

Veyne, Paul, *Die Originalität des Unbekannten. Für eine andere Geschichtsschreibung*, Frankfurt 1988 (French original: *L'inventaire des différences*, Paris 1976).

Warde, I., 'Die Tyrannei des 'ökonomisch Korrekten'. In: *Le monde diplomatique – die tageszeitung/WoZ*, 12.5.1995, pp. 20/21.

Weiss, Konrad, 'Verlorene Hoffnung der Einheit'. In: *Der Spiegel* (46/1993) pp. 41–44.

Wilson, James Q., *Thinking about Crime*, New York 1985 (first publ. 1975).

Wilson, James Q., and Richard Herrnstein, *Crime and Human Nature*, New York 1985.

White, Harrison C., *Identity and Control: A Structural Theory of Social Action*, Princeton, N.J., 1992.

3

REMARKS ON SOCIAL CONTROL, STATE SOVEREIGNTY AND CITIZENSHIP IN THE NEW EUROPE[1]

Dario Melossi

In considering the question of social control in the New Europe, we should move from thinking of social control as an articulation of the many experiences of different European "States," to imagining social control as pertaining to a self-contained European political unity.

However, because such self-contained European political unity is in many respects a complete novelty, it is necessary to ask ourselves what political, social and economic project will be at the core of the New Europe and what the consequences will be from the perspective of social control.

In particular, the process of European construction is a process that is advancing together with the seeming decline of ideas of State and Sovereignty, ideas that are "withering away," I would submit, together with those European nation-states within which they first saw the light.

How can we conceptualize social control outside the figures of the State and Sovereignty? (I should hasten to add that I do not mean by this that we should think of social control as completely detached from its linkage with political power and the ability of that power to use coercive force.)

Here are a few important starting points toward answering such momentous questions:

1   From a sociological perspective, social control is foremost the ability to reproduce (or change) a system of social relationships, whether or not such system is represented within a set of legal norms.
2   A fundamental part of social control is to be found today in mechanisms of creation and maintenance of consensus, especially through the mass-media.
3   The creation of a real European unity and of a discourse of social control inherent therein, cannot be separated from the creation of a European Constitution, a European political system, and a European "public sphere" within which a common debate may be allowed to unfold.

4 Such public sphere is essential to the creation of a genuine European democracy.
5 The creation of a European citizenship both for intra- as well as extra-EU persons is inseparable from the process of European unification.

It is only within such wider processes of formation of a European polity that we can sensibly talk of social control at a European level.

Europe and the "withering away" of the "pale ghost"

It is a commonplace to hear statements today according to which the creation of a European Union would somehow limit the extent of individual states' sovereignties. I believe however that those who advance such a claim, fail to consider that, especially after World War II, Europeans have experienced a situation of limited sovereignty, with the United States exercising hegemonic power in its Western section, and the Union of Soviet Socialist Republics in its Eastern section. Whereas there is no doubt that the Western section showed much greater dynamism in proceeding toward a fully democratic mass-society of the kind that had been developing in the United States, it is hard to deny that there have been *de facto* constraints on European independence that made it quite difficult, for instance, for political Left parties in certain countries to reach positions of governmental power. At the same time, a related type of social control developed, the main characteristics of which have been increasing consumerism, advertising and technical potential for telecommunications. However, a coercive, State-centered system of social control, albeit not as apparent as in the Eastern section of Europe, was still very present.

I believe however that it was only with the dramatic turn of events of 1989 and the dissolution of the Soviet Union that finally the kind of social model that had been growing in the United States in the course of this century could be extended to Europe, reaching an unstable compromise with the political and cultural traditions of each European country.

Correspondingly, at the theoretical level, to the quickly changing Europe of the 1970s, Michel Foucault announced, in *Discipline and Punishment* (1975) and then especially in "La volonté de savoir" in *The History of Sexuality* (1976), that power should be considered from the perspective of its constitutive, and not merely censorial qualities, and that the concept of the State is basically an obstacle in thinking about power relationships. "In political thought and analysis we still have not cut off the head of the king" (Foucault 1976: 88). It seems to me that this invitation by Foucault acquired its full actuality with the breakdown of the Soviet Union in 1989, a breakdown which, by putting an end to the cold war, opened up unexpected avenues of democratic development, not only, as was obvious and as everybody noted, in Eastern Europe, but also in Western Europe (and probably, eventually, in the United States themselves!). Only after the blackmail of a nuclear holocaust had been at least partially removed, could the question of the creation of consensus, and government by public opinion, so to speak, occupy center-stage once again.

What is going on today in Europe, within each European country and across Europe, about control of mass telecommunications, for instance, may be understood only on that historical backdrop. In this connection, it is quite useful to recall the events of August 1991 in Moscow, when the hard-liners tried to play their last card against Yeltsin. On the one hand, one could watch on TV the tanks rolling down the main boulevards of Moscow, on the other hand a handsome journalist of CNN was interviewing Boris Yeltsin holed up in the building of the Russian Parliament. The line from one of Bertolt Brecht's most famous short poems, "tanks have one defect, they need a driver" (Brecht 1938: 289) had never been truer. Unfortunately for the Moscow putschists, and lovers of open coercion in general, tank drivers watch TV, just as their parents, friends, and superior officers do.

Of course in Western Europe there has also been a process of political unification under way, so that the old coercive State-centered style of social control was becoming obsolete, and a new form of social control was being prepared, not only because of long-term historical developments, but also because the European Union was on the agenda.

Indeed, the disorganization of European society, and societies, is approaching levels that had not been attained in a long time. If some time ago it was European unity itself which seemed to be once again in question, a longer-term trend seems to be an increasing disorganization of the old nation-states, corroded by internal conflict and corruption (for each European state the list would be long, and even if Italy would probably have a good chance of winning in such a dubious race, everybody could contribute a "cahier de doléances" for their favorite country).

All in all, there is no reason to see such developments as too worrisome: it is only natural that, with the emergence of a new over-arching political entity, Europe, the old political entities, the nation-states, somehow reduce and atrophy. It is also quite natural that, correspondingly, the *local* political communities, freed from the century-long suffocating influence of political organizations usually modelled on Napoleonic centralism, become politically more active and in some cases even insurgent. At the same time, a scenario has been suggested according to which, especially because of dire economic necessities, the European Union would be "irreversible" (Schaefner 1991). Whereas such a scenario may accurately reflect the opinion of business leaders, it also shows severe underevaluation of subjectivity or, in less abstract terms, of the role of culture. The fact is that, once we were brought to consider a unified Europe as a reality impinging on our lives and not only as a fashionable idea, we slowly came to realize that there is no *cultural* unity of Europe, indeed there is no European *cultural identity*.

Having lived in the United States for quite some time, it is difficult for me not to look at these problems in a comparative vein. In the history of Europe, there is, at the roots of national identities, the idea of the nation-state and the central, massive presence of the state. In American history, on the contrary, we find an idea of nation, to be sure, but its support system is not so much "the state" – a word that only American political scientists and philosophers may happen to use in the same way in which the average European does – but the law, the economy, and public opinion (de Tocqueville 1835), in other words what we usually refer to as "civil society." This should of course not surprise anybody who is aware of the intense Utopian nature of the American origins. All in all, the Puritans from England wanted to build a *New* England also in the sense that was to be a *new* society, built according to their religious inspiration (Erikson 1966: 68). All voluntary immigrant groups have somehow related to this idea of America. The pioneering project of a "New England Way" has produced a lasting impact on American identity and has become a fundamental element in the connecting fabric of the American covenant (still today, in spite of all the talk of multiculturalism . . .).

Maybe here there is an interesting and useful lesson for the "new" Europeans. When we look for our identity in the past, we regularly come out empty-handed, or holding materials we would rather not have found (Smith 1992; Schlesinger 1992; Balibar 1991; Losano 1991) It might be useful therefore to try and reformulate the question: why should we look for identity in the past and not in the future – why shouldn't identity be *constituted* around a European project (instead of the constitution of Europe having to rely on a pre-constituted identity)? Indeed, it has been noted by students of nationality that the past is always somehow reconstructed to be put to the service of a contemporary project (Anderson 1983, Hobsbawm and Ranger 1983). Should we not then make this conceptual trajectory explicit by recommending a project instead of a loyalty to the past? Even before Anderson's or Hobsbawm's contributions, it was quite clear that *socio-political-economic* projects and *national-political-constitutional* projects are always intertwined. The American Constitution was so analyzed in Charles Beard's classic An *Economic Interpretation of the Constitution of the United States* (1913), where the main federal institutional framework is reconstructed as an attempt by the Federalists to prevent what de Tocqueville would have called "the tyranny of the majority," an attempt, in other words, at limiting the harm that democracy may cause to the propertied classes. A more homely example is the case of the Northern Leagues in Italy today, where the push toward self-determination is dependent on economic and fiscal considerations made from the perspective of well-off economic strata in the North (*Telos* 1991–2). The very politico-constitutional structure of the state always embodies different roles and opportunities for different strata in society (Schaefner 1991: 692–3).

At the very least, if we really wanted to look into the past, we might want to look for our Utopian past, the project of that Europe of the future that was imagined as an alternative to the grim reality of war in the thinking of authors between the two wars, from Georg Simmel (1917) to the progressive European Federalism of Silvio Trentin's *Stato, Nazione, Federalismo* (1945) or Altiero Spinelli and Ernesto Rossi's *Manifesto di Ventotene* (1941). Trentin's *Stato Nazione Federalismo* (1945) was published in an underground edition just a few days before the liberation of Northern Italy in 1945, and a year after its author, who had come back from France to organize the resistance in the Venetian area and had been captured, died after being released from Fascist jails. In his work, Trentin had already identified in the doctrine of the state – with all its accompanying elements – one of the most reactionary features of European tradition and one of the legitimating ideologies of recurring European conflicts and miseries. He had developed an impassioned plea for a future federalist European structure able to put an end to the succession of devastating European wars. A federal political community should be seen accordingly as an alternative to the centralized nation-state, with its *authoritarian* (Kelsen 1924) and, as it would appear later on, *patriarchal* luggage (Pateman 1988; Melossi 1990: 72–82 and *passim*).

This federalist tradition has been revived recently in the elaboration of those who, for the first time, have merged the issue of *European* federalism with that of federalism *within* what used to be the individual, European, nation-state, like the Basque legal theorist Gurutz Jauregui Bereciartu:

> Human collectivities have created diverse structures for organizing themselves in response to the social, economic, and other necessities of the moment. The nation-state appeared as the juridico-political structure that was adequate for a determinate type of society . . . Today it is abundantly clear that the existence of the nation-state is increasingly less synonymous with independence. At present, the nation-states lack meaning. I refer to those already constituted as much as to those that wish to be. The present national problem in Europe regards not the creation of new states but the disappearance of the existing ones, a disintegration that, in fact, should be accompanied by . . . social and economic transformations.
>
> (Jauregui Bereciartu 1986: 164)

In fact, the search for a new way of political being in Europe is slowly leading to an obfuscation, if not an obsolescence, of the role of the old nineteenth-century nation-states, and to the emergence of new entities, carrying a national or quasi-national identity but not necessarily aspiring to statehood. The principles of subsidiarity and proportionality adopted in the proposal for a European Constitution[2] seem to suggest that faculties and powers that traditionally resided with states, are being redistributed among different political subjects, the European Union and the Regions. However, the old state-centered ideology is still present today both with those who think in terms of a "Europe of Fatherlands," as is typical of most European conservative forces, and also with those who would like to project the sinister shadow of a centralized, "Napoleonic" Euro-State on the new European polity.

In fact, a clear contradiction exists between the efforts directed at building a political union and those directed instead at respecting the principle of sovereignty of the old nation-states, that very few really want to question openly. This is of course a more general problem that legal theorists who have dealt with the question of the protection of other than state-recognized rights (human rights, rights of self-determination) have well pointed out (Luban 1987, Ferrajoli 1995). This is quite clear in the project of European Constitution. The principle of subsidiarity is proclaimed loudly (art.10) but concerns only the individual nation-states, not the national-regional entities that are constituted within each state, and that also should take advantage of the subsidiarity principle, with relevant consequences inside each state in its relationship to its internal Regions. Citizenship is attributed only to citizens of the member nation-states (art. 3); more courageous proposals to recognize a concept of European citizenship independent from individual national citizenships, a citizenship therefore that could be independently extended to individuals from non-member states, were shelved (European Parliament 1993; Imbeni 1994).

Citizenship, immigration, and the European Constitution

Indeed, the issue of citizenship, and the related question of immigration, are a sort of acid test for social control in Europe today. In the same way in which social control of crime is a dependent variable of the much broader issue of social control, so in Europe today social control of immigration – that is becoming central to European policies in more than one way (Waever *et al.* 1993; Pastore 1993) – is strictly related to the concept of social control that is going to prevail in Europe, i.e. the kind of social and political *constitution* that is going to prevail.

Many years ago, an American sociologist, Kai Erikson, wrote an important book on the sociology of deviance, *Wayward Puritans* (1966). In it, he described three "crime waves," and as many types of deviants, that had shaken New England Puritans in the seventeenth century, the "Antinomian" heretics, the Quakers, and the most famous, the Salem "witches." He connected each of these cases to a given historical situation of identity crisis in the new colony. His theory was that a community publicly debates its norms and values through the notoriety of a famous case of deviance and its trial. Even if located in remote circumstances, Erikson's intentions were plain enough: he wanted to be able to draw a scenario that could be applied also to more contemporary events.[3]

I would like to follow Erikson's suit in submitting that, through the central and vexed issue of immigration – the crescendo of dramatic news related to the increasing numbers of "extracommunitarian" immigrants, the episodes of violence and racism, the general restrictions in immigration policies[4] – in a sense on the very skin of the immigrants, Europeans are conversing about themselves, who they are, and where they want to go.

The talk about immigrants' criminal and cultural deviance, with which European mass-media are replete (Van Dijk 1993; Ter Wal 1991), is not only a vehicle for controlling immigrants' behavior but is especially a vehicle for intra-European debate about the existence, nature and essential characteristics of a European identity that appears to be very problematic (Schlesinger 1992). Will the constitution of Europe go in the direction of a democratic and federalist society held together by loyalty to a "constitutional patriotism," as Habermas seems to suggest on the left (1992), or will it take the direction of a new European Empire, as Alain de Benoist (1991) seems to suggest on the right? This political-legal-constitutional backdrop is connected to the even broader problem that a "European public sphere" does not really exist, given the traditional connection between nation and democracy (Habermas 1992). And yet the existence of such a sphere is essential to the making of a European democracy. Only within it, a process of cultural identification may develop, that is strictly connected to the question of democracy, or, to be more precise, to the so-called "deficit" of democracy in Europe today. Guenther Schaefner has nicely summarized the problem:

> European law is made by Council and not by the European Parliament . . . This should surprise no one; the Community is not a political system that derives its authority from a constitution. It is a Community established by contract, by treaties of sovereign nations, and only what these member states decide in Council can become law.
>
> Legitimacy of EC law is based on the legitimacy of the decision of the contracting parties – the member states. Democratic control and legitimization is exercised, in theory, primarily by the parliaments of the member states. In fact, however, member state parliaments are ill equipped for this task. They are not capable of effectively controlling what their governments do in Brussels. It is a difficult task, given the lack of transparency and the extensive role of civil servants in the decision-making process. A transfer of democratic control to the European Parliament would imply a decrease in the role of national parliaments which they will probably resist. At the same time, it must be said that for a parliament to exercise effective control over an executive, it must rely on political parties to control this parliament and to control the executive. The political parties have to offer the voters, in this case the European citizens, clear alternatives in terms of European policy. In the European Parliament today, we do not yet have political parties with a European platform; instead we have political groups forming more or less loose association of national political parties.
>
> (Schaefner 1991: 686–7)

In fact the system in place today is more like a bureaucratic type of government, based on international treaties among the various European governments, than a true federal government. It is a system that may be offensive to feelings of national popular sovereignty without being able to secure an actual popular (European) legitimation for itself. The consequences that should be drawn from this analysis, it seems to me, are the necessities of a European Constitution and Bill of Rights, providing for a federal political and electoral system supported by that European "public sphere" that is indispensable in order to accompany such a complex legal and political change.

De Tocqueville, Durkheim and Gramsci (Melossi 1990 and 1996) all maintained that democracy, as a political form, is complementary to a high degree of development of communication. Democracy can only be constituted as a dialogic form, a conversational political mode. Both democracy and a common identity may grow only along with communication. Democracy and common identity are strongly connected because the fundamental premise of democracy is that we share something in common, something that cannot be made up by legal rules only, even if it has to be expressed in legal rules. As George Herbert Mead wrote in his 1920s and 1930s Chicago, "[t]he process of communication is one which is more universal than that of the universal religion or universal economic process in that it is one that serves them both" (Mead 1934: 259).[5] For him, social control is based on the capacity, for each one of us, to take the role of the other. The "generalized other," or social other, therefore controls our conduct (Mead 1925). In democracy, we have to be able to take the role of the larger community we become part of. Hence the importance of public opinion and especially of the media. According to Mead and the other authors of the Chicago school, a situation of continuous conflict, as the one which developed in the United States during the Progressive Era, can be governed only through the continuous re-establishment of a hegemonic balance – a view of democracy as the "institutionalizing of revolution" (Mead 1915: 150–1).

I believe therefore that developments in the field of the mass media of communication are destined to have a special impact on the process of European unification. The only level at which a "European public sphere" is being constituted today, is through such attempts as European newspapers and satellite TV channels where, ironically enough, substantial American interests are at stake (one has only to consider that the only actual worldwide "public sphere" of any sort is beamed from Atlanta, Georgia!). A process of European democratization will not only have to mean the extension of the actual legislative powers of the European Parliament to make laws and control their implementation, but also the expansion of the principle of freedom of speech, a principle that cannot be confined to the current radical *laissez-faire* interpretation without considering the problem of *plural access* to free speech.

In the case of the United States, Archibald Cox (1986) has observed that such access is seriously endangered by the growth of governments' near-monopoly of information on security matters, by concentration of private control on the mass media, and by the growing influence of political advertising. Consequently, critical legal theorists are questioning the supposedly "harmless" nature of free speech and are using arguments similar to those in J. L. Austin's "speech act theory" (1955) in order to show that speech is never really "unconsequential," and that there is therefore a legitimate public interest in its regulation (Fish, 1994; MacKinnon, 1993).

Conclusion: an answer to a "reactionary" critique

In Manchester, in his comments on my paper, Nils Christie defined his own position about Europe as "reactionary" and provocatively maintained that customs booths should be placed not only at the borders between different states but also at those between the different valleys of his beloved Norway. I agree with Christie that his position is indeed reactionary (and has on its side a good share of sound reasons, as solid reactionary positions usually have). Indeed the notion of a European democracy that I present in this chapter is a typically modernist, Enlightenment-oriented notion, not far from the positions usually taken by that paragon of Enlightenment, Jürgen Habermas. However, as Durkheim happened to suggest in his own times, the issue is not that Europeanization means destruction of old values and traditions. It is, rather, that what is required is the constitution of a European morality – a morality of European democracy, as it were – within which the protection of localities and their traditions will have to play a prominent role. Indeed, as I noted at the very beginning, I am convinced that each European citizen will acquire and not lose sovereignty with the development of a more united and stronger Europe. All individual European states, and therefore their citizens, hold very little power in themselves, *vis-à-vis* the international economic and political concentrations, but they will acquire much more weight when united.

Of course, because this is a political process the crucial requirement, for those who cherish the value of a democratic Europe (that is, a Europe not driven solely by bureaucratic and economic interests), is to find themselves *within the process*. This is particularly important, I believe, for England and Wales, and Scotland, which can bring to the European Union a precious tradition of political culture, what Walter Ullmann (1961) called an "ascending" concept of authority, opposite to a "descending" one on the European Continent. A decisive engagement of English political and legal traditions would be of paramount importance in structuring a European federation based on the concept of subsidiarity, on the idea of individual and communities being endowed with original rights of sovereignty, and on the protection of diversity, against the tendency of those who think in terms of a centralized "Euro-state." The paradoxical element therefore of a certain English shyness toward Europe, a shyness that is caused in fact by the fear of a powerful Euro-state that could somehow undermine the century-old English traditions, is that England might end up eventually being forced to join a Union that she has not contributed to shape and that therefore will be even farther from conforming to her most cherished ideals. A full participation of England in the process of the European Union is therefore not only in the interest of the hundred (state- and non-state-) European peoples, but is at the same time also in the highest interest of the peoples of the British Isles, in order to contribute to creating a European Union that is less of a Leviathan and more of a free community of free communities. I believe that in the decades to come, we will not be able to conceptualize social control in Europe in a way that is separate from a choice between the horns of this dilemma.

Notes

1 This is a revised version of the paper that was presented at the Meeting on "Crime and Social Order in Europe," Manchester, on 7–10 September 1996. I would like to thank the Center for German and European Studies of the University of California at Berkeley, and the Italian Institute of Culture of San Francisco that in different ways contributed to getting my research on this topic off the ground. I would also like to thank Nils Christie who, in Manchester, asked a very provocative and useful question. Inquiries and comments are welcome and should be directed to Professor Dario Melossi, Facoltà di Giurisprudenza, Università di Bologna, Via Zamboni 22, 40126 Bologna, Italy.

2 In 1994 the European Parliament examined and discussed a proposal for a Euopean Constitution (Oreja Aguirre 1994), elaborated within the Committee on Institutional Affairs. It decided to defer further discussion to its successor, the Parliament elected in 1994, with a view to submitting a proposal to the intergovernmental conference of 1996 (Resolution on the Constitution of the European Union, A3–0064/94, 10 February 1994).

3 See the reference to McCarthyism in the Foreword to his book, as a way to signal to the American public the shifting alliances from World War II to the Cold War.

4 However the last time "more severe" immigration policies were adopted, in 1973, a clamorous case of "unintended consequences" resulted in much higher numbers of immigrants, especially in Germany. The connection between immigration and crime, hypothesized both by official agencies of control and professional "myth-makers," is further evidence of this role of new "deviants" for extracommunitarian immigrants (see Tournier and Robert 1995).

5 It goes without saying that it is not possible to think of a European identity and culture without asking the question about a tendentially common European language. One small indicator of the centrality of language in all this is the fact that one-fourth of the 22,000 people staffing EC institutions are involved in translation (Schaefner 199: 684).

References

Anderson, Benedict (1983) *Imagined Communities: Reflections on the origin and spread of nationalism.* London: Verso.

Austin, John L. (1955) *How to Do Things with Words.* Cambridge, Mass.: Harvard University Press.

Balibar, Etienne (1991) "Es Gibt keinen Staat in Europa: Racism and Politics Today," *New Left Review* 186: 5–19.

Beard, Charles A. (1913) *An Economic Interpretation of the Constitution of the United States.* New York: Macmillan.

Brecht, Bertolt (1938) *Poems 1913–1956.* New York: Methuen, 1976.

Cox, Archibald (1986) "First Amendment," *Society* 24:1: 8–15.

de Benoist, Alain (1991) "The Idea of Empire," *Telos* 98–9 (1993–1994): 81–98.

Erikson, Kai (1966) *Wayward Puritans.* New York: John Wiley.

European Parliament (1993) *Report of the Committee for Public Liberties and Internal Affairs on the European Union Citizenship* (by the Hon. Renzo Imbeni), 21 December 1993.

Ferrajoli, Luigi (1995) "The Idea of Sovereignty at the End of the Twentieth-Century." Address delivered at the 17th IVR World Congress, Bologna, Italy, 16–21 June.

Fish, Stanley (1994) *There's No Such Thing as Free Speech . . . and It's a Good Thing, Too.* New York: Oxford University Press.

Foucault, Michel (1975) *Discipline and Punish.* New York: Pantheon, 1977.

—— (1976) *The History of Sexuality. Volume 1: An Introduction.* New York: Random House.

Habermas, Jürgen (1992) "Citizenship and National Identity," pp. 20–35 in Bart van Steenbergen. (ed.), *The Condition of Citizenship,* London: Sage, 1994.

Hobsbawm, Eric and Terence Ranger (1983) (eds) *The Invention of Tradition.* Cambridge: Cambridge University Press.

Imbeni, Renzo (Ed.) (1994) *La cittadinanza europea.* Bologna: Gruppo del Partito del Socialismo Europeo.

Jauregui Bereciartu, Gurutz (1986) *Decline of the Nation-State.* Reno: University of Nevada Press, 1994.

Kelsen, Hans (1924) "The Conception of the State and Social Psychology," *The International Journal of Psychoanalysis* 5: 1–38.

Losano, Mario G. (1991) "Contro la società multietnica," *Micromega* 5: 7–16.

Luban, David (1987) "The Legacies of Nuremberg," *Social Research* 54: 779–829.

MacKinnon, Catharine A. (1993) *Only Words.* Cambridge (Mass.): Harvard University Press.

Mead, George H. (1915) "Natural Rights and the Theory of the Political Institution." in G. H. Mead, *Selected Writings*: 150–70. Indianapolis: Bobbs-Merrill, 1964.

—— (1925) "The Genesis of the Self and Social Control." in G. H. Mead, *Selected Writings*: 267–93. Indianapolis: Bobbs-Merrill, 1964.

—— (1934) *Mind, Self, and Society.* Chicago: University of Chicago.

Melossi, Dario (1990) *The State of Social Control: A Sociological Study of Concepts of State and Social Control in the Making of Democracy.* Cambridge: Polity Press.

—— (1996) "State and Social Control à la Fin de Siècle: From the New World to the Constitution of the New Europe." in R. Bergalli and C. Sumner (eds), *Social Control and Political Order:* 52–74. London: Sage.

Oreja Aguirre, Marcelino (ed.) (1994) *La constitucion europea.* Madrid: Actas.

Pastore, Massimo (1993) "Frontiere, conflitti, identità: a proposito di libera circolazione e nuove forme di controllo sociale in Europa," *Dei delitti e delle pene,* 3(3): 19–37.

Pateman, Carole (1988) *The Sexual Contract.* Cambridge: Polity Press.

Schaefner, Guenther F. (1991) "Institutional Choices: The Rise and Fall of Subsidiarity," *Futures* 23(7): 681–94.

Schlesinger, Philip (1992) "A Question of Identity," *New European* 5(1): 10–14.

Simmel, Georg (1917) "The Idea of Europe." in Georg Simmel: *Sociologist and European*: 267–71. Sunbury-on-Thames: Nelson.

Smith, Anthony D. (1992) "National Identity and the Idea of European Unity," *International Affairs* 68: 55–76.

Spinelli, Altiero and Ernesto Rossi (1941) "Manifesto di Ventotene," in A. Spinelli, *Il manifesto di Ventotene:* 37–57. Bologna: Il Mulino, 1991.

Telos (1991–2) Special Section on: *The Leagues in Italy.* 90: 3–88.

Ter Wal, Jessica (1991) "Il linguaggio del pregiudizio etnico," *Politica ed Economia* 4: 33–48.

Tocqueville, Alexis de (1835) *Democracy in America.* Volume One. New York: Schocken, 1961.

Tournier, Pierre and Philippe Robert (1995) "La délinquance des étrangers en France: analyse des statistiques pénales." Paper presented at the first European meeting on deviance and crime among immigrants (Réseau COST/A2, Milan, October 19–20).

Trentin, Silvio (1945) *Stato nazione, federalismo* (Edizione clandestina). Milano: La fiaccola.

Ullman, Walter (1961) *Principles of Government and Politics in the Middle Ages*. London: Methuen.

Van Dijk, Teun A. (1993) *Elite Discourse and Racism*. London: Sage.

Waever, Ole, Barry Buzan, Morten Kelstrup and Pierre Lemaître (1993) *Identity, Migration and the New Security Agenda in Europe*. London: Pinter Publishers.

4

FROM INCLUSIVE TO EXCLUSIVE SOCIETY

Nightmares in the European Dream[1]

Jock Young

My task in this essay is threefold: first to trace the transition between the Golden Age of the post-War period within the First World to the crisis years of the late 1960s onwards. This is a shift from modernity to late modernity, from a world whose accent was on assimilation and incorporation to one which separates and excludes. It is a world where, I will argue, the market forces which transformed the spheres of production and consumption, relentlessly challenged our notions of material certainty and uncontested values, replacing them with a world of risk and uncertainty, of individual choice and pluralism, and of a deep-seated precariousness both economic and ontological. And it is a world where the steady increment of justice unfolding began to falter: the march of progress seemed to halt. But is a society propelled not merely by rising uncertainty but also by rising demand. For the same market forces which have made our identity precarious and our future unsure have generated a constant rise in our expectations of citizenship and, most importantly, have engendered a widespread sense of demands frustrated and desires unmet.

Second I wish to ground the dramatic changes that occurred in levels of crime and in the nature of deviance and disorder in the material changes which occurred within both the spheres of production and consumption, or the transition which, metaphorically at least, has come to be seen as the movement from Fordism to post-Fordism (see Lea, 1997). It is important that the lines of causality between changes in work and leisure, the levels and nature of crime, the impact on the crime-control apparatus and eventually criminology are made clear, at the very least for the reason that criminologists persistently attempt to disassemble them. Thus those of the right frequently attempt to suggest that levels of crime have no relationship to the changes in work and leisure but are rooted in the supposedly autonomous areas of child rearing, drug use or a world of free-floating moral values. On the other hand, those on the left repeatedly attempt to suggest that changes in imprisonment, patterns of social control, the emerging actuarialism, etc. are political or managerial decisions unrelated to the problem of crime. Indeed, their critical edge is often based in an overt denial of a relationship. And both left and right tend to downplay the level to which *their* criminology, at least, is affected by the external world outside of the academy.

Lastly, I want to stress how such changes, although occurring throughout the developed world, occur in specific circumstances. The contrast I want to make here is between the material and cultural situation in Western Europe and that in the United States: between the European Dream and the American Dream.

The modernist paradigm: a world at one with itself

The modernist project has, over the century, involved the greater and greater incorporation of the population into full citizenship. Such a social contract is based on the notion of a citizenship, not merely of formal rights, but of substantive incorporation into society. In the terms of T. H. Marshall's famous essay, citizenship should involve not only legal and political rights, but social rights: a minimum of employment, income, education, health and housing. In these terms, the full-employment, high-income economies of the Western World in the post-War period up to the recession, were well on the way to achieving full citizenship for the mass of the population. Let us examine the major premises of modernism:

1   **Citizenship resolved:** The long march of citizenship is either resolved or is on the brink of resolution. The incorporation of blacks and women into full citizenship in a formal sense of legal and political equality is accompanied by the achievement of social equality for the vast majority of citizens.

2   **The interventionist State:** The role of the State is to intervene in order to achieve in a piecemeal fashion social justice as a part of a meta-narrative of progress. It is Keynesian in economics and Fabian in its social policy. The twin pillars of modernity are the Rule of Law and the Welfare State as represented by neo-classicist legal theory and social positivist notions of planning. The State protects and the State delivers.

3   **Absolutist social order:** The vast number of citizens accept the given social order as the best of all possible worlds. Unemployment is low, the level of wealth is the highest in the history of humanity and the average income has annually increased since the War. The social order is viewed not only as just but as obviously in the interests of all, the major institutions of work, the family, democratic politics, the legal system, and the mixed economy are accepted without much question. The rules are seen in absolute terms: they are obvious, clear cut and uncontested. The end of ideology is at hand and Western values represent the end point of human progress.

4   **The rational conforming citizen and the determined deviant:** The vast majority of people are rational and freely embrace the consensus of values. The exceptions are a tiny minority of professional criminals and a

larger, but still small, number of criminals and deviants who are determined by psychological and social circumstances. The large-scale rational criminality and dissent possible prior to the modern advances in citizenship ceases to exist. No longer is the rational criminal, the spectre which haunts the work of Beccaria, a large-scale threat or possibility. People by and large do not choose deviance – they are propelled into it.

5   **The narrow conduit of causality:** Causality is reserved for those who deviate; conformity to absolute rules is, of course, unproblematic – aetiology is after all only necessary when things go wrong. Deviance occurs because of problems located not so much in the present as in the past: the conduit of causality is individualised and sited frequently in the family. The notion of sizeable, socially distinguishable groups occupying identifiable space is replaced by the atomistic individual, a random product of some unusual family background. The dangerous classes of pre-modernity become the individual deviant in modernity; it is not till late modernity that the spatial and social pariah re-occurs with a vengeance in the concept of the underclass.

6   **The assimilative State:** The role of the Welfare State is to assimilate the deviant back from the margins into the main body of society. To this end a corpus of experts builds up, skilled in the use of the therapeutic language of social work, of counselling, of clinical psychology and allied positivistic disciplines.

Nowhere was such an inclusive society embracing the citizen from cradle to grave, insisting on full social as well as legal and political citizenship, so developed as in the Welfare States of Western Europe: in Germany, France, Scandinavia and the Benelux countries. If the coming decades made the American dreamer fitful and listless, in Europe the events conjured the beginnings of a nightmare.

The deviant other in the inclusive society

This is a society which does not abhor 'the other', nor regard him or her as an external enemy so much as someone who must be socialised, rehabilitated or cured until he or she is like 'us'. The modernist gaze views the other not as something alien, rather as some thing or body which lacks the attributes of the viewer. It is lacking in civilisation, socialisation or sensibilities. It is a camera which is so strangely constituted that it can only take negatives of the photographer.

The deviant 'other' is thus:

1   a minority;
2   distinct and objective;
3   lacking in values which are absolute and uncontested. Indeed, contesting one's ascribed deviance is itself a sign of lack of maturity, sensibility;

4   deviance is, therefore, ontologically confirming rather than threatening. Our
      own certainty of values is confirmed by seeing the precariousness of those
      who lack our standards;
5   the goal is to assimilate and include these individuals. The discourses both
      penal and therapeutic are, therefore, of integration. Criminals 'pay their debt
      to society' and then re-enter, the drug addict is cured of his or her sickness,
      the aberrant teenager is taught to adjust to a welcoming society;
6   the barriers to outsiders are thus permeable: they encourage a cultural
      osmosis of the less socialised towards the well socialised.

From inclusive to exclusive society

The cultural revolution was followed by the economic crisis: If the first moment
in the 1960s and 1970s was that of the rise of individualism, the creation of
zones of personal exclusiveness, and the unravelling of traditionalities of community and family, then the second, counterpoised on top of it, lasting through
the 1980s and 1990s, involved a process of social exclusion. This is a two-part
process involving, first, the transformation and separation of the labour markets
and the massive rise in structural unemployment, second the exclusion arising out
of attempts to control the crime which arises out of such changed circumstances
and the excluding nature of anti-social behaviour itself.

The transition from modernity to late modernity can be seen as a movement
from an *inclusive* to *exclusive* society. That is from a society whose accent was on
assimilation and incorporation to one that separates and excludes.[2] This erosion
of the inclusive world of the modernist period, what Hobsbawm (1994) calls *The
Golden Age*, involved processes of disaggregation both in the sphere of community
(the rise of individualism) and the sphere of work (transformation of the labour
markets). Both processes are the result, as we shall see, of market forces and their
transformation by the human actors involved. It behoves us here, however sche-
matically, to attempt to spell out the links between changes in market relationships which bring about this shift and which ultimately underscore the changes,
conceptions and expectations of citizenship which, in turn, have transformed
contemporary developments of criminality and its control.

The most fundamental undercurrent is the familiar, although hotly debated,
movement between Fordist and post-Fordist modes of production. Fordism in the
post-War period involves mass standardised production, near-total male employment, a considerable manufacturing sector, massive hierarchical bureaucracies, a
sizeable primary labour market of secure jobs and standardised career prospects,
clearly demarcated roles, corporatist government policies and mass consumption
of fairly uniform products. The world of work is paralleled by the sphere of
leisure and the family; underwritten by the division of labour between the sexes;
the family becomes the site of consumption, the celebration of an affluent life-
style, the essential-demand side of Keynesianism, and presents an ever-expanding
array of standardised consumer goods by which to measure individual success

and to mark out the steady economic progress of an expanding economy. Such is the consensual world where the core values centring around work and the family present themselves like absolutes and where the modernist project of citizenship seems within a breath of resolution. It is an inclusive world, a world at one with itself, whose accent is on assimilation whether it is towards wider and wider swathes of society (the lower class, women, youth) or towards immigrants entering into a monocultural society. It is a social order which abhors 'the other' not as an external enemy as much as something or someone which must be transformed, socialised, rehabilitated into 'one of us'.

All of this interwoven and buttressed structure was to unfold. If we start with a structure seemingly monolithic and all embracing: its basic elements undergirding and stoutly maintaining the weight of the absolute certainties of biography and aspiration of its members, we end with a world which is more chaotic; its structure begins to unravel, its constituents fragment and the everyday world of its members seems problematic, blurred and uncertain. The major institutions of work and the family no longer provide the cradle-to-grave trajectories which embrace, engulf and insure. The strains, always there, between for example inherited wealth and merit, between equality of citizenship and inequality of gender, between formal and substantial equality were contained for a while by the sheer success of the 'never-had-it-so-good societies'. The seeds of change were already present in the contrast between the primary and secondary labour markets (Harvey, 1989) whilst the rise of individualism heightened demands for fuller and more developed citizenship as well as registering protest at the lack of equalities inherent in the system. That is a movement both of rising aspiration and thwarted expectation.

The market economy emerging in post-Fordism involved a qualitative leap in the levels of exclusion. The downsizing of the economy has involved the reduction of the primary labour market, the expansion of the secondary market and the creation of an underclass of structurally unemployed. Will Hutton in *The State We're In* (1995) describes this as the 40:30:30 society. Forty per cent of the population in tenured secure employment, thirty per cent in insecure employment, thirty per cent marginalised, idle or working for poverty wages. We may quarrel with his proportions but the percentage of the population who are part of J. K. Galbraith's 'constituency of contentment' (1992) is a minority and ever-shrinking.

If we picture contemporary meritocracy as a racetrack where merit is rewarded according to talent and effort, we find a situation of two tracks and a motley of spectators: a primary labour market where rewards are apportioned according to plan but where there is always the chance of demotion to the second track where rewards are substantially inferior, only small proportions of the track are open to competitors, and there is always the chance of being demoted to the role of spectators. As for the spectators, their exclusion is made evident by barriers and heavy policing: they are denied real access to the race but are the perpetual spectators of the glittering prizes on offer.

Yet it is not only that opportunities to enter the race are available without any but a contingent relationship to talent, the prizes have also become more unequal. For in the recent period income inequalities widen (Joseph Rowntree Foundation, 1995; Hills, 1996) Such a gradient of inclusion and exclusion engenders, according to Edward Luttwak (1995) both a chronic relative deprivation amongst the poor which gives rise to crime and a precarious anxiety amongst those better off which breeds an intolerance and punitiveness towards the law-breaker. The sphere of distributive justice, of merit and reward is thus transformed by the rise of the exclusive society. But let us now turn to the other sphere of order, that of community, and trace how the personal exclusiveness of individualism has its roots in post-Fordism. Here we are concerned more with the arena of consumption rather than production. David Harvey begins his treatise on post-modernity (1989) with a discussion of Jonathan Raban's *Soft City* published in 1974. Like so many other interesting works, at this point of change, Raban overturns the conventional depiction of the city as the epitome of rationalised mass planning and consumption; the iron cage where human behaviour is programmed, where the mass of humanity is channelled and pummelled through the urban grid of suburbs, downtown, offices, factories, shopping zones and leisure facilities. Rather than being the site of determinacy, Raban sees the city as the arena of choice. It is an emporium where all sorts of possibilities are on offer, a theatre where a multiplicity of roles can be played, a labyrinth of potential social interactions, an encyclopaedia of subculture and style.

The shift from the stolid mass consumption and leisure of Fordism to the diversity of choice and a culture of individualism involving a stress on immediacy, hedonism and self-actualisation has profound effects on late-modern sensibilities. The Keynesian balance between hard work and hard play, so characteristic of the Fordist period (see Young, 1971) becomes tipped towards the subterranean world of leisure. 'Modern capitalism', as Paul Willis nicely puts it, 'is not only parasitic upon the puritan ethic, but also upon its instability and even its subversion' (1990: 19). Out of such a world of choice, whether it is in the urban emporium or the wider world of cultural communities, people are able to construct identities: although springing from commercial, market forces they are transformed by the human actors. The new individualism which emerges on the back of the consumer society is concerned with pluralistic choice (it freely creates new subcultural styles bricollaging both from the present and the past), it is concerned with self-actualisation (the individual creates a life-style and a personal identity through choice), it is hedonistic and immediate (the old Keynesian personality involving a balance between work and leisure, production and consumption, deferred gratification and immediacy, becomes tipped towards the latter) and it is, above all, voluntaristic (choice is valued, freedom is seen to be possible, tradition is devalued). (See Campbell, 1987; Featherstone, 1985). Such expressive demands augment the instrumental demands for monetary sources and status which are the staple of the modern period. By late modernity the frustration of expressive demands becomes a source of strain in the system and, together with relative deprivation in the material world, a potent source of deviancy. (For early sightings of this phenomenon see Downes, 1966; Young, 1971.) What is without doubt is the rise of a culture of high expectations both materially and in terms of self-fulfilment, one which sees success in these terms and one which is far less willing to be put upon by authority, tradition or community if these ideals are frustrated.

Out of such frustrations arise both positive and negative consequences. *The Soft City* of Jonathan Raban is soft more in its plasticity than in its kindness:

> The city our great modern form, is soft, amenable to a dazzling and libidinous variety of lives, dreams and interpretations. But the very plastic qualities which made the city the great liberator of human identity also cause it to be especially vulnerable to psychosis ... If it can, in the Platonic ideal, be the highest expression of man's reason and sense of his own community with other men, the city can also be a violent ... expression of his panic, his envy, his hatred of strangers, his callousness.
>
> (Raban, 1974: 15–16)

There is, as one writer remarked, room for the flâneur but not for the flâneuse (Woolf, 1985). Here we have the paradox of the new individualism. The demise of consumer conformity gives rise to a dynamic, diverse pluralism of lifestyles. Such a release of human creativity has clearly liberative and progressive possibilities yet each diverse project has the potentiality to contradict and impede each other. Subcultures are frequently in collision: diversity may impede diversity. Discontent about one's social predicament, the frustration of aspiration and desire may give rise to a variety of political, religious and cultural responses which may open up the possibilities for those around one but they may well, often purposively, close up and restrict the possibilities of others. They may also create criminal responses and these very frequently bear the currency of restricting others. Let me give a couple of examples. The downsizing of the manufacturing base, discussed in the last section, generates relative deprivation throughout the class structure but, in particular, amongst those unskilled workers clustered around the empty factories, and on the desolate estates. Although young women in these areas can find a role for themselves in child rearing and, very often, work in the service sector, young men are bereft of social position and destiny. They are cast adrift; a discarded irrelevance locked in a situation of structural unemployment, not even available to offer the stability of 'marriageable' partners (see Wilson, 1996). They are barred from the racetrack of the meritocratic society yet remain glued to the television sets and media which alluringly portray the glittering prizes of a wealthy society. Young men facing such a denial of recognition turn, everywhere in the world, in what must be almost a universal criminological law, to the creation of cultures of machismo, to the mobilisation of one of their only resources, physical strength, to the formation of gangs and to the defence of their own 'turf'. Being denied the respect of others they create a subculture that revolves around masculine powers and 'respect'.

Paul Willis, in his classic *Learning to Labour* (1977), traces the way in which 'the lads' through the irrelevance of their schooling for the labouring jobs to which they are heading construct a subculture of resistance against the school and the wider middle-class world. But their reaction to being excluded from the primary labour market, from career, good prospects and a promising future is to rubber-stamp their own exclusion, which also serves to exclude equally vulnerable others. Thus their subculture of resistance elevates toughness and physical strength to a prime virtue: it is sexist, frequently racist and avowedly anti-intellectual.

Thus the excluded create divisions amongst themselves, frequently on ethnic lines, often merely depending on what part of the city you live in, or, more prosaically (yet to some profoundly), what football team you support. Most importantly, as Willis points out, this creates problems of safety and security for other members of the community, particularly women. They are excluded, they create an identity which is rejecting and exclusive, they exclude others by aggression and dismissal, and they are, in turn, excluded and dismissed by others – whether school managers, shopping mall security guards, the 'honest' citizen, or the police officer on the beat. *The dialectics of exclusion* is in process, a deviancy amplification which progressively accentuates marginality, a Pyrrhic process involving both wider society and, crucially, the actors themselves, which traps them in, at best, a series of dead-end jobs and at worst, an underclass of idleness and desperation.

As our second example, let me turn from a situation where exclusion creates crimes to one where attempts at inclusion are met by violence and aggression. The entry of women into the labour market and their fuller participation in public life, whether in leisure, politics or the arts, is perhaps the most profound structural change of the post-War period. Yet this process of inclusion involves, as Ulrich Beck puts it, 'erupting discrepancies between women's expectations of equality and the realm of inequality in occupations and the family' which 'it is not difficult to predict . . . will amount to an externally induced amplification of conflicts in personal relationships' (1992: 120). It is not, however, merely the increasing expectations of women but the challenge of these expectations to male preconceptions and the resistance to them which encapsulates the rising conflict. Here, surely, Giddens is right to point to violence being a more frequent occurrence in the family, *as in politics*, where hegemony is threatened, not where patriarchal, or state domination is accepted. Widespread violence is the currency of hegemony *breaking down* not of hegemony *in control* (see Giddens, 1992: 121–2). In the case of patriarchy it is when the ability of the man to dictate, without question, the unequal and marginal status of the womenfolk within his family, is challenged and severely weakened. Thus domestic violence increases whilst simultaneously, as Sandra Walklate argues, 'women are less likely to tolerate violent relationships . . . than they once were' (1995: 99). Thus the violence which has always occurred in domestic relationships is less tolerated whilst the amount of conflict increases.

It is commonplace to think of violent crime as the product of exclusion, the young men of my first example, but it is important to stress that much violence occurs because of conflicts over inclusion (i.e. of equality and modernity against subordination and tradition).

Pluralism and ontological insecurity

I have traced how changes in the economy have given rise on the one hand to increased relative deprivation and economic precariousness, and on the other hand to a more rampant individualism. But there is a further force for destabilisation and that is the emergence of a more pluralistic society, one in which people's sense of personal security, the stability of their being, becomes more insecure.

As Anthony Giddens graphically delineates, the situation of late modern life is characterised by heightened choice (stemming both from the opportunities of consumption and the flexible demands of work), by a constant questioning of established beliefs and certainties, a raised level of self-reflexivity, a lack of embedded biography and life trajectory and the constant confrontation with a plurality of social worlds and beliefs (1991: 70–88). Such a situation breeds ontological insecurity, that is where self-identity is not embedded in our sense of biographical continuity, where the protective cocoon which filters out challenges and risks to a sense of certainty becomes weakened, and where an absolute sense of one's normality becomes disoriented by the surrounding relativism of value. Individualism, with its emphasis on existential choice and self-creation, contributes significantly to such insecurity, whilst the pressing nature of a plurality of alternative social worlds, some the result of such incipient individuality, manifestly undermines any easy acceptance of unquestioned value.

The pluralism which the actor encounters can be seen as stemming from three major sources:

1   the *diversification* of lifestyles which are a result of growing individualism;
2   the closer *integration* of society, including the narrowing of travelling times through physical space and the implosion of glimpses of other societies and cultures provided by a growing and ever-proliferating mass media. Business, tourism, television, all bring us together;
3   the *immigration* of people from other societies.[3]

In Europe, in the last twenty years, such a pluralism has been pronounced on all three levels: mass immigration has occurred, increased European integration is a palpable fact, however disorganised the political process and limited nature of a common identity (see Melossi, 1996), whilst the process of diversification characteristic of advanced industrial societies has proceeded apace.

Such a situation has considerable effect on our perception of and reaction to deviance. In modernity, as we have seen, the deviant other appears as a distinct, minority phenomenon which contrasts with the vast majority consensus of absolute values which it lacks and, thus, by its very existence, confirms rather than threatens. In late modernity the deviant other is everywhere. In the city, as Richard Sennett (1991) writes in *The Conscience of the Eye*, everyone is a potential deviant. The distinct other is no longer present, cultures not only appear plural but they blur, overlap with each other. Youth cultures, for example, do not form distinct ethnic groupings but are hybrids constituted by bricolage rather than by ethnic absolutism (see Gilroy, 1993; Back, 1996).

In such a situation of ontological insecurity there are repeated attempts to create a secure base. That is to reassert one's values as moral absolutes, to declare other groups as lacking in value, to draw distinct lines of virtue and vice, to be rigid rather than flexible in one's judgements, to be punitive and excluding rather than permeable and assimilative. This process can be seen in various guises in different parts of the social structure. The most publicised attempts at redrawing moral lines more rigorously are the 'back to basics' initiative of the British Conservatives in 1995, which was a replay of the Back to Family Values campaign of the US Bush Administration. Lower in the structure this can be seen in the attempt by the socially excluded to create core and distinct identities. Part of the process of social exclusion, as Jimmy Feys argues, is: the inability 'to cast their anchor in a sea of structure prescribed by society' (1996: 7). That is, social exclusion produces a crisis of identity. And one could point to the policies of such groups as Black Muslims, Fundamentalists in émigré communities, and perhaps even the tawdry traditionalism of supporters of the far right, as an indication of this. That is, a reaction to exclusion by heightened commitment to past values, to create imaginary nationalisms where the present precariousness is absent, and, often, to ape the conventional or, at least, some imagined image of it. Lastly, amongst the intelligentsia, part of the process of political correctness involves a decline in tolerance of deviance, an obsession with correct behaviour and speech, and an insistence on strict policing of moral boundaries (see Moynihan, 1993; Krauthammer, 1993). Whatever the rights and wrongs of such pronouncements – and there is undoubtedly much that is genuinely progressive in such debates – it is remarkable that the self-same strata who expanded tolerance of deviance to the point of recklessness in the 1960s now restrict it like characters from a Victorian etiquette book in the 1990s.

The dyad of crime

The changes, then, in the sphere of production and consumption and their development and reinterpretation by the actors involved have effects both on the causes of crime and deviance and the reactions against it. That is both sides of the dyad of crime.

The combination of relative deprivation and individualism is a potent cause of crime in situations where no political solution is possible: it generates crime but it also generates crime of a more internecine and conflictful nature. The working-class area, for example, implodes in upon itself: neighbours burglarise neighbours, incivilities abound, aggression is widespread. The old-style crime of the

Table 4.1 The dyad of crime

The dyad of crime	Sphere of economy	Sphere of personal life
Causes of crime and deviance	Relative deprivation	Individualism
Reaction to crime and deviance	Material precariousness	Ontological insecurity

1950s and 1960s, which was to a large extent directed at commercial targets and involved the judicious use of violence to control the 'manors' of each 'firm', becomes replaced with a more Hobbesian spread of incivilities. 'We never harmed members of the public' muttered one of the Kray gang, lamenting the decline in civilised values within the East End of London. Some indices of this are that in the Metropolitan district of London, from 1950 to 1990, burglary and robbery rose from being 6 per cent of all crime to 14 per cent and domestic burglary in 1950 was 40 per cent of all burglary (domestic and commercial), whereas by 1990 it was 66 per cent (Harper *et al.*, 1995).

The contribution of economic precariousness and ontological insecurity is, of course, an extremely inflammable mixture in terms of punitive responses to crime and the possibility of scapegoating. We have already seen Lutwak's discussion of the likely impact of economic precariousness, in which those tenuously included in the job market are set up against those transparently out of it. Ontological insecurity adds to this combustive situation the need to less tolerantly perceive deviance and to reaffirm the virtues of the in-group. It is important, however, to distinguish tendencies from necessities and to specify the precise social scenario where such dynamics will be played out. I will return to this at the end of this essay, but first of all I will document the impact of crime on patterns of exclusion within our society.

Rising crime and social exclusion

Elsewhere I have written extensively on the rise in crime which occurred in the latter part of the twentieth century in most advanced industrial nations and its impact both on the public and on criminological theory itself (Young, 1997a, 1995).

The major motor in the transformation of public behaviour and attitudes, in the development of the crime control apparatus and in criminology, is the rapid rise in the crime rate. This has had profound effects from the perspective of exclusion:

On public avoidance behaviour

Rising crime rates fuel public fear of crime and generate elaborate patterns of avoidance behaviour, particularly for urban women. The isolated problem area of early modernity becomes in late modernity an intricate map of no-go zones, of subways and parks to be avoided, of car parks to be navigated and of public space to be manoeuvred. And for many women these possibilities of the day become a curfew at night. (See eg Painter *et al.*, 1989.) This is not the place to enter into the 'reality' of such fears, let alone to explore what 'realistic' risk calculations might look like; suffice it to point to the exclusion which crime generates and that its impact varies greatly by age, class, gender and ethnicity.

On penal exclusion

The rise in crime results in an increase in those incarcerated. Of course there is no linear relationship, but the absence of such does not obviate the fact that in the long run prison populations have in most countries risen in a response, perhaps mistakenly, to the need for crime control.[4] Indeed, the seemingly large differences between US and European imprisonment rates are less a matter of politics than actual differences in the crime rates. The frequent mistake here is, of course, to simply look at rates per population: thus James Lynch found that, when levels of crime and seriousness were allowed for, 'the extreme differences in incarceration between the United States and several other Western democracies are lessened considerably and in some cases disappear. To a large extent differences in . . . incarceration rates cross-nationally are due to differences in the types and levels of crime across countries' (Lynch, 1988: 196) Significant differences do remain, however, particularly between Germany and the United States, although much less between the latter and England, and these are due to differences in the administration of justice.

In the United States those in prison constitute a significant excluded population in their own right. Approaching 1.5 million people are imprisoned, which would create a city as large as Detroit if all were brought together in one place (Currie, 1996). Furthermore, 5.1 million adults are under correctional supervision (prison, parole or probation), one in 37 of the adult residential population (Bureau of Justice Statistics, 1996). Indeed, the American gulag is now the same size as the Russian gulag and both contrast with a situation in Western Europe, the total prison population of which is in the region of 200,000 (Council of Europe, 1995).

On exclusion from public space

The rise in crime generates a whole series of barriers to prevent or manage crime. Thus we have a privatisation of public space in terms of shopping malls, private parks, leisure facilities, railways, airports, together with the gating of private residential property. These now commonplace precautions are backed by stronger outside fortification, security patrols and surveillance cameras. The security industry, whose very job is exclusion, becomes one of the major growth occupations (South, 1994). The city, then, becomes one of barriers, excluding and filtering, although it must be stressed that such barriers are not merely an imposition of the powerful; systems of exclusion, visible and invisible, are created both by the wealthy and the dispossessed. Some of the latter can be as discriminatory as that of the powerful (Ruggiero and South, 1997) but much can be seen as *defensive exclusion*. For example, within Stoke Newington, the area of London that I live in, one finds gated communities of Kurds who live in constant threat of violence, of Hasidic Jews who face widespread anti-Semitism, there are women-only leisure centres, schools with intensive precautions against vandalism, etc. Furthermore, we must remember that the most commonplace physical barrier and by far the most costly are those that we are forced to erect to protect our own houses.

Impact on the criminal justice system

The rise in the number of crimes results in an increase in arrests which represents a dramatic rise of potential demand upon the criminal justice system. The reaction to this, as in any other bureaucracy, is first to attempt to take short cuts and second to decrease the possible number of clients. To take short cuts first, an institution like the police faces a growing number of cases per police officer. For example, in England and Wales, despite large increases in personnel, the number of crimes reported by the public per police officer rose from 10 in 1960 to 40 in 1990. The temptation here, particularly given government pressure to maintain an economic and efficient service, is legitimately to engage in plea-bargaining, illegitimately to engage in corruption (e.g. by manipulating clear-up figures through 'tic' (i.e. 'taking into consideration other offences'), by 'fitting up' suspects, by ignoring the gap between 'theoretical' and 'empirical' guilt) (See Kinsey *et al.*, 1986).

But it is the second strategy of increased selectivity or 'pickiness' with regard to prospective clients which is perhaps of greatest interest. At the level of suspicion the police shift from suspecting individuals to suspecting social categories. For example, in terms of stop and search: it is more effective to suspect those categories deemed likely to commit offences (eg blacks, the Irish, young working class men) rather than to suspect individuals. You trawl in waters with the likeliest, richest harvest rather than take the rather 'pea in a pod' chance of making an arrest by proceeding on an individual-by-individual basis (see Young, 1995). The old invocation 'round up the usual suspects' becomes transformed into 'round up the usual categories': individual suspicion becomes categorical suspicion.

The criminal justice system itself, from police through to judiciary, when faced by too many offenders and too few places to put them, has to engage in a process of selectivity: to distinguish the dangerous, the hardened, the recidivist from the less recalcitrant offender. The proportion of people sent to prison declines (in England and Wales in 1938, 38 per cent of those committing indictable offences were sent to prison, by 1993 this had fallen to 15 per cent) and the process of selectivity based on risk management increases. Thus, although the overall number of prisoners increases, the chance of an offender going to prison decreases.

There is little surprise in this, it is a process of expediency rather than leniency. A parallel could be, that as the Health Service faces the increasing pressure of patient numbers, hospitals refuse to deal with minor ailments and accidents and attempt to move elderly patients out to nursing homes. Alternative care and alternative medicines, like alternatives to prison, flourish in this predicament.

The impact on the offender of this process of corruption, plea-bargaining and selectivity is to *problematise justice*. The justice one receives becomes a result not of individual guilt and proportional punishment but is more a negotiated process, the result of political or bureaucratic pressure rather than absolute standards. The chaos of reward encountered in the field of distributive justice becomes echoed in the chaos of punishment occurring within the criminal justice system.

The new administrative criminology and actuarialism

The rise in crime and the increase in the number of offenders had a profound effect on the working principles occurring in the criminal justice system and the academic theory occurring within criminology. The widespread nature of crime, its very *normality*, makes the search for causes less attractive. The new administrative criminology openly criticises 'dispositional' theories; rather it explains crime by the notion of a universal human imperfection when presented with the opportunity (Young, 1995). The task is to create barriers to restrict such opportunities and to be able to construct a crime-prevention policy which minimises risks and limits the damage. An actuarial approach occurs which is concerned with the calculation of risk rather than either individual guilt or motivation (Feeley and Simon, 1992, 1994; van Swaaningen, 1997). Both the modernist discourses of neo-classicism and positivism are discarded. There is interest neither in liability nor pathology, in deterrence nor rehabilitation. The focus is prior to the event rather than after the event, on prevention rather than imprisonment or cure. It is not an inclusionist philosophy which embraces all into society until they are found guilty of an offence and then attempts to reintegrate them. Rather it is an exclusionist discourse which seeks to anticipate trouble whether in the shopping mall or in the prison and to exclude and isolate the deviant. It is not interested in crime *per se*, it is interested in the possibility of crime, in anti-social behaviour in general, whether criminal or not, in likely mental illness or known recalcitrance: in anything that will disrupt the smooth running of the system. Such an administrative criminology is concerned with managing rather than reforming, its 'realism' is that it does not pretend to eliminate crime (which it knows is impossible) but, rather, to minimise risk. It has given up the ghost on the modernist aims at change through social engineering and judicial intervention, it seeks to separate out the criminal from the decent citizen, the troublemaker from the peaceful shopper and to minimise the harm that the addict or alcoholic can do to themselves rather than proffer any 'cure' or transformation.

Table 4.2 Neo-classicism and actuarial criminology

	Neo-classicism	Actuarial criminology
Focus	Crime	All anti-social behaviour
	Actual event	Risk
	Intent	Behaviour
	Proof	Balance of probability
Goal	Elimination	Damage limitation/harm minimisation
Suspicion	Individual	Categorical
Method	Deterrence	Prevention
Agency	State	Private
Locus	Public space	Mass private property
Solution	Reparation	Insurance
Sentencing	Proportionality	Dangerousness

Towards an exclusive dystopia?

We cannot imagine a Europe that continues to be divided, not by the Iron Curtain this time, but economically, into a part that is prosperous and increasingly united, and another part that is less stable, less prosperous and disunited. Just as one half of a room cannot remain forever warm whilst the other half is cold, it is equally unthinkable that two different Europes could forever live side by side without detriment to both.

(Havel, 1996; 40)

Are we heading towards a dystopia of exclusion, where divisions occur not only between the nations of Europe, as Havel suggests, but within the nations themselves? Can one part of a room remain forever warm whilst the other half is perpetually closed off and cold? For many authors such a division between worlds has its own inevitability and forms a functioning, if oppressive, whole. Let us look at its components:

A central core

A sizeable section of the population are in full-time work, with career structures and biographies which are secure and embedded. Here is the realm of meritocracy, of equality between the sexes (both partners work), of the stable nuclear family, of a working week which gets longer just as joint salaries get higher. It is here that neo-classicism operates within the criminal justice system just as meritocracy occurs within work and school. It is a world graded by credit ratings and consumer profiling (it is *the* prime market place after all) but it is, on the face of it, kind and gentle in its relationships where social control increasingly, both in work and leisure, takes on a casual, almost Disney-like aspect (see Ericson and

Carriere, 1994). It is a world where the exigencies of biography are covered fully comprehensively by insurance whether it is from ill-health, accident, job loss or, indeed, criminal victimisation. It is a world which holidays in the Third World outside its custom barriers whilst shunning the Third World enclaves within it.

But it is an ever-shrinking core. The largest, and growing part of the labour market becomes that of the secondary market where job security is much less secure, where career structures are absent and where life is experienced as precarious.

The cordon sanitaire

A clear line is created between the core group and those outside by a whole series of measures: by town planning, by road networks which divide cities, by the gating of private estates, by the blocking off of areas from easy access, but above all by money – the cost of public transport downtown, the price of goods in the shops, the policing of the core areas whether it is suburban shopping mall or inner-city development, and whether it involves private or public police, is aimed at removing uncertainties, of sweeping the streets clean of alcoholics, beggars, the mentally ill and those who congregate in groups. It is an actuarial police calculating what is likely to cause disorder and discontent, and moving on the inappropriate rather than arresting the criminal. It is aided by the widespread introduction of CCTV (which in fact is more effective in dealing with incivilities than with serious, planned, crime) and by the enforcement of numerous pieces of legislation to control disorderly behaviour.

The outgroup

The outgroup becomes a scapegoat for the troubles of the wider society; its members are characterised as the underclass, who live in idleness and crime. Their areas are the abode of single mothers and feckless fathers, their economics that of drugs, prostitution and trafficking in stolen goods. They are the social impurities of the late modern world, whom David Sibley, in his eloquent *The Geographies of Exclusion* (1995), sees as a victim of sanitising and moralising geographies reminiscent of the nineteenth-century reformers. But unlike the reformers from the late nineteenth century, up until the 1960s, the new goal is not to physically eliminate their areas and integrate their members into the body politic, rather it is to hold at bay and exclude.

Up until the 1980s the word 'marginalisation' is used for such an outgroup: they are the people that modernity has left behind, pockets of poverty and deprivation in the affluent society, but from them 'social exclusion' becomes the phrase (see Feys, 1996), encompassing as it does a more dynamic expulsion from society and, most importantly, a decline in the motivation to integrate the poor into society. The neo-liberalism of the late 1980s and 1990s does not only attempt to draw back the limits of the state, it (perhaps more successfully) allows the limits of civil society to recede. It is not public policy but the market which is seen as the only possible salvation of the poor, yet the chance of such an increased labour market is extremely unlikely. This section of the population has a large ethnic-minority constitution, creating the possibility of easy scapegoating and of confusing the vicissitudes of class for those of race.

The future of exclusion

Of course, all this talk of exclusion might be easily dismissed as a temporary problem. The hopes of politicians of both the Left and the Right often hinge on a return to full employment, to the inclusionist societies of the 1950s. Unfortunately it is this nostalgia, however bi-partisan, that is likely to be temporary rather than any long-run change in reality. The future does not augur well for two reasons that I have already touched upon. First, the demand for unskilled and semi-skilled manual labour has contracted in all the countries of the First World. The globalisation of capital has meant that the factories of South-East Asia can compete much more cheaply than those in Europe and North America. The poor are isolated in inner-city ghettos, in orbital estates, and in ghost towns where capital originally led them, then left them stranded as it winged its way elsewhere, where labour was cheaper and expectations lower. This exclusion is on a large scale: in Will Hutton's (1995) estimation it is perhaps 30 per cent of the population and is a radically different problem from the marginalised pockets of poverty characteristic of the immediate post-War period. Furthermore, the full entry of China into the world economy will create reverberations which will vastly eclipse those created by the Asian tigers. Second, the introduction of more and more sophisticated computer software will eliminate many lower-middle-class jobs as well as making many lower-rung professional jobs increasingly precarious. The successful company nowadays is one that increases productivity whilst losing workers, not one which increases the size of its personnel.

Yet, on the face of it, it might be difficult to understand how such a dystopian society could maintain itself. How is it possible for it to contain within its frontiers a permanently dispossessed minority, particularly one which views citizenship, in the broadest sense of social as well as political equality, as a right rather than as something which is achieved? That is, a society which holds firm to the values of meritocracy yet denies so many participation in the race. As I have shown, the actuarial cordon sanitaire which separates the world of the losers from that of the winners is an attempt to achieve this: to make life more tolerable for the winners while scapegoating the losers.

To some extent the dangers and disruptions created by the excluded are delimited. Most significant are the sporadic riots which take place across the First World. In London, Birmingham, Paris and Marseilles, etc. they represent riots of citizenship. They occur constantly with the same pattern: a section of people who are economically marginalised are subject, over time, to stereotypical suspicion and harassment by the police. That is, not only are they denied their social rights as citizens of access to the labour market on fair terms, they are treated on the streets in a manner which palpably denies their legal rights (Lea and Young, 1993). Interestingly the exclusion of the market-place is matched by the actuarial exclusion of policing which I have described earlier. A single incident of prejudiced policing usually provides the trigger for the riots: which are quite clearly *riots of inclusion*, as compared with race riots, which are of an exclusionary nature, or insurrections where the fundamental aim is to redraw the nature of citizenship.

In terms of targets, however, such riots are invariably contained: they involve the destruction of the local community, the rage is directed implosively rather than explosively. The poor no longer threaten the Gentlemen's Clubs of St James', they terrorise the small shopkeepers of Brixton and Handsworth. Meanwhile, those areas are consumed by what one might call *the slow riots* of crime, incivilities and vandalism. A world turned in upon itself and, at times, each person against each other. And the actuarial line of differential policing, zoning and crime prevention, helps maintain this. Indeed, to the extent that it *displaces* crime from well protected middle-class to less protected lower-working-class areas, it actually increases the problem (see Hope, 1997; Trickett *et al.*, 1995; Hope, 1995). There are limits, however, to such an exclusionary project. This involves, as we have seen, a package with two components: material and cultural. That is, an actuarial process of exclusion and risk management coupled with a cultural mechanism of scapegoating: the creation of a spatially and socially segregated deviant other.

But let me first make the distinction between the material and cultural situation in Western Europe and in the United States, because there are important differences.

The American Dream and the European Dream

The American Dream has very particular notions both of community and of opportunity. Although the process of exclusion occurs in all developed industrial countries, it is important to stress the exclusionary nature of American ideology when compared to European ideals. In the American Dream the ideal is equality of opportunity: all get a chance to compete in the meritocratic race, but it is the winners who get the prizes and the losers who naturally do not. And losers fail because of individual qualities, it is *their* fault that they have lost (Merton, 1938). The notion of citizenship has, therefore, a strong stress on legal and political equality and much less on social equality. It is a cocktail glass society where social and cultural focus is on the successful and where winners, more and more, take all (Frank and Cook, 1996). In a way, then, social citizenship is something to be earned by hard work and forthrightness ('the American way'): it is not a right of citizenship.

In the European Dream, in contrast, there is much greater stress on rights of inclusion. In the post-War settlement the Welfare State stresses that social citizenship is as important as legal or political citizenship. In this race all get rewarded commensurate to their merit, and even those at the end of the race get compensation prizes to allow themselves the basic necessities of life. Failure is seen not so much as an individual fault as a fault of the system.

Such a more ready acceptance of economic exclusion in the United States is backed up by a far greater social and spatial exclusion. The famous Concentric Rings of the Chicago School are a symbol of this symmetry between economic and social exclusion. And such a vertical segregation is reinforced by a much greater horizontal segregation between different communities even when at the same level of affluence.

The United States is a quite exceptional exclusionary society. The notion of the ethnic segregation of suburban development scarcely causes criticism. Indeed the word 'community' becomes to be used as the singular form of a plural entity and even Amitai Etzioni's (1993) much vaunted 'communitarianism' is not one of integration but of overarching values and shared sentiments (see also Wilson, 1985). Ironically, Marcus Felson (1994), with rather amusing ethnocentricity, sees the 'divergent' cities of suburban sprawl and segretation of North America as the future when compared to the 'convergent' cities of urban villages and downtown heterogeneity of Europe and the American past (including Manhattan). Indeed he instructs his students to compare Los Angeles with the 'old convergent cities of Europe – for example Paris, Amsterdam, Brussels, Copenhagen and Stockholm' (p. 171). It takes a radical critic such as William Julius Wilson (1996) to point to the need to reverse the levels of suburbanisation and to repair the neglect of city centres characteristic of American cities in order to emulate those of Europe and to do away with spatial isolation of deprived groups.[5]

The public and social policies which, in the United States, have allowed unrestricted suburbanisation, the flight from the city and the deterioration of city centres, have not, on the whole, been present in Europe. Without such segregation, the ability to give spatial bearings to a distinct underclass is absent as, indeed, is the social setting on a large scale where there is a lack of any reference points to the workaday world. Overall, spatial and social exclusion has not occurred in Europe on the scale that it has in the United States.

With these caveats in mind, let us turn now to the general problems which limit material and cultural exclusion.

The cordon sanitaire

The heterogeneity of the city, both in respect of urban dwelling and also in terms of the need to transit the urban sprawl for reasons of work and leisure, makes it very difficult to isolate different populations. Indeed, the city, whether Manhattan, Paris, Barcelona or Rome, is something which is attractive in its own right, where the frisson of difference constantly amazes, bemuses and sometimes alarms: 'The rapid crowding of changing images, the sharp discontinuity in the grasp of a single glance, and the unexpectedness of onrushing impressions', as George

Simmel (1950) put it in *The Metropolis and Mental Life*. And, as we have seen, the emporium of roles and possibilities is a key attraction of the 'soft city'. The actuarial line, the cordon sanitaire of control, is, therefore, difficult to achieve and perhaps more so in a world which emphasises diversity, pluralism and choice.

But there is another important reason why the cordon sanitaire is unable to protect the 'honest' citizen from crime and disorder. The notion that the criminal is an external enemy 'out there' is fundamentally flawed. Relative deprivation and individualism occurs through the class structure: the existence of widespread white-collar crime (Lea, 1992) and crimes amongst the 'respectable' working class scarcely allows us to cordon off the criminal from the non-criminal. And in terms of violence, as Mooney has shown (1996), not only is it widely distributed throughout the class structure, but one half of all violence against men and women occurs in the home. The cordon sanitaire must, therefore, fail because the fifth column of offenders is in the suburbs, at work, or in one's local streets. Indeed, the chances of violence are greater from a close friend or member of the family than from a stranger.

The scapegoating function

It might appear that this problem . . . has been largely eclipsed by forces which have breached old boundaries and created a world of fractured, hybridised and fused identities. For example, the end of the cold war has rendered a particularly powerful rhetoric which supported a boundary between 'good' and 'evil' redundant. Migrations of peoples and cultures have given the South a much more influential presence in the North than in the past and not just in established cosmopolitan centres like London, Paris or New York. In the academy, post-modern texts have blurred previous subject identities.

I doubt, however, whether these cultural, political and social transformations have really made people less fearful, less concerned about keeping a distance from others, less exclusionary in their behaviour. The world political map in 1994 is replete with new, strong boundaries which are designed to secure cultural homogeneity, and, at the local level, hostility towards outsider groups like New Age Travellers in England and Wales and ethnic minorities in much of Europe is no less acute than it was before 'the passing of the modern world'. The desire for a purified identity, which requires the distant presence of a bad object, a discrepant other, seems to be unaffected by cross-currents of culture which are characteristic of recent global change.

(Sibley 1995: 183–4)

David Sibley, in the above quote, makes, I believe, the error of believing that the rhetoric of the time reflects reality. It is easy to mistake the siren voices of basic values for current melody, but they are singing songs that have long been out of fashion, they celebrate a world which will never return, their very insistence is because of incipient failure, they are signs of a world being lost rather than a hegemony triumphant. It is an irony that it is at the point when widespread exclusion occurs and when the existing system needs to justify itself more that traditional ideology begins to lose its currency.

Such ideas become all the more necessary at precisely the point where they become all the more implausible. It is difficult to create the notion of a 'deviant other' when:

1   *The size of the problem*: crime is so 'normal and extensive a problem that it is *implausible* to assume that it is all or largely due to an underclass or to immigrants or to a special group of people called 'criminals';
2   *The mass media*: are only too ready to focus not only on fecklessness at the bottom of the social structure but also on sleaze at the top. It would be a naive citizen today who believed that crime and deviance were a monopoly of the lower classes;
3   *The causes*: are too widespread to be able to allocate them to a particular outgroup. Who does not know a family that has broken up, a single mother bringing up her children, a friend who has become unemployed? In a precarious world it would be a foolhardy person who could not see the possibility 'that there but for fortune' they might be in the same predicament;
4   *Lack of segregation*: As we have seen, the relative lack of segregation in Europe compared to the United States makes it much less possible to spatially locate an isolated deviant other.

A clear sign of this collapsing hegemony is the phenomenon of moral panics: Angie McRobbie and Sarah Thornton have pointed recently to the transformation of moral panics in the late modern period. They point to the following features:

> *frequency*: moral panics increase in frequency;
> *disputation*: they are disputed, experts and pressure groups disagree both as to the nature of the panic and, more importantly, as to whether there is a basis to the 'panic' at all, (eg the moral panic about single mothers is strongly contested);
> *difficulty*: moral panics become more difficult to set off, not only that they are disputed, but 'the hard and fast boundaries between "normal" and "deviant" would seem to be less common'.
> (McRobbie and Thornton 1995: 572–3)

McRobbie and Thornton attribute such changes to the vast expansion and diversification of the mass media. There is no doubt that such a competition for audience has vastly increased the rate at which attempts at panic are made, but we must look to demand as well as supply if we are to understand this proliferation. The level of ontological insecurity of audiences in a pluralistic society make such revelation of deviance followed by reassurance of the limits of normality extremely attractive. Indeed, a plethora of chat shows from Oprah Winfrey to Ricki Lake, tackle daily a host of problems. They attempt to firm up normality in a world which is, as McRobbie and Thornton point out, increasingly uncertain. The revelation industry is thus coupled with a personal advice and therapy service (see Giddens, 1992).

The centre cannot hold: the periphery fragments

Jimmy Feys (1996) talks of the process of exclusion resulting in a crisis of identity for the excluded. This is certainly true, but the crisis is not only of those on the edge of society, but of those at its core. The ontological insecurity of a plural world, where biographies no longer carry the actors on time-honoured tracks and where reflexivity is a virtue, does not allow for any self-satisfaction of place or smugness of being. Nor is there a fixed 'deviant other' out there who grants one certainty by being the reverse of all that is absolutely correct and virtuous. The gaze of late modernity looks at the world seeking the firm and reassuring contours of the other but the gaze wavers, the camera is supposed to produce hard focus but the pictures of the other come out blurred and mosaic, at times some fragments look like pictures of one's own friends and family; the hand steadies resolutely, but the pictures keep on blurring.

Conclusion: the news from Gent

I have in this paper traced the transition from an inclusive to an exclusive society. That is, the move from a society which both materially and ontologically incorporated its members and which attempted to assimilate deviance and disorder to one which involves a great deal of both material and ontological precariousness and which responds to deviance in terms of separation and exclusion. Such a process is driven by changes in the material basis of advanced industrial societies from Fordism to Post-Fordism, and represents the movement into late modernity.

My second task was to root changes in crime and disorder to changes in the material base. The fundamental dynamic of exclusion is a result of market forces which exclude vast sections of the population from the primary labour market and of market values which help generate a climate of individualism. Such a situation has an effect both on the causes of crime (through relative deprivation and individualism) and in the reactions against crime (through economic precariousness and ontological insecurity). The exclusions which occur on top of this primary process are an attempt to deal with the problem of crime and disorder which it engenders. *They are often based on misperception but they are a misperception of a real not an imaginary problem.* Crime itself is an exclusion as are the attempts to control it by barriers, incarceration and stigmatisation. Such processes often exacerbate the problem in a dialectic of exclusion: but the changes which occur in the burgeoning apparatus of crime control are in the long run a response to this predicament. So too are the theories of crime which evolve during this period: the new administrative criminology with its actuarial stance which reflects the rise of risk management as a solution to the crime problem. James Q. Wilson's popular zero-tolerance theory of eliminating incivilities in selected areas, Charles Murray's notion of an underclass of single mothers and feckless fathers which gives an ideological basis to exclusion. Thus exclusionist theories occur at times of social exclusion. None of this suggests a reductionism but it insists that there is a strong continuity of influence between the material basis of society, levels of crime, the crime control apparatus and criminology itself.

Lastly, I have heeded the demands of specificity and contrasted the material and cultural situations in Western Europe and the United States. No doubt such contrast is over-schematic, for the differences within Western Europe are immense, but the constant tendency to generalise from the United States to Europe without acknowledging the profound cultural differences, has to be resisted.

As to the future, the scenario presented by Edward Luttwak is clear, the combination of increased lawlessness and economic precariousness is a formula which could lead to an ever-increasing punitiveness and scapegoating, probably with a strong racist undercurrent. The pre-war history of Europe is a grim portent for such a scenario. I have suggested, in this paper, that there is certainly no inevitability in this process, indeed, that there are strong forces which undermine the delivery of a 'successful' exclusionary policy whether actuarial or cultural. It is on these that a progressive politics must be based. In a world where more and more jobs are precarious, where families are frequently unstable, and where there is widespread knowledge of those from other cultures, it is surely not difficult to understand the predicament of the unemployed, to sympathise with the single mother, to empathise with and, indeed, enjoy cultural differences. The creation of folk devils is not facilitated by the late modern world. But what is necessary is a politics which embraces the excluded and those whose positions are precarious. We need a politics which starts at the edges and goes in as far as is palatable (which is a long way) rather than that which starts at the centre and goes out as far as is charitable (which is not very far). The social-democratic nostalgia for the inclusionist world of the 1950s with full (male) employment, the nuclear family, and the organic community is an impossible dream. As our friends from Gent have pointed out (Hofman, 1993; Lippens, 1994, 1996) any realism which has as its fundamental agenda the reduction of crime by a return to those times is doomed to failure. The task of devising new forms of community, employment which is not totally dependent on the whims of the market place and new and emerging family structures is another matter which takes us far beyond the remit of this paper.

Notes

1 This article draws upon helpful discussions with Stan Cohen, Tim Hope, John Lea, Roger Matthews, Jayne Mooney, John Pits and Nigel South.

2 Zygmunt Bauman has argued that the most exclusionary episode of modern European history, the Holocaust, is a direct product of modernity: 'I propose to treat the Holocaust as a rare, yet significant and reliable test of the hidden possibilities of modern society' (Bauman, 1989: 12). The bureaucratic efficiency of the operation, the industrialisation of the slaughter, even the eugenic ideas which underpinned the travesty, were part and parcel of modern ideas detachable from the specific circumstances of Adolf Hitler and the Third Reich. In terms of more recent history Nils Christie (1993) argued that the prison Gulag of the present period, particularly in the United States, represents a contemporary manifestation of such tendencies inherent in modernity. Bauman himself is, perhaps, less sure of this linkage talking of a 'totalitarian solution without a totalitarian state' (Bauman, 1995: 205) with regard to the present period, and of Hitler's camps as 'a modern invention even when used in the service of anti-modern movements' (*Ibid.*: 206). Clearly the distinction between fascism and liberal democracy has to be reiterated, as has the line between Enlightenment values and the industrial and organisational structures concomitant although not coincident with modernity. The ideals of the Enlightenment were radically inclusivist. They, moreover, as Tod Gitlin (1995) has strenuously indicated, were intended to ensure inclusion and equality despite difference.

The exclusions of fascism (and Stalinism) and of present-day liberal democracies are thus of a different nature. The inclusive post-War period of this essay points to what was to some extent a historical high point of liberal democracy: involving the widening political and economic base of citizenship. But as it was an inclusion which did not recognise difference, difference became deviance from absolute standards. It managed to achieve a high degree of inclusion but at the expense of diversity. Exclusion when it occurred was at a very high threshold. The exclusive society that follows it is much more ready to both accept differences *and* exclude. Diversity of 'lifestyle' is an ideal, and cultural pluralism a cherished value: exclusion is based not on difference but on risk. Acceptable society is thus differentiated and unacceptable society excluded in an actuarial gradient. We have, if you wish, a littoral society stretching from differences in credit rating to differences of assessed dangerousness.

The modern period saw itself as on the road to solving the problem of communality of interests but could not cope with difference of identity, the late modern period exalts differences but cannot cope with the differences of material interest which exist between citizens. The problem lies in the fundamental contradiction of liberal democracy between a system which legitimises itself in terms of equality of opportunity, and reward by merit, but which is unequal and grossly unmeritocratic in its structure. In the United States for example 1 per cent of individuals own one-third of the wealth, and large segments of the population are denied access to the primary labour market. It is such a criminogenic situation which generates the possibility of mass imprisonment. The present increase in the prison population builds on the basis of the chronic rise in crime that occurred throughout the Western World in the late modern period. It is a direct result of the rising rate of relative deprivation coupled with increasing individualism which present-day market economies engender. Thus it is, at core, the result of the *detraditionalisation* of modern societies (see Beck, 1992; Giddens, 1991); People are no longer willing to accept their place in the hierarchy or to unthinkingly place collective over individual interests. The glue that stuck together an unfair and oppressive situation has begun to lose its powers of adhesion. The process of exclusion which has reached its epitome in the American Gulag is, therefore, very much a product of the present moment of liberal democracy and the contemporary development of late modernity. It is a grossly inappropriate reaction to a very real problem: crime. It is thus qualitatively different both in its origins and nature from anything that happened in the exclusionary regimes of Hitler and Stalin.

3 Although it is commonplace to see immigration as the key factor in the formation of more pluralistic societies in the West, I do not think that this is the major influence on the level of pluralistic debate or on ontological insecurity. Indeed many of the values of immigrant cultures are traditional and form little challenge to the diverse values of late modernity. Rather it is the indigenously generated process of diversification which has been at the cutting edge of the new pluralism: witness the debates around women's role, violence, sexual orientation, the environment, animal rights, etc. Thus the debate is as acute in Dublin with little immigration as it is in London or Paris. The role of the immigrant is, as argued in this essay, more a scapegoat, an outgroup set up to assuage ontological insecurity rather than a cause of such (see Vidali, 1996).

4 The mistake here, surely, is that reacting against the empirical fact that there is no simple linear relationship between level of recorded crime and imprisonment, fear of crime and risk of crime, etc., we assert that imprisonment, fear and crime-prevention measures are autonomous of crime rates and, hence, caused by other factors (eg displaced anxiety about economic security, urban development, race). Undoubtedly such displacement occurs (indeed is described in detail in this paper) but this certainly does not allow us to eliminate crime itself from the equation. It must be remembered that human actors (whether manning the social control apparatus or citizens walking the streets) are not positivistic creatures who are simply reflexes of risk rates or crime levels. The human capacity is to assess and make sense of the social world. It would be surprising, therefore, if one ever found a simple linear relationship or the high correlations typical of the natural sciences. Let me give two examples:

(a) Imprisonment: the response to an increase in crime might be to bemoan the high cost of imprisonment and its ineffectiveness and to enter into a period of decarceration (perhaps involving the diversion of juvenile offenders and a pleth-ora of alternative schemes). This might be followed by a period of punitiveness and increased incarceration as a reaction to the fact that reported crime con-tinues to increase. Such a change of policy would ensure that there is no linear relationship between crime rates and imprisonment but the shifts in policy, the diversion schemes, the number and nature of the alternatives, and the scale and nature of the subsequent prison-building programme could not be understood without acknowledging the major influence of the problem of crime.

(b) Fear of crime: one response by lower-working-class men in cities to social exclu-sion is to create a machismo-based culture. This involves, as a matter of manli-ness, a low fear of crime despite a climate of mutual hostility which spills over frequently into crime. Thus a high risk rate is combined with a low fear of crime. Urban women, on the other hand, in the same environment, may become less tolerant to crime, may actively disdain violence, and may demand a better qual-ity of life. This will manifest itself in higher 'fear' (or at least annoyance, indigna-tion, etc). Thus two urban groups will develop diametrically opposite reactions to the risk of crime. To complicate matters further, the elaborate avoidance behaviour developed by sections of urban women to tackle crime may lead to lowered risks and allow criminologists to comment how they have unnaturally high levels of anxiety about crime given that their actual risk is low. Thus there is no conceivable way that one could expect a linear relationship between crime and fear of crime in a survey of such an urban population.

5 Loic Wacquant (1995) in his incisive comparison of Woodlawn on the South Side of Chicago and La Courneuve in the outer ring of Paris points to the crucial role of the State in the process of exclusion. The semi-Welfare State of the US props up rather than deflects market society. In Chicago 'state abandonment' and withdrawal of public institutions occurs to this spatially segregated 'racial reservation'. In Paris, if anything, La Courneuve suffers from an 'over-penetration' of state agencies and public organisations. It is, furthermore, mixed ethnically and socially. 'Racial enclaves such as Chicago's South Side', are, he notes, 'unknown in France – and in all of Europe for that matter'. (p. 560).

References

Back, L. (1996) *New Ethnicities and Urban Culture* (London: UCL Press).

Bauman, Z. (1989) *Modernity and the Holocaust* (Oxford: Blackwell).

Bauman, Z. (1995) *Life in Fragments* (Oxford: Blackwell).

Beck, U. (1992) *Risk Society* (London: Sage).

Beirne, P. (1993) *Inventing Criminology* (New York: State University of New York).

Bureau of Justice Statistics (1996) *Correctional Populations in the United States 1994* (Washington: US Department of Justice).

Campbell, C. (1987) *The Romantic Ethic and the Spirit of Modern Consumerism* (Oxford: Blackwell).

Christie, N. (1993) *Crime Control as Industry* (London: Routledge).

Council of Europe (1995) *Penological Information Bulletin* 19–20 (Brussels: Council of Europe).

Currie, E. (1996) *Is America Really Winning the War on Crime and Should Britain Follow its Example?* (London: NACRO).

Downes, D. (1966) *Delinquent Solution* (London: RKP).

Ericson, R. and Carriere, K. (1994) 'The Fragmentation of Criminology' D. Nelken (ed.) *The Futures of Criminology* (London: Sage).

Etzioni, A. (1993) *The Spirit of Community* (New York: Crown Publishers).

Featherstone, M. (1985) 'Lifestyle and Consumer Culture' *Theory, Culture and Society* 4: 57–70.

Feeley, M. and Simon, J. (1992) 'The New Penology: Notes on the Emerging Strategy of Corrections and Its Implications' *Criminology* 30(4): 449–474.

Feeley, M. and Simon, J. (1994) 'Actuarial Justice: The Emerging New Criminal Law' in D. Nelken (ed.) *The Futures of Criminology* (London: Sage).

Felson, M. (1994) *Crime and Everyday Life* (Thousand Oaks, California: Pine Forge Press).

Feys, J. (1996) 'Social Exclusion and Identity Politics', ERASMUS Common Study Programme, Critical Criminology and the Criminal Justice System, University of Gent (November).

Frank, R. and Cook, P. (1996) *Winner Takes All Society* (London: Routledge).

Galbraith, J. K. (1992) *The Culture of Contentment* (London: Sinclair-Stevenson).

Giddens, A. (1991) *Modernity and Self-Identity* (Cambridge: Polity).

Giddens, A. (1992) *The Transformation of Intimacy* (Cambridge: Polity).

Gilroy, P. (1993) *The Black Atlantic* (London: Verso).

Gitlin, T. (1995) *The Twilight of Common Dreams* (New York: Henry Holt).

Harper, P., Mooney, J., Pollack, M., Whelan, E. and Young, J. (1995) *Islington Street Crime Survey* (London: Islington Council).

Harvey, D. (1989) *The Condition of Postmodernity* (Oxford: Blackwell).

Havel, V. (1996) 'The Hope for Europe' *New York Review of Books* 43(8) (20 June): 38–41.

Hills, J. (1996) 'New Inequalities: the Changing Distribution of Income and Wealth in the United Kingdom' (Cambridge: Cambridge University Press).

Hobsbawm, E. (1994) *The Age of Extremes* (London: Michael Joseph).

Hofman, H. (1993) 'Some Stories of Crime Prevention' Paper given to the Common Study Programme in Criminal Justice and Critical Criminology, University of Gent, 2 November.

Hope, T. (1995) 'The Flux of Victimisation' *British Journal of Criminology*, 35: 327–342.

Hope, T. (1997) 'Inequality and the Future of Community Crime Prevention' in *Crime Prevention at a Cross Roads* ed. S. Lab, American Academy of Criminal Justice Sciences Monogroup in Series (Cincinnati, OH: Anderson Publishing).

Hutton, W. (1995) *The State We're In* (London: Cape).

Jacoby, R. (1994) 'The Myth of Multiculturalism' *New Left Review* 208: 121–126.

Joseph Rowntree Foundation (1955) *J.R.F. Inquiry into Wealth and Income* Vols 1 & 2 (York: Joseph Rowntree Foundation).

Kinsey, R., Lea, J. and Young, J. (1986) *Losing the Fight Against Crime* (Oxford: Blackwell).

Krauthammer, C. (1993) 'Defining Deviancy Up' *The New Republic* (22 Nov.): 20–25.

Lea, J. (1992) 'The Analysis of Crime' in J. Young and R. Matthews (eds) *Rethinking Criminology* (London: Sage).

Lea, J. (1997) 'Post-Fordism and Criminality' in N. Jewson and S. MacGregor (eds) *Transforming Cities* (London: Routledge).

Lea, J. and Young, J. (1993) *What is to be Done About Law and Order?* (London: Pluto).

Lippens, R. (1994) 'Critical Criminologies and the Reconstruction of Utopia. Some residual thoughts from the good old days' ERASMUS *Common Study Programme, Critical Criminology and the Criminal Justice System, University of Bari* (May).

Lippens, R. (1996) 'Hypermodern Progressive Social Policy: A view from Belgium' Conference on *Crime and Social Order in Europe* Manchester 7–10 September.

Luttwak, E. (1995) 'Turbo-Charged Capitalism and Its Consequences' *London Review of Books* 17 (21) (2 Nov.): 6–7.

Lynch, J. P. (1988) 'A Comparison of Prison Use in England, Canada, West Germany and The United States: A Limited Test of The Punitive Hypothesis' *Journal of Criminal Law and Criminology* 79(1): 180–217.

McRobbie, A. and Thornton, S. (1995) 'Rethinking Moral Panic for Multimediated Social Worlds' *British Journal of Sociology* 46(4): 559–74.

Melossi, D. (1996) 'Social Control in the New Europe' Conference on *Crime and Social Order in Europe* Manchester 7–10 September.

Merton, R. K. (1938) 'Social Structure and Anomie' *American Sociological Review* Vol III: 672–682.

Mooney, J. (1996) 'Violence, Space and Gender' in N. Jewson and S. MacGregor (eds) *Transforming Cities* (London: Routledge).

Moynihan, D. P. (1993) 'Defining Deviancy Down' *American Scholar* 62: 13–16.

Painter, J., Lea, J., Woodhouse, T. and Young, J. (1989) *The Hammersmith and Fulham Crime Survey* (Middlesex University: Centre for Criminology).

Raban, J. (1974) *Soft City* (London: Hamilton).

Ruggiero, V. and South, N. (1997) 'The Late-Modern City as a Bazaar' *British Journal of Sociology* 48: 55–71.

Sennett, R. (1991) *The Conscience of the Eye* (London: Faber & Faber).

Sibley, D. (1995) *The Geographies of Exclusion* (London: Routledge).

Simmel, G. (1950) 'The Metropolis and Mental Life' in K. H. Wolff (trans.) *The Sociology of Georg Simmel* (New York: The Free Press).

South, N. (1994) 'Privatising Policing in the European Market: Some Issues for Theory, Policy and Research' *European Sociological Review* 10(3): 219–27.

Trickett, A., Ellingworth, D., Hope, T. and Pease, K. (1995) ' Crime Victimisation in the Eighties' *British Journal of Criminology*, 35: 343–359.

Van Swaaningen, R. (1997) *Critical Criminology: Visions from Europe* (London: Sage).

Vidali, S. (1996) 'Selectivity, Police Activity and Internal Enemies in Greece' Paper given at the ERASMUS Common Study Programme: *Critical Criminology and Criminal Justice* University of Gent, November.

Wacquant, L. (1995) 'The Comparative Structure and Experience of Urban Exclusion: "Race", Class, and Space in Chicago and Paris' in K. McFate, R. Lawson and W. J. Wilson (eds) *Poverty, Inequality and the Future of Social Policy* (New York: Russell Sage Foundation).

Walklate, S. (1995) *Gender and Crime* (Hemel Hempstead: Prentice Hall).

Walton, P. and Young, J. (eds) (1997) *The New Criminology Revisited* (London: Macmillan).

Willis, P. (1977) *Learning to Labour* (Aldershot: Gower).

Willis, P. (1990) *Common Culture* (Milton Keynes: Open University Press).

Wilson, J. Q. (1985) *Thinking About Crime* (New York: Vintage Books).

Wilson, W. J. (1996) *When Work Disappears* (New York: Knopf).

Woolf, J. (1985) 'The Invisible Flâneuse' *Theory, Culture and Society* 2(3): 37–46.

Young, J. (1971) *The Drugtakers* (London: Paladin).

Young, J. (1995) *Policing the Streets* (London: Islington Council).

Young, J. (1997a) 'Writing on the Cusp of Change: A New Criminology for the Twenty-First Century' in P. Walton and J. Young (eds) *The New Criminology Revisted* (London: Macmillan).

Part II

PENALITY AND CRIMINAL JUSTICE

5

A CRISIS OF YOUTH
OR OF
JURIDICAL RESPONSE?

Francis Bailleau

Introduction

For a number of years now, the issue of young people has been at the centre of controversy, particularly in respect of the troubled debate over law and order. More specifically, the growth of crime, and nearly all references to the perceived increase in the use of violence within social relationships, are attributed to young people. In several European countries, all kinds of penal and social policies that had previously been implemented with respect to young people have been subject to questioning and modification, as we will see in this discussion of the situation in France.

This paper will address the capacity of the French penal system to regulate the deteriorating situation of young people in a rapidly changing society. But our remarks will hopefully also be relevant to other countries, where similar attempts may be taking place 'to contain' the excesses of a weakened social order, perhaps by modification of traditional penal policies (Bailleau, 1996).

The current tension between the feeling of insecurity and the responses by the state apparatus is only one side of a more general questioning. Indeed, since justice is the secular arm of the state, it is the role of the state itself which is currently at stake within Western societies. The state's dominant role in making, applying and managing norms is being contested. This weakening of normative systems has been encouraged through a blurring of the previously distinct roles of the private and public spheres, on the one hand, and the absence of a clear border-line between these spheres, on the other (Ehrenberg, 1995).

Following the period often referred to as 'Les Trente Glorieuses' (the thirty glorious years) – during which the state was particularly active in order to ensure the social protection and the everyday safety of its citizens – today's state can no longer impose its rule, correct the behaviour of particular individuals and/or minorities, or facilitate the integration of poor or deviant people into mainstream society (Bailleau *et al.*, 1995). Previous forms of public policy, which maintained public order whilst also ensuring that citizens left behind continued to be focussed on the hegemonic model of waged employment, have been replaced. These policies or models of government action are succeeded by a situation in which a range of different job-creation and order-maintenance projects are funded and implemented by a variety of public or private bodies, run either by the central or local government.

- Can and should the mode of regulation established in France in 1945 (whereby the magistrate is granted exceptional power within the juvenile court), respond to this new orientation?
- Is it its role to do so?

Authorities of socialisation and juvenile law

In order to answer these questions, it is necessary to think more broadly, so as to include all the institutions in charge of young people. Actions by the juvenile court cannot be isolated from the influence of other agencies, which are equally important for their role in 'teaching the norm' and in social regulation (the family, schools, the health services, culture, sports). Juvenile-court magistrates maintain close relationships with these authorities, even though their courts are sometimes isolated both geographically and institutionally – i.e. through their specifically legal role. The magistrate, however, very often relies on members of other institutions to take specific action. More precisely, the magistrate depends on police or social workers for obtaining information prior to any court case, as well as on community and residential workers, and others who play key roles, later, in the treatment phase. Without them, the magistrate could possibly not act, and vice versa.

The majority of the young people dealt with by the juvenile court have not committed any more serious offence than other youngsters. However, they usually have a heavy burden of 'institutional past' – marked by a series of experiences of rejection and/or exclusion at the hands of one or other socialisation authority. Even before the final intervention – the mechanism of segregation itself – young offenders have been identified for education, re-socialisation, retraining and some kind of follow-up. These mechanisms are constituent elements – known procedures and practices – of the national Department of Education, the national Department of Health or local authorities.

Like the majority of the institutions dealing with the young, the juvenile court (and juvenile law as such) still trades in a notion of education which identifies the young offender as an 'adult-to-be'. The juvenile magistrate mainly intervenes as a state agent, so as to control the socialisation and educational experience of a young person still under the purview of his or her family and local neighbourhood. The juvenile magistrate operates as the representative of the state in the sense that the behaviour of some young person (and sometimes his or her family) is deemed to have been disruptive to public order as a whole, and the magistrate sees it as his or her role to encourage acceptable behaviour and successful re-education. His or her intervention in these cases is based on an individual order which may, in some circumstances, demand the segregation of the young person from his/her environment and categorise the young person, in effect, as 'a distinctive problem to be solved'.

The specific position of the juvenile court and its unique functioning (from both a judicial and legal point of view) are justified in so far as their action is limited in time. Their aim is to bring a teenager *to the age of majority* in conditions respecting public order. The judge's assigned role as a 'mentor' casts light on the prevalent notion of negotiation, based on a personalised relationship with the young offender (at least in a first stage).

Social and economic changes, however, we will argue, have started to render this distinct category of youth indistinct, and this has contributed to a weakening of the institutions themselves. After having benefited from a long period of social consensus, the exceptional practices of the juvenile magistrate have increasingly been contested by the public as well as by elected representatives and professionals.

Two main trends can be distinguished in the attempt to regulate the consequences of the deterioration in the social situation for youngsters and to compensate for the loss of credibility of the institution. The first answer to this difficult situation, at least in France, has been state-led, beginning in the early 1970s. In the passage of the 'Liberty and Security Law', the Gaullist Government attempted to strengthen the traditional repressive apparatus available to the state. In 1981, the new (socialist) government engaged itself in a new direction : in contrast to their predecessors, they repealed the Liberty and Security Law and also put an end to the death penalty.

A new role for justice?

In accordance with their accustomed and familiar ideological predispositions, the Socialist Government located the issue of crime (especially juvenile delinquency) alongside a bundle of other social problems, at least to begin with, which it intended to tackle through a series of reformative measures. In particular, it argued that these problems were to be understood as resulting from conditions of economic crisis, to which its own economic strategy was a response. But events such as 'the hot summer' in 1981[1] forced the Government to launch more specific and immediate policies aimed at reducing popular feelings of insecurity. The main response was the production of a new policy of security and delinquency-prevention at the local level.

The promotion of this new orientation in 1982 resulted from the work of a Commission of Mayors chaired by the Deputy-mayor of a commune within the Paris region, Gilbert Bonnemaison. Bonnemaison was in effect put in charge of the political management of this re-making of social-democratic law-and-order policy, taking into account the context of decentralisation of legal powers voted in by the new government.

The report by the Commission of Mayors was based on the following principles:

1   the legitimacy of the prevention-repression couplet,
2   the search for a consensus between the various political trends,
3   the power of locally elected politicians,
4   the significance of the local level in the pragmatic management of illegality, and
5   the importance of a strategy of communication.

Central to this strategy was an emphasis on the improvement of living conditions, a struggle against segregation, the promotion of crime-prevention mechanisms and other means to ensure security in the city, especially in the so-called 'difficult' areas. However, the police, the 'gendarmerie' and the legal system did not lose their pre-eminence. They still remained central to the enactment of the new policy, in some cases acting as a major obstacle preventing change in the definition of public order and the conception and strategic management of public order. Justice is a concept, a moral doctrine, but it is first and foremost an idea that is bound up with old and hierarchical forms of administration, deemed necessary in an earlier period to the routine functioning of the state. It is also a system and hierarchy that is extremely jealous of its prerogatives and capable of mounting strong resistance to any programme of change. The reformist ideas of 1982 were not strong enough to overcome this resistance, and the new approaches to the regulation of delinquency identified with Bonnemaison (emphasising local processes in particular) failed to be generalised throughout France and also failed to foster significant change in the legal machinery.

But the new responses implemented in some parts of France at the local level did encourage a broader rethinking of the role of the state. Local authorities began to look in a more concrete way at different means of underwriting the security to which all citizens are entitled. Many authorities found ways of creating and extending alternative and intermediate solutions to 'crime problems' other than the legal or specifically penal response. Nowadays, the expectation in many areas is that the law should not only define the parameters of social order and acknowledge the limits to morally acceptable behaviour (through the courts), but also that it should initiate systems for protection of the people and their goods, that it should manage systems of restitution and make up for damage through mediation and reparation.

Defining 'public order' (and describing systems for its effective implementation) was not an easy task for the Mayors and Local Delinquency Prevention Councils (Conseils Communaux de Prevention de la Delinquance). It may well be, however, that the main causes of difficulty are the internal problems of these institutions, the problems its agents face in translating their concerns into legal language, rather than the actual mobilisation of the practices themselves.

In the 1990s, there is a suggestion that the very concept of law and order ('ordre public') (together with the responses to delinquency associated with it) are becoming obsolescent. The evidence for this is the contradiction between the insecurity felt by the population faced with certain types of offence-behaviours and the limits of the action that both the police and legal system can take in such cases.

A new delinquency?

In order to understand the new role of the state, it is necessary to look beyond the classic idea of the public order–youth delinquency relationship, as it is expressed in the stance of the local authorities. Most laypeople now have a new definition of the insecurity they feel in relation to young people's behaviour, irrespective of the official definitions of delinquency, police function, police and legal action.[2] The new expression 'incivilités' (which in part owes its origins to surveys mounted by criminological and social researchers) illustrates this mismatch. The idea involves explicit or implicit reference to a whole set of behaviours and incidents found disturbing by the population. However, up until now, the word has not been advanced in any legal form. Hence accusations of 'incivilité' still cannot lead to a legal procedure or to incrimination as such. The expression particularly references activities committed by young people in groups or gangs, especially when visible in public or semi-public spaces – juvenile misbehaviour, various types of threatening behaviour, vandalism, suspected drug-trafficking, verbal abuse, disturbing the peace or just minor offences. It can also be a reference to what often are simply called local neighbourhood problems.

Juvenile law is faced with the challenge of adapting to this new 'security environment', and this does not prove easy. Two key problems present themselves.

The first element refers to the role of a judicial intervention within stigmatised areas of the city. Such areas are commonly characterised by the heavy concentration of unemployed and/or idle adults and youth. A relatively restricted space, once conceived of as a space to which an employed workforce returned in the evenings and at the weekend, is now 'occupied' 24 hours a day. These people can only base their identity and intimate personal knowledge of the world on their experience of this same area, by contrast with the rest of the city, of which they know relatively little. Their access to the larger city (for example, its shopping malls or arcades) may actively be denied (e.g. by private security guards) and/or they may be alienated in other ways from that larger city, which they may feel reinforces a negative image of themselves. Indeed, the reaction of many residents of marginalised areas to the larger city may take the form of aggression – a way of rejecting a city that is not theirs.

In many cases, the resulting acts of violence cannot be specifically codified as an infraction of law. The court may often find itself in a position whereby it is unable to take up these cases and start proceedings, and may instead have to make use of the description of them as 'incivilités' instead of offences.

The second element relates to the current situation of young people. Generally speaking, two trends can be stressed. On the one hand, there is a rapid rise in schooling rates (more than 80 per cent of 18 to 19 year olds in France are still in school) and on the other hand, the vast majority of the remaining 20 per cent are unable to find any kind of stable job and hence to be financially independent. This postponement of adult autonomy in the labour market can easily continue to the age of 25. The 20 per cent (school dropouts) are mainly concentrated geographically in the 'sensitive districts'. They are young people who might previously have been dealt with by the juvenile courts through some kind of educational or treatment order – for a fixed period of time during their adolescence: now they must remain – for at least twice as long a period of time as any supervisory or treatment order in the earlier historical period – within the confines of their own run-down areas, without any guaranteed income, beyond minimal levels of state benefit, and without any accommodation of their own. Such conditions make it hard for teachers or social workers to do any serious work with them, over and above that of managing the extended period of inactivity.

The new situation can be summarised in the form of three questions:

1   How to implement a judicial order when the facts of the case cannot directly lead to legal incrimination?
2   Should it always be the role of the juvenile court to regulate the transition from the status of 'needy young people' to the status of autonomous adult?
3   How to implement an educational or treatment order when the age limit of 18 is the cut-off point for projects directed at the young?

Defining a new social order

The suburbs and the 'cités' (high-rise estates) have become the defining symbols of the new social issues that have emerged in the last few years. The 'social question' is now nearly always formulated by reference to this population that has been 'alienated' from society. Of course, there were the tramps and beggars before the Industrial Revolution, impoverished or lumpenproletariat workers and alcoholics later, but in France we now have an excluded, marginal population contained within 'balkanised' areas on the urban periphery. Accordingly, political discussions of 'social problems' are nearly always traced or reduced to the individuals who reside, and/or the conditions which obtain, in these types of areas. In this process the media play a major role, increasingly presenting any manifestation of disorder in geographical or spatial metaphors – as emanating from 'those areas' – the high-rise estates left behind by public authorities.

Social workers engaged in community activity within these areas are overwhelmed. They cannot cope with such a concentration of social tension, and are no longer able, even with the most imaginative 'preventative' endeavours, to reduce the number of violent incidents in these confined, overcrowded balkanised areas. Social workers in France used to be able to monitor the transition of young people to adulthood in a personalised way, especially after the imposition by the courts of individual supervision orders. Nowadays, in the balkanised urban areas, this kind of individual regulation of young people and their transition to adulthood is highly problematic. It is no longer that young people are having problems simply with their parents, or with the 'storm and stress' of adolescence, to which social workers can respond by acting as a tutor and a friend. The problem increasingly is one of a confrontation between young people in these areas and all Others – i.e. those who have access to regular, official and waged work, proper education and accommodation. The authorities are not only confronted with a significant increase in individual delinquency, but with a continuing deterioration of the living conditions in these districts situated in the core or on the periphery of industrial cities. The real issue is that of long-term marginalisation, and the question of whether groups cut off from the classic process of inclusion in society (through waged work) will indeed participate within the established normative arena (Castel, 1995).

This new situation demands a reassessment of the problem beyond traditional frames of reference. In the first place, this reappraisal must take into account the widening gap between behaviours that constitute an offence in law (and are therefore acted upon by the police and legal systems) and popular views on youth behaviour. This discrepancy between legal and social conceptions also finds expression, it should be said, in major conflicts in relation to the use of public space.

These tensions and conflicts cannot be treated in the traditional legal context. Increasingly, in fact, the situation is one of opposition between different social groups (street people versus adults etc.) creating the conditions for unending general insecurity. There are no solutions to this through individualised treatment, and, as we have already argued, the impact of law is reduced by the fact that so many of the incidents of trouble finish up being defined as 'incivilités' rather than offences.

Underlying all these processes, of course, is the evolution in the behaviour of 'excluded youth'. Since the 1970s, the statistical evidence suggests, there has been a significant increase in youth suicides, and in many other examples of self-destructive behaviour. The consumption of alcohol and drugs, for example, has increased significantly during the last twenty years – and the consumption of both types in combination is also on the increase – in parallel with the increase in marginalisation. So also have other forms of risk behaviour (cars, motorbikes, violent sports).

These changes in youthful behaviour patterns are more relevant to the issue of exclusion than the actual increase in classic types of juvenile offences committed by idle young people. The increase in self-destructive behaviours may be explained in terms of the scarcity of financial resources, the geographical divide between the areas where the marginalised young people are most heavily concentrated and the larger city (a separate world), and the absence of positive prospects.

In addition to this, in many of these balkanised areas, access to the minimum wage necessary for survival is increasingly difficult or impossible. Instead, there is evidence of the development of a parallel economy based on barter, drugs, the sale of stolen objects, illegal work, and prostitution. The idea of employment in a traditional sense (involving a salary, independence and social protection) has no clear reference. There are some individual examples of success and/or escape, but the overwhelming collective adaptation emerging in the balkanised areas is evidence of a new 'culture of poverty', akin to that first defined by Oscar Lewis in 1961 (Lewis, 1993) but in different historical and structural circumstances, in which survival in conditions of general worklessness is the paramount consideration. In particular, within this new culture of poverty, the boundaries between the legal and the illegal are blurred, and they are not widely used as a cultural reference. Social integration requires conformity to the culturally dominant models and living standards. Since the culture of poverty cannot clearly be separated from the cultural aspects of a struggle for survival, this tends to render the traditional distinction between exclusion and delinquency meaningless.

This general estrangement from mainstream society of marginal young people in the balkanised urban peripheries – and the increasing embeddedness of these young people in a separate community – is rarely analysed as such. Instead, current legal and political discussion and treatment of the delinquencies of marginal young people – which never address the conditions that produce such marginalisation in the first instance (no matter that they are intensifying in their effects) – only serve to reinforce the phenomenon. In many ways, these legal responses actively contribute to its institutionalisation. Criminologists have often said that there are no legal solutions to social problems: it is particularly clear that the new policies currently being developed in France to combat crime and offenders *cannot* solve the specific kinds of social problems (of marginalisation and the institutionalisation of the balkanised urban peripheries) that have been produced by contemporary socio-economic transformation, especially as these changes have impacted on the transition from youth to adulthood amongst the residualised populations. The state remains the traditional warden of public order through the mechanics of its judicial apparatus. But it has not yet been able to react to the widespread feeling of insecurity – insecurity which arises, on the one hand, from the emergence of new behaviours (and cultures of survival) on the part of young people, and, on the other, from the state's own inability to respond with any effectiveness to these changed circumstances (Bailleau *et al.* 1989).

Juvenile law historically tried to provide individual and collective responses to situations of social dysfunction, through an educational strategy. But such a response in juvenile law has now encountered its limits, not least because of its continued adherence to a classic definition of the judicial function. Vainly thriving to preserve its traditional role in a changed society, the law is unable to play a significant and useful role in the protection and enhancement of public order.

Notes

1 The first event – a violent riot of young people – took place in the eastern suburbs of Lyon during the summer of 1981. Following this first outburst, references to the idea of a 'hot summer' became commonplace and served to foster several exceptional procedures, often identified as 'operations against a hot summer' implemented by Local Authorities to prevent further occurrences (Jazouli, 1992).

2 'The feeling of insecurity helps redefine the limits of those who are considered to belong to society, to redefine the "social contract" – a basis for accepting the presence of other human beings, who have rights and duties' (Roché, 1993: 15).

References

Bailleau, F. (1996), *Les jeunes face à la justice pénale. Analyse critique de l'application de l'ordonnance de 1945*, Paris: Syros.

Bailleau, F. and Garioud, G. (1989) 'Violence et insécurité : l'impossible partage' in *L'état de la France et de ses habitants*, Paris: La Découverte.

Bailleau, F., Castel, R. and Joubert, M. (1995) 'La réduction des risques, peau de chagrin des politiques sociales?' *Journal du Sida* 73, Paris.

Castel, R. (1995), *Les métamorphoses de la question sociale*, Paris: Fayard.

Ehrenberg, A. (1995), *L'individu incertain*, Paris: Calmann-Levy.

Jazouli, A. (1992), *Les années banlieues*, Paris: Seuil.

Lewis, O. (1993), *Les enfants de Sanchez. Autobiographie d'une famille mexicaine*, Paris: Gallimard.

Roché, S. (1993), *Le sentiment d'insécurité*, Paris: PUF.

6

PRISON: BETWEEN THE LAW AND SOCIAL ACTION

Claude Faugeron

Two remarks inspired me to write this chapter. The first came from a prison psychiatrist who, during a conversation, posed the question, 'Why can't we care for people whilst in prison since we can't do so in the outside world?'. The other remark was taken from an interview with a magistrate:

> Each time we could possibly pass an alternative sentence, either deferred or with probation, we did so. But it is not always possible. These drug addicts who crawl out of the gutter in the early hours of the morning, thin, haggard, freezing cold in their little suits and shirts, what should be done with them? Leave them outside on a suspended sentence and probation which would probably not work? Or indeed send them to prison where they can get warm, eat and wait for better days.
>
> (Greilsamer and Schneidermann 1992: 214–215)

These two remarks give rise to the following thoughts – in today's democratic Western societies, should prison not be the last place to give charity, care, education, training, entertainment, in brief, social action? If we were to stretch this reasoning to its extreme, could we not say that prisons have a real function in taking charge of the mentally disturbed and the under-privileged sectors of the population?

I would like to concentrate on these questions by referring to three points – quantitative and qualitative changes in the use of imprisonment in Western societies; the current way of thinking on the function of prisons; and finally the evolution of prisoners' rights in the context of the constraints on prison management.

The majority of points that I will make are taken from recent French studies. Indeed, the period of Socialist rule has enabled prisons to be opened to research, which had never been the case in France. I do think, however, that we must be able to recognise the reasoning which may be revealed in empirical studies, in the context of different cultural traditions, provided that these contexts are not too economically and politically distant. This is, in any case, the conclusion that I can draw from examining the international literature on the subject.

Prison confinement in European democratic societies

Without going too far with analogies which could be misleading – having taken into account cultural differences and contrasting histories – several similarities between the countries of Western Europe can be found, particularly if we were to speak of trends. Indeed, we can note symptoms linked to difficulties encountered by national budgets, a slowing down of growth in the majority of these countries, difficulties transferring from the Welfare State to neo-liberalism (Rosanvallon 1995), a crisis of confidence in institutions and political representation, as well as a trend towards a dualisation of society.

The changes which affect the penal systems have also shown similarities, which are certainly not unrelated to the aforementioned points – increased sentences for certain crimes (notably in relation to the battle against drugs, terrorism, violent crimes, etc.), remodelling of the penalty scale, creating new crime categories, and the fight against unauthorised immigration. More often than not, these legislative reforms are carried out according to a logical step-by-step response, as problems arise, when it is felt that public opinion is affected, or even for electoral reasons. The modification of legislation has become a matter of interest for the general public in which current affairs and the press play a supporting role (cf. Ehrel and Garapon 1993). The practice of remand, sentencing and release on parole come under the 'lowest risk' category (the risk being understood here as releasing someone who could commit a crime). Imprisonment is clearly becoming more and more a means of neutralisation. The result is a rising number of inmates, and this is exacerbated by the lengthening of prison sentences (Tubex and Snacken 1995 and 1996).

In this chapter, I will not try to uncover explanations for these changes, in part suggested by the previous remarks, which you will find in greater depth in Ruggiero, Ryan and Sim (1995) amongst others. I would just like to underline the following points:

1   European countries' support for the Convention for the Protection of Human Rights and Personal Freedom is leading to the abolition of the death penalty. In most countries such an innovation is accompanied by the concern to retain an instrument of an exemplary nature and of long-lasting neutralisation. The neutralisation tool is all the more necessary since the sphere of activity of psychiatric confinement is dwindling: imprisonment becomes the only solution for cases of mental disorder for which psychiatric institutions do not have any immediate answer (Langlais and Géronimi 1993. Laberge *et al.* 1995).

2   Strategies to combat illegal immigration are leading to a reinforcement of

repressive tools or even to the creation of short terms of imprisonment in case of deportation, which we know, in a number of countries, even those renowned for being the most democratic, presents scandalous imprisonment conditions, as the CPT reports show (cf. also Observatoire International des Prisons 1996, and in addition, for France, Ganoux 1996, Perrin-Martin 1996). In this context, we also use prison sentences, even short-term, as a form of arrest and as a pretext for expulsion. As an example for France, there are the charter flights to the country of origin, which are filled to a large extent with foreign prisoners at the end of their sentence, picked up as they leave prison.

3　Policies to fight against drug use and illicit drug trafficking have led to increased 'tariffs' for drug trafficking, without making the distinction between traffickers and drug dealers.

4　At the same time a general trend can also be observed towards carrying out changes in the penal policies of 'bifurcation' and researching new methods of open supervision (Community Service, Electronic Tagging,[1] etc.). These innovations have not always provided the expected results with regard to the decrease in prison populations (Landreville 1994): they have probably had the unintentional effect of extending the sentences actually served, where previously sentences would have been carried out in the community. What-ever the case, we know that such sentences are rarely applied to crimes committed by people who are in precarious situations – such as drug addicts and foreigners.

5　Finally, a trend towards developing and rationalising police operations and customs control, within a national context or on a European level (cf. for example the Schengen agreement and the Maastricht Treaty (Brion 1996)). Although the integration of European policing is proving to be a slow and difficult process to implement, this movement accentuates the trend towards using remand in the same way as in the nineteenth century, that of a public order policing tool, supporting, with the aid of the law, unstable, drifting, mobile populations, or even those in an illegal situation.

With these developments, we can see certain characteristics related to the use of imprisonment which are found in many countries: the trend towards an increase in remand prisoners, an increasing length of time spent in prison and the over-representation of foreigners in prison. National characteristics must be considered, for example, with regard to the fight against terrorism or organised crime. However, unification of criminal policies at a European level is being carried out as well as can be expected. On the one hand there are humani-tarian intentions outlined in policies developed within the framework of the European Council (Faugeron and Hulsman 1996); on the other hand, policies are being developed from a policing point of view and under the pretext of public order.

However, the extensive use of imprisonment to deal with the problems of serious criminality, mental disorders, public order, drug-addiction, insecurity and illegal immigration, causes serious difficulties with regard to penitentiary policies: over-population, tensions within prisons and amongst the staff, continually inadequate budgets, without mentioning the sanitation aspects linked to the imprisonment of marginalised individuals, drug-addicts and often those infected with the HIV virus, hepatitis or tuberculosis (Haut Comité de la Santé Publique 1993). The difficulties which arise come under two categories. The first is of a symbolic nature: how do we justify the use of criminal law and, in particular, the decision to use imprisonment to deal with social problems which could be dealt with in the outside world? 'Bifurcation' policies provide one of the answers to this question. The second difficulty is of a practical nature: how do we maintain order in these over-populated prisons, in the context of toughening criminal policy? The truth is that it is this second point in particular which has held the attention of politicians. There have been numerous investigations following violent incidents or staff strikes in prisons. They have not all had the same widespread publicity as in Great Britain. However they all show the particular concern of the management with regard to maintaining calm in prisons.

I would suggest that there is a constant retrospective effect and reciprocal adjustments between the matter of legitimisation and matters regarding prison management conditions. We cannot have one without the other. Indeed, in sup-posedly democratic regimes, we cannot maintain law and order for long periods purely by force alone. This requires methods which do not conflict too much with public opinion and which to some extent manage to justify the use of imprison-ment. Here, I support the arguments of Sparks (1994): the crisis of the penal model is essentially a legitimacy crisis. However, I do not support Sparks' argu-ments which focus essentially on punitive imprisonment, as I believe that since the invention of prison, practices of imprisonment have been justified through social defence and neutralisation (Faugeron and Le Boulaire 1992; Faugeron 1994 and 1995).

At the same time, democratic rules can only be applied in the context of forced imprisonment in which by definition individuals are deprived of the main charac-teristic of their citizenship: the freedom to come and go as they choose. It is therefore necessary to create other rules which clash with the logic of closed environments.[2]

I would like to further develop these points, dealing with studies about normal-isation and rehabilitation, the interaction between the two extremes of prison management – security, and the maintenance of law and order – and finally the very way in which rights evolve within this context.

Rehabilitation versus normalisation

With reference to the typology of Adler and Longhurst (1994), in Europe we can identify similarities among the analyses of the ends and of the means of imprisonment. Certainly, national and cultural differences are even more perceptible on this point than on the former, particularly with regard to the specific points being debated. Thus, for example, the rehabilitation and normal-isation debate in France has never gone beyond a small number of initiates,[3] whilst it has gone much further in the United Kingdom and countries of North-ern Europe. Rehabilitation remains the key phrase of magistrates, of prison administration (largely dominated by magistrates in France) and professionals. Yet, the policies put into effect by the prison service are governed by the notion of normalisation, probably for management reasons, particularly in regard to the establishments for prisoners on remand and for short sentences, which are largely overpopulated. The idea of control is linked to the increase in long prison terms. Even if 'control' is a major concern of prison management – always reactivated during collective demonstrations by prisoners – this concern only ever extended beyond the prison service into the broader society during the period of great revolts at the beginning of the 1970s.

I am not going to linger over the arguments here – based mainly on neutralisa-tion, the defence of public peace and the security of citizens – which are used by politicians to justify the increase of sentences for certain crimes. Parties of the left and right mostly agree on such arguments, just as they agree on the need for a penal policy of 'bifurcation'. It is true that in France politicians are particularly interested in sentences and criminal procedures (from a legislative point of view), and are hardly interested in the conditions and practices of enforcing the sen-tences (from an executive point of view). I would like to consider the 'legitimacy' argument which is being used increasingly by advocates of the dignity of prisoners or by practitioners (magistrates, social workers, doctors and psycholo-gists, volunteers, etc). This argument could be classified as being humanitarian, as it concentrates on two themes: that of the 'prisoner-citizen' (Favard 1994), and that of punishment as 'a reminder of the law' (Garapon and Salas 1995). The first theme touches on normalisation: the prisoner must have the same rights and duties as the ordinary citizen, with the exception of freedom. The second is a new metamorphosis of rehabilitation: in order to become a good citizen, the 'person being punished' must learn where the limits are set and must know which social boundaries must not be crossed.

Indeed, these two arguments are not contradictory. Furthermore, we can observe that they are often elaborated upon by magistrates and doctors. The former argue: 'remind them of the law and I can work with them', whilst the latter state: 'in order to create a state of mind suitable for reinsertion or accept-ance of treatment, I must first of all remember the law'. In both cases, it seems to me that it is only a question of justifying professional practices and we cannot disguise the fundamental failure: the prevention of recidivism.[4]

Against the background of these arguments, the question of physical and moral misery of the majority of prisoners arises. This question, which is not completely new, has allowed the implementation of social and health services in prisons, even more so when the imprisonment of drug addicts and the Aids epidemic have given rise to the fear that the prisons are becoming new sources of infection. Thus a new argument of legitimacy has been developed: to imprison an ill person, a drug addict, an illiterate, etc., is to act for their well being, since they will be given care, food, educational programmes, professional training, etc. We are coming to a kind of paradox: the quality of the action carried out on behalf of these 'captive' individuals sometimes goes beyond that of the programmes addressed to similar individuals outside prisons. We must also emphasise the energy and dedication demonstrated by many voluntary organisations and social workers in implementing these services.

Previously, I mentioned the role of management within a climate conducive to the expansion of the penitentiary system as a whole. A constantly increasing budget can only be defended by arguing for the social use of prison, or by mobilising the notion of security through neutralisation and the fight against recidivism. As a result, the arguments used by international and non-governmental organisations, which pursue humanitarianism, and those used by prison administrations when asking for funds, come together on this point. In both cases, the question is to provide prisoners with decent living conditions. If we add to this the fear that a supposedly excessive liberalism towards prisoners alienates the electorate, who then risks being tempted by the Extreme Right, the objectives of prison can only vary slightly between rehabilitation (how to change the individual for the better), normalisation (how to treat him/her as an ordinary citizen), and neutralisation[5] (how to detain him/her for as long as possible to protect society, without causing further problems for the other prisoners and especially for the staff).[6]

The problem is, therefore, that only neutralisation can prove its effectiveness, provided prison sentences are long enough and calm reigns in the establishments for long-term prisoners. On the other hand, the validity of rehabilitation cannot be proven. In order for rehabilitation to prove effective prison would have to improve conditions in the outside world, a task which is beyond its remit. The remaining prison function which may have any credibility is normalisation We can argue that the increase in individuals suffering from some form of social disadvantage should be dealt with through the expansion of 'care in prison', which ought to be brought to the standards of care provision outside the institution. Furthermore, since the funds destined for penal administration are always delayed, one is forced to resort to other organisations[7] or voluntary intervention. In this context, arguments about normalisation and rehabilitation have a common cause: some reference to the fight against recidivism is always useful to obtain external help and new investments. We can also understand that this combination of arguments is found in the discourse of the authorities responsible for prison management.

Notions of security and maintenance of law and order

Whatever the form and quantity of the rights and services that we try to bring into force in prisons, the difficulty remains of adapting such rights and services

to a population deprived of freedom. Research has shown that two major concerns govern prison actions: security, understood in the sense where the prisoner must not escape, and the maintenance of law and order (Faugeron *et al.* 1996). Deprivation of freedom through a judicial decision is the first major concern. In addition – contrary to what we often believe (or say) – it is not only the safety of citizens which is under question, but primarily state authority: escape is a defiance of this authority just as arbitrary imposition of detention is a defiance of human rights. Of course these two ideas of security and maintenance of law and order are also at the heart of the functioning of civil society, but each is related in a different way. Maintaining law and order can be understood from a different perspective. In civil society freedom pre-exists, is given freely to all, and can only be taken away in order to protect the freedom and safety of citizens. Everything which is not forbidden is allowed. In prison however, this perspective is reversed, since the deprivation of freedom is the first condition to be imposed. It means therefore that everything which is not authorised is forbidden. Maintaining prison order differs from maintaining public order in that the former is an end in itself, whatever the means may be – calm must prevail in prison – whilst maintaining public order is a means of ensuring freedom and protecting citizens. Imprisonment itself is a means of ensuring public order and/or public safety.

In this respect, and unlike the majority of organisations, the prison organisation cannot have a clear objective (whatever it may be called: amendment, treatment, rehabilitation, re-socialisation, etc.), in particular when, under pressure from the demand for neutralisation, the prison must cope with increasingly long periods of detention. It can only have one objective, determined from outside as directly relevant by state authority, that of keeping prisoners in a closed environment. It is then the responsibility of the prison to ensure that there is no overcrowding. Furthermore, the safeguards which society has by way of maintaining law and order – for example, resorting to organised mediators or recognised experts – do not exist.

But the notion of security is not clearly defined and has no legal content, dependent as it is on individual feelings and judgements. However, the idea of security does not have the same limitations as those relevant to the democratic organisation of society, except when in the name of security we undermine the freedom to come and go (as in the case of identity checks or police custody measures or administrative detention of foreigners). In prison, security has only moral limits, and it is this that international organisations and in particular the CPT try to lay down, with notions of inhumane and degrading treatment, or even the European Council with European penitentiary rules. However everything is possible in the name of security, as clearly demonstrated by prison overcrowding, the increase in surveillance technology impinging on human dignity, the practice of body searches, and the limitation of communication and space for prisoners. In brief, prison treatment is heavily dependent on the prevailing concerns for security. With this, we touch upon the limits of the law according to which, in the name of the protection of society, democratic societies deny individuals the fundamental possession which is freedom. We also touch upon the limits of control outside the prison, in particular juridical appeals.

Returning to the ruling function of the State, security is at the heart of penitentiary rules and its bureaucratic inflation. Anything that is not authorised is forbidden, and the internal penitentiary rules are not satisfied with listing what is authorised and what is forbidden, but are constantly amended, often in a contradictory manner, to formalise new authorisations or restraints, according to the place, the context or the incident.

The maintenance of law and order involves particular rules which are exempt from these regulations. The staff know – and say – that if they were to respect the regulations to the letter, they would lay themselves open to numerous incidents (Chauvenet *et al.* 1994, Chauvenet 1996). But their margin for interaction is small, insofar as the hierarchical bureaucratic organisation characteristic of prisons exposes them to punishment if there is the least suspicion of autonomous behaviour. In particular, in the name of security, relations between warders and prisoners, other than by more or less benevolent authority, are forbidden (Rostaing 1994). But we know that no society can survive in a state of relative social peace, without the existence of social relations based on exchanges and reciprocal obligations. Chauvenet (1996) has shown that in the prison society, social relations between warders and prisoners could only be established on the model of exchange of offers of cooperation, in a rather similar way to certain societies studied by anthropologists, and that social peace can only be maintained thanks to the respect of the given word, outside of any regulatory order. The violation of this implicit code also leads to confrontations which can only be resolved by an appeal to authority.

The prison society, in which one person holds the power to allow access to goods and services and the other person, in return, can only offer information and the promise to remain quiet, is a non-domestic society based on the model of favour. The context of relative deprivation and moderate resources makes 'the favour' a much more effective tool for maintaining law and order than pure force.

But, in such a society which is not supported, like traditional societies, by traditions passed down from generation to generation and where mistrust is endemic (the staff amongst themselves, the guards and their officers, the prisoners amongst themselves and with the staff), there is a fragile balance. The introduction of rights or service-use always comes up against unwritten rules or even rules profusely dispersed in texts which are not very well known and are therefore questioned. The model of favour is not recognised in penal codes. It is not ever, or very rarely, discussed even by those who use it. It can put both the staff and the prisoners in danger.

The evolution of rights

The practice of – and discourse about – normalisation concerns the status of the prisoner, with regard to the rights he can have, which, following the example of Pires (1991) and other authors, 1 will divide into two categories: resistance rights (right to do something) such as the right to move, to vote, to enter into contracts, etc., which aim to secure an area of individual autonomy; and credit rights (right to get something) right to education, to health, to leisure, etc., which aim to promote a greater standard of living and indeed include access to services.

But although resistance rights and credit rights could be equally guaranteed, particularly with reference to articles 22 to 27 of the Universal Declaration of Human Rights, credit-rights – in the form of services rather than formally guaranteed rights – have changed more rapidly than the former, for reasons which pertain to the particular structure of social relations in prison which I have briefly described above.

Resistance rights

Indeed, social relations between warders and prisoners are governed by a formal principle of hierarchical authority, determined unilaterally, and are as constraining for the staff with regard to the hierarchy, as for the prisoners towards the staff. This principle does not authorise either negotiation or contractual relations. Consequently, scope for civil legal regulations is minimised. Social relations in prison are not based on rights but on authority (Bourmanne 1988). Tribunals, aware of this, usually do not want to intervene in a so-called administrative decision. Strictly speaking, with regard to penal codes, they leave a lot of scope for the arbitrary. It is for this reason that Herzog-Evans (1994, 1996) speaks of the 'blurred' penal laws, of the weakness of the sources of this law, of the illusion of procedural guarantees modelled on those in force outside but without offering all the guarantees. As Loucks (1996) showed when comparing Sweden, France and England, the penitentiary rules impose few limits on the interpretation of the rules.

International sources of law are hardly better. European rules are very general, and not opposable, and can only be considered as recommendations (de Jonge 1994). As for the European Court in charge of enforcing the European Convention for the protection of Human Rights and Personal Freedom, not only are the procedures so lengthy that they discourage many people, but also their jurisprudence remains very restrictive.[8]

The weakness of the legislation explains why appeals are almost exclusively internal, and are submitted for an out-of-court settlement. The judicial procedures remain extremely slow and the prisoner, except if he/she is condemned to a very long sentence, has a good chance of being freed before any decision has been reached.[9] Besides, the courts are not aware of what goes on in prison on a daily basis.

Consequently, social relations in prison cannot conform to the rules of democracy which involve equality and reciprocity. This is what makes resistance rights either non-existent, or in certain cases (disciplinary procedures for example) difficult to control through ordinary operations (civil and administrative courts). Relations cannot be based on reciprocity, and anything which is acquired can only be in the form of a favour which may be granted but is never certain.

Credit rights

If the matter of resistance rights brings to the fore the lack of guarantees for prisoners, as it does the reluctance of the legislator and the courts to grant these guarantees, credit rights find their place more easily inside prisons. Indeed they can be directly managed by the prison administration. They are especially easy to develop since they are situated between the arguments for normalisation and rehabilitation, and the logics for maintaining law and order – occupying the prisoners, trying to motivate them, rewarding them for good conduct as well as allowing them, in a number of countries, to obtain a reduction of the sentence and early release. With this, they easily fit in with the model of favour, the golden rule for controlling prisoners. Positive discrimination which we hear about now and then (for example in the Annual Report of the French penitentiary administration) could well be no more than an archetype of favour. The punishment is to go down in status, that is to say, to be deprived of certain activities. In the previous model based on access to work, the loss of status was the deprivation of work and certain prerogatives of the individual. In the current model where work is rarely done and is sometimes no longer obligatory (as in France), the loss of status concerns all activities, whether paid or unpaid. Certainly, this disciplinary tool has to be handled with caution – we know that in terms of maintaining law and order the prisoners are more sensitive to the threat of degrading their living conditions than to a reward (Ditchfield 1990). The benefit of this kind of punishment-reward is that there is no need to go through the procedures. The allocation of activities is related directly to the prison administration's discretionary power and is not susceptible to appeals other than internal submissions for an out-of-court settlement, which once again take the form of a favour and not a right.

The introduction of services which could give rise to the development of credit rights is similar to – or is often an extension of – the system put in place outside for individuals with a socio-economic profile identical to that of the majority of prisoners (for example, social policies for disadvantaged areas). Just as in the outside world, where these policies are supposed to reduce tensions between the underprivileged youth and their environment, the development of credit rights in prison is supposed to cause the reduction of tensions between inmates and prison officers.

However, even when these services and rights are granted, they observe the less-eligibility principle whereby there must be a gap between the living conditions outside and those inside the prison. Furthermore, to aid the transition of these services from 'favours' to rights, as some would wish, would at least involve applying the rules in force in the outside society. For example, it is hard to imagine, in the current situation, a prisoner challenging the prison administration for deficiencies with regard to medical provisions. Let us see another example. Work contracts do not exist in French prisons, and the inmates are not subject to the common work legislation. Moreover, a law passed in 1987, which repealed the obligatory nature of prison work and established that training activities be regarded as 'proof of good behavoiur and rehabilitation', exacerbated the discretionary nature of work allocation inside the institutions (Talandier 1994).[10] Legislation such as this compound the problem of identifying the purpose of the prison sentence, and moreover do not take into account remand prisoners. But again, one can always argue that material problems and the lack of funds limit the prisoner's access to such services or programmes.

Under the regime of favour we do something for the prisoner and in return, the prisoner must always prove that he deserves what has been done for him, through good behaviour. We must hereby take certain ambiguities into account which many authors have referred to, in the matter of the allocation of social benefits and allowances or even the 'Minimum Integration Income' (MII).[11] As in previous centuries, the poor have to prove that they are 'the deserving poor' (Castel 1995), by demonstrating that they are in favour of basic rules of decorum and that they show respect for social institutions. But if, outside, these *credit rights* are part of social redistribution and of civil society, especially if they can appear as a 'due' (even if the reality of social resettlement does not really correspond to basic principles and if the access to certain services is a sign of 'being a lesser member' of society), in prison the access to these services is always 'granted'. It is only in terms of health that receiving care once again becomes a 'due'. I would hypothesise that, in fact, behind this debt to society is a hidden obligation, to prevent the risk of contamination which the poorly cared-for released prisoners would spread, as well as a justification of medical knowledge.

Conclusion

The specificity which the *credit rights* take in prison is more characteristic of the prison organisation than of the actual individuals imprisoned. Furthermore, the desire on the part of prison management to introduce measures of social action and services, or cultural programmes and training is not restricted to prison governors. Over and above the possibility of obtaining additional resources, there is a powerful argument for justifying the use of imprisonment not only in the eyes of the practitioners (as seen in the two quotations at the beginning of this chapter), but also in the eyes of the legislators and the general public. Certain campaigns carried out by organisations, for example, which argue in favour of continuity, on release, of the care received in prison, or of the training begun in prison, can only help to reinforce this argument.

One of the problems created by this evolution, in particular in France, but also in other countries, is that these measures have not really been thought out and transformed into doctrines which can be used by the staff, by the prison governors or by the prisoners themselves. Social relations within the prison remain dominated on the one hand by a principle of hierarchy which is typical of crisis-response mechanisms and on the other hand by the maintenance of law and order. However, outside, the maintenance of law and order is entrusted to specialised and flexible organisations, whilst in prison the warders are in a fixed location and have a variety of tasks: they are responsible for security and maintaining order as well as the daily lives of the inmates; they must also ensure that the prisoners do not self-mutilate (in their vocabulary do not 'cut themselves'). On the other hand, the trend towards bureaucratisation of roles, more common in Western penitentiary systems, is in conflict with the trend towards increasing the services and programmes offered.

A second problem is the normalisation of the way in which prisoners are taken care of. If prison becomes an everyday fact of life, a metamorphosis of sanitation and social services, there will no longer be any reason not to use it as a way of dealing with undesirables, or with precarious sectors of the population. The bifurcation policies are going to face certain limitations which can only be overcome by injecting extra funding into community-care programmes. This is hardly likely within the framework of neo-liberal politics, in which social budgets are among the first to be affected. Certainly, we can see limitations to this work on normalisation and even more so in studies carried out on 'the citizen prisoner'. On the other hand we can see certain advantages in terms of legitimisation, which the promoters of penal law can extract from such studies and put into practice, albeit in a limited way. However in view of the context of criminal law in democratic states, as well as the structural illegitimacy of forced confinement, the objective of complete legitimacy can never be achieved. We can also see, and this is a point to campaign for, the advantages that the prisoners can gain from the normalisation programme. From this perspective, I would support Sparks' (1994) argument that all prison systems have serious problems of legitimacy, and that these problems can be used in a critical way to generate change.

Notes

1 For France, the introduction of the use of electronic tagging is advocated to try to reduce prison overcrowding and to 'fight against the problem of recidivism' (Cabanel 1996).

2 It must be understood that it would be impossible to not refer to Goffman at this point. I would refer to more recent work carried out in France (notably Chauvenet et al. 1994, Chauvenet 1996, Rostaing 1994, Fabiani 1995, Marchetti 1996, Jaeger and Monceau 1996, Combessie 1996).

3 Particularly at the beginning of the 1980s by the left-wing trade union for state prosecutors and certain professional organisations co-operating in the Coordination Syndicale Pénale (COSYPE) (Penal Trade Union Co-ordination).

4 The failure of imprisonment is marked by recidivism, which allows them to justify the deprival of freedom in the first instance, except when justification in terms of neutralisation suffices on its own, which can only occur in exceptional circumstances (e.g. terrorists, sex offenders).

5 I am using the term 'neutralisation' here rather than that of 'control' used by Adler and Longhurst (1994) and by myself in a previous paragraph because the term calls to mind both the intended objective of the sentence and a concern with prison management.

6 In France, notably, the warders' trade unions have been hostile to the introduction of fixed sentences for the sake of internal security in the prisons.

7 In France such organisations include the Ministry of Culture, Work and National Education, the Health authority and a number of Municipal authorities (see the Rapport annuel de l'Administration Pénitentiaire).

8 In this respect, see the enquiry carried out by the ONG Prison Reform International (PRI), National Association for the Care and Resettlement of Offenders (NACRO), Association Nationale des Visiteurs de prison (ANVP) for the control of prison conditions presented at the conference at Marly 25–27 October 1996, as well as Reynaud (1986).

9 See the results of the enquiry mentioned above: this delay can be found in countries where court appeals are possible, unless emergency interim proceedings are allowed in this regard.

10 Although the law states that management must provide work for whoever demands it, in times of crisis in the work force, it is not always easy to respect this.

11 The 'Minimun Integration Income' is given with the condition that there is a certain level of resources available. It is supposed to be at odds with practices of traditional assistance, as it combines the idea of a regular income with the receiver committing himself to a reinsertion contract (for an analysis of the application of this measure and its contradictions see Collectif 1991). Prisoners do not benefit from this despite the efforts of the prison service in this regard.

References

Adler, M., Longhurst B. (1994) *Discourse, Power and Justice. Towards a New Sociology of Imprisonment*, London: Routledge.

Bulletin d'Information Pénologique, Strasbourg: Conseil de l'Europe.

Bourmanne, M. (1988) 'Armée, prison: institutions totalitaires' *Revue Interdisciplinaires d'Etudes Juridiques*, 20: 89–166.

Brion, F. (1996) 'Les menaces d'une forteresse. Citoyenneté, crime et discrimination dans la construction de l'Union Européenne', in F Tulkens, H. D. Bosly (eds) *La justice pénale et l'Europe*, Bruxelles: Bruylant.

Cabanel, G. P. (1996) *Rapport au Premier ministre. Pour une meilleure prévention de la récidive*, Paris: La Documentation Française, Collection des rapports officiels.

Chauvenet, A (1996) 'L'échange et la prison', in Faugeron *et al.*: 45–70.

Chauvenet, A. Benguigui, G., Orlic, F. (1994) *Le monde des surveillants de prison*, Paris: Presses Universitaires de France.

Collectif (1991) *Le RMI à l'épreuve des faits*. Paris: Syros Alternatives.

Combessie, P. (1996) *Prisons des villes et des campagnes*, Paris: Editions de l'Atelier.

COSYPE (1982) *Le lobby pénitentiaire*, Paris: Syndicat de la magistrature.

De Jonge, G. (1994) *The European Prison Rules. Sleeping Beauties in Need of the Kiss of Life*, paper presented at Prisons 2000, Leicester, 8th–10th April 1994.

Ditchfield, D. (1990) *Control in Prisons: A Review of the Literature*, London: HMSO.

Ehrel, C., Garapon, A. (1993), 'La loi et le fait divers', *Esprit*, 211: 103–117.

Fabiani, J.-L. (1995) *Lire en prison. Une étude sociologique*, Paris: Centre Pompidou, Bibliothèque Publique d'Information.

Faugeron, C. (1994) 'Légitimité du pénal et ordre social', *Ethique, démocratie et droit pénal, Carrefour*, 16, 2: pp. 64–89.

—— (1995), La dérive pénale, *Esprit*, 215: 132–144.

—— (ed.) (1995), *Prisons et politiques pénitentiaires, Problèmes politiques et sociaux*, nos 755–756, Sept.–Oct., Paris: La Documentation Française.

Faugeron, C., Houchon, G. (1987) 'Prison and the Penal System: from Penology to a Sociology of Penal Policies', *International Journal of the Sociology of Law*, 15: 393–422.

Faugeron, C., Hulsman, L. (1996) 'Le développement de la criminologie au sein du Conseil de l'Europe: état et perspectives', in F. Tulkens, H. D. Bosly (eds) *La justice pénale et l'Europe*, Bruxelles: Bruylant.

Faugeron, C., Le Boulaire J.-M. (1992) 'Prisons, peines de prison et ordre public', *Revue française de sociologie*, 23: 3–32.

Faugeron, C., Chauvenet, A., Combessie P. (eds) (1996) *Approches de la prison*, Bruxelles–Ottawa–Montréal: De Boek-Presses de l'Université d'Ottawa – Presses de l'Université de Montréal.

Favard, J. (1994) *Les prisons*, Paris: Flammarion.

Ganoux, F. (1996) 'Rapport sur les conditions de détention et le traitement des personnes privées de liberté en France', *Les Cahiers de l'Institut des Droits de l'Homme*, no. 2, Université Catholique de Lyon: 33–193.

Garapon, A., Salas, D. (1995) 'Pour une nouvelle intelligence de la peine', *Esprit*, 215: 145–161.

Greilsamer, L., Schneidermann, D. (1992) *Les juges parlent*, Paris: Fayard.

Haut Comité de la Santé Publique (1993) *Santé en milieu carcéral*, Rennes: Ecole nationale de la santé publique.

Herzog-Evans, M. (1994) *La gestion du comportement du détenu. L'apparence légaliste du droit pénitentiaire*, unpublished PhD thesis, Université de Poitiers.

—— (1996) 'Le droit pénitentiaire: un droit faible au service du contrôle des détenus?', in Faugeron., *et al.* 273–296.

Jaeger, M., Monceau, M. (1996) *La consommation de médicaments psychotropes en prison*, Ramonville Saint-Agne: Erès.

Laberge, D., Landreville, P., Morin, D., Robert, M., Soullière, N. (1995) *Maladie mentale et délinquance, deux figures de la déviance devant la justice pénale*, Bruxelles–Ottawa–Montréal: De Boek-Presses de l'Université D'Ottawa – Presses de l'Université de Montréal.

Landreville, P. (1994) 'Compensatory Work Programme, A Way of Limiting Prison Use? The Quebec Experience', *The Howard Journal of Criminal Justice*, XXXIII, 3: 236–245.

Langlais, J.-L., Géronimi, J. (1993) *L'emprisonnement prolongé des détenus difficiles et dangereux*, Paris: Inspection Générale de l'Administration, Inspection Générale des Services Judiciaires.

Loucks, N. (1996) 'La gestion de l'indiscipline en prison: une étude comparative de la Suède, de la France et de l'Angleterre', in Faugeron *et al.*: 297–321.

Marchetti, A.-M., avec la collaboration de Combessie P. (1996) *La prison dans la cité*, Paris Desclée de Brouwer.

Observatoire International des Prisons (1996) *Rapport 1996*, Lyon: Observatoire International des Prisons.

Perrin-Martin, J.-P. (1996) *La rétention*, Paris: L'Harmattan.

Pires, A. (1991) 'Ethiques et réforme du droit criminel: au-delà des philosophies de la peine', *Ethica*, III, 2: 47–78.

Rapport annuel de l'Administration Pénitentiaire (annuel), Paris: la Documentation française.

Reynaud, A. (1986) *Les droits de l'homme dans les prisons*, Strasbourg: Conseil de l'Europe.

Rosanvallon, P. (1995) *La nouvelle question sociale. Repenser l'Etat-providence*, Paris, Seuil.

Rostaing, C. (1994), *Prisons de femmes. Les échanges et les marges de manoeuvre dans une institution contraignante*, unpublished thesis, Ecole des Hautes Etudes en Sciences Sociales.

Ruggiero, V., Ryan, M., Sim, J. (eds) (1995) *Western European Penal System. A Critical Anatomy*, London: Sage.

Sparks, R. (1994) 'Can Prison Be Legitimate? Penal Politics, Privatization, and the Timeliness of an Old Idea', *British Journal of Criminology, Special Issue*, XXXIV: 14–60.

Talandier, J. (1994) 'La problématique travail-prison: les intentions à la peine', *Economie et Humanisme*, 329: 43–49.

Tubex, H., Snacken, S. (1995) 'L'évolution des longues peines. . . Aperçu international et analyse des causes', *Déviance et Société*, XIX, 2: 103–126.

—— (1996) 'L'évolution des longues peines: sélectivité et dualisation', in Faugeron *et al.*: 221–243.

118

7

BETWEEN CIVILITY AND STATE

Nils Christie

Two pictures on how rules are created

We know the story: Moses came down from the mountains. Under his arm he carried the rules, engraved in granite, dictated to him by one even further up than the mountains. Moses was only a messenger, the people – the *populus* – were the receivers, controlled from far above. Much later, Jesus and Mohammed functioned according to the same principles. These are classical cases of '*pyramidal justice*'.

And then the other picture: females gathering at the water-fountain, the well, or at natural meeting places along the river. Here they come, often every day at the same time. Fetch the water, wash the clothes – and exchange information and evaluations. The point of departure for their conversation will often be concrete acts and situations. These are *described*, *compared* to similar occurrences in the past or somewhere else, and *evaluated* – right or wrong, beautiful or ugly, strong or weak. Slowly, but far from always, some common understanding of the occurrences might emerge. This is a process whereby norms are *created*. It is a classical case of horizontal or '*equalitarian justice*'.

The growth of Moses

In modern societies, Moses has got the upper hand. The legal apparatus is bulging. In Denmark a count was made. Hans Henrik Brydensholt[1] reports the existence of some 7,000 laws, 10,000 ministerial instructions, and then of course an abundance of books and articles on legal questions. In addition these days electronically conveyed messages come in. With the morning coffee, the latest legal decisions can be called up on the screen by all legal experts who are connected to a legal data-bank. And they will all soon *have* to be connected if they want to be taken seriously. The courts are under continuous electronic upgrading in all highly industrialized countries. In the case of the penal courts, sentencing tables of the USA type will soon be outdated. Detailed information on offender and offence can be fed into the electronic system, and out come details on the 'profile' – distributions of sentences in 'similar' cases, and an overview of previous judicial action in such cases. From carvings on a stone to a diagram of what is a normal sentence on the screen, the electronic revolution has not created equalitarian justice but a pyramidal one.

In the meantime, the water-well is abolished. We had in modernized countries for a while some small shops with coin-operated Laundromats where we could come with our dirty linen and leave with it clean. In the interval, there was some time for talk. Now the Laundromats are gone, ruined by private affluence. Huge shopping malls might give some opportunities for encounters, but mostly they are too large for the creation of horizontal justice. Too large to find old acquaintances and too busy and crowded for the prolonged chats needed for establishing standards for behaviour. Television is of course no functional alternative to the water well. On the contrary, TV is a pyramidal device, allowing the many to look at the few[2] and thereby receive their implicit messages.

More tasks for the state

In this situation, Moses and his functionaries become even more important. In the 1950s, the police of Norway became aware of some 20,000 acts they called crimes. Today, they register 300,000 such acts. This does not necessarily mean that the amount of such unwanted acts has increased, even though this probably also is the case. But what is indisputable is *that the use of penal law classifications has multiplied*! 300,000 deplorable acts called crime. But that is of course only the tip of that famous floating iceberg. What would happen if it all was revealed, if all deplorable acts were processed by the official apparatus of the state?

No natural limits

There are no natural limits. As the women at the water-well were so clearly aware, social life is filled with unwanted acts and occurrences – as also is filled with highly wanted and appreciated acts. It is the sorting of bad from good that makes for some of the excitement in social life.

- The act might be seen as malicious, he broke her window; but maybe it broke because the pathway was slippery, or
- he took away money from another man's drawer; but that other man had not paid him decently for last season out at the fisheries. And it was not his habit to remove other people's money. And he really needed that money, or
- he was hitting his comrade; but was it more than he himef had been hit? And was it a strong blow, compared to his strength, or
- he inspected her genitals, and she his penis, and they were siblings; but was it more than six- and seven-year-old children usually do when they train for adult life, or
- as reported from Stockholm the other day[3]; a man drugged his wife, and then suffocated her. Then he wrote to the police, told them what he had done, and

also what would be the end of the story. He would board the ship to Finland, weight his body with heavy stones and jump. The letter reached the police two days later. They found the door to the apartment unlocked, as the man had said in his letter. They also found the wife, as he had said. The body had been laid out in the old-fashioned way, cleaned, and with a linen cloth above her face. She was 86, he 78. She had Alzheimer's. He had nursed her for a long time and she was about to be sent away. 'They were very close,' said the family doctor. 'We look for the man, he is under strong suspicion for having committed premeditated murder', said the police.

Moses and his functionaries might put names on much of this: violence, theft, indecent behaviour, murder. They might apply the general term 'crime'. They might distribute roles as 'victims', 'offenders' and 'witnesses'. And they would see to it that pain was delivered to those designated as offenders.

The females at the water-well would often look differently at much of this. It is as if they are not so sure in their classifications. What is what, and who is who?

Maybe we can understand them better if we put it all upside down, and take as our point of departure the following subtitle.

Crime does not exist!

Acts are not, they *become*. So also with crime. Crime does not exist. Crime is created. First there are acts. Then follows a long process of giving meaning to these acts.

With this as our point of departure, we have to frame our questions in another way than the usual. Let me give you a summary of a life story by putting the story in a diagram (Table 7.1).

In our diagram, we might let the acts become known within four different systems for understanding. In the family, the taking of the money and the blow directed at the brother is seen as a result of an overwhelming first love – and a kindly formed correction is expressed. Among young friends, the necessity of his acts is obvious, and admiring questions follow. In the health-system – let us think of

Table 7.1 The meaning of acts

Social system	Family	Friends	Health	Law
Type of evaluation	First love	An act of necessity	Neurotic behaviour	Theft Violence
Type of reaction	Kindly formulated oral correction	Words of appreciation	Treatment	Police action, Punishment

an extreme case of panicked parents and insensitive professionals – the acts might be seen as an indicator of an emerging deviant personality, and some sort of psychiatric counselling might follow. While the legal system might see it all as theft and violence where police, courts and possible punishment will follow. The other examples above, for example the man who killed his wife, might be analysed using similar categories.

Two types of justice

With rules engraved in granite, an idea of the existence of general validity is created. Equal cases have to be treated equally. But cases never are equal, if everything is taken into consideration. Therefore, *everything cannot be taken into consideration* in formal law. It becomes necessary to eliminate most of the factors surrounding any act to be able to create cases that can be presumed to be similar or equal. This process is called eliminating what is *irrelevant*. But what is irrelevant is of course a matter of values. To create equality it is necessary to create rules for irrelevancy. That is what we train law students to know and apply.

The fiction of equality and its control through relevance is essential as a protective device if pain is to be delivered. But at the same time it makes penal law into a clumsy instrument – clumsy through all the information lost.

But that clumsiness is not so important in modern societies. Modernity means to a large extent a life amidst people we do not know, and never will come to know. This is a situation where penal law can be applied without restraint.

Retribution versus compensation

At the water-well, justice becomes of another sort. Three differences are of core importance:

1   Decisions are locally anchored. How cases are solved in villages far away is of limited interest. What matters is here and now, compared to before, and with concern for the future.

2   Questions of relevance are handled in a radically different way to what happens in the legal system. Relevance is seen as a central concern, but one without ready-made solutions. Agreement must be created among all interested parties that something is relevant, how relevant, or eventually not relevant. That Kari 15 years back in time was humiliated by Per, might be seen as of considerable importance by all interested discussants when Kari's little sister now has covered Per's little brother with tar and then rolled him in feathers.

3   At the water-well, compensation becomes more important than retribution. This is related to several structural elements in small-scale societies; such societies are often relatively egalitarian. Not necessarily in the sense that all are equal in wealth or prestige, but in the sense that *if* conflicts appear, parties

will move into alliances with relatives and friends and thus mobilize until they become somehow equal to their opponents. Many such societies also exist far away from external authorities with power at their disposal. This means they themselves will have to cope with the conflicts. This is in a situation where they know each other from far back in time, and also know that they will have to live together in the future. They cannot behave as other modern people do, just break off relationships and move to another social system when conflicts loom. Punishments are particularly dysfunctional in such systems. Punishment, or infliction of pain, may lead to civil war in close-knit societies. With distant external authority, with nowhere else to move, and with no superiority in power, compensation rather than pain becomes the natural answer.

The females at the water-wells have disappeared. But a functional alternative is about to appear in many industrialized societies. This is the so-called mediation-board, or council for alternative conflict-solutions as it sometimes is called. It appears in different forms, but mostly built on the same basic idea: parties in conflict must meet; some outsiders must come to their help; the purpose of this encounter must be to create an evaluation of the conflict and compensation to the suffering party, but not pain to the other participant.

Survival of the civil society

Where will the development of mediation and alternative conflict resolution bring us?

It is a cultural–political question. Maybe we can draw up two major scenarios. The first is in continuation of recent developments.

More and more conflicts are moved into the institution of penal law. The USA has more than tripled its prison population, from half a million fifteen years ago, to the 1.7 million of 1 January 1997. If this continues, they will pass 4 million in another fifteen years. At present there are 4 million on parole and probation in the USA. If that population also triples, there will be 12 million on parole and probation in 2012, and in total 16 million under the control of penal law, which means that 6 per cent of the population will come under that form of control. If Russia double their present prison figures, they are back to their peak figures from the most extreme GULAG times. Great Britain follow their leader across the Atlantic. At present England and Wales increase their prison population by 1,000 a month. The prisons bulge; even a ship is bought to be used as a prison. There are no natural limits. And there are so many rewards in following this pathway of expansion. Profit, work, and total control of the supposedly dangerous classes. Our present penal policy is an indicator of a general expansion of the state-control systems.

But there are also some indicators of growth in the civil elements. New Zealand, Australia, Finland, Norway, – they are all experimenting with mediation and alternative conflict-solutions. And in a related field – drug-control – there are also civilizing influences. Very important is the so-called 'large cities initiative'. Frankfurt, Amsterdam, Hamburg, Baltimore – they are not any longer willing to obey state-commands for a punitive drug policy. Of importance might also be the renewed interest in the USA in local government. The rich are moving out of the cities and are creating ghettos for themselves, ghettos for the rich. Back in town are the ghettos for the poor. This paradoxical situation might lead to civil solutions in the countryside, but then more state power in the inner city. A strengthening of the civil side might also result from the dissemination of an understanding that crime control is based on choices. It is a cultural phenomenon. To incarcerate large segments of the population is the result of political decisions. Awareness of this might give some hope for a reversal of the present developments.

Notes

1 Jura på mange måder pp. 71–84 in: *Festskrift til Børge Dahl*. Copenhagen 1994.
2 Cf. Thomas Mathiesen (1997): 'The viewer society; M. Foucault's 'Panopticon' revisited', *Theoretical Criminology*, 1(2): 215–234.
3 *Dagens Nyheter*, March 13 and 14 1997.

8

THE 'SENSITIVE PERIMETER' OF THE PRISON

A key to understanding the durability of the penal institution

Philippe Combessie

Preamble

I have been interested for many years now in the interaction between prisons and the outside world (Combessie, 1996). In this chapter I would like to present a previously unexplored approach, involving research on four French prisons, each situated in environments with very different characteristics.

The oldest establishment dates back to 1808 – that is to say, practically from the earliest period of development of penitentiaries. This is an institution for prisoners serving long-term sentences, and it is set in a rural area, currently in economic decline. The second prison, slightly newer, was built almost a century ago in the countryside surrounding Paris. It was originally planned as a replacement for the prisons in the capital which were to be razed to the ground before the World Fair in 1900. Since the Second World War the Parisian suburbs have developed, and this penitentiary, which currently holds more than 3,000 prisoners, is now surrounded by blocks of high-rise flats and small houses. The third prison is also situated in the Parisian suburbs, but this one was constructed after much more significant urbanisation in the urban periphery: it dates from 1975. The fourth prison is even more recent: it is part of a new prison-expansion programme managed in part by private businesses.[1] These establishments are governed by ordinary prison staff and the social workers are the same as in the other prisons. But everything else (prison food, the health of the prisoners, heating, work, and, of course, the maintenance of the buildings) is entrusted to private firms. There is, however, in these prisons, a director who has authority over the state employees and an external manager who is responsible for all of the activities managed by the private companies.

During the course of research I completed in 1996, I was surprised to discover that these four different establishments, each in very different localities and of very different vintage, have many similar relationships with the outside world and many other common traits. These traits are so distinctive that I propose to try and capture their provenance conceptually in terms of the idea '*périmètre sensible de la prison*', which I feel can be translated into English as the '*sensitive perimeter* of the prison'.

Introduction: what is the sensitive perimeter?

The relationship between prisons and their environment is marked by a tension, defined, on the one hand, by a powerful logic emphasising security and public order (a logic that works to separate prisoners off from the world, and indeed from each other) and, on the other, a logic we can call socio-educational (which is focused, to one degree or another, on the eventual reintegration of prisoners into society as a whole). This second logic is in many ways more widely valued in society at large, and is therefore more central to the legitimacy of the prison institution. The imposition of the first logic, however, works to separate prisoners off from the wider society, and renders the stigmatisation and the demonisation of the (invisible) incarcerated population over time that much more effective.

Around any prison there is a type of no man's land, which demarcates the institution both materially and symbolically from its broader environment. This is the zone that I want to call the *sensitive perimeter*. The symbolic power of the perimeter extends far beyond the obvious material aspects of the prison – its high surrounding wall, and other defining architectural features.

One of the key findings in my recently completed research highlights the infrequency of contact between the population living in the prison, and the local population. Contacts between the prisons I studied and the outside world generally took place over some considerable distance. Those few contacts which were established with people or agencies living or working in close proximity with the prison were frequently disguised, camouflaged or very indirect.

The extent of the *sensitive perimeter* of the prison seems to vary: in general, it is larger when the area in which the prison is established is poorly urbanised. From the perspective of the local community itself, of course, the *sensitive perimeter* around the neighbourhood's prison is a kind of symbolic block or barrier, 'containing' the local presence of a foreign body – the penitentiary itself. As for the prison community, the perimeter acts as a sort of quarantine line, I would argue, which reinforces the isolation of those within the walls.

Constituted by and through a mix of these different logics, the *sensitive perimeter* can be seen to operate along many different perspectives. In this chapter I want to describe five different areas: the development of voluntary activities, relations with businesses outside, relations with local councillors, the impact of the prison on property values and the social composition of the local neighbourhood, and finally the routine discursive positions adopted by key managers and decision-makers in the penal system with respect to the isolation of prisons and their relations with the outside world.

Prison and voluntary activity

The development of voluntary activities among prisoners is a good illustration of the dynamics which outline the *sensitive perimeter.*

Volunteers working in prisons do not come from the immediate vicinity

All prisons need volunteers, but it is noticeable that in general volunteers are particularly difficult to find in the immediate environment of prisons. Local residents from the area immediately surrounding the prisons, especially, do not want to hear about it. To recruit volunteers, prison managers generally have to move away from the establishment. This phenomenon is more apparent in rural areas than in urban areas, and my own research suggested that the newer prisons evoked a stronger negative reaction than the older ones, although this phenomenon was seen everywhere. There was even one instance, it must be said, of a priest who refused to visit prisoners, although the prison was in his parish. So I was told by a chaplain working in prison that: 'Ordinary men from the area round the prison won't come here . . . and priests are just ordinary men'.

The search for money

Particularly when it comes to preparing for Christmas for the prisoners, prisons need extra money. Once again, this is far easier the further the prison authorities move, in their appeals for support, from the vicinity of the prison itself. In the Paris region one prison governor told me that he thought it useless to ask for money for prisoners within approximately a 10-kilometre circumference of the prison.

Publicity at a geographical distance from the prison may be the only solution when attempting to recruit volunteers, but when it comes to money, certain stratagems allow the route which the money takes to be artificially disguised. For example a prison chaplain explained to me how he took collections outside of the prison on behalf of a sub-branch of Catholic Aid. The money he collected went to the departmental office of Catholic Aid and at this departmental level the money can quietly be directed towards purchases on behalf of the prison. It could be argued that routing the money from collections in this way constitutes a form of money-laundering (or more accurately, 'money-laundering in reverse' since it is not where it comes from that is covered up, but rather where it is going).

Concern for other poor people

In another prison, when a Chairman of the Association for Prisoners came to appeal to the regional council for a grant, elected members strongly advised him to modify the statutes of his association and to concern himself with other 'have-nots' in the area – people with no links to the prison. In practice, of course, this solution also allowed some councillors to disguise the destination of the funds granted. In this instance, the grant which was awarded – to an organisation which declared itself concerned in general with the poor in the area – was in fact partly spent in the prison. Ideally, however, many prison governors told me, it was better for money, like voluntary activities, to be seen to come from afar, and certainly for it to be so presented. We are now going to see that money which takes the opposite channel – from the prison towards the outside world – follows a path which is often just as long and indirect.

The prison and local business

Prison purchases

When there is talk of a prison being opened in a particular area, the majority of mayors and local councillors almost always appear resistant. In order to convince them, national authorities very often promise that the opening of the prison will carry considerable economic effects for the locality. Local building firms, for example, will profit from work on the important new local building project. Many other benefits are promised (for local taxi firms, hoteliers, etc.). But research suggests that the medium- to long-term benefits of prisons on local economies are negligible. After the initial building phase, hardly any significant profit accrues to local business.

In prisons which are entirely managed by the Prison Service, the rules of the procurement process (particularly with regard to invitations to tender, where corrupt practices are widespread) often specifically prohibit local retailers from bidding. In many of the semi-privatised prisons, free competition rules and small retailers find themselves ousted from the market in favour of larger national or regional businesses.

The only remaining direct economic repercussion from the prison on the surrounding environment is the small-scale market in tobacco. French tax laws force each prison to stock up at the local tobacconist rather, for example, than by bulk mail order. Our research suggested that in the majority of cases, the local retailer very rarely publicises his or her entry into the prison market and the guaranteed income so received. In cases where there were disputes with the client (the prison), the supplier would usually use indirect methods to rectify the situation, in order that the retailer could avoid being seen publicly in negotiation with prison managers.

An additional regular market for local retailers potentially involves visitors to the prison, especially the families of prisoners. Mostly, prisoners' families pass through local towns and villages and do not stop, spending very little in the area. Local residents often chafe that the visitors arrive having bought their provisions elsewhere (and local residents as a whole complain that they then leave their rubbish behind). The only establishments that these people sometimes visit are bars and in some cases, cheaper local hostels. In such cases, there is a particularly dramatic instance of the management of relations between the prison and its immediate vicinity. Hostels offering accommodation to prisoners' families almost always house them separately, at a distance from the 'ordinary' clientele. In a few hostels, indeed, a separate entrance is provided so that they do not come into contact especially with tourists from whom there is a great desire to hide the proximity of the prison. Most importantly, all contact between the prisoners' family and prison staff must be avoided. So in some prisons, a further measure of segregation is evident – one bar serves the prisoners' families, whilst another serves the warders. In this way, the prison divide is repeated in the surrounding community. Everyone must remain in their place: it would be quite inappropriate for warders to mix with the relatives of prisoners. So, also, when the members of the prison staff go shopping, they mostly do so by car – often in the hypermarkets which are often quite far away from the prison, rather than in the small shops in the neighbourhood. It is to these small shops that prisoner's families will occasionally revert during their visits, never likely to encounter there any member of the prison staff.

So this empirical enquiry into financial flows between prisons and their environment confirms and reinforces the analysis of what I have named the *Sensitive Perimeter* and confirms the rarity of contact between different parties in the prison. A similar kind of divide overshadows the relationship between any companies who could give work to the prisoners.

Companies and prison employment

Our investigations revealed that business people working near prisons are often warned against offering work to inmates in the local prison. Warnings are given both by the local leaderships of trade union managers and local MPs as well as by the authorities in charge of local employment exchanges, or otherwise involved in the local labour market. The employment of prisoners (especially at a low wage) is considered unfair competition to local 'free workers' – just as it was in the last century (Petit, 1990). The officer in charge of employment training and work programmes in a new prison told me:

> We realised that from the moment we enquired about work opportunities in the area all the doors closed on us. So we enquired in neighbouring regions and that worked. Companies came from far away, which increased production costs due to transport, but it was the only solution to get work for the prisoners.

For prisons, the labour market can only be opened up outside their immediate area, and this can be quite an extended distance, given that many prisons are situated in areas where the economy is already quite weak and where there is a shortage of work.

The prison and the local councils

Without doubt, these logics have their own specific features, but we can see that their convergence of each of them reinforces the distance between the local society and the prisons. This does not encourage councillors to take action on behalf of prisons when there is one in their constituency (Villette, 1991). When asked about funding for prisoners' activities or about any kind of direct contact with local prisons (and even their governors) local mayors of French cities are in general very reserved.

The various organisations which approach the council for grants often meet with categorical refusals, under the pretext that it is the State's responsibility to take charge of the prisons and their residents: the mayors always insist, in this respect, that prisoners are not part of the local community. Yet when they send the statistics to be taken into account in the calculation of the amount for central-ised state funding payable to the municipality (on the basis, in part, of their population), the municipal authorities almost always add local prisoners onto the total number of inhabitants, though of course this is not 'shouted from the roof-tops'. In this sphere, the local prisoners are certainly given the status of full citizens. On the other hand, prisoners are almost certainly not included in the count when the same municipality is asked to contribute, on a *per capita* basis, to a regional fund for social service support, usually on the argument that prisoners already benefit from their own social workers. When grants are directly requested for prison activities, they are often refused or are very modest, or even, as I specified above, only allocated under the proviso of a joint programme with the poor people in the community, who seem a more worthy cause than the prisoners.

Sometimes, a local councillor will delegate responsibility for any relations with the prison to one of his assistants. Several mayors explained their reluctance, for example, to go and celebrate a marriage in prison, arguing that they would be regarded as an intruder or, alternatively, that they resented being searched before entering the prison and sometimes regarded with suspicion. This show of dis-interest from the local councillors for prisons within their constituency is one of the key aspects which distinguishes the prison from other public establishments, such as hospitals or schools.

Perhaps no other circumstance can better illustrate the consensus on keeping the prison at a distance than the annual meeting of the Prison Warders' Commission. Here, the local authorities are technically called upon to evaluate the prisons, but in fact the meeting of these commissions usually turns into a social event among colleagues. Even when the Mayors themselves participate in the meetings of the Prison Warders' Commission, their rare interventions normally concern the impact of prisons on their surrounding environment (the warders' accommodation, escorting the prisoners back when they go beyond their constituency, etc.). They hardly ask any questions about the internal functioning of the prison over which they are supposed to be keeping watch. The local authorities willingly confirm all actions taken by the director who has the authority in this particular field, yet does not belong to the local community. This, of course, does not prevent the prison from having an effect on the surrounding environment, as far as the value of property is concerned.

The impact of the prison on local property values

At first glance, analysis of the evolution of home prices around prisons reveals quite contradictory situations. As Hawes (1985) and others have also noted, the stigma attached to prison does tend to depreciate the market value of surrounding property in urban areas, whilst in rural and depopulated areas, a more pragmatic economic logic leads to a revaluation of the market value of property over time.

Beyond these seemingly contrasting trends, we can see that when prisons are first established in urban areas, local property prices are driven closer together – usually at a lower level than before. The change in prices then attracts a different, usually rather poorer population into the area. But it can also happen that this reduction in the price of housing enables prison warders and other staff to buy in the area, and a certain balance between the locality and the prison can thereby be encouraged. What is clear is that there will be no significant settlement in the area by the bourgeoisie (for this to happen the prison would have to close, and other more noble buildings erected) and it is precisely this which prevents a rapid trend towards a middle-class outlook in a community. We can see once again, for different reasons, these two opposing trends operative at different levels (between a prison which attracts and a prison which rejects, one prison that has got to be hidden and another that tries to be integrated into the community).

The 'perimeter' in the discourses of the authorities

We can see the sensitive perimeter at work again, for example, in the discursive arguments of those responsible for penitentiaries and penal policy generally, and here too there is evidence of significant contradiction. Figure 8.1 illustrates this. In general, political authorities, on a national level, speak about prisons in a fairly abstract, theoretical discourse (which may sometimes even recommend that prisons should become more open to the outside world). But in complete contrast, at local level, civic authorities usually speak about prisons in a practical and particularistic fashion: insisting that they should not be in the town centre, not too near to a tourist or prestigious place, etc. Prison governors and administrators of

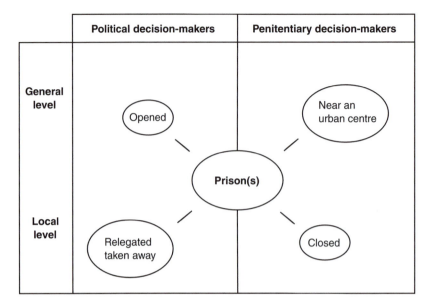

Figure 8.1 Official discourse on prisons

the penal system generally would ideally like to situate some of their establishments, especially the short-term detention centres, near to town centres and
would also like to encourage partnership with the surrounding society (cf. for
example, the report of the Study Commission on 'Architecture and Prisons'
chaired by Madame Myriam Ezratty, published in 1985). The senior managers
of one particular prison, however, have tried to resist this opening up on security
grounds. The closer we get to the individual establishment, indeed, the more we
lose sight of the rhetoric of the political and administrative elites, and the more
we are confronted with the immediate concerns of local managers and local
citizens, and the more the ideological arguments in favour of the opening up of
prison give way to pragmatic and unspoken practices which work in the other
direction. These practices aim to ensure a certain 'keeping of distance' between
the prison and local community rather than active collaboration, participation
and openness. These practices are clearly linked to the identification of prisoners,
in effect, as the 'undeserving poor', particularly since they are not working and
are not of the local parish or local community (Castel, 1995: 63).

In this way, the Sensitive Perimeter works in two opposite directions, on the
one hand creating attraction and mystique, and, on the other, ensuring that a
good distance is maintained between the prison and its locality. The resulting
tension (between those exhortations which operate on a general level to open the
prisons, and the daily management of relations between this establishment and
its environment) builds the Sensitive Perimeter both in the direction *prison* →
environment and in the direction *environment* → *prison*. In this respect we could

say that the environment treats the prison in the same way as the prison treats the prisoners. And we can also say, taking an opposing point of view, that the prison imparts on its host locality a stigma similar to that which affects the prisoners.

Conclusion

It should not be believed that this suppression of relations between the prison and the outside world works to conceal the prison completely. Indeed – and this may seem paradoxical – I want to argue it accentuates the prison's visibility. Our argument, obviously, is that this visibility is more symbolic than real. The symbolic aspect of the prison and its disturbing presence in the midst of the community make it possible to project images onto the prison which have even more strength (since they are constructed on top of the social divisions the prison's perimeter has erected). In this way, the *sensitive perimeter* contributes to the *success* and the *durability* of the *prison*. I am not a historian – I do not know if, as Michel Foucault (1975) argued – the prison was 'born of a takeover by force'. But I do think that prisons have enjoyed an unexpected success, and their life-expectancy is not threatened. And I think that these phenomena which constitute what I called the *sensitive perimeter* are partly the cause of this longevity since they confuse the image of the prison. As a magician conceals from the public the very thing which allows the trick to function, these phenomena in the same way con-tribute to disguising the ordinary running of the prison. In front of a magician, the public can be led to believe that they are not watching a feat born of a skill worked on for a long time, rather that it really is magic. When faced with the penitentiary institution, those who are highly ignorant of prison reality can create an image of the prison which they believe to be more suitable. For some, this image will be of a three-star hotel or a holiday club. For others it may appear to be a concentration camp. Others again can be led to believe that these high walls conceal an organisation which, temporarily separating certain individuals of society, could eventually allow them to find a better place for themselves in soci-ety. These three opposing images depend upon the status held in society by the person producing the image and on the path which he has taken in life. These three images are diametrically opposed in discussions of prison reform. In the first instance the argument would be that penal reform should consist of toughen-ing up the conditions of imprisonment (examples of which can be seen in the United States). In the second case the image is pushing for the ideal of prison *abolition* 'on principle'. In the third case we would like to reform prison to allow it 'finally' to function (Faugeron, Le Boulaire, 1992). Confronting these three images is futile in my view insofar as they are all based on a lack of knowledge about the reality of prison.

An analysis of the *sensitive perimeter of prison* has enabled me to show that certain relations which exist between the prison and its neighbourhood are often seen to be kept out of sight, under the seal of secrecy, and confidential. In 1989, French

Socialist MP Gilbert Bonnemaison drew up a report which advocated for a vast opening up of prisons. He concluded his report with the words:

> the time of ignorance, suspicion, and thoughtlessness of putting individuals into oubliettes, without making any distinction, could, in fact, come to an end.

Without doubt, however, Mr Bonnemaison underestimated the power of this *sensitive perimeter*, and the force of the different social and ideological relationships constructing a popular ignorance towards prisons.

In concluding, let me try, in order to avoid any misunderstanding, to highlight the following point: the sensitive perimeter around prison is the source of obfuscation of prison reality resulting from the practical activities of prison authorities. The sensitive perimeters of the prison would not have such mystificatory power if the prison itself did not so severely limit its relations with the outside world. In a world where suspicion is endemic, the slightest interference is seen as a disturbance. Whether it is the volunteers, a temporary replacement, an elected councillor, or a sociologist carrying out research – whoever enters the prison must arm themselves with patience and much humility. The long and difficult task of taming this environment is necessary. But it is never enough: the danger facing those having contact with prison (volunteers, temporary replacements or researchers) – other than elected local councillors – is always that they can be banned from entering the prison.

As long as these phenomena (which I grouped under the concept of *sensitive perimeter*) exist, they will continue to recur, because, it must be noted, they strengthen and reinforce each other. In this way, the durability of the prison will be guaranteed, due to the ignorance of prison reality which these phenomena perpetuate.

Notes

1 In France, there are currently no completely private prisons.

References

Bonnemaison, G. (1989) *La modernisation du service public pénitentiaire*, Rapport au Premier Ministre et au Garde des Sceaux, Paris: Ministère de la Justice.

Castel, R. (1995) *Les Métamorphoses de la question sociale, une chronique du salariat*, Paris: Fayard.

Combessie, Ph. (1996), *Prisons des villes et des campagnes*, Paris: Editions de l'Atelier – Editions Ouvrières, coll. Champs pénitentiaires.

Commission d'Etude 'Architecture et Prisons' présidée par Madame Myriam Ezratty (1985) *Architecture et prisons: rapport présenté à Monsieur le Garde des Sceaux par la commission d'étude*, Paris: Direction de l'administration pénitentiaire.

Faugeron, C., Le Boulaire, J. M. (1992), 'Prisons, peines de prison et ordre public', *Revue française de sociologie*, vol. XXXIII, no. 1, pp. 3–32.

Foucault, M. (1975) *Surveiller et punir: naissance de la prison*, Paris: Gallimard. coll. Biliothèque des Histoires.

Hawes, J. A. (1985) *Cities with prisons: do they have higher or lower crime rates?*, Report to Senator Robert Presley, Los Angeles: Senate Office of Research.

Petit, J.-G. (1990) *Ces peines obscures, la prison pénale en France, 1780–1875*. Paris: Fayard.

Villette, A. (1991) *J'étais maire de Fresnes*, Paris: Editions Ouvrières.

9

"THE BIG THIEVES HANG THE SMALL ONES"

Equality before the criminal law in an unequal society

Amedeo Cottino

"The big thieves hang the small ones"

(Piedmontese proverb)

Preface

Everywhere one looks in Europe, the rhetoric of government is that there is "equality before the law." Research tends to show otherwise but public opinion does not seem to be particularly affected by this fact. Apparently, nothing or very little has been done in the realm of justice to dismiss Saint Matthew's famous statement: "to them that hath shall be given: from them that hath not will be taken away" (Matthew 12.13). The rhetoric also speaks of equality of treatment of the population by the criminal system itself, but countless studies provide evidence that police abuse of their powers is most common in respect of "the most marginalized groups (unemployed, the poor and the immigrants) who suffer most from whatever abuse of power takes place" (Sanders and Young 1994: 304). Needless to say, the voices of these people are not counted as critical public opinion. Conversely, the evils of justice cover the front page of the daily press when victims of presumed abuse are powerful and/or popular persons. As to criminal policies, governments, by and large, are overwhelmingly interested in adopting measures which improve the efficiency of the legal system, rather than strategies oriented toward a reduction of injustice. Moreover, the invoked "better efficiency" is more often than not just a cover for repressive policies (Christie 1993; Chambliss 1995).

As to the goal of this paper, I want to reflect upon two related issues: first of all I will discuss two different notions of equality – the legal and the sociological – and the different implications in terms of political and penal action depending on the notion which is chosen; second, following the sociological definition of equality, I will illustrate through my own data the ways in which inequalities of treatment are constructed during a typical penal trial. Moreover, concrete although sketchy references will be made to the Italian legal system and in particular to a recent penal reform.

The 1989 penal reform

The reform of the criminal procedure system in Italy in 1989 was intended to replace the existing practices of courts (the inquisitorial system, where, at least in theory, the court played the dominant role) with an adversarial system (where the burden of preparing the case falls on the parties themselves).

Two main points were made in favor of the reform: first of all it was argued that the new system would help the traditional weakness of the defense *vis-à-vis* the power of the prosecution, typical of the inquisitorial style; second, it was believed that the adoption of the adversarial system would contribute to reduce the extremely high number of cases committed to court for a trial.

In fact, for a number of reasons, the original project was modified in several respects. The final result is a system in which significant inquisitorial traits are preserved.[1]

In an overall evaluation of the reform, and with specific reference to the courts of first instance, the Italian legal scholar G. Neppi Modona has argued that "according to the new perspective adopted by the code of penal procedure, there should be some sort of incompatibility between the *probation of evidence*, or admission of responsibility, on the one hand, and *trial*. Conversely, the prosecutor should never forward the case to trial, unless he is reasonably sure to get a verdict of conviction" (Neppi Modona 1991: 472).

Another circumstance which has further undermined the adversarial character of the penal process is a Supreme Court decision (n.255/1992) according to which evidence collected by the police and the prosecutor in the pre-trial phase can be utilized during the trial.

Notions of justice

To discuss and to investigate equality means to deal with both models of justice and normative models of penal process. For one thing the penal process is the site where resources are allocated among defense and prosecution (and the allocation can be more or less fair), and where "commodities" such as the penal sanction are distributed (and the distribution can be more or less fair). But the penal process also reflects the two contrasting ideologies of crime control and due process, where

> crime control values prioritise the conviction of the guilty, even at risk of the conviction of some (fewer) innocent, and with the cost of infringing the liberties of the citizen to achieve its goals, while due process values prioritise the acquittal of the innocent, even if risking the frequent

acquittal of the guilty, and giving high priority to the protection of civil liberties as an end in itself.

(Sanders and Young 1994: 18)

Now, the notion of justice currently employed by Italian legal scholars (Ferrajoli 1995: 43; Neppi Modona 1995: 41), does not seem to refer to the concept of distributive justice but rather to the idea of just allocation, defined as a proper balance of power between defense and prosecution. It is a notion that covers most of what may happen to a citizen from the first police interrogation, through the trial to sentencing and eventually to imprisonment As Ferrajoli, commenting on the Italian penal system, has recently observed, problems of inequality can be studied and found "in all the three elements which constitute the phenomenology of the criminal law: crime, process and punishment" (Ferrajoli 1995: 40).

This is undoubtely a legitimate concern, and one cannot but agree with the many authors who, having observed the frequent imbalance of power between defense and prosecution, have pointed out the various loopholes through which the system violates the due-process principles established by the formal law. Thus, as Sanders and Young have recently noticed:

> in both England and America, the great majority of defendants plead guilty and forego their right to an adversarial trial. The prosecution evidence is never tested, witnesses are not cross-examined and the case is not proved beyond reasonable doubt.
>
> (Sanders and Young 1994: 19)

And similar remarks hold true for the Italian case as well.

The crux is that this preoccupation with power balance between defense and prosecution does not concern the problems of inequality raised by "unjust distributions," basically, the fact that socially different types of prosecuted or suspected persons are treated differently. And it cannot do it simply because the problem has been formulated in terms of allocative justice: is the "exchange" between defense and prosecution fair? Can the adversarial parties conflict with comparable means?

Put in slightly different terms, the problem amounts to asking where on the spectrum between crime control and due process a given legal system is located. However, whether to adopt one definition of inequality or another, is not without concrete implications. For, if we reason in terms of allocative justice, equality will be easily restored, at least in principle, by providing the party which is weaker with more power. In other words the problem can be solved through legislation.

But we can formulate the quest for equality by asking where on the social-class spectrum the two normative models are located. And if we look at the Italian case we may find that the two models, though unevenly distributed, coexist. In this sense it would be wrong to conclude that the prevailing model is that of crime control (unless we are reasoning in quantitative terms). As I will show below, the due-process model does function fairly well in the present Italian adversarial system (it worked fairly well for that matter under the previous inquisitorial system), but it constitutes the privilege of the well-off. However, we don't "see" it, unless we reason in terms of distributive justice. Clearly, this is a case which well exemplifies the often forgotten truth that different concepts lead to different constructions of reality.

One of the reasons why data from distant countries and historically different periods consistently show an overrepresentation of the lower social classes either in terms of severity of punishment (Aubert 1964) or in terms of conviction (Cottino 1986), is that the due-process model has been reserved to the higher social classes. What happens, is that within the frame ensured by the due process, this "obstacle course, with each successive stage presenting formidable impediments to carrying the citizen any further along the process" as it has been defined by Packer (1968), the members of the higher classes can fully display their resources (e.g. in terms of qualified defense) and exploit their social position (e.g. in terms of the culture they have in common with prosecutors and judges).

The general frame of reference of the investigation

Seron's and Munger's opinion that "research without a structural concept of class impoverishes our understanding of law and inequality" (Seron and Munger 1996: 206) is most convincing. However, as the authors show in their recent review of sociolegal research, unfortunately almost exclusively concerned with English-speaking literature, the "analysis of class has declined in importance and the recent interpretive research on law and inequality has abandoned the institutional and social organizational perspectives of earlier research" (Ibid: 197). They believe that this may be due to to "skepticism about the concept of structure"; others may argue that the concept of class is no longer a useful tool for analyzing what is currently called the post-modern society. Both suggestions are probably true, but this is not to deny that, as I have discussed in detail elsewhere,[2] there are at least two more, very concrete reasons which explain why the structural perspective has (albeit temporarily) lost ground.

The two difficulties I am thinking of, which any scholar dealing with the issue of inequality before the law is familiar with, both pertain to the core of the research design. One problem is methodological and raises the question of how to construct a valid measure of inequality. We all know that it is extremely difficult to compare socially different offenders because they commit different crimes. We also know that the severity of sanctions is unevenly distributed among the different social classes. Thus, the circumstance that members belonging to lower social classes are punished more severely, can be simply explained by the fact that the crimes they commit are considered by the law as more serious than the crimes committed by members of the higher social classes. A way to overcome these objections is to compare the judicial outcome for socially different offenders and then ask why should white-collar criminals be acquitted significantly more often than blue-collar criminals, unless some type of discriminatory mechanism is at work.

To state that courts discriminate between socially different offenders is almost a truism. One wishes to go a step further to understand precisely what these mechanisms are. And here we come to the second problem. It is one thing to state that there is a correlation between social class on the one hand and outcome of the penal process on the other, but another is to explain why this correlation occurs. To provide an answer in this direction it is essential to look at the penal process not primarily as a stage where different narratives compete for success,[3] but above all as a place where the unequal distribution of economic, social and cultural resources due to the societal division in classes, determines the significance of the various roles involved in the process. Direct observation becomes the key instrument.

The investigation presented below represents an attempt to carry out a project within this perspective.

The context of the investigation

During 1993, one hundred criminal cases, commited to a Turin court of first instance, were observed. There were several reasons to observe a court active in this town. After Milan, Turin is the most important town in northwestern Italy, marked in its history by the vicissitudes of two different dynasties: the royal one represented by the Savoia family – who unified the country in 1860 – and the bourgeois one, namely the Agnelli family, founders of the car manufacturer FIAT.

Thus Turin can be considered a living laboratory where several positive and negative experiences have occurred. Let me briefly mention the major ones. To begin with, an accelerated development based upon a monoindustrial culture and the related massive migration initially from the deep North (mainly the mountainous areas) and later from the South. Between the 1950s and the 1970s the population has more than doubled, reaching a million inhabitants. And this urban growth – more or less unplanned – has brought about peripheral districts with all the attributes of the classic slum.

Second, and obviously not disconnected from the process of industrialization, the rise of a strong labor movement with the first experiences of workers' councils in a period when Antonio Gramsci, the communist leader who himself lived in Turin, was politically active until he was jailed by the fascists.

Third, Turin has experienced advanced models of solidarity, quite often of Catholic inspiration. Already in the nineteenth century a priest called Don Bosco promoted initiatives oriented to the care of children and of sick people. Today the Gruppo Abele is leading the battle against social exclusion. Similarly, the Local Juveniles Criminal Court is experimenting with alternative paths to incarceration.

Today the crisis in the automobile industry has had a severe impact on the local level of unemployment. Unemployment now is around 10 percent and the population size has decreased in ten years by 5.5 percent. Consequently, the recent, often clandestine, immigration from non-European countries (Morocco, West-African countries, South America, etc.) finds it hard to gain access to the official labor market. In such a situation, it can be tempting for the local authorities, including the courts, to tackle the issue with traditional law-and-order measures.

The penal process may provide an opportunity to see if significant changes are occurring also in this direction.[4]

The investigation

The one hundred cases which became the object of observation, were not sampled randomly, because we were interested in having a fair proportion of both white- and blue-collar trials. On the contrary, the cases, which were observed between April and October 1993, were selected on the basis of two variables: type of crime and social position of the defendant. Blue-collar crimes included theft and fencing; white-collar crimes included violations of industrial safety regulations and violations of environmental legislation.

The defendants' social position was not measured in terms of profession (which was often difficult to detect) but according to whether they possessed a regular occupation or not. Then the defendants were split into two groups: a group labelled "*integrated*" (those with a regular occupation) and a group labelled the "*marginal*" (those without one). Needless to say, we found an extremely high correlation between occupational situation on the one hand and type of charge on the other: while marginals were tried for blue-collar crime, the integrated were tried for white-collar offenses.

All defendants were males. The variable "gender" was excluded in consideration of the limited number of female defendants.

Another variable taken into account was what we called "procedural resources." The idea was to evaluate the quality of the defense, by observing the extent to which formal and informal strategies were used by the defense. For example, we paid attention to indicators of the quality of the defense such as the occurrence of cross-examination, the exchange of information between the defendant and the defense attorney, and the length of the defense's closing address. Finally we registered the length of different trials.

The overall results[5]

The three variables mentioned earlier – the social position of the defendant, the quality of the defense and the length of the trial – have enabled us to have an 80 percent correct estimation of the outcome. As one can see in Table 9.1, we have been able to predict 48 cases of acquittal out of 60, and 32 cases of conviction out of 40.

A logistic regression showed that the probability of acquittal increased enormously when moving up from the group of "marginals" to the group of "integrated".

These overall results – although based on limited material – suggest that there are two sorts of justice, or, if we prefer, two sorts of process: the due process and the crime-control process and that these two sorts coexist. This is what we actually find at a closer look at the data.

Table 9.2 shows how length of time of trial is distributed among socially different types of defendants. While the majority of the marginals got a trial which lasted less than 30 minutes, the overwhelming majority of the intergrated got a trial which lasted longer than 30 minutes and for almost half of this group the time was three hours and longer.

Table 9.3 gives a rough measure of the quality of the defense: the length of the closing address of the defense attorney is cross-tabulated with the social position of the defendant.

Again time appears to be the critical variable: in most cases, the system does

Table 9.1 Outcome of trials estimated according to the social position of the accused and the number of procedural resources

	%		%
Acquittals	60	Convictions	40
Predicted acquittals	48	Predicted convictions	32
Correct estimation	80	Correct estimation	80

Table 9.2 Type of defendant and length of trial (in minutes)

Type of defendant	Length of trial (in minutes)			
	Less than 30	30–90	Over 180	Total
Marginal	38	24	3	65
Integrated	5	15	15	35

Table 9.3 Type of defendant and length of the defense closing address (in minutes)

Type of defendant	Defense's closing address (in minutes)				
	Less than 1	1–5	6–15	Over 16	Total
Marginal	20	31	13	1	65
Integrated	7	8	11	9	35

Table 9.4 Number of "procedural resources" utilized and type of defendant

Type of defendant	Resources utilized				
	None	1	2	3 or more	Total
Marginal	49	10	3	3	65
Integrated	15	9	4	7	35

not "allow" the defense of the marginals to speak longer than five minutes. The opposite situation holds true for the defense of the intergrated.

Table 9.4 shows how the "procedural resources" are distributed among different types of defendants.

Table 9.4 really speaks for itself. It shows that in the cases involving marginal defendants hardly anything was said on the part of the defense. In almost 80 percent of the cases the defense utilized no "procedural resources." The defendants were there because they were guilty. One may add: they were stupid enough not to understand that they should have pleaded guilty.

It is quite clear by now that time is one of the strategic variables. It is strategic because its systematically different use acts both directly and indirectly upon the outcome. It acts directly, for example, to the extent to which the judge openly interrupts the defense (one judge turning to the defense: "make it short . . . (there are other trials waiting . . . "), or the defense attorney excuses himself for taking the judge's time. It acts indirectly through the principles which regulate the activity of the court. Thus it is standard practice, at least in Turin, that while the various cases are randomly distributed among the different judges, the length of each trial is established in advance by the chief judge and blue-collar offenses are supposed to need lesser time than white-collar offenses. We have been told that the latter trials are estimated, on the average, to last three times longer than the former.

Conclusion

From the viewpoint of a research design, there is not much to say except that, if the problem of equality before the law is defined in terms of distributive justice and not of allocative justice, the remedies to be adopted cannot be exhausted by reducing the imbalance between defense and prosecution. "My" white collar criminals did actually enjoy a due process. But what happened to the majority of the defendants? So the question is whether the emphasis on due process is the right emphasis.

We can also reformulate the issue in the following terms: we have been dealing with two perspectives on justice and equality, respectively the legal and the sociological. And it has been clear that legal scholars and sociologists deal with different realities. Whether one reality is more "real" than the other cannot be empirically determined, but it can easily be empirically determined that there are gains – in terms of insight – which are provided by one perspective but not by the other. Is there any alternative?

Right now some of us fear a society where the law and the judge may become much like the ones depicted by Samuel Butler. In Erewhon, the imaginary country described by Samuel Butler, it is considered highly criminal and immoral to be ill. This is how solemnly and severely the judge speaks, having just found a young man guilty "of the great crime of labouring under pulmonary consumption":

> It is all very well for you to say that you come of unhealthy parents, and had a severe accident in your childhood which permanently undermined your constitution; excuses such as these are the ordinary refuge of the criminal . . . I am not here to enter upon curious methaphysical questions as to the origin of this or that – questions to which there would be no end were their introduction once tolerated . . . There is no question of how you came to become wicked, but only this – namely, are you wicked or not? This has been decided in the affirmative . . . You may say that it is not your fault . . . that if you had been born of healthy and well-to-do parents, and been well taken care of when you were a child, you would never have offended against the laws of your country . . . If you tell me that you had no hand in your parentage and education, and that it is therefore unjust to lay these things to your charge, I answer that whether your being in a consumption is your fault or not, it is a fault in you . . . You may say that it is your misfortune to be a criminal. I answer that it is your crime to be misfortunate.
>
> (Butler 1909: 113).

We know that we don't want that law and that judge.

However, there is another type of judge, "the most acute and forcible of the English judges" described by G. K. Chesterton (1963) in his book "*The Club of Queer Trades.*" What happened with this judge at the end of his career was that he "seemed to have lost interest in the law," and that "he talked more like a priest or a doctor, and a very outspoken one at that." Most interesting of all was what he said, initiating a series of trials whose style forced him to retire, "to a man who had attempted a crime of passion": "I sentence you to three years' imprisonment – he said – under the firm, and solemn, and God-given conviction, that what you require is three months at the seaside" (Ibid.: 9).

Whether or not we consider priests or doctors as particulary suited for solving conflicts, Chesterton's message is clear: to find the solution to criminal conflicts, find somewhere else to look, beyond the realm of the penal law.

Whether we like it or not, equality before the law is not a legal problem. Whether we want it or not, we are at a crossroads: we can either perpetuate our self-deception by refusing to see that equality before the law is an impossibility in our societies, or invent new paths as alternatives to the existing legal system.

Notes

1 I will not go into other problematic aspects of the reform, such as, for example, the fact that the lawyers' and judges's legal culture is still very much marked by the inquisitorial model.
2 A. Cottino and M. G. Fischer (1996) "Pourquoi l' inégalité devant la loi? in *Déviance et Société. vol. 20. 3: 199–214.*
3 The reference is to Bennett and Feldman's (1984) in many respects stimulating work.
4 The variable of ethnicity will be taken into account in the next phase of the investigation.
5 I owe Nicola Negri a great debt for his methodological suggestion.

References

Aubert, W. (1964) *Likhet og rett*, Pax, Oslo

Bennett, L. W. and Feldman, M. S. (1984) *Reconstructiong the Reality in the Courtroom. Justice and Judgment in American Culture*, New Brunswick, Rutgers University Press.

Butler, S. (1909) *Erewhon or over the Range*, London, Fifield. First published 1872.

Chambliss, W. J. (1995) "Controllare le classi pericolose: l'istituzionalizzazione dell' Apartheid negli Stati Uniti d'America," in Cottino and Sarzotti: 151–180.

Chesterton, G. K. (1963) *The Club of the Queer Trades*, Penguin, Harmondsworth.

Christie, N. (1993) *Crime as Industry*, Routledge, London.

Conso, G. and Grevi, V. (eds) (1991) *Profili del nuovo codice di procedura penale*, Padua, Cedam.

Cottino, A. (1986) "Peasant Conflicts in Italy," *Journal of Legal Pluralism*, 24: 77–100.

Cottino A. and Sarzotti, C. (eds) (1995) *Diritto, Uguaglianza e Giustizia Penale*, Turin, L'Harmattan Italia.

Ferrajoli, L. (1995) "Uguaglianza Penale e Garantismo," in Cottino and Sarzotti: 39–48

Neppi Modona, G. (1991) "Procedimento davanti al Pretore (artt. 549–567)" in Conso and Grevi, (1991).

Neppi Modona, G. (1995) "Crisi del processo penale e del principio di uguaglianza tra accusa e difesa" in Cottino and Sarzotti: 191–200.

Packer, H. L. (1968) *The limits of the Criminal Sanction*, Stanford University Press.

Sanders, A. and Young, R. (1994) *Criminal Justice*, Butterworths, London, Dublin, Edinburgh.

Seron, C. and Munger, F. (1996) "Law and Inequality: Race, Gender . . . and, of Course, Class," *Annual Review of Sociology*, 22: 187–212.

10

PRISON AND ALTERNATIVES TO PRISON IN SPAIN

José Cid and Elena Larrauri

Introduction

This chapter provides information on the evolution of the prison population and alternatives to prison in Spain. We distinguish and discuss the Franco dictatorship (1939–1975), the democratic constitutional period (1976–1995), and the new criminal code (1995) enacted under the socialist government. We then endeavour to provide an explanation for the enormous increase in the prison population in the 1980s. In addition, we seek to explain the alternatives to prison established in the latest criminal code and relate them to debates elsewhere in Europe.

The prison situation during the dictatorship (1939–1975)

At the end of the Spanish Civil War, the prison population stood between 213,000 and 280,000 people (Roldán 1988: 187), most of these being political prisoners. By 1944, this population had been reduced to 50,000 and by 1968 the prison population had fallen to 10,500. This is very low by European standards and was accomplished despite the heavy reliance of the criminal justice system on prison as the principal form of punishment.

The main penalties laid down by criminal legislation in this period were: the death penalty, terms of imprisonment (from one day to thirty years), house arrest and fines. Fines and house arrest were prescribed for very few offences. House arrest was a substitute sentence for prison sentences and could be imposed for up to one month. Fines were rarely prescribed as the *only* penalty for an offence and were normally added to prison sentences. Hence the usual penalty was a prison sentence.

The only permissible alternative to imprisonment was the *suspended sentence*, which tended to be automatically granted to non-recidivist offenders who had committed crimes punishable with a one-year prison sentence. The maintenance of a suspended sentence had as its sole condition that no crime was committed for two to five subsequent years.

146

Regarding penitentiary law, the practice which most affected the length of sentence – and therefore the size of the prison population – was *remission*. Ordinary remission was 'formally' granted to prisoners engaged in work in the prison, but in practice automatically applied to all prisoners; while extraordinary remission was a reward for being loyal to the prison staff and participating in rehabilitation activities (going to church, attending educational classes, etc).

A second device that regulated and, in time, helped reduce the prison population, was *parole*. This was a benefit conceded to all prisoners who had served three-quarters of their prison sentence if they had demonstrated 'good behaviour'. This applied to all sentences regardless of their length. The 'adding up' of remissions and parole, which usually shortened sentences by a minimum of one half and sometimes even more, had considerable impact in keeping the prison population low.

It is our view that the low prison population achieved during the later stages of Franco's dictatorship can be explained by the following factors:

1   the low level of criminality, perhaps related to the *general* poverty of the country;[1]
2   the informal violence and repression exercised by the police which resulted in much crime being unrecorded or unprosecuted (Roldán 1988: 201);
3   the policy of awarding 'pardons', which Franco delivered to mark special occasions such as Christmas, or the anniversary of the civil war;
4   the penitentiary policy of remissions.

The prison situation during democracy (1976–1995)

The increase in Spain's prison population began precisely at the moment of the end of the dictatorship, a period when Europe generally, and Spain in particular, suffered the economic crisis of the 1970s. All of this coincided with the first few years of democracy after Franco's death in 1975.

As one can see in Table 10.1, at the end of the 1970s and the beginning of the 1980s there were several factors at work that *decreased* the prison population before the recent, steady increase began in the mid-1980s. The first relevant development that affected the prison population after Franco's death was an amnesty which affected only political prisoners. Although no alternatives to prison were introduced and the system of punishments remained the same,[2] the reforms in criminal law and in procedural law also had important decarceration effects. At the beginning of the new socialist government of 1983, there was a reduction in the length of penalties that could be imposed[3] for property crimes and drug-related offences, and a reform of the system of remand imprisonment (this could now only be imposed for serious crimes and for up to four years).

These changes, initially leading to a very low prison population, were followed by further change as Spanish society experienced an increase in criminality and in feelings of insecurity. By 1984, these developments featured among the most important topics covered by the mass media. The subsequent 'reforms' proposed by the same socialist government were now aimed at increasing penal severity. These measures included: increasing the time that could be spent whilst held in a remand prison; and increasing the number and the length of sentences for drug trafficking offences. The result of such 'reforms', which were referred to as 'counter-reforms', was – unsurprisingly – an enormous increase in the prison population.

This evolution can be seen in Table 10.1.[4]

With such an increased prison population[5] and the lack of alternatives to incarceration, the mechanisms available to contain prisoners had to receive some reconsideration. This was recognised as a problem since there had been serious prison riots in 1977–1978, mainly caused by a feeling of discrimination because amnesty was only granted for political prisoners. The new special penitentiary benefits which were added to the possibilities of remission and parole, were the *open regime* (in which a person could work outside the prison but had to return at night) and *temporary licences*, allowing leave from prison for a few days or a weekend, granted to prisoners with a record of good behaviour.

Table 10.1 Prison population in Spain 1976–1996

Year	Prison population	Prisoners/100,000 inhabitants
1976	9,937	28
1977	9,392	26
1978	10,463	29
1979	13,627	37
1980	18,253	49
1981	21,185	56
1982	21,942	58
1983	13,999	36
1984	17,713	46
1985	22,802	59
1986	25,256	66
1987	27,073	70
1988	29,468	76
1989	31,473	81
1990	33,119	85
1991	36,539	94
1992	41,013	105
1993	45,416	116
1994	48,212	123
1995	47,219	121
1996	44,199	113

The new criminal code

What is surprising during this steady growth of the prison population is that there was no sensitivity to the problem of prison overcrowding. The introduction of alternatives to imprisonment, found in the new Spanish Criminal Code of 1995, was mainly a response to the idea that prison, and especially short sentences, do not rehabilitate. Additionally, however, this development also reflected a wish to move into line with standards elsewhere in Europe.

Table 10.2 summarises and depicts the new punishment system.

The principal means of punishment within the Spanish criminal code are now: prison, weekend arrest, fines, and restriction of rights (disqualification).[6] To elaborate upon these:

Prison: continues to be the main penalty for most crimes. The minimum length of custody is 6 months and the maximum 20 years, with some exceptions permitting an increase to 30 years.

Weekend arrest: this possibility was unknown in the previous criminal code, and it has been introduced for a select few crimes as an alternative to penalties of imprisonment of less than six months. It is worth noting however, that this penalty will actually be implemented within prisons as the previous penalty of 'house arrest' has been abolished. Such prisoners are to be held in individual cells, though this is not a recognition of 'rights', privacy or dignity, but a requirement and policy based on the 'criminal contagion hypothesis', which would suggest that the 'redeemable' should be kept separate from the 'irredeemable', lest the latter further corrupt the former.

Fines: This penalty has undergone two major changes. On the one hand, it may now be imposed as a 'main' penalty, although this is so for very few crimes and, as in the past, a fine is normally added to a prison sentence; on the other hand, the 'unit fine system' has been introduced.[7] The payment of fines is ensured by use of imprisonment, but as an alternative, imprisonment can be replaced by weekend arrest or community service (see below).

As regards *alternatives* to prison, legislators have not passed many sanctions

Table 10.2 Spanish punishment system under the Criminal Code 1995

Main penalties	*Alternative penalties (for sentences up to 2 years)*
Prison (6 months to 20 years)	Suspended sentence (with or without
Weekend prison (1 to 24 weekends)	supervision)
Unit-fines (1 day to 30 months)	Interchange sentence (weekend arrest, unit
Disqualification	fine, community service)

other than prison, but have relied mainly on suspension or interchange mechanisms to avoid the custodial penalties ordered by the law. In this sense they have transferred responsibility for finding alternatives to custodial sentences to the judges. It should be noted that in the continental system, the law prescribes penalties for every crime, therefore the suspension or interchange of a prison sentence at the discretion of the judges is an exception in the legal system.[8] This can now happen via:

1   *Suspended sentence*: sentences of up to two years' imprisonment may be suspended for a period of between two and five years. To this alternative to prison, which already existed in the previous criminal code, has been added the possibility of attaching 'behaviour rules' or 'conditions' (for example, bans on going to some places, curfew orders, and a 'catch-all' clause to include any other obligations that the judge considers necessary). These are in addition to the previous single condition of 'not committing a crime during the period of suspension of the sentence'.
2   *Interchange of custody*: this alternative is totally new and consists of the possibility of sentences of up to two years' imprisonment being interchanged by other penalties. If the main penalty is prison it can be converted into 'weekend custody' or fines, while if the main penalty is 'weekend custody' it can be converted into fines or community service.

In penal law the mechanisms that previously favoured a shortening of sentences have also undergone some transformation. The main change worth noting is the *abolition of remission*, on the grounds that this was considered to undermine the aims of sentencing, since it could result in a large reduction in the sentence imposed by the judge. *Parole* has been maintained for cases where three-quarters of the sentence have already been served in custody, but in order to compensate for the abolition of 'remission through work', an exceptional category of parole has been established which may apply where the prisoner has served two-thirds of their sentence. A second new development is the possibility of adding to parole 'behaviour rules' or conditions (similar to those attached to suspended sentences).

Problems for debate

One concern about the state of penological discussion in Spain is the lack of attention paid to the question of how the prison population might be reduced. The low level of debate currently pursued in Spain,[9] noticed and remarked upon by non-Spanish observers (Huber 1994), has focused more on how to achieve 'rehabilitation through alternatives' rather than on how to reduce the prison population.

Alternatives and rehabilitation

In the English-language literature one can identify at least two approaches to alternatives to prison. One could be called the rehabilitation approach and the other the desert approach. According to the first, alternatives should be promoted and defended because of their greater potential for rehabilitation; while according to the second, alternatives to prison should be promoted and defended because they represent intermediate punishments which may be applied according to the severity of the offence (Wasik and von Hirsch 1988).

In Spain the model of alternatives to imprisonment is heavily influenced by the rehabilitation model. This can be seen in the following ways:

1   Alternatives are not considered as the main punishments in law but are awarded by judges according to an individualised assessment of the dangerousness of the offender.
2   The possibility of suspending or interchanging imprisonment is available only in the case of short sentences. This reflects the influence of a model of rehabilitation which holds that short periods of imprisonment are too short to allow prison treatment programmes to rehabilitate.
3   The introduction of behaviour rules attached to suspended sentences or substitute sentences allows the judge to tailor the sentence to the offender.
4   Suspension and interchange of prison sentences are highly unlikely to be available for re-offenders, as they clearly have not been 'rehabilitated'.

The international debate as to whether the rehabilitation or the desert model will have the least impact on the achievement of significant prison decarceration, of course, continues.

Alternatives and decarceration

This leads us to our next point. A well-known theme in the English-language literature is the scant impact that alternatives have had in achieving prison decarceration (Bottoms 1987; Ashworth 1995: 288). This same result may follow in Spain for the following reasons.

A first reason is that the 'normal response' to every crime (with the few exceptions responded to by use of a fine and/or weekend house arrest) is always, in the first instance, prison. In some cases, the judge is then placed in the position of being asked to suspend or interchange a sentence of imprisonment. In this sense alternatives are considered to be 'privileges': measures that permit the offender to avoid what they really deserve. Alternative punishments like probation or community service are not considered as penalties in their own right.

A second reason is that even the discretionary possibility of judges imposing sentences that are alternatives to prison is very restricted. This follows from the fact that the maximum penalty has to be no more than two years in order for it to be suspended or substituted. If one considers that the most frequent crimes are against property and that, for example, burglary has, as an average penalty range, from two to five years, while drug-trafficking has an average from three to nine years, it is not difficult to foresee that these alternatives will be inapplicable in the cases of the very crimes which are committed most frequently.

A third reason might be the fact that all the alternatives retain prison as a 'back-up'. In Spain, there is no model of, for example, scaling community sentences according to their severity (Wasik and von Hirsch 1988), or the use of different back-ups in cases of a breach of the alternative. Moreover, since the alternatives now include more conditional requirements, the chances of breaching these and ending up in prison anyway, increase, and hence the prospect of decarceration recedes further.

Alternatives and net-widening

The term 'net-widening' (Austin and Krisberg 1981; Cohen 1985) in the English-language literature tends to refer to the observation that alternatives do not actually result in fewer offenders being sent to prison since they tend to be applied to offenders who would not normally have been imprisoned anyway. This scepticism also reflects the fact that alternatives have come to be more intrusive, since many behaviour rules have to be added in order to make them credible as punishments.

The first of the two problems concerning net-widening might be seen as the risk that the people who face the imposition of the additional requirements of the new alternatives will be people who would previously simply have received suspended sentences. Therefore in some cases, the new alternatives will indeed be employed instead of the old provisions, but *nonetheless* the people actually sent to prison will remain the same. The second of the above problems relates to the severity of the alternatives, which follows from a requirement that they match the severity of prison as punishment. Hence, community service may last up to 386 hours (when the usual maximum in Europe is 240 hours), with similar harshness in the use of unit-fines.

Increased severity can also be observed in the case of suspended sentences. Whereas previously the only requirement was that the person should not commit a further crime, now there is the possibility of adding multiple behaviour rules that also have to be complied with. These behaviour rules are not only 'control' rules, in the sense of obligations *not* to do something (for example not to go to some places), but are also 'positive' rules in the sense that they require participation in cultural, sexual-health, educational or detoxification programmes.

Concluding comments[10]

In general, rather than promoting alternatives to prison or contributing to decarceration, the new penal code has increased the level of penal severity. In some cases, the scale of punishment has been reduced but: (a) this does not compensate for the abolition of remission; and (b) for crimes against property, which previously received sentences of less than six months of imprisonment, the penalties have been *increased*, precisely in order to avoid the decarceration effect that would have resulted from abolishing prison sentences of less than six months (Mir 1993).

Alternatives to imprisonment in Spain are very few (for example there are no restitution or compensation orders),[11] crimes punished by sanctions other than prison (fines, weekend arrest) are also very few, and new institutions (such as community service) are not designated as main punishments under the law but, as we have described, are only conceded as privileges awarded through judicial discretion. Finally, since prison is still seen as the central punishment, even when alternatives are contemplated, they are designed to match perceived levels of prison severity. Hence, their characteristics are long duration, the addition of many conditional requirements, and the fall-back of imprisonment.

This unsatisfactory situation probably reflects a lack of critical debate among progressive forces in Spain, before and following the approval of the new criminal code, under a socialist government which did not embrace a reductionist approach toward use of the prisons (Rutherford 1984). Instead, progressive groups in Spain have tried to promote new reforms through the use of criminal law. This has been a strategy which implies the use of criminal law as a pedagogic aid to rehabilitation and has therefore opened up further routes by which people may end in prison!

Notes

General Note. Some aspects of the prison system in Spain and details of use of non-custodial punishment are beyond the scope of this paper. For a literature review concerning relevant recent research, see pp. 56–58 (and *passim*) in Giminez-Salinas and Funes 1995.

1 Toharia (1974: 79–141) notices that convictions did not increase substantially even during the economic boom of the 1960s when there was an increase in recorded criminality (offences against property).
2 As we have seen, prison is the main penalty and the suspended sentence is the only alternative in the criminal code and remission and parole the only alternatives in the penal law.
3 For the influence of different factors on prison populations see Kuhn (1996).
4 From 1976 to 1984, figures express the prison population at the end of every year. Since 1985, they express the average of prison population during the year. (Sources: Dirección General de Instituciones Penitenciarias, Ministerio del Interior, and personal elaboration. We thank Eulalia Luque, from the Centro de Estudios Jurídicos y Formación Especializada, for her help).
5 It is worth remarking that women in prison increased from 361 in 1976 to 4,217 in 1995, more than double the increase in the male prison population (Figures: prison

153

population at the end of each year. Source: Dirección General de Instituciones Penitenciarias. Ministerio del Interior).

6 For example for civil disobedience to military service, the penalty is restriction of rights which includes not being eligible for any job in the public Administration.

7 The system of the unit fine is to impose 'so many days' of fine (units) according to the severity of the offence, with the price of the day set according to the means of the offender (the mimimum being 200 pesetas and the maximum 50,000 pesetas).

8 To the two mentioned possibilities one should also add expulsion. This is a (so-called) 'alternative' to prison for illegal foreigners which consists of the possibility of being expelled from the country when the court sentence would be up to six years' imprisonment.

9 The reasons for this low level of discussion might be that the previous dictatorship did not favour criminal-policy debates; the influence of German scholarship, better known for elaborating a system of 'when' to punish, than 'how' to punish; and the lack of empirical studies, since criminology is confined to law faculties. The most recent books on alternatives to prison are: Luzón (1979); Sola *et al.* (1986); Valmaña (1990). A short review of the Spanish debate in English is found in del Rosal (1986).

10 For a fuller evaluation of the new system see Cid and Larrauri (1997).

11 It might be worth commenting that electronic monitoring has been introduced in the new penal law of 1996 for people who were allowed to work outside prison and had to return at night (open regime). This obligation can be avoided if people accept monitoring at night. The scheme has not yet been implemented.

References

Ashworth, A. (1995) *Sentencing and Criminal Justice*, 2nd ed. London: Butterworths.

Austin, J. and Krisberg, B. (1981) 'Wider, Stronger and Different Nets: the Dialectics of Criminal Justice Reform', *Journal of Research in Crime and Delinquency*, vol. 18, 165–196.

Bottoms, A. (1987) 'Limiting Prison Use: Experience in England and Wales', *The Howard Journal of Criminal Justice*, 26/3: 177–202.

Cid, J. and Larrauri, E. (eds) (1997) *Penas Alternativas a la Prisión*. Barcelona: Bosch.

Cohen, S. (1985) *Visions of Social Control*. Cambridge: Polity Press.

del Rosal, B. (1986) 'Alternatives to Imprisonment in the Spanish Criminal Justice System: The Current Situation and Outlooks for the Future', in *Papers on Crime Policy 2*. Helsinki: HEUNI.

Giminez-Salinas, E. and Funes, J. (1995) 'Research during crises, research on crises: ten years of research on order and the control of crime in Spain', pp. 47–69 in Robert, P. and van Outrive, L. with Jefferson, T. and Shapland, J. (eds) *Research, Crime and Justice in Europe*, Centre for Criminological and Legal Research, Sheffield.

Huber, B. (1994) 'Sanciones intermedias entre la pena de multa y la pena privativa de libertad (Sobre la discusión en torno a las penas ambulatorias y de contenido comunitario)', in *Anuario de Derecho Penal y Ciencias Penales*, 47/1: 155–176.

Kuhn, A. (1996) 'Incarceration rates: Europe versus USA', *European Journal on Criminal Policy and Research*, 4/3: 46–73.

Luzón, D. M. (1979) *Medición de la pena y sustitutivos penales*. Madrid: Instituto de criminología de la Universidad de Madrid.

Mir, S. (1993) 'Alternativas a la prisión en el borrador de Anteproyecto de Código Penal de 1990', en M. Cobo del Rosal (ed.): *Política criminal y reforma penal. Homenaje a la memoria del prof. Dr. D. Juan del Rosal*. Madrid: Editorial Revista de derecho privado, 843–854.

Roldán, H. (1988) *Historia de la Prisión en España*. Barcelona: Instituto de Criminología.

Rutherford, A. (1984) *Prisons and the Process of Justice. The Reductionist Challenge*. London: Heinemann.

Sola, A. de, García-Arán, M. and Hormazábal, H. (1986) *Alternativas a la prisión. Penas sustitutivas y sometimiento a prueba*. Barcelona: PPU.

Toharia, J. J. (1974) *Cambio social y vida jurídica en España*. Madrid: Cuadernos para el diálogo

Valmaña, S. (1990) *Sustitutivos penales y proyectos de reforma en el Derecho Penal español*. Madrid: Ministerio de Justicia.

Wasik, M. and von Hirsch, A. (1988): 'Non-Custodial Penalties and the Principles of Desert', *The Criminal Law Review*, September: 555–572.

11

ANOTHER ANGLE ON EUROPEAN HARMONISATION: THE CASE OF THE EUROPEAN COMMITTEE FOR THE PREVENTION OF TORTURE

Rod Morgan

In their introductory chapter to *Western European Penal Systems: A Critical Anatomy* (1995), Sim, Ruggiero and Ryan stress the importance for analysts of criminal-justice policy of the structural links being developed within Europe which are influencing the direction and shape of domestic policy within states. They high-lighted the Council of Europe and European Union mechanisms and processes and pointed out the arguably contradictory nature of some of the initatives being pursued. But in the final analysis the burden of their discussion was critical. They stressed the illiberal nature of the emergent European state, its relative unaccountability and the repressive policy focus in Europe on a number of powerless and 'dangerous' marginal populations – particularly illegal migrants and asylum seekers.

This attention to possibly harmonising processes is important, though how potent some of the processes Sim, Ruggiero and Ryan identify will prove to be, remains to be seen. The strength of local cultural traditions should not be under-estimated. Moreover, it is far from clear to what extent policies being pursued domestically in common can be attributed to the emerging supra-national struc-tures. Socio-economic and ideological currents are exercising a powerful influ-ence on domestic policy *in spite of* any assistance from the, as yet, relatively weak institutions being erected in Europe. Moreover, as I wish to emphasise in this paper, any analysis of the institutions that might promote harmonisation of crim-inal justice policy within Europe must also include scrutiny of those mechanisms that, contrary to Sim, Ruggiero and Ryan's emphasis, may promote human rights and greater accountability – both aspects of criminal justice policy which have in many respects been conspicuous by their absence from the domestic policies of many European states. It would be a mistake to view the processes of European harmonisation from a standpoint which, implicitly if not explicitly, assumes some

156

past Golden Age of national sovereignty during which the rule of law prevailed, human rights were assured and accountability was guaranteed. It was never so in many European states.

I wish to illustrate my theme – the positive aspect of harmonisation and the negative tradition of national sovereignty – by considering one of the transnational mechanisms of which Sim, Ruggiero and Ryan made no mention – the Council of Europe Committee for the Prevention of Torture (the CPT). It is necessary to begin with a brief outline of the origin, constitution and method of this recent piece in the jigsaw of possibly harmonising influence in Europe.

The CPT: constitution, *modus operandi* and standards

The CPT is the creation of a European Convention of the same name which came into force in 1989 and, at the time of writing has been ratified by 30 Council-of-Europe member states (Council of Europe 1996*a*). The Convention is the latest in a long line of international provisions designed to outlaw and prevent the re-emergence of torture following the rise of totalitarian states in Europe in the first half of the twentieth century (see Rusche and Kirchheimer 1939, 179–80; Peters 1987; for a comparison between the CPT and other international mechanisms, see Morgan and Evans 1994), though the CPT, working in a European context, has fortunately largely to concern itself with 'inhuman or degrading' treatment.

The Convention creates no new norms, though, as we shall see, the Committee formed under the Convention may develop safeguards and standards which exercise wider norm-setting influence. The Convention strengthens by non-judicial means of a preventive nature the existing obligation in Article 3 of the European Convention for the Protection of Fundamental Human Rights prohibiting torture or inhuman or degrading treatment or punishment. It does this by means of visits based on a principle of co-operation. The CPT has no sanctions at its command other than the possible publicity of its findings and it is not bound by the case law of the European Commission or Court of Human Rights. It may use that case law, and other human rights instruments, as a reference point.

The CPT is made up of persons from a variety of backgrounds and may undertake visits for any number of reasons as a result of information received from any number of sources. The Committee works on the basis of strict confidentiality. Its visits are thorough and the Convention requires signatory states to provide unimpeded access to any place within their jurisdiction where persons are deprived of their liberty by a public authority. The Committee is therefore able to speak to detained persons in confidence and does so. This includes suspects and other persons detained in police stations (for a full account of the *modus operandi* of the CPT see Evans and Morgan 1992).

Reports on visits, including any recommendations the CPT considers it necessary to make, are confidential to member states. Only 'if the Party fails to co-operate or refuses to improve the situation in the light of the Committee's recommendations' may the CPT decide, by a two-thirds majority, 'to make a public statement on the matter' (Article 10). This is the Committee's only sanction, so far used only twice, on both occasions with respect to Turkey in December 1992 (Council of Europe 1993*a*) and December 1996 (Council of Europe 1996*e*). To date, however, only two countries – Turkey and Cyprus – have failed to publish their CPT reports and most governments have published their responses to the CPT. It follows that there is now a substantial body of CPT-collected information and 'jurisprudence' available for analysis – currently some 45 country inspection reports in all. Before briefly considering both what practices and conditions CPT visits have revealed, what recommendations the Committee has made, and what response those recommendations have elicited, I should say a few words about definitions.

Defining torture and inhuman or degrading treatment

The CPT has two main tasks. First, to establish whether there is torture or inhuman or degrading treatment or punishment. Second, to make recommendations to reduce the likelihood of ill-treatment occurring.

'Torture' is a relatively less contentious term than 'inhuman and degrading' simply because there is more agreement about its meaning in international law (for a general review see Rodley 1987). Current definitions build on a distinction between torture and inhuman or degrading treatment developed in the jurisprudence of the European Court of Human Rights (see the *Greek* [1969] and *Northern Ireland* [1976] cases). According to this approach torture is not merely the extreme end of an ill-treatment continuum. Though all torture is inhuman and degrading and all inhuman treatment is degrading, it is generally agreed that torture is inhuman treatment which has a purpose, such as the obtaining of information or confessions, or to induce terror or to inflict punishment. It is an aggravated form of inhuman treatment. But it is specifically purposive in a way that inhuman or degrading treatment may not be. Thus torture mainly – though not exclusively – occurs during the initial phase of police custody and often involves established, almost traditional, techniques. In the *Greek* case it involved *falanga* (otherwise known as *falaka*), the beating of the soles of the feet.

Precisely when the boundary of torture is reached was considered in the highly controversial *Northern Ireland* case. Here the question concerned the use of violence and five interrogation techniques against terrorist suspects by the security forces. The Commission found that use of the five techniques in combination – forced prolonged standing in a stress position against a wall, hooding, subjection to white noise, deprivation of sleep, and deprivation of food and drink – did amount to torture. But the Court disagreed. Both the violence and the interrogation techniques were judged to constitute inhuman or degrading treatment but:

although their object was the extraction of confessions, the naming of others and/or information and although they were used systematically they did not occasion suffering of the particular intensity and cruelty implied by the word torture as so understood.

(Council of Europe, 1994*d*)

Needless to say this judgement has been heavily criticised. But this and other cases mean that the CPT has a clear set of benchmarks to follow. If the Committee chooses to. For, as we have noted, the CPT is obliged neither to define the terms 'torture' and 'inhuman and degrading' nor to follow the jurisprudence of the ECHR. Nor has the Committee defined these terms, except by way of example.

The term 'inhuman and degrading' raises altogether more difficult questions. Assuming that the five Northern Ireland interrogation techniques are indicative of the boundary between torture and inhuman or degrading treatment, where have the lower levels of inhuman and degrading treatment been found by other authorities to lie? The ECHR has judged that this:

is, in the nature of things, relative; it depends on all the circumstances of the case, such as the duration of the treatment, its physical or mental effects and, in some cases, the sex, age and state of health of the victim, etc.

(*Northern Ireland*, para 162)

In the *Northern Ireland* case detainees had been made to do strenuous physical exercises. Whether this was inhuman *or* degrading depended on the age and fitness of the persons involved: neither the Commission or the Court found there to have been a breach of Article 3 in this respect. Also in the *Northern Ireland* case 'comparatively trivial beatings' leading in one case to a perforated eardrum and minor bruising, and being 'made to stand spreadeagled against a wall' and being 'severely beaten or otherwise physically ill-treated', *was* found to be inhuman and degrading [*Ibid.*, para 174]. In the *Greece* case detainees were found to have received 'slaps and blows during, or shortly after, their arrest'. But, the Commission noted, the detainees had 'tolerated . . . and even taken for granted . . . a certain roughness of treatment' [*Greece*, para 11]. Thus in his extended review of this issue Rodley concludes that the minimum of what constitutes inhuman or degrading treatment cannot be and has not been precisely drawn. It is in part cultural and in part subjective. What is acceptable and normal in one country, may not be in another.

When do the conditions in which prisoners are kept amount to inhuman or degrading treatment? No clear-cut answer can be given to this question because both the ECHR and the UN Human Rights Committee have found breaches of prohibitions when a combination of circumstances have applied. Further, the UN Human Rights Committee has relied on both the prohibition of inhuman and degrading treatment *and* the requirement that prisoners be treated with respect for the inherent dignity of the human person (under the International Covenant of Civil and Political Rights 1966).

In the *Greek* case, where conditions in both a police station and prisons were found to have breached Article 3, the judgement relied on a complicated combination of factors. In the police station these included: severe overcrowding; incommunicado detention for up to thirty days; no access to open air; limited light; no exercise; all for a period of nine months. When more specific conditions – such as solitary confinement with a degree of sensory isolation – have been involved, both the Commission and ECHR have been reluctant to find a breach of Article 3. As Rodley has put it: 'the task of balancing humane treatment with exceptional security needs is a difficult one, but it seems that, for the Commission, the balance can tilt a long way towards security concerns before article 3 comes into play' (Rodley 1987: 232).

It follows that whatever conditions the CPT finds to be 'inhuman or degrading' are almost bound to be contentious. Member states on the receiving end of reports claiming that there is 'inhuman and degrading' treatment within their jurisdiction, particularly in relation to physical custodial conditions, will almost certainly contest the appellation, not least because to do otherwise might stimulate a flood of applications to Strasbourg for breach of Article 3.

CPT fact-finding

In this context it is possible only to illustrate what the CPT has found during its visits of inspection. Let us take the example of physical ill-treatment of suspects, or psychological pressure brought to bear on suspects, during pre-trial custody by or at the behest of the police or prosecution – the context in which torture classically occurs.

The CPT has developed phrases which summarise how common are allegations of physical ill-treatment by the police. The continuum ranges from 'none' to 'hardly any' or 'a few', to 'a certain number' or 'a number', to 'a fairly large number' or 'numerous', to 'a considerable number' or even an 'extremely large number'. This continuum generally, though not invariably, corresponds closely with the continuum of phrases developed to convey the degree to which the Committee concludes that ill-treatment does take place and the severity of that ill-treatment. The Committee customarily assesses the risk of ill-treatment. This ranges from a 'little' or 'small risk', to 'a risk', to a 'risk not negligible' or 'not inconsiderable', to a 'serious risk'. What is risked ranges from 'ill-treatment', to 'severe ill-treatment' to 'torture', though on the few occasions that the latter two terms have been used, it has generally been only a tentative conclusion due to the high evidential standard which it is clear the Committee has set for reaching the most serious of the findings that it can record.

Regarding both prevalence and seriousness the most unequivocal and damning conclusion yet reached by the Committee has been about the situation in

Turkey following visits in 1990, 1991 and 1992. The CPT concluded that 'the practice of torture and other forms of severe ill-treatment of persons remains widespread in Turkey' (Council of Europe 1993*a*: Appendix 4, para 21). This conclusion was reached following receipt of a large number of consistent and serious allegations, subsequently corroborated through medical examination, and concordant physical evidence, namely, incriminating equipment found in specific police sites where victims had described torture taking place. In Turkey the types of ill-treatment described were so severe, and the context so self-evidently purposive, that they would satisfy any definition of torture:

> suspension by the arms; suspension by the wrists which were fastened behind the victim (so-called 'Palestinian hanging', a technique apparently employed in particular in anti-terror departments); electric shocks to sensitive parts of the body (including the genitals); squeezing the testicles; beating of the soles of the feet ('falaka'); hosing with pressurised cold water; incarceration for lengthy periods in very small, dark and unventilated cells; threats of torture or other forms of serious ill-treatment to the person detained or against others; severe psychological humiliation.
>
> (*Ibid.*: para 5)

In December 1996 the CPT publicly announced that torture remained 'widespread' in Turkey (Council of Europe 1996*e*).

Elsewhere, however, the Committee has adopted a more qualified form of words, particularly where serious allegations have been received. With regard to Spain, for example, the question of whether there is continuing torture has been left largely open. The Committee concluded, following a visit to Spain in 1991, that they were:

> satisfied that recourse to torture or other forms of severe ill-treatment . . . is no longer a common practice. . . . However, its delegation did hear a certain number of allegations of very recent torture or severe ill-treatment, and not only, it should be stressed, from persons detained on suspicion of offences of a terrorist nature. It would therefore be premature to conclude that the phenomena of torture and severe ill-treatment have been eradicated.
>
> (Council of Europe 1996*c*: 23, para 25)

This conclusion was repeated following further visits to Spain in 1994 though on this occasion, after investigating a few allegations closely, the Committee reported that the allegations were not stereotyped (the Committee recognised the problem of false allegations made, particularly by members of politically motivated organisations, in order to undermine the legitimacy of state law-enforcement agencies) and that some medical evidence had been found consistent with allegations which had 'the ring of truth' about them. (*Ibid.*: 203, para 29). The Committee called on the Spanish authorities to undertake an immediate investigation into the methods employed by the Guardia Civil for questioning suspects held under Spanish preventive detention anti-terrorist legislation.

In Greece also the Committee received allegations and found evidence of torture. The Committee concluded that:

> it appeared that the ill-treatment of detained persons by police officers remained fairly commonplace for at least certain types of criminal suspects (notably those suspected of drug-related offences) and that in the case of persons suspected of very serious crimes, resort could still be had on occasion to severe ill-treatment/torture.
>
> (Council of Europe 1994*a*: para 15)

During the 1993 visit to Greece the CPT interviewed separately five prisoners who alleged they had received electric shocks in a particular police station. Two of these prisoners described the device used. It was, they said, 'a rod . . . some 40–50 cm in length with two small points at one end' (*Ibid.*: para 21). Whereupon the delegation went without notice to the police station concerned and, following a lengthy process of what can only be interpreted as prevarication by officers in the station, discovered in the personal locker of an officer

> who had been identified to the delegation as someone who had inflicted electric shocks . . . a 29 cm long plastic rod equipped with two small electrodes at one end. The pressing of a button in the middle of the rod resulted in a spark passing between the electrodes.
>
> (*Ibid.*: para 22)

During the same mission to Greece allegations were received of beatings with wooden sticks, and two detainees were found by medical members of the delegation to have 'contusions consistent with the allegations' of beating. It was significant, therefore, that the delegation discovered in the different offices of one police station:

> a variety of wooden sticks and batons as well as a baseball bat. Police officers present offered a number of conflicting explanations for the presence of these objects. By the time of the delegation's second visit two days later, all the above-mentioned items had disappeared, a situation for which, once again, different reasons were proffered.
>
> (Council of Europe 1994*a*)

Physical ill-treatment falling short of torture at the hands of the police has been found by the CPT to be relatively commonplace in a number of European states. After a visit to Portugal in 1992 the Committee said it could 'only conclude that the ill-treatment of persons in police custody is a relatively common phenomenon' (Council of Europe 1994*b*: para 15). In Austria in 1990 the Committee concluded that 'there is a serious risk of detainees being ill-treated while in police custody (Council of Europe 1991*a*: para 48). The ill-treatment 'ranged from slaps with the flat of the hand to punches, kicks or being struck with truncheons or heavy books during interrogations' (*Ibid.*: para 42). When the Committee returned to Austria in 1994 they discovered, as we shall see, evidence of even more severe ill-treatment (Council of Europe 1996*f*). In France, following a visit in 1991, the Committee found that 'persons deprived of their liberty by the security forces on the orders of the court run a risk which is not inconsiderable of being ill-treated' (Council of Europe 1993*b*: para 11).[1]

> The delegation heard a large number of allegations of ill-treatment, some of them serious. . . . The allegations related to the police in particular. The allegations included: punches and slaps; blows on the head with telephone directories; psychological pressure; verbal abuse; and deprivation of food and medicine. The allegations concerned: males and females; foreigners, young persons and other vulnerable detainees; and they related to police stations in both Paris and the provinces. The allegations were corroborated from so many sources that they merited belief.
>
> (*Ibid.*: para 11)

Almost identical conclusions were reached regarding Italy, both with respect to the Carabineri and the police (Council of Europe 1995*a*: paras 18–23), and Eire, particularly with regard to Garda stations in Dublin (Council of Europe 1995*b*: para 20).

In most countries the CPT reports having heard some allegations of mistreatment by the police, but generally not of a serious nature. This mistreatment has comprised slaps, kicks, failure to provide food, and so on. Quite often particular groups of suspects are identified as being vulnerable to this sort of treatment. In Belgium, for example, foreigners are identified and it is notable that the two examples of ill-treatment cited in the Belgian report both relate to Africans, one from Morocco and the other from Guinea (Council of Europe 1994*c*: para 20). In Sweden also, the few allegations of ill-treatment came mostly from foreign nationals (Council of Europe 1992: para 9).

Generally speaking the CPT has not found much evidence of physical ill-treatment of suspects in custody at the hands of the police in Northern Europe, that is throughout Scandinavia, Germany, the Netherlands and the United Kingdom, though, following a visit to Northern Ireland in 1993, the Committee concluded that the information it had received regarding the holding centres for terrorist suspects was 'sufficient to give rise to legitimate concern about the treatment of persons detained' in them (Council of Europe 1994*e*: para 36).

A different picture is emerging from Eastern Europe, however, most of which states have ratified the Convention only in the last year or two,[2] have been visited for the first time only recently; the reports on these visits are only beginning to be published. In Hungary in 1994, for example, the visiting CPT delegation heard 'numerous allegations of physical ill-treatment inflicted by the police on detained persons, both at the time of arrest and during subsequent interrogations (Council of Europe 1996*b*: para 17).

> The majority of the allegations ... were remarkably consistent as regards the precise form of ill-treatment involved. In most cases, the persons concerned alleged that, after their hands had been handcuffed behind them (or their ankles attached to an item of furniture), they had been struck with truncheons, punched, slapped or kicked by police officers. The delegation found that, in a number of cases, the allegations made were supported by medical evidence.
>
> (*Ibid.*: para 17)

As in other countries in Eastern and Southern Europe the Committee concluded that, in Budapest at least, 'persons deprived of their liberty by the police . . . run a not inconsiderable risk of ill-treatment' (*Ibid.*: para 22).

Conditions of custody

Generally, though not invariably, those countries in which the CPT has found suspects' risk of physical ill-treatment in police custody to be greatest, have also been those countries in which the conditions of police custody are worst. Police accommodation in Scandinavia, Germany, the Netherlands, and the United Kingdom has generally been found to be good – in these countries there are normally well-sized, reasonably furnished, lit and ventilated cells, the provision of clean matresses and blankets, in-cell sanitary arrangements, cell alarms, and so on – whereas in Southern and South-Eastern Europe the CPT has found much to criticise. In the space available a few brief examples will have to suffice.

In Turkey the material conditions of detention were described as 'extremely poor'. Incarcerating suspects 'for lengthy periods in very small, dark and unventilated cells' is clearly an integral part of the serious widespread ill-treatment of suspects (Council of Europe 1993*a*: Appendix 4, para 5). In Greece in 1993 conditions in police detention were found to range from 'adequate to extremely poor' and the CPT employed possibly its most severe judgement to date in a published report. At Piraeus Police Station, for example, the delegation encountered severe overcrowding of prisoners held for several days in cellular conditions where the toilet and washing facilities were described as 'appalling' and no mattresses had been provided. Moreover, conditions at the Piraeus Transfer Centre were described as 'inhuman', a judgement arrived at following a description of an overcrowded, dirty, badly lit area which was a cross between a yard and a room in a generally poor state of repair (Council of Europe 1994*a*: paras 52–89).

Custodial conditions almost as bad have been found much closer to home. Following a visit to France in 1991, for example, the CPT considered that the conditions in police detention ranged from 'acceptable' to 'bad' to 'deplorable' (Council of Europe 1993*b*: para 16). Two sites were thought to raise issues sufficiently serious for them to be made the subject of immediate observations to the French authorities at the end of the mission. The cells at Aubagne Gendarmerie Headquarters, for example:

> were in a very dilapidated state and the cells for men smelt strongly of urine. The walls were running with condensation. There was very limited natural light (through a grill at the height of the ceiling) and there was no artificial lighting. The ventilation was inadequate. Finally there was no alarm system, a vital facility in the circumstances, since the two cells were in a barracks block separated from the other buildings.
>
> (*Ibid.*: para 17)

The CPT delegation announced that they thought this and another police detention area so 'unacceptable' that it should be closed forthwith, a recommendation with which the French authorities quickly agreed. Elsewhere in France some police cells were judged to be too small for overnight use, were insanitary or insufficiently ventilated, or were found to lack mattresses or blankets for prisoners held overnight.

Such strictures have not been uncommon. In Spain in 1991 and again in 1994, police accommodation was found to range from the very good to the extremely poor. In some police stations the delegations found rotting food, flea-ridden and dirty mattresses, blood-stained walls or sleeping blocks, very inadequate lighting, poor access to lavatories and a lack of ventilation. In one Madrid station in 1991 the CPT recommended that the Spanish authorities explore the possibility of withdrawing from service a labyrinth of underground cells, a request that had to be reiterated at the end of the 1994 visit following the delegation's discovery that they were still being used and that no significant improvements had been made to them. Elsewhere in 1994 cells were inspected, use of which the CPT considered 'quite unacceptable . . . for any form of detention' (filthy, unlit, poorly ventilated and excessively small or narrow). Again the delegation recommended at the conclusion of the visit that police accommodation be closed forthwith (Council of Europe 1996*c*: 25–8 and 116–23).

CPT safeguards against torture and other ill-treatment

Early in its life the CPT promulgated fundamental safeguards against ill-treatment in police custody and has since repeatedly intoned those safeguards as a more or less standard formula (the wording sometimes varies slightly):

The CPT attaches particular importance to three rights for persons detained by the police:

- the right of those concerned to have the fact of their detention notified to a close relative or third party of their choice of their detention,
- the right of access to a lawyer,
- the right to a medical examination by a doctor of their choice (in addition to any medical examination carried out by a doctor called by the police authorities).

The CPT considers that these three rights are fundamental safeguards against the ill-treatment of persons in detention, which should apply from the very outset of custody (i.e. from the moment when those concerned are obliged to remain with the police).

(Council of Europe 1996b: para 40)

In this regard the CPT has gone beyond anything established in the jurisprudence of the European Court of Human Rights. The European Court has failed to consider deprivation of liberty of a suspect for interrogation a 'deprivation of liberty' in terms of Article 11 (the right to freedom of association), and has had difficulties deciding when legal representation is called for (see Murdoch 1994: 245).

The implementation of these rights, which in the CPT's view serve as fundamental safeguards against ill-treatment, is elaborated in detail and supplemented by other recommendations – an obligation on the police to notify suspects of their rights; comprehensive custody records on which all events and decisions relevant to detainees' welfare should be recorded; the electronic recording of police interviews; rules on the practice of police interrogation; rules on the treatment of particularly vulnerable suspects such as juveniles, the mentally disordered, etc; an independent complaints mechanism; and so on – depending on the risks, procedural shortcomings and resources found in different states. This is not to suggest that the CPT's standards are inconstant: rather that the Committee's standards appear to be prioritised and applied with more or less vigour depending on the circumstances.

What is clear is that very few European countries meet the three fundamental safeguards, let alone the elaborated code, recommended by the CPT. In this regard, England and Wales is a conspicuous exception – indeed, the CPT code might almost have been based on the provisions of the Police and Criminal Evidence Act 1984 (see Morgan 1996). Once again, a few brief examples will have to serve to illustrate the point.

In Portugal the CPT found that the right of detained persons to have a third party notified of their detention is only expressly guaranteed in Portuguese law 'when a court order involving deprivation of liberty becomes effective', that is, not from the outset of custody (Council of Europe 1994<i>b</i>: para 38). Further, though the CPT found that detainees' right to choose and be assisted by counsel *was* guaranteed by Portuguese law, the delegation learned.

> that it was extremely rare for a detained person to have access to a lawyer during the initial period of police custody and that, in practice, access to assistance from a legally qualified person was often not available even during later stages of the proceedings.
>
> > (*Ibid.*: para 44)

The CPT has found the situation in Portugal to be replicated in several countries. In France the CPT found that suspects held during the initial period of custody (*garde à vue*) had no statutory right to inform a third party of their detention, or to have access to a lawyer, or to be examined by an independent doctor of their choice. The French police maintained that it was their practice to allow suspects, where there was no fear of collusion, to inform third parties about their detention. But there was no statutory right to be able to do so (Council of Europe 1993*b*: para 38–46). In Austria the CPT found that there was a legal right to have third parties informed and for some suspects to have access to a lawyer. But in practice the evidence was that the former was often denied and the latter so seldom happened that the provision was almost a dead letter. There were in Austria no legal services to provide 'legal advice free of charge and at short notice to persons in police custody' (Council of Europe 1991*a*: paras 48 and 59). In some of the Viennese police stations visited police officers confessed that they could not recall any suspect held in custody receiving a visit from a lawyer.

This disjunction between the law and practice, or the absence of a clear right to legal advice during the initial phase of police custody, is true of most European countries. These countries include several where the CPT has found little or no evidence of ill-treatment by the police. In Germany, for example, a person apprehended by the police on *suspicion* of having committed a criminal offence (a *'Verdachtiger'*) has no right of access to a lawyer and is rarely allowed access. Not until the suspect becomes the *subject* of a criminal inquiry (a *'Bechuldigter'*) – that is, at the start of the first interrogation – does a suspect have the right to consult a lawyer. Further, it appears that persons held only on suspicion are rarely allowed to inform third parties of their detention, and suspects who are the subject of criminal inquiries are allowed to have a near relative or a third party informed only 'if this is considered compatible with the needs of the inquiry' (Council of Europe 1993*e*: paras 32–3).

A similar situation regarding legal advice appears to exist in Sweden (Council of Europe 1992: para 25–7) and in Norway, though in Norway the law accords every arrested person right of access to a lawyer at every stage in criminal proceedings: in practice, however, it appears that suspects are not told of the fact or granted access until first interviewed (Council of Europe 1994*e*: paras 32–3) which means that initial interrogations take place without the benefit of legal advice. In Finland also there is a right of access to a lawyer at all stages though there is legal provision for the police to exclude lawyers during interrogations for 'important reasons related to the investigation', an ambiguous qualification about the use of which the CPT sought clarification. Further the CPT noted that 'it was extremely rare for a lawyer to become involved' during the initial phase of detention following apprehension (Council of Europe 1993*d*: para 34).

A particularly telling example is to be found in the CPT report on the Netherlands and in the published response of the Dutch government. The Dutch Code of Criminal Procedure provides that:

> the suspect may, in accordance with Part III (legal counsel), request the assistance of one or more legal counsel. As far as possible, he shall be granted the opportunity, whenever he so requests, to communicate with his legal counsel.
>
> (Council of Europe 1993c: para 41)

However, the CPT found that though 'the formal position under Dutch law . . . seems quite favourable' the actual 'situation (during the initial period of detention for up to six hours allowed to the police) appears less satisfactory. . . . The official interpretation, which is said to be widely applied, is apparently that access to a lawyer may be granted, but is not a right' (*Ibid.*). Since it is the CPT's view that it is precisely during the *initial* period of detention that suspects are most vulnerable to ill-treatment – a conclusion about which everyone with experience of jurisdictions in which ill-treatment by the police is common is agreed – the CPT recommended to the Dutch 'that persons held for interrogation by the security forces be entitled to have access to a lawyer as from the outset of their deprivation of liberty' (*Ibid.*).

The Dutch government response on this issue is robust and includes a double message, though it is quite clear which message carries the most weight. The Dutch point out that there is an unequivocal right for suspects to be assisted by legal counsel 'during interrogation by the public prosecutor or his deputy preceding possible remand in police custody' – the stage *following* the initial six hours – but:

> The police interrogation may begin before that period. There are often practical difficulties in finding a lawyer who is available at short notice. Moreover, *it is not considered desirable for the legal counsel to be present during the police interrogation, when the investigating officer is intent on creating an atmosphere in which the person concerned is prepared to co-operate in establishing the facts and clarifying his role in the suspected crime.* The presence of legal counsel at this stage *could have the effect of lessening his willingness to co-operate*, which would oblige the police to make more frequent use of other measures to establish the truth such as searching the premises of third parties. As measures of this kind take more time than interrogation, it could mean prolonging the period of pre-trial detention. There

is no evidence to suggest that the police make improper use of interrogation procedures.

(Council of Europe 1994*d*, 23–4, emphasis added)

This is a frank rebuttal which we can speculate many Turkish officials would publicly endorse, though it is doubtful, given the inference that would undoubtedly be drawn from such a statement, they will do so. Turkish law does not guarantee the right of a suspect to have a lawyer present during police interrogation as such, but does guarantee a general right (with the exception of persons suspected of collective offences) of access to a lawyer during police detention. The difference is that in the Netherlands there is little or no suspicion that the Dutch police misuse their limited powers during this initial six hours, whereas in Turkey periods of police detention are much longer and there is a widespread apprehension, and a considerable body of evidence, that even the limited legal guarantees for suspects are ignored and police powers abused:

> These long detention periods are, according to the reports, a major factor in the continued use of torture [in Turkey] . . . lawyers are reportedly constantly denied by the police or security forces an opportunity to see their clients . . . in practice relatives spend days trying to learn the whereabouts of a detainee and are neither informed about the place of detention nor helped by the authorities in their search for such information.
>
> (United Nations 1992: para 480)

It appears, therefore, that in Scandinavia, as in Germany and the Netherlands – let alone the countries of Eastern and Southern Europe where there is widespread evidence of police ill-treatment of suspects in custody – the presence of lawyers during the initial stage of police custody is generally not encouraged and seldom occurs. Furthermore, most of the additional safeguards on which the CPT places reliance – comprehensive custody records, the electronic recording of police interviews, a detailed code for the conduct of interrogations, and so on – are either lacking or are only partially in place in the majority of the countries on which the CPT has reported.

In Germany, for example, the Basic Law provides that detained persons shall not be subject to physical or mental ill-treatment and the German Code of Criminal Procedure states that 'an accused person's freedom to determine and exercise his will shall not be impaired by ill-treatment, fatigue, physical constraint, the use of medicines, torture, deception or hypnosis' (Council of Europe 1993*e*: para 40). German police officials told the CPT that it was the practice of the police to allow persons being interrogated to have a break when requested 'in order to eat, rest or discuss matters with their lawyer'. Any break in the proceedings would be recorded in the written account. There were no rules about these matters, however, and 'prisoners could be questioned for up to 12 hours, on condition that they showed no signs of fatigue' (*Ibid.*: para 41). The CPT took the view that there should be more detailed guidance and that the German authorities should examine the possibility of making the electronic recording of police interrogations a standard practice, something which no country in Europe, other than the United Kingdom, currently provides for. The Committee has found it necessary to make similar recommendations in the vast majority of the European countries on which it has reported.

Similar shortcomings have been found by the CPT with regard to custody records. Seldom are police custody records comprehensive in that they record medical information, or details of requests for visits or visits themselves, or whether prisoners have been fed, or when they have been questioned, and so on. In Norway the custody registers contained 'scant information' (Council of Europe 1994*e*: para 42). In Belgium the information in police registers and other records 'étaient variables' ('were variable') (Council of Europe 1994*c*: para 52). In Sweden police records 'were not being scrupulously completed' and in any case they 'contained no details of such matters as the holding of interrogation sessions and the granting of rights' (Council of Europe 1992: para 36). In Italy the police kept rudimentary records about detainees' time of arrest and liberation but the carabinieri appeared to keep no registers (Council of Europe 1995*a*: para 52). In Slovenia the Criminal Investigation Department told the visiting CPT delegation that no record at all is made of the custody of someone detained for less than six hours (Council of Europe 1996*d*: para 42).

Psychological pressure applied to suspects held in custody pre-trial

One further angle on police custody is worth emphasising. A survey of CPT reports reveals a custodial pattern that will come as no surprise to any analyst familiar with penal systems world-wide: the worst living conditions in prison systems are generally found in remand establishments for unconvicted prisoners awaiting trial. However, the CPT has brought to the fore another aspect of pre-trial detention which has received rather less attention – namely the degree to which in some countries remands in custody are to police accommodation, or, where remands are to prison establishments, the police or the prosecution are able to determine the restrictiveness of that custody and, potentially, use it to bring pressure to bear on accused persons. Though, arguably, all pre-trial custody *serves* to bring pressure to bear on accused persons, the systems described below greatly increase the scope for manipulative use of psychological pressure that, in the view of some critics, sometimes amounts to psychological torture. This phenomenon has several aspects and a few examples will illustrate the point.

First, the system of repeated transfer back into police custody. During their 1990 visit to Austria the CPT delegation encountered a prisoner held in a Vienna remand prison who alleged that he had been ill-treated by the police (punched and struck on the head with a heavy book). The prison medical records were consistent with the prisoner's allegation. They showed that on reception from the police the prisoner had:

> bruising . . . on the right hand side of the . . . chest, large red marks on both kneecaps and bleeding on the outside of both his thighs. This part of his body was very painful when touched. The prisoner complained of headaches. The top of his head was painful when touched and a slight swelling was found on his scalp.

> According to a report . . . consulted by the delegation, the prisoner said that when he was questioned at the Lower Austria Security Bureau he received blows to the head, the chest, the kidneys and the legs, that he was forced to kneel for a long period and was dragged by his hair, that he eventually lost consciousness, and that when he recovered consciousness, he was examined by a police doctor, after which the questioning renewed, and that at no time was he served any food.
>
> (Council of Europe 1991*a*: para 44)

These injuries, the delegation satisifed themselves, were not sustained *prior* to reception into prison. The prisoner had been released by the prison *back into police custody for further interrogation*: when first received by the prison the reception medical record indicated that he had no injuries. Nor was this a lone example. Another prisoner in the same Austrian remand prison had a perforated eardrum after being received back into the prison following further police questioning (*Ibid.*: para 43). The same pattern of alleged ill-treatment, some of it 'amounting to torture' by the Vienna Security Bureau, emerged during the CPT's second periodic visit to Austria in 1994. On this occasion allegations, for some of which there was supporting medical evidence, were received involving suspects: having plastic bags placed over their heads; being subjected to electric shocks with electric shock batons; threatened with 'bathtub treatment' (i.e. having their head held under water); and being physically beaten (Council of Europe 1996*f*: paras 12–17).

This possibility – release of prisoners back into police custody for further questioning – exists in many continental European jurisdictions and in some, it appears, the arrangement offers additional opportunity for police ill-treatment.

Second, there is the system of using police accommodation for remand prisoners. This is a routine arrangement in several European countries. In Hungary, for example, the CPT found that the Prison Rules provide that remand prisoners may be accommodated on police premises until the conclusion of the period of pre-trial investigation, which in principle means two months, but may be extended for an additional two months by the district prosecutor and a further two months by the county prosecutor. The maximum period in police accommodation can therefore last six months (Council of Europe 1996*b*: paras 14–15). The delegation found that periods of remand on police premises for 'several months' were 'common' and that it 'was not unusual for persons who had been transferred to remand prisons to be returned to police premises for further questioning. Such transfers took place at the request of the police and subject to the approval of the competent public prosecutor' (*Ibid.*). In Hungary, therefore, the police and the prosecutorial authorities exercise total control as to where the suspect is held for up to six months: they may keep their suspects at will in police stations after the court has initially approved a remand in custody. It will be recalled that in Hungary the CPT received 'numerous' allegations of physical ill-treatment by the police on persons detained in police stations. These allegations related both to detention at the time of arrest *and* 'during subsequent interrogations' following a court appearance (*Ibid.*: para 17). Thus the CPT conclusion that detainees in Budapest 'run a not inconsiderable risk of ill-treatment' applies also to remand prisoners. Moreover, these prisoners are held for 23 hours a day in overcrowded police cells, with little or no opportunity for physical exercise, few opportunities for visits, no access to a telephone, and so on – a regime the CPT found totally inappropriate for lengthy detention (*Ibid.*: paras 35–6).

A more subtle use of police accommodation to exert pressure is to be found in Finland. In Finland suspects remanded in custody may be detained either in a remand prison or in 'another place suitable for long-term detention'. Some police stations are designated for these purposes, and considerable numbers of remand prisoners were being held in these police stations for normally four but sometimes up to six weeks when the CPT visited Finland in 1992. The decision initially to remand to a police station is taken by the court, but the police have discretion to transfer the prisoner to a prison before expiry of the order (Council of Europe 1993*d*: para 10). Though the material conditions in Finnish police stations were generally found to be of a 'very high standard' none, in the opinion of the CPT delegation, 'offered a suitable regime for people detained for lengthy periods' (*Ibid.*: paras 16 and 22). Remand prisoners were allowed exercise for thirty minutes each day in cages of 'oppressive' design and, apart from showers, visits or interrogation sessions, had no other out-of-cell activities. They were confined in isolation to their 'featureless' cells for 23 hours per day. This regime was much more restrictive than that in the remand prisons where prisoners could associate with each other. As far as the remand prisoners in the police stations were concerned the prospect of a transfer to a remand prison 'was seen as an inducement to provide information' to the police (*Ibid.*: paras 23–4).

Third, in other Scandinavian countries remands were always to prisons, but the prosecution authorities were able to determine the nature of the custodial regime within the prison. In Denmark in 1990, for example, the CPT 'encountered a large number of persons who had been held on remand for periods varying between 6 months and 2 years . . . (a) matter all the more noteworthy as a remand period was often accompanied by a fairly lengthy solitary confinement measure' (Council of Europe 1991*b*: para 4). This restriction, which is determined by the court, concerns communication with other prisoners and may be total (no contact with any prisoner) or partial (no contact with certain prisoners). The duration of a solitary confinement order may not exceed eight weeks at any time (though it can be renewed) unless the foreseeable penalty is a prison sentence of more than six years which, in the case of persons accused of drug-related offences, it invariably is.

The CPT heard allegations that isolation is invariably ordered for particular types of cases 'and subsequently prolonged without any real verification of the need to continue it', allegations 'to some extent supported by the remarks of police officers whom the delegation met' (*Ibid.*: para 23). Prisoners complained that the total-isolation regime was harsh and 'could ultimately lead to the individual's psychological destruction', a view corroborated by prison staff, doctors, lawyers and NGO representatives (*Ibid.*: para 24). Total-isolation prisoners were locked in their cells for 23 hours a day, had little contact with uniformed or other staff due to other calls on their time, and were frequently also subject to either prohibition or strict regulation of letters and visits. The latter, which either take place in the prison in the presence of a prison officer or in a police station in the presence of a police officer, are often very infrequent.

The CPT interviewed prisoners who had been isolated for periods of two to twenty one months. The prisoners complained of 'psychological torture' and described various psychological consequences of their isolation, complaints that were confirmed by medical staff who referred to an 'isolation syndrome' (*Ibid.*: para 25). Use of the term 'torture' was consistent with the allegation, made not just by prisoners, 'that solitary confinement was used by the police as a means of pressure to obtain statements' and that it 'would end as soon as "acceptable" confessions had been made' (*Ibid.*: para 26). In its conclusions the CPT went no further than saying that 'solitary confinement *could* amount to inhuman and degrading treatment' (emphasis added) (*Ibid.*: para 29), but various groups and critics in Denmark have accused the authorities more forcibly, some describing the Danish use of pre-trial isolation as 'civilised psychological torture' (Dansk Retspolitisk Forening 1980, 1983; Koch 1986; Koch and Petersen 1988).

In Sweden in 1991 the CPT encountered a parallel system of restrictive custodial remands, albeit the Swedish system appears to have attracted less attention and criticism within Sweden than in Denmark, despite the fact that the Swedish prosecutors' powers were at that time greater and appeared to be used more widely. In Sweden in 1991 the public prosecutor might, in the interests of the investigation, limit or prohibit contact between detainees and other persons, or restrict contact between detainees and the outside world (preventing visits, letters, telephone calls, access to television, newspapers, etc) and might continue to apply those restrictions throughout the whole period of arrest and remand in custody, and even after conviction in the event of an appeal being lodged (Council of Europe 1992: para 63 and Appendix III, para 12). There was no provision for appeal to the court against the prosecutors' decisions.

In the two remand prisons visited by the CPT there were few out-of-cell activities for pre-trial prisoners, subject to restrictions or otherwise. It followed that the application of prosecutorial restrictions made 'the sitation worse; they can result in the solitary confinement of prisoners for very long periods' (*Ibid.*: para 64). Prisoners subject to restrictions would typically be confined to their cells for 22 hours a day, often for months on end. One prisoner seen by the delegation, for example, had been held for eight months subject to a total prohibition of all visits (including his wife and children) save those with his lawyer, was allowed no contact with fellow prisoners and 'had only very limited contact with prison staff. He was allowed to write to his wife, subject to censorship. He had recently been sentenced and the restrictions continued pending the outcome of an appeal' (*Ibid.*: para 58). The delegation found that fifty per cent of all pre-trial prisoners at Stockholm's main remand prison were subject to such restrictions, and staff within the prison not only 'expressed disquiet about the effects of the isolation' but 'were of the opinion that resrictions were applied too frequently'. The CPT reiterated, following the precedent of the Danish report, that 'solitary confinement can . . . amount to inhuman and degrading treatment', judged that there was 'prima facie evidence that . . . restrictions are being applied too liberally', and recommended: that the Swedish authorities take steps to ensure that restrictions are resorted to only in exceptional circumstances; that such decisions be reviewed at regular intervals and be subject to independent appeal; that the reasons for restrictions being imposed in any particular case be set out in writing; and that when any prisoner subject to restrictions requested to see a doctor, a doctor be called without delay to conduct a medical examination (*Ibid.*: para 66).

In 1994 the CPT returned to Sweden, on this occasion to conduct a short *ad hoc* visit specifically to the Stockholm remand prison. This visit was prompted because information received by the CPT in Strasbourg suggested that, in spite of responses from the Swedish government describing, *inter alia*, changes in the legal framework, 'conditions . . . had not improved to the extent which the Committee would have wished' (Council of Europe 1995*c*: para 5). It is clear from this second report that a major consideration for the CPT was the continued use of pre-trial restrictions in Sweden.

Following the 1991 visit an official Swedish inquiry, conducted by a former ombudsman, into the use of pre-trial restrictions recommended that in future the decision should rest with the court rather than with the public prosecutor. The recommendation was enacted and became law in January 1994. However the decision as to *which* restrictions should apply, the duration of their application, and their variation, remained with the prosecutor. The result, it appeared to the CPT, was that little had changed, though the new system had been in operation for only eight months. The proportion of remand prisoners subject to restrictions remained between 45 and 50 per cent, restrictions were still applied for lengthy periods including, sometimes, following conviction, and their pattern remained the same (*Ibid.*: para 22). The CPT concluded, therefore, that their recommendation that restrictions be applied only in exceptional circumstances had not been met, the Committee was not satisfied that any regular and effective independent review of the application of restrictions was in place, and they were not satisfied that the tick-box proforma on which decisions to restrict were now recorded, provided any real explanation or justification for their imposition. 'It remained commonplace for public prosecutors to apply restrictions throughout the whole of a person's period of remand in custody' (*Ibid.*: paras 25–6). The Committee concluded, therefore, 'that the current system in Sweden does not strike a proper balance between the needs of a criminal investigation and the imposition of restrictions, and that it fails to accord a number of important safeguards to persons on whom restrictions are imposed'. The Committee recommended, *inter alia*, that the Swedish courts be given a more hands-on responsibility for determining the need to apply particular restrictions, and for reviewing those decisions.

It is noteworthy that neither of the CPT reports on Sweden, unlike that on Denmark, so much as hint that the extensive use of pre-trial restrictions in Sweden is employed by the police and prosecution as a coercive means to extort compliance (confessions, co-operation, information, pleas of guilt) from the accused, though this obvious function is discussed at length by at least one Swedish commentator (Bylund 1993). In Norway, however, this coercive purpose *is* referred to by the CPT.

The 1993 CPT delegation to Norway met many remand prisoners 'held in conditions of virtual solitary confinement' and was told 'that this practice was routinely applied to prisoners on remand during their first four weeks of imprisonment' Council of Europe 1994*f*: para 59). Though such restrictions were subject to periodic court review (at least every four weeks) they could continue for months. The delegation heard of one case lasting fourteen months. Pre-trial restrictions, known in Norway as *forbud* or *kontroll*, were invariably requested by investigating police officers and the CPT was informed by, among others, police officers, that police recommendations were generally followed by the courts. Not surprisingly the psychological pressure represented by restrictions was said to be exploited by the police and some prisoners told the delegation that the 'officers in charge of their investigations had explicitly stated that "forbud/kontroll" measures would be eased or lifted if they co-operated' (*Ibid.*: para 60), a statement which may constitute a probable fact and is said by the Norwegian authorities to be legally permissible (Council of Europe 1994*f*: paras 16–17), but is almost certainly used and interpreted as a threat, pressure or inducement, something forbidden by the Norwegian Prosecutorial Code (Council of Europe 1994*f*: paras 15 and 60).

Remand prisoners in Norway subject to restrictions were confined to their cells for 23 hours each day, took their exercise alone in small concrete enclosures with metal grille roofs, and in the case of two prisoners 'the delegation's psychiatric expert observed serious medical implications arising from solitary confinement by court order'. Both prisoners were depressed and felt suicidal, one displayed symptoms of psychosomatic disorders and the other was psychotic. In the latter case the risk of suicide had been judged by the prison medical officer to be so great that he had contacted the prisoner's lawyer and investigating police officer, following which intervention the prisoner had been transferred to a specialised psychiatric clinic (*Ibid.*: para 64). This example seems fully to bear out the serious fears expressed by Danish critics of what we may reasonably describe as the Scandinavian system – albeit that the administrative and judicial mechanisms differ from country to country – of pre-trial isolation and psychological pressure on suspects.

Conclusion

This fairly detailed account, which has focused almost exclusively on police custody rather than psychiatric, immigration, military and penal custody, demonstrates two things. First, the coming into force of the European Convention for the Prevention of Torture and Inhuman or Degrading Treatment or Punishment, and the operation of the Committee (the CPT) established under the Convention, has established beyond all doubt that there is continued use of torture in Europe (albeit probably in relatively few countries) and that physical and psychological ill-treatment of suspects held in custody during criminal proceedings – some of which ill-treatment arguably amounts to inhuman and degrading treatment – is relatively widespread in many European jurisdictions. Second, many of these jurisdictions have not in place basic legal and procedural safeguards to protect suspects against ill-treatment at the hands of the authorities. Or, if they have those safeguards in place, the safeguards are not accompanied by an infrastructure of resources, inspection and accountability to ensure that they are complied with. The result is that the police are able widely to ill-treat suspects with impunity.

The CPT constitutes an example of a European harmonising mechanism promulgating preventive, human-rights-based, rule-of-law recommendations to sovereign states which, to a greater or lesser extent, have implicitly, if not explicitly, pursued illiberal, unaccountable and repressive criminal-justice procedures.

This does of course beg the question as to the impact of the CPT, in the face of domestic resistance to its recommendations from member states and the possibly more potent countervailing influence being exercised by the other harmonising mechanisms, like common drugs and immigration policies, to which Sim, Ruggiero and Ryan (1995) have drawn attention. It is too early to form judgements on this question of relative influence. Not surprisingly there is evidence that member states generally respond fairly speedily and positively when CPT recommendations involve relatively simple and resource-neutral issues such as the closure of a few squalid police cells. However, much that the CPT is recommending questions fundamental cultural practices and legal traditions and would, if implemented and made meaningful, involve significant expenditure – the creation of legal aid schemes or equipping the police with training and bureaucratic recording systems, for example. Such structural reforms typically take years to implement even when recommended by domestic official enquiry bodies established by government in the wake of some major domestic scandal. Such reforms are bound to take even longer when they emanate from an international body whose do-gooding interference in domestic affairs is no doubt widely resented by local practitioners and politicians whose first reaction is often to deny, privately at least, the validity of the evidence the CPT has gathered (see Cohen 1993). My current research is focusing on this process of reaction.

Notes

1 CPT reports are written in French or English. That on France in 1993 was in French: all translations from the French are by the author and are not authorised by the Council of Europe.
2 Hungary in 1993, Bulgaria, Poland, Romania, the Slovak Republic and Slovenia in 1994, and the Czech Republic in 1995. Estonia, Lithuania, Moldova, Russia, 'Tyfro' Macedonia and the Ukraine have signed the Convention but not yet ratified it.

References

Bylund, T. (1993) *Tvångsmedel I*, Uppsala: Iustus Förlag.

Cohen, S. (1993) 'Human Rights and Crimes of the State: the Culture of Denial', *Australian and New Zealand Journal of Criminology*, 97–115.

Council of Europe (1991a) *Report to the Austrian Government on the Visit to Austria from 20 May 1990 to 27 May 1990*, (CPT/Inf(91)10), Strasbourg: Council of Europe.

Council of Europe (1991b) *Report to the Danish Government on the Visit to Denmark carried out by the European Committee for the Prevention of Torture and Inhuman or Degrading Treatment or Punishment (CPT) from 2 to 8 December 1990*, (CPT/Inf(91)12), Strasbourg: Council of Europe.

Council of Europe (1992a) *Report to the Swedish Government on the Visit to Sweden from 5 to 14 May 1991*, (CPT/Inf(92)6), Strasbourg: Council of Europe.

Council of Europe (1993a) *3rd General Report on the CPT's Activities Covering the Period 1 January to 31 December 1992*, (CPT/Inf(93)), Strasbourg: Council of Europe.

Council of Europe (1993b) *Rapport au Gouvernement de la Républic Française relatif à la visite effectuée par le Comité européen pour la prévention de la torture et des peines ou traitements inhumains ou dégradants CPT en France du 27 octobre au 8 novembre 1991*, (CPT/Inf(93)2), Strasbourg: Council of Europe.

Council of Europe (1993c) *Report to the Dutch Government on the visit to the Netherlands carried out by the European Committee for the Prevention of Torture and Inhuman or Degrading Treatment or Punishment from 30 August to 8 September 1992*, (CPT/Inf(93)), Strasbourg: Council of Europe.

Council of Europe (1993d) *Report to the Finnish Government on the visit to Finland carried out by the European Committee for the Prevention of Torture and Inhuman and Degrading Treatment or Punishment (CPT) from 10 to 20 May 1992*, (CPT/Inf(93)8), Strasbourg: Council of Europe.

Council of Europe (1993e) *Report to the Government of the Federal Republic of Germany on the visit carried out by the European Committee for the Prevention of Torture and Inhuman and Degrading Treatment or Punishment from 8 to 20 December 1991*, (CPT/(93)13), Strasbourg: Council of Europe.

Council of Europe (1994a) *Report to the Government of Greece on the visit to Greece carried out by the European Committee for the Prevention of Torture and Inhuman or Degrading Treatment or Punishment from 14 to 26 March 1993*, (CPT/Inf(94)20), Strasbourg: Council of Europe.

Council of Europe (1994b) *Report to the Portuguese Government on the Visit to Portugal carried out by the European Committee for the Prevention of Torture and Inhuman or Degrading Treatment or Punishment from 19 to 27 January 1992, and Response of the Portuguese Government*, (CPT/Inf(94)9), Strasbourg: Council of Europe.

Council of Europe (1994c) *Rapport au Gouvernement de la Belgique relatif à la visite effectuée par le Comité européen pour la prévention de la torture et des peines ou traitements inhumains ou dégradants (CPT) en Belgique du 14 au 23 novembre 1993*, (CPT/Inf(94)15), Strasbourg: Council of Europe.

Council of Europe (1994d) *Response of the Netherlands Government to the Report of the European Committee for the Prevention of Torture and Inhuman and Degrading Treatment or Punishment on its visit to the Netherlands from 30 August to 8 September 1992*, (CPT/Inf(94)), Strasbourg: Council of Europe. [The English language version of the original in Dutch published on 20 December 1993.]

Council of Europe (1994e) *Report to the Government of the United Kingdom on the visit to Northern Ireland carried out by the European Committee for the Prevention of Torture and Inhuman or Degrading Treatment or Punishment (CPT) from 20 to 29 July 1993*, (CPT/Inf(94)17), Strasbourg: Council of Europe.

Council of Europe (1994f) *Report to the Norwegian Government on the visit to Norway carried out by the European Committee for the Prevention of Torture and Inhuman or Degrading Treatent or Punishment (CPT) from 27 June to 6 July 1993*, (CPT/Inf(94)11), Strasbourg: Council of Europe.

Council of Europe (1994g) *Response of the Norwegian Government to the Report of the European Committee for the Prevention of Torture and Inhuman or Degrading Treatment or Punishment (CPT) on its visit to Norway from 27 June to 6 July 1993*, (CPT/Inf(94)12), Strasbourg: Council of Europe.

Council of Europe (1995a) *Rapport au Gouvernement de L'Italie relatif à la visite effectuée par le Comité européen pour la prévention de la torture et des peines ou traitements inhumains ou dégradants (CPT) en Italie du 15 au 27 mars 1992*, (CPT/Inf(95)1), Strasbourg: Council of Europe.

Council of Europe (1995b) *Report to the Irish Government on the visit to Ireland carried out by the European Committee for the Prevention of Torture and Inhuman and Degrading Treatment or Punishment (CPT) from 26 September to 5 October 1993*, (CPT/Inf(95)14), Strasbourg: Council of Europe.

Council of Europe (1995c) *Report to the Swedish Government on the visit to Sweden carried out by the European Committee for the Prevention of Torture and Inhuman and Degrading Treatment or Punishment (CPT) from 23 to 26 August 1994*, (CPT/Inf(95)5), Strasbourg: Council of Europe.

Council of Europe (1996a) *6th General Report on the CPT's Activities covering the period 1 January to 31 December 1995*, (CPT/Inf(96)21), Strasbourg: Council of Europe.

Council of Europe (1996b) *Report to the Hungarian Government on the Visit to Hungary carried out by the European Committee for the Prevention of Torture and Inhuman or Degrading Treatment or Punishment (CPT) from 1 to 14 November 1994* (CPT/Inf(96)5), Strasbourg: Council of Europe.

Council of Europe (1996c) *Report to the Spanish Government on the visits to Spain carried out by the European Committee for the Prevention of Torture and Inhuman or Degrading Treatment or Punishment (CPT) from 1 to 12 April 1991, 10 to 22 April 1994 and 10 to 14 June 1994*, (CPT/Inf(96)9), Strasbourg: Council of Europe.

Council of Europe (1996d) *Report to the Slovenian Government on the visit to Slovenia carried out by the European Committee for the Prevention of Torture and Inhuman or Degrading Treatment or Punishment (CPT) from 19 to 28 February 1995*, (CPT/Inf(96)18), Strasbourg: Council of Europe.

Council of Europe (1996*e*) *Public Statement on Turkey*, (CPT/Inf(96)30), Strasbourg: Council of Europe.

Council of Europe (1996*f*) *Rapport au Gouvernement autrichien relatif à la visite effectueé par le Comité européen pour la prévention de la torture et des peines ou traitements inhumains ou dégradants (CPT) en Autriche du 26 septembre au 7 octobre 1994*, (CPT/Inf(96)28), Strasbourg: Council of Europe.

Dansk Retspolitisk Forening (1980) *Vidnesbyrd om de psykiske og sociale følger af dansk isolationfaengsling: En dokumentation fra Isolationsgruppen*, Haarby: Forlaget.

Dansk Retspolitisk Forening, Isolationsgruppen (1983) *Isolation under varetaegtsfaengsling (II): En ny henvendelse til Folketingets Retsudvalg, Justitsministeren og Den danske Dommerstand*, Copenhagen: Dansk Retspolitisk Forening.

Evans, M. and Morgan, R. (1992) 'The European Convention for the Prevention of Torture: Operational Practice', *The International and Comparative Law Quarterly*, 41, 590–614.

Koch, I. (1986) 'Mental and Social Sequelae of Isolation: the evidence of deprivation experiments and of pre-trial detention in Denmark' in *The Expansion of European Prison Systems, Working Papers in European Criminology No 7*, The European Group for the Study of Deviance and Social Control, 121.

Koch, I. and Petersen, M. W. (1988) 'Isolation af waretaegtsfaengslede' in H. Lohdam and F. Balvig (eds), *Retspolitisk Status*, Copenhagen: DJOF Forlag.

Morgan, R. (1996) 'Custody in the Police Station: How do England and Wales Measure up in Europe?', *Policy Studies*, 17, 1, 55–72.

Morgan, R. and Evans, M. (1994) 'Inspecting prisons: the view from Strasbourg' in R. D. King and M. Maguire (eds), *Prisons in Context*, Oxford: Clarendon Press.

Murdoch, J. (1994) 'The Work of the Council of Europe's Torture Committee', *Journal of International Law*, 5, 2, 220–248.

Peters, E. (1987) *Torture*, Oxford: Basil Blackwell.

Rodley, N. (1987) *The Treatment of Prisoners Under International Law*, Oxford: Oxford University Press.

Rusche, G. and Kirchheimer, O. (1939) *Punishment and Social Structure*, New York: Columbia University Press.

Sim, J., Ruggiero, V. and Ryan, M. (1995) 'Punishment in Europe: Perceptions and Commonalities' in V. Ruggiero, M. Ryan and J. Sim (eds), *Western European Penal Systems: A Critical Analysis*, London: Sage.

United Nations (1992) *Report of the Special Rapporteur: torture and other cruel, inhuman or degrading treatment or punishment*, Commission on Human Rights, 49th Session, United Nations: Economic and Social Council.

179

12

VICTIMS' PERCEPTIONS OF POLICE SERVICES IN EAST AND WEST EUROPE

Rob Mawby

Abstract

The extent of crime in post-Communist societies is the subject of some debate. In general it seems that levels of recorded crime have escalated but it is arguable that at least some of the increase is due to changes in reporting and recording practices. Victim survey data moreover suggests that there are marked differences in crime rates, both between post-Communist societies and for different offences. What is clear, though, is that public concern about crime is evident throughout Central and Eastern Europe and the public sees crime as a major problem. This raises a number of questions about crime control. Principally, how feasible is it to move towards more liberal policies when public concern is so great?

The research reported on here is a cross-national study of one crime, burglary, that occurred in 1993–4. Six cities in four countries were originally covered: from Western Europe, Salford and Plymouth (England) and Mönchengladbach (Germany), from Eastern Europe, Warsaw and Lublin (Poland) and Miskolc (Hungary). Research is currently taking place in a seventh city, Prague. Victim samples were drawn from police records; victims were interviewed about crimes and their subsequent experiences with agencies such as the police. Discussions also took place with representatives of the police and other agencies such as victim support.

This paper focuses on victims' feelings about the crime and their assessments of the police, by addressing two general questions:

1   How far do victims from East and West share similar experiences and perceptions?
2   To what extent are their assessments of the police influenced by policing traditions, to what extent by their perceptions of the crime problem and to what extent by the services provided by the police today?

Victims' perceptions of police services in East and West Europe

In recent years, the position of the victim in the criminal justice process has been considerably enhanced and a number of studies have identified the emergence of victim services both in the UK and other Western societies, such as the US and Canada (Mawby and Gill 1987; Rock 1986, 1990). Developments in Europe, particularly in the West but also in Eastern Europe, have also been noted and accelerated through Council of Europe and United Nations initiatives as well as groups specifically created to promote international co-operation, such as the European Forum for Victim Services (First European Conference of Victim Support Workers 1989; HEUNI 1989; Joutsen 1987; Mawby and Walklate 1994; Waller 1988).

A number of studies have indicated that victims have very clear ideas about police performance and in many cases see the police as failing to address their own priorities *vis-à-vis* the crime situation (Maguire 1982; Shapland *et al.* 1985), and in England and Wales British Crime Surveys (BCS) provide recent evidence of growing public dissatisfaction with the police, albeit among a minority of victims (Mawby 1991; Mayhew, *et al.* 1989; Mayhew, *et al.* 1993; Skogan 1990). Yet, with the notable exception of the Netherlands (Hauber and Zandbergen 1991; Wemmers and Zeilstra 1991; Winkel 1989), we know very little about alternative models of service provision by the police in other societies outside the Anglo-Saxon/North American experiences. It is difficult, therefore, to assess how far alternative police systems may be better adapted to providing services that the public appreciate. In particular, little is known of victims' perspectives in Continental police systems, in both Eastern and Western Europe.

The last 30 years has also seen the development in the UK of a range of victim services, including criminal injuries compensations, compensation orders, rape crisis centres, refuges for battered women, and victim support schemes (Mawby and Gill 1987; Mawby and Walklate 1994; Rock 1990; Shapland *et al.* 1985). Similar, but not identical, developments have occurred in North America (Lurigio *et al.* 1990; Mawby and Gill 1987; Rock 1986) and elsewhere (First European Conference of Victim Support Workers 1989; HEUNI 1989; Joutsen 1987). However, whilst much of the literature provides a general outline of such policies and tends to stress the broad similarities, as yet no focused comparative analysis has taken place to assess and explain the precise variations in victims' experiences. For example: how far do different social structures and cultures influence the impact of crime on victims, and the ready availability of informal help; how do different legal and welfare systems influence the structure of services on a formal level; and how are political changes affecting future developments? Such questions are of particular salience in the context of the transformation of political and social structures in Eastern Europe.

The dramatic political changes in Eastern Europe have impacted upon law and order in at least four ways. First, widespread public unrest has led to a challenge to legal authorities in an explicit fashion, something that would not have been contemplated a few years ago. Second, changes to the political structure have made the problem of crime more of an issue than in the past, whether because of an actual increase in crime, a more open review of the extent of crime, or a mixture of both (Mawby 1990). Third, these political changes have implications for the criminal justice system and its organisation; for example, with major reviews of the operation and functioning of the police. Finally, shifts away from state monopolies towards a market economy raise a number of questions about the adequacy of welfare policies and the role of the state, private sector, voluntary sector and local community in meeting needs, in the context of the criminal justice system *vis-à-vis* victim services. At the same time, the implications of 1992 for countries within the European Union have raised questions about international co-operation between agencies, centralisation and co-ordination of service planning and delivery, and equality of provision between countries, in areas such as policing and victim services (Fijnaut 1992; 1993; King 1993), an issue of wider concern if Eastern European countries join the EU.

While official statistics have often been used to provide some comparisons between different countries, variations in definitions of crime and in the way victims, police and other agencies deal with 'their' crime make such comparisons hazardous. Comparison of national victim surveys is equally problematic (Block 1993), but until recently comparative victim surveys have been rare (for one exception see Arnold and Korinek 1991). The international crime survey (ICS), first carried out in 1989 (Van Dijk, Mayhew and Killias 1990) and repeated in 1992 (Del Frate *et al.* 1993) and 1996/7 (Zveric 1996) therefore makes a major breakthrough by providing a more valid picture, one that is not distorted by variations in definitions of crime and reporting practices. Further, it allows for some comparative assessment of victims' experiences of their crimes, including their views on police involvement and the intervention (or non-availability) of other agencies.

In fact, the 1989 survey focused on western capitalist countries. Japan was the most notable exception to this, although the survey also incorporated samples from one Eastern (Indonesia) and one Eastern European (Poland) capital city. Rather fewer Western-European countries were covered in 1992. However, capital cities were covered from a range of developing societies and from Eastern and Central Europe. Poland, Czechoslovakia and parts of the former Soviet Union were included. In addition, the international team also sought to incorporate data from national surveys: for example one carried out in 1990 in what were formerly East and West Germany (Kury *et al.* 1992). The most recent ICS has attempted to include all former Eastern Bloc countries and former members of the USSR, although it is as yet incomplete (Zveric 1996).

Of course, the ICS incorporates many of the methodological problems associated with national victim surveys, and provides only a partial view of crime in an international context. For example, data on domestic violence are problematic, and, as Lahore *et al.* (1993) note, some victims and offences such as those involving street children, are inevitably missed. Moreover, the methodology assumes that respondents in different societies and different cultures will be equally likely to interpret similar events as crimes, and also equally ready to talk about them to an interviewer. Bearing these qualifications in mind, the overall picture painted by these surveys is of marked variations in crime throughout the world. For example, in developing societies rates appear relatively high in Africa and South America, lower in Asia. In developed capitalist societies, the US, Australia, New Zealand and Canada appear to have high rates, whilst Switzerland, Finland and Japan have comparatively low crime rates. Most countries of Western Europe, in comparison, have rates somewhere between these extremes, yet somewhat higher than those in Central and Eastern European countries.

As well as providing a general framework within which national crime patterns can be located, the international surveys provide further information, for example on reporting behaviour, fear of crime, attitudes towards the police and public views on alternative sentences. Nevertheless it is almost inevitable that such surveys can only address these issues on a very basic level. In order to curtail costs, in developed societies the surveys have used telephone interviews with relatively small samples. Whereas one result of telephone interviewing is a variable response rate, poor in some countries such as England and Wales, a more fundamental restriction is the limited number of questions that can be asked. Moreover, while targets of 1500 completed interviews in most countries sound impressive, the fact that only a minority of respondents have suffered specific types of crime recently has two consequences. First, most international comparison of recent crime is restricted to overall crime levels; second, where international differences in specific crimes are addressed, data are used for crimes over a five-year period. A further restriction in response details is imposed by the research design, where in the first two surveys victims were only asked about their experiences of their most recent crime. Consequently, differences in response between countries may be due as much to the different types of crime experienced as to differences caused by national influences. Take, for example, burglaries, excluding attempts, which are defined as affirmative answers to the question, 'Did anyone actually get into your house or flat without permission and steal or try to steal something?'. On average, the 1992 survey unearthed about 50 burglaries per country. Drawing inferences on the *nature* of burglary in a given country is thus hazardous. Moreover, since not all these burglaries will have been reported to the police and not all those that have been reported will be included in the follow-up questions, police response to burglaries in different countries cannot be assessed with any certainty through the international survey.

Another limitation arises when we seek to explain differences that do emerge. Just as the British Crime Survey has been criticised for providing an overall picture that fails to identify, much less account for, small-area patterns (Crawford *et al.* 1990), so the international survey tends to restrict itself to description and avoid explanation of national patterns. Thus, for example, variations in reporting rates and attitudes towards the police are noted, but are not related to different police structures and traditions in the countries under review.

It would be unfair to criticise the international survey for this. It was not intended as a mechanism for explaining national patterns, but rather as a means for allowing national experiences to be located in a wider context. Indeed, for this reason it provides an excellent backcloth to more detailed comparative analysis, using a more focused approach. It is, moreover, pertinent to consider how far the findings of different research strategies are similar.

The current research

In contrast to the international survey, we decided to compare the experiences of crime victims by concentrating on one specific offence in a limited number of countries. The choice of countries was to a certain extent fortuitous, coming as it did from discussions among the team (to be) at an international conference in Warsaw in 1991.[1] However, there seemed to us a certain logic in comparing two countries from Western Europe (England and Germany) with two countries from Eastern and Central Europe (Poland and Hungary). The fact that the latter two countries also had centralised police forces, whilst England and Germany had, to some extent, elements of local control (Mawby 1992), was an additional point of contrast. Furthermore, specialist agency support for victims varied between the four countries. At one extreme, Poland had no specialist agencies concerned with helping victims, other than the Foundation for Assisting Victims of Crime which provides some financial compensation for a small number of victims. At the other, Victim Support in England has developed as *the* specialist agency providing counselling, support and advice, initially for burglary victims, and more recently for victims of a wide variety of crimes. Somewhere between, the Weisser Ring is well established in Germany where it provides some help (largely but not exclusively financial) for victims of serious crimes, and more recently it has been introduced to Hungary (Mawby and Walklate 1994).

Having decided to concentrate on four countries, we then decided to focus on a small number of cities in these countries. One of our reasons here was practical, in that we did not have the resources for national coverage. On the other hand though, we felt that by restricting ourselves in this way we would overcome some of the difficulties experienced by the British Crime Survey and international surveys. We could consider victims' experiences in the context of the areas in which they lived and relate them to local policies and local agencies with which they might (or might not) have had contact. We therefore took two cities in each of England and Poland and one from Germany and Hungary. Mönchengladbach in Germany and Miskolc in Hungary are both industrial cities of some quarter of a million inhabitants. In England, Plymouth is a similarly-sized city with a rural hinterland, while Salford is a city of 230,000 within the Manchester metropolitan area. In Poland, Lublin is, like Plymouth, a city in more rural surroundings although with 330,000 inhabitants somewhat larger. In Warsaw we originally intended to focus on one of the seven police districts, which again has a population of about 250,000, but for operational reasons subsequently included the whole city.

In addition we decided to restrict our survey to one offence, household burglary, using the international victim survey definition. We excluded burglary when associated with more serious offences (e.g. rape or robbery), aggravated burglary of corporate premises, and attempted burglary, that is, where entry is attempted but not effected. By so doing we were concerned to ensure that variations in the findings were not artefacts of the different crimes experienced in different countries. By choosing burglary, we concentrated on an offence which is considered relatively serious, has marked effects on many victims and is commonly reported to the police.

Our survey was also restricted to crimes reported to the police. This meant that we were unable to consider unreported crimes or control for reporting variations between countries. However, we were most concerned both with the impact of the crime on the victim and the experiences of victims at the hands of the police and other agencies, rather than crime rates and saw our survey as complementary to the international victim survey.

Members of the research team met with representatives of the police and victim service agencies. These meetings were used both to conduct semi-structured interviews with key people and to ensure that the research was being set up in similar ways in the different countries and cities. These semi-structured interviews provided us with a fuller grounding in the work of police and victim-service agencies, and the perceptions certain key workers held of burglary and its victims. However the main research methodologies involved analysis of police records and extensive structured interviews with samples of victims drawn from police records.

The questionnaire was designed to relate to the experiences of burglary victims in all of the countries. Open-ended questions were included, but pre-coded questions were most common because of their practicality. In some cases, pre-coded alternatives varied between countries. However, such exceptions apart we aimed to ask the same questions throughout and, to ensure accuracy in translation, we aimed to have questionnaires translated from English into each of the other languages and then back into English by a different translator to enable cross-checking. What then of the questions?

The English version of the questionnaire contains 100 questions plus three interviewer assessments.[2] Broadly, ten areas of inquiry were covered:

1 Social characteristics of victim and victim's household: occupational status, home type, marital status, household composition, general levels of affluence and lifestyle patterns. Given the problems of international comparison we did not include any questions on social class. However, we did tap 'spending power' by asking whether the household owned a car, video or computer and had been on holidays abroad, and we also asked respondents to rate

themselves in comparison to others in their city on a scale varying from 'very well off' to 'very poor'.

2   Details of the nature of the crime: when it occurred, the extent of theft or damage.
3   Insurance details and experiences of claiming insurance.
4   The impact of the crime on the victim and other household members.
5   Details of police actions and victims' assessment of these.
6   More general attitudes towards the police.
7   Details of help received from family or friends or agencies other than the police, and assessment of these.
8   Views on appropriate sentencing for 'their' crime.
9   Security measures taken before or since the burglary.
10 Views on the area in which they lived and feelings of safety.

In Germany and Hungary, a further series of questions on the public prosecutor were added, mainly by adapting existing questions on the police.

The difficulties associated with carrying out comparative international research are legion, but are multiplied when we attempt to make international comparisons based on secondary data analysis and limited to a reading of authors (or even just English-writing authors) covering a particular topic (Mawby 1990). To date two problems have surfaced that we feel that our approach has enabled us to overcome.

The first of these concerns the problem of drawing together background material on which to base the current study. As already noted, the international victim survey provides a general overview and included Germany (in 1989 only) and Poland, but did not cover Hungary. The most recent ICS does include both Poland and Hungary, but with the exception of Zverik's (1996) article little has been written on it as yet. There is little else available in English on victims' experiences in these countries. In Poland, Ostrihanska and Wojcik (1993) carried out a survey on a small number of burglary victims and there are some more general discussions of victim policies (Bienkowska 1989; Wojcik 1995); in Hungary material deals almost exclusively with victim policies and particularly the emergence of the Weisser Ring as a victim-support agency (Gorgenyi 1993; Vigh 1991). With regard to policing, there is no tradition of any critical evaluation, with research largely confined to general reviews by government officials or visiting academics (for Hungary, see Rudas 1977 and Ward 1984). While this has changed in recent years (see for example Fogel 1994; Jasinski and Siemaszko 1995; Pagon 1996; Shelley and Vigh 1995; Timoranszky 1992, 1994) the amount of research based on primary data is still minimal. A collaborative project of this kind therefore allows us to draw on the specialist knowledge of researchers in each of the countries, incorporating everyday experiences with awareness of relevant material not translated into English. One of our early tasks, therefore, was to ask each of the team to provide a summary of material within their countries on the cities concerned, crime, victim's experiences, relevant policies and policing. One difficulty commonly encountered in comparative studies concerns the difficulty of being expert on a range of different societies. Yet being able to appreciate victims' experiences requires an understanding not just of the crime situation but of the particular setting within which crimes are experienced; that is the social, cultural and political contexts. While some would justifiably claim to be expert on one society in addition to their own, few would claim detailed expert knowledge of more societies. Our research design clearly overcame such potential difficulties by drawing in specialists from each of the countries concerned. Moreover, by focusing on specific cities we were able to make use of the team's more detailed local experiences. This also enabled local situations to be more tangible to other members of the team – it's easier for an outsider to get to know a city than a country – and the design allowed for study visits to cities in the research sample by different members of the team.

The second problem we encountered relates to the question of definition. While the international victim survey uses a British definition of burglary, legal and practical definitions of burglary or breaking and entering vary markedly between countries, and thus the extent of burglary as defined in police statistics makes for misleading comparison. Indeed, definitions influence the data at two stages: in law and in the classification of crimes in police statistics. To illustrate the difficulties we may take the English and German definitions as examples.

In English law, burglary is covered by the 1968 Theft Act and attempted burglary by the 1981 Criminal Attempts Act. According to section 9 (i) of the former, it covers illegal entry to premises followed by theft or with the intent to commit an offence. Aggravated burglary (as defined in section 10) which is excluded from our study, occurs when the offender commits the burglary while in possession of a firearm, explosive or other weapon. 'Burglary' does not depend on the use of physical force to enter the property: merely that the offender had no legitimate or general right to be there at the time the offence occurred. Offences where the offender gained entry through trickery or false pretences are thus also defined as burglaries. Attempted burglaries are distinct from this in that while the offender has to have acted in a manner that is more than merely preparatory to the commission of the offence, he or she would not have entered the dwelling. Our survey was restricted to burglary as defined in section 9 (i) and confined to burglary *of a dwelling*. In police statistics, these are classified under section 28 (iii). However attempted burglaries are also included here, so we were forced to exclude these through further scrutiny of the cases.

Overall, then, in England the definition of burglary includes the following:

1   Break in to home through door or window.
2   Use other method (e.g. plastic card) to enter through locked door or window without causing damage.
3   Enter through an open window.
4   Enter through an open door.
5   Enter without permission, where the offender used trickery to gain access.

In contrast, in Germany, only the first three examples given here are defined by law and statistical classification as the same, falling (for crime against dwellings) under legal code 243 and classification 435; in fact, while entry through an open window is categorised in this way, it is commonly referred to as 'einsteigen' rather than burglary. Moreover, examples (4) and (5) are covered by legal code 242 and classified as 335, being generally defined as simple theft.

While in Hungary and Poland definitions of burglary were rather more like those in Germany, they also differed in some respects. For the purposes of our research then, the development of a sampling frame proved more difficult in some countries than in others and required scrutiny of cases defined as simple theft as well as burglary. In a wider context, though, this one example demonstrates the difficulties in drawing international comparisons based on secondary material. If studies use different definitions of burglary, then it would not be surprising to find not only that *rates* of burglary appeared to vary, but also that victims' experiences differed between countries.

This paper focuses on findings from the interview survey. In total, 1194 interviews were conducted, 200 in Plymouth, 134 in Salford, 257 in Mönchengladbach, 198 in Warsaw, 200 in Lublin and 207 in Miskolc, although in the latter 63 per cent involved break-ins to weekend homes and have been excluded from this analysis.[3] The data have also been reweighted to allow for the different sample sizes and slightly different gender balances. Analysis is therefore based on readjusted totals of 100 men and 100 women from each of the cities.

In the following three sections some of the key findings are presented. First, the crime problem is discussed in terms of the extent of crime, the impact of the crime on victims and concerns about the future. Then victims' perceptions of the police are considered. Finally the similarities and differences between the four countries are discussed and some attempts made to explain them. The chapter then concludes with some reflections on cross-national research on victims' experiences of policing.

The crime problem

It is difficult to assess the extent of the crime problem in one society; cross-national comparisons are fraught with additional difficulties. Police statistics, notoriously unreliable at the best of times, are especially problematic in a comparison of post-Communist societies, where in the past data were either unavailable or massaged to create a favourable picture (Szumski 1993). The overall impression, however, is that recorded crime rates were generally lower in Eastern-European countries than in Western Europe, but rose dramatically at the end of the 1980s (Bartnicki 1989; Farkas 1996; Fogel 1994; Jasinski and Siemaszko 1995; Kalish 1988; Sessar 1996; Vigh 1987), scarcely surprising given the dramatic social, political, economic and cultural changes taking place (Jasinski 1995).

Victim survey data available from Germany (Kury 1993) confirm this picture *vis-à-vis* differences between East and West Germany. However ICS data for

England and Wales, Germany and Poland provide a slightly different impression. For example at the time of the 1992 survey the burglary rate appears highest in England and Wales, lowest in Germany, but Poland had a relatively high victimisation rate for some offences such as pick-pocketing (Del Frate *et al.* 1993). Zverik (1996), however, suggests that between 1992 and 1996 victimisation rates levelled out in societies in transition, and for some offences such as burglary they may have fallen. Nevertheless, research findings also suggest that fear of crime and public concern over crime are considerable in post-Communist societies. Sessar (1996) argues that under a repressive policing system crime was not perceived as a problem in the GDR and that the public from the old East Germany are less likely to accept crime as normal than are their West German counterparts. Equally, as Szumski (1993) and Siemaszko (1995) argue for Poland, in the past crime statistics were manipulated, often to give the impression that crime was under control, whereas they are now made public and the object of media attention. Findings from the 1992 ICS that show high levels of fear of crime in Poland and Czechoslovakia (Del Frate *et al.* 1993) are thus scarcely surprising.

Our own research supports some but not all of these findings. Impressionistically it seemed that reported burglaries were most common in England, least in Hungary and Poland. While some of the difference here may be due to under-reporting or under-recording, it appears unlikely that these account for all of the difference. For example, when we asked victims whether or not they had been the victim of another burglary within the preceding five years, the proportions answering in the affirmative was about twice as high in England as in the other three countries. While not conclusive, this at least suggests that burglary may be less common in Hungary, Poland *and* Germany.

Be this as it may, our survey findings indicate that victims in Poland and Hungary were at least as affected by the crimes as were those from England and Germany. For example in each city over 90 per cent of respondents said that they or someone else in their household had been emotionally affected by the crime, and while 54 per cent overall said they themselves had been personally affected 'very much' those from Lublin (72 per cent), Warsaw (65 per cent) and Miskolc (61 per cent) were most likely to say this. The financial impact of the crime was also most evident in Poland where a significantly lower proportion of victims were covered by insurance. Thus while overall 61 per cent were covered, this fell to 39 per cent in Lublin and 35 per cent in Warsaw; and while 21 per cent of all victims said that insurance fully covered their loss, only 3 per cent and 0 per cent respectively said this in Lublin and Warsaw.

Victims from Hungary and especially Poland were also more likely to express feelings of lack of safety or worry about future crime. For example they were more likely to say they felt unsafe at home alone or walking out alone after dark, and were also more worried about the prospect of a future burglary, robbery or vandalism to the home. This is illustrated in Table 12.1 for concern about burglary.

Concerns about crime were to some extent underpinned by concerns about

Table 12.1 Percentage of victims worried about 'having your home broken into and something stolen'

	Plymouth	Salford	Mönchen	Warsaw	Lublin	Miskolc	Total
Very worried	25	34	42	45	50	43	40
Fairly worried	45	41	37	44	43	45	43
Not very/not at all worried	29	25	21	11	7	12	17

the wider environment within which victims lived. Polish victims were least positive about the locality. For example 18 per cent of respondents overall said they were definitely likely to move, but 30 per cent from Warsaw and 26 per cent from Lublin said so. And although 25 per cent of all respondents felt they lived in an area where people generally helped each other, in Warsaw and Lublin only 11 per cent and 7 per cent respectively said so. It seems then that, overall, victims from Poland especially were most likely to be affected by the crime, most likely to express concern about the prospect of future crime, and most likely to see their area of residence as providing least support against crime.

The police

If crime is a problem, the police may be seen as part of the solution. But public expectations of the police, and perceptions of appropriate policing policies and practices, may vary considerably between societies. While interaction with burglary victims is only one aspect of police work, we might nonetheless expect to find variations between countries with different policing traditions and different public expectations.

In almost all cases the police visited the crime scene. However the speed of response varied. Overall 28 per cent of victims said the police responded within 20 minutes of the crime being reported, with this being most common in Miskolc (42 per cent) and Salford (41 per cent), least in Warsaw (15 per cent) and Lublin (16 per cent). In 23 per cent of cases the police did not attend for at least 80 minutes, such delays being most common in Warsaw (44 per cent) and Plymouth (32 per cent). On average police response was quickest in Miskolc, slowest in Warsaw.

There was also considerable variation in the *nature* of police response. It seemed that bureaucratic procedures were most extensive in Hungary and especially Poland, with victims having to attend the station to sign statements and – in Poland – in many cases locks were removed for 'analysis' and premises sealed. Such measures may sometimes be interpreted as meticulous policework, but our impression was that in Poland victims often saw this as a nuisance (Mawby *et al.* 1997). Certainly there was no evidence that detection rates improved in such circumstances. Overall only 7 per cent of victims said the police cleared up their burglary. Detection rates were highest in Miskolc (17 per cent) and Lublin (12 per cent), lowest in Mönchengladbach (1 per cent) and Warsaw (3 per cent).

Speed of response and detection methods underpin victims' evaluations of police performance. We asked a number of questions specifically about the way police dealt with the complaint. For example, we asked whether victims had been kept well informed of police progress and if they felt they should have been kept better informed; whether the police had put sufficient effort into the case; whether the police had responded quickly enough; and how satisfied they were overall. Responses to this last question are given in Table 12.2. We then constructed a scale based on these four items, where those critical of the police on all four would score 4, those uncritical on all four would score 0 (Table 12.3).

Tables 12.2 and 12.3 illustrate the marked variations between victims in the different cities. In general victims from Poland expressed considerably more criticism than those from the other three countries, including Hungary. Moreover while lack of feedback was one of the most common criticisms in all four countries, in other respects the emphasis was different. Most notably, whereas in England victims were also most likely to criticise the police because they 'did not do enough' or were 'not interested', in Poland the most common complaints were that the crime was not cleared and that property was not recovered.

These findings broadly correspond to Zverik's (1996) analysis of burglary victims in societies in transition, using preliminary data from the 1996/97 ICS. Thus levels of satisfaction were considerably higher in Hungary than in Poland. Furthermore, discussing the nature of victims' complaints, Zverik (1996: 54) concludes: 'In countries in transition, many victims complained that the police "didn't find the offender", "did not do enough" or did not recover the property.'

Criticisms of the way the police dealt with a specific complaint are of course intimately bound to overall feelings about the police. We asked a number of

Table 12.2 Percentage of victims expressing different levels of overall satisfaction

	Plymouth	Salford	Mönchen	Warsaw	Lublin	Miskolc	Total
Very satisfied	19	7	17	1	3	20	11
Fairly satisfied	58	54	56	17	20	55	44
Fairly dissatisfied	14	22	11	45	39	13	24
Very dissatisfied	8	9	8	21	20	3	11
Too soon to say	0	2	0	6	7	5	3

Table 12.3 Mean scores of criticism of police on scale 0–4

Plymouth	Salford	Mönchen	Warsaw	Lublin	Miskolc	Total
1.18	1.53	0.96	2.47	2.61	0.79	1.6

questions on this, which generally suggested that victims in the Western-European cities were more positive in their evaluations than those from Central and Eastern Europe. For example, we asked respondents to select up to three occupations from a list of twelve that they most admired. In England and Germany the police ranked third on this list, being selected by 24–27 per cent of respondents; in Poland and Hungary they ranked rather lower, being selected by 15 per cent of victims in Miskolc, 11 per cent in Warsaw and 7 per cent in Lublin.

It seems that Hungarian victims were less positive about the police in general than they were about the way the police dealt with their complaint. This is confirmed where we asked whether contact had made respondents 'feel more or less favourable to the police in general'. In Poland almost four times as many victims responded in the negative compared with the positive; in Hungary 30 per cent said their contact had improved their views of the police while only 9 per cent said they now felt more critical.

However, in both post-Communist societies it seemed that victims felt the police were now more likely to be considerate in their treatment of victims. For example, we asked respondents how sympathetic they felt the police were when dealing with victims of (a) burglaries (b) disasters like fires and floods (c) rape and sexual assault. Although responses varied with each situation, overall, respondents from Poland and Hungary were about as likely as those from England to see the police as sympathetic and it was in Germany, with its militaristic policing tradition, that victims were least likely to consider the police sympathetic (Mawby and Kirchoff 1996). We then asked whether, over the last few years, 'the police have got better or worse at handling the victims of crime'. As is clear from Table 12.4, victims from Poland and (especially) Hungary were likely to register an improvement rather than a deterioration in this respect.

What is clear from Table 12.4 is that police practices, and recent changes in police response to burglary victims, vary in a number of ways between the four countries and that victims' perceptions of the police, both in general and regarding this particular incident, also vary. There are, indeed, at least as many differences between Poland and Hungary as there are similarities and some differences are also evident between England and Germany. The next section therefore covers two related issues: how do we account for victims' perceptions of the police in Central and Eastern Europe, and how do we explain the marked differences between Poland and Hungary?

Table 12.4 Percentage of victims who felt that police handling of victims had changed

	Plymouth	Salford	Mönchen	Warsaw	Lublin	Miskolc	Total
For the better	31	32	15	29	22	37	28
For the worse	21	34	13	4	9	5	14

Discussion: towards an explanation

There would appear to be at least three ways in which the distinctive patterns might be explained. First there is the argument that public perceptions of the police in some post-Communist societies might be influenced by tradition; that the 'repressive' police of communist societies are thought to have survived the transition. Second is the suggestion that different perceptions of the police reflect different standards and levels of police performance. Third is the claim that perceptions of the police are closely linked to perceptions of the crime problem.

The first argument is persuasive in explaining the lower public esteem enjoyed by the police in both Poland and Hungary. Despite concerted attempts in both countries to change police personnel, the structure of the police, political connections, roles and accountability (Fogel 1994; Jasinski and Siemaszko 1995; Szikinger 1994; Timoranszky 1992), changes are inevitably slow and difficult. It is however possible that public perceptions may be affected by 'defining moments'; that is, high-profile events in which the police are clearly identified as supporting the old or new order. One such example from Hungary concerns the refusal by the police in 1990 to contemplate the use of firearms to disperse a protest by striking taxi-drivers.[4] This rejection of what was interpreted as possible direct political interference may well have led to the 'new' police gaining public credibility and may partially explain the different public perceptions we found between Hungary and Poland. On the other hand, both quantitative analysis and more qualitative examination of our interviews suggest that in both countries victims drew a clear distinction between the 'old' and 'new' police. On one level this is illustrated by the example of 'victim-proneness', where many victims identified improvements in police response. On another level it is reflected in verbatim comments made in the course of the interviews. For example:

'They were nicer and kinder than seven years ago.'

(MISK4069)

'They are more kind. They don't consider themselves to be above everybody now.'

(LUB6027)

'They are more tolerant and gentle.'

(WAR23)

If public perceptions of the police are not entirely explained in terms of memories of the repressive police of communist regimes, how far is it possible to explain differences in terms of actual variations in the quality of police services? In some respects this is plausible. For example, in Warsaw at least police response was slow, leading to victim criticism, and in Hungary and especially Poland (see Mawby *et al.* 1997) the bureaucracy involved in filing a complaint was considerable. Detection rates were also higher in Miskolc than in Poland, which might provoke more criticism in the latter. Moreover, where inadequacies were compounded by the attitudes expressed by the police at the time, it is easy to understand victims' complaints. Take for example two Warsaw cases where victim criticisms centred on, respectively, slow police response and an apparent unwillingness to investigate the crime:

> 'Five to six hours – very late. They explained that they had something very important to do.'
>
> (WAR9)

> 'Police's declaration that practically nothing can be done in this case. So they left you with such an attitude, what can you expect?'
>
> (WAR618)

However while poor police services combined with an inappropriate attitude in explaining inadequacies may partly account for differing levels of criticism, it is scarcely adequate as the sole explanation. For example, detection rates in England and Germany were at least as bad as in Poland, and response times in Lublin were not particularly poor. What then of the third explanation: that perceptions of the police are related to concern over the crime problem?

The fact that victims in Central and Eastern Europe, and Poland in particular, were more concerned about the crime problem, more worried about future crime, and more affected by their current burglary, has already been noted. It is thus not surprising to find that those on whom crime had the most impact, those most worried about crime, and those most dissatisfied with their current residences, are most critical of the police. For example, those who were insured averaged 1.16 on the scale of police criticism, those who were not insured 2.05. Victims from Poland were most likely to say they had been seriously affected by the burglary; those most affected were most critical of the police; Polish victims were most critical of the police. Polish victims were least likely to be covered by insurance, uninsured victims were most critical of the police; not surprisingly, then, Polish victims were not only most critical of the police but focused their criticisms on the inability of the police to clear up the crime and recover their property.

This is however only one strand to the link between crime and evaluations of the police. Another is the extent to which the police may be blamed for the crime problem. One element here is the feeling that respondents are vulnerable because the police are ineffective – even if they are more sensitive than in the past! For example: 'They were polite, but they didn't find the perpetrator' (MISK5076). As one victim said when asked what was the worst thing about the burglary: 'Lack of feeling safe. The police's inefficiency and ineffectiveness of the work' (LUB7).

A key feature here is the implication that the former repressive police, for all their faults, were at least efficient. While this is questionable, the inefficiency of the police in communist society was certainly not as *public*. A second, crucial element here though is the feeling that the police in post-Communist societies have lost power and are thus less well equipped to respond to the crime problem:

'We ain't in a safe area and the police are powerless.'

(MISK6031)

'Feeling of harm, hopelessness, frustration. There is nobody that can help. The police are helpless; they have the excuse that the law is too lenient and they can do nothing.'

(LUB113)

'There was someone we suspected but the police didn't act. They told us they can't enter anybody's house without the prosecutor's consent and he wouldn't give it.'

(WAR224)

This was most evident in relation to questions taken from the British Crime Survey, where we asked victims if they felt the police treated people they suspected of crimes 'more fairly than a few years ago, or less fairly'. For many Polish respondents, this question was meaningless: the key issue was that the police were now *too* soft on suspects/offenders, as the following quotations illustrate:

'The rights of the police are too limited.'

(LUB25)

'The policemen take care of the criminals and not the victims.'

(LUB6016)

'The rights of the police are too little. Offenders feel exempt from punishment.'

(WAR219)

'From my point of view they are less fair – unsuccessful and helpless.'

(WAR315)

'Now if they don't have any definite evidence against the offender, they do nothing.'

(WAR630)

In one sense, ironically, it seems that concern over crime in post-Communist Poland has led to the public reacting with a nostalgic reinterpretation of the work of the 'old' police, when crime was apparently under control. In another sense, though, it is easy to identify similar concerns in Western society, but where public blame is directed at the courts and the criminal-justice process as a whole, not the police.[5] That is, the low public esteem enjoyed by the police in the past in Poland may mean that they are more readily blamed for the problems victims experience; in England where the police have traditionally enjoyed high public esteem, so-called 'lenient' courts and 'soft' sentencing may bear the brunt of criticisms.

Clearly this does not fully account for the differences in public perceptions of the police, especially the marked differences between Poland and Hungary. However, while police traditions and current practices may to some extent account for present patterns, it seems that differences are more adequately explained in terms of victims' concerns about crime and their willingness to blame the police for failing to resolve the crime problem.

Conclusion: cross-national research in perspective

Given the problems involved in cross-national research, it is not surprising that so little research of this kind has been undertaken. The chief exception here, of course, is the ICS, which is currently completing its third sweep. The ICS offers the considerable advantage of being large-scale and allowing a broad comparison of crime, and attitudes and responses to it, in a range of different countries. However, because numbers who have been victims of specific crime types and have reported those crimes to the police are limited, and because the survey is designed as a telephone interview survey, its application is strictly limited. Moreover, it is very expensive.

Our approach is more limited but, we would argue, has considerable advantages. By focusing on one specific offence-type we have attempted to compare like with like, although different legal definitions of burglary and different 'working' practices by burglary offenders mean that even this strategy is limited. Concentration on a limited number of cities has allowed us to build up a team approach to the research, where the local and specialist expertise of colleagues has been used to maximum benefit. Finally, our approach has enabled us to incorporate a number of open-ended questions into the interview schedule and so elicit victims' feelings 'in their own words'.

In one respect, we are able to directly compare our own findings with those from the ICS. Zverik (1996) has contrasted burglary victims' perceptions of police performance for those societies in transition included in the early phase of the third sweep of the ICS, and identified marked differences between countries. Our own distinction between Polish and Hungarian victims is broadly in line with this, although in our survey the latter were even more positive towards the police than the ICS would suggest. It is reassuring, nevertheless, to note similar findings from very different research approaches.

We would therefore advocate additional research based upon collaboration between academics from cities in different countries throughout Europe and further afield. To this end we have modified the questionnaire we used so that it can be deployed in other countries so as to provide a picture of local victims' experiences that can be located in a cross-national context.

Our project has also raised a number of other issues that could be addressed in future research. Three examples might be mentioned here. First, we are aiming to carry out a new study into victims of corporate burglary. Given the expanding private sector in post-Communist countries, crimes against small businesses might be particularly threatening. Moreover, the response of the police, most notably in terms of crime-prevention advice, may have a significant impact on future victimisation. We have argued elsewhere (Wojcik *et al.* 1997) that crime prevention strategies are less evident among household victims in Central and Eastern Europe than in England; how far does a similar situation exist among corporate victims?

Second, we have noted the apparently lower rates of repeat burglary for our samples from Poland, Hungary *and* Germany. To date, much of the international emphasis on repeat victimisation has been on North America (Farrell 1992; Polvi *et al.* 1991). Is the situation different in former Eastern Bloc countries, and if so does this apply to crimes other than burglary? Further, will repeat victimisation feature more prominently as crime rates rise in societies in transition, and if so what impact will this have on victims' perceptions of crime?

In this context, our research in Hungary, where weekend homes were inadvertently included in the sample, revealed considerably higher rates of burglary *and* repeats in such property. It is notable that no research has, as yet, been undertaken into second-home burglaries. This is surprising, since both opportunity theory and the relationship between lifestyle and risk suggest that such properties would be relatively vulnerable. Additionally, it is interesting to query the impact that second-home burglaries have on victims and the extent to which victims' experiences differ and impact upon the desirability of owning a second home.

Cross-national research is in its infancy. We would argue that the research reported here suggests that it is both possible and productive and that collaboration between academics in different countries may help minimise the costs and methodological problems associated with this type of research. Additionally, as has been illustrated here, such research may raise further questions to address in new research and identify and explain variations in the experiences of crime victims in different societies.

Notes

1 The research team comprises Rob Mawby (Director), University of Plymouth and Sandra Walklate, Manchester Metropolitan University, England; Dobrockna Wojcik and Zofia Ostrihanska, Polska Akademia Navk, Warsaw, Poland; Ilona Gorgenyi, University of Miskolc, Hungary; Gerd Kirchoff, Abeilung, Mönchengladbach, Germany. The Project was funded by the Central European University; contract 7/91–92, total award $55,200. Additional travel funds were supplied by NATO: contract CRG 920530, total award 277,000 BF.

2 A number of questions were taken from the British Crime Surveys of 1984, 1988 and

1992. We are grateful to Pat Mayhew of the Home Office for permission to use these. Other questions were written specially for this project.

3 More details of *dacha* (i.e. weekend-home) burglaries are contained in Mawby and Gorgenyi (1997).

4 I am grateful to István Szikinger for clarification of this point.

5 In England and Wales public confidence in the police fell between 1982 and 1992, but then stabilised. It is, however, still relatively high, with 82 per cent rating the police's performance very or fairly good (Bucke 1995).

References

Arnold, H. and Korinek, L. (1991). 'Victimisation, attitudes towards crime and related issues: comparative research results from Hungary', pp. 99–121 in G. Kaiser, H. Kury and H.-J. Albrecht (eds), *Victims and Criminal Justice*. Freiburg: Max Planck Institute.

Bartnicki, S. P. (1989). 'Crime in Poland: trends, regional patterns and neighbourhood awareness', pp. 135–60 in D. T. Evans and D. T. Herbert (eds), *The Geography of Crime*. London: Routledge.

Bienkowska, E. (1989). 'Declaration of basic principles of justice for victims of crime and abuse of power – the Polish experience', pp. 46–65 in HEUNI (ed.) *Changing victim policy: the United Nations declaration and recent developments in Europe*. Helsinki: HEUNI.

Block, R. (1993). 'A Cross-national Comparison of Victims of Crime: Victim Surveys of Twelve Countries', *International Review of Victimology*, 2: 183–207.

Bucke, T. (1995). 'Policing and the public: findings from the 1994 British Crime Survey', *Home Office Research and Statistics Department, Research Findings* no. 28.

Crawford, A., Jones, T., Woodhouse, T. and Young, J. (1990). *Second Islington Crime Survey*. London: Middlesex Polytechnic.

Dijk, J. J. M. van, Mayhew, P. and Killias, M. (1990). *Experiences of Crime Across the World: Key Findings of the 1989 International Crime Survey*. Deventer, the Netherlands: Kluwer.

Farkas, A. (1996). 'New problems of controlling crime in Hungary', paper to *Ninth Baltic Criminological Seminar*. Tallinn, Estonia.

Farrell, G. (1992). 'Multiple victimisation: its extent and significance', *International Review of Victimology*, 2: 85–102.

Fijnaut, C. (1992). 'International Policing in Europe: its present situation and future', paper to International Conference Policing Systems and Police Co-operation in Europe, Paris.

Fijnaut, C. (1993). 'The Schengen treaties and European police', *European Journal of Crime, Criminal Law and Criminal Justice, 1*.

First European Conference of Victim Support Workers (1989). *Guidelines for Victim Support in Europe*. Utrecht, the Netherlands: VLOS.

Fogel, D. (1994). *Policing in Central and Eastern Europe*. Helsinki: HEUNI.

Frate, A. A. del, Zvekic, U. and Dijk, J. J. M. van (1993). *Understanding Crime: Experiences of Crime and Crime Control*. Rome: UNICRI.

Gorgenyi, I. (1993). 'Hungarian aspects of victimology', pp. 212–218 in S. P. Singh Makkar and P. C. Friday, (eds) *Global perspectives in victimology*. Jalhandar, India: ABS publications.

Hauber, A. R. and Zandbergen, A. (1991). 'Victim assistance in Police Stations on the Move', *International Review of Victimology*, 2: 1–13.

HEUNI (1989). *Changing Victim Policy: the United Nations Declaration and Recent Developments in Europe*. Helsinki, Finland: HEUNI.

Jasinski, J. (1995). 'Crime Control in Poland: an overview', pp. 6–10 in Jasinski and Siemaszko (1995).

Jasinski, J. and Siemaszko, A. (eds) (1995). *Crime Control in Poland*. Warsaw: Oficyna Naukowa.

Joutsen, M. (1987). *The Role of the Victim of Crime in European Criminal Justice Systems*. Helsinki, Finland: HEUNI.

Kalish, C. B. (1988). 'International Crime Rates', Bureau of Justice Statistics Special Report, NCJ-110776, Washington, US Department of Justice.

King, M. (1993). 'Towards Federalism? Policing the borders of a "new" Europe', Discussion Papers in Federal Studies, Faculty of Social Sciences, University of Leicester.

Kury, H. (1993). 'Germany', pp. 537–45 in Del Frate *et al.* (1993).

Kury, H., Dormann, U., Richter, H. and Wurger, M. (1992). *Opfererfahrungen und Meinungen zur Inneren Sicherheit in Deutschland*. Wiesbaden, Germany: BKA – Forschungsreihe, (summary in English, pp. 413–435).

Lahore, K., Taylor, M., Veale, A., Hussein Ali, A. and Elamin Bushra, M. (1993). 'Victimisation amongst street children in Sudan and Ethiopia: a preliminary analysis', pp. 343–347 in Del Frate, *et al.* (1993).

Lurigio, A. J., Skogan, W. G. and Davis, R. C. (eds) (1990). *Victims of Crime: Problems, Policies and Programs*. Newbury Park, Calif: Sage.

Maguire, M. (1982). *Burglary in a Dwelling*. Heinemann: London.

Mawby, R. I. (1990). *Comparative Policing Issues: the British and American Experience in International Perspective*. London: Routledge.

Mawby, R. I. (1991). 'Responding to Crime Victims', Final Report to Home Office (unpublished).

Mawby, R. I. (1992). 'Comparative police systems: searching for a continental model', pp. 108–132 in K. Bottomley, T. Fowles and R. Reiner (eds) *Criminal Justice: Theory and Practice*. London: British Society of Criminology.

Mawby, R. I. and Gill, M. L. (1987). *Crime Victims: Needs, Services and the Voluntary Sector*. London: Tavistock.

Mawby, R. I. and Gorgenyi, I. (1997). 'Break-ins to Weekend Homes: research in an Hungarian city. Forthcoming.

Mawby, R. I. and Kirchoff, G. (1996). 'Coping with crime: a comparison of victims' experiences in England and Germany', pp. 55–70 in P. Francis and P. Davies (eds) *Understanding Victimisation: Themes and Perspectives*. Newcastle: University of Northumbria Press.

Mawby, R. I., Ostrihanska, Z. and Wojcik, D. (1997). 'Police response to crime: the perceptions of victims from two Polish cities', *Policing and Society*, forthcoming.

Mawby, R. I. and Walklate, S. (1994). *Critical Victimology*. London: Sage.

Mayhew, P., Elliott, D. and Dowds, L. (1989). *The 1988 British Crime Survey*. London: HMSO (Home Office Research Study 111).

Mayhew, P., Maung, N. A. and Mirrlees-Black, C. (1993). *The 1992 British Crime Survey*. London: HMSO (Home Office Research Study 132).

Monaghan, L., Taylor, I. and Walklate, S. (1994). *Crime Audit Salford 1994*, Salford City Council.

Morris, A., Findlay, A., Paddison, R. and Rogerson, R. (1989). 'Urban quality of life and the north–south divide', *Town and Country Planning*, *58(7/8)*: 207–210.

Ostrihanska, Z. and Wojcik, D. (1993). 'Burglaries as seen by the victims', *International Review of Victimology, 2.3*: 217–226.

Pagon, M. (ed.) (1996). *Policing in Central and Eastern Europe: comparing firsthand knowledge with experience from the West*. Ljubljana, Slovenia: College of Police and Security Studies.

Polvi, N., Looman, T., Humphries, C. and Pease, K. (1991). 'The time course of repeat burglary victimisation', *British Journal of Criminology, 31*: 411–414.

Rock, P. (1986). *A View from the Shadows*. Oxford: Clarendon Press.

Rock, P. (1990). *Helping Victims of Crime*. Oxford: Clarendon Press.

Rudas, G. (1977). 'The changing role, responsibilities and activities of the police in a developed society', *International Review of Criminal Policy, 33*: 11–16.

Sessar, K. (1996). 'Social Transition and fear of crime', paper to *Ninth Baltic Criminological Seminar*, Tallinn, Estonia.

Shapland, J., Willmore, J. and Duff, P. (1985). Victims in the Criminal Justice System. Aldershot: Gower.

Shelley, L. and Vigh, J. (1995). *Social changes, crime and the police*. Chur, Switzerland: Harwood Academic Publishers.

Siemaszko, A. (1995). 'The media and crime', pp. 20–27 in Jasinski and Siemaszko (1995).

Szikinger, I. (1994). 'The police in Hungary today', pp. 23–35 in Timoránszky (1994).

Skogan, W. G. (1990). *The Police and the Public in England and Wales*. London: HMSO.

Szumski, Z. (1993). 'Fear of Crime, Social Rigorism and Mass Media in Poland', *International Review of Victimology, 2*: 209–215.

Timoranszky, P. (1992). *Rendészeti, Tanulmányok*. Budapest: BM Rendeszeti, Kutatointezet.

Timoranszky, P. (1994). *Rendészeti, Tanulmányok*. Budapest: BM Rendeszeti, Kutatointezet.

Vigh, J. (1987). 'Thoughts about the essence of socialist criminology', *Annales Universitatis Scientiarum Budapestinensis-Sectio Juridica, 29*: 151–173.

Vigh, J. (1991). 'Information on the organisation and activity of the Hungarian White Ring Association', paper to the Annual Conference of the European Forum for Victim Services, Mainz.

Waller, I. (1988). 'International Standards, National Trail Blazing and the Next Steps', pp. 195–203 in M. Maguire and J. Pointing (eds) *Victims of Crime*, Buckingham: Open University Press.

Ward, R. H. (1984). 'Police and criminal justice in Hungary', *Police Studies, 6*: 31–34.

Wemmers, J. M. and Zeilstra, M. I. (1991). 'Victim Services in the Netherlands', *Dutch Penal Law and Policy, Bulletin 3*.

Winkel, F. (1989). 'Responses to Criminal Victimisation: evaluating the impact of a police assistance program and some social psychological characteristics', *Police Studies, 12.1*: 59–72.

Wojcik, D. (1995). 'Juvenile delinquency and victims of crime', pp. 73–76 in Jasinski and Siemaszko (1995).

Wojcik, D., Walklate, S., Ostrihanska, Z., Mawby, R. I. and Gorgenyi, I. (1997). 'Security and crime prevention at home: a comparison of victims' response to burglary in England, Poland and Hungary'. *International Journal of Risk, Security and Crime Prevention, 2.1*: 38–48.

Zverik, U. (1996). 'Policing and attitudes towards police in countries in transition', pp. 45–59 in Pagon (1996).

Part III

CRIMINAL BUSINESS

13

SOME OBSERVATIONS ON ILLEGAL MARKETS

Pino Arlacchi

Illegal markets may be defined as places within which goods and services are exchanged whose production, sale and consumption are forbidden or strictly regulated by the majority of national states and/or by international legislation. The exchange of such goods and services is regarded as an inherent threat to human dignity and the public welfare. Markets in hard drugs, in armaments being sold outside official agreements, in human beings reduced to economic or sexual slavery, in capital generated by crime, and in secret information are examples of this type of exchange.

Because they originate from formal judicial prohibitions, illegal markets can be regarded, to a large extent, as artificial creations, spawned by international legislation which accompanied economic growth and regulation in the wake of the two World Wars (Cassese 1984: chapter 3).

Multilateral treaties for the protection of human rights, international conventions on slavery and on drugs, the outlawing of violence in intra-state disputes, the increasingly restrictive regulations of the production and sale of certain weapons, are some examples of legal provisions which, while aiming at the enhancement of collective security and the protection of human rights (Bull 1977: 135–53, Hoffmann 1983: 33–34; Cassese 1984: 321–57) have contributed to the creation of contemporary illegal markets.

Such markets, therefore, cannot solely be analysed from an economic perspective, according to which they are the result of an increase in supply and demand for some specific goods and services. Illegal markets are also to be examined as the result of the growth of the instruments aimed at protecting society from the destructive effects of market forces themselves (Polanyi 1974). The notion that the trade in certain goods and services should be placed under strict control, or should be completely banned, in the name of humanitarian concerns relating to the psycho-physiological integrity of society, began to develop in the eighteenth century, in response to the slave trade (Scelle 1934) and large-scale opium smuggling (Chang 1964: 95; Johnson 1975).

In this respect, it is interesting to note that from the outset both international legislation and political debate over slavery simultaneously took into account issues surrounding the regulation of arms and drugs trafficking. During the nineteenth century, the English Anti-Slavery movement included in its campaign for the abolition of slavery the prohibition on the British selling opium to China (NIDA 1978: 175–8). Similarly, the 1890 Brussels Treaty on the repression of the African slave trade – which was signed by 17 countries including the USA and 13 European States – also banned the sale of arms in large areas of Africa (SIPRI 1971).

It is only in the years following World Wars I and II that prohibition or regulation of the manufacture and sale of goods that today we regard as illegal began to be applied (Lowes 1966; Stanley and Pearton 1972). Prior to this century, the production, circulation and sale of arms and drugs, for example, were neither prohibited nor subjected to significant restrictions (Harkavy 1975; Gregg 1974). It should also be noted that only over the last twenty years or so have some Western States introduced legislation preventing the investment of illegally accumulated capital in the official economy.

The increasingly tighter web of prohibitions and controls over provision of illegal goods has resulted in a dramatic increase in the related rates of profit and has contributed to the re-emergence in illegal markets of 'archaic' economic behaviours. Alongside the calculating mentality of contemporary finance and industry, criminal markets are characterised by the violent spirit of primitive capitalism.

Dynamics and peculiarities

The internal dynamics of illicit markets are often described by the popular press as being typically obscure and inspired by a mysterious logic ultimately eluding analysis. In fact, a number of studies have shown that we are faced with rational economic phenomena and well-structured 'industries'. Illegal markets have much in common with their legal counterparts. There are buyers and sellers, wholesalers and retailers, go-betweens, importers and distributors, priced structures, balance sheets, profits and, though less frequently, losses.

In a broad distinction, two main sectors typifying illegal markets can be identified. First, a competitive sector, which is occupied by a multiplicity of small and medium-sized, semi-independent firms supplying goods and services to final consumers. Second, an oligopolistic sector, occupied by a limited number of enterprises of varying national background and composition which supply the former sector. These oligopolistic enterprises are usually unknown to the majority of final consumers and often to the very firms operating in the competitive sector.

Each of these sectors, in its turn, can be divided into sub-sectors whose number is determined, among other things, by the need to maintain a given degree of secrecy, the nature of the goods traded, and the kind of entry barriers in place in the specific market considered (Moore 1970). Actors engaged in illicit markets appear to be motivated by the same goals usually ascribed to legal businesspeople: the pursuit and re-investment of the highest profits possible.

However, a closer examination of criminal markets reveals the existence – *vis-à-vis* a modern system of legal transactions – of a series of peculiarities and anomalies. The following are among the most relevant:

1   the frequent presence, within the oligopolistic sector, of multifaceted organisational entities, in respect of their sociological composition and their use of resources;
2   high transaction costs that imply the adoption of organisational frameworks based on 'clans' or 'families', and that foster invisible exchange networks rather than formal and impersonal ones;
3   the absence of a formal apparatus aimed at ensuring the smoothness of transactions.

The multifaceted nature of criminal enterprises

The multifaceted characteristics of the enterprises occupying the higher levels of illegal markets relate to their ability to combine economic, political and military resources. The largest criminal organisations possess economic and political resources which enable them to act as powerful pressure groups in the official arena. On the other hand, unlike their legitimate counterparts, they can resort to the use of violence and intimidation against their competitors and opponents. Although such organisations are oriented towards the acquisition of profits and/or political power, they are rarely inspired either by political or economic goals exclusively, as they are 'polymorphous' entities endowed with sufficient flexibility to shift from one arena to another. The internal relationships amongst their members, as well as the relationships of members with individuals and institutions of the legitimate world, do not merely consist of either business, political or military pacts. Such relationships are of a more complex nature.

The multifaceted character of illegal enterprises is largely determined by the particular nature and conditions of illicit business. For this type of business to take place, three main items must be available: capital, violence and inaction of law enforcement agencies and the judiciary. The share of the market controlled by each enterprise, the duration of its presence in the oligopolistic sector, and the volume of its business are closely related to the capacity of the enterprise to gain access to the items mentioned above and to combine them effectively.

The multifaceted nature of criminal enterprises is exemplified by the confederation of Sicilian families known as Cosa Nostra (Arlacchi [1992] 1993, 1994), and other major criminal coalitions operating in the Italian Mezzogiorno, namely the Calabrian 'Ndrangheta (Ciconte, 1992, Paoli, 1994), and the Campanian Camorra (Sales 1993). According to recent estimates by investigators, Cosa Nostra is composed of about 90 mafia families mainly based in the Palermo and Trapani provinces with an overall number of members around

3,000 (Ministero dell' Interno 1995). The 'Ndrangheta is understood to be formed by approximately 85 families mainly based in the Reggio Calabria province, and with ramifications in other parts of Italy and abroad; its estimated number of members is also around 3,000 (Ministero dell' Interno 1994: 212). Finally, the Camorra is said to include around 145 criminal groups operating in the Campania region, 90 of which are based in the Naples province (Ministero dell' Interno 1995).

These three criminal organisations constitute the most powerful and destructive component of Italian large-scale illegality. Their superiority to other illegal firms derives from the large economic scale of their activity, the number and expertise of their affiliates, their ability to manipulate public institutions, and the complexity of their organisational structure.

The ability of the mafia coalitions to muster economic, political and military resources is unmatched by any other actor involved in illegal business. For example, speculators and illicit financiers may own banks, companies and huge amounts of finances, but they are hardly in the condition to mobilise and manage a specialised criminal labour-force. Networks of illicit power such as masonic and para-masonic sects may be extremely dangerous politically, but they are unlikely to base their power on financial and military resources. Urban gangs may sometimes display high levels of violence, but their sphere of influence and power rarely extends beyond the local context.

The power of the mafia coalitions and families is due to their multifaceted nature, namely to the fact that they are not simple entities such as, respectively, a party, or company or an army. As a consequence, their strategy, along with its logic and aims, is rarely straightforward and transparent. The 'real motives' of certain mafia exploits, and their deep meaning, are often difficult to decode even to the very members of the organisation.

Resources consisting of capital, violence and the ability to paralyse law-enforcement agencies are irregularly available to the different criminal firms or groups of firms. A rapid accumulation of economic strength, stemming from the opening of new business opportunities or fresh sources of illicit wealth, may alter the position of a family business in the criminal market, encouraging the ascending groups to call for a redefinition of power relationships with other groups and a new territory division which reflects the changed conditions. Because the search for new areas of illicit activity mainly characterises less consolidated and younger criminal coalitions, the shifts in power relations which can be observed in criminal markets can be mistaken for generational conflicts. These are frequently and erroneously described as 'conflicts between old and new criminality' or 'wars between old and new mafias'.

A rise in the supply of criminal labour in a given market can benefit groups capable of absorbing such an increase. An increase in military power, due to a wider availability of hit-men, or an increase in the availability of extortionists and dealers, may allow for the expansion of criminal activities for some groups at the expense of weaker ones. Similarly, the identification of common economic interests with corrupt politicians, for example, in monopolising legal resources such as public finances or services, or the establishment of alliances with legitimate institutions such as the secret services, the police and other governmental bodies, may lead to an increase in the degree of impunity for a given criminal group.

Inequalities in the ability to manipulate parts of the criminal-justice system and sectors of government administration are crucial for the establishment of criminal hierarchies. Groups which are evenly endowed with military and economic power may find in the criminal-justice system an important arena in which to compete. For example, the manipulation of the justice system for about a decade – from the early 1970s to 1982 – by the Corleonese mafia coalition, through their connections with central-government agencies and the P2 masonic lodge, gave the Corleonesi the opportunity to destroy their powerful Inzerillo-Bontade-Badalamenti competitors. The manipulation of criminal-justice agencies allowed the Corleonesi to re-direct the investigations towards their competitors in respect of killings they themselves had committed.

Conditions of 'double integration' into legality and illegality offer a series of additional advantages which derive from privileged access to confidential information. Tip-offs regarding the decision of the US government to re-supply Iran with military equipment enabled a group of seventeen businessmen and shady intermediaries to conduct transactions to the value of 2 billion dollars before the Irangate scandal broke out.

Unequal availability of, and unequal access to, resources creates an endemic imbalance between illicit enterprises that generates internal conflicts and fosters a continual re-definition of alliances and a constant re-drawing of the power map.

The cost of transaction

The cost of transactions was once defined by Kenneth Arrow as 'the functioning cost of the economic system'. Within the illicit economy the costs of transactions are much higher than those determined by the pursuit of efficiency, as they include additional expenses relating to the illegality in which they take place. These additional costs are due to the attempt to minimise the risks connected with potential arrest, theft or fraud to which illicit actors are exposed (Rottemberg 1968).

The huge difference between actual cost and market price of commodities exchanged in criminal markets is largely due to the risk of interception of such commodities. The need to restrict the amount of information available to participants in illegal exchanges and to conceal the identity of the real 'principals' makes such exchanges incredibly tortuous and time-consuming, often requiring a disproportionate number of participants. Therefore, every criminal enterprise which succeeds in shortening the supply chain will gain an important advantage over competitors. Chances of detection will be reduced, while the number and costs of transactions will be lowered.

Segments of market operations can be 'internalised' and turned into a co-operative effort by members of a group or clan. In this way, associations are created which can be likened to Durkheimian organic solidarity groups, with members relating to each other on a kinship or non-kinship basis. The frequent superiority, in most global illicit markets, of groups based on ethnic, political or religious solidarity lies in their ability to eliminate parts of the transaction costs while, simultaneously, discourage opportunistic behaviour and defection among members (Ouchi 1980). A sense of moral obligation towards one's own group and associates plays a more important role than discipline imposed through threats of retaliation.

That transactions occur more effectively between clan-type groups than between bureaucratic organisations lacking organic solidarity represents a 'typical' but by no means an 'exclusive' feature of illicit economies. Ouchi, Jaeger and others have shown that a variety of official firms, in conditions characterised by advanced technology and rapid growth, are also structured as clans. The clan structure helps reduce the distance between individuals and enterprise, and creates a strong community spirit which makes expensive surveillance mechanisms redundant.

However, in the case of official firms, clan ties and co-operative relations are restricted to the firm itself and to its productive process. The distribution and marketing of the commodities produced in such a co-operative atmosphere are then left to impersonal strategies and organisations. Although in the initial phases of their development or when poised to penetrate new markets official enter-prises may also resort to protected business conduits and may be favoured by political-institutional circles, these enterprises will have sooner or later to compete in the market with other businesses.

Illicit markets may be distinguished from licit markets for their failure to adopt impersonal forms or internal communication and distribution of goods. The illegal nature of the industry generates a constant risk that shipments may be seized or participants identified. This means that a detailed knowledge of the background and 'curriculum vitae' of every business party is essential. Detailed information on the trustworthiness of illegal actors would be almost impossible to obtain in conditions of open exchange or would be extremely costly even for large-scale illicit organisations. It is therefore safer and cheaper for the organisa-tion to entrust its external relations to other actors who can guarantee the suc-cessful conclusion of criminal transactions and, most importantly, who can ensure a 'standard of illegal reliability' among participants in the exchange. These actors are located in, and constitute 'illicit networks', and act as intermedi-aries between a clan and a bureaucracy. Such networks can combine some typical traits of both formal organisations and primary groups.

A member of a mafia family, a unit of the intelligence service, a group of corporate criminals, and a chain of illicit arms dealers can rely upon a web of allies for support and protection. This may have multi-national and multi-cultural ramifications, and may combine the advantages of a permanent standardised bureaucracy with the flexibility and reliability of an informal group. Illegal goods, services, obligations and counter-obligations circulate in these networks with relatively low costs and risk. The very admission to the network guarantees for the reputation of those involved.

Criminal networks adopt further forms of camouflage because they tend to engage in a much wider set of relationships. These wider systems consist of:

1　commercial diasporas;
2　communication links created by extensive migration;
3　power networks.

The size of the networks and of these wider systems in which the organisations operate determine the position of criminal groups in the interactional hierarchy. For example, organisations endowed with remarkable economic power and the ability to manipulate the state apparatus, such as the Japanese Yakuza and the Colombian cocaine cartels, may nevertheless find it difficult to spread their operations at the international level because, unlike their Italian and Chinese counterparts, they cannot rely on multi-continental networks of associates, or on enclaves of expatriates, which disguise their illicit dealings.

The absence of such enclaves in Western Europe (with the exception of Spain) has prevented the cocaine cartels from inundating the European market, as one might have expected a few years ago after the saturation of the North America cocaine market. In fact, the establishment in Spain of affiliates to these cartels in 1985–6 was not followed by the development of an efficient distribution network in other major European countries. As for power networks, the third set of relationships mentioned above, they are formed by a variety of voluntary organisations such as friendship and affinity groups, charitable trusts, lobbies engaged in the promotion of religious or cultural values, and so on. These organisations pursue legitimate objectives but tend to cover their activities and membership with confidentiality or secrecy. Masonic lodges, the Knights of Malta and of San Sepolcro, and Opus Dei are important examples of such power networks.

Criminal sub-networks specifically aiming at illicit lobbying often associate themselves with such networks, usually ignoring the identity of most of those who compose them. Over the last two decades, such sub-networks have helped tighten the connections between large criminal organisations and the world of legitimate power. For instance, some years ago it emerged that the Sicilian mafia had used the Knights of San Sepolcro and some secret masonic circles to facilitate contacts between criminal bosses and representatives of the state in Trapani, Palermo and Cefalù. These contacts were then extended into a wider web of connections on the national level.

The preferability of informal networks as opposed to structured bureaucracies arises not only from the necessity to ensure the trustworthiness of participants in illegal transactions, but also from the need to adapt to variations in the nature of these transactions.

The multifaceted character of illegal networks partly compensates for their limitations in terms of the number of transactions conducted. It is rare for a specific network to be used for a one-off operation or a one-off set of operations. The trial for the 1981 attempt to murder the Pope started according to the 'Bulgarian Connection' hypothesis: the killing had been commissioned by the Bulgarian secret services on behalf of their Soviet counterparts, and entrusted to a coalition of Turkish neo-fascists and professional criminals.

Investigations carried out during the public hearings focused on a very different reality: a complex network involving the Grey Wolves, a Turkish Islamic fundamentalist movement extending across two continents and half a dozen countries. This network was used: (a) to export morphine base and heroin from Turkey and Southeast Asia to the West; (b) to move war material and illicit capital in the opposite direction; (c) as an espionage network to promote political terrorism. The presence of the Grey Wolves among the million-strong Turkish population of Germany enabled them to establish a heroin distribution system in the major German cities, to consolidate contacts with neo-Nazi paramilitary groups and arms dealers, and to gain access to the European circles of financial speculators and adventurers.

Security of contracts

As I have already suggested, the third characteristic of illegal markets is their lack of formal rules and enforcement bodies which guarantee respect for the terms of transactions. Illegal markets, in other words, are devoid of external authorities and written regulations, and they cannot rely on arbitration or mediation to bring up complaints and seek redress for the damage suffered. Moreover, unlike some important sectors of the official market such as the financial market, they are devoid of informal mechanisms of self-regulation which bind members and penalise deviants with exclusion from certain circles (Clarke 1985).

The conditions under which illicit exchanges take place resemble those prevalent in primitive societies described by anthropologists (Bohannan 1967). So long as a sovereign power is lacking, individuals and groups pursue different interests and feel deeply justified in doing so. There is no use of signed contracts, nor of written records of transactions. There is no monopoly of force. Violence is decentralised and owned as a right by all groups and individuals. Moreover, there is no everlasting social contract. The social contract is a constant, everyday creation. It is a process that goes through all socio-economic relations.

A permanent tension between trust and violence seems to be present in every illicit transaction. Trust should be understood here as the reliability of the parties regarding their present and future intentions. Violence is employed as a sanction when contracts are violated, and as an instrument to solve disputes and to regulate the market activities. In some contexts, primary bonds between members of the organisation, based on kinship, ethnicity, family, nationality and locality, guarantee the security and continuity of illegal transactions and minimise the need or the threat of violence. Well-established illicit markets usually rely more on trust than violence. Moreover, in the more industrialised countries, where a state monopoly of force is firmly established, the use of violence by criminal groups tends to become increasingly counter-productive.

However, participants in some specific illegal markets are unable to avoid the threat or the use of violence. This is usually the case in racketeering, in large-scale illicit financial activity and the trade of confidential information conducted by secret agents and 'agents provocateurs'.

Johnson *et al.*'s ethnographic account of the retail market of heroin in New York suggests that acts of violence following the violation of contracts, theft and fraud are more common, between rival gangs, than violent conflicts over terri-torial control. In this context violence and the threat of violence constitute the major tool for the maintenance of order in a specific illicit market (Johnson *et al.* 1985: 174).

Trust and violence, while representing alternative ways of guaranteeing mar-ket security, are more closely tied than might first appear. Markets based on trust may rapidly deteriorate and turn into violent battlegrounds following the breach of contracts between former allies or business partners. Markets originally built on sub-cultural or friendship loyalties – like the heroin market in Rome in the early 1970s – can evolve in such a way that they become dominated by fraud and coercion.

A common line of development can be identified from: (a) an initial phase in which illicit markets are dominated by reciprocity, friendship, trust and 'political-cultural' commitment among participants, to: (b) a 'mature' phase, characterised by increasing volume and diversification of transactions, in which the contractual dimension of relationships takes over and exchanges become increasingly formal and rigidly controlled.

Trust and violence may be present in a fluid state as principles which express themselves in different ways, or may have a fixed and institutionalised form. The description of the business ethic of the 'man of honour' given by Tommaso Buscetta, in his landmark statement to investigative magistrate Giovanni Falcone, seems to be inspired by the principle of double standards: an ethic of responsibility within mafia circles and a tendency to the opposite with regard to the outside world.

The drive towards the unification and consolidation of illicit markets, along-side a trend towards interdependence and specialisation, forces some actors to multiply contacts at such a rate that it becomes difficult for them to rely on trust or violence exclusively. In some cases, therefore, a third party assumes the risks of transactions: hence the emergence of professional mediators in recent years. In particularly complex markets, such as the trade in Western-produced arms dir-ected at developing countries, the legal standing of the protagonists can be very mixed (professional criminals, agents of arms producers, speculators, terrorist groups, official and semi-official representatives, etc.). Here, transactions tend to be few and involve very large sums. The security of contracts is therefore increas-ingly entrusted to a special kind of mediator, whose role is to make up for the lack of trust between the parties involved. These mediators facilitate a deal that is in the interest of both sides, while making the deal impossible to take place without their own intervention. See for example the following case mentioned in the Tower Report:

> The United States had agreed (to the clandestine sale of arms to Iran), the Israelis had agreed, and the Iranians had agreed to do a little business. But nobody trusted anybody else. The Iranians would not have paid a cent without first having received and inspected the merchandise, from what I knew of previous transactions in which they had paid for shipments in advance, and then opened the containers to find rocks. The Israelis, on the other hand, would ship nothing without payment in advance.
>
> There was an impasse until Kashoggi arrived and said: 'OK, I'll trust the Iranians, I'll trust the Israelis and the Americans, and I'll put the money needed upfront'.
>
> In this way the first deal that I knew about took off with a million dollars deposited by Kashoggi in a numbered account indicated by the Israelis.
>
> (Tower Report 1987: 135–6; see also U.S. Senate 1991)

Furthermore, as stated by an 'expert' before an Italian investigating magistrate, the responsibility for the payment of bribes to state officials and political leaders of the countries involved in a specific arms deal lies with such mediators.

The activities of the P2 masonic lodge provides a good illustration of the demand for protection and guarantees within the spheres of illicit exchange which are based on the institutionalisation of trust and violence. Between the early 1970s and 1981, an international masonic lodge called Propaganda Due (P2) operated as a cover, as well as in its own right, for a large number of illegal economic and political activities, ranging from the trafficking in arms and drugs to terrorism, from illegal lobbying to fraud and corruption. Italy was one of its major centres, where according to many commentators it took on the form of a clandestine political party. However, given the analysis above, P2 appears to have been something far more complex. This masonic lodge could carry out a variety of operations such as:

1   the internalisation of illegal networks and the professional use of violence;
2   the transferral of its practices into the legitimate political and economic arena, thus maximising its competitive position;
3   the mediation and resolution of conflicts occurring within the ambit of both clandestine and legal transactions (Commissione P2 1984).

Trends

The analysis of the rise and fall of organisations such as the P2 lodge raises the issue of the future of illegal markets. Which direction are these markets taking? Will they continue to oscillate between conflict and regulation? Between centralisation and dispersion, control of violence and promotion of armed conflict?

It is impossible to give an unequivocal answer. Within some criminal markets forces seem to be in place which encourage the creation of regulative bodies and stable means for the administration of trust and violence. Such bodies of 'governance' are the product of the unification process experienced by illegal markets, a process triggered by the growing economic interdependence of the actors involved on the one hand, and the increasing vulnerability of criminal firms to law enforcement agencies on the other.

There is a growing tendency for participants in illegal business to give rise to semi-formal institutions for the prevention and control of conflict. This is exemplified by the so-called Provincial and Regional Commission of Sicilian Cosa Nostra. According to statements given by several mafia turncoats, the former Commission was founded in the late 1950s on the model of the American Cosa Nostra Commission (Tribunale di Palermo 1985; Arlacchi 1994). Another example can be found in the regrouping and centralisation of the Yamaguchi-gumi syndicate within the Japanese Yakuza. According to estimates of the Japanese police, in 1992 the Yamaguchi-gumi syndicate dominates over 1,300 smaller groups and managed to include almost 40 per cent of the total Yakuza affiliates, while in 1980 it only included 11 per cent (Iwai 1986: 225; National Police Agency 1989: 5).

Illegal business is replicating developments which took place among nation-states since World War I, namely it is moving from a condition of anarchy and absolute sovereignty of individual firms to an international system placing strict limitations on them (Bonanate 1976: VII–XXI; Cassese 1984).

Are we witnessing a shift from a kaleidoscope of criminal enterprises potentially at each other's throats to a web of interdependent firms operating against the background of rules and accords? Will this development, which is due to greater enforcement pressure and the growing scope of illegal business, transform criminal organisations into bodies with relative rather than absolute sovereignty? Is there an embryonic 'international law' regulating illicit markets? This may well be happening. However, the frequent failure of attempts to impose some kind of control on illicit economies suggests the inadequacy of the primitive regulation methods adopted in such economies. This author believes that this inadequacy constitutes one of the greatest internal obstacles to the further development of illegal markets on a domestic and international scale.

Growing public awareness in a number of countries regarding the trafficking in drugs, arms and human beings, along with the rise of popular protest movements against particularly dangerous forms of large-scale crime and political corruption, constitute another obstacle to such development. However, the capacity displayed by criminal business to reproduce itself, and the institutional complicity enjoyed by such business, force us to keep an open mind about the future.

References

Arlacchi, P., *Men of Dishonor. Inside the Sicilian Mafia: an account of Antonino Calderone*, New York, William Morrow and Company [1992], 1993.

—— *Addio Cosa Nostra. La vita di Tommaso Buscetta*, Milano, Rizzoli, 1994.

Bohannan, P., *Law and Warfare. Studies in the Anthropology of Conflict*, Austin, University of Texas Press, 1967.

Bonanate, L., *Il Sistema delle relazioni internazionali*, Torino, Einaudi, 1976.

Bull, H., *The Anarchical Society: a Study of Order in World Politics*, New York, 1977.

Cassese, A., *Il diritto internazionale nel mondo contemporaneo*, Bologna, Il Mulino, 1984.

Chang Hsin-pao, *Commissioner Lin and the Opium War*, Cambridge, Mass, Harvard University Press, 1964.

Ciconte, E., *'Ndrangheta dall' Unità ad oggi*, Bari, Laterza, 1992.

Clarke, M., *Regulating the City. Competition Scandal and Reform*, Milton Keynes, Open University Press, 1985.

Commissione P2, *Commissione parlamentare d'inchiesta sula Loggia Massonica P2. Relazione finale*, Roma, Camera dei Deputati, 1984.

Gregg, R., 'The International Control System for Narcotic Drugs', in L. Simmons and A. Said, eds, *Drugs, Politics and Diplomacy*, London, Beverly Hills, Sage, 1974.

Harkavy, R., *The Arms Trade and International System*, Cambridge, Ballinger, 1975.

Hoffmann, S., 'Reaching for the Most Difficult: Human Rights as a Foreign Policy Goal', *Daedalus*, n. 112, 1983.

Iwai, H., 'Organized Crime in Japan', in R. J. Kelly (ed.) *Organized Crime. A Global Perspective*, Totowa, Rowman and Littlefield, 1986.

Johnson, B. D., 'Righteousness before Revenue: the Forgotten Moral Crusade Against the Indochinese Opium Trade', *Journal of Drug Issues*, n. 5, 1975.

Johnson, B. D., Goldstein, P., Preble, E., Schmeidler, J., Lipton, D., Spunt, B. and Miller, T. *Taking Care of Business: The Economics of Crime by Heroin Abusers*, Lexington Books, Lexington, 1985.

Lowes, P., *The Genesis of International Narcotic Control*, Genève, Droz, 1966.

Ministero dell' Interno, *Rapporto annuale sul fenomeno della criminalità organizzata per il 1993*, Roma, Camera dei Deputati, doc. XXXVIII-bis, n. 1, 1994.

—— *Rapporto annuale sul fenomeno della criminalità organizzata per il 1994*, Roma, 1995.

Moore, M., *Economics of Heroin Distribution*, Croton-on-Hudson, Hudson Institute, 1970.

National Police Agency, *White Paper on Police: Organized Crime Control Today and Its Future Task*, excerpt, Tokyo, Ministry of Justice, 1989.

NIDA, National Institute on Drug Abuse, *Perspectives on the History of Psychoactive Substance Use*, Rockville, 1978.

Ouchi, W.G., 'Markets, Bureaucracies and Clans', *Administrative Science Quarterly*, vol. 25, March 1980.

Paoli, L. 'An underestimated criminal phenomenon: the Calabrian 'ndrangheta', *European Journal of Crime, Criminal Law and Criminal Justice*, vol. 2, 3: 212–38, 1994.

214

Polanyi, K., *La grande trasformazione. Le origini economiche e politiche della nostra epoca*, Torino, Einaudi, 1974.

Rottemberg, S., 'The Clandestine Distribution of Heroin, its Discovery and Suppression', *Journal of Political Economy*, January, 1968.

Sales, I., *La camorra. Le camorre*, Roma, Editori Riuniti, 1993.

Scelle, G., *Précise de Droit des Gens*, vol. II, Paris, 1934 (cit. In Cassese 1984, 65).

SIPRI, Stockholm International Peace Research Institute, *The Arms Trade and the Third World*, New York, Humanities Press, 1971.

Stanley, J. and Pearton, M., *The International Trade in Arms*, The International Institute for Strategic Studies, London, Chatto and Windus, 1972.

Tower Report, *The Tower Commission Report. The Full Text of the President's Special Review Board*, New York, Bantam Books, 1987.

Tribunale di Palermo, Ufficio Istruzione Processi Penali, *Ordinanza-sentenza di rinvio a giudizio nel procedimento penale contro Abbate Giovanni + 506*, Palermo, Novembre 8, 1985.

U.S. Senate, *Permanent Subcommittee on Investigations of the Committee on Governmental Affairs, Arms Trafficking, Mercenaries and Drug Cartels, Hearing*, Washington D.C., Government Printing Office, 1991.

14

DRUGS, WAR AND CRIME IN THE POST-SOVIET BALKANS[1]

Roger Lewis

Summary: War conditions in the Balkans provided new opportunities for illegal business. The war generated the most unlikely alliances, fostering criminal activity and organisation in the former Yugoslavia and beyond. The flow of drugs was not hindered. Innovative routes and arrangements circumvented and exploited areas of conflict while the social distress created by war has generated further demand.

Introduction

Following the outbreak of war in the former Yugoslavia, it might have been thought that the disruption of trafficking routes through the Balkans would hinder heroin supplies to Western Europe. In fact, new conduits were rapidly established that circumvented areas of combat and took advantage of political change both domestically and in adjacent countries. While military conflict clearly disrupted supply lines, it also encouraged the development of routes to the north and south of the combat zones. War conditions provided additional opportunities for illegal business. Prior to the outbreak of war, trafficking was already a means of raising funds and purchasing weapons. Moreover, social and political destabilisation proved advantageous to illicit entrepreneurs as economic liberalisation in eastern Europe facilitated, rather than hindered, the availability of heroin locally and in western Europe. During the course of 1995 over one ton of heroin was seized by British customs, an 80 per cent increase on 1994. Most shipments were organised by Turkish-controlled organisations and had been routed through Bulgaria, the former republic of Yugoslavia, Hungary, Slovakia, the Czech republic and Germany (Travis 1996).

Geopolitics of the post-communist period

War in the former Yugoslavia, the break-up of the former Soviet Union, and the licit and illicit business opportunities that have arisen in eastern Europe and the near East had a profound impact on European drug markets in the 1990s. A report on illicit drug trafficking by the secretariat of the UN Commission on Narcotic Drugs (UNCND) concluded that 'the processes of political and economic change set in motion by the breakup of the former USSR and the drive to liberalise the international economy and domestic economic transactions have significantly increased the magnitude and complexity of illicit drug trafficking' (1995: 23). Such changes and the effect of armed conflict on the region through which the Balkan Route has historically passed have had immediate consequences.

Andreas (1995,1996) has argued that the loosening of government controls over the flow of goods, services, information and capital encourages both legal and illegal economic activity. As trade liberalisation and economic integration help traffickers penetrate Western markets, simultaneously the privatisation of state-owned enterprises and deregulation of banking systems facilitate the laundering of profits and provide an influx of hard currency. Labour migration and the drugs trade have helped to cushion economic crises in Latin America and may yet do so in the Balkans, the Caucasus and Russia's southern rim.

The UNCND secretariat recently observed that a special danger, emerging in countries that aim at rapid privatisation of state-owned assets, is that such assets become a target for criminal finance (UNCND 1995a). At times of profound social and political change, distinctions between the legal and illegal in a privatised world become unclear and the magnitude of funds under criminal control in some countries poses a direct threat to the state and to the community. These problems are aggravated by conditions of armed conflict, or civil war, when criminalised paramilitary and state-intelligence organisations invest in, sponsor, or directly enter the drug traffic. Unemployment within the security services in eastern Europe has resulted in reports of bodyguard services being provided for the new business class and for black marketeers. Civil corruption in the contemporary Balkans, combined with relatively lax controls and under-resourced enforcement, has meant traffickers may have a relatively clear run until they reach Hungary, Slovakia, the Czech Republic and Poland. Some eastern European states have retained long-term police personnel, who may be experienced but politically compromised, while others have employed uncompromised, but less experienced, new staff. It is likely that employees of intelligence units formerly guided by the Russians may be frustrated in aspiration and susceptible to corruption.

Useful, if not particularly insightful, parallels have been drawn by Sterling (1994) between the presence of organised criminals in the new bureaucracies and economies of the former Soviet bloc, and the role of mafia in Italian society. In eastern Europe an endemic cynicism about public service was and continues to be accompanied by flourishing parallel economies in licit and illicit products. The consequences of promoting self-interest over ideals of public service have not been limited to eastern Europe as publicly owned enterprises are sold off at knockdown prices to mediocre bureaucrats, formerly employed within such bodies, across the continent.

A Europol document (1993) recently concluded that endemic corruption, the displacement of peoples, and the collapse of social infrastructures provide major opportunities for long-established, well-organised and entrepreneurial criminal networks in Russia and eastern Europe. Black market networks that formerly dealt in consumer goods and hard currency are ideally placed to expand their operations, with local populations becoming increasingly involved as living standards fall and demand increases for psychoactive substances.

The Balkan route: diversification and innovation

While drug trafficking through the Balkans has been conducted for decades (Newsday 1975: 2; Sundaralingham 1988), a marked diversification of transit routes into Western Europe took place following the outbreak of war in 1991. Overland transport channels via Bulgaria, Romania, Hungary, Poland, Slovakia and the Czech Republic were established, as well as maritime routes accessing Venice, Koper, Trieste, Durres and the Dalmatian coast on the Adriatic, and Puglia and Calabria on the Ionian sea. While some heroin entering Serbia, Bosnia, Croatia and Macedonia is intended for internal consumption, Macedonia and Albania have become particularly important as zones of production and transit. Following the Dayton accord and the ending of sanctions, there have been reports of reactivated land routes through the former Yugoslavia. The potential for trafficking by river along the Danube–Rhine axis has also raised concerns.

Taking advantage of connections in European-based Turkish communities, Turkish traffickers prefer to retain overall control over bulk transport to key distribution points such as London and Amsterdam, while 'short networks' purchasing from Turkish suppliers in the southern Balkans run smaller consignments west on their own behalf. Major roads running from Turkey to European destinations carry thousands of vehicles, including TIR trucks, every day, which makes control difficult (INCB 1994). Airports in central and eastern Europe are regularly utilised (INCB 1995). The bankruptcy of chemical and pharmeutical companies in the former Soviet bloc has left skilled chemists with no income. These factors plus the expansion of trafficking via Belarus, the Russian Federation, and the Ukraine into Poland and central Europe, using operational bases in Prague and Warsaw, together with spillage, diversion and direct sales on local markets, has contributed to diversification from the historical heroin route through the former Yugoslavia (INCB 1994).

The death of Yugoslavia

Silber and Little have argued that federal Yugoslavia did not die a natural death but was deliberately and systematically killed off (Silber and Little 1995: xxiii). The Balkan wars have been marked by civil conflict within and between communities and exacerbated by career politicians and criminalised paramilitaries. It was trouble in the economically disadvantaged regions of Macedonia and

Kosovo that sparked the disintegration of the Yugoslav federation and where its consequences in terms of trafficking became particularly evident. While Belgrade later demanded far-reaching autonomy for Serbs in a new Croatia, it adamantly opposed similar claims by Albanians in Kosovo, even though the latter composed 90 per cent of the population prior to 1990 (ibid.: 213). A logic of secession and partition, which with tacit Western approval has succeeded in the northern Balkans, sowed the seeds of violence in the southern Balkans where heroin trafficking and consumption have become particularly florid (Glenny 1996).

Before 1991, Yugoslavia earned US $2 billion per annum from arms exports (Silber and Little 1995: 59). The availability of weapons in the former Yugoslavia was partly the result of Tito's defence policies and the nation's role as a major arms producer and exporter, and partly the result of the prevalence of a popular gun culture in many rural and mountain communities (Glenny 1993). Weapons were also sought externally by Kosovo Albanian militants and Slovenian, Croatian, Bosnian Serb and Bosnian Muslim forces. This frequently required entering spheres of semi-legal and illegal exchange entailing more than one commodity. UN embargoes further encouraged Budapest-based cross-border trading systems that involved sanctions-busting on a grand scale specialising in oil and other products. Inevitably, wars create the conditions for black marketeering in controlled or prohibited goods and services. Trade in all directions across the confrontation lines continued in spite of sanctions. A blockade imposed on Macedonia by Greece, like the blockade imposed on Serbia by the United Nations, nurtured a profiteering black-market culture in which distinctions between licit and illicit commodities became increasingly academic.

While an arms embargo applied to all combatants in the former Yugoslavia, it particularly penalised the Bosnian Muslims, who were strong in foot soldiers but weaker in military hardware. Arms factories in the Bosnian mountains and the withdrawal of troops controlled by Belgrade from Slovenia and Croatia provided the Bosnian Serbs with almost a surfeit of heavy ordnance. Arms shipments intended for the Bosnian Muslims were skimmed by the Croatians and then by Bosnian Croats before being passed to their putative allies. The Croatians through the Croatian diaspora, the assistance of some major powers, and efficient smuggling via their lengthy seaboard, succeeded in building a well-equipped army in spite of embargoes. The smuggling of weapons from Hungary and elsewhere to arm Croatia's own forces as they broke with the Yugoslav federation is a matter of public record. Slovenia, using similar foreign sources, had ensured from the beginning that it also had a military capacity, including anti-tank weapons.

While Kosovo, Albania and Macedonia have been particularly associated with heroin production and transport in recent years, smuggling, black marketeering and gangsterism have been evident in all disputed territories. Convicted criminals and former secret policemen have been prominent in the leadership of para-military groups, both professions having a complex involvement in the evolution of the Balkan route over many years that has included heroin trafficking and assassination (Newsday 1975: 51–58). Misha Glenny (1996) points out that a 'culture of atrocities' was greatly encouraged by the practice of drafting criminals into the police and military. Gangsters organised ethnic cleansing in order to accumulate vast fortunes from looting and from taking over industries that were part of the war economy. They prolonged the war in order to maximise their profits.

Rivals in war, partners in business, brothers in crime

Serbia helped pay for the war by inflationary funding, destroying the wealth base of Yugoslavia's once-strong, professional elite and giving rise to a new elite which became rich through war-profiteering and sanctions busting. 'While Serbian society was criminalised, tens of thousands of educated people fled the country – escaping mobilisation or searching for a way to make a living' (Silber and Little 1995: 386). Such developments were evident in all the warring republics. The spoils of war impoverished the vulnerable and enriched the unscrupulous (Traynor 1995). 'Official' pressure, as well as paramilitary and gangster coercion, resulted in people signing away their property and rights of residence across Bosnia and Croatia. It is widely believed that the secret services in Belgrade entered the drug trade with their criminal associates and are still involved (OGD 1996a). There are similar concerns, that have been directly expressed to the author by drugs workers, about ex-military and police involvement in Croatia, where Zeliko Raznjatovic, a Serbian gangster otherwise known as 'Arkan' also has business connections. There is little doubt that paramilitary groups worked closely with government agencies in Belgrade, Zagreb and Sarajevo, most notoriously those led by Raznjatovic and Vosislav Selelj, an extreme Serbian nationalist militia leader, whose 'weekend Chetniks' committed systematic atrocities (Bell 1995: 159). Such warlords have 'trafficked shamelessly in the misery of their captives, and in bodies both live and dead' (Berger 1995). (There have been darker unconfirmed reports in French press circles of a trade in human organs (Giordano 1996).) As a respected Serb commander and former social worker observed 'this is a war, and in wars bad things happen. We have emptied our prisons and asylums, what did you expect?' (Bell 1995: 130–2).

Allegations of corrupt business practice have been made not only between warring factions but also internally within national political bodies. Dobrica Cosic, president of the Federal Republic of Yugoslavia in 1992–3, spoke out in the national assembly warning of the corruption and disorder that would inevitably follow such behaviour (Owen 1996: 53–72). However, war increased politicians' special privileges and the obduracy of the Bosnian Serbs and others reflected a reluctance to give them up (Bell 1995: 109). While oil and economic sanctions directly or indirectly damaged the formal economies of the Balkan region and its immediate neighbours, war and the black market was good for illegal business.

Kiseljak on the western edge of Sarajevo became a Bosnian 'Casablanca'

(Silber and Little 1995: 328) as hard-line Croats who had been trading with Serbs besieging Sarajevo, as well as with Muslim black-marketeers within Sarajevo, exploited their position as middlemen. Croats bought from Serbs and sold on to Muslim profiteers operating a cartel system that kept black-market prices artificially high. Despite turf wars dressed up in patriotic guise, Muslim gangsters, Croat middlemen and Serbian suppliers all had a vested interest in maintaining the siege. Similar reports of paramilitary gangster collaboration have emerged in eastern Bosnia, Slavonia, Montenegro, Bosnia and Kosovo (Rumiz 1994).

Military units as well as paramilitaries engaged in unconventional trading. On one occasion, bargaining was monitored between a Muslim commander and his Serb counterpart over the Deutschmark price of Serbian shells which the Muslims wished to buy to fire at Croats in Mostar. After a price was agreed and lorry supply routes arranged, the Muslim commander inquired whether the Serbs, if they were given a little extra money and the cross-bearings, would fire the shells themselves. After further haggling, the Serbs duly fired the shells on behalf of the Muslims. In early 1995, fuel was supplied to the Bosnian Serb army with Croat complicity at a time when Serbia itself was prohibiting oil to the Bosnian Serbs. The Croats sold fuel to the Bosnian Serbs, partly in return for the protection of Bosnian Croats against Muslim attacks and partly to underwrite Bosnian Serb assistance to the Bihac Bosnian Muslim leader, Fikret Abdic, who had strong links with the Croat financial community. Occasional payments were made to local commanders to persuade them to stop fighting while fuel trucks passed through combat lines (Owen 1996: 380–384).

In the same way as opium caravans are taxed by insurgent forces in Burma's Shan states, informal levies were applied by paramilitary and official forces on embargoed materials, arms, oil and humanitarian aid transiting disputed territory. For instance, one oil tanker in ten making legitimate deliveries might be confiscated by paramilitaries from whatever side. In early 1993 UNHCR was forced to suspend operations until all sides in Bosnia-Herzegovina honoured commitments to allow urgently needed convoys of food and medicine through without obstruction or theft. Nevertheless, in the summer of 1993 UNHCR was obliged to pay a toll of US $350 for each aid truck passing through Serb-held territory (Almond 1994: 402). UN contingents, such as the Egyptian and Ukrainian UN battalions, sold food, fuel and equipment on the black market despite the efforts of senior officers (Bell 1995: 175–189).

The arms trade

Arms and ammunition factories throughout ex-Yugoslavia continued production throughout the war, including those in Muslim-held Sarajevo, Zenica and Gorazde. The US, Russia and the European Union knew about sanction-busting and embargo-breaking by all sides, and the smokescreens that were employed to conceal them. A number of governments helped arm the Croats and Bosnian Muslims. The Russians, in comparison, generally maintained their embargo against the Serbs, who were largely self-sufficient in arms. Black-market spare parts were obtained by both Serbs and Croats directly through Russian generals operating on their own account (Owen 1996: 382–383). Embargo-busting involved a variety of legal and illegal goods including arms and drugs. The tendency of governments to place less emphasis on weapons-trafficking than on drug-trafficking, and the inevitable ambivalence of combatant and supplier states, meant that actual seizures were a poor reflection of real levels of activity.

The pre-war arming of the republics could not be formally condoned by public officials within the Yugoslav federation, hence private deals were struck between the various governments and other suppliers (Moder 1994). As open warfare approached, Customs officials on the Italian–Swiss border noted that automatic weapons, usually procured for Italian criminals in Switzerland, were increasingly destined for Yugoslavia (Auchlin 1993). The outcome of Operation Benjamin conducted by Swiss police in 1991 linked Kosovo Albanian couriers and heroin-distribution networks in Zurich to the purchase of firearms in Switzerland and Czechoslovakia (Vastano 1994). Switzerland remains an important brokerage centre. Intelligence sources suggest a meeting was held in Prague in 1992 between Italian and Russian organised-crime figures to discuss drug traffic and money-laundering with follow-up meetings in Warsaw, Moscow and Switzerland (Jamieson 1995).

It seems likely that drugs may have been given free passage within the Balkans in exchange for arms or hard currency (Jamieson 1994: 116; Moder 1994). Operation Dinero, initiated by the US Drug Enforcement Administration in 1992 to follow global drug and hot-money networks, resulted in the arrest of 100 traffickers in Spain, the USA and Italy in 1994, the sequestration of US $33 million in assets, 9 tons of cocaine and a shipment of arms destined for Croatia. A Sicilian principal was identified with ownership of 14 navigation companies in Cyprus, Gibraltar and Croatia, a bank in Zagreb and another in Puglia. Other mafia figures involved in the arms trade have taken refuge in Croatia. Both the Santapaola and Fidanzati Cosa Nostra families have been involved in arms-trafficking with citizens of the former Yugoslavia (Jamieson 1995). However, seizures in Milan, Slovenia and elsewhere indicate that more recently there may have been a greater outflow of light weaponry from the Balkans than there has been inflow. An investigation in Trieste in 1994 exposed a Puglian-Croatian network dealing in machine guns, anti-tank rockets and ammunition that is probably representative of other undetected arrangements. Major shipments of arms and explosives are known to have been made from Slovenia and Croatia to Sicily (Longo and Moder 1995).

Exiles, migrants and disposable labour

The Balkan conflict helped create and was strongly influenced by migrant populations and diasporas. Germany's pro-Croat policy was partly determined by Croatian residents and political activists and Germany, as subsequent host to over

400,000 refugees, was particularly keen to see the wars terminated (Moder 1996). In Italy few Balkan refugees now wish to return home, and the smuggling of migrants from and through the Balkans is a thriving business. Important issues arise for all European countries that encounter drug suppliers operating within different diasporas. The use of national origin as imprecise shorthand for different criminal formations in itself may heighten xenophobia and perpetuate institutionalised racism.

Ruggiero and South have identified a general increase in organised forms of drug-related crime (1995). While business skills are increasingly required for importation and wholesale distribution, they argue that a 'mass' criminal labour pool, easily deployed and dispensed with as required, can be utilised for mundane tasks requiring minimal expertise. Dealing by Slovenes, Croats, Albanians, Macedonians and Serbs has been identified in Germany. Increasing numbers of Kosovo Albanians and Macedonians have become involved in distribution in Croatia and Slovenia, with political and economic refugees in Switzerland, Germany and Italy being drawn into distribution and retail sales. It seems that Turkish retail dealers have been supplanted increasingly by individuals from the former Yugoslavia in Germany and Switzerland (Koutouzis 1995). In Italy and Switzerland, reliable heroin user/dealers are offered intermediary tasks by mid-level wholesalers (Grosso 1993).

Highway E5 revisited, Albania and 'short-network' systems

Turmoil in the former Yugoslav republics and the opening of borders in eastern Europe contributed to shifts in the main Balkan route away from Yugoslavia's E5 highway. Diversification resulted in heroin being moved: first, through Bulgaria and Romania, with Hungary, the Czech Republic and Slovakia acting as warehousing and transshipment sites; second, through Bulgaria and Macedonia to the Albanian ports and Italy; third through CIS member states, Belarus and the Ukraine, to Poland and Germany; and, fourth, via maritime routes to the Italian Adriatic and Ionian ports (INCB 1994; Rumiz 1994). High-speed boats and hydrofoils ply between Italy and the Balkan litoral from Istria to Greece carrying drugs, cigarettes, plundered valuables, small arms, refugees and other migrants (Rumiz 1994a). Freighters and ferries transport heavier weaponry, cars and other cargo. With the ensuing profits, duty-free shops, restaurants, casinos and marinas have been purchased in the former Yugoslavia at remarkably low prices.

Albanian and Macedonian 'short networks' have fully exploited their access to suppliers in Turkey and the Caucasian republics, the relative tranquillity of Macedonia, Albanian access to the Adriatic, and their own established presence in Switzerland, Italy and Germany. Detailed interviews and enforcement data confirm the extent of Kosovan and Macedonian involvement in central-European distribution reported by Koutouzis (1995). Tight, traditional, family-based networks are active throughout the former Yugoslavia and its immediate neighbours. Adherence to value systems built on respect, silence and blood feud makes them difficult to penetrate. Refineries appear to be operational in Macedonia, Kosovo and Albania. Skopje, Macedonia's capital, has experienced a boom inconsistent with prevailing legitimate economic conditions, as well as significant heroin seizures.

Albania's poverty, its conversion to free-market economics, the breakdown of formal controls, and its coastline, have provided ideal conditions for two-way trading in weapons, oil, drugs, tobacco, stolen vehicles and migrant smuggling. The subjection of Serbia to an internationally agreed arms, oil and economic embargo, and Macedonia to a blockade imposed by Greece, resulted in smuggling on a grand scale (Observatoire 1994; OGD 1995). On the fringes of the war theatre from Trieste to southern Hungary, there was a steady outflow of heroin and low-cost small arms during the conflict, and the inward delivery, via the Adriatic and the Danube, of electronic materials, heavy weapons, surface-to-air missiles and other sophisticated equipment. The Albanian port of Durres continues to be the destination of hundreds of vehicles for the transportation and bartering of heroin and other products through the Balkans and via the ferry to Italy. Protected warehousing is provided in Albania itself, with consignments earmarked for Italy, Switzerland and Germany. While traffickers from the former Yugoslavia, particularly Kosovo Albania and Macedonia, have established themselves in Italy, Italian criminals have also set up entrepreneurial outposts in Albania (Jamieson 1995).

Drug markets and heroin consumption

The pattern of heroin use in most Western European countries is reported as stable or showing a slight increase. However, the UN Commission on Narcotic Drugs suggests that there has been a dramatic increase in the number of heroin users in some republics of the former Yugoslavia, with a higher incidence of use than elsewhere in Europe. It is likely that spillage in countries used as trafficking routes has contributed to increased consumption (UN Commission 1995b). Fieldwork reports indicate that retail distribution will become increasingly commercialised and criminalised as time goes by. With political and economic difficulties increasing in adjacent countries such as Bulgaria, markets have expanded as has the influence of criminals and shady businessmen well-connected to Serbian war profiteers (Smale 1996).

Problem drug use in the former Yugoslavia first became evident in the early 1970s in Belgrade, Zagreb and parts of the Adriatic coast. While the federal republic initially served as a transit country for heroin, domestic markets eventually developed (Sakoman and Hecimovic 1991). Plans to strengthen prevention, treatment and care were seriously affected by the outbreak of fighting. High levels of alcohol and drug use became particularly evident in combat zones as well as the brutal consequences. Similar high levels of drug use by US troops in Vietnam and by Russian troops in Afghanistan indicate an important area for study. Although Macedonia had been a traditional opium producer, there was little evidence of problem usage until the 1990s. Domestically produced heroin is now readily available, and a boom in consumption has been reported. Wholesale shipments involving hundreds of kilos are negotiated in Skopje. Processing and marketing is largely controlled by ethnic Albanians, a group that is also most affected by drug dependence (OGD 1996b).

Slovenia and Croatia

Slovenia, with 35 land border-crossings, one airport, one seaport, and a 600-kilometre frontier with Croatia, became independent in 1991. With the disintegration of Yugoslavia and the outbreak of war, crime was characterised by an organised market in weapons and drugs and the illegal transfer of state-owned assets and companies into private hands. Although overall crime figures fell in 1993, professional criminals appeared to be more violent and better prepared. These trends persisted in 1994 as career criminals linked in with foreign crime groups, particularly with respect to drug and weapons trafficking. The impact of the conflict to the south on social conditions in Slovenia appeared to perpetuate these trends, although while drug-related crime continued to rise in 1994, the recorded number of offences related to arms-trafficking actually decreased from 1991 (Svetek 1995).

Drug use emerged as a major problem in the latter half of the 1980s. Falling heroin prices were accompanied by growing acceptability of its use among young people. Social deprivation, unemployment and socio-political change played their part. There was a marked increase in the supply and demand for heroin in 1990–91, with an estimated 1,500 injecting drug users by 1992 and 3,000 in 1994 (Nolimal 1992; Krek 1994). In reviewing Slovenia's response to the need for harm-reduction policies, Nolimal indicates how priorities related to economic difficulties, political intrigue, refugee problems and war took precedence over those related to HIV infection and addiction.

Krek (1994) suggests that Slovenia's location at the western end of the traditional Balkan route meant that spillage would inevitably occur. A dynamic link between the bordering markets of Slovenia and Northeast Italy has evolved with Slovenes selling in Italy and Italians seeking cheaper heroin in Slovenia. Overland traffic has historically passed through Gorizia, and a new maritime route has opened up to the port of Koper. Low-cost heroin also enters Slovenia from Croatia and Bohemia. Drug users frequently travel from Slovenia to Croatia to buy heroin. While bulk transit routes into western Europe, particularly via Hungary, have been developed since war broke out, supplies for local consumption pass through Zagreb and Ljubljana. Slovenian and Croatian observers strongly suggest that there has been an intrinsic connection between the military conflict, dealing and drug consumption (ibid.).

Turks, Kosovo Albanians and Macedonians are most commonly involved in transit trafficking. Kosovo Albanians also deliver two- to four-kilo units of heroin directly to the Slovenian market with collateral payments being made in Macedonia, Albania or Italy. Turkish heroin bought in Macedonia is markedly cheaper than purchases made in Slovenia or Croatia (Sakoman 1992; Sakoman and Hecimovic 1991). While Slovenians rank first among local users in Slovenia, enforcement sources believe that Croats, Albanians and Bosnians are more frequently involved in distribution. There is a clear element of distrust between the republics of the former Yugoslavia, reflecting wider conflicts.

As in Slovenia, spillage and the pressures of war have contributed to the growth of Croatia's internal drug market. Its strategic position, sharing landward frontiers with Slovenia, Hungary, Serbia, and Bosnia-Herzegovina, and its lengthy coastline have been exploited by traffickers and have made heroin supplies readily available. There may be as many as 4,000–5,000 regular opiate users in the country (Sakoman 1992). The loosening of social controls, deprivation and anxieties created by war conditions have contributed to increased adolescent heroin use and the emergence of a cocaine market. Heroin is particularly evident in the ports of Split, Zadar, Rijeka, Pula and Sibenik which have seen increases in drug-related crime. Historically, Split and Pula have had busy markets with drug users also travelling to make purchases from other towns and republics. Split, in particular, has experienced a mixture of repression and complicity that has contributed to its drug problem (Sakoman 1992). While the war situation reduced police and prevention activity, smugglers in tobacco, arms, drugs and migrant people have been active along the litoral from Trieste in the north to Albania in the south.

There has been a significant increase in local drug consumption in Mostar since the heavy fighting of 1993–4. There is also a flourishing cannabis agribusiness in the surrounding area. Split became a major trafficking centre during the war, importing embargoed fuel and arms as well as drugs. In Dubrovnik, too, drugs were linked to weapons trading through Bosnia, Albania, Macedonia and a criminalised military. Subsequently, criminal groupings have invested profits in hotels and businesses through Croatia's privatisation programme (OGD 1996c; Middleton 1994). The extensive overlapping of political, military and criminal structures created a form of warlordism evident in many of the combat zones. This, combined with a loss of policing controls, the use of drugs as a form of currency to trade in weapons, and a recourse to dealing by the dispossessed, gave further impetus to retail markets.

Conclusion

Social and political destabilisation within the Balkans and beyond has proved advantageous to illicit traffickers, opening up new markets and opportunities for the delivery of drugs, weapons, and other commodities. Innovative routes and arrangements have been developed that both circumvented and exploited areas of conflict. War conditions have hindered international enforcement, while generating the most unlikely alliances.

Conflict and war have directly affected drug distribution and other criminal activities in the former Yugoslavia and beyond. Conditions in Macedonia, as well as trading opportunities that arose, meant that Kosovo Albanians were already active in Swiss and other heroin markets well before war broke out. Changes in their home environment had helped to create a pool of émigré criminal labour, promote the development of the 'short-network' delivery system and encourage the purchase of arms with heroin profits. Elsewhere, recent important developments in Italian organised crime arose within the context of the Balkan conflict. The Puglia-based Sacra Corona Unita (SCU) through its domination of seaborne contraband made a qualitative and quantitative leap in power and influence. Albanian and Macedonian trafficking groups with subsidiary or independent bases in Rome acquired the standing to negotiate with Italian mafia-type organisations on an equal footing. Criminal ethnic Chinese groups also became increasingly active in Italy, utilising the Silk Route via the central Asian republics and Albania to enter the peninsula. Nor has this been a one-way process. Casinos and other forms of enterprise with a money-laundering capacity in the former Yugoslavia have attracted both Italian and Turkish criminal investment (Longo and Moder 1995).

Transit spillage of heroin occurred in Yugoslavia in the past, unlike in some other eastern-European countries where markets have been less developed and currency has not been convertible (Hartnoll 1989; Ruggiero and South 1995: 69). The direct targeting of purchasers has created established markets in Slovenia and Croatia that require more organisation and skill than the opportunistic transactions associated with unplanned leakage. The Croatian coast continues to experience high levels of smuggling and consumption. User/dealers have benefited from price differentials between Croatia, Slovenia and northeast Italy, but not to the extent that user/dealers profited in northeast Italy from high product availability in the early 1980s. This may be because bulk supply in Slovenia and Croatia is largely controlled by career criminals from the southern republics.

The Balkan conflict did not hinder the flow of drugs to Slovenia, Croatia and their neighbours. It seemed to do quite the reverse. The social distress that accompanies war may continue to generate further demand. It is hard to predict what the long-term consequences of the increased demand will be in terms of the future development of organised criminality in the region, and its impact on the general population. Political change and the determination of public-health officials to implement efficient and effective harm-minimisation policies may help to reform the criminal justice and health systems and limit potential damage.

Notes

General note: while this paper focuses specifically on drugs, war and illegal enterprise in the Balkan region, it was influenced and informed by a wider study of the conflict's impact on heroin supply and consumption throughout Europe. A detailed literature review was carried out and in-depth interviews conducted with specialists in a variety of fields.

Research visits were made to Italy, Switzerland, Austria and Slovenia, and the cities of Verona, Zurich and Ljubljana selected as sample drug market sites. Quantitative criminal justice, treatment and other relevant data were collected where available, as were policy and planning documents, analyses of local activity, and qualitative descriptions of illicit markets by enforcement officers, health-care staff and drug users themselves. Given the nature of the subject matter, care has been taken to ensure that contemporary accounts of events in the Balkans that validated the study's findings are cited wherever possible.

1 The author would like to thank the Council of Europe Pompidou Group Fellowship scheme for funding the research visits that contributed to this paper.

References

Almond, M. (1994) *Europe's backyard war*, London: Mandarin.

Andreas, P. (1995) 'Free market reform and drug market prohibition: US policies at cross-purposes in Latin America', *Third World Quarterly* 16, 1: 75–87.

Andreas, P. (1996) 'U.S.–Mexico: open markets, closed border', *Foreign Policy* 103, 2: 51–69.

Auchlin, P. (1993); 'Per favore; mi incarti quarantanove kalashnikov', *Narcomafie* 1, 4: 27–8.

Bell, M. (1995) *In Harm's Way*, London: Penguin.

Berger, J. F. (1995) *The humanitarian diplomacy of the ICRC*, Geneva: ICRC.

Europol (1993) 'The drugs threat from eastern Europe', unpublished report, Strasbourg.

Giordano, A. (1996) 'Paraboloide, un'inchiesta pagata cara', *Narcomafie*, 4, 6: 35.

Glenny, M. (1993) *The fall of Yugoslavia*, London: Penguin.

Glenny, M. (1996) 'Why the Balkans are so violent', *New York Review of Books* 43, 14: 34–9.

Grosso, L. (1993) 'Quant' era scomoda l'eroina al caramello', *Narcomafie* 1, 4: 15–16.

Hartnoll, R. (1989) 'The international context', in S. MacGregor (ed.) *Drugs and British society*, London: Routledge.

INCB (1994) *Report of the International Narcotics Control Board for 1993*. Vienna: United Nations.

INCB (1995) *Report of the International Narcotics Control Board for 1994*, Vienna: United Nations.

Jamieson, A. (ed.) (1994) *Terrorism and drug trafficking in the 1990s*, Aldershot: Dartmouth.

Jamieson, A. (1995) 'Geografia criminale del made in Italy', *Narcomafie* 3, 8: 15–26.

Koutouzis, M. (1995) 'L'eroina sulle vie della seta', *Narcomafie* 3, 7: 21–4.

Krek, M. (1994) 'General review of the sphere of the IV drug addicts in Slovenia', unpublished paper, 2nd Pan-European Ministerial conference on co-operation on illicit drug abuse problems, Pompidou group, Strasbourg.

Longo, F. and Moder, M. (1995) 'Con la lira debole alla fiera dell'Est', *Narcomafie* 3, 3: 6–7.

Middleton, J. (1994) 'Drug misuse in Croatia', *Lancet* 344, 8921: 64.

Moder, M. (1994) 'L'Europa al mercato dei cavalli di Frisia', *Narcomafie* 2, 4: 11–13.

Moder, M. (1996) 'A casa no si puo, in Italia nemmeno', *Narcomafie* 4, 1: 9.

Newsday (1975) *The heroin trail*, London: Souvenir Press. (In particular, see the account of the role of the Bulgarian Kintex import–export company during the 1970s.)

Nolimal, D. (1992) 'Drug Abuse and the HIV/AIDS situation in Slovenia', paper prepared for the 36th International Congress on alcohol and drug dependence, Glasgow.

Observatoire Geopolitique des Drogues. (1994) 'L'ombra della Grande Albania', *Narcomafie* 2, 7: 42–3.

OGD Correspondent. (1995) 'Italy: Mafia overhaul in the north', *Geopolitical Drug Dispatch* 5, 45:1–4.

OGD Correspondent. (1996a) 'Serbia: the three state pillars of the drugs trade', *Geopolitical Drug Dispatch* 8, 58: 1–3.

OGD Correspondent. (1996b) 'Macedonia: heroin precursors', *Geopolitical Drug Dispatch* 7, 57: 5–6.

OGD Correspondent. (1996c) 'Bosnia-Herzegovina: 'federating' criminal-political networks', *Geopolitical Drug Dispatch* 6, 56: 1–5.

Owen, D. (1996) *Balkan Odyssey*. London: Indigo.

Ruggiero, V and South, N. (1995) *Eurodrugs: drug use, markets and trafficking in Europe*, London: UCL Press.

Rumiz, P. (1994) 'Le rotte del traffico nello spazio jugoslavo', *Narcomafie* 2, 4:14–15.

Rumiz, P. (1994a) *La linea dei mirtilli*, Trieste: Ote-Il Piccolo.

Sakoman, S. (1992) 'Drug abuse and addiction control programme in Croatia', paper for 17th meeting of epidemiology experts in drug problems, Pompidou Group, Strasbourg.

Sakoman, S. and Hecimovic, A. (1991) 'Drug addiction and AIDS in the republic of Croatia and Yugoslavia', in N. Loimer (ed.) *Drug addiction and AIDS*, Vienna: Springer Verlag.

Silber, L. and Little, A. (1995) *The death of Yugoslavia*, London: Penguin.

Smale, A. (1996) 'Politicians dither as Bulgaria slides', *Guardian*, July 27.

Sterling, C. (1994) *Crime without frontiers*, New York: Little Brown.

Sundaralingham, R. (1988) 'The Balkan route 1986–87', *National Drugs Intelligence Unit Bulletin*.

Svetek, S. (1995) *The battle against crime in the republic of Slovenia*, Ljubljana: Ministry of the Interior.

Travis, A. (1996) 'Heroin dealers target lucrative UK', *Guardian* March 19.

Traynor, I. (1995) 'Tide of desolation floods Croatia', *Gaurdian* August 16.

UN Commission on Narcotic Drugs (1995) *Illicit Drug Trafficking: report of the secretariat*, Vienna: E/CN.7/1995/7.

UN Commission on Narcotic Drugs (1995a) *Economic and social consequences of drug abuse and illicit trafficking: an interim report, Note by the secretariat*, Vienna, E/CN.7/1995/3

UN Commission on Narcotic Drugs. (1995b) *Reduction of illicit demand for drugs: report of the secretariat*, Vienna, E/CN.7/1995/5

Vastano, L. (1994) 'Geografia industriale della guerra di Bosnia', *Narcomafie* 2, 4, 23–6.

15

THE MARKET AND CRIME IN RUSSIA

Yakov Gilinskiy

Introduction

The social situation in Russia

In any given society, the level and character of crime (as well as the distribution of other types of deviant behaviour – drug addiction, alcoholism, suicide, etc.) depend on the social, economic, political and demographic processes at work in that society.

It is impossible to single out any one reason for the extremely serious and total crisis currently affecting Russian society. Much of it has historical roots: the lack of a democratic tradition in Russia; the country's marginality (and also its proximity) to the west; the nature of the Orthodox religious ethical system as opposed to Protestant religion; the centuries-long tradition of despotism, etc. The immediate source of today's problems begin in October 1917 with the unique social experiment to forcibly establish a social utopia (the slogan on the gate of the Solovki Labour Camp read 'Happiness for Everyone Through Violence').

The attempt to build utopia was accompanied by an unprecedented 'process of negative selection' which saw those who were most proficient in their field (scientists, writers, philosophers, workers, artists, 'kulaks' [property-owning peasants], military leaders and political activists) undergoing repression, exile or destruction whilst the grey, mediocre (often criminally-minded) elements of society were championed. This process of repression did not stop short of genocide, and the Soviet State (and Russian society) eventually confronted a situation of catastrophe. The main symptoms of this catastrophe were the disintegration of production and the economy; the loss of trade skills; the de-professionalisation and de-qualification of the majority of the working population; the lumpenisation of the people; the lack, and non-development of, a middle class which might have provided some kind of social stability; continuing crises in the health, education, transport and other social services; a sequence of inter-ethnic conflicts resulting in large numbers of deaths; a series of political crises; crises in spirituality and morality; the increase in various forms of deviant behaviour (crime, drug addiction, suicide, etc.), and the growth of Mafia-type organised crime.

Gorbachev's Perestroika was a necessary attempt to save existing power structures through a process of internal reform. A similar attempt had previously been made by Khrushchev (the 'Thaw'). However, all previous attempts at such reform ended with the actual or political death of their propagators and were followed by 'Stagnation'.

With all due credit to Gorbachev, his reforms turned out to be the most radical (Glasnost, the multi-party system, the release of those states occupied by Stalin – Latvia, Lithuania and Estonia – the lifting of the Iron Curtain, and the right to hold private property) but even these did not turn out to be fully satisfactory. The symptoms of socio-economic catastrophe we mentioned above remained untreated. Power was still returned to the ruling nomenclatura; corruption, quite familiar in Russia, continued (and still continues) on a monumental scale in all organs of power and the Establishment, and the militarisation of economics and politics continues; inter-ethnic conflicts have given rise to vast numbers of deaths; nationalist, anti-Semitic and neo-fascist groups have re-formed and meet with little or no resistance (Laquer, 1994). The criminal war in Chechnya is a terrifying evidence of the neo-totalitarian impulse. The ever-growing economic polarisation of the population – visible in the stark contrast between the poverty-stricken majority and the wealth of the 'New Russians' (a criminalised, nouveau-riche minority) – is a guaranteed source of continuing social conflict.

The country is also witness to masses of human-rights abuses, particularly in the army and in penitentiaries and other penal institutions, where tyranny and torture are widespread. Confirmation of this may be found in the research completed by Amnesty International, as well as in research undertaken by Russian observers themselves (White Book of Russia, 1994; Amnesty International Newsletter, 1995; Abramkin, 1996).

It is hardly surprising that this kind of socio-economic and political situation in the country has led to a growth in crime and other types of deviant behaviour.

The market in Russia

The economic reform under way in Russia, involving a rapid transition from a planned state-run economy to a market economy, is without doubt a necessary and progressive move. Side by side with it, however, as many observers have noted, very many 'criminogenic' consequences can be observed.

The redistribution of property, for example, is being carried into effect not only by lawful means, but also by the widespread use of illegal methods (bribery, murder, threats).

There is also a process of sudden and deep economic and social polarisation of the population, with a large and pauperised majority on the one hand, and a minority which has grown very rich on the other. The distribution of income between the most and least prosperous widened significantly in just the three years between 1991 and 1994; where the ratio of the most to least prosperous stood at 1:4.5 in 1991, it had widened to 1:15 by 1994 (*Financial News*, 1992; Social and Economic Situation in the Russian Federation, 1994: 139). This rapidly widening gap between rich and poor is one major reason for the social instability and conflicts now engulfing Russia.

Implicit in the growth of poverty is the emergence of overt (explicit) unemployment and of partial (incomplete) employment in Russia. On official figures, the unemployment rate in Russia is by no means high, particularly when compared to many western societies. In 1992 some 4.7 per cent of the able-bodied population (3,588,000 people) were registered as unemployed – a figure that had risen by 1995 to 7.7 per cent (about 5.5 million). Still fewer Russian people are classified officially as being unemployed on a long-term basis: in 1994, only 0.5–0.7 per cent of Russians (61,759 people in total) actually received the unemployment allowance allowed in such circumstances (Russian Annual of Statistics, 1994). But it is important to note that the Russian people are not accustomed to unemployment. In the Soviet period, state subsidies ensured a condition of near-to-full employment (though there was always some latent structural unemployment). Second, of course, the recent statistics recording those in work in Russia do not themselves reveal how few of those able-bodied Russians currently registered as employed are employed *on a full time basis*. Very large numbers are working only on a part-time basis, for only a part of the day or week. Third, structural unemployment is growing. Fourth, given the low per-capita income of the majority of population, the current increases in unemployment add significantly to the psychological fear of becoming jobless. Opinion-poll data collected in St Petersburg shows that whilst in 1991 only 19 per cent of the respondents spoke of a fear of unemployment, by 1992 and 1993 the figure admitting to such fears had increased some 33–40 per cent.

According to other, national surveys, the number of crimes committed by able-bodied people *who had neither studied nor worked* increased from 110,018 in 1987 to 720,889 in 1995 (an increase of 650 per cent) (Crime and Delinquency, 1992; Crime and Delinquency, 1996). There is also a large number of people whom we may call the hidden employed or semi-employed, who are not caught in the official statistics. All the existing evidence suggests that the increase in their numbers runs parallel to the increase in the numbers of the officially unemployed.

In the course of the recent reforms, the technological backwardness of the Russian economy, especially in the spheres of production and services, has become absolutely clear. One consequence of this is a growing inferiority complex on the part of many Russian workers, newly aware of their own lack of qualifications, and the threat of their marginalisation and 'lumpenisation'. In the meantime, the disintegration of public services and of the social infrastructure has entailed further difficulties for the population. A study in St Petersburg by Kassinov, for example, highlighted the complete unreliability of local municipal transport and the contribution this makes to low levels of public morale and often to incidents of violence – the products of frustration and anger amongst citizens.

Similar stresses and strains can easily be observed in respect of the provision of heating and light, and other services providing for fundamental human needs.

The virtual neglect of children and teenagers, by parents too busy with the daily acquisition of subsistence is also a major problem in contemporary Russia. Publicly-run out-of-school centres for children and teenagers have largely been closed down because of lack of state financing, whilst private ones charge exorbitant tariffs, which very few can afford. Alongside all that, however, the amount and range of 'temptations' (fashionable youth clothes, audio and video appliances, sweetmeats) has grown sharply, thus encouraging the adoption of illegal means for acquiring them. The rate of recorded juvenile delinquency (per 100,000, age group 14–17) has gone up from 1510 in 1987 to 2420 in 1995 (160 per cent), and the amount of 'hidden delinquency', unrecorded by the police, is extremely high (Crime and Delinquency, 1992; Crime and Delinquency, 1996).

As Durkheim himself would have understood, the sheer speed of the changes occurring during the reform period has itself produced considerable disorientation in respect of social values and norms – and, indeed, a state of anomie. There is an obvious contradiction between the old sets of values (with their core emphasis on equality) and the new (emphasising wealth and enterprise), between old legal ideas and norms (private enterprise is a crime – article 153 Criminal Code, 1960) and new (private enterprise is the norm), between old moral norms (wealth is evidence of vice and evil) and new norms (celebrating personal wealth), between civil and criminal law, as well as between the Constitution of the Russian Federation and the other legislation. There are many spheres of social life in which the writ of the law does not run, and many areas of life where there is, in effect, a vacuum of values and ideals.

There is widespread recognition and popular discussion of mistakes on the part of the country's leadership in carrying the economic reforms into effect, and also considerable evidence of corruption – not least, the suspicion that the nomenclatura from the Soviet period has successfully positioned itself to take personal advantage of the process of privatisation (for example by its application of public funds, late in the Soviet period, for use in the creation of private banks, now trading on the open market).

Crime in Russia

The incidence of recorded crime in Russia has risen from 987 offences per 100,000 people in 1985 to 1,857 in 1995 (Table 15.1).[1] The increase in violent crime over the last decade has been particularly significant: the incidence rate for *premeditated murder*, for example, rising from 8.5 in 1985 to 21.4 in 1995 (153 per cent increase), and the recorded incidence of *serious bodily harm* from 19.9 to 41.6 over the same period (109 per cent) (Table 15.1). Such an explosive growth in the level of violent crime, measuring, as it does, only those offences reported to the police, indicates the severity and depth of the process of criminalisation in Russia, and should be seen as an index of the severity of the condition of social

Table 15.1 Trends in Crime in Russia 1985–1996

	1985	1986	1987	1988	1989	1990	1991	1992	1993	1994	1995	1996
Premeditated murders (including attempts), absolute number	12,160	9,434	9,199	10,572	13,543	15,566	16,122	23,006	29,213	32,286	31,703	29,406
Rate	8.5	6.6	6.3	7.2	9.2	10.5	10.9	15.5	19.7	21.8	21.4	19.8
Grievous bodily harm, absolute number	28,381	21,185	20,100	26,636	36,872	40,962	41,195	53,873	66,902	67,706	61,734	53,417
Rate	19.9	14.7	13.9	18.2	25.0	27.7	27.8	36.2	45.1	45.7	41.6	36.0
Larceny-theft, absolute number	464,141	380,582	364,511	478,913	754,824	913,076	1,240,636	1,650,852	1,579,600	1,314,788	1,367,866	1,207,478
Rate	324.7	264.4	251.1	372.2	512.1	616.8	837.3	1,110.2	1,065.2	888.4	888.4	814.8
Robbery, absolute number	42,794	31,441	30,441	43,822	75,220	83,306	101,956	164,895	184,546	148,546	140,597	121,356
Rate	29.9	21.8	21.0	29.9	51.0	56.3	68.8	110.0	127.3	100.4	94.7	81.9
Aggravated assault, absolute number	8,264	6,018	5,656	8,118	14,551	16,514	18,311	30,407	40,180	37,904	37,631	34,584
Rate	5.8	4.2	3.9	5.5	9.9	11.2	12.4	20.4	27.0	25.6	25.4	23.3
Total number of registered crimes (in thousands)	14,169	13,384	11,859	12,204	16,192	18,394	21,679	27,606	27,996	26,327	27,557	26,251
Rate (per 100,000)	989.8	929.9	816.9	833.9	1,098.5	1,242.5	1,463.2	1,856.5	1,887.8	1,778.9	1,856.9	1,771.0

Sources: Crime and Delinquency (1992); Crime and Delinquency (1996).

crisis in the country.[2] The growth in the incidence of *robbery* has been particularly sharp – from 21.0 in 1987 to 94.7 in 1995 (a 351 per cent increase), whilst the incidence of *assault* increased by 650 per cent from 3.9 in 1987 to 25.4 in 1995 (Table 15.1). The suspicion is that the fall in the rate of recorded crime in 1994–1995 was primarily the product of new recording practices introduced by police management which are, in effect, a way of covering up the extent of crime in contemporary Russia. There are several different rationales for this interpretation. First, the growth in serious violent crime, which is much more regularly reported to the police than other offences, remains quite marked (premeditated murder by 10.5 per cent, grievous bodily harm by 1.2 per cent between 1994 and 1995) meaning that the reported decrease in crime as a whole is said to be occurring amongst those crimes with the least frequently reported incidents. So, for example, in St Petersburg, while the overall crime level 'decreased' by 12.7 per cent between 1994 and 1995, the incidence of premeditated murder increased by 13 per cent.

Second, it is well known that the level of premeditated murder, taken as a percentage of overall crime, is relatively stable (around 0.7–0.8 per cent of all recorded crime during the 1980s and 1990s in Russia). In 1994, this proportion increased by a factor of 1.6 (reaching 1.2 per cent of the total amount of recorded crime), which can only be explained by the artificial reduction in the number of other crimes.

Third, whilst the lack of professionalism (and also corruption) within the militia is ever on the increase, we are asked to believe that the number of crimes solved by the militia increased from 46.9 per cent in 1992 to 64.5 per cent in 1995. However, this increase in the 'clear-up rate' is surely to be explained in terms of the selective recording or registration by the militia of those crimes that are the least difficult to solve.

Fourth, in St Petersburg – according to the Victims Survey we mentioned earlier – some 26 per cent of respondents reported having been victims of crime in 1994. Three years earlier, in a similar survey, only 12 per cent had reported being victims of crime. So we have a doubling of the rate of self-reported victimisation over those three years, a period in which, according to official figures, crime had declined some 12 per cent.

The problem of organised crime

There has been an explosion, in very recent years, of scholarly and journalistic interest in the growth of organised crime, and particularly the growth of the 'Mafia' in Russia – and a significant amount of mythology, as well as mystery, has been created. We want to offer a few words on the character of organised crime in Russia as we see it.

Organised crime in any society involves the functioning of stable hierarchical associations, engaged in crime as a form of business whilst setting up a system of protection from public control, usually by means of protection rackets and other forms of corruption.

Criminal associations are a *kind of social organisation* of a 'working (labour) collective body' type. The growth of criminal associations is a natural process, in the sense that they are a manifestation of the social systems in which they develop as well as of specific features of their own 'subsystemic' development. Studies of organised crime have shown that the factors influencing the level of development and the specific form of organised crime are world-wide: they are not confined to Russia or even Sicily. The high degree of adaptivity of criminal associations (resulting from their strict labour discipline, their careful selection of staff, the high rate of profit and return, etc.) is a major factor in the survival of organised crime in any society, particularly once they are well established within that specific social system.

The members of criminal gangs – professional criminals – are generally not heroes, but neither are they 'the scum of the earth'. They are people engaged in their own business. In his pioneering essay on the economics of crime, for example, Gary Becker, the award-winning American neo-classical economist, argued that criminal activity is as much a profession or trade as joinery, engineering or teaching. As an activity, he argued, crime is chosen when the profit (the revenue minus the costs of production) involved in it exceeds that which can be realised in legal occupations (Becker, 1967). This process does not necessarily involve, or correspond with, the abstract moral or juridical laws of society, though it *is* on the other hand an activity akin to those in the legitimate economy, concerned with the satisfaction of routine social and economic needs. In this sense, the idea of drawing distinction between legal and criminal business according to accepted criteria of morality and legality is hardly possible in contemporary Russia.

I want to argue that the three specific models of organised crime acknowledged in the literature (hierarchical; local or ethnic models; and organised crime as a business) (Helly, Ko-Lin Chin and Schatzberg, 1994: 78–87) actually complement each other in practice. 'Business enterprise' constitutes the *content* of the organised crime activities, whereas hierarchical, local and ethnic models manifest the *organisational forms* of this activity. As we have already suggested, the literature of criminology throughout the world is increasingly recognising organised crime as a form of *business enterprise* (Helly, Ko-Lin Chin and Schatzberg, 1994: Arlacchi, 1986, 1998, in this volume). But in the Russian case, it is also important to recognise the way in which organised crime, through lobbying and direct infiltration, *directly attempts to influence Government and state*. Moreover, in Russia, we think it important to recognise the relatively high efficiency of organised crime particularly when compared with the forms of state-owned industry which went before: criminal associations, for example, are very careful in their selection of staff and very demanding in the discipline they impose on this newly-selected workforce. Generally speaking, they employ only the youngest, bravest and most enterprising of people with the greatest strength of character, and they do so strictly on the basis of 'payment by results'. The very high fees involved in organised crime, importantly, are several times higher than the remuneration on offer in nearly all the legitimate structures of Russian civil society, including the police itself.

Organised crime in Russia

Organised crime has a long history in Russia. Even in the aftermath of the 1917 revolution, the presence of a form of organised gangsterism was well-known to most Russians, and from the 1930s onwards, a curious but well-organised association known as the Thieves' Code or the Thieves' Parliament achieved ever greater prominence (the thief-in-law is a professional thief or swindler, who has chosen crime as a permanent way of life, who is well known in the local criminal world, obeys the 'thief's law', and even upholds this law in prison). In the 1950s there was much talk of the activities of the so-called 'tzechovici' [criminal groups within professions] at work in different places of employment; and, according to modern scholars, the 1970s witnessed the infiltration of the so-called 'tyenyevecki' [shady dealers] into existing state structures. It was during the tumultuous 1970–1990 period that some kind of contact was established and collaboration initiated between traditional 'white-collar' criminals (misappropriators of 'Socialist property'), dealers working in the hidden economy of crime, corrupt party and state functionaries, and the more committed criminals. Contemporary organised crime is a result of this process of amalgamation oriented to the pursuit of heightened levels of profit. The ongoing process of economic reform and privatisation in Russia takes place against this kind of background, and in this sense it is not surprising that one of the defining features of contemporary organised crime is its involvement, and the advantageous position it occupies, with the culture of enterprise. In present circumstances, indeed, it makes sense to see criminal enterprise as being *hegemonic* in many spheres of legitimate business – for example, in the official arms trade or in the provision of private protection and security, as well as in most illegitimate spheres (like the drugs trade,[3] the hidden economy in arms, or in other forms of protection).

The term mafia is widely used as a description of these developments, though it is not strictly scientific. In a broad sense the word 'mafia' serves as a synonym for any kind of structured association dedicated to the pursuit of crime in an organised, professional and full-time capacity. In a narrower sense, the term refers to criminal organisations akin to the originating example in Sicily, characterised, first, by a high degree of organisation and hierarchy and, second, by a regular resort to the use of force for attaining its goals. Both types of activity are quite common in contemporary Russian cities. Business activities in St Petersburg (and in many other regions of Russia) are closely overseen by groups that are locally referred to as 'mafia'. These are organised criminal groups with excellently organised informational services enabling them to track down and monitor most commercial transactions taking place in the city and, in particular, to identify the moment when a new commercial structure begins to make a profit. At this point, these mafia groups begin, on fear of retribution, to demand a tribute or perhaps, even, a controlling role within the commercial enterprise. Business people in St Petersburg have reported to us that this 'racket' has penetrated all enterprises, except for the old military-industrial complex and a few more sophisticated foreign firms.

The payment of 'tribute' operates at high levels of commerce, but also at street level. Organised criminal gangs, also referred to locally as 'mafia', will demand protection money from the tenants of the small kiosks that occupy vacant space on most city centre streets in St Petersburg (usually run by family members working together for many hours a day, trying to subsist on small-time trading). The mafiosi will tend to take care directly of more successful commercial enterprises by including their own representatives in the business, just as they do at a higher level. People cannot object, as first, the criminals have power, and second, who else can force a debtor to pay, even when the decision of the arbitration court is available? The main fields of activity of Russian criminal organisations include shady banking transactions with counterfeit letters of advice; fictitious transactions with real estate; hi-jacking and reselling of cars; illegal export of non-ferrous metals; black-market transactions with 'humanitarian aid' (bribing city functionaries); the production of, and trafficking in, contraband home-made alcohol; arms sales; counterfeiting money; control over gambling; and agencies for supplying sexual services and 'narcobusiness'.

The Mafia display a keen interest in privatisation. One respondent in St Petersburg, for example, insists that 'their goal is to take hold of real estate'. They obtain information about forthcoming auctions, come to the auctions accompanied by armed men and dictate who buys what property and at what price. Potential competitors from rival and legitimate business spheres are deterred from making any purchase for fear of trouble, or alternatively from fear for their own personal safety. Another quite widespread method for laying hands on real estate is to buy up company shares from workers fired from munitions plants and thereby to acquire a controlling interest.[4] There is also widespread suspicion that the growth of the massive network of banks and other financial institutions heavily involves the mafiosi, often on the board of such banks. There is a widespread sense of what we may call the criminalisation of all business.

Interviews we conducted in St Petersburg describe the enormous pressures on anyone entering into business to participate in different forms of illegal dealing. This is symbolised most of all in the universal payment of bribes. Bribes are required, for example, when registering enterprises, when taking the lease of premises from state bodies, when acquiring licences for utilisation of such premises from state bodies, when obtaining a favourable bank credit rating, when reporting to the tax inspectorate, when engaging in any customs formalities. Business people *have* to try to bribe the tax authorities; given the current taxation rate, amounting to 80–85 per cent, even an honest business person could not pay and survive. Most non-state-owned enterprises in contemporary conditions also pay money for the 'protection' of gangsters (mafia) i.e. they are 'guarded' by some gang, basically on the basis of a bribe, against others.

Conclusion

Levels of reported crime in Russia have been increasing with great rapidity during the 1990s, and the rate of violent crime, in particular, is now spectacularly high. Much of this has to do with the presence of highly organised forms of criminal activity, closely bound up with the forms assumed by the processes of privatisation during the 1992–1995 period. Organised crime in Russia, typically, is very closely implicated in the dominant areas of business activity and trade (one estimate is that it has a controlling interest in 40 to 60 per cent of all banking institutions and commercial enterprises). Very large rates of profit are also typically involved, far in excess of the salaries and other incentives that can be paid to the police or other legitimate state authorities. The state system is therefore prey to widespread corruption at all levels, with the payment of the bribes as the main, publicly-understood signifier of this widespread and fundamental corruption. In the sphere of businiess and commerce, the idea of honest business practice is almost a chimera. We describe the process as one of the criminalisation of the economy and of politics. On all present evidence, Russia seems to be heading further along this road of extended criminalisation, both in dominant areas of the economy and political life, and also at the level of everyday economic and social life. The process of democratisation and reform initiated by perestroika is in fundamental jeopardy.

Notes

1 The decrease in crime in 1986/87 was due, we would argue, to the initial impact of 'Perestroika' on the consciousness of the people. Following this, the social and political crisis caused the crime rate to rise again, in 1989, by 32 per cent and in 1992, by 27 per cent.

2 Health and morbidity statistics for Russia give a measure of the under-estimations involved in these particular police statistics. According to these data, the incidence of death by murder, for example, rose from 13.4 per 100,000 people in 1990 to 32.6 in 1994 – an increase of 146 per cent in three years (Russian Statistical Annual, 1996).

3 The drugs trade or 'narcobusiness' is one of the most well-organised dimensions of the hidden economy of crime in Russia, though it is not the main focus of this paper. One measure of the prevalence of drugs in Russian life is the number of registered users of narcotics: according to official sources, the number of such registered users increased from 48 per 100,000 people in 1991 to 105 in 1995, a period of just four years. Table 15.2 details the numbers of crimes which, in official records, were defined as being 'drug-related'. The bulk of these offences relates to possession, manufacturing and sale for personal use, without intention to sell (offences under the Russian Criminal Code, Article 224 parts 3 and 4). But in 1995 there were also some 3,734 recorded cases of intentional sale of narcotics. Research conducted in St Petersburg by the Institute of Sociology in 1994 suggested that some 7 per cent of children aged 12–14 had personally consumed narcotic or toxic substances, and 26 per cent of older children in a vocational school and 33 per cent of teenagers in a police reception centre admitted to doing so. In St Petersburg itself, there was some evidence of cocaine consumption, in addition to an

Table 15.2 Drug-related crime in Russia 1987–1996

	1987	1988	1989	1990	1991	1992	1993	1994	1995	1996
Drug thefts	823	470	439	413	433	315	475	529	691	546
Manufacture, sale, carriage, trafficking and acquisition	15,506	9,527	10,594	13,646	17,036	27,115	49,249	70,420	72,457	89,803
Persuade to drug use	503	194	130	182	187	190	338	613	648	666
Keeping 'drug dens' – premises for drug use	444	252	171	206	181	324	499	721	750	909
Forgery, making forged documents (prescriptions) for drug acquisition	602	248	277	222	296	*	285	162	129	112
Illegally growing poppies or cannabis	136	74	5	76	76	91	343	593	666	727
Breaking stock-taking and storage laws	365	776	793	642	488	813	1,066	1,690	1,886	2,335
The percentage of drug related crimes to common crime	1.6	1.0	0.8	0.9	0.9	1.1	1.9	2.8	2.9	3.7
The percentage of drug-addicts' crimes to common crime	.	0.2	0.1	0.1	0.1	0.2	*	*	*	*
The percentage of crimes which was committed at the condition of drug intoxication	0.3	0.2	0.2	0.2	0.2	0.2	0.7	0.5	0.4	0.4
Total	18,534	12,553	13,446	16,255	19,321	29,805	53,152	74,798	79,819	96,645
Rate (per 100,000) citizens	12.7	8.6	9.1	10.9	13.0	20.0	35.7	50.3	54.7	67.9

Sources: Crime and Delinquency (1992); Crime and Delinquency (1996).

increase in use of hallucinogenics in both natural (the 'liberty cap' – a small mushroom found in the local forests) and synthetic forms (phencyclidine) – but opiates continue to have the greatest popularity. The main sources of narcotics in Russia as a whole are either the traditional sources within the territory of the former Soviet Union (Uzbekistan, Tadzhikistan, Turkmeniya, Kazakhstan and Kirgizya), but Russia is now a key transit point for drugs emanating from the Golden Triangle in South-East Asia en route to Europe.

4 Workers' ownership of shares arose from the way in which the privatisation of the bulk of state industry in Russia (some 8,000 larger industrial plants) was handled during the period between 1992 and 1995. With the encouragement of various advisors from the West, and under the leadership of Yegor Gaidar, economic policy advisor to President Yeltsin, workers were offered the choice of receiving vouchers to the value of 25 per cent of each firm's share capital for nothing, or alternatively of clubbing together to buy 51 per cent of the firm's shares. The vast bulk of these share vouchers have subsequently been bought up from share-owning workers by reputable and 'disreputable' financial institutions, and these institutions – not the workers – are now widely recognised to have been the main beneficiaries of the privatisation process. Robert Cottrell, 'Russia: The New Oligarchy' *New York Review of Books XLIV* (5) 27 March 1997: 28–30.

References

Abadinsky, H. (1994) *Organized Crime*, Fourth Edition. Chicago, Nelson-Hall.

Abramkin, V. (1996) *In Search of a Solution. Crime, Criminal Policy and Prison Facilities in the Former Soviet Union*, Moscow: Human Rights Publishers.

Amnesty International Newsletter (1995) *CIS: List of Facts*. London: Amnesty International.

Arlacchi, P. (1986) *Mafia Business: The Mafia Ethic and the Spirit of Capitalism*, London: Verso.

Becker, G. (1967) 'Economic Analysis and Human Behaviour', in *Advances in Behavioural Sciences*, Norwood, NY: Ablex.

Crime and Delinquency: Statistical Review, 1991 (1992) Moscow: Finansi I statistike (in Russian).

Crime and Delinquency: Statistical Review, 1995 (1996) Moscow: MVD RF (in Russian).

Financial News 1992 No. 2 (in Russian).

Gilinskiy, Y. (1996) 'The Penal System and Other Forms of Social Control in Russia' *Nordisk Tidsskrift for Kriminalvidenskab*, 124–128.

Gilinskiy, Y., Podkolzin, V and Kochetkov, E. (1994) 'The Drug Problems in St Petersburg' in *Petersburg in the Early 90's: Crazy, Cold, Cruel*, St Petersburg: Nochlezhka Foundation, 218–222.

Helly, R., Ko-Lin Chin and Schatzbery, R. (eds) (1994) *Handbook of Organized Crime in the United States*, Greenwood Press.

Laquer, W. (1994) *Black Hundred: The Rise of the Extreme Right in Russia*, New York: Harper.

Russian Annual of Statistics (1994) Moscow: Gosstat (in Russian).

Russian Statistical Annual 1995 (1996) Moscow: Statistika.

Social and Economic Situation in the Russian Federation (1994) Moscow: Gosstat (in Russian).

White Book of Russia: (Observations and Recommendations in the Field of Human Rights) (1994) Frankfurt am Main: Internationale Gesellschaft für Menschenrecht.

16

RUSSIAN ORGANISED CRIME

Moving beyond ideology

Patricia Rawlinson

The failed coup of August 1991 saw the final collapse of the Soviet structures of power, an ironic end to the ambitious reforms of perestroika and democratisation which had aimed at strengthening the very system they ultimately helped to destroy. The subsequent euphoria on the part of the reformers and their ideological allies, the Western capitalist states, translated into the assumption that Russia now would be able to complete the transition to a full market economy and adopt Western-style liberal democratic style of governance. Few were naïve enough to believe that the transition would be easy. But even fewer could appreciate the extent to which negative social phenomena, particularly organised crime, would flourish under the new conditions and, as they had done under Gorbachev, threaten the development of Yeltsin's 'new Russia'. Less than two years after the coup, crime, and particularly organised crime, was acknowledged as 'problem number one' in Russia (*Pravda*, 13 February 1993). Organised crime, or the 'mafiya' as it became known,[1] had infiltrated every sector of the economy, threatened significantly to undermine the move towards political democracy and had such an impact on social consciousness that it became one of the key issues upon which political parties based their programmes and manifestos.[2]

The total transformation of the economy did not, as the reformers of the Gorbachev era had hoped, reduce organised criminal activity by legitimising the ubiquitous operations of the black market. Indeed crime, particularly in the economic sphere, continued to spiral upwards.[3] Organised crime became a politically explosive phenomenon. Die-hard communists became more vociferous in their condemnation of the capitalist reforms, pointing to the growth of organised crime as an inevitable consequence of the inherent exploitation of such a system, while the pro-market government and its Western supporters continued to blame the old regime for deep-seated corruption which they realised would be impossible to eradicate in a short period of time. Both sides argued their case from an ideological standpoint, that is, they concentrated on the 'who' rather than the 'what' of organised crime. It was also a stance taken by many Western commentators, including Claire Sterling (1994), Stephen Handelman (1994) and the media at large. The fact that organised crime has proliferated under two ideologically opposing systems belies the accusations each camp has hurled at the other in reducing the debate to empty Cold-War rhetoric. Such an approach acts as a dangerous diversion away from one of the major problems of studying and dealing with organised crime, that is, how to define and identify it. Assumptions are made regarding the nature of organised crime, and as a corollary, the nature of the market mechanisms within which it operates. Dwight Smith, in his study of organised crime in the US, offers a caveat which has particular significance for Russia:

> The observer who first looks at events and then at the persons associated with them is more likely to adopt a scientific, value-free and causal analytic style. The observer who defines a universe by the people it contains is more prone to bias and to non-testable assumptions – in short, to conclusions that are based more on ideology than logic.
>
> (Smith 1991: 136)

Alerted by Smith's observations this chapter argues that the nature and extent of organised criminal activity in contemporary Russia is not solely the result of failed Soviet Communism (ideology). More significant is an analysis of the interactive relationship between Soviet and Russian legitimate and illegitimate structures (organised crime), and how this relationship became dangerously balanced in favour of the latter as a consequence of major political and economic upheavals. Hence it is the nature of this relationship rather than the actors involved which has encouraged the present criminogenic condition of Russia. Further, by concentrating on ideological definitions of organised crime and the more orthodox representation of the 'gangster', as depicted in the Western and Russian media, we detract attention away from what is arguably the most critical area of organised criminal activity, that is, where licit and illicit business interface. From this viewpoint we can extricate the argument from the limitations of ideology and culture, whilst maintaining their significance, and broaden the debate beyond national differences. This would therefore imply that we in the West should not assume a complacent attitude regarding the extent to which our own dominant systems are immune to an interactive relationship with organised crime, irrespective of the ideology which underpins them.

The nature of this interactive relationship is described through a model I have called the Chameleon Syndrome (see Figure 16.1). The model demonstrates that it has been the *response* of the legitimate structures towards the presence of organised crime which has determined the development of the latter. Organised crime cannot, as Mike Woodiwiss points out, 'operate in a vacuum' (Woodiwiss 1993: 28). Some of the literature on the American-Italian Mafia has indicated the existence of such a relationship, both at local and national level, between US politicians, law enforcement and business, and organised crime (Block 1993, Chambliss 1996, Pearce 1976, Woodiwiss 1990). However the strength and

ORGANISED CRIME		LEGITIMATE STRUCTURES
Bandits, teenage groups. No desire or ability to negotiate and break into the legitimate structures.	**Reactive** ↓	Usually strong. Political and economic stability. No need to negotiate.
Integration into *legitimate* structures, usually as informant or low level bribery. Restricted level of money laundering.	**Passive assimilative** ↓	Subtle weakening of structures, e.g. economic slump, law enforcement not in full control. Prepared to negotiate on prescribed terms.
Integration now more controlled. Bribery moves into higher level of *legit* structures. Money-laundering widespread. Active and significant participation in *legit* economy	**Active assimilative** ↓	Political and economic structures significantly weakened. Power vacuums. Grey areas between *legit* and *illegit* increases. Negotiation strength on a par with organised crime.
Significant control of *legit* structures, particularly economic and law enforcement. Manipulation in politics.	**Proactive**	Anomie. Acquiescence replaces negotiation.

Figure 16.1 The Chameleon Syndrome

stability of the American system has, so far, ensured that this relationship is controlled by the legitimate structures.

Organised crime needs to interact with the legitimate structures in order to expand its activities. At various stages of this interaction the legitimate structures become the dominating force behind the dynamics of the relationship. The condition of the legitimate structures determines their response to organised crime. This response can vary from antagonism to compromise or even encouragement. The type of response depends on the strength and needs of the legitimate structures at any one time. When the dominant system is stable it can control its response to organised crime by choosing to eradicate or manipulate it. More than likely it will opt for the latter as there exists a risk in negotiating with a criminal group, either on moral or expedient grounds, which by its very nature is hostile to the laws of the dominant system. However, if the legitimate structures begin to weaken, and in the case of the Soviet Union this occurred most notably in the economic sector, the pressure to negotiate with illegal organisations increases particularly if the services they offer can be used to the advantage of the dominant system. This was very much the case from the 1970s with the shadow economy and its quasi-acceptance by the Soviet authorities in the hope of offsetting the shortages within the official economy. The problem with prolonged negotiation is that both sides become increasingly interdependent. From the point of view of the lesser partner – organised crime – such interdependence is advantageous. For the legitimate structures however their negotiating position becomes increasingly fragile as they begin to lose their dominant position. The further they are forced to negotiate with organised crime the weaker they become. When a point of equilibrium is reached between the two the most obvious tendency is for the legitimate structures to further weaken as their claim to legitimacy demands that they operate within prescribed parameters, a restriction not placed on organised crime, which can behave according to its own rules. From this stage on, the balance of power shifts and organised crime becomes an active, or even, proactive partner, inextricably bound up with the legitimate structures and hence almost impossible to identify as a separate entity. In turn, the legitimate structures are increasingly pressurised to adopt criminal behaviour in order to survive. Organised crime now acts like a chameleon, blending into the very structures whose management it seeks and achieves.

This negotiation can go through four stages of development, impacting on the nature of organised crime. These four stages describe the capacity for organised criminal activity. They are: *reactive, passive assimilative, active assimilative* and *proactive*. It must be noted that these phases do not indicate a natural progression for every organised crime group. Some only develop as far as the reactive stage, others are immediately propelled into the proactive stage. Where and how a group develops depends upon its relationship to the appropriate legitimate structures and the condition of the latter. The four stages can be described as follows:

Reactive

This refers to organised crime when it operates outside of or contiguous to the dominant political, economic and legislative structures. The reactive phase occurs either when there is political stability and a relatively strong economy or when the organised crime group is insufficiently developed to impact on the legitimate structures. At this stage the legitimate structures refuse to negotiate as it is not in their immediate interests to do so. As the balance of power lies squarely with the legitimate structures organised crime can only respond or react according to the conduct of the former. Organised crime groups at a primitive stage of development tend to fall into this category, in particular youth gangs which lack the hierarchical sophistication and stability of the more complex formations.

Passive assimilative

This describes the first phase of negotiation with organised crime by the legitimate structures. It indicates an initial weakening of the dominant system which needs to acquire from illegal sources that which the legal sector cannot provide. This can be either goods or services. At this stage control remains very much with the legitimate structures which dictate the terms of negotiation, limiting the extent to which organised crime can be assimilated into the system. Organised crime remains the passive partner but having been allowed a certain degree of contact with legitimate bodies it can start to push from within to acquire more control. Small-scale bribery, limited extortion and coercion mark the characteristics of organised crime at this level. It is possible to trace this phase back through most of Soviet (and occasionally Tsarist) history. It was evident in the GULAGs or camps and is particularly pertinent to the evolution of the shadow economy.

Active assimilative

This third stage has proven to be most significant for the development of organised crime in Russia. This involves penetration into the legitimate structures to a point at which a degree of autonomous action is reached in specific areas. It is at this stage that the balance of power between the two moves towards a dangerous equilibrium. The distinction between licit and illicit becomes increasingly ambiguous as both sides are actively involved in negotiation. From around 1987 until the August coup of 1991, the period during which Gorbachev introduced his Draconian political and economic reforms, most notably the Law on Individual Labour Activity (1987), the Resolution on Joint Ventures (1987) and the Law on Co-operatives (1988) organised crime began to dominate the economic life of the emerging socialist market. Bribery, corruption, protection rackets and numerous shady businesses which facilitated money-laundering flourished in an environment of uncertainty and instability. Organised crime was becoming ubiquitous as the old system began to crumble under the weight of failing reforms. The symbiotic relationship, most significantly between organised crime and the economic sector and criminal justice system, seriously weakened the legitimate structures rendering them increasingly impotent to curb the criminal influence.

Proactive

The final phase of development describes organised crime as the major holder of power. It now has the ability to influence policy-making, to terrorise those who oppose it without fear of redress and to penetrate major institutions such as the media, banking and ultimately, politics. At this stage it is impossible to distinguish between legitimate and illegitimate activities and institutions. If detection does occur the more powerful groups can buy or threaten their way around the judicial system, or in the case of high level economic activity, eradicate those who obstruct their operations. Law enforcement can tackle only those groups which remain at the lower stages of development. Organised crime has become the chameleon, blending into the background of any enterprise or institution it desires, and acting with impunity in its desire to fulfil its own goals.

A brief history of organised crime

Alexander Konstantinov's advice 'To understand organised crime in Russia today you need to go back to Tsarist Russia' (Konstantinov 1994) is applicable to an understanding not just of organised crime but of the evolution of those dominant structures which helped shape contemporary politics and society and now struggle to survive. The history of organised crime in Tsarist Russia and the early years of Soviet communism can be roughly divided into two categories: political banditry[4] and underworld gangs. Of the two, it was political banditry which had the greatest influence on the perception of criminal organisations, an understanding which dominated the criminal justice system until the recent reforms of the Criminal Code in 1995. Up until this time organised crime was described as Banditism, a state crime of which Article 77 of the RSFSR Criminal Code offered the following ambiguous definition:

> the organisation of armed gangs having the intention to attack government or public enterprises, institutions, organisations or private individuals, and in like manner, the participation in such gangs and the carrying out of such attacks.
>
> (*Ugolovni Kodeks RSFSR* 1987)

No mention was made of economic types of crime such as the sale of illegal goods and services or racketeering. In an autocratic or totalitarian system, crimes threatening the state, which controlled all or most of the institutions and functions of the country, were regarded as the most heinous. Economic and other non-political crimes would therefore have lower priority.

In the seventeenth and eighteenth centuries banditry was endemic in Tsarist Russia but remained localised and of little real threat to the status quo. The two exceptions were the rebellions led by the bandit leaders Stenka Razin and Emelyan Pugachev, both of whom incited hordes of supporters to protest at the harsh conditions endured by their Cossack communities. The Tsars' response was uncompromising and hostile and both were executed. A century after Pugachev's death in 1775 another wave of armed resistance emerged to challenge Tsarist authority. This time however rebellion took on a revolutionary tone. Political groups were well organised and their activities often orchestrated by leaders exiled abroad. Some revolutionaries formed alliances with members of the traditional underworld in a symbiosis of 'the criminal' and 'the political' which would be echoed in the latter period of the Soviet regime. The Bolsheviks were particularly active in this liaison, with known criminals carrying out armed robberies of banks, post-offices and mail trains as a means of funding their organisation. Unlike their peasant forebears however, they met with little resistance from Tsar Nicholas II who had been severely weakened by widespread social discontent culminating in the devastating impact on Russia of the First World War. When they took the reins of power in 1917, the Bolsheviks, knowing the strength and tactics of armed resistance, set about ruthlessly eradicating all counter-revolutionary groups. As attention was heavily focused on political criminal groups, the more traditional underworld gangs were able to not only survive, but in the case of those individuals who had worked with the Bolsheviks before the revolution, were promoted into the new positions of authority under the Communist government, including those involved in law enforcement (Ovschinskii 1994).

The criminal underworld flourished in the pre- and post-revolutionary social and economic chaos. Murder and theft showed dramatic rises alongside gang violence (Gernet 1991: xxv). One bandit leader, Misha Kultyapi, was alleged to have taken part in seventy eight gruesome murders (Gernet 1991: xxvii). Other groups such as the Black Mask Gang Band (*Shaika Chornoi Maska*), the Band of the Forest Devil (*Band Lesnogo Dyabola*), and Your Money Will Be Ours (*Vashi Dengi Budut Nashi*), carried out armed robberies against individual householders and businesses (Golinkov 1971: 76) There was a certain ambivalence towards those who offended against private property as the state itself was now in the act of appropriating industries and businesses under the nationalisation scheme known as War Communism (1918–20). Of more importance to the authorities was the protection of these assets newly acquired from their previous owners, many of whom banded together to form organised groups involved in sabotage and terrorist activities. These groups offered the greatest threat to the new regime and, as with Razin and Pugachev under Tsarism, were automatically executed, in many instances by the Cheka,[5] without a trial. The reactive response by the dominant structures to this type of crime ensured that, while the appropriate ruling governments were strong, such types of organised criminality, in the broadest sense of the word, could be either eradicated or contained. By the end of the 1920s the majority of political banditry, with the exception of that in some Central Asian states, had been eradicated.

The response by the Soviet authorities to more traditional forms of organised crime and professional thieves, the latter whom became known as *vory v zakone*, literally 'thieves-in-law', was more tolerant – particularly in the GULAGs or labour camps where the *vory* served as unofficial agents of control, policing the ever-increasing numbers of inmates who were sent to the camps during Stalinism. Prisoners who broke the unwritten laws or codes of the underworld were severely punished by the *vory* or *pakhany*. The War of the Bitches (*suki*) – an internecine conflict which involved the deaths of hundreds of inmates across the country – was an extreme example of the punitive measures taken against apostasy and betrayal of the code (Gurov: 1995, Konstantinov and Dixelius: 1995). Few of the *vory* however would consider their role in the camps as an act of collusion with the authorities. Unlike some of their successors the idea of infiltrating the legitimate structures as a means of wealth and power acquisition was anathema to them. Allegiance lay with the *vorovkoi mir*, or thieves' world. However as new and more violent groups began to control the camps after the divisive War of the Bitches, old traditions were replaced by a new breed of criminal and ambitions. Years later old *vory* were to lament the passing of the good old days:

> And this is how it has now turned out. A thief-in-law now works as the head of a co-operative, as a businessman, acting legally. . . To be 'in-law' for us meant simply to be a professional thief.
>
> (Gurov and Riabinin: 1991)

The new gangs and leaders were more materially ambitious. Norms which had preserved the honour of the underworld were replaced by those which filled the pockets of its elite. It was in many ways a mirror image of what was happening in the legitimate structures. The two worlds were soon to be united in a common goal: self preservation and self advancement.

The centre cannot hold

Growing corruption and a proliferating black market became the hallmarks of the Brezhnev era and have been described in detail by Soviet writers in exile (Simis: 1982, Chalidze: 1977). The ubiquitous presence of these negative phenomena signified the weakening of the Soviet regime even at this point in time. Corruption within the nomenklatura grew unchecked by a law enforcement structure that was totally subservient to the ruling elite, that is, the Communist Party. Agencies such as the KGB and the MVD (Ministry of Interior) were constantly required to cover up the malfeasance of their bosses and in doing so betray the ideology upon which the system claimed its legitimacy. The gulf between theory and practice grew ever greater, resulting in a dangerous cynicism and disregard for Marxist–Leninist dogma, particularly amongst the young. The weakness of the ruling structures was further exacerbated by a drop in the country's productive output, especially from the end of the 1970s. By the early 1990s, one economist estimated that growth had gone into reverse (Hanson 1992: 12). Economic failure was a particular disaster for the USSR. The legitimacy of the state had previously rested heavily on an economic foundation, on the idea of wealth creation by the people for the people. Centralised planning was intended to 'increase the total of productive forces as rapidly as possible' which would be 'concentrated in the hands of a vast association of the whole nation' (Marx 1978: 490). Hence economic failure meant the political failure of the Communist Party. Shortages were not just a sign that the economy was dysfunctional but that the political elite was failing to fulfil its claims to legitimacy. The authorities were therefore forced into a tolerance of the shadow economy which was helping to offset potential social explosions resulting from the inefficiencies of the legitimate economy. However in so doing they further exacerbated the shortages, as more and more goods were being misappropriated from the legitimate sector to be sold on the black market. Effectively the shadow economy was simultaneously supplementary to and parasitic on the legal economy. Toleration of economic crime meant toleration of its operators. An unarticulated negotiation was in process between the authorities and the underworld but the longer this negotiation continued the weaker the official partner became.

Heralding free enterprise

The powerhouse of illegal economic activity from the mid 1970s was to be found in the underground factories run by the *tsekhoviki*, managers of illegal enterprises which produced millions of roubles worth of goods in short supply. The majority operated under political patronage (*krysha*) or by directly bribing local officials and members of the criminal justice system. By the 1980s they had become an inexpendable part of the economic life of the country but continued to remain dependent on the good will and continuing status of their patrons. The disruption of some political-criminal alliances during Andropov's anti-corruption campaign broke a few of the top-level networks but made little impression on corrupt practice as a whole, so systemic had it become (Vaksberg 1991).

Increasing wealth accumulation in the underworld was to create the ideal environment for racketeering. Gangs like the Dnepropetrovsk group, led by the Matross (Sailor), freely extorted money from vulnerable *tsekhoviki* and black marketeers, confident that there would be little response from law enforcement. As rivalry between underground businesses became fiercer, gangs were now called upon to work with their erstwhile victims by helping to eliminate competition, thus bringing the element of violence into the commercial world. It was not long before the more able gang bosses went into partnership with the *tsekhoviki*, accumulating expertise in the market and substantial amounts of capital, both of which were to become a vital pre-requisite for the assimilation of organised crime into the legitimate economy during perestroika and beyond.

Gorbachev's reforms: a Criminal Klondyke

Gorbachev's Russia did not give birth to organised crime, but it certainly provided the hothouse conditions for what was already well embedded in Russia's social and economic soil. When Gorbachev became General Secretary of the Communist Party in March 1985 the USSR was facing a number of crises, *inter alia* an increasingly apathetic workforce, frustrated by shortages, shoddy goods and a general lack of choice which increasingly turned to the black market on a daily basis. Even the Russian language accommodated the two-tier economic system. *Kupeet'* was to buy from legitimate outlets; *dostat'* meant to purchase (literally 'acquire') from illegal sources. Gorbachev prefaced his cautious move towards a socialist market with a disastrous anti-alcohol campaign, which was an attempt to increase labour efficiency. The lessons of American Prohibition were ignored and the consequences for the spread of organised crime more devastating. Bootleg alcohol transferred the much-needed government tax revenue, especially from vodka, into the pockets of underground distillers. As a further gift to organised crime, perestroika provided a plethora of opportunities for laundering its growing wealth. The Law on Individual Labour Activity (1987), the subsequent Law on Co-operatives (1988) and the resolution on the creation of joint ventures (1987) which included foreign partners, made private ownership, albeit within a limited framework, a legal reality. Rather than kick-starting the economy with the growth of incentive-driven enterprise, the new reforms became entangled in the old bureaucratic and economic systems. The remit was a contradiction in terms. The new ventures were supposed to provide those goods and services which were unavailable from the state sector, operating more efficiently since they would be run by self-motivated parties in the pursuit of profit. In reality many co-operators were forced into the illicit world of business by having to obtain the materials they required on the black market either through marketeers or by bribing officials. Both required considerable amounts of capital before business could even be established (Jones and Moskoff 1991: 78–86). Naturally those most advantaged possessed sufficient capital, market know-how and the ability to efficiently circumvent the law. All this was essential for economic growth. It was only a question of time before organised crime made significant inroads into this newly emergent market.

The rackets

In 1989 a Jewish colleague announced that he was leaving Leningrad with his father because of the danger they both faced. Believing his fear to be motivated by the recent spate of anti-semitism in the city it came as a complete surprise to hear the word 'racket', *reket*. Their newly established business, he explained, was under threat from the 'mafia'. The inevitable transition of 'the mafia' from protection of small-scale underground business to flourishing large-scale business enterprise had been rapid and ruthless.

Varese's study of illegal protection in Russia (Varese 1995), based on Gambetta's model of the Sicilian Mafia, posits the idea that 'the mafia is a specific economic enterprise, an industry which produces, promotes, and sells private protection' in the absence of clearly defined property rights (Gambetta 1993: 1). Certainly, Soviet and post-coup Russia have not experienced the legislation or implementation of these rights. As Varese comments, 'such a situation reduces trust in the state and fosters a *demand* for alternative forms of protection' (Varese 1995: 258). As Gilinskiy shows in this volume, however, protection is usually only one of many services offered by Russian organised crime groups and there is a suggestion we need a broader definition of the nature of organised crime in Russia.

It is worth noting another factor which encouraged the growth of protection rackets. Once again the 'blindness of ideology', this time in placing constraints on the work of the militia, compounded the problem of identification and control.

When the first private co-operatives began under perestroika, in the 1980's, we were ideologically trained to see them as enemies; so when they needed protection from racketeers the only place they could find it was in the arms of other racketeers.

(Handelman: 1996)

The protection industry flourished, and continues to flourish, in conditions of lack of trust and in circumstances in which the line between licit and illicit security has been blurred. Ex-militia and former KGB employees are able to utilise their expertise, contacts and resources in what are often very dubiously advertised as legitimate companies such as SKAT (*World in Action*: 1995). Placing too great an emphasis on the rise of this market in protection as an expression of the rise of the 'mafia' itself deflects attention away from more complex forms of organised criminal activity, that is, where it interfaces with legitimate and semi-legitimate business. Although protection has evolved to an active assimilative level in relationship to the legitimate structures, in other words, in its ability to undermine commercial autonomy and competitiveness and to weaken the position of the criminal justice system through bribery, or tempt the poorly paid members of the militia into its extremely lucrative employment, protection constitutes only a small part of organised criminal activity prevalent throughout the country. For obvious reasons protection rackets dominate representations of Russian organised crime and have been the main focus of media attention as images of heavily built, tough-looking bodyguards are both photogenic and enhance the orthodox Hollywood representation of organised crime as the mafia gangster.[6] Less distinct and yet, it can be argued, more deleterious to the health of Russia's legitimate structures, are invisible aspects of organised crime operating in the world of business.

Close encounters

The liaison between organised crime and business at a sophisticated level began in the latter days of perestroika. As the legal remit for economic relations broadened, large co-operative associations were formed bringing together underground entrepreneurs, corrupt officials and muscle from gangs. The patron–client relationship between officials and entrepreneurs developed into a more symbiotic one as the emphasis on power concentration moved from the political to the economic sphere. Entrepreneurs operating in both legitimate and non-legitimate sectors still required political *krysha* to facilitate the signing of contracts and export documents, to facilitate tax evasion and so on, but in turn, officials were becoming increasingly dependent on their alliances with criminal businesses as the political structures began to weaken under conflict and pressure for reform. The abrogation of Article 6 of the Constitution in 1990, which had granted the Communist Party political monopoly, signalled the ineluctable decline of the old power structures.

Rather than supplementing the deficiencies of the dominant economy, criminal groups were now becoming a formative part of economic development, capable of introducing their own codes of behaviour – for example, high levels of violence, mistrust, corruption and ruthless competitive tactics – into business practice as the norm. In 1988 official figures for recorded crime in the co-operative sector stood at 1500; for the first nine months of 1989 it had increased to 5700 (Jones and Moskoff 1991: 79). The balance between the legitimate structures and organised crime was being tipped in favour of the latter. Groups like the Association of the 21st Century, well known to have a strong criminal base, operated with impunity in Moscow, opening the first co-operative bank, laundering money through a myriad of business ventures (including insurance, pensions, oil, as well as more traditional business such as extortion, prostitution, etc.). In the mid-1990s, its activities continue to expand (Dunn 1996: 69–70).

Crime and politics: the battle of ideologies

When glasnost (openness) gave the media greater freedom to act as investigative journalists they finally exerted their long denied right to investigate, vigorously pursuing their exposure of many hidden and negative features of the USSR. Organised crime became one of the more sensational topics, allowing correspondents such as Arkady Vaksberg, Vitaly Vitaliev, Lev Feofanov and Yuri Shchekochikin to write, often with threats hanging over them, on a topic which officially did not exist. The impact of Shchekochikin's article 'The Lion has Jumped', published in July 1988, was considerable – not only because it provided a detailed account of the geographical location and characteristics of indigenous organised crime, but more significantly because this information was proffered by a member of the MVD, Colonel Alexander Gurov (Shchekochikin 1988). Organised crime, he stated in the interview, was prolific and systemic. The subsequent flood of articles on the 'mafia', a phenomenon normally associated with the 'jungles of capitalism', infected the consciousness of the Soviet public with fear and anger. Although at that time few of the ordinary public had had any direct contact with organised crime, the word 'mafia' became part of the vernacular and began to be used indiscriminately as a term of abuse against any organisation, business group or even the government.

Once in the public domain organised crime became political currency for the growing split between pro- and anti- reformist groups. For the hard-line faction, those opposed to the pace of reform, including Ligachev, an erstwhile supporter of Gorbachev, and Polazkov, a particularly vociferous opponent of co-operatives, the proliferation of organised crime provided the perfect vindication of their continuing loyalty to traditional Soviet Communism. The easy infiltration of organised crime into the newly created business structures was seen as a clear indication that capitalism was inherently exploitative and criminal. The counter-argument led by the reformist factions, including Yeltsin, maintained that the burgeoning of organised crime was a direct result of the pervasive corruption within the Party structures. Once liberal democracy and full market relations were established, they argued, corrupt elements within the economy would be forced to comply with the new dominant mode of production. Further, the creation of healthy fiscal relations meant that the economy would respond to the laws of supply and demand rather than to the whims of an elite motivated by nepotism and bribery.

Identifying organised crime on ideological grounds served only to obfuscate an understanding of its activities. 'Alien conspiracy' theory, that is, the creation of a dangerous 'other', usually as a means of uniting disparate and antagonistic groups or individuals behind a leader or government, has dominated interpretations of organised crime in the West, most of which have been heavily influenced by American thinking and policy. The Kefauver Committee proceedings in 1950–1, an investigation into interstate organised criminal activities across the US, had come to much the same conclusions as the Soviet factions in Gorbachev's government (Kefauver 1952). Organised crime, or the mafia, was conspiratorial, international and covert, seeking to destroy the country within which it operated. Collusion with such an organisation was nothing less than treachery. While the American government was able to single out Italian ethnic groups as the most representative examples of the mafia, the Soviet government, even though it would speak of ethnicity in relation to lower forms of organised crime, made wholesale and destructive use of the idea of conspiracy by one or other warring factions within the bureacratic and political apparatus, and, of course, in so doing, destroyed the legitimacy of their own bureacratic sphere. By 1991 the legislature was inoperable, law enforcement ineffective and the economy chaotic. The aftermath of the abortive August coup appeared to offer a resolution to the crisis as the old Soviet structures were removed from the conflictual equation. The reformers, led by Yeltsin, assumed power with promises of democracy and an equitable free market. The continuing proliferation of organised crime guaranteed their dismal failure.

New Russia, old problems

The unity of the new government was, at its inception, fragile. It agreed on the need to take Russia out of the ruins of a failed centralised economy, but hardly showed unanimity on how this was to be achieved. Unlike its predecessor however it now had the backing of its erstwhile enemy, the West. Of the various forms of economic transition already adopted by Eastern European States, Russia's Prime Minister, Yegor Gaidar, opted for 'shock therapy', which had been applied with varying degrees of success to Poland and Czechoslovakia. This would involve rapid privatisation and price liberalisation, a reform programme constructed and encouraged by Western economists such as Richard Layard and Jeffrey Sachs (Rutland 1994). The creation and adoption of this course was based on what could arguably be stated as two erroneous premises assumed by all parties (Russian and Western – firstly, that the total demise of communism would now enable the economy to proceed unhindered towards a healthy state of capitalism (in other words, an assumption based on the perceived value of different ideologies). Secondly, it was assumed that capitalism, operating in tandem with a liberal democratic government, ultimately operates for the public good by inspiring good business practice. Even if in the initial stages the capitalist system proves to be less than equitable, it was assumed that its adherents would eventually use it judiciously at a more 'civilised' phase, as the advantages of doing so will become self-evident. Mancur Olsen takes this argument a stage further by equating a 'good economy' with law and order:

> the self-interest of the individuals and firms in a market economy with good economic policies and clearly delineated property rights is a major force for crime prevention, lawful behaviour and law enforcement.
>
> (Olsen 1995: 15)

Hence, the logic follows, gangster economics, or wild capitalism, which prevails in contemporary Russia, will eventually adapt to the most expedient long-term alternative, that is, the legitimisation of its activities. That this has not yet occurred, and in fact seems to be less the case now than then, casts serious doubt on this conjecture.

By July 1992 Russia had embarked on its privatisation programme, having liberalised prices the previous January. One of the main aims was to relocate the ownership of large state enterprises to managers, workers and the remaining populace, the latter acting as outside shareholders. This was carried out through a citizen-wide distribution of vouchers intended to stimulate the economy in a competitive, self-motivated environment. It was assumed that the 'real' owners would be those which could invest and reactivate idle production, in other words, now that they stood to directly benefit from the profits of increased output and sales, the management workers would have the incentive to increase standards and performance. The programme provoked a range of hostile responses. Many political groups opposed the scheme seeing it as an opportunity for organised crime to:

> acquire vouchers and/or stocks from common Russian citizens, gaining controlling interests in Russia's most valuable properties, and then sell the assets of these enterprises for a quick profit without reference to the individual firm.
>
> (McFaul 1995: 229–230)

It was an alarmingly accurate prognosis. Only months after the launch of the scheme, vouchers which had been valued at 10,000 roubles per shareholder in October 1992, were sold at half or even less their original value as continuing inflation and price liberalisation forced many holders to use the vouchers as currency, given that they had used up any personal savings in an attempt to keep pace with prices. Those best placed to buy up the vouchers, often from desperate shareholders on the streets, were naturally the capital-holders from perestroika, that is, co-operative owners, joint-venture employees and black marketeers. Voucher purchase also provided another ideal opportunity for money-laundering.

Other assumptions were quickly discredited. Placing faith in market forces it was supposed that the larger shareholders would invest in the rehabilitation of their enterprises and get them to work in response to consumer demand. Instead, economic growth in large industry was blocked, machinery was left to rot and workers laid off. Insider dealing, the resale abroad of shares for huge profit margins, tax evasion, and so on, became endemic. Referred to as 'nomenklatura privatisation' this was the first stage of the consolidation of 'grey' business, the political elite (many of whom had formerly held posts in the old government) and criminal organisations, a repeat of the tri-alliance under Gorbachev, under the auspices of the free market and democracy. (After all, no-one had been coerced into selling their vouchers.) Further, the world's leading financial institutions such as the World Bank and International Monetary Fund pledged to continue their fiscal support for the programme without questioning too deeply how privatisation was being executed. Svetlana Glinka has suggested that many of the Communist Party's 'missing millions' were invested in privatised commercial ventures (Glinka 1995) probably with the tacit approval of the government and certainly with little objection from the West. When the need to create and implement effective legislation to prevent such abuse was acknowledged, it was too little, too late.

It was not long before a saga of economic scandals was reported in the media. Even though some of it was politically motivated, as with the Rutskoi affair (in which the former Vice-President was accused of criminal liaisons and owning offshore accounts with illicitly acquired funds) few doubted the fact that the criminalisation had taken place within the privatisation programme. There were numerous examples. The Kolo conglomerate, had it succeeded, intended to take over large state institutions including the news agency TASS and a Siberian coalfield. The private companies within the conglomerate had as their directors many former managers of the acquired state enterprises. The Moscow real-estate company MOST was involved with the purchase and resale of city property, bought at ludicrously low prices with a huge mark-up when leased or sold and the inevitable cut going to 'helpful' councillors (Handelman 1994: 132). Almost mind-boggling in its attempted range of dubious business activity was the UKOSO deal, whose agenda was the privatisation of a whole district council, *ispolkom*, in the Oktyabrski region of Moscow (rather like privatising the whole of Islington). The intention was to turn the area into an investment haven, free from 'bureaucratic bias'. Social centres and residential accommodation were either sold off or relocated to business parties. This included new flats originally built to re-house large families. There was no consultation with the local residents – many of whom would have been forced to move out. Complaining to the Moscow City Council, Mossoviet, would have proved futile as some of its members had been invited in as shareholders. Anticipating a political backlash against such an obvious abuse of state property, the Mayor, Yuri Luzhkov, closed the firm down in late 1992 (Djokaeva 1992).

Businessmen gone wrong?

We have three types of capitalists in our (city). There are entrepreneurs who have been given the chance to make real money, thanks to the changes in our system, and there are criminals who launder their dirty capital in legitimate business. But the first and second types are mere kids in comparison with our 'biznessmen' in the official structures of power. They, in disguise, are the true masters of Moscow.

(Shchekhochikin 1994: 134)

Varese has argued, powerfully, that the conflicts and confusions between licit, semi-licit and illicit business are explicable in terms of the absence of clearly defined property rights and an effective criminal-justice system to protect those rights (Varese 1995). But to attribute the causes of this ambiguity solely to the dearth of property rights fails to appreciate other factors which have contributed to the crisis of organised crime in Russia.

In one sense, Russians were no strangers to the idea of capitalism. With the exception of the current younger generation, the Russian population had been educated to see the world from a Marxist–Leninist perspective. At its centre lies a damning critique of private ownership. Capitalism was seen as the exploitation of the masses by the bourgeoisie. The overnight legitimisation of capitalism did not necessarily inculcate a sense of moral responsibility into those who pursued its path. Many simply responded to the opportunities offered by a free market unconfined by legislation. Nor was there any reason why a sense of morality should be linked to capitalism. It is purely a system of economic relations. And yet a moral righteousness, or perhaps more accurately, a sense of justified economic colonialism, from the West has accompanied the implementation of a capitalist market in Russia. Most twentieth-century thinking has been dominated by the two ideologies of capitalism and communism – a naïve dichotomy which has determined the character of international politics since the 1920s. In this ideological battle the demise of communism was therefore seen as a moral victory for capitalism, even more so because it was seemingly self-induced. From this moral high-ground the West as the victor could push, and Russia as the loser accept, a programme based on the cornerstone of capitalism, that is privatisation, without due regard for any positive elements that might have been present in the Soviet system, and also without cautious consideration for the conditions of Russia's weakened legitimate structures. The proposed hasty transition from a centralised to a market economy was driven by a blind acceptance of the inherently successful economic performance and hence the moral superiority of capitalism. Organised crime, entrepreneurs and the nomenklatura, were doing little more than they had done under the old system: feverishly pursuing the goals of material success, regardless of the [exploitative] means used to justify the [owner-ship] ends. The difference was that what had once been illegal was now legal. Although the West muttered disapproval at some of the means it nevertheless encouraged, and continues to do so, these aims. Comparatively little has been done to ameliorate the social hardship which has resulted from privatisation. In the pursuit of establishing a 'good economy' the West has ignored those forms of organised crime which have now become a proactive part of Russian society. This is based either on expediency or on a genuine inability to recognise organ-ised criminal influences on business practice, so concerned is commerce with profit margins.

Ian Taylor's analysis of Merton's essay 'Social Means and Social Structure', a damning critique on the prescribed cultural goals of American society, could be equally applied to the situation in contemporary Russia:

> The enormous value placed on money as a value itself – without regard to the intrinsic value of the activity through which pecuniary success had been realised – *was accompanied by no obvious moral or legal qualification on such success:* Al Capone was by no means an unwelcome guest in all social circles (especially the baseball park) in 1930's Chicago. Americans of all backgrounds were, in effect, invited to pursue material success even by illegitimate means without fear of social exclusion.
>
> (Taylor 1994: 248, emphasis added)

The wild capitalism of contemporary Russia may be seen as a temporary moral blip on the economic landscape – symptoms of an economically under-developed culture, capitalism gone bad, racketeering gone mad and businessmen gone wrong. Merton himself would certainly interpret the contemporary condi-tion of Russia as more of a peculiarity and, like President Yeltsin and his sup-porters, argue for the capacity of the market eventually to produce social stability. But this may ignore the lengthy history of organised crime in Russia and also underestimate the extent to which organised crime is now complicit in legitimate structures of capitalist Russia. The images of Chicago mobsters are visible on the streets of most large Russian towns and cities. Less visible are the boardroom criminals who, in the pursuit of self-interest, manipulate politics, legislation and the criminal-justice system to suit their ends. These are the people with whom entrepreneurs form the West feel they 'can do business' and do. The Canadian journalist, Stephen Handelman's impressively detailed account of the rise of organised crime in Russia is similarly unable to countenance the widespread criminalisation of legitimate business or to analyse the role of Western business in giving succour to this process of criminalisation of commerce in the new Russia:

> Yekaterinberg's tragedy is only compounded by the fact that its 'liberal' economic environment has made it a magnet for Western investment. Without realising it – *or at least so one would hope* – Western businessmen

flocking in to exploit the rich resources of Central Russia end up providing a cover of legitimacy to Russia's comrade criminals.

(Handelman 1994: 80, emphasis added)

Criminal society

Edward Luttwak, in his article 'Does the Russian mafia deserve the Nobel prize
for economics?' describes the present state of organised crime as part of the
evolutionary process of capitalism, following its early patterns of development in
the US and Japan. Most telling is the role organised crime has played in Japan:

> its Yakuza gangsters have certainly been of great economic benefit to
> Japan . . . Because of the extreme fragmentation of landownership into
> a huge number of tiny house plots, developers usually find it impossible
> to legally buy up sites big enough for apartment blocks or office buildings
> of economic size. Only with the help of hired gangs and their colourful
> repertoire of threats and vandalism (bodily violence is rare) can house-
> owners be persuaded to sell, even at very, very high prices. Many of the
> modern buildings one sees in Japanese cities could never have been built
> without Yakuza help.
>
> (Luttwak 1995: 7)

Organised crime in Russia is equally as functional, operating as an effective
means of kick-starting the country's cumbersome and monopolistic economic
machinery into action. This sentiment is also held by the Organisation for Economic Co-operation and Development which claims in its report on the state of
the Russian economy that 'a degree of criminal activity . . . "could in a certain
sense be thought of as providing a necessary service to business"' (*The European*
5–11 October 1995). Collusion between the legitimate structures and organised
crime, it would appear, has become an acceptable means of promoting a
'healthy' economy. The question that needs to be asked here is, does this negotiation process not bring with it the same dangers as it did to the USSR? Regarding this type of collusion as situation-specific, that is, that once the organised
crime group has fulfilled its function, it can be switched off and replaced by
'normal' business practice, assumes the continuing ability (and commitment) of
the legitimate structures to control its negotiating partner. Such a relationship
pays no heed to ideological factors. It is not a specific ideological system which
attracts organised crime or creates an environment conducive to it. Rather it is
the extent to which any dominant structures, regardless of the underlying ideology, are prepared to go down the road of expedient compromise and how far
they are capable of holding the balance of power on their side.

The proliferation of semi-licit and illicit business practice in Russia's developing economy is far more detrimental than the much-publicised gangsterism of
the rackets and mobs. It is in the sphere of grey business that tolerance of and

collusion with criminal structures allows them to inimically penetrate the legitimate economy and exert a negative influence on society. More destructive however is the tendency to adapt behaviour according to the most advantageous, profitable, outcome. Vincenzo Ruggiero describes how 'learning processes appear to cross the boundaries of social groups, as criminal know-how is transmitted to a variety of actors. In other words, techniques are exchanged and skills enhanced within an economic arena inhabited by legal, semi-legal and illegal businesses' (Ruggiero 1996: 154). On current evidence, the hope that organised crime in Russia will eventually legitimise itself into decent business practice looks merely utopian. Instead we are witnessing the criminalisation of politics, of the criminal justice system and of society as a whole, as organised criminal influences have become proactive, encouraged by definitional ambiguities of what constitutes organised crime and in turn, legal business.

Conclusion

Ideological debates on the causes and character of organised crime in Russia have offered little understanding of the real problems that have given rise to what has now become the 'Russian criminal state'. Dwight Smith's statement that 'if businessmen and gangsters behave like each other, what is the sense in having two categories, that, by definition, are not mutually exclusive?' offers a different 'entry point' into the study of organised crime. Its proliferation in Russia and the unique social conditions that exist there offer an invaluable opportunity to reappraise not just trends in organised criminal behaviour but those of legal business. The development of organised crime in Russia has been a history of responses by the legitimate structures to the presence of the former. In Western states the existence of civil society and the gradual evolution of a market economy within stable legal parameters (with the exception possibly of Italy) have allowed the dominant structures to contain organised crime, or manipulate it for expedient ends. This containment is however contingent upon maintaining the strength and balance between the various legitimate structures. Strain theorists would argue that the very essence of capitalism – that is, competition – encourages malpractice as the need to get ahead supersedes legal limitations placed on business activities. But this is only part of the problem. The success in being able to restrain semi-licit and illicit business practice, which if unrestricted as in Russia, become organised forms of crime, depends on the ability to maintain equilibrium of power between political, legislative and economic structures. As the balance of power shifts further into the economic domain and continues its incursion into all spheres of society warning bells should start to sound, particularly as technological advances and economic globalisation render control of business and commerce more problematic. The BCCI affair and the Maxwell Pension Fund scandal are just two of numerous examples of the extent to which legal business can become criminalised. Economic recession has also become a reality for many wealthy states which were initially complacent in their optimism for continuing growth, with the result that a willingness to compromise with grey or even black business practices and structures becomes even more attractive. The line between licit and illicit has proven to be dangerously fine. After all, organised crime and legal business are engaged in the pursuit of the same goals. Should we continue to be complacent when estate agents, across the world, accept cash payments from wealthy Russians for top-quality property, in the interests of the economy, or when city banks find the quantity of invested capital more attractive than the quality? Russia has been down the path of negotiation between legitimate and illegitimate markets – a journey on which many Western legitimate institutions have now embarked. A genuine commitment to curtailing organised crime involves a clear understanding of its relationship with legitimate business and politics, but also a clear and strong definition so that organised crime can no longer blend chameleon-like into normal business practice. This is an urgent and immediate task for Russia, but also anywhere the impacts of global economic transition are being encountered.

Notes

1 Throughout the text the term 'organised crime' will be used in preference to 'mafia'. The latter will follow the orthodox spelling rather than the Russian version, unless directly quoted.

2 A survey taken by a Russian public opinion poll, Vsyerossiski Tsentr Obshchestvyennogo Mneniya, in September 1995, reported that in answer to the question 'What problems do you consider to be the most pressing in your city/town/village?' 54 per cent (the highest response) quoted rising crime (*CTE Briefing*, December 1995, No. 1).

3 The Ministry of the Interior reported a 19.8 per cent growth in crime (including economic crime) for 1992, the first year of Yeltsin's government (*Shchit' i Myech*, February 11, 1993). Figures for 1995 continued to show an increase of 5 per cent. Out of the 2.7 million reported cases, 200,000 were economic crimes. This, the report admits, is a gross underestimation (*Kommersant*, March 26, 1996).

4 This definition when applied to the Russian bandit leaders Razin and Pugachev is at odds with that put forward by Hobsbawm (1972: 17) who prefers the term 'social bandit' as they were not motivated to change the status quo. Nonetheless from the point of view of the authorities they were regarded as a threat to the Tsar and duly executed.

5 The Cheka (Extraordinary Commission for Combating Counter-revolution and Sabotage) were the first secret police formed under the Bolsheviks. They were (in)famous for their brutality and ability to take the law into their own hands.

6 The question arises as to how far the image adopted by Russian protection rackets relates to their perception of the Hollywood mobster through films like 'The Godfather'. Our expectations of the stereotypical gangster are constantly reaffirmed through the media as one newspaper demonstrates: 'They look exactly like a Slavic mobster should: guys with big muscles and designer suits' ('A New Mob on the Waterfront' *Independent*, 9 April 1996).

References

Block, A. (1993) 'Defending the Mountaintop', in F. Pearce and M. Woodiwiss (eds) *Global Crime Connections*, London: MacMillan.

Chalidze, V. (1977) *Criminal Russia*, New York: Random House.

Chambliss, W. (1996) 'Toward a Political Economy of Crime', in J. Muncie *et al. Criminological perspectives*, London: Sage.

Djokaeva, T. (1992) 'Poliekonomika at Il'I ili Fenomenon UKOSO', *Rossiiskaia Gazeta*, September 26.

Dunn, G. (1996) 'Major Mafia Gangs in Russia', *Transnational Organized Crime* (Special Issue) Summer/Autumn 1996, London: Frank Cass.

Gambetta, D. (1993) *The Sicilian Mafia*, Cambridge: Harvard University Press.

Gernet, M. N. (1991) *Prestupni Mir Moskvi*, Moscow: MKHO'Lyukon'.

Golinkov, D. L. (1971) *Krakh vrazhevskogo podpolia*, Izdatel'stvo Politicheskoi literaruri.

Glinka, S. (1995) 'The Shadow Economy in Contemporary Russia', *Russian Politics and Law*, March–April, 46–76.

Gurov, A. I. and Riabinin, V. N. (1991) *Ispoved' 'vora v zakone'*, Moscow: Rosagrompromizdat.

Gurov, A. I. (1995) *Krasnaia Mafia*, Moscow: Samotsvet MIKO Komercheskaia Vestnik.

Handelman, S. (1994) *Comrade Criminal: The Theft of the Second Russian Revolution*, London: Michael Joseph.

Handelman, S. (1996) 'Can Russia's Mafia be broken?', *New York Times*, 9 November 1996.

Hanson, P. (1992) *From Stagnation to Catastroika*, New York: Praeger.

Hobsbawm, E. (1972) *Bandits* Harmondsworth, Middlesex: Penguin.

Jones, A. and Moskoff, W. (1991) *Koops*, Bloomington: Indiana University Press.

Kefauver, E. (1952) *Crime in America*, London: Victor Gollancz.

Konstantinov, A and Dixelius, M. (1995) *Prestupni Mir Rossii*, St Petersburg: Bibliopolis.

Luttwak, E. (1995) 'Does the Russian mafia deserve the Nobel prize for economics?', *London Review of Books*, Vol. 17, No. 15.

McFaul, M. (1995) 'State Power, Institutional Change and the Politics of Privatization in Russia', *World Politics* 47, 210–43.

Marx, K. (1978) 'Manifesto of the Communist Party' in R. Tucker (ed.) *The Marx–Engels Reader*, New York: Norton.

Olsen, M. (1995) 'The devolution of Power in Post-Communist Societies: Therapies for Corruption, Fragmentation and Economic Retardation' in R. Skidelsky (ed.) *Russia's Stormy Path to Reform*, London: Social Market Foundation.

Ovschinskii, V. S. (1994) Interview with author in Moscow, November 3.

Pearce, F. (1976) *Crimes of the Powerful: Marxism, Crime and Deviance*, London: Pluto

Ruggiero, V. (1996) *Organized and Corporate Crime in Europe*, Aldershot: Dartmouth.

Rutland P. (1994) 'The Economy: The Rocky Road from Plan to Market' in S. White *et al.* (eds) *Developments in Russian & Post-Soviet Politics*, London: Macmillan.

Shchekhochikin, Yu. (1988) 'Lev Prignul', *Literaturnaia Gazeta*, July 20.

Shchekhochikin, Yu. (1994) Quoted in Handelman.

Simis, K. (1982) *USSR: Secrets of a Corrupt Society*, London: J. M. Dent.

Smith, D. (1991) 'Wickersham to Sutherland to Katzenbach: Evolving an "official" definition for organized crime', *Crime, Law and Social Change*, 16, 2, 135–154.

Sterling, C. (1994) *Crime Without Frontiers: The world-wide expansion of organised crime and the Pax Mafiosa*, London: Little, Brown and Company.

Taylor, I. (1994) 'The Political Economy of Crime' in M. Maguire, R. Morgan and R. Reiner (eds) *Oxford Handbook of Criminology*, Oxford: Oxford University Press.

Ugolovni Kodeks RSFSR (1987) Moscow: Yuridicheskaia Literatura.

Vaksberg, A. (1991) *The Soviet Mafia*, London: Weidenfeld & Nicolson.

Varese, F. (1995) 'Is Sicily the future of Russia? Private protection and the rise of the Russian Mafia', *European Journal of Sociology*, xxiii(2), 224–258.

World in Action (1995) 'Dealing with the devil', Granada Television.

Woodiwiss, M. (1990) 'Organized Crime, USA: Changing Perceptions from Prohibition to the Present Day', *BAAS Pamphlets in American Studies*.

Woodiwiss, M. (1993) 'Crime's Global Reach' in F. Pearce and M. Woodiwiss (eds) *Global Crime Connections*, London: Macmillan.

17

THE PENTITI'S CONTRIBUTION TO THE CONCEPTUALIZATION OF THE MAFIA PHENOMENON

Letizia Paoli

The present article investigates the contribution made by former mafia affiliates – the 'pentiti' (literally, penitents), as they are popularly called in Italy – to the knowledge of the Italian mafia, and the impact of their statements on the conceptualization of the mafia by academic and other commentators. The paper is organized as follows. The first section briefly summarizes the growth of the phenomenon of 'pentitismo', drawing from Tommaso Buscetta's cooperation with Judge Giovanni Falcone in 1984. The second section outlines the two paradigms of the mafia that have dominated academic and social commentary up to the early 1990s: the ideal-typical representation which characterizes the mafia simply as a set of attitudes and general behaviours, *vis-à-vis* the alternative representation of the mafia as an enterprise. Some of the precautions which are necessary when dealing with pentiti's statements will be discussed. Each of the three subsequent sections then deals with a thematic area where the pentiti's statements openly contradict the core arguments of one or other of the two dominant paradigms on the mafia. These sections respectively revolve around the topics of structure, culture and the relevance of a force-using, power-oriented action *vis-à-vis* a profit-oriented one. A brief summary of the main points and some final considerations then follow.

The phenomenal increase in the number of pentiti

In the summer of 1984 the Sicilian mafia boss, Tommaso Buscetta, started to cooperate with the Giudice Istruttore (Investigating Judge) Giovanni Falcone of the Palermo Court, and revealed that what was known by public opinion and law enforcement officials as mafia was in reality a secret society, named Cosa Nostra. At the beginning of the following autumn, on 29 September, the so-called anti-mafia pool of the Palermo Court, headed by the Consigliere Istruttore (Investigating Counsellor) Antonino Caponnetto, delivered 366 arrest warrants to alleged Cosa Nostra members on the basis of the confession made by Buscetta. Soon afterwards, thanks to the collaboration of another mafioso, Salvatore Contorno, the same investigating body issued another 127 arrest warrants for the crime of 'mafia association' (Stille, 1995).

The confessions of Tommaso Buscetta and Salvatore Contorno became the primary sources on which the investigating judges relied in order to weave the charges against most of the members and the leaders of the Palermo mafia families associated with Cosa Nostra, and to reconstruct the history of the organization itself over the previous fifteen years. Their patient work resulted in the indictment of Abbate Giovanni and 706 of his associates. This marked a turning point in the history of the investigations and the knowledge of the mafia phenomenon in Italy, proving the existence in its core of a permanent and structured group. 'This is a trial', the judicial documents stated, 'against the mafia organization named Cosa Nostra, a most dangerous criminal association which, with violence and intimidation, has sown and sows death and terror' (TrPA, 1986, vol. V: 713).

Buscetta and Contorno's decision to 'cooperate with Justice' was followed by many others. From the mid-1980s onwards, hundreds of mafia adherents started to report about their crimes and experiences in the underworld to policemen and magistrates. After a drop in the late 1980s, the rate of confessions and collaborations with the judiciary rapidly increased, at first in Sicily and subsequently in the other high-density mafia regions of the Continental Mezzogiorno. According to data published by the Ministry of the Interior, which is in charge of the collaborators' protection, their number was 1,177 as of 30 June 1996 (Ministero dell'Interno, 1996). Thanks to the information provided by contemporary 'Justice collaborators' and the personal commitment of some judges and police officials, knowledge about the phenomena of the mafia and organized crime in Italy has reached its highest level ever.

It may be interesting to recall that, contrary to what is frequently believed, Tommaso Buscetta is not the first 'pentito' of the mafia history. Even in the past there were cases of mafiosi who confided their experiences to law enforcement officials or journalists. Research shows that several trials carried out in the nineteenth century made use of mafia turncoats (Lupo, 1993; 1994). Even in the present century, both in Sicily and Calabria, there have been cases where affiliates broke the veil of silence surrounding the inner mafia world. Due to the 'disorganized' images of the mafia prevailing in the academic community, however, the confessions of these precursors of 'pentitismo' were usually overlooked and quickly forgotten.

The two dominant paradigms of the mafia

It is unfortunate that the statements of contemporary 'pentiti' have been so far relatively neglected in criminological and other social-scientific analysis. The reasons for this neglect are to be found in the different (but equally constraining)

265

perspectives imposed by the conceptual paradigms that have succeeded one another in the study of the mafia and organized crime. In extreme simplification, we can say that the post-war scientific discourse on the mafia produced two dominant ideal-typical images. Until the early 1980s, the predominant view was one of the mafia as a set of cultural attitudes and behaviours, a view which denied the existence of a corporate dimension in the organization. Thus, there were mafiosi, namely individuals behaving in a specific 'mafia way', but there was no permanent mafia organization. From the beginning of that decade onwards, when judicial investigations started to provide solid and abundant proof of the existence of mafia groupings, attention shifted towards their economic activities. In a way that challenged the 'culturalist' perspective, the mafia was conceptualized as an enterprise and the mafiosi's economic activities started to receive unprecedented attention.

The creation of the former paradigm was mainly due to a group of non-Italian scholars who went to Sicily, conducted their field work in the late 1960s or early 1970s and published their essays within a short timespan: the German sociologist Henner Hess ([1970] 1973); the Dutch anthropologist Anton Blok ([1974] 1986); and North-Americans Jane and Peter Schneider (1976). Although with different emphasis, these four scholars described the mafia as a method involving the private use of violence. In their view, the mafia was an offspring of the social division of labour and distribution of power connected to the 'latifundium' (large land ownership), and tended to be the prerogative of some typical figures of large estates, the 'gabellotti', who rented whole properties from inactive landowners and sub-rented to farmers. Mafiosi were also other lower, intermediate figures of the 'latifundium' economy, such as estate guards ('campieri') and chief herders. 'Most, if not of all, of the first mafiosi were rural entrepreneurs' (1976: 9), Jane and Peter Schneider claimed. None of these researchers, however, considered the mafia as a legacy of the feudal past but, on the contrary, they all saw a strong causal connection between the rise of the mafia and the incapacity of both the Bourbon and the Italian states to effectively accomplish the transition from a feudal to a modern order, and to impose and legitimize their own monopoly of violence. Hence, in all the three studies just mentioned, the use of private violence characterizing the mafia was regarded as legitimate within the specific local sub-culture: the mafiosi shared with the surrounding society the basic cultural codes among which the most relevant was the 'code of honour', which justified the use of private violence. On these codes, the mafiosi founded their power, by claiming to be 'the men of honour': the exclusive repositories of such codes.

The mafia group was perceived as being of a non-corporate nature. According to Hess, for example, the network surrounding each mafioso was constituted by a series of dyadic relationships which, though variously based on work, clientelism or kinship, remained independent of one another. Such a relationship was allegorically represented in the word 'cosca' (artichoke), where the mafioso represented the core and the men grouped around him the leaves of an artichoke.

Referring to the definition of 'quasi-group' given by Adrian C. Mayer (1966), Hess argued that 'the cosca is not a group; interaction and an awareness of "we", a consciousness of an objective to be jointly striven for, are absent or slight' (1973: 76; cf. 75–82).

In the early 1980s, the emphasis shifted onto the economic dimension of mafia members and their role on the domestic and international illegal markets. Frequently, academic investigation adopted and reinterpreted concepts developed in the North American scientific debate on organized crime. As Santino and La Fiura argue:

> In the last years the analysis of the mafia as enterprise is increasingly establishing itself, a not completely original approach if already Franchetti and Sonnino [nineteenth-century writers] talked about the 'industry of crime'. However, this type of analysis has moved a step forward towards overcoming the stereotypes of traditional and modernized 'mafiology' and to frame a more scientific analysis.
>
> (1990: 17–18)

The scholar who instigated this change, and whose writings represent a link between the 'old' and the 'new' ways of analysing the mafia, is Pino Arlacchi. On the one hand, he elaborates on the analysis provided by Hess, Blok and the Schneiders, and adopts their definition of the mafia as a type of behaviour and a type of power, rather than a formal organization ([1983 and 1986], 1988: 3). On the other hand, Arlacchi argues that, following a crisis in the 1950s and 1960s caused by processes of economic and cultural modernization, the mafiosi underwent an entrepreneurial transformation, abandoning the traditional roles of mediators and devoting themselves to the accumulation of capital. Therefore, he maintains, 'only by turning to the Schumpeterian concepts of enterprise and entrepreneurial activity (or entrepreneurship), rather than to more strictly sociological or criminological categories' (1988: xv), can an understanding of the modern mafia be developed.

The breakthrough provided by Arlacchi was subsequently followed by other researchers who were faced with the growing evidence of the mafia involvement in economic activities, both legal and illegal. With few exceptions (Centorrino, 1986; 1989) however, most of the subsequent analyses of the mafia differentiated themselves from Arlacchi's work on a major point, as they denied an 'entrepreneurial transformation' of the mafia, and tended to ascribe a primarily economic-oriented behaviour to traditional mafiosi as well as to contemporary ones. According to Catanzaro, for instance, 'the only commonly agreed upon identifying characteristic is that the Mafia exists to make profits illegally' ([1988] 1992: 3), while the element shared by the mafia and organized crime that distinguishes them from social bandits is 'their organizational stability, their being shaped in the form of a "firm" within the ambit of normal economic activities' ([1988], 1991: 4). In order to prove his thesis, Catanzaro then identifies the mafiosi with the 'gabellotti' and the 'campieri', and concludes that all the traditional ways of exploiting farmers in the 'latifundium' system were forms of mafia accumulation (1992: 31–4). In his view, contemporary mafia enterprises are, instead, all those 'that perform legal . . . [and] illegal production activities and employ violent methods to discourage competition' (1992: 203), and the so-called 'screen enterprises' which hardly perform any productive activity, whose main aim is to launder dirty money (ibid.: 203–9; see also 1986).

Similar two-tier conceptualizations of the mafia phenomenon became standard in the subsequent literature. As far as the past is concerned, the mafiosi are defined as the social class of 'homines novi', the only true expression of the Sicilian bourgeoisie (Recupero, 1987b), and they are generally equated to the 'gabellotti' and 'campieri', that is the figures that most clearly show a 'modern' acquisitive attitude in the traditional economic and social system of the latifundium. When attention is focused on the last forty years, the model of the mafia enterprise is put forward (see Santino, 1988; 1994a; Santino and La Fiura, 1990). This model, however, ends up reducing the mafia groups to an enterprise by denying any other dimension but profit. The mafia, therefore, becomes indistinguishable from large sectors of the Sicilian bourgeoisie and, at the same time, loses any peculiarity *vis-à-vis* other types of organized crime.

The studies carried out since the 1960s highlight important facets of the mafia culture and economy. Nonetheless, their accounts are partial, because they overlook some relevant aspects pinpointed by the 'pentiti', thus leaving many questions unanswered. For instance, the analyses inspired by economic assumptions, which are today by far the prevailing ones, rightly underline the growing economic power of the mafia, denouncing the threats to the economic and social development of large areas of the country (Centorrino, 1990; 1995; Becchi and Rey, 1994; Zamagni, 1993). What these analyses totally neglect is the symbolic dimension of the mafia, thus preventing any real understanding of what it means to be a ritually affiliated member of a mafia family, or to be part of the social basis granting legitimation to the mafia itself. At the same time, these analyses overlook the political aims and means adopted by mafia groups and fail to explain the terrorist strategy staged by Sicilian Cosa Nostra in 1992–93. Moreover, the scholars deeply committed to such an economic framework of analysis are often unable to explain the recent dramatic increase in the number of mafia turncoats and the underlying legitimacy crisis that today is shaking Cosa Nostra so violently.

Some methodological considerations

Not all that is revealed by former mafia affiliates can be taken at face value. The statements made by the 'pentiti' should be handled with caution and a degree of scepticism, in order to avoid the risk of uncritically accepting and reproducing the mafia ideology or of giving legitimacy to confessions which, at times, are meant to penalize one defendant and benefit another. We need to remember that the first assessment of the confessions is made by the police and the prosecutors, and subsequently by judges. However, social scientists are also involved in assessing the reliability and consistency of turncoats. It is necessary, in particular, to be aware that even in the case of 'pentiti' of proven 'judicial trustworthiness', their statements on and judgment of their former life experiences are greatly influenced by the particular psychological conditions in which they find themselves. No matter what their motivations (that is, whether or not their choice to collaborate is self-serving expediency), the decision to start cooperating with the judges always represents a dramatic life-style change for a mafioso. Frequently, this leads the 'pentito' to idealize the traditional principles to which the secret association once inspired its actions, and to drastically contrast them with its present choice. In other words, the 'pentito' tries to come to terms with his whole life story and to rationalize both his former choice to become a mafia member and his current choice to betray the prime obligation imposed by the mafia association, namely the vow of silence (cf. Di Maria and Lavanco, 1995: 70–88).

Nonetheless, the use of pentiti's confessions for analytical purposes poses fewer difficulties than those they pose to law enforcers. The information which is more likely to interest academic scholars is also the least 'dangerous' for informants; it is the least likely to trigger judicial proceedings or retaliation on the part of former acolytes. Hence, with regard to some topics, 'justice collaborators' have few incentives to lie. Conversely, that these themes are frequently only marginally investigated by the magistrates carrying out the pentiti's questioning is a major research drawback. Despite this, written reports of the turncoats' questioning and judicial proceedings based on this material represent a major source of information, given that social scientists are usually denied direct access to the 'pentiti'

Theoretically, one cannot rule out the possibility of a collective 'conspiracy' plotted by the 'pentiti' to give a distorted view of the mafia or to achieve some other goal. Yet, there are several reasons that justify a positive – though not unconditional – approach towards this type of source. First, there are a multiplicity and a variety of informants. Second, a high degree of objectivity is guaranteed by the high number of law-enforcement officials and independent observers who have gathered confessions as well as the similarity of accounts over time. Furthermore, there are surprising analogies between these reports and descriptions of the mafia dating as far back as last century. Finally, it must be remembered that the information disclosed by 'justice collaborators' is confirmed by what is still regarded by some 'suspicious' scholars as the only source of objective information: that is, the recording of conversations between the mafiosi themselves. In addition to the famous talks bugged in Paul Violi's bar in Montreal in the early 1970s (TrPA, 1986, vol. V: 845–72), several interesting and detailed conversations between two mafiosi of the Altofonte family, a village in the outskirts of Palermo, were taped in 1994. After their arrest, one of the persons involved committed suicide in prison, realizing the relevance of the information he had unwittingly disclosed to law-enforcement agencies, while the other chose to cooperate with the judges. As the Palermo prosecutors put it:

these wiretappings confirm – though they are only 'ordinary conversations between two men of honour, who are not even of the highest rank – all the information on the structure and the activity of the criminal organisation named Cosa Nostra which have been unanimously provided by "justice collaborators", and which nonetheless somebody still finds doubtful'.

(PrPA, 1993: 109)

Structure

The information provided by the 'pentiti' has a great impact on the debate surrounding the mafia organizational form. While the image of a powerful secret society has been informing much of the official discourse on the mafia since the last decades of the nineteenth century in Italy and the United States (Smith, [1975] 1990), academics, almost invariably, have fiercely opposed such a view, and have promoted a 'disorganized' notion of the mafia. Yet, most Sicilian justice collaborators claim to be 'ritually affiliated members' of mafia families belonging to a consortium known as Cosa Nostra. The 'inside' accounts provided by the 'pentiti' also prove the existence of another secret consortium of mafia families, located in Southern Calabria and known under the label of 'ndrangheta. Over the last decade, the existence of the two mafia consortia has been confirmed in several judicial proceedings, some of which – and among them the first Palermo 'maxi-trial' – have undergone the scrutiny of the highest Italian judicial body, the 'Corte di Cassazione'. According to the latest police estimates, there are about 90 mafia families, made up of 3,000 men, associated with the Sicilian Cosa Nostra, which are mainly based in the Palermo and Trapani provinces, and to a minor extent in smaller Sicilian towns. Around the same number of units and associates is also estimated for the Calabrian 'ndrangheta, whose base is in the Reggio Calabria province and the surrounding area (Ministero dell'Interno, 1994 and 1995). Although the term mafia remains an ambiguous, ill-defined term, having a stratified and contrasting variety of meanings, these two 'cosca' groupings can be regarded as the hard core of the wider organisation described as the mafia.

The existence of two sets of Sicilian and Calabrian mafia families is not only supported by the accounts of former mafia members and by the judicial investigations that have been accomplished on the basis of the contributions of the former. It also finds corroboration in several, varied documents, mostly dating back to the pre-World-War-I period, which have been retrieved thanks to the painstaking research of a new generation of historians. One of these historians, Paolo Pezzino (1987: 954) states:

if it is true that these sources have to be examined with great prudence. It is also true that the statements on the existence of well structured associations are so many, finding confirmation in several judicial proceedings, that it would be difficult to deny their plausibility.

For a similar opinion see Lupo, 1988.

Such a recognition, however, does not imply the endorsement of the view that Cosa Nostra and 'ndrangheta are two rigid and hierarchical criminal bureaucracies. As the 'pentiti' themselves point out, the emergence of central coordinating bodies in both consortia is a recent evolutionary change. This development took place in Sicily with the establishment in the late 1950s of the Commission for the families of the Palermo province, subsequently followed by the creation of a Regional Commission in the mid-1970s, while in Calabria a similar body was created at the beginning of the current decade (TrPA, 1986, vol. V; Arlacchi, 1994; PrRC, 1993 and 1995). On the other hand, the mafia turncoats are unanimous in stressing the unity of Cosa Nostra and 'ndrangheta consortia even before the establishment of superior bodies of coordination. 'Substantially', Francesco Marino Mannoia, a former associate of the Palermitan family of Santa Maria del Gesù, states, 'Cosa Nostra, as the word itself implies, is a single and unitary organization . . . I am therefore staggered by reading in the newspaper that there is somebody doubting this elementary truth, that each of us learns at the moment of joining the organization' (TrPA, 1989: 63).

A way to acknowledge the unity of the two mafia consortia on the one hand, and the autonomy of the individual families on the other, is to consider Cosa Nostra and 'ndrangheta as segmented societies (Smith, 1974: 98). In this way, we can appreciate the unitary nature of both Cosa Nostra and 'ndrangheta, without overemphasizing their centralization. As in traditional societies, it is the extensive replication of corporate forms which defines the unit as a separate system.

Since these groups have managed to remain largely unknown to national public opinion and the law-enforcement agencies until the early 1980s (though, especially in Calabria, they were long clearly visible to the local population), it does not seem inappropriate to label them as secret societies. According to several historians, the assumption of secrecy was originally induced by the emulation of associative models prevalent in Southern Italy in the first half of the nineteenth century, such as Freemasonry and the 'Carboneria' (Pezzino, 1990; 1992; Recupero, 1987a). Secrecy was mainly adopted as a tool to increase group cohesion and to strengthen its collective identity. Eventually, however, the commitment to secrecy increasingly became a necessary choice to escape the process of criminalization staged by the state apparatus in order to assert its monopoly of violence. The commitment to secrecy thus assumed the twin function of uniting and protecting the society.

While the Sicilian Cosa Nostra and the Calabrian 'ndrangheta have always asserted the need to hide themselves completely from the public view, in actual fact considerable differences between the two organisations are noticeable. With respect to secrecy, it is necessary to distinguish: first, between Cosa Nostra and the 'ndrangheta; second, between the type of the 'public' concerned; and third, between different time periods (Paoli, 1997).

First, the rule of secrecy has historically been observed by Cosa Nostra much more strictly and successfully than by the Calabrian 'ndrangheta. Though the veil of secrecy surrounding Cosa Nostra was occasionally broken by some judicial investigations and by some rare confessions of its members, by and large the myth of the non-existence of a formal mafia organization survived until 1984, when the existence of Cosa Nostra was revealed by Tommaso Buscetta.

On the contrary, the units that compose the segmentary society named 'ndrangheta have been for a long time fully recognized. In the local contexts, some of its members limit themselves to excluding strangers from direct participation in their associative life. The visibility and the local consensus enjoyed by Calabrian 'cosche' are confirmed by several sources. For example, in an article published in the 'Corriere della Sera' back in 1955, the Calabrian writer Corrado Alvaro recalled the presence of the mafia in the following way:

> The *Fibbia*, *'ndrina*, *'ndranaheta*, the *Onorata Società.* in short the mafia, of which one talks in these days, I have known since the age of reason. A precise memory is when, having come home for the holidays, my mother, coming towards me, told me that my father was busy in the room upstairs with those of the association. I cheered up saying: 'Is there finally an Association in this village?' I had just finished my studies and I believed that it was an association for the promotion of local interests. My mother immediately made me change my mind: 'It is the criminal association'. I don't know what my father had to do with these people but I was not surprised.
>
> (Alvaro 1995)

The men affiliated to Cosa Nostra are aware of the gap between their own organization and their Calabrian counterpart in terms of secrecy, a circumstance which leads them to consider the 'ndrangheta with contempt and an ill-concealed feeling of superiority. The 'ndrangheta – Tommaso Buscetta remembers – 'represented a slack entity, because of its lack of seriousness in recruiting and its very low, almost non-existent, secrecy' (Arlacchi, 1994: 53).

The different commitment towards secrecy between the two organizations can be explained by the considerable difference in the attention that has been devoted by public opinion and law-enforcement institutions to them. Since the unification of Italy the Sicilian mafia became a topic of nationwide debate and investigations to the point that the local ruling class risked exclusion from the national elite (Pezzino, 1987). In contrast, the attention received by the 'ndrangheta has always been limited, whereas in many Calabrian villages and towns the existence of a criminal organization recruiting the most prominent and/or violent local men has long been widely known and accepted.

Second, even though the boundary marked by secrecy is subjectively felt by the mafiosi as sharp and insurmountable, each mafia family is surrounded by concentric circles within which secrecy, in objective terms, nuances gradually. The innermost circle consists of those who, although not (yet) ritually initiated, continuously cooperate with the mafia, in most cases hoping to join it in the future:

'around every man of honour of a certain rank', Calderone argues, 'there is always a circle of twenty or thirty kids – nobodies who want to become something' (Arlacchi, [1992] 1993: 149; see also CPM, 1993a; TrMI, 1994).

The second circle is constituted by individuals linked by bonds of biological or artificial kinship to the components of the nucleus. These are persons belonging to different social classes – from self-employed professionals to public administrators – who maintain a non-systematic but fully trustful relationship with the members of the inner circle. They provide information, favours, and protection to the organization. Then there are individuals who, though unrelated to the members of a mafia family, gravitate around it in an intermittent way on the basis of specific interests. These may be part of the underworld, such as thieves, loansharks, swindlers, or representatives of the upperworld, such as corporate criminals, 'friendly' politicians and public administrators.

The concentric circles surrounding the secret nucleus perform a protective function for the organization, and at the same time contribute to the expansion of its power and influence.

Lastly, throughout the decades, there have been considerable variations in the way in which the principle of secrecy has inspired the internal setup of Sicilian and Calabrian mafia families. There has been a tendency towards an increase in secrecy. This tendency was caused by two external factors: first, the loss of popular legitimacy faced by mafia consortia in their own local communities and, second, the strengthening of law-enforcement action. Since the early 1970s, due to external factors, secrecy became of paramount importance. Both the mafia and the 'ndrangheta applied important organizational innovations aimed to strengthen the protection of their internal nucleus. They reduced the internal circulation of information and widened the bosses and lower-rank members. In a sense, secrecy became increasingly reflexive within the organization (Luhmann, [1984] 1991: 450–5): that is the strategies initially adopted for the protection of the organization from outside threats began to be applied within the organization itself. As a consequence, secret societies within the very secret society were established, such as the 'Santa' formed by an elite of 'ndranghetisti' invisible to, and isolated from, the majority of 'ndranghetisti (PrRC, 1995; Ciconte, 1996).

Culture

The relevance of cultural codes for the mafiosi's legitimation in their local contexts was well understood by the scholars who elaborated the first paradigm of the mafia. However, as we have seen, their analyses remain unfocused, given their denial of a corporate dimension in the mafia. As a consequence, neither this first generation of scholars, nor their successors, largely constrained by a utilitarian perspective, have been able to single out and thoroughly analyse the culture of the mafia, and thus to appreciate adequately the meaning that individuals attach to their belonging to the organization. Mafia rituals, symbols and codes have been described since the late nineteenth century in trials and scientific texts, as well as in popular publications. Despite the scepticism of scholars with respect to the existence of such rituals and symbols, these are described in detail by contemporary pentiti. From their accounts, it is clear that symbolic action plays a relevant role in, transmitting and imposing the role of 'man of honour' upon each new member, and in constructing the group's collective identity.

Given their commitment to secrecy, the mafia associations do not bind their members through a mere purposive contract – as a 'modern' firm or bureaucracy would do – but they claim their whole personality, their whole self throughout their life. As Leonardo Messina, a former affiliate to the San Cataldo family in the Caltanisetta province, puts it, 'the membership of Cosa Nostra, involving the way of being and thinking of the individual, can neither be suspended nor interrupted by any event' (PrPA, 1992: 248; see also TrPA, 1984, I: 23). As secret societies, mafia associations set themselves as 'total institutions' (Goffman, 1961). It is for this reason that they have to resort extensively to symbolic tools. By combining a particular image of the universe with a strong emotional attachment to that image, symbolic action is particularly well suited to exert an absolute and unconditional claim upon individuals. This symbolic action has an impact not only at the normative, but also at deeper cognitive and emotional levels (Cohen, [1974] 1976).

In joining a mafia family, the new affiliate signs a 'pact for life', what Weber ([1922] 1978: 672) defines as a 'status contract'. As opposed to purposive contracts, which characterize the market economy, status contracts 'involve a change in what may be called the total legal situation (the universal position) and the social status of the persons involved'. With the initiation into either Cosa Nostra or 'ndrangheta, each new affiliate is expected to assume a completely new identity, 'to make a new "soul" enter his body'. As in a religious conversion, the mafia novice undergoes an 'alternation', that is, a process of re-socialization which implies an almost-total transformation of his identity and a redefinition of all his previous allegiances (Berger and Luckmann, [1966] 1967: 156–63). As judge Giovanni Falcone pointed out, the admission to Cosa Nostra 'commits a man for all his life. Becoming a member of the mafia is tantamount to being converted to a religion. You never stop being a priest; nor being a mafioso' (1991: 97).

The ceremonies of mafia affiliation may thus be seen as *rites de passage* (van Gennep, ([1909] 1960), as they mark the change of position of the initiates and the acquisition of a new status as member of a secret society. The initiation ceremony represents a symbolic representation of death and resurrection through which the initiate is reborn as 'a new man, with a new outlook, and a personality reshaped by the values of his new environment' (MacKenzie, 1967: 18). 'When I entered', the 'pentito' Gaspare Mutolo recalls, 'it was for me a new life, with new rules. For me there existed only Cosa Nostra' (CPM, 1993a: 1225). Serafino Castagna, remembering his formal entrance into the Calabrian Honoured Society, confesses, 'at the end of the meeting, I felt as if I had almost grown in rank; I was no longer a nobody, but a camorrista, somebody who had to respect the law of honour and make it respected by everyone' (1967: 37).

Every new member of the mafia families swears an oath of absolute secrecy and faithfulness during his rite of affiliation. In the families associated to Cosa Nostra the oath, which is to be pronounced by the neophyte while holding the burning image of a saint, was reported by a turncoat as follows: 'I burn you as paper, I adore you as a saint. As this paper burns, so my flesh must burn if I betray Cosa Nostra' (TrPA, 1984: 3). This oath seems to have remained almost unaltered over the decades. In 1885 Tommaso Colacino reported that a similar formula was used to initiate the novices into one of the largest mafia associations investigated in the late nineteenth century, 'La Fratellanza' of Agrigento (Colacino, 1885: 180; see also De Mauro, 1962).

Secrecy shapes every moment of the mafioso's life. 'In Cosa Nostra', Francesco Marino Mannoia states, 'it is obvious to everybody that, when one betrays the organization, death is the only retribution, and this haunts the traitor for the rest of his days' (TrPA, 1989: 88).

As with the majority of status contracts, the pact sanctioned by a ceremony of affiliation is also a 'fraternization contract' (Weber, 1978: 672). That is, the rite of mafia initiation establishes a ritual kinship between each new adherent and the rest of the group; the members of a mafia family are bound to consider themselves as brothers, part of a single collective entity. Through the symbolic representation of death and rebirth accomplished during the initiation, the new member is bound to identify himself totally with the mafia collective, to become part of a common body, to enter into almost religious communion with the other adherents in the mafia community with whom he becomes 'the same thing'. This is the phrase, not by chance, used by Cosa Nostra members when introducing 'men of honour' to one another ('He is the same thing') (TrPA, 1986, vol. V: 822; 879). Such a common belonging is also stressed by the name adopted by the Sicilian organization at least in the last three decades, Cosa Nostra, 'our thing', whereas the basic units of the organization are termed families. Here, the words have the magical power to establish barriers and to constitute groups (Bourdieu, [1980] 1990: 170).

The revaluation of the cultural aspects of the mafia may be easily misunderstood as an idealization of the mafia itself. This is not the case. Through symbolic action, mafia consortia are able to impose the role of 'men of honour' on their members as an inevitable fate, and to legitimize themselves in the eyes of both insiders and outsiders through a diversified and sophisticated use of symbolic codes and rituals. Through these means, both Cosa Nostra and the 'ndrangheta manage to build and preserve what Max Weber terms a communal social relationship, namely a relationship based on feelings of common belonging (1978: 40), in order to enhance the mutual confidence among associates. The preservation of this confidence is an essential condition for the existence of any secret society.

As with other 'ritualized relationships', those in place in the mafia appear to be characterized by 'a peculiar and distinct type of combination of instrumental and solidaristic relationship, in which the solidarity provides the basic framework, yet within this framework various instrumental considerations, albeit very diffusely defined, are of paramount importance' (Eisenstadt, 1956: 91). In other words, mafia organizations combine specific exchanges with what anthropology describes as a 'generalized exchange'. This last expression, created by Marcel Mauss in his essay *Sur le don*, and then elaborated by Claude Lévi-Strauss, is today employed to point out the non-utilitarian and unconditional relationships which are necessary to establish conditions of basic trust and solidarity in society, and to uphold what Émile Durkheim called the 'pre-contractual elements of social life' (Eisenstadt and Roniger, 1984). Belonging to a mafia group is characterized by a mixture of opportunism and solidarity, of personal selfishness and unconditional involvement.

It is exactly the necessity to maintain a balance between these two different elements, namely to prevent selfish calculation overtaking group solidarity, that causes fragility and potential disorder in mafia consortia. In the daily life of Cosa Nostra and 'ndrangheta, the prescription of group fraternity and solidarity is constantly weakened or betrayed by the conflicts of interests, the rivalries and the personal ambitions of the members, who attempt to exploit the strength of the mafia family's relationships for the achievement of specific, personal or factional goals.

The failure to maintain this balance was the primary cause for the multiplication of the number of 'pentiti' in Cosa Nostra and to a lesser extent in its Calabrian counterpart (Paoli, 1997).

Power versus profit

As the 'pentiti' report, in the 1970s both Cosa Nostra and the 'ndrangheta became involved in licit and illicit economic activities, orienting themselves towards the speedy enrichment of their members. This process was already clear in the previous decades, and mainly involved mafiosi of the larger towns, most notably those of Palermo. Such a trend was associated with the progressive withering of the 'subculture of honour' in society at large, a subculture upon which the mafiosi had traditionally founded the legitimation of their power. In the common perception of the 1950s and 1960s wealth became the basis for reputation and a readily recognizable proof of success. Being wealthy was imperative for anyone who wanted to enjoy a position of respect (Arlacchi, 1988: 57–61). In order to adapt to this cultural change and to avoid the loss of a preeminent position in their local communities, in the 1950s a growing number of mafia associates progressively 'bent' mafia brotherhood bonds with a view to accumulating wealth.

Such a 'mimetic' process (Di Maggio and Powell, 1983) was encouraged by two circumstances which were already at work in the 1960s, but reached full potential in the following decades. The mafia groups in Sicily and in Calabria took the opportunity of accumulating wealth thanks to the expansion of world illegal markets, most notably of tobacco and illicit drugs, and thanks to the growth of public spending in South Italy. A number of 'pentiti' told of the effect caused by the sudden potential for huge profits arising from the development of heroin trafficking. For example, in Antonino Calderone's recollection: 'richness came, everybody became rich. With cigarettes we earned well, but it was not a strong source of income; drugs really changed Cosa Nostra; everybody went crazy and all began to earn huge amounts of money' (CPM, 1992a: 319). This notwithstanding, the growing emphasis on economic activities is misleading for the understanding of the mafia as an enterprise. 'In reality, the mafia has not become a set of criminal *enterprises*' (Becchi and Turvani, 1993: 156; italics in the original). Although 'men of honour' routinely form coalitions in illegal markets and own myriads of officially registered companies – that is, they act time and again as entrepreneurs – their action (as well as the danger they pose) cannot be appreciated in mere economic terms.

First of all, neither Cosa Nostra nor the 'ndrangheta have given up their potential and actual use of violence. For this reason, despite their increasing relevance as economic actors, these organizations cannot simply be conceptualized in economic terms. The use of economic concepts should be limited to the description of organizations oriented to the realization of profits by means of peaceful methods. As Weber (1978: 640) put it: 'the appropriation of goods, through free, purely economically rational exchange . . . is the conceptual opposite of appropriation of goods by coercion of any kind but especially physical coercion, the regulated exercise of which is the very constitutive element of the political community'.

Like the actors involved in the creation of 'oceanic commerce' in the sixteenth century (admirably studied by the historian Frederick Lane), the mafia associations cannot be classified as either governmental or business enterprises. In both, profit- and power-oriented activities are simultaneously present and closely intertwined. 'The way', noted Lane, 'in which force was applied to secure gain determined the economic success or failure of many innovating enterprises that created oceanic commerce' (1966: 402). Violence is not a marginal element in the mafia enterprise, as its very success in the economic arena has always been dependent on the use of such a resource. Violence played an essential role in the establishment of local monopolies in a situation characterized by a lack of resources. Furthermore, violence was instrumental for the mafia groups to access international illegal markets.

It should be borne in mind that government and business have not always existed as separate organizations. Under feudalism, for example, the activities that are ideal-typically associated with the two institutions were often simultaneously carried out by the feudal lord (Lane, 1966). The separation of force-using enterprises from profit-seeking enterprises did not take place at the same time throughout Europe. Southern Italy was one of the European areas where this separation was delayed, as still in the nineteenth century feudal vestiges were clearly visible and the spirit and the legal forms of feudalism shaped most social relationships, especially in the countryside. Looking at the mafia associations, one could argue that such separation, even in current times, has not been achieved. The mafia groups evolved in a context where the use of violent means was an almost inescapable pre-condition of social ascent and, as a result of their criminalization, they were excluded from the wider process of diversification between force-using and profit-seeking enterprises. To the mafia members, violence is, on the one hand, an effective means to gain power, profits and social prestige. On the other hand, due to their exclusion and increasing secrecy, to them violence is a means by which they enforce their own internal normative code, sanction other members' violations, and defend themselves from competitors and state agencies.

Through the threat or the actual use of violence, mafia associations also attempt to impose – often successfully – their rules on their territories of influence. In a Weberian sense, mafia organizations can be properly defined as political organizations, in that they assert the validity of their own legal order within a given territorial area through the threat and the use of physical force (Weber, 1978: 54). Each 'cosca' associated either to Cosa Nostra or to the 'ndrangheta claims sovereignty over a well-defined territory which usually corresponds to a town or a village. Only in big urban conglomerates – such as Palermo and Reggio Calabria and few other Calabrian localities, does the territory of each mafia family correspond to a neighbourhood. The sovereignty that each Sicilian or Calabrian mafia unit claims to exercise is total: as the Sicilian mafia turncoat, Leonardo Messina, explained to the Antimafia Parliamentary Commission:

> You have to take into account that the families have their own businesses and that these concern everything related to the territory of the families themselves. For example, if in the community of Rome there were a family, everything that belongs to the community would be of interest, from the point of view of politics, of public works, extortions, drug trafficking, etc. In practice, the family is sovereign, it controls whatever happens on that territory.
>
> (CPM, 1992b: 516)

The exercise of a territorial dominion finds its most evident exemplification in the imposition of extortion rackets in wide areas of Sicily and Calabria. Indeed, the imposition of a tax, termed 'tangente' or 'pizzo', has always been one of the preferred ways for the mafia to secure resources. Extortion is a type of financing that, as Weber noted with explicit reference to the Sicilian mafia and the Neapolitan camorra, is only intermittent on the surface, because it is formally illegal. In practice, it often assumes the character of a periodic 'subscription', paid in exchange for the delivery of certain services, notably of a guarantee of security (Weber, 1978: 194–5).

Such an exchange has recently led Diego Gambetta to conceive of the mafia as 'a specific economic enterprise, an industry that produces, promotes and sells private protection' (1993: 1). This approach has the merit of pointing out one of the most important functions carried out by mafia groups. This is a quintessential one, since it derives from their claim to legitimately exercise violence in their areas of influence, denying the legitimacy of the state monopoly of force. It is, however, regrettable that, for polemical reasons, Gambetta overlooks the analogies between the mafia and the state, thus denying the status of political organization to the former. This analogy was outlined by Charles Tilly in the following terms: 'if protection rackets represent organized crime at its smoothest, then war making and state making – quintessential protection rackets with the advantage of legitimacy – qualify as our largest examples of organized crime' (1985: 169). Gambetta's analysis has also been criticized for his one-sided emphasis on protection and his denial of the multi-faceted nature of the mafia. According to him, in fact, 'mafiosi as such deal with no good other than protection. Joining the mafia amounts to receiving a license to supply protection rather than simply consuming it' (1993: 9). Nonetheless, the pentiti's accounts as well as a large number of judicial and non-judicial sources prove that members of Sicilian and Calabrian 'cosche' not only 'sell' protection but are also active on a plurality of other legal and illegal markets. As Nelken put it, 'Gambetta's insistence that the Mafia is and has always been in the protection business is somewhat essentialist. The vast range of activities in which the Mafia plays a part makes generalization difficult' (1995).

There is an inextricable mixture of power- and profit-oriented activities which clearly emerges in the investment strategies developed by both the Sicilian mafia and the 'ndrangheta. Throughout the last fifteen years, both organizations have exploited large shares of their drug trade to acquire a dominant position over the local public-works market, discarding safer and possibly more profitable investments abroad. Though these last have not entirely been neglected, 'men of honour' of both Cosa Nostra and 'ndrangheta have preferred to consolidate their control over a local market that has consistently grown over the post-war period as a result of increasing state intervention:

> The practical goals are three: to gain kickbacks, to place their work force in the sub-contracts, and to let 'friendly' companies win the tenders. But the general objective has been more ambitious: with the hands on public tenders, Cosa Nostra is able to control the essential aspects of the political and economic life of the territory, because it conditions entrepreneurs, politicians, bureaucrats, workers and professionals. This aspect contributes to strengthen their territorial domination, consolidates social consensus, makes individual mafia families more powerful in their own territory, as well as in the political and administrative apparatus.
>
> (CPM, 1993b)

With these aims, members of both organizations have employed their large financial surplus to buy – either directly or through fronts – a large number of small and medium-sized companies and vast pieces of land in their areas of dominion (PrRC, 1992). Notwithstanding the growing involvement in economic activities, it is thus evident that, today as in the past, a primary goal of mafia action remains the establishment of power over the local community, to which the attainment of the highest investments returns is subordinated. Even from a psychological point of view power remains the decisive element:

> The true goal is power. The obscure evil of organization chiefs is not the thirst for money but for power. The most notorious fugitives of the mafia could enjoy a luxurious life abroad until the end of their days. Instead, they remain in Palermo, hunted, in danger of being caught or being killed by internal dissidents, in order not to lose the territorial control and not to run the risk of being deposed. Marino Mannoia once told me: 'Many believe that you enter into Cosa Nostra for the money. This is only part of the truth. Do you know why I entered Cosa Nostra? Because before in Palermo I was Mr. Nobody. Afterwards, wherever I went, heads lowered. And this for me was priceless.
>
> (Scarpinato, 1992: 94)

Far from having diminished the mafia's political role, the accumulation of wealth since the 1970s appears to have fostered the systematic exercise of political violence, particularly on the part of Cosa Nostra. According to Buscetta: 'in the early 1980s they seemed to be convinced that they could either buy or kill all state officials that intended to fight them, and that their power was untouchable' (Arlacchi, 1994: 222). Since 1978, Cosa Nostra has killed several policemen, judges and politicians who had 'betrayed' mafia friendships or endangered mafia interests (Stille, 1995), whereas in the past the targeting of state officials and representatives had been much less frequent. Without any type of economic consideration, fully-fledged terrorism has also been organized by the Sicilian mafia organization. In 1992, after the definitive confirmation of the Palermo maxi-trial sentence by the Corte di Cassazione, Cosa Nostra put aside the traditional strategy of 'mediation and cohabitation' with state institutions (PrPA, 1995, vol. 3: 15–18). In addition to murdering the two main political pawns, Salvo Lima and Ignazio Salvo, who were punished for having failed to influence the court, Cosa Nostra organized the spectacular murder of the two judges regarded as responsible for their conviction: Giovanni Falcone and Paolo Borsellino. The subversive strategy of direct confrontation with both state institutions and civil society went on into 1993, when Cosa Nostra staged alarming acts of terrorism in some major cities of mainland Italy. These acts of terror remain unintelligible if one equates mafia groups with contemporary business enterprises. In fact, they promoted the mobilization of large strata of the civil society as well as a determined response on the part of law-enforcement institutions, which produced the highest volume of anti-mafia activities in the last 30 years. As a result, the major mafia bosses were arrested and illegal trades were considerably hampered. The impressive display of their own military potential was, however, judged by Sicilian 'capimafia' as an indispensable measure to reassure Cosa Nostra's imprisoned 'people', to force colluding politicians to respect the pacts (by opposing newly introduced antimafia legal provisions), and to secure the support and silence of the local population.

Concluding remarks

The statements and confessions of the 'pentiti' constitute an unprecedented source of information about the world of the mafia. As a 'ndrangheta turncoat put it, mafia affiliates cooperating with the judiciary describe the mafia 'from the inside and not only from the outside, as it has so far been done through the investigative work of the police and carabinieri' (PrRC, 1995: 361) as well as scholars. Thanks to their contributions, starting with Buscetta's confession to Judge Falcone in 1984, the knowledge of the mafia has increased in a phenomenal way. This new knowledge allows us to supersede the two main paradigms that have been constructed in the last thirty years.

In recent years, several scholars and observers have begun to utilize such knowledge. The existence of corporate mafia actors has, for example, been acknowledged by many authors who previously denied it (Arlacchi, [1992] 1993; 1994; Hess, 1995). Similarly, authors who had more intensely stressed the economic dimension of mafia groups, have recently paid more attention to their political dimension (see, for example, Santino, 1994b; Catanzaro, 1988; 1994a and b). Although remaining in a strictly economic perspective, Gambetta's analysis has contributed to overcoming the standard version of the enterprise paradigm, by hinting at the political functions of mafia actors and by beginning a reassessment of mafia rituals and symbols. Cultural concerns have also been powerfully raised by the activists of antimafia movements that have flourished since the early 1980s in Palermo. Their exposure of widespread attitudes and behaviours favouring the perpetuation of mafia power, and their efforts towards cultural regeneration in Sicily have stimulated the work and debate among social scientists and cultural-studies experts (Schneider and Schneider, 1994). The culture of the mafia as well as the culture of the surrounding society colluding with it are now on the agenda of pedagogues (Casarrubea and Blandano, 1991; 1993) and psychologists (Di Vita, 1986; Di Maria et al., 1989; Di Maria and Lavanco, 1995). Finally, similar emphasis on the mafia culture has inspired a series of studies dealing with the relationship between women and the mafia (Puglisi, 1990; Puglisi and Santino, 1996; Siebert, 1994).

The present paper has tried to add to such contributions. It has focused on three aspects in relation to which the information provided by the 'pentiti' is most relevant: the internal structure of the mafia, the components of its subculture, and its intertwining political and economic activities. With respect to the first aspect, it should be reiterated that at the core of the mafia there are some organized groups. Although these groups are called families by their members, they can neither be reduced to a simple aggregation of biological or acquired relatives around a mafioso, nor to a loose network of patron–client relations. The 90 or so mafia families associated respectively to the Sicilian Cosa Nostra and the Calabrian 'ndrangheta are closed, formalized organizations, whose membership is regulated through ceremonies of initiation. Since the nineteenth century, the boundary dividing the group from the outside world is provided by secrecy, and secrecy represents the first commitment of each affiliate.

Rituals, cultural codes and symbols shape the mafia groups' life and define the role of 'men of honour'. Although regarded by most academic observers with suspicion, these rituals and codes play a central function in the reproduction of the mafia organizations, in that they secure and reinforce members' loyalty and create a 'feeling of belonging' which constitutes a pre-condition for the maintenance of secrecy.

In conclusion, despite the growing involvement in economic activities since the early 1970s, the mafia groups cannot be regarded as mere business enterprises. On the one hand, these groups differ from other enterprises for the life-long unconditional commitment they require from their members. On the other hand, they differ from their official counterparts for their use of violence, which allows them to claim sovereignty over the territories in which they inhabit. In mafia groups the use of force coexists with power-oriented and economic-oriented activities.

References

Alvaro, C. (1955) 'La fibbia', *Il Corriere della Sera*, 17 September.

Arlacchi, P. ([1983 and 1986] 1988) *Mafia Business. The Mafia Ethic and the Spirit of Capitalism*, Oxford: Oxford University Press.

—— ([1992] 1993) *Men of Dishonor. Inside the Sicilian Mafia: An Account of Antonino Calderone*, New York: William Morrow.

—— (1994) *Addio Cosa Nostra. La vita di Tommaso Buscetta*, Milano: Rizzoli.

Becchi, A. and Turvani, M. (1993) *Proibito? Il mercato mondiale della droga*, Roma: Donzelli.

Becchi, A. and Rey, G. M. (1994) *L'economia criminale*, Bari-Roma: Laterza.

Berger, P. L. and Luckmann, T. ([1966] 1967) *The Social Construction of Reality: A Treatise in the Sociology of Knowledge*, New York: Anchor Books.

Blok, A. ([1974] 1986) *The Mafia of a Sicilian Village, 1860–1960: a Study of Violent Entrepreneurs*, New York and Oxford: Basil Blackwell.

Bourdieu, P. ([1980] 1990) *The Logics of Practice*, Cambridge: Polity Press.

Casarrubea, G. and Blandano, P. (1991) *L'educazione mafiosa*, Palermo: Sellerio.

—— (1993) *Nella testa del serpente. Insegnanti e mafia*, Molfetta: La Meridiana.

Castagna, S. (1967) *Tu devi uccidere*, edited by A. Perria, Milano: Il Momento.

Catanzaro, R. (1986) 'Impresa mafiosa e sistemi di regolazione sociale: appunti sul caso siciliano', in G. Fiandaca and S. Costantino (eds.) *La legge antimafia tre anni dopo*, Milano: Franco Angeli.

—— ([1988] 1991) *Il delitto come impresa. Storia sociale della mafia*, Milano: Rizzoli.

—— ([1988] 1992) *Men of Respect. A Social History of the Sicilian Mafia*, New York: The Free Press.

—— (1988) 'Il governo violento del mercato. Mafia, imprese e sistema politico', *Stato e Mercato*, n. 23, agosto: 177–211.

—— (1994a) 'La mafia tra mercato e stato: una proposta di analisi', in G. Fiandaca and S. Costantino (eds), *La mafia, le mafie*, Bari-Roma: Laterza.

—— (1994b) 'Violent Social Regulation: Organized Crime in the Italian South', *Social and Legal Studies*, vol. 3: 267–79.

Centorrino, M. (1986) *L'economia mafiosa*, Soveria Mannelli: Rubbettino.

—— (1989) 'La mafia come impresa', *Politica ed economia*, n. 9.

—— (1990) *L'economia 'cattiva' del Mezzogiorno*, Napoli: Liguori.

—— (1995) *Economia assistita da mafia*, Soveria Mannelli: Rubbettino.

Ciconte, E. (1996) *Processo alla 'ndrangheta*, Bari: Laterza.

Cohen, A. ([1974] 1976) *The Two-Dimensional Man. An Essay on the Anthropology of Power and Symbolism in Complex Society*, Berkeley and Los Angeles: University of California Press.

Colacino, T. V. (1885) 'La Fratellanza. Associazione di malfattori', *Rivista di discipline carcerarie in relazione con l'Antropologia, col Diritto Penale e con la Statistica*, xv, 5–6: 177–189.

CPM, Commissione Parlamentare d'inchiesta sul fenomeno della mafia e sulle altre associazioni similari (1992a) *Audizione del collaboratore di giustizia Antonino Calderone*, 11 novembre, XI legislatura.

—— (1992b) *Audizione del collaboratore di giustizia Leonardo Messina*, 4 dicembre, XI legislatura.

—— (1993a) *Audizione del collaboratore di giustizia Gaspare Mutolo*, 9 febbraio, XI legislatura.

—— (1993b) *Relazione sui rapporti tra mafia e politica*, doc. XXIII, n.2, XI legislatura, 6 aprile.

De Mauro, M. (1962) 'La Confessure del dott. Melchiore Allegra: come io, medica, diventai mafioso', *L'Ora* 22–3 Jan.

Di Maggio, P. J. and Powell, W. W. (1983) 'The Iron Cage Revisited: Institutional Isomorphism and Collective Rationality in Organizational Fields', *American Sociological Review*, 48: 147–160.

Di Maria, F. Di Nuovo, S. Di Vita, A. M., Dolce, C. G. and Pepi, A. M. (1989) *Il sentire mafioso*, Milano: Giuffré.

Di Maria, F. and Lavanco, G. (1995) *A un passo dall'inferno. Sentire mafioso e obbedienza criminale*, Firenze: Giunti.

Di Vita, A. M. (ed.) (1986) *Alle radici di un'immagine della mafia*, Milano: Angeli.

Eisenstadt, S. N. (1956) 'Ritualized Personal Relations. Blood Brotherhood, Compadre, etc.: Some Comparative Hypotheses and Suggestions', *Man*, 96: 90–95.

Eisenstadt, S. N. and Roniger, L. (1984) *Patrons, Clients and Friends. Interpersonal Relations and the Structure of Trust in Society*, Cambridge and London: Cambridge University Press.

Falcone, G. (in cooperation with M. Padovani) (1991) *Cose di Cosa Nostra*, Milano: Rizzoli.

Gambetta, D. (1993) *The Sicilian Mafia. The Business of Private Protection*, Cambridge and London: Harvard University Press.

Gennep, A. van ([1909] 1960) *The Rites of Passage*, Chicago: University of Chicago Press.

Goffman, E. (1961) *Asylums*, New York: Anchor Doubleday.

Hess, H ([1970] 1973) *Mafia and Mafiosi. The Structure of Power*, Westmead: Saxon House.

—— (1995) 'Parastato e capitalismo corsaro. La mafia siciliana dal 1943 al 1993', *Incontri meridionali*, 1–2: 41–71.

Lane, F. C. (1966) *Venice and Its History*, Baltimore: The Johns Hopkins Press.

Luhmann, N. ([1984] 1991) *Social Systems*, Standford: Standford University Press.

Lupo, S. (1988) 'Il tenebroso sodalizio. Un rapporto sulla mafia palermitana di fine Ottocento', *Studi storici*, 29, n. 2: 463–489.

—— (1993) *Storia della mafia dalle origini ai giorni nostri*, Roma: Donzelli.

—— (1994) 'Pentitismo, ieri ed oggi', in G. Fiandaca and S. Costantino (eds) *La mafia, le mafie*, Bari-Roma: Laterza.

MacKenzie, N. (ed.) (1967) *Secret Societies*, London: Aldus Book.

Mayer, A. C. (1966) 'The significance of quasi-groups in the study of complex societies', in M. Banton (ed.) *The Social Anthropology of Complex Societies*, ASA monograph no. 4, London: Tavistock

Ministero dell'Interno (1994) *Rapporto annuale sul fenomeno della criminalità organizzata per il 1993*, Roma, Camera dei Deputati, doc. XXXVIII-bis, n. 1, XII legislatura.

—— (1995) *Rapporto annuale sul fenomeno della criminalità organizzata per il 1994*, Roma, XII legislatura.

—— (1996) *Relazione sui programmi di protezione, sulla loro efficacia e sulle modalità generali di applicazione per coloro che collaborano alla giustizia* – 1996, Roma, Senato della Repubblica, doc. XCI, n. 1, XIII legislatura.

Nelken, D. (1995) *Review of 'The Sicilian Mafia. The Business of Private Protection'*, by Diego Gambetta, *British Journal of Criminology*, vol. 35, no. 2: 287–9.

Paoli, L. (1997) *The Pledge of Secrecy, Structure, Culture and Action of Mafia Associations*, Ph.D. thesis, Firenze: European University Institute.

Pezzino, P. (1987) 'Stato violenza società. Nascita e sviluppo del paradigma mafiosoö, in M. Aymard and G. Giarrizzo (eds.) *La Sicilia*, Torino: Giulio Einaudi Editore.

—— (1990) 'La tradizione rivoluzionaria siciliana e l'invenzione della mafia', *Meridiana*, 7–8: 45–71.

—— (1992) *La congiura dei pugnalatori. Un caso politico-giudiziario alle origini della mafia*, Venezia: Marsilio.

PrPA, Procura della Repubblica di Palermo, Direzione Distrettuale Antimafia (1992) *Dichiarazioni rese da Leonardo Messina*.

—— (1993) *Richiesta di applicazione di misure cautelari contro Agrigento Giuseppe + 60*, 20 May.

—— (1995) *Memoria depositata dal pubblico ministero nel procedimento penale n. 3538–94, instaurato nei confronti di Andreotti Giulio*.

PrRC, Procura della Repubblica di Reggio Calabria, Direzione Distrettuale Antimafia (1992) *Richiesta di ordini di custodia cautelare in carcere nel procedimento contro Mammoliti Saro + 12*, 31 July.

—— (1993) *Richiesta di ordini di custodia cautelare in carcere nel procedimento contro Morabito Giuseppe + 161*, 5 November.

—— (1995) *Richiesta di ordini di custodia cautelare in carcere e di contestuale rinvio a giudizio nel procedimento contro Condello Pasquale + 477*, July.

Puglisi, A. (1990) *Sole contro la mafia*, Palermo: La Luna.

Puglisi, A. and Santino U. (1996) 'Appunti sulla ricerca del Centro Impastato su Donne e Mafia', unpublished typescript.

Recupero, A. (1987a) 'La Sicilia all'opposizione (1848–74)', in M. Aymard and G. Giarrizzo (eds) *La Sicilia*, Torino: Giulio Einaudi Editore.

—— (1987b) 'Ceti medi e "homines novi" alle origini della mafia', *Polis*, 2: 307–328.

Santino, U. (1988) 'The Financial Mafia: the Illegal Accumulation of Wealth and the Financial-Industrial Complex', *Contemporary Crises*, 12: 203–243.

—— (1994a) *La borghesia mafiosa. Materiali di un percorso di analisi*, Palermo: Centro siciliano di documentazione Giuseppe Impastato.

—— (1994b) *La mafia come soggetto politico*, Palermo: Centro siciliano di documentazione Giuseppe Impastato.

—— (1994c) 'La mafia come soggetto politico. Ovvero: la produzione mafiosa della politica e la produzione politica della mafia', in G. Fiandaca and S. Costantino (eds.) *La mafia, le mafie*, Bari-Roma: Laterza.

Santino, U. and La Fiura, G. (1990) *L'impresa mafiosa. Dall'Italia agli Stati Uniti*, Milano: Franco Angeli.

Scarpinato, R. (1992) 'Mafia e politica', in Various Authors, *Mafia. Anatomia di un regime*, Roma: Librerie Associate.

Schneider, J. and Schneider, P. (1976) *Culture and Political Economy in Western Sicily*, New York: Academic Press.

—— (1994) 'Mafia, Antimafia and the Question of Sicilian Culture', *Politics and Society*, vol. 22, no. 2: 237–258.

Siebert, R. (1994) *Le donne, la mafia*, Milano, Il Saggiatore.

Smith, D. C. ([1975] 1990) *The Mafia Mystique*, New York: Basic Books.

Smith, M. G. (1974) *Corporations and Society*, Duckworth.

Stille, A. (1995) *Excellent Cadavers. The Mafia and the Death of the First Italian Republic*, London: Jonathan Cape.

Tilly, C. (1985) 'War Making and State Making as Organized Crime', in P. B. Evans, D. Rueschemeyer and T. Skocpol (eds) *Bringing the State Back In*, Cambridge: Cambridge University Press.

TrMI, Tribunale di Milano (1994) *Ordinanza di custodia cautelare in carcere nei confronti di Abys Adriano + 394*, 6 June.

TrPA, Tribunale di Palermo (1984) *Verbali di interrogatorio reso dal collaboratore di giustizia, Tommaso Buscetta*, vol. 3.

—— (1986) *Sentenza-ordinanza di rinvio a giudizio nei confronti di Abbate Giovanni + 706*, November.

—— (1989) *Verbali di interrogatorio reso dal collaboratore di giustizia, Francesco Marino Mannoia*.

Weber, M. ([1922] 1978) *Economy and Society*, edited by G. Roth and C. Wittich, Berkeley and Los Angeles: University of California Press.

Zamagni, S. (ed.) (1993) *Mercati illegali e mafie. L'economia del crimine organizzato*, Bologna: Il Mulino.

Part IV

THE INTERNATIONAL AND THE LOCAL

18

GLOCAL ORGANISED CRIME:
CONTEXT AND PRETEXT

Dick Hobbs and Colin Dunnighan[1]

Introduction

This chapter challenges the empirical adequacy of a recent conceptual trend in criminological research that is best described as the global mapping of organised crime and criminal organisations. A serious shortcoming of global-transnational-international studies of organised crime is that they ignore or substantially under-estimate the importance of the local context as an environment within which criminal networks function. Based on the case studies of an ongoing ethno-graphic investigation (Hobbs and Dunnighan, 1997), this chapter suggests that improved understanding is gained by exploring the dynamics of the local context of trading networks and transformative systems of criminal and legitimate com-mercial activity that facilitate sources of innovative mediation between a matrix of local places, flexible spaces, local and global networks and negotiated criminal collaborations. The case-study abstracts enter the lifeworlds of organised crime from two perspectives: first, the concept of locality is explored, paying particular attention to the reflective trajectories and mirrored dissolution of urban working-class populations and the traditional organised family firm, and secondly, the criminal careers of various deviant identities are examined. Following on, the paper presents an analysis of the key thematic issues raised in these studies and discusses their implications for contemporary understandings of organised crime. As the final discussion evolves, it will become increasingly apparent that our experience of crime is grounded in the local, a dynamic mapping context that, when perceived in terms of a collectivity of experiences, constitutes a funda-mentally different way of seeing and defining organised crime.

This is crucial at a time when European policing systems are merging, amal-gamating and mutating, while continuing to compete within a bewildering mael-strom of political and legal jurisdictions (Sheptycki,1995). The knee-jerk shift towards the adoption of variations upon post-modern narratives, tends to cast aside powerful enacted histories, in favour of tales of historical fissure which are located in state-fixated, post-Marxist analysis. For while forms of formal government are in a state of constant shift, the illegal market place merely will continue to negotiate new boundaries with the same adeptness that it used in negotiating the old.

The problem with global paradigms of organised crime

Both the destruction of formal national boundaries and the redundancy of cold-war narratives have led to an increasing concern with the nature and implications of transnational organised crime (see Godson and Olson, 1993; Labrousse and Wallon, 1993; Williams, 1993; 1994; Williams and Savona, 1995; Sterling, 1994; Calvi, 1993). The term 'transnational' is particularly problematic when referring to organised crime because it speaks in a language that normally relates to cross-border activity and operations that explicitly exclude the State (Hobsbawm, 1994). The relationship between the State and serious crime however, is now so ambiguous that the term 'transnational organised crime' can only be meaningful when situated within the political-science-inspired moral panics that have emerged as a response to the fragmentation of the Eastern Bloc, and situated within the fiscal civil wars of declining western states (Naylor, 1995). Further, transnationality suggests a crucial 'otherness', an essentially alien pollutant (cf. Cressey, 1972) that denies the home-grown nature of serious crime (see Potter, 1994). Crucially this denial allows for the development of transnational policing systems (cf. Bresler, 1992) and their enabling legal instruments (Commonwealth Secretariat, 1993), with little regard to the nature of the criminal activities they were designed to combat.

Relations between the local and global

It is crucial therefore, to be sceptical of models of organised or serious crime that rely heavily upon transnationality, cross-border, international or other metaphors of globalisation at one end of the spectrum, and 'local street gangs' (Rider, 1990) at the other. Such a model fails to embrace the complexity of 'local contextualities' (Giddens, 1991: 22), and although the essential connectedness of contemporary organised crime is necessitated by the existence of trading relationships that stretch across the globe (Harvey, 1989), this does not indicate either a local/global – action/reaction polarity, or a cultural homogeneity that will override difference. As Robertson notes, 'it makes no good sense to define the global as if the global excludes the local . . . defining the global in such a way suggests that the global lies beyond all localities, as having systematic properties over and beyond the attributes of units within a global system' (1995: 34). In fact, current research indicates that even 'international' criminal organisations function as interdependent local units (Hobbs and Dunnighan, 1997), and as the following case studies illustrate (in particular, see 'Bill and Ben'), the incorporation of locales into overlapping networks of legal and illegal commerce is a more accurate description of criminal activities than the compression of criminal action into a legalistically framed world order of transnational corporations.

The dialectic between the local and the global suggests that the indirect nature of the power wielded by large multinational organisations confirms elements of flexibility, autonomy and independence that were once unimaginable. This indirect power and its associated flexibility is also a major factor in serious/ organised crime, for as current research indicates, there are enormous variations in local crime groups (Hobbs and Dunnighan, 1997), which function and prosper within the distinctiveness and viability of different localities, where the organisation of criminal labour tends to mirror general trends in the organisation of legitimate labour (Hobbs, 1997; Ruggiero, 1995). It will become apparent, as the paper evolves into a discussion of the different localities of Downton and Upton, that it is possible to draw close parallels between local demographic patterns, local employment and subsequent work and leisure cultures with variations in organised crime groups.

Criminal lifeworlds

Local places and negotiated spaces

Downton

Downton has witnessed the transformation of the local criminal neighbourhood firm during the second half of this century from traditional family-based associations, deeply entrenched in the traditional overtones of working-class parochialism, to a networked system displaced from the resonance of nostalgic criminal locales. The firm becomes re-invented in the form of temporary collaborations, momentarily suspended within the trading networks of a market environment drained of any capacity to translate territorial control into market sovereignty. Contextualised within Downton as a locality, the transformation of the traditional family firm into either individualistic mutations or actively disorganised deviant scavengers, is reflective of dramatic economic changes that the region has sustained since the turn of the 1960s. Stripped of the traditional industrial contours that once shaped and structured community life (local labour market, neighbourhood ecology, extended family networks and leisure time), Downton's working-class population began to fragment against the backdrop of a redundant industrial landscape, fracturing the community's material base and creating new crucially blurred socio-economic coalitions.

These consist of loosely structured informal collectivities of ad hoc groupings, local social systems that can no longer rely on forms of parochial dominance previously enjoyed by the feudal warlords of the 1950s and 1960s (such as the Krays, Billy Hill, Jack Comer and the Richardson brothers). The disappearance of the traditional working-class milieu, along with its highly specific domestic arrangements, its organised leisure, and its well established neighbourhood patterns and oral networks (Pakulski and Walters, 1996), has meant the dissolution of traditional forms of organised crime that were so reliant upon this milieu and its dominant familial structures. With this in view, it is evident that a contemporary interpretation of organised or serious crime, like a traditional reading of working-class populations, is meaningless if and when analysed only within the languid boundaries of traditional cultures and subcultures (Horne and Hall, 1995). New dynamics of bureaucratic and technological capital are influencing new rhythms of lifestyle consumption that have consequentially led to the emergence of the 'market place' as the primary societal dynamic and the ultimate framework for contemporaneous conceptualisations of organised and serious crime.

Upton

The above account of Downton, a site of disused industrial landscape, shifting populations and dispersed working class neighbourhoods, discusses the changes incurred when the foundations of traditional industry are uprooted. Unlike in Downton, the destruction of Upton's industrial base has not resulted in a similar cultural destination for the region, as it is a locality of static population grounded in traditional notions of the family and neighbourhood, both of which have managed to remain coherent and relatively intact. Clearly, the ecological relationship between the demographic dynamics of a location, including the structure of populations and design of housing settlements, and features of economic-technological development, is central to any contemporary interpretation of the transformation of organised crime. In the case of Downton, the dissolution of traditional forms of organised crime occurred among a shifting and ethnically diverse population structure. For Upton, an active but stationary population facilitated the preservation of a cultural inheritance that enabled its principal crime groups to reflect the city's traditional profile (family based and territorially orientated) in a way that has become a persistent feature of the local landscape across generations.

Upton is a city characterised by a highly concentrated leisure industry. Engagement with these indigenous leisure markets has generated two central commercial concerns for crime: the drug trade and the protection business. Criminal groups in Upton interact with market contingencies such as commodities, networks, localities and consumption points, in an overtly identifiable style representative of acknowledged images of heavily localised organised criminality that are in accordance with the city's cultural inheritance (Ianni, 1971). The persistence of forms of retrospectively styled localised criminality is best represented by the protection business. In the case of traditional neighbourhood-crime groups in Upton, their continued existence has been fuelled by the use of violence or violent potential in an effort to control and regulate the amphetamine and ecstasy market in and around the city's pubs and clubs. Acknowledged reputations, long-standing tenure in local neighbourhoods and their illegal markets (as well as the cultural authority they propagate), inspires a sense of trust that is crucial to the continued prosperity of any old established firm (Hobbs, 1995: Ch. 3 & 6), and simultaneously enhances the firm's future prospects by expanding its operations beyond the confines of the old neighbourhood and into the leisure ghettos of the post-industrial city (Hollands, 1995). The provision of physically imposing uniformed security staff for the policing of pubs and clubs helps create an elevated and highly marketable profile for criminal entrepreneurs seeking to gain a monopoly in the bountiful terrains of the illegal market place – a business profile that rides high on the image of 'super-competency', implicit to the working of any market, and leans heavily upon the marketing of trust (Gambetta, 1988 and 1993).

The nature of protection as practised by traditional firms in Upton is extremely ambiguous in that the entity being protected is essentially a mutant of both market and territorial domains. For although local crime groups engage in the policing of leisure establishments, they seldom own the premises within which they work. Consequently when a sector of the leisure market is manifested as a field of contested space, it can become both an arena for the rejuvenation of old feuds, and a primary context for the translation of territorial concerns into market prerogatives.

It is evident that the style of organised crime in Upton – one that is firmly entrenched in the locations, working practices – occupational cultures and oppositional strategies of the industrial working class, represents an ideal synergy with the past. Such a graphic reaffirmation of local heritage is a way of maintaining the internal order and identity of traditional cultures, features that play a role in retaining coherent leisure market potential purely because they are able to 'lift out' (Giddens, 1991:18) the symbolic impressions of routine traditional strategies such as leisure time, and rearticulate them in the place of the locale and space of pragmatic consciousness (see Horne and Hall, 1995; Davis, 1990: Ch. 5; Hobbs, 1988).

An ecological appreciation of the city's demographic structure facilitates an interpretation of organised crime on a plane of analysis that differs greatly from approaches that are harnessed to a global model of organised crime with a focus on essentially corporate organisation. There are, it is believed, bigger money makers than the local firms in Upton, but in terms of the effect on the local order of this city, the impact is made by the traditional neighbourhood firms rather than the serious crime entrepreneur, as the former provide a form of spatial governance that is coherent with the immobility of the working-class population, the continuity of neighbourhood boundaries and the relevance of familial ties. Compared to Downton, the city of Upton relays a very different and highly simplistic situation, and one in which it is possible to conduct mapping exercises that elucidate the origins, nature and operations of the city's organised crime groups. The mapping of organised crime in Downton has been a futile activity for nearly a quarter of a century.

Traditions and the heritage of locales

The heritage of locales such as that of Upton are steeped in traditional notions of criminality, and whilst they are established by the precedents of indigenous markets, these locales succeed in simultaneously engaging with contemporaneous criminal opportunities – a move which is representative of an explicit acknowledgement of the distinct characteristics inherent in local demographics, of variations of demand, of the indigenous utility of space, and of the power intrinsic in the notion of a distinctly homogeneous and identifiable enacted environment of local serious criminal activity. Cumulatively, this empowers organised crime with the capacity to summon some retrospective order and inject it into a life-world that is prone to chaotic, apparently incoherent interludes (Reuter, 1984) of criminality. Through blending experiences within the enacted environments of contemporary serious crime markets with an acquired sense of 'retrospective unity' (Bauman, 1992:138), a generalised recipe of locality (Robertson, 1995: 26) that relies heavily upon an understanding of invented traditions is created (Anderson, 1983).

In Downton, however, the territory that once defined and shaped organised crime groups has disintegrated and serious crime has become removed from the territories that spawned elementary forms of criminal organisation (King, 1991: 6). In particular, the delineation of Downton's traditional neighbourhoods and housing settlements has inspired a blurred and confused set of boundary distinctions that, due to its municipal housing policy and developments in the region's private housing market, has succeeded in distributing the local serious-crime community and its progeny over a wide, amorphous territory. Along with the globalisation of legitimate commercial markets, this fragmentation has speeded up the disintegration of traditional cultures (Bursik, 1986), and the growth of a global drugs market has contributed to the widespread destruction of traditional criminal territories and their accompanying historic practices, feuds and alliances. Consequently, organised crime groups as social systems have been stretched across time and space, its practitioners residing upon a socio-economic terrain indistinct from that occupied by civilians, and contrasting with all prior forms of criminality 'in respect of their dynamism, the degree to which they undercut traditional habits and customs, and their global impact' (Giddens, 1991: 1). Yet such a macro view, although vital to an understanding of the negotiations between the historical, geographical, familial and market forces that are central to our understanding of serious crime networks, is in danger of bypassing the career trajectories of those who constitute the criminal workforce.

Criminal careers

Bill and Ben

The criminal careers of Bill and Ben began separately as local teenage burglars. In their late teens, they had started to rob offices and factories whilst operating within various amorphous coalitions of part-time thieves. In his early twenties, Bill had received two years imprisonment for theft and receiving stolen goods, and on his release he teamed up with Ben and an associate from prison to plunder building sites. Working in league with building workers and contractors, they managed to progress the scope of their thieving operations from building supplies to equipment and light plant machinery. Because they had secured a close collaboration with the contractors, the success of their money-making enterprises over a five-year period generated a degree of wealth that allowed Bill and Ben to invest in property. Ben moved into property development funded partly by a series of fraudulent mortgage deals using family members on his wife's side as a front. During the property boom, Ben invested in the importation of cannabis and by the time his property business collapsed, he was borrowing money to invest in dope. His marriage failed, and the fallout of involvement in the mortgage scams by certain members of Ben's family gave a certain edge to the ensuing divorce proceedings. This, together with a lack of available funds and the problems of an unrelated dispute with his business partners, assured the decline of the dope importation business, an enterprise which had been located within the framework of a legitimate transport company, and consigned Ben to the massed ranks of small-time local dealers.

Meantime, Bill's career had favourably progressed with his acquired share in a thriving pub, and he teamed up again with Ben as part of a loose collectivity of thieves who plundered vehicles parked at all-night lorry parks. The activities of this deviant collaboration were simplistically organised, but effective. They would borrow a lorry, display false registration plates on the vehicle, enter the lorry park, pay the fee to the security guard and park the lorry, at which point the driver would leave the scene – leaving behind the thieves he had smuggled into the park in the back of the lorry. During the night, the thieves would exit the vehicle, locate a target or targets to plunder and load up their own lorry with goods. At dawn, the lorry driver would return to the scene and drive away both the thieves and the plunder to the goods yard of Ben's dope-business partner. Once the registration plates on the lorry were changed back to the original, the nature of the deviant collaboration turned from goods acquisition to commercial marketing and distribution via a network of outlets constituted mainly of legitimate businesses.

It was apparent to Bill that his investment in the pub was proving to be a prosperous move. Doing business in the leisure market uncovered opportunities for Bill to pursue in the drugs industry, and he struck up an association with a group of men importing and dealing in amphetamines. Networking within a myriad of associations among the pub-and-club fraternity was more profitable than the plundering game, from which he was soon to retire. His career followed on with a move into the second-hand-furniture business, and the contacts and trading network footholds that he acquired from his work on the leisure scene enabled him to move on large quantities of stolen CDs and designer clothes. Bill, lost in drink, remarried and left the area, and Ben's business partners have become heavier in style as his wealth has prospered.

There are no key players in this network, no ring leaders, bosses or godfathers. The criminal collaborations of Bill and Ben are essentially co-operative, a series of temporary arrangements of ever-changing actors, forged around the common pursuit of money.

Dave Peters

Dave Peters was an all-purpose thief who by the late 1970s regularly collaborated with various criminal coalitions to import and wholesale cannabis. His criminal career has featured a long-term relationship with Gary Smith, and during the early 1980s he was involved with the administration of a team of burglars who worked freelance for Gary Smith. Peters later went on to assist in the management of a number of prominent pubs that now form a chain across Downton. In the early years of the 1990s, Peters moved to Spain, acquiring commercial and residential property on the Costa Del Sol, and set up a business as a shipping agent. Smith is the owner of several clubs in Europe and has, for some time, been involved in the business of drug importation and distribution. For at least eight years, his trade has involved ecstasy and amphetamines, and for about five years Smith has been involved in importing cocaine. Aside from his illegal trading in Europe, Peters also owns warehouses on the periphery of Downton, which apart from their legitimate use, are also used by thieves as a 'slaughter', a venue for the dispersal of stolen goods.

Ned

In many respects, Ned's lifestyle is not dissimilar to any other successful middle-aged businessman. He lives with his second wife and their two children in a £100,000 house, drives a new Mercedes car, is being pursued by the Inland Revenue for unpaid tax, is a member of his local sports/health club and has a mistress. What differentiates Ned from the mainstream of business careers, however, is the diversity of his income-generating activities, which span a spectrum of legal and illegal concerns.

Born into a family who had, for several generations, been successfully involved (both legally and illegally) in taking bets on horse races, Ned's years as a young man were lived in a style that was accustomed to having access to large sums of ready cash. On leaving school with a handful of GCEs and CSEs and taking on the position of a trainee shop manager, he soon realised that the wage he received was insufficient to satisfy his developing fondness for women, gambling, drinking bourbon and smoking cannabis. With requests for cash rebuffed by his father in the tone of 'you've got to stand on your own two feet', Ned sought out additional sources of income. He became a regular visitor to greyhound racing 'flapping' tracks where he quickly became involved in the doping of dogs and the fixing of races. Using pseudonyms and travelling widely, his betting on fixed races started to generate the kind of income he desired. However, he sought greater rewards. Using the proceeds of a win on a fixed race, Ned bought enough cannabis to set himself up as a dealer initially dealing to friends and close acquaintances. Within months he had established a small distribution network that warranted the direct employment of three others and saw him comfortable enough to leave his legitimate job. Through that drug network, Ned met Angus who introduced himself as part of an active burglary team targeting 'good quality houses'. Over the next two years, he bought stolen property from Angus and others who had learned of his abilities to dispose of virtually any item through the extensive network of contacts he had developed whilst trading in drugs and gambling at dog and horse-race tracks throughout the UK and Ireland.

Ned's good fortune ran out when someone whom the police had caught in possession of ten crates of stolen whisky informed on him as having been the supplier. Ned was sentenced to nine months imprisonment for handling stolen goods. On his release, he re-invented himself as a jobbing plumber (having learned the basics from a family friend) and soon became reasonably prosperous. Within two years, Ned's career change was proving itself to be fortunate one. He was able to employ a dozen or so men and by paying backhanders to 'oil the wheels' of commerce, he managed to successfully tender for large plumbing contracts. At the same time, Angus introduced him to a wider circle of criminal contacts, some of whom were part of a gang involved in armed robberies at sub-post offices.

Having found prison a 'devastating experience', Ned believed that it might be useful, should he be arrested in the future, to have a bargaining tool at his side to alleviate the consequences of capture. He decided therefore to inform on the robbery team. Having approached a police detective he had once met at a social event Ned, over a period of months, began to provide information that eventually led to the arrest of a number of gang members. Although financial gain was not his sole motivation for doing so, the money he received from the police for 'paid information', proved itself to be a useful addition to his income. Ned has maintained relationships with police officers since that time, informing on an 'as and when necessary' basis. His informing activities went undetected by his criminal acquaintances and throughout the 1970s and 1980s, Ned continued to dispose of stolen property – anything from an industrial generator to a lorryload of toys. During this period, his legitimate business activities had their ups and downs and, while continuing to run the plumbing business, he briefly diversified into the hire of plant equipment and the selling of upholstery. Neither avenues proved viable concerns and, after selling his businesses at a loss, Ned refocused his energies on consolidating the plumbing business he had built.

Through the success of his tendering bids and the plumbing contracts he secured within the UK and elsewhere, Ned's network of contacts expanded. Many of those he met through legitimate activities were wealthy, and it was not unusual for Ned to be invited to their homes. Sometimes, if he thought he could make a reasonable amount of money, he later arranged for their homes to be broken into and have the items he specified stolen. Believing that dealing in drugs was 'too risky' and likely to get him a substantial prison sentence if caught, Ned had not resumed the dealing role on his release from prison. However, during the 1980s whilst on a contract in Holland, he was approached by a group of criminals whom he knew by reputation only. 'You could not refuse these people unless you wanted to end up badly beaten or worse,' and with this thought in mind, on two occasions he allowed a works van to be driven into the UK by a third party. Although he was never directly told what cargo was being smuggled, he had little doubt concerning its contents, and was 'well rewarded' for his 'assistance'.

By the end of the 1980s, Ned was relatively well off. Nevertheless, during the 1990s, while continuing with his flourishing legitimate business activities, he has persistently been on the lookout for supplementary sources of income. Ned will still buy and sell stolen property, dabble in selling counterfeit currency or any other commodity that will return a profit. However, most days of the week Ned can be found at his health club where he is considered by the staff as a businessman reaping the rewards of a successful career.

Networked crime

Contemporary organised criminality is expressed through local trading networks (Dorn *et al.*, 1992: 3–59; cf. Piore and Sabel, 1984), and appropriate commercial viability is assured (cf. Hobbs, 1995: ch. 7) by the continual realignment of local precedents in the context of global markets (Giddens, 1991: 21–2; cf. Hobbs, 1995: ch. 5) In order to co-ordinate relations between individuals and groups (Giddens, 1979: 65–6), both organised crime and its legitimate counterpart are involved in 'constant mediations and re-negotiations that are duplicated as perpetually mutating social systems of culturally indeterminate extraction and eclectic commercial destination' (Hobbs, 1997). The scope and extent of this activity depends upon the degree of connectivity between groups and individuals, and it is this connectedness rather than corporate identity that forms the structural connotation inherent in 'organised crime'. The connection between sets, the relationships that lie at the core of serious crime groups, can be based upon familial, interpersonal, geographic or commercial sets, and often some combination of some or all of the above. These combinations, with their multi-dimensional faces, 'form stars connected by hubs made up of shared vertices' (Gould, 1991: 25; cf. Johnson, 1986). By the term hubs we (Hobbs and Dunnighan, 1997) mean those individuals who, by virtue of their interconnectedness with these multi-dimensional sets, combine flexibility and mobility with crucial qualities of relationality. The power of these individuals that may be defined as 'hubs' should not be underestimated. Even within environments that feature established, traditional crime groups, network hubs are licensed to operate in an infinite variety of deviant collaborations. The biographical case studies on the criminal careers of Bill and Ben, Dave Peters, and Ned are associated with a whole gamut of criminal entrepreneurship and with numerous combinations of networked interactions serving as the springboard for the trajectories of criminal careers.

These individuals were free to seek out money-making opportunities both as individual operators, and as collaborators with established criminal firms, functioning within multiple cross-cutting networks of criminal and legitimate opportunity. They are not 'gang members', nor have they pledged their allegiance to some permanent structure of criminal destiny, but constitute hubs of action and information-link networks featuring webs of varying densities. In some cases these individuals are better money-makers than the household names of criminal identities that would be recognisable to any local cab driver.

It must be emphasised however that networked criminal careers do not necessarily follow a relentless ascent. Ben's criminal life at the time of writing is all but over, while Bill's has yet to peak. Dave's entrepreneurial activities are so well spread across Europe and so entwined with legitimate commercial activity as to make it impossible to weed out the good notes from the bad money, while Ned's past collaborators are rather more exotic and indeed venomous than the punters to whom he now sells training shoes from the back of his car. Peaks and troughs, expansion and retraction all inform the destiny, strength and spread of networks that must be understood as much for their flexibility and subsequent interactive qualities as for their criminal content.

Conclusions

Organised crime is, to paraphrase Latour, 'local at all points' (Latour, 1993) yet simultaneously realigns itself in progressive negotiations with global markets. Unlike previous eras, contemporary organised crime, with its emphasis upon drugs, fraud and counterfeiting, is able to occupy both a local and global context. These criminal activities are also enabling devices for passage from one sphere to another forming a transition of cross-cultural interests that is an expedient dynamic for the criminal career of contemporary serious-crime personnel such as Bill and Ben whose career trajectories are no longer limited to specific, often stereotyped, geographic locations of some urban underworld (Hobbs, 1997). Rather they are committed to a reorientation of their practices to the temporality of the commercial overworld. New networks of criminal entrepreneurs, some with ancient affiliations, no longer limit themselves to the parameters of specific neighbourhoods, but operate across different locales. The dilution and eventual disappearance of the legitimate employment market in cities like Downton and Upton, has redefined criminality in the context of a new decentred and unpredictable trading economy (Ruggiero and South, 1997), which is essentially a mutation created by the harsh post-industrial thrust of urban society, 'emptied' of its marketable labour and traditional forms of governance (Wilson, 1987). Consequently, the ever-evolving ecology and 'ecological communities' (Burgess, 1929 (cf. Thrasher, 1927); Landesco, 1968; Morris, 1957: Ch. 2,4,11) of late twentieth-century urban Britain are as influential in spawning deviant coalitions as they were in the writings of Mayhew (1861) or Booth (1889) (cf; Chesney, 1968).

Contemporary criminals who subscribe to the histories of a past order, as was evident in the case of Downton, engage with 'cultural chaperones from previous eras' (Hobbs, 1997) to inform their practices and provide reference points for their own activities and those of civilians for whom the notion of a distinct homogeneous and identifiable proletarian-based milieu is no longer part of their enacted environment. Any touchstone with the past, with a social order that resonates of traditional working-class community, empowers those that constitute the debris of de-industrialised locales with the ability to derive a sense of order, albeit retrospective, and implant it in a culture that is disordered, inchoate and episodic (Pileggi, 1987) 'where there were no rules, where cheating, lying, and stealing were accepted, even expected' (Anastasia, 1991: 279).

In contemporary society, 'the same processes that destroy autonomy are now creating new kinds of locality and identity' (Wilk, 1995: 130), and the recurrence of sacred myths concerning traditional deviant strategies and iconic deviants, preserves a mirage of a resilient, expert, essentially local social system. In Upton, where the symbiotic relationship between the traditional community and its serious-crime prodigy has been retained, the enacted environments of contemporary serious-crime markets are blended with a sense of 'retrospective unity' (Bauman, 1992: 138), creating an imaginary community that despite its heavy reliance upon an invented tradition (Anderson, 1983), succeeds in retaining its power as a defined local order located within a post-industrial milieu that is also embued with extra-territorial organisational characteristics.

This paper seeks to reiterate that organised crime is not experienced globally or transnationally, for these are abstract fields devoid of relations (Strathern, 1995: 179). Organised crime is essentially a tangible process of activity that is manifested in the context of locality. We experience crime as global only via the manufactured outpourings of media or control agencies (NCIS, 1993a, 1993b; Sterling 1994). Cumulatively such images constitute a global way of seeing organised or serious crime, affording a sense of scale and the capacity to measure (Strathern 1995: 179), and transcend the local to create perceptive scales, thereby lending licence to a universalist discourse that creates the resource-ripe scenario of a global expert system.

Our perception of the local clearly must transcend dated national and economic boundaries, while as this paper has suggested acknowledging the manifestation of serious crime as a phenomenon bounded by powerful indigenous histories and highly specific locales that have been defined by parameters imposed by legitimate socio-economic forces. As we continue to realign the resources of police and security agencies in the aftershock of the curtailment of the cold war (see Godson and Olson, 1993), such politically motivated rhetorics should be resisted as: 'For the moment we are not only without an adequate cartography of global capitalism, we lack political maps of our own backyards'. (Cooke, 1988: 489)

Note

1 The authors wish to acknowledge Jenni Lewis for her input, and the ESRC who funded the project 'Serious Crime Networks'.

References

Anastasia, G. (1991) *Blood and Honor*, New York: Zebra Books.

Anderson, B. (1983) *Imagined Communities*, London: Verso.

Bauman, Z. (1992) *Intimations of Modernity*, London: Routledge.

Booth, C. (1889) *Labour and Life of the People*, London: Williams and Norgate.

Bresler, F. (1992) *Interpol*, London: Mandarin.

Burgess, R (1929) 'Urban Areas' in Smith, T. V. and White, L. D. (eds) *Chicago: an experiment in Social Science*, Chicago: University of Chicago Press.

Bursik, R. J. (1986) 'Ecological Stability and the Dynamics of Delinquency', in Reiss, A. J. and Tonry, M. *Communities and Crime*, Chicago: University of Chicago Press.

Calvi, F. (1993) *Het Europa Van de Peetvaders. De Mafia Verovert een Continent*, Leuven: Kritak Balans.

Chesney, K. (1968) *The Victorian Underworld*, Harmondsworth: Penguin.

Cooke, P. (1988) 'Modernity, Postmodernity and the City', in *Theory Culture and Society* 5: 2–3.

Commonwealth Secretariat (1993) *Action Against Transnational Criminality* Vol. 3. Papers from the 1993 Oxford conference on International and White Collar Crime.

Cressey, D. (1972) *Criminal Organisation*, London: Heinemann.

Davis, M. (1990) *City of Quartz*, London: Verso.

Dorn, N., Murji, K. and South, N. (1992) *Traffickers: Drug Markets and Law Enforcement*, London: Routledge.

Douglas, M. (1995) 'Forgotten Knowledge' in Strathern, M. (ed) *Shifting Contexts: Transformations in Anthropological Knowledge*, London: Routledge.

Gambetta, D. (1988) 'Fragments of an Economic Theory of the Mafia' *Archives Européennes de Sociologie*, 29: 127–45.

Gambetta, D. (1993) *The Sicilian Mafia: The Business of Private Protection*, Cambridge Mass: Harvard University Press.

Giddens, A. (1979) *Central Problems in Social Theory*, London: Macmillan.

Giddens, A. (1991) *Modernity and Self-Identity*, Cambridge: Polity.

Godson, R. and Olson, W. (1993) *International Organised Crime: Emerging Threat to U.S. Security*, Washington: National Strategy Information Center.

Gould, P. (1991) 'Dynamic Structures of Geographic Space', in Brunn, S. D. and Leinbach, T. R. (eds) *Collapsing Space and Time*, London: Harper Collins.

Harvey, D. (1989), *The Condition of Postmodernity*, Oxford: Blackwell.

Hobbs, D. (1988) *Doing the Business: Entrepreneurship, Detectives and the Working Class in the East End of London*, Oxford: Clarendon Press.

Hobbs, D. (1995) *Bad Business*, Oxford: Oxford University Press.

Hobbs, D. (1997) 'Professional Crime: Change, Continuity and the Enduring Myth of the Underworld', *Sociology*, February.

Hobbs, D. and Dunnighan, C. (1997) *Serious Crime Networks*. Final Report to the ESRC Crime and Social Order Research Programme, University of Durham.

Hobsbawm, E. (1994) *The Age of Extremes*, Harmondsworth: Penguin.

Hollands, B. (1995) 'Friday Night, Saturday Night: Youth Cultural Identification in the Post Industrial City' *Working Paper No 2*: Dept. Of Social Policy, Newcastle University.

Horne, R. and Hall, S. (1995) 'Anelpis: a preliminary expedition into a world without hope or Potential', *Parallex*, 1: 81–92.

Ianni, F. (1971) 'Formal and Social Organisation in an Organised Crime "Family": A Case Study', *University of Florida Law Review*, 24: 31–41.

Johnson, R. (1986) *On Human Geography*, Oxford: Blackwell.

King, A. D. (1991) 'Introduction' in King, A. D. (ed.) *Culture Globalisation and the World System*, London: Macmillan.

Labrousse, A. and Wallon, A. (eds) (1993) *La Planète des Drogues*, Paris: Seuil.

Landesco, J. (1968) *Organised Crime in Chicago*, 2nd edn, Chicago: University of Chicago Press.

Latour, B. (1993) *We Have Never Been Modern*, London: Harvester Wheatsheaf.

Mayhew, H. (1861) *London Labour and the London Poor*, 4 Vols, London: Dover, facsimile edition 1968.

Morris, T. P. (1957) *The Criminal Area*, London: Routledge.

Naylor, R. T. (1995) 'From Cold War to Crime War', *Transnational Organised Crime*, 1, 4, 37–56.

NCIS (1993a) *An Outline Assessment of the Threat and Impact by Organised/Enterprise Crime Upon United Kingdom Interests*, London: NCIS.

NCIS (1993b) *Organised Crime Conference: A Threat Assessment*, London. NCIS.

Pakulski, J. and Walters, M. (1996) *The Death of Class*, London: Sage.

Pileggi, N. (1987) *Wise Guy*, London: Corgi.

Piore, M. and Sabel, C. (1984) *The Second Industrial Divide*, New York: Basic Books.

Potter, G. W. (1994) *Criminal Organisations*, Illinois: Waveland Press.

Reuter, P. (1984) *Disorganised Crime*, Cambridge Mass.: MIT Press.

Rider, B. (1990) *Organised Economic Crime*. Working Paper, University of Cambridge.

Robertson, R. (1995) 'Glocalisation: Time-Space and Homogeneity–Heterogeneity', in Featherstone, M., Lash, S. and Robertson, R. (eds) *Global Modernities*, London: Sage.

Ruggiero, V. (1995) 'Drug Economics: A Fordist Model of Criminal Capital'. *Capital and Class*, 55: 131–150.

Ruggiero, V. and South, N. (1997) 'The Late Modern City as a Bazaar'. *British Journal of Sociology*, 48, 1: 54–69.

Sheptycki, J. (1995) 'Transnational Policing and the Makings of a Postmodern State', *British Journal of Criminology*, 35, 4: 613–615.

Sterling, C. (1994) *Crime Without Frontiers*, London: Little Brown.

Strathern, M. (1995) 'Afterword: Relocations', in Strathern, M. *Shifting Contexts: Transformations in Anthropological Knowledge*, London: Routledge.

Thrasher, F. (1927) *The Gang*, Chicago: University of Chicago Press.

Wilk, R. (1995) 'Learning to be Local in Belize: global systems of common difference', in Miller, D. (ed.) *Worlds Apart: Modernity Through the Prism of the Local*, London: Routledge.

Williams, P. (1993) *The International Drug Trade: An Industry Analysis*, Pittsburgh: Ridgway Center for International Security Studies.

Willlams, P. (1994) Transnational Criminal Organisations and National Security, *Survival*, 36: 96–113.

Williams, P. and Savona, E. (eds) (1995) The United Nations and Transnational Organised Crime, *Transnational Organised Crime*, 1: 3.

Wilson, W. J. (1987) *The Truly Disadvantaged*, Chicago: University of Chicago Press.

19

CRIME AND THE SENSE OF ONE'S PLACE: GLOBALIZATION, RESTRUCTURING AND INSECURITY IN AN ENGLISH TOWN

Evi Girling, Ian Loader and Richard Sparks

In a recent advertising campaign Barclaycard (a leading brand of VISA card in Britain) deployed the following slogan:

> For instant cash around the world (including Macclesfield) all you need is your Barclaycard.

In the ads two Englishmen abroad (they are comic sub-Graham Greene types of middle-class anglos) try to obtain money and services in a variety of exotic foreign locations. The comic hook of each vignette is the refusal of one of them (the pompous all-knowing one) to believe that credit cards work in such remote places. He therefore attempts various arcane and always disastrous forms of barter and bribe, whilst his junior colleague sorts it all out with his Barclaycard.

Of more pressing interest here than the use (part satirical, part complicit) of assumed English attitudes to all things foreign is the introduction of the name of Macclesfield into this scenario, since it is in this place that the work reported in this chapter has been conducted. 'Macclesfield' seems to work in the ads as an ironic counterpoint to 'foreign parts' – if they are comically and excessively alien, it is comically and excessively English. By extension it is also *parochially* English: the expression 'around the world (including London)' would be baffling. So some degree of surprise (and amusement) must also attach to the idea that Barclaycard works *in Macclesfield*; that is, to the fact that this seemingly obscure English town (tucked away in the Cheshire countryside some 180 miles north of London and twenty miles from the nearest metropolis, Manchester) is part of the global system of financial services.

Barclaycard have done some of our work for us. We set out to study some aspects of people's fears and feelings about crime in Macclesfield against the context of the town's recent experience of economic and cultural change.[1] In other words, we wanted to show (a) that public apprehensions of crime and sensibilities towards criminal justice were best grasped in an ethnographically intensive way and with careful attention to the question of *place*; but also (b) that such a way of working, far from being parochial, might in fact have something to contribute to broader theoretical and substantive debates – not least in respect of an emergent European criminology.

We expressly sought to bring the analysis of 'fear of crime' into dialogue with the cultural theory of risk (Giddens 1991; Douglas 1992).[2] This does not mean over-arguing the 'representativeness' of the place in which we happened to work (though as Hoggart (1993) points out such studies are always caught in suspension between the claims of uniqueness and representativeness), even within one national cultural frame let alone across Europe. Rather it means exploring, within the dense thicket of historical and cultural particularities that go into the constitution of any given place, the bearing upon it (filtered in however specific a form) of aspects of contemporary social organization and disorganization that may be quite general in scope, if not indeed pervasive. The Barclaycard example – more neatly and fortuitously than we could have hoped – reminds us that the little town whose fortunes matter so much to our respondents is indeed caught up willy-nilly in the global flows of capital and culture (cf. Lash and Urry: 1994). We can establish that this is so without much difficulty. What remains to be shown is that this has any bearing on the bundle of sensibilities and anxieties known conventionally as the 'fear of crime'. Later we flesh out in some detail how we think the fears of crime of Macclesfield residents connect with their sense of their place in the wide world.

To pose the matter in this way does not suggest any lack of interest in the distribution of crime risks or their relation to the traditionally-studied axes of social stratification. Neither is it to impute irrationality or gullibility to those citizens for whom the danger of crime has become a besetting worry. As Mary Douglas (1992: 29) comments, an interest in the cultural analysis of risk perception is not an assertion of agnosticism about the reality of risks. It does, however, mean exploring the social and personal consequences of people's feelings about crime and justice and their connections with other dimensions of social life. As Douglas further suggests, a risk is anyway not a 'thing' but a way of thinking – not just the probability of an event 'but also the probable magnitude of its outcome, and everything depends on the value that is set on the outcome' (1992: 31). In other words, crime is not just something that bashes us over the head out of ill-luck, like a falling branch. It is something for which we seek explanation and accountability – and how we explain it and whom we blame may be highly symptomatic of who we are and how we organize our relations with others (Douglas 1992: 6–7). In this respect crime may be one of those forms of 'danger on the borders' which gives form to a community's sense of itself and its distinctiveness from others. But it may also provoke anxieties that turn inwards, towards a sense of division from others who are socially and geographically close.

In general outline this much has probably been well known to social scientists since Durkheim and to criminologists perhaps in particular. It seems arguable, for instance, that proponents of 'deviancy amplification' and 'moral panic' were in some sense doing the social theory of risk twenty years or so *avant la lettre*; and Sumner's sociology of 'censures' (1994), for example, re-works that concern in a contemporary way. What Douglas's version of cultural theory brings into special focus, however, is the way in which the identification of particular sources of threat and blame refracts a given community's dispositions towards order and authority:

> There is no way of proceeding with analysing risk perception without typifying kinds of communities according to the support their members give to authority, commitment, boundaries and structure.
>
> (Douglas 1992: 47)

The presentiment of risk, therefore, is inherently political: it galvanizes action and prompts discourse. Studying the connections between risk, fear and blame can thus never be solely an activity of quantitatively cataloguing dangers and allocating responses to risk into boxes marked 'rational' and 'irrational' (Sparks 1991). Risk-perception is cultural, to borrow philosopher Richard Rorty's phrase, 'all the way down'. In principle this suggests a daunting and exciting research agenda (and as such a potential fruitful way of pursuing a European criminology). It draws attention to the weight that attaches to the dangers of crime, and to some crimes rather than others, in the social and political conversations that go on in particular times and places – the social construction of their differential visibility. It also gives a clue as to why, amidst the proliferation of technical means of risk assessment in the administrative culture of modern societies (the generic 'probabilization' of which Hacking speaks (1990)), the social discourse of crime and punishment still 'falls into antique mode' (Douglas 1992: 26) and refuses to shed 'its ancient moral freight' (*ibid.*: 35). At least under certain conditions – and Melossi (1994) suggests that those conditions are currently most characteristic of the free-market individualism of the Anglo–American world – crime and punishment still occupy the centre-stage of social concern and political competition. Examining how and why this is so is a key task for comparative criminology, raising as it does significant questions about the varying sensibilities towards crime and order prevalent both across and within the constituent nations of Europe (Nelken 1994; Zedner 1995). But it also demands an understanding of how these issues bear upon the life-world of Europe's differently-located citizens, something that requires us to proceed ethnographically and in relation to *place*.

Placing the 'fear of crime'

In the course of *The Wind in the Willows* (an emblematic fiction in its way of a certain pastoral vision of Englishness) Mole asks Ratty what lies beyond the wild wood. Ratty replies: 'Beyond the wild wood, my dear Mole, lies the wide world, and that is something that is of no concern to you or me.' Of course, Ratty is here giving comic voice to a distinctly anti-modern nostalgia – one known to be losing plausibility even at the time of writing. By contrast the joke in the Barclay-card ads is that nowhere, not even Macclesfield, is outside modernity.

For contemporary social theory 'place' has become problematic (indeed 'phan-tasmagoric' in Giddens's (1991) view) and so by extension (and this may be more the rub from the point of view of fear of crime) has the concept of 'home' (Robertson 1995: 35). In Giddens's view this is intrinsically a consequence of modernity with profound psychic implications for individuals and their search for security. For Giddens 'localities are thoroughly penetrated by distanciated influences' (1991: 188). Thus:

> Processes of change engendered by modernity are intrinsically con-nected to globalising influences, and the sheer sense of being caught up in massive waves of global transformation is perturbing. More important is the fact that such change is also intensive: increasingly it reaches through to the very grounds of individual activity and the constitution of the self . . . No one can easily defend a secure 'local life' set off from larger social systems and organizations.
>
> (*ibid.*: 184)

This argument is somewhat complex and cannot be rehearsed fully here. For present purposes its most relevant implications would seem to be that places are no longer inhabited in the manner attributable to traditional or pre-modern societies – they do not confer an unquestioning sense of identity or membership. Rather they are – at least by some and to some degree – 'chosen' for what they offer in terms of commitment to a certain lifestyle and the continuity of a rea-sonably coherent 'narrative of self-identity'. For this reason among others the 'protective cocoon' which sustains trust and buffers the individual against 'radical doubt' is comparatively more 'brittle' and prone to various forms of personal crises, including the danger of 'engulfment' by a sense of powerlessness.

Although Giddens's remarks on the significance of place have at times a somewhat grudging tone ('Everyone still continues to live a local life . . . Yet the transformations of place and the intrusions of distance into local activities radi-cally change what "the world" actually is.' [1991: 188]), they may be capable of being extended and revised in ways directly relevant to the present discussion. As Giddens recognizes, the very fragility of the 'compromise package' of con-temporary personal security ('routine and commitment to a certain form of life-style' (*ibid.*: 196)) engenders needs for its defence. Moreover the very brittleness of trust as a bulwark against feelings of 'dread' may itself give rise to a preoccupa-tion with order and propriety (*ibid.*: 202). If, as Giddens argues, the 'frontiers of sequestered experience' (criminality included) are 'battlegrounds' then the intru-sion of unmastered or unassimilable behaviour is likely to be seen as especially threatening. This suggests a certain intensity in the demand for order and, more-over, a high expectation upon the responsible 'expert systems' to deliver it. As Giddens further comments, behaviour which is not 'integrated into a system' is thus especially likely to be seen as 'alien and discrete' (*ibid.*: 150).

In our view, therefore, there are clearly grounds for expecting fears of crime to figure amongst the penumbral worries of late-modern European citizens, espe-cially as regards behaviour in public places: and it may be possible to theorize criminologists' traditional concern with 'incivilities' in these terms. Moreover, the fact that local life cannot 'easily be defended' hardly means that people do not attempt so to defend it – indeed current criminology and urban sociology are replete with instances of such defensiveness, most famously Davis's (1990) account of the fortress suburbs of Los Angeles. In this sense Giddens tends to understate the likely emotiveness of the politics of place under the very condi-tions that he outlines. As Robertson (1995) points out, 'home' (like 'nation') may be one kind of invented tradition in late-modernity, but this hardly drains it of significance. Rather it draws attention to the various kinds of investment in place (in both the emotional and the literal financial senses of that term) that people may make.

Giddens also pays little attention to the kinds of difference between places in terms of their dangerousness (Sherman *et al.* 1989; Hope 1995; Trickett *et al.* 1995), their proneness to disorder, and their symbolic significance (Shields 1991) that criminologists and urban sociologists routinely discover. Such issues are sug-gestively raised in Tim Hope's recent analysis of variable participation in 'com-munity' crime-prevention projects (Hope 1997). By the same token Giddens has little to say on national cultural and political variation in the identification and visibility of dangers of the kind that have been identified across Europe (Melossi 1994; Nelken 1994; Zedner 1995). We argue instead that perceived threats to place from crime are some of the most acute examples of the kind of politicization of risk and blame of which Douglas speaks.

We have conducted a case-study of public feeling about crime, place and security in one middle-sized and criminologically ordinary English town – the self-same Macclesfield that is the butt of the ad-people's metropolitan sneer. Of course Macclesfield was caught up in processes of economic and cultural restructuring long before the world of marketing condescended to notice it. Once a single-industry silk-weaving town, Macclesfield has from the 1960s onwards become host to a number of multi-national companies, especially the pharma-ceutical giants Zeneca and Ciba-Geigy. It thus embarked on a period of hitherto unknown prosperity, and has retained relatively high employment and compara-tively high property values even through the recession of the late 1980s and early 1990s. Though surrounded by yet more affluent places (the Manchester com-muter belt of Knutsford, Wilmslow, Alderley Edge and, perhaps most elite of all, its immediate neighbour Prestbury – see Figure 19.1) it increasingly represents itself, for example in the promotional literature produced by its moderately entrepreneurial local authority, as a comfortable place with an 'enviable

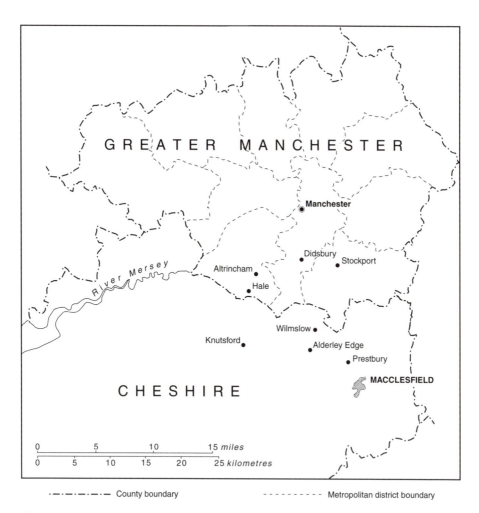

Figure 19.1 Macclesfield and the south Manchester 'commuter belt'

life-style'. It claims to combine the lifestyle attractions of modern amenities and transport (a mainline railway link with London, proximity to an international airport) with the 'heritage' orientation of a former mill-town on the edge of the beautiful open spaces of the Pennine foothills. The influential Henley Centre for Forecasting recently numbered Macclesfield amongst the thirty British towns with the brightest economic prospects.

In the course of the last three decades Macclesfield has both spread geo-graphically and become more socially diverse. In brief and summary terms it is possible to identify three primary groupings: (a) 'old', 'born and bred' families of two or more generations' standing (known locally as 'Maxonians'), a substantial proportion of whom either live in one of the town's five public-housing estates or occupy the nineteenth-century terraced houses close to the town centre; (b) an influx of working people who since the 1960s have arrived to take up jobs in the pharmaceutical industry or the burgeoning service sector; and (c) incoming professionals working in the new industries, or the administrative sector, or commuting to Manchester. For some of the latter group, moving to Macclesfield was merely a fact of occupational life and 'company moves'; for others it would have been a reflexive lifestyle decision – a flight from Manchester and towards the countryside. In these respects the town has grown by the twin processes of industrial regeneration and suburbanization.

We have conducted in this place a research effort that we call an ethnography of anxiety. This has comprised the following modes of enquiry: an analysis of publicly available information on economic, social and demographic change within the town, and of patterns of crime and demands for policing; an analysis of local representations of crime-related matters as contained in the local press and crime-prevention literature; a series of focus-group discussions with different sections of the local population; individual and group discussions with criminal-justice professionals and other local-interest groups and 'opinion-formers'; a small number of biographical interviews; and numerous hours devoted to informal conversations and observation, attending meetings, hanging around police stations and travelling in police cars. Our aim in interpreting the perspectives thus generated is to construct a detailed and nuanced account of the competing sensibilities towards crime and insecurity prevalent within this particular English town. In this chapter we examine in some detail one micro-location within this place (namely, the group of streets composing the 'old town') and one focus of anxiety, albeit the one that we found to be most pervasive (namely, the behaviour of young people in public space).

Low life on the High Street: interpreting teenage disorder in 'old Macclesfield'

Asked in a recent Cheshire County Council (1996) survey how their quality of life could be improved, Macclesfield Borough residents made 'reducing crime' their top priority. Some 52 per cent of the Borough's respondents placed this in their 'top three', followed some distance behind by 'reducing air pollution' (34 per cent) and 'improving education standards' (33 per cent). Our research suggests that this evident concern about crime in large measure attaches itself to children and young people.[3] The 'crime-talk' (Sasson 1995) of our focus-group participants either proceeded on the taken-for-granted assumption that crime was a youth problem, or explicitly referenced young people as primary sources of anxiety. The most apparent concerns included: alcohol-related public violence in the town centre at weekends; the prevalence of drug-consumption among the town's youth; (parental) worries about the physical and moral safety of children and young people while out in public, and problems of graffiti, vandalism, petty theft, and general noise, nuisance and disorder caused by groups of unsupervised teen-agers 'hanging around'.

Inter-generational conflict (ostensibly over the use of public spaces) appears to represent one of the main social cleavages in Macclesfield, and across the town it is possible to identify a number of 'hot spots' (Sherman *et al.* 1989) where teen-agers routinely congregate, where (adult) residents are routinely bothered and annoyed, and where the police are routinely called (see further, Loader *et al.* 1996; Girling *et al.* 1998). But what are the precise contours of such conflict? Why should young people represent such a powerfully-felt source of anxiety among older Macclesfield residents? How is teenage behaviour interpreted by those residents?

We want to explore these questions by examining in some detail one such site of inter-generational tension: the area just south of the town centre around the old High Street.[4] Designated a 'Preservation Area' by Macclesfield Borough Council, this dense network of two- and three-storey nineteenth-century weavers' cottages (interspersed with old silk mills mostly now converted into 'designer' flats) is the part of town from which much of Macclesfield's reputed charm and inherited self-representation as an historic silk town derives. This physical charm is not unrelated to the High Street area's recent fortunes. The area remains home to some long-standing elderly residents, many of whom live in rented accom-modation; some equally established working- and lower middle-class residents, many of whom have been there for decades, and a scattering of young families with children. But in recent years these have been joined by a burgeoning num-ber of young professionals, as the area has made at least a nod in the direction of gentrification (it is best characterized as an area altered yet not entirely colonized by mainly 'marginal gentrifiers' (Rose 1984)).

For these young professionals – mostly incoming first-time buyers who work in Cheshire or Manchester – the High Street area seems altogether a pleasant place. As one such young professional – an émigré from Didsbury in south Manchester – put it: 'I'm very much more aware of a sense of community here. [The neigh-bours] are not my best friends but they're good acquaintances. It's friendly.' It is also – as this resident proceeded to illustrate – taken to be a haven of relative safety:

> I lived in Didsbury temporarily for six months, which is five miles outside the city centre, and I got broken into, cars were always getting broken into. When I moved back, the difference in the premiums for insuring my car for example, it was two-thirds of what it cost in Manchester, there was enormous difference. I felt a palpable sense of risk in Didsbury compared to Macclesfield.

However, for some of the more established residents things do not appear so rosy. Following the property-boom of the late 1980s, when house prices in the area soared, and many of the larger properties were bought by private landlords for conversion into bedsits, the area has also become home to a shifting population of what are seen as 'undesirable' incomers: 'the homeless', people released 'into the community' from Parkside [psychiatric] hospital, 'drug-takers', 'DSS [social security] cases' and former residents of Victoria Park flats, Macclesfield's most 'notorious' housing estate. For some – including Dawn Jones, proprietor with her husband Ray of a local grocer's – the area has spiralled into decline:

> We have a transitional population round the corner. In the bigger [owner-occupied] houses here, things are more stable. But the ones that have been converted to bedsits they are a complete mish-mash of every-thing at the bottom end, the drones of Macclesfield. They are the people from Victoria Park who live very close to the legal line, and when they put the surveillance system into the flats they opted to move out . . . That is what we got down here.

The High Street area has in recent years become an attractive meeting point for congregations of young people – mainly, according to residents, from one of what the Jones's described as Macclesfield's 'three naughty areas' – the council estates of Victoria Park, the Weston and nearby Moss Rose.[5] Especially during the summer, the school holidays, and in the weeks surrounding Guy Fawkes' night firework festivities in early November, these teenagers are to be found main-ly in and around the grocers (the Jones's claim that on occasions 'up to sixty youths' hang around in the street in front of the shop); or in the children's play-ground from whence the intended younger users are said to have been usurped:

High Street focus group I.
*Cast: **Margaret**, 36–50, child-minder, 44 years in Macclesfield, 31 years in the area, married to **Tom**, 51–65, retired, born in Manchester, 31 years in the area.*

MARGARET: It's supposed to be for little ones, they're not allowed to go in it, the big ones are in it. The big ones are doing God knows what in it . . .
TOM: They dominate the play area to the exclusion of infants who are supposed to be using it. If you go in there Thursday, Friday, Saturday morning, and have a look at all the milk cartons that have been thrown about. . . . They're putting tablets in the milk cartons.

Among these long-standing High Street residents the presence in the area of what they see as 'unruly' groups of teenagers (from elsewhere) is a source of considerable anger and disquiet – Tom and Margaret, both resident in the area for some thirty-one years, came to the focus group with the sole and express purpose of venting their frustrations. The disturbances the youths are reputed to cause ('they're either drunk, they're on drugs, or they're fighting', as Margaret put it), are clearly felt to have a detrimental impact upon the life of the local community. For some the combined effect of the teenagers and the 'undesirable' occupants of the bedsits is a desire to vacate the area entirely.

These kinds of worries are rather less evident among the recently-arrived young professionals who live in the High Street area.[6] Tom and Margaret's immediate neighbour (a 25-year-old woman architect working in Altrincham, south Manchester) thus professed herself ignorant of the disorder that was alleged to be happening on her doorstep (much to the consternation of the former). Another local professional admitted to complete surprise when the subject of teenage drug-use in the area arose: 'It's come as a revelation to me. I've been here five years and I work away from Macc, and I go away for weekends, so I'm only here for a relatively small amount of time. I'm in the house and out again. I'm quite surprised listening to your concerns and experiences'. Yet another managed to describe the 'incivilities' that so concern and anger her more established neighbours in the following dead-pan terms:

High street focus group I.
Cast: **Fiona**, *late 30s, chartered planning consultant working in Knutsford, born in south Wales, lived in Macclesfield for 4 years.*

FIONA: When I've been to the shop I have seen a group hanging around on the opposite side to the shop. I don't go to the shop that often. When I was walking back along High Street a couple of days before bonfire night, the other week, I noticed that there were a lot of kids in the children's play area, and somebody had set off a rocket which had gone into the wall on the opposite side and narrowly missed a lady walking past. That's about it, the biggest incident that I have seen or heard.

We have then starkly juxtaposed in the High Street area social groupings with markedly different relationships to 'place' and divergent responses to the same group of teenagers. These teenagers appear to impact minimally on the lives and consciousness of residents for whom the area provides something of a (pleasant) retreat from a life lived fulfilingly elsewhere. While for those whose lives derive much meaning from their local attachments, the presence of the youths (and the seeming reluctance of anyone to do anything about them) is seen as being deeply entangled with and implicated in the decline of the area and its 'community spirit'. The following exchange not only captures this well; it also reveals at their starkest the differences (in biography, orientations to place and *Weltanschauung*) between older, established residents and more mobile, professional incomers. People can – as Patrick Wright (1985) has observed – inhabit the same locality, but live in different worlds:

High Street focus group I.
Cast: **Jane**, *25, architect working in south Manchester, born in Macclesfield, returned to live there following university, 1 year in the area.* **Margaret**, *see above* **Fiona**, *see above.*

IL: Would you describe Macclesfield as a friendly place?
JANE: Yes.

MARGARET: So-so, it rather depends. It can be, but then again not necessarily. People I speak to I've spoken to years, you get people in now and they just don't bother any more.

FIONA: I think it's a friendly place, it's one of the friendliest places I've lived, and I don't want to move. I've lived in Wales, southern England, middle England, northern England, and I think Macclesfield is great. It's small enough to get to know people. Yes, it's a friendly place.

MARGARET: I think the people now keep themselves to themselves. Any trouble, people lock themselves in now and pretend it doesn't go on. They don't get involved, they don't get together to stop it. They pretend, hide behind their curtains. That didn't happen.

FIONA: Isn't that because it was a tighter close-knit community and you knew everybody along your street, and now you don't, because people have to move around for their jobs, and they have to go to Manchester for a job, they have to move if they're made redundant. We're in a society that moves around a lot more than we did thirty years ago.

'Crime-talk' among High Street residents is not only entwined questions of biography, however. It is also culturally encoded in particular ways, serving as a vehicle for registering and making sense of other, unsettling changes in the social and moral order, both locally and nationally. But in what frames of meaning is teenage behaviour situated? What wider aspects of economic, social or moral life is such behaviour taken to be entangled with? How does talk about youth relate to people's sense of the past, present and possible futures of their area, their town and the world beyond?

Foremost among the 'frames' (Sasson 1995) used to account for teenage disorder is the erosion or – as is more often implied – collapse of familial discipline.[7] Among both High-Street-area residents, and our focus-group discussants more generally, the 'crisis of the family' was commonly – and in terms that resonate closely with many current tropes of British political discourse on 'law and order' – held to account for the presence of unruly teenagers on the streets. Often this was a discourse of blame, a means of talking about 'bad' or 'irresponsible' parents, who (unlike 'us') are unconcerned about the whereabouts or behaviour of their teenage offspring. But it can also take a more sympathetic form, a reference to parents struggling to cope, or else quite innocently unaware of the problems their children cause. As Tom put it: 'I'm very, very sure that most of the parents of the teenagers that congregate outside our house don't know what they're doing at all, they're oblivious to the fact that they're creating damage.'

A second – rather less common, but still apparent – 'frame' addresses the failure of public provision, and corresponds to what Sasson (1995) terms the 'blocked opportunities' framework. Here teenage crime and disorder is seen as flowing from the deprivation, frustration and low or unfulfilled expectations associated with joblessness:

High Street focus group II.
Cast: **Simone**, *51–65, retired psychiatric nurse, born in Switzerland, lived in Macclesfield for 8 years.*

Why do they need to go again and again and drink so much, take drugs, why is there such a malaise all round? There is a fear of the future, the youngsters don't have a future unless they have training of some sort, and even with this training and qualifications, they can't find a job, so they feel desperate, they feel frustrated because they can't do what they would wish to do, they have to do anything that is going, or they're unemployed.

This 'frame' also takes a more local idiom and becomes a commentary on the emergent social divisions that globalization is seen to be creating in Macclesfield:

High Street focus group II.
Cast: **Peter**, *41, psychiatric nurse, Macclesfield-born.* **Simone**, *see above.*

PETER: I know, two, three generations of certain families in Macclesfield, like on the Moss estate . . . What they see is people coming from outside, doing very well, going through Macc, who are not Macc people. All these people working for ICI, and they've nothing to do with Macc, and here's me stuck on my estate, and my dad's never had anything, and his dad has never had anything, and they live on the Moss, and they all live on the Moss, and they see nothing, and all they do is see these people from out of the corner of the window . . . They think what are these people doing, I'd like to do that, I'd like to go to Tytherington [golf and social] Club. But these people from Macc, you try and get some of those youths and let them try and get into Tytherington Club: 'I'm sorry, you haven't got twenty thousand or whatever for your BMW, go away, go back to your Weston estate' and . . .
SIMONE: Yes, it's a prosperous town and I think if we go on prospering and there's an air, yes, of a booming town . . .
PETER: For some.
SIMONE: For some.

Talk of public provision more readily connects teenage disorder with a lack of things for young people to do. The following exchange is especially interesting in this regard, not only because the discussants are keen not be come across as 'soft' on youth crime (hence demonstrating the currently marginal political status of the position in Britain), but also because of their evident doubt as to whether received forms of youth provision are in fact what 'today's teenagers' really want:

High Street focus group II.
Cast: **Peter**, *see above.* **David**, *25–30, nurse at Parkside hospital, lived in Macclesfield for 8 years, son of* **Simone**.

PETER: Nobody is bothering to say, I'm not defending the kids, but say why they are doing it in the first place. There's nothing, there's just nowhere to go, nothing to do. I'm not saying it should be given to them on a plate, but there isn't anything at all, no facilities.

EG: What kind of facilities would you like to see?

PETER: I know some of those, where they want anything really just to toss around. A youth club seems an old-hat sort of thing now, they don't want that sort of thing now, so I wouldn't even know. My youth and what they want now are probably a bit different.

EG: What would you say that the younger people in Macclesfield want?

DAVID: It's a bit difficult because attitudes have completely changed from what it was ten years ago. They seem to grow faster, they seem to be doing a lot of the things that we used to do when we were eighteen. When they're twelve and thirteen, they seem to be smoking. I'm not saying we should give them what they want, but we should ask them what they want first.

A further significant means of framing the question of youth crime (and one not unrelated to that of public provision) concerns the failure – or, once again, collapse – of legal authority; in particular, the seeming inability of the police to deal adequately with teenage disorder. This in fact was one of the most recurrent themes of our focus-group discussions (with adults) across Macclesfield, with participants voicing generally high levels of abstract support for the police, coupled with evident disquiet over their increasing and improper remoteness from everyday life.[8] The by-no-means unusual frustrations of High-Street-area residents included: the apparent lack of a visible police presence on the streets; the police's failure to respond sufficiently urgently to calls about nuisance youths; a failure to recognize the seriousness of the situation, and a reluctance on the part of the police to involve parents. Above all, there was an uneasy sense that the police were no longer able either to command the respect of young people, or to cope with the demands placed upon them. As Tom put it: 'They're under-powered and under-staffed. You can't expect one young PC [police constable] to deal with twenty or thirty kids shouting verbal abuse'. One resident even wondered whether current difficulties might augur some significant shifts in the nature of policing provision:

High Street focus group II.
Cast: **David**, *see above.*

DAVID: Attitudes have changed now. Police today have got so much to do. They've got to like sort out not just theft, but drug problems, violence, domestic violence. They've got such a wide range. Police twenty–thirty years ago, they would have to deal with theft, but now they have to cover a whole range. They'll have to change, and perhaps the community will have to change. Perhaps we'll have to do our policing ourselves, in a minor way, we may have to patrol.

It is thus apparent that 'crime-talk' about local youth is not merely a response to actual teenage misconduct (though of course it is also that). The assessments people make of the problem of 'unruly teenagers', and the impact it has upon their lives and consciousness, is intricately bound up with their sense, both of the 'place' in which they live (its past, present and possible futures); and their 'place' in the wider world, with all its attendant opportunities, pitfalls and uncertainties. There is perhaps no better illustration of this than the case of Ray and Dawn Jones. For them the High Street area appears to have declined hand-in-hand with the fortunes of their shop. As trade has dropped and profits fallen, life has become hard. The certainties they recall their parents enjoying are gone. The things they believed would be the reward for hard work – security, stability, the opportunity to 'ease off' in later life – have not been forthcoming. They anticipate their futures with some trepidation. Against this backdrop, the presence of 'disorderly' teenagers in the local streets is not just in some material sense the last straw; it also powerfully exemplifies a world gone horribly wrong:

IL: How do you feel about the next ten years of your life?
RAY: Apprehension. We are living, not looking very far ahead, we can't, we daren't, it's bleak. We hoped we'd be semi-retired by now. I thought I'd be working 25–30 hours a week and enjoy it. I am working 68–70 hours a week and I am not enjoying it.
DAWN: And if you have the problems with the youngsters we had last autumn that was the final straw. If everything else is okay you can cope with it, but when you are already in a situation of under stress, that stress affects people's attitudes, and the customers do not want to come in because of the kids outside, and you have to watch them because they are stealing and causing trouble. It's another pressure that you don't want.

Conclusion: crime in and out of place

In showing that many of the mundane crime-worries of adult citizens attach with special vehemence to young people in public spaces we are reiterating a well-attested and ostensibly rather unsurprising criminological finding. Of all the inward community divisions which, as Douglas notes, sharpen the sense of danger and the identification of dangerous others, the boundary between youth and age is probably one of the more commonplace (as Pearson (1983) famously demonstrates). Moreover, under conditions of modernity – to whose febrile sense of disruptive change nostalgia and privatism are frequent defensive reactions – the 'youth–crime connection' figures frequently as 'a controlling metaphor of social change and social breakdown' (Pearson 1994: 1194). What we want to add here is that this attribution is variably made in relation to the values and meanings that attach to particular places and in turn to the 'life-plans' of those who inhabit them. In this sense the language of risk and blame remains in some degree tied to the language of place. The social divisions of which Douglas writes are in part conceived and enacted in spatial terms, as communities map zones of safety and danger, improvement and decay and so on.

Under the press of globalizing economic pressures and the 'disembedding' tendencies of modern culture and communications, what it means to live in any given place has surely changed. But those who seem to suggest that modernity has emptied out place and eroded 'community' *completely* arguably reiterate a classic mistake in sociology; as Robertson (1995) suggests, the pervasively globalizing influences and the various ways in which they may be locally inflected and received is actually an empirical issue. In our view the key issue concerns not how place has 'evaporated' but rather how different places have fared in terms of their 'urban fortunes' – their dynamics of reconstruction and decline, inclusion and segregation (Logan and Molotch 1987). Criminologists have lately had much to say on these matters (Sampson and Wilson 1995; Trickett *et al.* 1995), and, moreover, it is part and parcel of the uneven relation between place and security under modern conditions that different places may be differently conceived of and inhabited by 'old' residents and incomers, adults and youth, those free to leave and those who are trapped, and so on (Elias and Scotson 1994; Butler 1995; Urry 1995). In this paper, we have turned this concern in a 'microscopic' direction.

It also seems clear therefore that the modes of risk perception across 'community' boundaries that Douglas identifies have *infrastructural* dimensions, so that the changing political economy of place and ideational divisions of the social landscape interlace, in ways that have intimate and sometimes fateful consequences for each of us in our attempts to maintain a personal sense of security or to make a 'home' out of the choices and constraints that we confront.

Why then are the kids on the corner of such compelling interest and concern to some (but apparently not all) of the High Street residents. We see here an instance of the classic sociological crossroads between history and biography (Wright Mills 1959). The High Street we have suggested represents a case of 'marginal gentrification' – its 'improvement' (part of which involves the arrival of new owner-occupiers) has remained partial, incomplete – the area neither able to purify itself of undesirable elements, nor to seal its borders against disreputable neighbours. The presence of the youth on local streets is thus for some a sign and embodiment of their inability to make of this part of 'Old Macclesfield' the kind of home and refuge they want it to be, or take it to have once been. The youth are thus an exceptionally *visible* problem; particularly 'out of place'. And those residents for whom this is true are especially disposed to 'read' the youth in terms of Pearson's 'controlling metaphor' for social change (and decay). Their sense of exposure and their tendency to assimilate notions of dangerous and disorderly youth that come from 'outside' (in political rhetorics and media discourses) are part and parcel of the same experience of insecurity, and their consequent bleak vision of the future.

Epilogue: another kind of European criminology

In the emergent project of European criminology (to which this volume seeks to contribute) a number of strands can thus far be discerned. One relatively well-established body of work endeavours – by way of comparison – to advance understanding of either the policies and practices of the constituent criminal justice and penal systems of Europe, or of the ways in which 'crime' is constructed and responded to within Europe's various political and institutional cultures (Downes 1988; Nelken 1994; Ruggiero *et al.* 1995). A second strand draws upon a rich (if – in the English-speaking world at any rate – somewhat neglected) vein of theorizing about crime and law, in order to 'Europeanize' and thus breath new life into the project of critical criminology (van Swaaningen 1997). A third more emergent corpus of work focuses on some pressing matters to do with transborder crime (around, for example, trafficking in drugs); or, alternatively, seeks to address the shift of decision-making power within areas of criminal justice from nation-states to supra-national institutions (Ruggerio and South 1995; Anderson *et al.* 1996).

These genres of research and reflection will, it seems safe to assume, figure prominently within whatever criminology of Europe emerges in the coming years. And quite properly so. But we have in this chapter taken a somewhat different path and tried to put in a word for another (albeit complementary) kind of European criminology; one that is committed to documenting and understanding the criminological implications of global flows of capital and culture on the life-worlds of Europe's differentially-situated citizens (see also Åkeström this volume). What though does this way of doing the criminology of Europe have to contribute? Or, to put it another way, in what ways are studies of public feeling about crime and risk that are expressly grounded in place relevant to projects of comparison or synthetic theorizing?

There are several ways of answering these questions and we want to conclude here by briefly signalling what some of them might be. First, in designedly conducting our research in a place that is criminologically obscure (that is, which does not suffer from an exceptional crime rate, which has no great ghettos of the most abject poverty), we are *already* joining a 'junior branch' of the tradition – outside the urban core and in the relative *terra incognita* of the suburbs and smaller towns. This in itself represents an extension of disciplinary focus of the kind that might assist European criminology in avoiding the pitfalls and limitations of what Robert Merton once called 'slum-encouraged provincialism'.

Second, the theoretical resources on which we have drawn (especially Douglas's account of ways of thinking about risk as relative to the constitution of community) not only raise matters of substantive importance regarding the construction of literal and symbolic borders around and across Europe. By postulating risk judgments as forms of 'local knowledge' (Geertz 1983), they also implicitly raise issues of interpretive strategy (cf. Nelken 1994). We have been and remain relative strangers in our research setting, and our efforts at making sense of local people's constructs of crime and danger (their 'translation' as it were *in situ*) at least pose the question of their intelligibility to a notional cultural outsider. We have as such come up against the kinds of pressing (methodological) questions that seem likely to confront European criminology in the coming years – and not only in its explicitly comparative forms.

Third, the vagaries of place and local attachment under conditions of modernity are thus *in principle* comparative – they can be posed anywhere to different conclusions. In this sense, the kind of criminology of Europe to which we hope to contribute is not a 'placeless' or homogenizing discourse (cf. Shapland 1991). Rather, it would be one that sought to comprehend the particular experiences of crime and risk, trust and fear that characterize the 'places' of Europe in terms of their differing trajectories into and through modernity (Therborn 1995a, 1995b) and their *englobement* within distinct local, regional and national economies and political cultures. Such a project begins in some sense 'at home', albeit a problematic and intrinsically 'permeable' modern home.

Notes

1 The research was supported by the Economic and Social Research Council under its Crime and Social Order Research Programme (award no. L210252032).

2 This ambition seems common to a number of colleagues currently; see especially the work of Taylor (1995), Taylor *et al.* (1996), Evans *et al.* (1996) and Hollway and Jefferson (1997).

3 In national terms Macclesfield experiences a relatively low recorded crime rate (roughly some sixteen times lower than the not so geographically distant Salford in Greater Manchester – see Evans *et al.* 1996). In 1995, Cheshire Police recorded 4150 offences for the town's six beats; of the 3120 calls made to the police in April/May 1995, 440 (14 per cent) concerned nuisance/suspicious youths.

4 In so doing, we rely principally on material drawn from two focus groups with residents of the area, one with a group of pupils attending the nearby secondary school, and a biographical interview with Ray and Dawn Jones, proprietors of a local grocer's. All names have been changed.

5 In 1995 819 offences were recorded for the police beat covering the High Street and Moss Rose. In April/May 1995, residents of High Street/Moss Rose made 868 calls to the police, 176 (20 per cent) of which concerned nuisance/suspicious youths.

6 It is also worth noting that the young people concerned view matters somewhat differently from many established local residents: 'If we go into the park we always had the people coming round complaining that we're making too much noise. Like there was a fight a couple of weeks ago, and these people from a house come out and said, 'Will you just eff off' and ended up hitting someone who was about half their age. It ended up in a big argument and all they had to do was come and ask us to move on. You get that all the time, but we weren't doing anything wrong, it's just because we were there.'

7 In the Cheshire County Council survey mentioned above, 54 per cent of Macclesfield Borough respondents thought that 'family breakdown' was a 'very significant' cause of youth crime. This compared with 26 per cent for 'young people not involved in community activities', and 20 per cent for 'lack of moral teaching/no respect'. All of the

above would be implicated in the 'social breakdown' frame which Sasson (1995) found to predominate amongst his respondents in Boston, USA.

8 The Cheshire County Council (1996) found that 'putting more police on the beat' was the most common solution to the crime problem proffered by Macclesfield Borough residents – 48 per cent had it as their top priority, 71 per cent as one of the 'top three'.

References

Anderson, M., den Boer, M., Cullen, P., Gilmore, W., Raab, C. and Walker, N. (1996) *Policing the European Union: Theory, Law and Practice*, Oxford: Oxford University Press.

Butler, T. (1995) 'Gentrification and the Urban Middle Classes' in T. Butler and M. Savage (eds) *Social Change and the Middle Classes*, London: University College London Press.

Cheshire County Council (1996) *Our Cheshire (Volume C – Crime and Concerns About Crime)*, Ellesmere Port: Cheshire County Council Research and Intelligence Unit.

Davis, M. (1990) *City of Quartz: Excavating the Future in Los Angeles*, London: Vintage.

Douglas, M. (1992) *Risk and Blame: Essays in Cultural Theory*, London: Routledge.

Downes, D. (1988) *Contrasts in Tolerance: Post-War Penal policy in the Netherlands and England and Wales*, Oxford: Oxford University Press.

Elias, N. and Scotson, J. (1994) *The Established and the Outsiders*, London: Sage.

Evans, K., Fraser, P. and Walklate, S. (1996) 'Whom can you Trust?: The Politics of "Grassing" on an Inner-city Housing Estate', *Sociological Review* 44, 3: 361–380.

Geertz, C. (1983) *Local Knowledge: Essays in Interpretive Anthropology*, New York: Basic Books.

Giddens, A. (1991) *Modernity and Self-Identity: Self and Society in the Late Modern Age*, Cambridge: Polity.

Girling, E., Loader, I. and Sparks, R. (1998) 'A Telling Tale: A Case of Vigilantism and its Aftermath in an English Town', *British Journal of Sociology*, 49 (in press).

Hacking, I. (1990) *The Taming of Chance*, Cambridge: Cambridge University Press.

Hoggart, R. (1993) *Townscape with Figures: Farnham – Portrait of an English Town*, London: Chatto.

Hollway, W. and Jefferson, T. (1997) 'The Risk Society in an Age of Anxiety: Situating the Fear of Crime', *British Journal of Sociology* 48/2: 255–266.

Hope, T. (1995) 'Community Crime Prevention' in M. Tonry and D. Farrington (eds) *Building a Safer Society*, Chicago: University of Chicago Press.

—— (1997) 'Inequality and the Future of Community Crime Prevention', in S. P. Lab (ed.) *Crime Prevention at a Crossroads*, Cincinnati, OH: Anderson.

Lash, S. and Urry, J. (1994) *Economies of Signs and Space*, London: Sage.

Loader, I., Girling, E. and Sparks, R. (1996) 'Youth, Community and Demands for Order in an English "Middletown"', paper presented to *American Society of Criminology Annual Meeting*, Downtown Marriott Hotel, Chicago, November.

Logan J. and Molotch, H. (1987) *Urban Fortunes: The Political Economy of Place*, Berkeley: University of California Press.

Melossi, D. (1994) 'The Economy of Illegalities: Normal Crimes, Elites and Social Control in Comparative Analysis', in D. Nelken (ed.) *The Futures of Criminology*, London: Sage.

Nelken, D. (1994) 'Whom can you Trust?: The Future of Comparative Criminology', in D. Nelken (ed.) *The Futures of Criminology*, London: Sage.

Pearson, G. (1983) *Hooligan: A History of Respectable Fears*, Basingstoke: Macmillan.

—— (1994) 'Youth, Crime and Society', in M. Maguire, R. Morgan and R. Reiner (eds) *The Oxford Handbook of Criminology*, Oxford: Oxford University Press.

Robertson, R. (1995) 'Glocalization: Time–Space and Homogeneity–Heterogeneity', in M. Featherstone, S. Lash and R. Robertson (eds) *Global Modernities*, London: Sage.

Rose, D. (1984) 'Rethinking Gentrification: Beyond the Uneven Development of Marxist Urban Theory', *Environment and Planning D: Society and Space* 2: 47–74.

Ruggiero, V. and South, N. (1995) *Eurodrugs: Drug Use, Markets and Trafficking in Europe*, London: University College London Press.

——, Ryan, M. and Sim, J. (1995) *Western European Penal Systems: A Critical Analysis*, London: Sage.

Sampson, R. and Wilson, W. J. (1995) 'Towards a Theory of Race, Crime and Urban Inequality', in J. Hagan and R. Peterson (eds) *Crime and Inequality*, Stanford: Stanford University Press.

Sasson, T. (1995) *Crime Talk: How Citizens Construct a Social Problem*, New York: Aldine de Gruyter.

Shapland, J. (1991) 'Criminology in Europe', in F. Heidensohn and M. Farrell (eds) *Crime in Europe*, London: Routledge.

Sherman, L., Gartin, P. and Buerger, M. (1989) 'Hot Spots of Predatory Crime: Routine Activities and the Criminology of Place', *Criminology* 27, 1: 27–55.

Shields, R. (1991) *Places on the Margin: Alternative Geographies of Modernity*, London: Routledge.

Sparks, R. (1991) 'Reason and Unreason in "Left Realism": Some Problems in the Constitution of Fear of Crime', in R. Matthews and J. Young (eds) *Issues in Realist Criminology*, London: Sage.

Sumner, C. (1994) *The Sociology of Deviance: An Obituary*, Buckingham: Open University Press.

van Swaaningen, R. (1997) *Critical Criminology: Visions from Europe* London: Sage.

Taylor, I. (1995) 'Private Homes and Public Others: An Analysis of Talk about Crime in Suburban South Manchester in the mid-1990s', *British Journal of Criminology* 35, 2: 263–285.

——, Evans, K. and Fraser, P. (1996) *A Tale of Two Cities Global Change, Local Feeling and Everyday Life in the North of England: A Study in Manchester and Sheffield*, London: Routledge.

Therborn, G. (1995a) *European Modernity and Beyond*, London: Sage.

—— (1995b) 'Routes to/Through Modernity', in M. Featherstone, S. Lash, and R. Robertson (eds) *Global Modernities*, London: Sage.

Trickett, A., Ellingworth, D., Hope, T. and Pease, K. (1995) 'Crime Victimisation in the Eighties: Changes in Area and Regional Inequality', *British Journal of Criminology* 35, 3: 343–359.

Urry, J. (1995) 'A Middle Class Countryside?', in T. Butler and M. Savage (eds) *Social Change and the Middle Classes*, London: University College London Press.

Wright, P. (1985) *On Living in an Old Country: The National Past in Contemporary Britain* London: Verso.

Wright Mills, C. (1959) *The Sociological Imagination*, Harmondsworth: Penguin.

Zedner, L. (1995) 'In Pursuit of the Vernacular', *Social and Legal Studies* 4, 4: 517–534.

20

THE MORAL CRUSADE ON VIOLENCE IN SWEDEN

Moral panic, or material for small-talk indignation?[1]

Malin Åkeström

> Much of the international comment on the assassination in Stock-
> holm on February 28th dwelt on Sweden's peaceful peculiarity.
> True, until last week, Stockholm was one of the few capital cities
> where it was still imaginable that a prime minister and his wife
> would walk home through the streets late at night and unescorted.
>
> (*The Economist*, 8 March 1986: 16)

The assassination referred to in *The Economist* was the murder in 1986 of the then Prime Minister of Sweden, Olof Palme, and the typical comment emphasized the speaker's astonishment that such a thing could occur in that country. In *Newsweek*, a girl is reported to have said, 'You know, this never happens in Sweden' (10 March 1986: 29). Comments such as these were representative in the Swedish media and also in other forums. For example, a biography published at the time contained this statement concerning the assassination: 'Now the violence has come to Sweden' (Bratt, 1988: 140).

This particular manifestation of violence, however, was not the start of a focus on violence but was embedded in a rhetoric typical of the time; the reference to the violence was no coincidence.[2] Violence, at this time, seemed to be regarded as something more than mere violent behaviour: it was seen as a foreign social force with a life of its own. Many other murders and various violent acts were widely publicized at this time, even though Sweden – compared to most other Western countries – had then a rather low rate of violent crime (Ahlberg, 1994; Deane, 1987; Dolmén, 1994). An increase in violence might explain the change. According to a national longitudinal poll, however, only a very slight increase had taken place during the previous ten years.[3] During this period a certain increase in reported violence has occurred. According to Swedish criminologists, this could be attributed to an increase in the tendency to report (mirroring the current climate of opinion), as well as reflecting a real increase (Olsson and Lindström, 1994; Wikström, 1994). Thus, a high statistical increase in the rate of youth violence during the last two decades could be explained by a greater tendency towards bringing people into the judicial system, since there was no corresponding increase in *deadly* violence for this category (von Hofer, 1995). In this case, Estrada concludes that the drastic increase occurred after the great attention paid to youth violence [dating this to 1986] (1996:13).

The descriptions above in the media were thus probably more concerned with the image (and self-image) of Sweden as an orderly, calm, peaceful and safe society, than with describing real, dramatic changes. Still, violent crimes and the issue of victims were brought to the fore, and various actions and campaigns against violence were mounted.

Moral panic – yes and no

Such intense public concern regarding the designation of a social problem has often been referred to as a moral panic, a concept coined by Cohen (1972/1980). He used a detailed case study of the English youth groups during the 1960s who were called Mods and Rockers, to formulate an account of social reaction and control. According to Cohen, the process of a moral panic takes the following course: first of all, one or more dramatic event(s) take place. This event elicits moral entrepreneurship, which leads to a mobilization of the control apparatus. The function of the mass media is to make the public conscious of (sensitized to) the problem and its potential consequences by establishing a focus on crime within the current milieu.

Researchers who have studied moral panics, or who have worked in the related tradition of studying the construction of a social problem, have concentrated on the panic or on the problem that is constructed, scrutinizing its processes, moral entrepreneurs, consequences, etc. (Best, 1989; Goode and Ben-Yehuda, 1994; Schneider, 1985). Seldom has the public's reaction to these panics been at the centre of such studies. In the analyses researchers generally content themselves with discussing the lack of proportion that they themselves see between the scope of the problem and the anxiety of the public. In spite of this, Goode and Ben-Yehuda (1994: 36), for example, claim that this disproportion is a constituting characteristic of a moral panic. The authors, however, do not make it clear what is special about 'the public'. This seems to be 'just there', resembling the conceptually fictive public that Blumer (1969: 195–208) once described as an artifact of public-opinion research. A lack of clarity, perhaps due to a confusion occurring between the actors directly engaged, who are often public figures, and the so-called 'general public'. In this article I shall concentrate on the social psychological attitudes of the latter.

Moreover, I would question the very concept, or rather its implications. A synonym dictionary equates panic with 'alarm, terror, horror, fear, fright, dread, trepidation; stark horror, abject fear, scare of one's life; hysteria', etc. (Rodale, 1978). This is also the way in which researchers in this tradition have used the concept. The implications can be found in Cohen's book. He referred to 'mass delusion' (1980: 148), made comparisons with disaster research (1980: 144–45), and also used the concept of 'mass hysteria' (1980: 33, 62, 78), (even if his main interest was the focusing on and mobilization of as well as the interaction with, the demonized). In Goode and Ben-Yehuda's book *Moral Panics* the associations are explicit. One of their chapters deals with 'collective behavior', a concept used in studies of mobs, riots, etc. The authors compare moral panics to such phenomena:

> One of the essential defining aspects of the moral panic is an exaggerated
> fear; in this sense, the moral panic is a kind of mass hysteria.
> (Goode and Ben-Yehuda, 1994: 111)

This statement, however, is not supported by any evidence. In their description of concrete cases, the authors also portray an image of a semi-hysterical public. They write for example about 'many Americans' believing that many more children were being kidnapped than by any possible count could have been kidnapped, and that 'many' Christian fundamentalists believed that satanists were torturing children. These statements are not supported by any evidence either.[4] Are so-called moral panics about mass hysteria, implying strong emotional involvement – or are they a social formation which may be used, on the level of the public's everyday discourse, among other things, as stories exchanged by concerned voices during everyday conversation?[5]

The recent focus on violence in Sweden could have led to emotional mobilization in the form of fear, which is what I have studied. (Other feelings such as anger may also be typical reactions to moral panics, but fear was emphasized, as we saw above, as a constituting characteristic.) Judging by available empirical data, 'panic' seems, however, to be too emotionally charged a word to the reactions provoked by the attention to violence. A national longitudinal poll including questions about fear of crime revealed no dramatic increase during the period under study.

Furthermore, with the aid of some results from different studies revealing discrepancies in the respondents' own attitudes and those they believe others to hold, I want to present the hypothesis that so-called moral panics above all inform us about other people's attitudes, emotions, and behaviour. These seem to me to be crucial to an interpretation of one consequence of a moral panic – that is, as transmitters of knowledge about others. Noelle-Neumann's (1986) theory about the spiral of silence will be used in this context.

Materials and methods

The study contains several different bodies of empirical material. One study specifically of adolescents in Halmstad concerns experiences of crime as well as fear of crime. Later on a postal questionnaire was sent to a representative population of the city of Helsingborg. A national longitudinal poll makes it possible to see whether the level of fear in society as a whole changed during the ongoing moral crusade against violence. This survey has been carried out every year since 1978 by Statistics Sweden. Among other questions, the survey contains a few items about crime and fear of crime.

The study of adolescents was carried out in Halmstad, a medium-sized Swedish town (approx. 50,000 inhabitants) and included a survey of students in grade 9 (age about 16) in junior high school, as well as the first and second year in senior high school (age about 17 and 18). The questionnaire was distributed to 542 students, of whom 528 answered, from 25 different classes among 11 schools. In addition, this study contained interviews, informal conversations, and observations during meetings with politicians, police and social-service officials. This material was collected during the autumn of 1986.

In the study conducted in Helsingborg, a medium-sized city, in 1994, the focus concerned the general public's attitudes to and experiences of the police (Folkesson *et al.*, 1995). It also contained questions about experiences of crime and fear of crime. A random sample of 1200 people aged 15 and over was drawn; 62 per cent of these completed and returned the posted questionnaire.

The mass media were studied by means of a monitoring of the media debate, performed by collecting newspaper articles[6] and – though this was done less consistently – recording relevant radio and television programmes.

Focusing on and mobilizing against violence

The attention given to violence during the period in question cannot be described like any other media 'crime wave', i.e., simply as an increase in news coverage. The topicality of the issue was manifested in the way in which the subject was written about and discussed, as well as in actual, concrete mobilization of different groups. Violence was referred to with the definite article. One front page thus stated 'The violence must be stopped now – on youth violence' (*Expressen*, 5 August 1986). In this way it was assumed that we all share the same definition of the meaning of the word 'violence'. New concepts were expressed and became well-known. Sub-categories appeared and were seen as new and/or especially upsetting – the unprovoked violence, the meaningless violence, etc. – and certain offence-types like wife-battering, had a renaissance in their 'degree of observability'. Furthermore, the media articles concentrated on victims, rather than on criminals, as had been common before.[7] So the attention to violence was specifically embedded in a discussion of victims – a process that has been occurring in most Western countries in this same period (Mawby and Walklate, 1994).

In Sweden, as elsewhere, hot lines for victims emerged and crime victim shelters were set up and given publicity.[8]

One illustration of the intense new media focus is the fact that articles on 'Violence' and 'Crime victims' (usually referring to victims of violence) came to be newly categorized in newspaper archives. Previously, violent crime and the few articles that existed on crime victims alone were filed under 'Crime'. The new way of filing at *Sydsvenska Dagbladet* and *Kvällsposten* (daily papers covering the south of Sweden) began during 1987, but involved a reorganization of articles from a few years back. Newspaper archives are of course organized in a set of categories that are expected to be useful in the future, in the belief that the subject will continue to feature later on. To acquire its own heading in this way, a subject must – according to one archive employee – 'qualify first'.

To study the form taken by the media attention over time, a simple quantitative survey was carried out. The front pages of *Expressen*, the daily evening paper with the largest circulation in Sweden, were studied for the period 1978–1993, the years chosen so as to be comparable to the data from the longitudinal national poll. This survey was rather crude.[9] The story on the front pages was often given considerable space inside the paper; it was not uncommon for the articles to fill several pages. Figure 20.1 shows the incidences of front-page headlines in which the term 'the violence' was explicitly used.

Other headlines which did not use the term 'the violence' can also be interpreted as being part of the focusing movement. Examples are: 'Minister: "Police must look after the young."' Violent youth gang burgles homes and robs people out walking alone at night' (28 November 1988); 'Every week a woman dies as a result of assault' (18 June 1990); 'How are we to protect our children? Phone in tonight about assault' (4 November 1990).

Estrada (1996) found the same pattern when examining the leaders of the

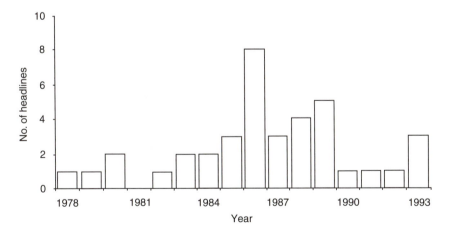

Figure 20.1 Front-page headlines on 'violence'

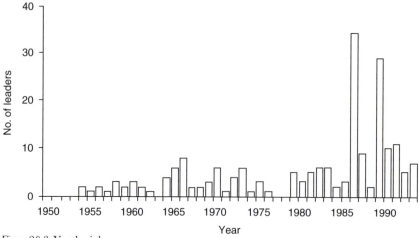

Figure 20.2 Youth violence
Source: Estrada 1996: 6

main Swedish newspapers on a specific category: youth violence. For comparison, his results are presented in Figure 20.2.

The fact that the problem of violence has assumed a central place in recent years not only meant that the area had become noticeable in the media, on talk shows, and so on; it also resulted in concrete action, i.e. in a *mobilization*. Several parliamentary commissions were set up and bills were drawn up, some of which resulted in new or revised laws.[10] The more visible manifestations of the mobilization were the various campaigns, rock concerts, etc. organized by action groups in which celebrities and politicians were often involved. One such campaign was described in *Sydsvenska Dagbladet* under the headline 'Prime Minister meets enemies of violence' (7 November 1989). The King of Sweden also stressed the importance of the issue during one of his traditional Christmas speeches during the period. The headline, 'The King at Christmas: Look after your children', shows one of the recommendations which was commonly proposed as a solution (*Expressen*, 26 December 1989).

All over Sweden the subject was discussed and integrated in different forums. Schools had theme days on violence. Parents were encouraged to take part in campaigns to 'reclaim the city'. Women were exhorted to 'reclaim the night'. Furthermore, new ceremonies emerged to commemorate the memory of those who actually had fallen victim to violence. People lit candles and put flowers in the streets on the spot where someone had been killed; torchlight processions and demonstrations opposing 'the violence' were held in the streets, and support funds were organized in the names of murder victims.

The attention to violence and its repercussion on fear

In the context described above, how did people react? One criterion of 'panic' is that people become more afraid. Evidence derived from the scientific literature in this field suggests that there are not necessarily any direct links between media attention to crime and fear of crime. According to Stinchcombe, objective factors, i.e. 'real risks' are associated with fear of crime, rather than media attention (1980: 37; 39–73). In their widely-referenced study *Coping with Crime*, Skogan and Maxfield found four factors significantly associated with fear: victimization, vulnerability, neighbourhood conditions, and vicarious experiences. The last was examined through two sources of secondhand messages, personal conversation and media. Even though the coverage of crime was extensive in the media in the studied areas, and their survey revealed widespread attention to crime news, they state:

> we could discern no impact of media exposure on fear of crime ... media effects are confined to more abstract and general perceptions of crime, and not to close-to-home assessments of risk.
>
> (Skogan and Maxfield 1981: 260)

An annually repeated Swedish national survey includes questions on fear and experiences of violence. Findings from this survey (Figure 20.3) can be used as an indicator as to whether the attention given to the subject resulted in people becoming more afraid or whether they reported being victimized to a higher degree than before.

During the time when there was special focus on violence, there was scarcely any dramatic difference in the number of people who stated that they were afraid, compared with other years. One may also note that in neighbouring Denmark (a country very similar to Sweden), where there was similar focus on violent crimes and victims, the fear of being a victim oneself actually declined in the late 1980s (Balvig, 1990).[11]

Attention to violence: conveying a specific message

However, there seem to be *some* consequences resulting from the attention to violence and crime victims, apart from the very real ones concerning changes in laws, etc. As the objects of attention were disseminated through different forums, they were transformed into topics of shared concern. Not only were they made into phenomena ('unprovoked violence', 'meaningless violence', 'youth violence') that people were distinctly aware of – people were aware of others being aware of them, too.

This was evident in several ways. At one point in the debate, for example, Swedish criminologists noted that there were no data to show that violent crime was actually increasing. Politicians and researchers nevertheless warned of the

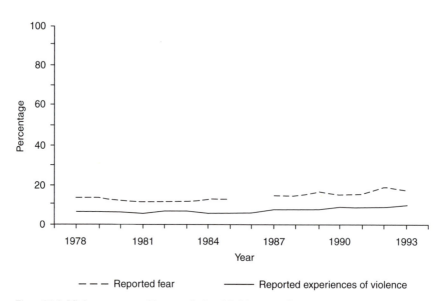

Figure 20.3 Violence reported by population 16–74 years of age
Source: SCB
Note: The question used by the Swedish Statistical Bureau in order to measure the experience of violence was, 'During the last twelve months, that is, since . . . have you yourself been exposed to one or more of the following occurrences?' A range of possible answers followed, including violence requiring medical attention, injuries manifested as bruises etc., and other types of violence or threats. (The question was not asked in 1986.) The question measuring concern or fearfulness was formulated as follows: 'In the course of the last year, did you refrain from going out in the evening because you were afraid you might be assaulted, robbed, or molested in some other way?' Those who answered those questions affirmatively are included in the figure above.

effect of the media coverage itself. The assumption they made was that the focus on violence led people to be more afraid.[12]

The results from the study of adolescents in Halmstad as well as from the study in Helsingborg provide another illustration of how moral crusades serve as communication transmitters of the attitudes of *others*. Some of the questions concerned whether the subjects were afraid of crime. These questions are admittedly crude and furthermore do not always measure the same dimensions, but they are consistent. Some examples: a much higher percentage reported that others were afraid, than that they were themselves afraid. In Helsingborg, 75 per cent believed that 'many' and 20 per cent that 'some' were afraid of becoming victims of violence, while only 6 per cent reported that they were themselves 'often' afraid and 39 per cent reported that they were 'sometimes' afraid of this. In answer to a question concerning whether the youngsters in Halmstad were afraid of specific groups 66 per cent reported that they were not afraid of any specific groups, while only 25 per cent thought that others were not too afraid of any specific groups. In answer to yet another question, on whether one was afraid of visiting certain places in Halmstad, the same pattern emerged: others are more worried than oneself.

Another indicator suggesting both the attention to the subject of danger and violence, and that this might result in the transmission of a communication about other people, was the phenomenon of the much-discussed 'Green Gang' in the Halmstad study. According to the police they had been a group of 'professional assailants', eight to ten teenagers from immigrant families, usually dressed in green army jackets. Even though the gang had been broken up about a year before according to the police, they were commented on by many youngsters at various places in the questionnaire as a real and threatening group. The gang thus seemed to have taken on something of a mythical character. It was mostly, however, not oneself but 'others' who were reported to be afraid of them.

One obvious interpretation would be that the results reflect a 'macho syndrome' (everyone else is afraid, but not me!). The results would then be an expression of a normal situation. One argument against this view is that it could then be assumed that these attitudes would be more common among boys than among girls – since such a 'macho attitude' is obviously inherent in the masculine role. This was not, however, the case. It is true that, in this as in other studies (for example Maguire, 1982; Skogan and Maxfield, 1981), fewer boys than girls responded that they were afraid; but with regard to opinions about others' fear compared to one's own, the gender differences were not in the expected direction.[13] Thus it seems reasonable to assume that the current climate of opinion could convince people that others are afraid.[14]

Defence strategies

Fear was described by different officials in terms not only of being an effect, but also a potential producer of violence among young people. A commonly-held belief among local politicians, social-welfare officials, recreation-department administrators, etc. was that many young people in Halmstad at that time carried weapons to protect themselves when they went out dancing or met friends in town. (In Helsingborg, eight years later, the same claims were made by the police.) Some even claimed that 'all' or 'almost all' carried some sort of weapon – a knife, chain, or something similar. These were quite spectacular opinions considering the earlier image of Sweden as a calm, peaceful society. Therefore, several questions were formulated as to whether the youngsters did carry some form of weapon, and whether they believed that other young people had them. The results were as in Tables 20.1, 20.2 and 20.3.

According to the results shown in the Tables, 37 per cent believed that 'young people nowadays' carry weapons of some sort when they walk downtown on a Friday or Saturday night. However, when asked if they know anyone who does carry a weapon, 25 per cent answered that they know of some, though they are not their friends, and 7 per cent say some of their friends do. Only 3 per cent say they do it 'often' or 'sometimes' themselves.

In a less highly charged social atmosphere, 37 per cent of young Swedish

Table 20.1 Young people and weapons 1

'People say that young people these days carry weapons (knives, chains, etc.) when they go downtown on a Friday or Saturday night, to be on the safe side if nothing else. Do you think that's basically true?' (Percentages)

Yes, I suppose many do	37
No, there aren't many who do that	39
No, I don't think that's true at all	4
Don't know, no answer	19
Total	100
(Number of replies)	(528)

Table 20.2 Young people and weapons 2

'Do you know anyone who does it?' (Percentages)

I know some who do, but none of my friends does it	25
Some of my friends do	7
No, I don't know of anyone	64
No answer	3
Total	100
(Number of replies)	(528)

Table 20.3 Young people and weapons 3

'Are you in the habit of doing so yourself?' (Percentages)

Yes, often	1
Yes, sometimes	2
It's happened once or twice	5
No, never	89
No answer	2
Total	100
(Number of replies)	(528)

Note: the response options were provided

people would probably not believe that others carry weapons. This rather seems to be yet another expression of the focus on violence giving clues as to other people's behaviour.

Few 'don't know' answers

Yet another result points in the direction of so-called moral panics as communicators of others' attitudes. The proportion of 'no answer' or 'don't know' in all tables from the Halmstad and the Helsingborg study may be held to be rather low with reference to the opinion of other people's experience of fear. As Noelle-Neumann (1986: 9–16) has argued, it is not clear that people are really secure about what others believe and experience. Therefore, it is significant that there is a low rate of 'don't know' answers given in opinion polls when a particular opinion appears to be socially dominant. Since this is visible and openly expressed one acquires leads and cues as to what 'everyone' thinks.

Food for talk – 'moral panic' on the level of social conversation

'Moral panics' are highly visible manifestations of interest in certain subjects that prevail in our milieu. The interest of people around us is bound to convey the message that others are upset, afraid, concerned, and so forth. During the last decade Swedes have been surrounded by horror stories about violence – we have seen films and plays in school about youth violence; there were articles in the newspapers about 'street violence', 'racist violence', 'woman-battering', 'child-battering', etc., as well as programmes on radio and television. Therefore, a specific interpretation of my results may be that the higher level for 'others' fear' in comparison to one's own, is due to the fact that people themselves had not been directly affected as victims, whereas the general impression that others were afraid remained.

A more general interpretation, and perhaps a more important one, is that the climate of opinion in itself creates issues which are functional on a level of 'social conversation'. At such a level one can include conversational topics such as the weather, high food prices, crime – 'it's terrible that people don't dare to go out these days' – stories about dramatic violent crime, etc. These are topics in which everyone can be included and upon which everyone can agree. Besides, agreement is actually not only possible but expected. In such a 'conversational atmosphere', one hardly violates the socially acceptable by voicing something akin to 'I don't believe it's that dangerous'. Perhaps one doesn't even reflect whether one is afraid oneself or not. Noelle-Neumann's (1986) theory about 'the spiral of silence' concerns the social control of opinions, attitudes and values that at a particular time seem to be improper or inappropriate. In this case it is not a question of dedicated views being split into two or more camps – with one or other falling silent. There is no stance which says 'I am not afraid'. Yet something of this mechanism may still be relevant. Noelle-Neumann's argument is that a consequence of very visible expressions of current opinion will be that one evaluates the attitudes in one's surroundings in accordance both with the clues one receives in conversation and with what is reflected in the general discussion at the time.

Discussion

During the last few decades, many studies of moral panics, as well as of the constructions of social problems, have been carried out. Through them we know a lot about the surface dynamics of how they are displayed in rhetoric and how mobilization from society through law and practices changes.

At the beginning, I stated that I wanted to question the concept of moral panic. McRobbie and Thornton (1995) in a theoretical way have questioned the old model (in Cohen's (1972/80) and Pearson's (1983) studies) where the concept seems to reference a consensual language for social control in a homogeneous society. Today, they state, 'folk devils' are less marginalized and their interests are defended in their own niches and micromedia; multiple representations are articulated. My concern is different: there seems to me to be a lack of studies seeking to investigate the actual response to moral panics.

We know fairly little about how 'moral panics' are dealt with in interaction and related to emotionally. We know a little bit about who claims-makers are and how they construct their objects. We know less about how they construct the problems in back-stage talk and their emotions *vis-à-vis* these objects of concern. In Best's (1989) words there are more 'contextual constructionists' than pure constructionists among researchers.

In parentheses, I would therefore like to dwell briefly on some impressions concerning the activists and executors of moral panics in my study. Some, but not all, moral entrepreneurs seemed to be deeply emotionally involved. Some might have used the issue strategically, i.e. for their own advancement, as Reinarman and Levine (1989) claimed that American politicians did in the case of the campaign against crack. Those responsible for implementation of policies on youth violence in Sweden – politicians and different officials – that we encountered talked about 'the problem' in quite different ways – some cynically, some probably paying lip-service, while others seemed honestly concerned. By and large, they seemed preoccupied with the necessity of doing something about it: appointing a commission, suggesting a suitable policy, and so forth. Questions were posed: are new leisure centres for youngsters a good idea? How can we increase parental involvement? Who shall we invite to give a speech on the subject of violence in school, in church? Their perspective, then, seems to me to be more of a practical nature *vis-à-vis* a social object forcing itself on one's attention – a 'this-has-to-be-acted-upon' attitude – than a strongly emotional one.

Many researchers have shown a moral indignation in their own writing, sometimes writing with irony about the disparities between a rational way of viewing and acting on a problem and the one moral panics force policy-makers and others to take. (This tradition of 'debunkery' is nicely analysed as rhetoric, using for example, hyperbole and irony as strategies, by Jaworski, 1994.) Like Mathiesen (1996), they have been upset because politicians, for example, have not been involved in communicative rationality. The concept – borrowed from Habermas – conveys a sense of principled and informed argumentation forming a basis for decisions and policies, as well as discourses and practices in society. Mathiesen assumes a more opportunistic mode of handling matters of criminal justice today. Perhaps this is so, but in that case we do not know how. If political strategies today are to a large extent equivalent to media strategies, as McRobbie and Thornton (1995) claim, closer studies might reveal how politicans and others construct a rational way of tackling these panics. Perhaps we should study them like – or at least compare them with – other phenomena that have similar traits (for example, of transience, e.g. fashion), or like any other opinion that forces all of us to somehow take a position, form a viewpoint, mobilize our consciousness and perhaps our feelings.

Even though the data presented above are meagre and were not collected with the aim of studying moral panics,[15] they nevertheless suggest that studies in this area can discern other aspects than have hitherto been common. One first, obvious issue is that of centrality.

The lack of centrality of 'crime' as a category of concern in people's everyday life is, for example, forcefully illuminated in Balvig's study of fear of crime. In a period of media attention to violence in Denmark (1986–1987) he organized a study where students went out asking people about general matters of concern in their everyday life. People spoke about work, food, travel, influenza, relatives, etc. Crime was conspicuous by its absence. Balvig concluded that: 'Private, everyday concerns on the one hand and general, societal concerns on the other seem to be two quite different notions' (1990: 124).

Second, however, we can surely go beyond the repetition of familiar refrains regarding 'moral panic'. I specifically want to link the emotional, social psychological response to the social form called moral panic. One such response might be that moral panics serve as communication transmitters giving clues about other people's emotions and are then used as food for talk in everyday conversation.

Notes

1 I would like to thank Stanley Cohen, Jack Katz, Ian Taylor and Harvey Molotch for helpful comments on this manuscript, and Alan Crozier and Marianne Thormählen for correcting the English.

2 According to Cohen a moral panic starts with one or more dramatic incidents taking place. This seems however to be a simplified notion. For example, Denmark has experienced the same attention to violence lately, without any such very special event (like the assassination of Palme) (Balvig, 1990). One interpretation of such changes might be that they are born out of a saturation process (Asplund, *Mättnadsprocesser*, 1967). 'New objects of concern' both satisfy media demand for something new, and give moral entrepreneurs the rhetorical weapon of claiming their object's previous lack of societal attention.

3 See Figure 20.3 (Reported experiences of violence and reported fear).

4 It is not only the conventional 'social problem' researchers who write about moral panics in this vein; lately postmodern theorists have been suggesting that the American public is in a fundamental and continuing panic about a range of issues: gender,

affluence, the future, a sense of secure values, etc.). Cf. Arthur Kroker (1988) and Stephen Pfohl (1992).

5 Another use may be that of integrating social relationships in a more direct way, such as when children can display their commitment to their elderly parents by warning them against going out at nights; examples of this were encountered in a recent qualitative study of fear of crime.

6 The systematically researched newspaper is Sweden's most sold daily, the evening paper *Expressen*. The less systematically researched include the local daily paper *Halmstadposten*, the daily morning paper *Sydsvenska Dagbladet*, and the daily evening paper *Kvällsposten*.

7 See, for example, Graber (1980) and Sherizen (1978), on crime news focusing on criminals rather than victims.

8 Women's shelters had existed previously, but during the mid- and late 1980s their number increased dramatically (Åkerström, 1990).

9 This is not the best way of illustrating the media coverage, but it was chosen since there is no easily available option. There is no equivalent for Swedish newspapers, for example, of the New York Times Index where one can fairly easily count references to different subjects.

10 See, for example, Statens Offentliga Utredningar, *Våld och brottsoffer*. (1990) (The Official State Investigation on Violent Crimes and Victims of Crime) 2; *Kvinnovåldskommissionen* (1995) (The Commission on Violence against Women): 60. For a review of different commissions and new legal policies concerning victims of crime, see *Brottsoffren i blickpunkten (Ds 1993: 29)*. The changes and revisions of laws are too broad a subject to be included here, but a prohibition on carrying knives in public places can be mentioned as an early result of the discussions. Several changes were also made aiming to help crime victims.

11 Balvig's interpretation of this deals with the reasons why people do not appear to be so afraid. His explanation involves a generational analysis: fear of the young as a potentially threatening category is perhaps not as great today as when there was a greater distance between the generations. The analysis is thus not about the social psychological consequences of moral panic.

12 The Minister of Justice, Laila Freivalds, warned for example, of such consequences in a television talk show (Talk show host Lasse Holmkvist. TV2. 23/2 1990).

13 Gender differences comparing own fear vs that of others (%):

	Girls	Boys
I am not afraid, others are	73	51
I am not afraid, others are not afraid	27	49
(Number of replies)	(150)	(158)

14 This is a suggested interpretation; I have not been able to find studies giving support for this, for example, comparisons between oneself and others regarding fear of violent crimes, whether during, before or after a moral panic or a media 'crime wave'. That is, the differences that appear might appear in less highly-changed situations as well. However, they do run counter to some findings pointing towards a tendency among adolescents to believe that others are tougher than oneself (e.g. Hauge, 1971) when

discussing drinking habits or Schank's (1932) classic study where the concept of pluralistic ignorance was coined, others being thought to be better than oneself.

15 The materials were originally collected as part of a straightforward study of fear of crime.

References

Ahlberg, J. (1994) 'Brottsstatistik är svår att jämföra' in *Brottsutvecklingen 1992 och 1993*, Brå-rapport 1994: 3, Stockholm: Brottsförebyggande rådet.

Åkerström, M. (1990) *Dilemman i frivilligjourer- exemplen kvinno- och brottsofferjourer*. Lund: Research reports. Department of Sociology. Lund University.

Balvig, F. (1990) *Mod et nyt kriminologisk samfundsbillede*, Copenhagen: Jurist- og Ekonomiforbundets forlag.

Best, J. (ed.) (1989) *Images of Issues: Typifying Contemporary Problems*, New York: Aldine de Gruyter.

Blumer, H. (1969) *Symbolic Interactionism*, Englewood Cliffs, NJ: Prentice-Hall.

Bratt, I. (1988) *Mot rädslan*, Stockholm: Carlssons.

Cohen, S. (1972/1980) *Folk Devils and Moral Panics*, Oxford: Martin Robertson.

Deane, Glenn D. (1987) 'Cross-National Comparison of Homicide: Age/Sex Adjusted Rates Using The 1980 U.S. Homicide Experience as a Standard', *Journal of Quantitative Criminology*, 3, 3: 215–227.

Dolmén, L. (1994) 'Brottsofferundersökningar', *Brottsutvecklingen 1992 och 1993*, Brå-rapport 1994: 3. Stockholm: Brottsförebyggande rådet.

Estrada, F. (1996) 'Ungdomsvåld: upptäckten av ett samhällsproblem: Ungdomsbrottslighet i svensk dagspress 1950–1994'. Kriminologiska institutionen. Stockholms universitet.

Folkesson, E., Gustavsson, H. and Johannesson, N. (1995) *Vad tycker allmänheten om polisen?* Research report. 1995: 2. Lund: Kriminalvetenskapligt nätverk. Sociologiska institutionen. Lunds universitet.

Goode, E. and Ben-Yehuda, N. (1994) *Moral Panics: The Social Construction of Deviance*, Oxford: Blackwell.

Graber, D. (1980) *Crime News and the Public*, New York: Praeger.

Hauge, R. (1971) *Kriminalitet som ungdomsfenomen*, Stockholm: Aldus/Bonniers.

von Hofer, H. (1995) 'Violence criminelle et jeunes en Suède: une perspective à long terme', Les Politique Sociales, nr. 3&4 33–45.

Jaworski, G. D. (1994) 'Debunking the Drug Scare: a Rhetorical Analysis', in J. Holstein and G. Miller (eds) *Perspectives on Social Problems* vol. 5: 55–71. Greenwich, CT: JAI Press.

Katz, J. (1987) 'What makes crime "news"?', *Media, Culture and Society*, 9: 47–75.

Kroker, A. (1988) *The Panic Encyclopedia*, New York: St Martin's Press.

McRobbie, A. and Thornton, S. (1995) 'Rethinking "moral panic" for multi-mediated social worlds', *British Journal of Sociology*, 46, 4: 559–574.

Maguire, M. (1982) *Burglary in a Dwelling: the Offence, the Offender and the Victim*, London: Heinemann.

Mathiesen, T. (1996) 'Driving Forces Behind Prison Growth: The Mass Media', *Crime and Social Order in Europe. Newsletter*, No. 4. London: ESRC, July: 3–5.

Mawby, R. I. and Walklate, S. (1994) *Critical Victimology*, London: Sage.

Noelle-Neumann, E. (1986) *The Spiral of Silence: Public Opinion – Our Social Skin*, Chicago: University of Chicago Press.

Olsson, M. and Lindström, P. (1994) 'Vad säger kriminalstatistiken?' in *Det obegripliga våldet*. Stockholm: Forskningsrådsnämnden: 13–28.

Pearson, G. (1983) *Hooligan: A history of respectable fears*, London: Macmillan.

Pfohl, S. (1992) *Death at Parasite Café*, New York: Macmillan.

Reinarman, C. and Levine, H. G. (1989) 'The crack attack: Politics and media in America's latest drug scare' in J. Best (ed.) *Images of Issues*, New York: de Gruyter.

Rodale, J. I. (1978) *The Synonym Finder*, Emmaus, Pa.: Rodale Press.

Schank, R. (1932) 'A Study of a Community and Its Groups and Institutions Conceived as Behaviors of Individuals', *Psychological Monographs*, 43, no. 2.

Schneider, J. (1985) 'Social Problems Theory' *Annual Review of Sociology*, 11: 209–229.

Sherizen, S. (1978) 'Social Creation of Crime News' in C. Winick (ed.) *Deviance and Mass Media*, Beverly Hills: Sage.

Skogan, W. G and Maxfield, M. G. (1981) *Coping with Crime*, Sage Library of Social Research. vol. 124. Beverly Hills: Sage.

Statens Offentliga Utredningar (1983: 31) Allmänna förlaget: Stockholm.

Statens Offentliga Utredningar (1990: 92) *Våld och brottsoffer* Slutbetänkande av våldskommissionen. Stockholm: Allmänna förlaget.

Stinchcombe, A. L. (1980) Crime and Punishment: changing attitudes in America, San Fransisco: Jossey-Bass.

Wikström, P-O. (1994) 'Utvecklingen inom olika brottskategorier', *Brottsutvecklingen 1992 och 1993*, Brottsförebyggande rådet. Stockholm.

21

YOUTH DEVIANCE AND SOCIAL EXCLUSION IN GREECE

Sophie Vidali

Youth, deviance and subcultures: the Greek case

One of the central themes in the field of criminology and the sociology of deviance has always been the formation and the constitutive elements of deviant subcultures among adolescent groups, as well as their corresponding influence on juvenile social behaviour.[1] The interaction between deviant culture and social control[2] is well established in the relevant literature. However, youth subcultures, even though they constitute 'a common way of solving problems', must not be theorised as if they were a homogeneous entity.[3] Consequently, dealing with these subcultures means that we are dealing with attitudes that may share a great deal in common, yet at the same time be very different. These differences have to do not only with the social context but also with personal attitudes.[4]

Until recently in Greece, attempts to explain criminality, deviance and subcultural styles among youth have mainly employed American, British and European theories of criminology and of the sociology of deviance. Most authoritative criminologists[5] also referred to the dogmatic application and interpretation of juvenile law.[6] On the other hand there are few studies of juvenile criminality and attitudes, beliefs, deviance and subcultures.[7]

This chapter focuses on the personal and collective attitudes of young people and the influence of these attitudes on criminal or deviant behaviour, as reported in Greece. More specifically our hypotheses are that:

1 There are some new tendencies, attitudes and beliefs among sections of Greek youth, mostly between 15 and 22 years old, related to criminal and deviant behaviour, which may mean that changes are taking place in the process of social integration.

2 These changes are related to the formation of new subcultures of youth in Greece, the constitutive elements of which are completely new in the social and historical context of this country.

3 If we take into consideration the social context and background factors in

Greece, the characteristics of the new subcultures may contribute to unexpectedly extreme forms of social integration or exclusion.

If there exists a typical and characteristic[8] element of Greek youth during the 1970s and 1980s it is surely its massive and strong politicisation.[9] The recent reversal of youth's politicisation (occurring between 1985 and 1989) and the subsequent rise in juvenile delinquency, are, among other developments, new elements in Greek society. The consequences and the repercussions of the above-mentioned phenomena have never been, until now, the subject of research or study in Greece.

During the last few years there have been periodic eruptions of violence involving groups of young people. These have had a quasi-political character but without any continuity and, often, without any concrete demands. At the same time, a common impression in public opinion and political analysis is that the influence of youth groups in political life is today insignificant. This is quite contrary to the influence of such groups during the years 1975–1985. Instead, in the last decade, the characteristic tendency among young people has been toward passive observation and self-exclusion from the social process.

The feeling of marginality

On the basis of the discussion so far, we can now formulate the hypothesis that new forms of social integration and of marginalisation are developing in Greece. This process concerns not only youth identified as socially and economically marginalised[10] but also youth groups of the Greek middle class, which are by no means deprived of opportunities for social and economic success. These young people constitute a 'grey area' of intermediate and heterogeneous groups situated between the marginalised and the conformist groups of society, even though, as I shall argue, they also are characterised by a peculiar kind of marginalisation.

By the term marginal or marginalisation, we usually refer to the social strata in a given society who do not participate in, or are deprived of the possibilities of participation in, the common social processes which have to do with the economy, the prevailing ideology (at a political and cultural level) and consequently with social adaptation.[11] Marginalisation, among other things, refers to the efficiency and character of social control, to deviance, to criminality, to situations of social exclusion and labelling phenomena, which are all currently very important in Greece.

In this chapter, I discuss some of these new youth groups and their ways of thinking and living. One basis for my approach is an interest in their deviant or criminal behaviour in relation to the places they 'hang around'; a secondary concern is with the identification of common constants which influence their way of life.

I will take, as examples of such groups, two subcultures of young people in Greece, with similarities and differences. These groups reflect two *different* sets of attitudes and socio-political behaviour yet may include the *same* young people, who may simultaneously belong (permanently or temporarily) to the two different groups. I will first describe a group of youth, commonly identified by the media and public opinion as associated with both common crime and political deviance. This is the so-called 'anarchists' group. The 'anarchists' frequent a lively central square of Athens and, from time to time, create problems of social nuisance and public disorder. The characterisitic element of this group is the *apparent* but not necessarily clear, political motivation underpinning its actions. What follows is based on my own observational research, as well as police and media reports on the everyday activities and behaviour of the 'anarchists' during riots and conflicts with the police.

The second group which I will describe comprises students from high schools and Universities. My sources regarding this subculture derive from other studies and from participation in the daily activities of such students.

Youth, marginalisation and deviance: the 'anarchists'

The mythical Exarchia

One of the best-known squares in the centre of Athens is the Exarchia square, and it is around this location that a variety of marginal and non-marginal groups of youth congregate. These groups have come to be seen as associated with the most charismatic and dynamic group – the so called 'anarchists'.

The characteristics of this group

In attempting to demystify this group and its activities we must first identify its typical characteristics. The 'anarchists' are neither a institutionalised nor homo-geneous political group, but are best seen as a constellation of groupings, repre-senting sub-groups with different perceptions of society and political activity. Most of their engagement and intervention in political and social protest has been regarded as political provocation.[12] However it has also been claimed that some members of para-political groups are also involved with the police (e.g. as informants), and/or with the underworld of organised crime. In other words, the participation of some may be more to do with other loyalties than with politics. Nonetheless, there are certainly some groups of young people who are genuinely committed to 'anarchism'.

The stigmatisation of the group

At the time of writing, one interesting point is that this constellation of groups constitutes the reserve of the 'usual suspects' held responsible for terrorism. Accord-ing to media portrayals and public perceptions, they constitute a kind of 'internal enemy' in Greece. From this point of view, criminal-justice responses and public stigmatisation of some members of these groups have effectively produced their social exclusion. During the last twelve years, the police and media have held the anarchists responsible for all of the major street conflicts in Athens (especially during the annual anniversary of the Polytechnic School revolt of 1973).

The point that interests us here is that we can distinguish, within this constellation of sub-groups, those groups that I have termed *intermediate* groups of young people, who display a contradictory stance in that they seem to both adopt and yet reject commonly accepted values.

The rejection of the myth

The street conflicts of November 1995 are generally associated with the occupation of the Polytechnic School by the 'anarchists' and with political provocation by other persons 'known and unknown'. For the first time in many years, the police intervened to arrest all those who had occupied the Polytechnic School of Athens.[13] No resistance was offered. Police estimates and media reports suggested that among those arrested there were about 50–100 persons of various political and para-political affiliations who could not, or would not, provide any age identification. With regard to social-class background, it has generally been assumed that members of the 'anarchist' groups come from the low social strata, that they were children of 'broken homes', deprived backgrounds, and with personal histories of being marginal delinquents, drug dependants, and so on.

The police arrested 512 young people; the majority being adolescent[14] students between 16 and 21[15] years old. Eye-witnesses and participants in the protest testified that about two thousand young people took part in the occupation.[16]

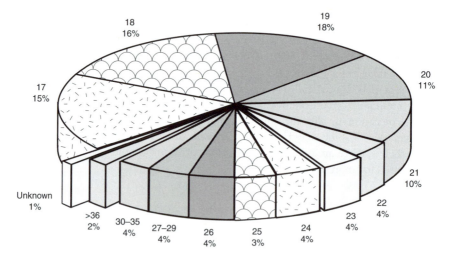

Figure 21.1 Age of those arrested.
Source: Eleftherotypia *data elaboration* S. Vidali

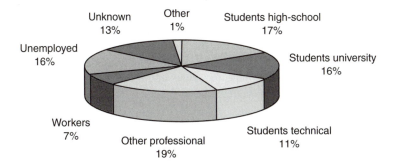

Figure 21.2 Persons arrested according to their occupation
Source: Eleftherptypia *Data elaboration* S. Vidali

In fact, those arrested did not come from deprived backgrounds and broken families. Their parents were aware of the conflicts and, for the first two days after the arrests, gathered outside the police station where their children were taken.[17] They also sought to help their children in every possible way. Furthermore, and contrary to common opinion, these young people came from a range of different social strata and not simply from the working class.[18] Again, contradicting the image of these young people as being persistently in trouble with the law, the majority of those arrested had not had any previous involvement with the police.

Importantly they also held no clear or concrete political ideology. Their behaviour during preventive detention reflected a general rejection of state authority, rather than an explicitly anarchist critique of society. Some of the spirit of this sense of 'rejection' may be illuminatingly conveyed by quoting a well-known journalist who participated in the occupation and was arrested with the youngsters.

> These events were the denouncement of the state's barbarism . . . they were an expression of resistance to the 'smoothness' [of modern life], a re-assertion of self-dignity in contrast to the 'convenient' way of life; an instantaneous feeling of an escaped liberty, a fury of life which struggles against a society in decline where the only solution is death: death through every-day alienation, through the illusion of the 'virtual' realis-ation of dreams. These events *fractured the boredom of the glass towers.* They were the reflection of some youngsters' desperation, which recorded their denial of a society which rejected them.[19]

Here we can identify a form of deviant behaviour, with a clearly political character, yet one which seems inconsistent and almost incomprehensible because its 'political' nature is not tied up with any clearly evident motive or agenda. We shall return to this point later.

Youth, deviance and conformism

As noted earlier, the education sector, particularly the high schools and Universities, are the second key location for the formation of youth subcultural groups in Greece. The results of past research on high school populations provide information on the forming of marginal subcultures in Greece.

Here I present findings from two such studies:[20]

> Study 1. 'Youth, free time and models of deviance' (hereafter denoted as r1). This was a project conducted by members of the scientific team of the Laboratory of Criminological Science of the Democritus University of Thrace.
> Study 2.'Destructiveness, school experience and political behaviour' (hereafter denoted as r2). This was a study carried out by a team of teachers in Athens.

Because of space limitations, I will only briefly refer to some of the conclusions of these projects:

1   The self-reports of vandalism and destructiveness are lower in percentage terms than the kind of figures alleged by the media [r2, p. 35]. We cannot necessarily talk here about the orchestration of moral panics[21] but it remains the case that such facts are neither reported systematically nor given prominence by the media. The media reporting that does occur contributes to the construction of a stereotypical portrait of young people as angry and deviant.

2   Adolescent deviance and criminality in Greece is not necessarily (as often assumed) associated with the working class or the lowest strata of society (the Greek 'underclass') [r1, r2 p. 35]. These results, as well as our discussion of the mixed nature of the Exarchia square groups, and the 'anarchists', lead us to suggest that in Greece we cannot identify concrete youth subcultures directly and specifically related to specific social-class groups.[22] Deviant behaviour simply seems to be a 'normal' aspect of general youth behaviour.[23]

3   The majority of adolescents who self-reported deviance and/or vandalism/destructiveness, attended 'technical high schools' and perceived schooling as 'repressive and a threat to their autonomy. School is outside of their interests and, because of this, a boring place and, even more, a place hostile to self-reflection' [r2 p. 35, r1]. Reporting of deviance within this group should not overshadow the fact that the majority of these adolescents usually spend their free time watching television, listening to music and going to pubs [r1].

4   The studies also indicated that negative school experience and 'problematic relations' with teachers contribute to acceptance of, and involvement in, activities involving violent behaviour and which have a wider social and political character. In turn, these latter problematic relations, and subsequent reactions, influence the personal, social and political *identity* of these young

344

people [r2]. Boredom, apathy and disinterest in the status quo seems to be the general and dominant feeling expressed by young people in these research studies.[24]

Summarising, we can suggest that: in *some* groups of Greek adolescents, regardless of specific class origin, there is a cultural, social and political 'impasse' which is expressed by disinterest, rejection and the absence of a sense of creativity and purpose.[25] This situation seems common among various groups of Greek youth independent of their subculture, their class origin, their level of political activity, or their objective life perspectives. This absence of creativity and purpose – not new as a phenomenon[26] in other countries – is a completely new phenomenon for Greek youth. This development seems to be mirrored in the way they spend their free time.

This apathy, disinterest and absence of creativity may be an attitude of life set to increase. As an attitude it also seems to be present in the older group of young people discussed in this essay, the University students. Formally empirical and also non-systematic observation of the daily life of the students, as well as many discussions, lead me to conclude that they too feel unmotivated and generally 'bored' by their lives and opportunities, seeing no alternatives available with the power to excite or to motivate them.[27]

Marginalised again

If such a sense of boredom, apathy and absence of creative activity or thinking are common features of the life of Greek youth today this is a significant development. This also has implications for how youth may view their future and their contribution to society. Marginalisation may lead to social exclusion, deviant behaviour and/or participation in criminality.[28] It is possible that Greek society is being confronted by the broad and diverse marginalisation of youth groups. The discussion so far has been intended to highlight and emphasise a peculiar form of social exclusion, a condition in which youth have lost their commitment to or ability to identify with a 'dream' for life. This is somewhat different to the more familiar and typical forms of social exclusion. The intermediate groups to which we have referred are integrated into their social context, yet they are marginalised on a psychological level, in terms of their perceptions of the future and the negative value they place on traditional hierarchies of objectives and rewards. The most characteristic feature here is a 'search for excitement' that may counter their state of boredom. These young people do not identify any clearly attractive or useful social or political model to underpin this search.[29]

It seems that for these adolescents the energetic 'expressivity' and 'aggressiveness' of youth can find no easy outlet. It also seems that they feel excluded from any means by which they could express their creativity or contribute on an individual or on a collective level. It is particularly in this respect that the sense of 'psychological exclusion' that influences their social life is constructed. The experience of this process is expressed through a general denial of the authority of the state and other institutions; by a denial of everything collective; and by contestation with the social system via the rejection of contemporary politics in Greece. All of these elements have been the subject of other studies in subculture-theory in other countries.[30] However, as I have already observed, the difference in the Greek case is the significance of the *reversal* of young people's attitudes toward politics and political *involvement* during recent years. This complete turnabout, and the cases illustrated, lead to my identification of a peculiar marginalisation and social process of self-exclusion, also identified on a psychological level.

This latent marginality and exclusion requires three levels of analysis in order to understand its influence on social reality, its influence in the forming of youth subcultures, and finally its influence on criminal and deviant behaviours.

On a macro-level we can say that the 'crisis of values' in Greek society 'permits' behaviours producing and promoting 'excitement'. On a mezzo-level, this crisis of values has resulted in the neutralisation of young people's interest in a broader sense in social life and in social problems. In consequence there has been an inward turning towards the 'self'. Finally, on a micro-level, the absence of a clear model and pattern for social and individual life makes both deviant *and* conformist patterns of life simultaneously and equally accessible and acceptable.

At this micro-level, experience of latent exclusion and marginality may be converted into a further drift towards commitment to a career of properly deviant or criminal behaviour.[31] Such behaviours may often seem incomprehensible[32] and need further investigation and refinement of appropriate methodologies. I must emphasise here that this essay is a first approach toward these various developments. A more penetrating study would have to answer the question of whether this kind of marginality and social exclusion is the result of ineffective social control or the result of its neutralisation.

Notes

Editors note: Readers more familiar with the portrait of youth culture found in transatlantic criminology and sociology of deviance may be unfamiliar with the situation in countries where there has been a history of the politicisation of youth. Traditional involvement in political activity has been giving way to 'western' patterns of youth activity more reminiscent of the 1960s images of 'drop-out' and 'hedonistic' youth in the USA. Vidali presents one example of this phenomenon; for discussion of the case of Italian youth and new patterns of hedonistic 'hyper-activity', see 'Interview with Giovanni Traverso', *Crime and Social Order in Europe*, Newsletter, 1: 4. London: ESRC.

1 See among others D. Downes and P. Rock, *Understanding Deviance*, Oxford, Clarendon Press, 1995; G. Pearson, 'Youth, Crime and Society', in M. Maguire, R. Morgan and R. Reiner, *Oxford Handbook of Criminology*, 1994, Oxford, Clarendon Press; S. Alexiadis, *Criminology* (in Greek), A.Sakkoulas, Athens-Komotini, 1989.

2 E. Lambropoulou, *Social Control of Crime* (in Greek), Papazisi, Athens 1994: 82 ff.; Chr. Nova: 'School socialisation and deviance (in Greek), *'Chroniques' of Laboratory of Criminological Sciences*, 1993, vol. 6: 3 ff.; S. Cohen, 'Social Control and the politics of reconstruction', in D. Nelken, *The Futures of Criminology*, Sage, London , 1994: 63–87; Y. Panoussis, 'Self-report Youth's Criminality', in Panoussis *The Message in Criminology* (in Greek), A. Sakkoulas Athens-Komotini, 1995: 419–420.

3 There is not a general theory about youth but different theories. Each one of them points out to a specific dimension of the phenomenon 'youth'. (S. Papaioanou, 'Youth's social situation and conscience' (in Greek), *Review of Sociological Research*, 1987, vol. 66: 10, 23). See for a classification of subcultures in the Greek bibliography: A. Astrinakis, *Youth Subcultures: Deviant Subcultures of the Working-class Youth. The British Approach and the Greek Experience* (in Greek), Athens, Papasissi, 1991: 11–16.

4 Downes and Rock : *op. cit.*: 185, where the approach of S. Cohen is mentioned, and S. Papaioanou, *op. cit.*: 19.

5 We have to mention here that in Greece Criminology is mainly a field of Law Schools' teaching. Consequently the majority of criminologists have a Jurisprudential background.

6 We mention indicatively : S. Alexiadis, *Criminology* (in Greek), *op. cit.*, K. D. Spinelli and A. Troianou, *Juvenile Legislation* (in Greek), Athens-Komotini, A. Sakkoulas, 1987. A recent study in the field is that of A. Pitsela, *The Penal Confrontation of Juveniles' Criminality* (in Greek), Thessaloniki, Sakkoula, 1996.

7 According to Y. Panoussis the reasons for the slow growth of empirical research in the fields of Criminology and Sociology of Deviance are to be looked for not only in the State's policy but also in the Criminologists' conformism (Y. Panoussis, 'Criminological research in Greece' (in Greek*)*, *Dikaio kai politiki*, 1989, vol.17–18, p. 112).

The greatest number of criminological studies in Greece are conducted in prisons, in schools and other institutions and in some cases in urban areas. They are orientated (through a quantitative data analysis) mainly to a macroscopic approach to juvenile delinquency. Among others we refer to the research of: S. Alexiadis, *Adolescents' Criminality at Thessaloniki*, (in Greek), Thessaloniki, 1966, D. Tsaoussis and E. Koppe-Crueger, *Adolescents' Criminality in the Capital* (in Greek), Athens, E.K.K.E., 1974, L. Besé, *Delinquance et Mass Media*, Thesis, Université Paris XIII, 1986, X. Kelperis, A. Mouriki, G. Myrizakis, and others, 'Youths: free-time and interpersonal relations' (in Greek), *The Greek Review of Social Research*, 1985, vol. 57: 83–144. Two more recent pieces of research on the issue of youth subcultures with a micro-sociological approach have been conducted by A. Astrinakis: The first is *Youth Subcultures, op. cit.*, and second is published under the title, *Heavy Metal – Rockabili and Fanatic Fans* (in Greek), Athens, Ellinika Grammata, 1996. The work of Astrinakis is focused on the subcultures of groups of youths in populous poorer neighbourhoods.

8 For historical reasons related to the cultural, political, economic and social background of the evolution of the Greek State, 'Greek society does not seem to be a society with a fixed class structure' S. Papaioannou, *op. cit.* 1987, *The Greek Review of Social Research*, vol. 67: 43. For a historical approach to the evolution of the Greek metropolitan cities see P. Pisanias, *The Poor of the Cities*, Athens, Themelio, 1993.

9 We must mention that crises in Greece up to 1989 were concerned mainly with economic development and, almost never, the values and expectations of Greek society. After the end of World War II, the majority of the Greek people lived with the expectation of a social or political change. This resulted in a massive politicisation and

the adherence of young people to left-wing political organisations, especially between 1975–1985. The new phenomena that appeared in Greek society after the middle of the 1980s – like the uprising of neo-liberalism, political corruption and crisis of credibility of politics and politicians – resulted in the frustration of the expectations of social change. This lead to the decline of politicisation and the massive abandonment of political organisations by teenagers. The secondary consequence was indifference and an apparent apathy about social and political problems.

10 Juvenile crimes are also phenomena that are registered independently of class origin (A. Pitsela, *op. cit.*, 344). The dimension of crime- (and deviance-) perception as a provocation or a joke is another variable that must be taken into consideration in the case of youth subcultures (Y. Panousis, 'Joke and provocation' (in Greek), in L. Besé (ed.), *Prevention et traitement de la delinquance juvenile (rieducation – insertion): rapports*, Athens – Komotini, A. Sakkoulas, 1990: 61–79.

11 A . Astrinakis, *Youth Subcultures*: 175.

12 Newspaper 'Eleftherotypia', 15.11.1995.

13 Newspaper 'Eleftherotypia', 18.11.1995.

14 Newspapers 'Avgi', 23.11.1995 and 'Ta Nea', 20.11.1995.

15 Original Data published in 'Eleftherotypia' on 20.11.1995, Data analysis-elaboration S. Vidali.

16 J. Sotirchou: 'Fracturing the boredom of the glass towers', in 'Eleftherotypia', 20.11.1995.

17 Newspapers 'Eleftherotypia', 20.11.1995 and 'Ta Nea', 21.11.1995.

18 Newspapers 'Ta Nea', 20.11.1995 and 'Eleftherotypia', 20.11.1995.

19 J. Sotirchou, *op. cit.*

20 The first was pilot research which was conducted on a sample of 110 adolescents from five schools in Athens. Although the results of this first piece of research cannot be perceived as final results, we can notice some general tendencies in relation to the use of free-time and the stereotypes of deviant behaviour. The relative conclusions will have to be tested at the end of the main research. From the second piece of research, which was conducted on a sample of 2530 adolescents from 52 schools in Athens we will mention the basic results concerning our theme. These results have been published (in Greek) in the review, 1995, *Sychroni Ekpaideusi*,1995, vol. 81: 32–41.

21 S. Cohen, *Folk Devils and Moral Panics: The Creation of the Mods and Rockers*, Blackwell, 1987: xxii–xxv, 191–198 and D. McQuail, *Mass Communication Theory*, Sage, 1994: 344.

22 Downes and Rock, *op. cit.*: 175–179. And G. Pearson, *op. cit.*: 1176 ff.

23 Chr. Nova, *op. cit.*: 27. G. Pearson, *op. cit.*: 1163, 1186.

24 Downes and Rock, *op. cit.*: 161.

25 N. Elias, J. L. Scotson, *The Established and the Outsiders*, London, Sage, 1994 (first ed. 1965): 110, 116 ff.

26 N. Elias, and J. L. Scotson, *op. cit.*: 114.

27 Downes and Rock, *op. cit.*: 161.

28 A. Astrinakis, *Youth Subcultures*,: 214 and S. Papaioannou, *op. cit.*: 18–19.

29 Downes and Rock, *op. cit.*: 166, D. Matza and G. Sykes, 'Juvenile Delinquency and Subterranean Values', *American Sociological Review*, n. 26/5: 716, and S. Vidali, 'The transfer of violence from the society to school' (in Greek), *Sychroni Ekpaideusi*, 1995, vol. 82–83: 116.

30 Downes and Rock, *op. cit.*: 148–186, S. Alexiadis: *op. cit.*: 118 ff, A. Cohen, 'The

delinquent subculture' in M. E. Wolfgang, L. Saziz and N. Johnston, *The Sociology of Crime and Delinquency*, J. Wiley & Sons, NY and London, 1970: 290, R. Cloward and L. Ohlin, 'Differential opportunity theory' in Wolfgang, Saziz and Johnston *op. cit.*: 310, Th. Sellin, 'Culture, Conflict and Crime' in J. Farsedakis: *Criminological Thought: From Antiquity to our days* (in Greek), Nomiki Bibliothiki, Athens, 1990: 477 ff.

31 A. Astrinakis, *op. cit.*
32 G Pearson, *op. cit.*: 1163–1164.

22

CRIMINALITY OR CRIMINALIZATION OF MIGRANTS IN GREECE? AN ATTEMPT AT SYNTHESIS

Vassilis Karydis

'The scourge of social exclusion' was the main theme of the French-language magazine of social and political commentary *Le Monde Diplomatique* in February 1995. The contents had to do mostly with migrant communities established in the advanced industrialized European countries, written about a topic familiar to the average Northern-European citizen. Yet very few people in Greece – or other Mediterranean countries like Italy (Palidda, 1996) – would have imagined a few years ago that the phenomenon could soon concern them, since these countries have traditionally been countries of emigration. After the collapse of the 'existing socialist' regimes in Europe – especially in the Balkans – the country received a large and continuing wave of migrants, who today total an estimated number of about 450–500,000 people, half of them Albanian citizens, in a total population of about 10 million people (Karydis, 1996a).[1] The Polish community in Greece is also large, consisting of about 100,000 people. Egyptians, Filippinos and Africans number also a few tens of thousands each (Linardos-Rylmon, 1993). The main employment of the migrants – many of whom are seasonal workers – is unskilled labour in the construction business (Polish, Albanians), catering to the seasonal needs of agriculture, fishing and tourist economy (Egyptians, Polish, Asians), house-helping (Filippinos, Albanians), and other household jobs like decorating, gardening etc. (Petrinioti, 1993). The average payment of the migrant workforce is half or even one third of the daily pay for a Greek worker, usually without social security or payment of overtime. According to estimates, about 70 per cent of the migrants are 'irregular' and stay illegally in the country (Katseli *et al.*, 1996). This feature – the illegal status of the large majority of the migrant community – distinguishes the Greek experience from developments in other advanced European countries, and, even more so, Northern America. Another differentiating feature, of course, is the geographic position of Greece in the turbulent Balkan peninsula and the consequent influence of narrow political considerations on immigration policies. We will return to these points later in the chapter.

The process of criminalization

The legal framework

The Greek Law for Aliens (L.1975/1991) is the defining origin of the collective victimization of the migrant community in Greece. This law is very much informed by a 'Fortress Europe' conception, later echoed in the Schengen Agreement, focussing on the protection of the single European entity from illegal migration and irregular asylum seekers. The Greek legal framework materializes this common policy[2] in three main directions:

1   drastic reduction of the number of petitions for asylum and curtailment of the rights of asylum seekers, using a strict visa policy, the 'safe third country' principle, a narrow definition of the refugees entitled to asylum, and the immediate rejection of 'obviously unfounded' petitions (Karydis, 1996b). Article 4 of the law allows for the immediate administrative repatriation of irregular aliens with no judicial remedy. The particular article has been employed by law enforcement agencies in hundreds of thousands of cases in recent years:[3]
2   deterrence of illegal entry by a set of provisions threatening penalties both for illegal entry and exit, punishing anyone who will help the illegal entry and imposing fines on carriers;
3   exclusion of irregular migrants from any public service, such as health care (except in emergency cases) and education, and punishment of those working without a permit as well as those who hire them, etc.

At the same time, the law provides for serious restrictions on regular immigrants, requiring an annual renewal of stay permits, five years as the maximum period of stay and dependence on the particular employer who invited them. Administrative authorities exercise wide discretion on serious matters like the granting and the renewal of stay and work permits, the recognition of refugee status, the immediate rejection of petitions deemed to be 'obviously unfounded', the setting up of the list of undesirable aliens and the procedures of administrative deportation and repatriation (Chlepas and Spyrakos, 1992).

I should mention at this point that the European Parliament has repeatedly criticized the central immigration policies of the member states – dictated mainly by inter-governmental agreements and the relevant non-accountable committees and groups of governmental functionaries – on the grounds of the violation of the human rights of asylum seekers and the existence of a significant 'democratic deficit' in the function of the European Union (European Parliament, 1993).

Popular opinion and the mass media

The enactment of a repressive legal framework was based on claims that migrant flows will create serious problems for the Greek economy and society, such as unemployment and serious criminality.[4] Collective social consciousness has internalized these assertions although, as we will consider later in the text, facts and data belie them.

In a survey of 1989 (conducted just before the first migrant wave), the Greek people exhibited an impressive level of tolerance and understanding about the presence and the rights of aliens in the country. Three years later, there was evidence that xenophobic attitudes were more widespread in Greece than in many other EC member states (*Eurostat*, 1989, 1992). Survey evidence reported by Voulgaris *et al.* in 1995 suggested that the percentage of people believing there were 'too many' foreigners in the country rose every year from 29 per cent in 1991 to reach 69 per cent in 1994. We would argue that this increase has nothing to do with an increase in the number of migrants *per se* (which remained more or less stable) or with changes in their social behaviour but with stereotypic reflections of the migrant community as a threat to public order and economy.

The mass media have contributed a lot to the shaping of collective social consciousness in this direction. A content analysis of the Greek press during the years 1990–1993 revealed that unemployment and criminality were the main issues connected to migration (Spinelli *et al.* 1993). Albanians were the ethnic group most frequently mentioned[5] and reports focus on the crimes against property and violations of drug legislation in which they are alleged to participate. Moreover, one also quite often encounters the characterization of migrants as 'killers' and 'assassins'. Headlines of a terrifying and frequently misleading nature are quite usual in newspapers and even on television news reports. I will mention just one example of such misleading information. The headline in May 1995 on the front page of an Athens-based paper with wide circulation read: 'HELP, save us from the Albanians'[6] and then included correspondence in the inside pages about crimes which (according to the paper) were being perpetrated by Albanian migrants. On an inside page the report was headlined, 'They kill us in our homes' but the text read 'the perpetrator went quickly down the stairs of the house and then disappeared'. So, the offender was actually unknown. The eye-witness account of the murder by the victim's wife said that the burglar turned his flashlight on their faces so that they could not see him. Nevertheless, it was reported that 'from the description of the wife, the police concluded that the offender was an Albanian migrant'! In the same issue, another report is entitled 'Robbery with blood … the ruthless Albanians did not hesitate to shoot and seriously wound a citizen who chased them'. However, a few lines below it is reported that the robbers disappeared and of course remain unknown. On the same page, another incident is reported as a 'wild crime by the Albanian Cosa Nostra'. In the text, the eye witness says that 'five people waited for us outside the cottage. Without saying a word they shot and killed Petros and then they left'. So the assassins were not arrested, were not identified and they did not even talk! What remains of the frightening front page headline is only the intention of the publisher to increase the circulation of his paper by exploiting and contributing to the creation of a moral panic about bloodthirsty Albanians who have collectively become the 'usual suspects' for any wild crime committed by unknown offenders.

Politics

Politicians are ready to amplify the stereotype for their own political gain. Remarks are often made about the raging criminality of the migrant community. The Minister of Public Order stated a few years ago, referring to administrative repatriation, that 'the practice of confronting the problem has been entirely ineffective . . . we have reached the point of sending Albanians on a free excursion to their country along with their prey from here'.[7] In one phrase are condensed all the different elements which are used in the demonization of Albanian migrants: illegal entry – criminality – mocking the authorities – insistence on deviance – lenient legislation. The same Minister on another occasion declared after a massive police operation against migrants that 'there is no one in the streets. Maybe some of them are hiding in kitchens or warehouses or restaurants and factories'.[8] This is a clear implication of the analogy between migrants and rats who used to frequent such places and calls forth the idea of the symbolic purification of public space from unwanted or dangerous creatures. In this way, what Benedict Anderson called the 'imagined community' in a single nation-state consolidates its racial boundaries, isolating institutionally and socio-politically the 'Alien-Other' (Anderson, 1983). It is characteristic that the policy of the Greek state is favourable to 'Albanian' migrants of Greek origin or towards those people of Greek origin born in regions of the ex-USSR. This resembles the policy of the German government in facilitating the acquirement of citizenship by people of distant German origin born in Poland and Russia, while children of 'Gastarbeiter' born in Germany face serious problems in that respect. Similar amendments to the formerly liberal relevant legislation concerning the naturalization of immigrants' children have taken place in France during recent years (Ventoura, 1994). This differential rejection of different groups of foreign migrants is now quite common throughout Western Europe.[9]

The leadership of the police are also happy with the situation since the low detection rates can be explained in terms of the criminal activity of the migrants. In a recent survey, 92 per cent of police respondents of all ranks believed that the big increase in crime rates could be attributed to the massive presence of illegal migrants in the country.[10]

We must also refer to the influence of politics in the strictest sense, since state and party policies in both Greece and Albania have introduced a peculiar policy we might refer to as 'hostage-taking'. On the Greek side there is the threat of immediate expulsion of all Albanian migrants, whilst on the other the Albanian government manipulates the issue of the human rights of a Greek minority in southern Albania as an instrument in its foreign policy (Karydis, 1993). Political–economic factors also allow for the creation of a cheap labour force. The illegal status of migrants provides the basis for such exploitation, mainly within the household-based farming economy. This partly explains why migrants still live and work in the country in their hundreds of thousands, despite their high visibility. Legalization would mean a much more expensive labour force for employers, which many small businesses cannot afford, while strict enforcement of the law could result in a loss of the cheap labour necessary for a crucial sector of the Greek economy. I must state at this point that, according to relevant research, migrants pose a threat of competition in very few other areas of employment. Generally speaking, migrants occupy roles in the labour market which Greek workers are unwilling to fill because these jobs are seen as heavy or dangerous (Katseli *et al.*, 1996, Linardos-Rylmon, 1993). Consequently, the argument that the presence of migrants is causing serious unemployment amongst the local workforce proves incorrect.

The stereotype

All these interacting factors result in the transformation of the category of 'foreigner' to that of an 'illegal migrant', but more specifically in the identification of the 'illegal migrant' problem mainly with the Albanian migrant. Then, the presence of Albanian migrants is quickly correlated with the rise of criminality, which is conceived as serious, extensive and dangerous in all its forms and circumstances of commission. Lastly, the rhetoric works to attribute all these features collectively to the Albanian migrant community. In this way, 'crime' acquires in a convenient way specifically ethnic characteristics through a socially constructed stereotype of the Albanian migrant as 'illegal – thief – violent – dangerous – criminal'. The particular stereotype certainly has to do first of all with the massive presence of Albanian migrants – constituting half of the migrant population in Greece. But it also results from the suddenness of the emigration from Albania after the collapse of the former regime in 1990, which changed the previous conception of migrants as low-profile individuals, confined to their communities. Of course, this change had also to do with the petty criminality employed by desperate illegal migrants trying to secure food and shelter. A similar 'moral panic' of the population took place in Germany, concerning the presence and activities of migrants from the former socialist countries after 1990, transforming the 'guest-worker' into an 'immigrant' and linking alien groups with organized criminal activities (Albrecht, 1991, 1995).

Moreover, in my view, there is another component of the stereotype with a cultural dimension, partially explaining the scapegoating of the Albanians compared to other ethnic migrant communities. Western Europe always shared a stereotypic attitude towards the Orient (Said, 1996), and in particular towards the

Balkans. Although – geographically – the Balkans are an intrinsic part of Europe, culturally they have been constructed as a negative 'Other' against whom a positive image of the 'European' and the 'West' was historically built (Tontorova, 1996). The idea of 'Balkanism' is a reference to an atavistic return to the primitive, barbarous, underdeveloped stage in European history and Balkan people are generally identified with a set of negative (stereo)typical characteristics, attached to them by the 'real' Europeans.

Greeks, although belonging to the Balkans, also have always shared the same 'European' positive and narcissistic image for themselves, applying negative cultural features to other Balkan nations. This attitude has been especially strong towards Albanians as citizens of a small, poor, newly-founded state, which tried to implement the socialist experiment in the worst possible fashion, even compared to the 'socialist' regimes of the other Balkan countries. This negative attitude was reinforced because of the repressive policy of the former Albanian regime towards a strong Greek-Orthodox minority located in southern Albania – an unresolved problem between the two countries even today (Tsouderou, 1994).

In this way, the Albanian migrant community easily becomes the 'Generalised-Balkan-Other' for the mass of Greek citizens themselves. The stereotypic picture, we mentioned earlier, of the Albanian migrant in Greece as 'illegal – thief – violent – dangerous- "Balkan"- criminal' is one way in which the 'identity' of the dominant Greek population is affirmed and valorized.

In order to verify the presence of the stereotype, I conducted research among first year students of the Law Department at the Democritus University of Thrace. I collected 150 completed questionnaires consisting of 25 questions each (Karydis, 1996a: 138–155). According to the findings of this survey, it is remarkable how widely the stereotypical representations of migrant Others are held, even amongst a university-student population.

As an indicative example, I will refer to the four more significant characteristics of the various ethnic migrant groups, according to the respondents. *Albanians*: dirty, 74 per cent; thieves, 70.7 per cent; dangerous, 70 per cent; impoverished, 67 per cent. *Polish*: men, 50.7 per cent; laborious, 47.3 per cent; young, 45.3 per cent; peaceful, 40 per cent. *Africans* (despite the colour): men, 50 per cent; peaceful, 43.3 per cent; young, 43 per cent; sympathetic, 42 per cent. *Filippinos* (despite the race): hardworking, 54.7 per cent; peaceful, 48.7 per cent; young, 45.3; per cent; sympathetic, 39.3 per cent.

The majority of the sample apparently believed that there is a big increase in serious criminality in the country, and Albanians scored 8.8 per cent out of a maximum possible of 10 to the question which ethnic group is responsible for that. Albanians also obtained by far the lowest score to the question (compared to other ethnic migrant groups): 'which of the following groups of the population would you sympathize with more? Mark from 1 – not at all – to 10 – very much'. Albanians scored 2.7, followed by the Muslim minority of Thrace (3.4) and the Gypsies (4.1),which are the only groups scoring below 5. I must note that both

Muslims and Gypsies are not migrants but Greek citizens, born in the country. Filippinos obtained 5.8 and Africans 6.5 to that question while to the question about 'the opinion' of the sample about ethnic groups (1 – very bad – to 10 – excellent) they scored even better, 6.2 and 6.7 respectively.

Victimization

The construction of this particular stereotype, of course, facilitates the victimization of the Albanian migrant community. Many of them have, indeed, been killed by police and army patrols at and near the frontiers. Many incidents of torture – even to death – have been reported at places of detention. Nobody has been punished for that so far. Moreover, an impressive number of serious incidents against migrants are perpetrated by civilians. In two cases, migrants were shot and killed because they tried to steal a bicycle. Another one was killed because he was stealing water-melons! A farmer shot at a group of Albanians and killed one without any reason, 'Because I became afraid of them', he said. The phenomenon of the 'fear of crime' is closely involved with such incidents (Kellens and Lemaître, 1993). However, I believe that no one would act this way if the conception of the migrant 'Other' as an inferior being did not exist. The criminal stereotype leads to the moral neutralization of the use of violence against migrants as objects not deserving respect and protection.

It can also be anticipated, from the reverse direction, that an almost institutionalized racism (Hudson, 1993) could trigger defensive violence by the migrants, constructing and consolidating in their turn a hostile, threatening and unjust Greek 'generalised Other' (Mead, 1964).

In this way, the presence of a 'criminal stereotype' of the migrant-Other is itself exerting a criminogenic influence upon Greek society and claims its share in shaping the social reality of crime in modern-day Greece.

Criminality of migrants

I have described so far a process of criminalization and collective victimization of the migrant community due to strict legislation, discretionary policy and law-enforcement activity, arbitrary media stereotyping, exploitation of them as a work-force, racist attitudes and behaviour. However, the issue cannot merely be closed at this point. Migrants *do* commit crimes and we must examine the extent, the structure, the qualities and the reasons of this criminality. Moreover, as we will discover, the degree of the involvement of the different ethnic groups with criminal activities is significantly different, and this calls for close examination of the facts and the social reality of crime. We will try to address these issues hereafter starting from the 'criminologist's Cross', criminal statistics.

Criminal statistics

From the moral statisticians of the nineteenth century until the 'heretic decade' of the 1960s, the consensus over the reliability of the official criminal statistics was more or less unchallenged. The picture has dramatically altered since, through a devastating, innovative and fascinating criticism of mainstream criminological certainties. The discourse in the field is quite well known and continues (Maguire, 1994) so I will confine myself to the approach towards the indices of reported criminality which I adopted during my research.

There is no doubt that official statistics about the criminality of migrants are influenced by parameters of societal reaction to their presence, like the willingness of the population to report even petty offences committed by migrants more readily than crimes by other (Greek) offenders. These are also more likely to name migrants as perpetrators of offences by unknown offenders. Also, the heavy policing of the migrant community inevitably results in the disclosure of more hidden criminality among them than among other segments of the population. It is true that the mechanistic conception of reported crime and even more the use of official statistics at face value for the shaping of policies can result in the distortion of the social reality of crime and to misleading conclusions. On the other hand, the nihilistic view that statistics are merely products of the activities of the law-enforcement agencies and explain nothing about actual criminality could deprive us of data which under certain conditions and proper elaboration can prove quite useful. In any case, arguments supposedly linking the migrant community with crime are often based on actual criminality and statistics. So we are obliged first to examine these claims on the same grounds.

The numbers of *migrant offenders* known to the police is 2–3 per cent of the total number of reported criminal offenders (Courakis, 1993; Karydis, 1996a) but migrants constitute only 5 per cent of the general population. It is also important to take into consideration the age variable, i.e. that two out of three of all offenders known to the police belong to the age group of 20–45 years old, in which group the vast majority of the migrants also belong. We must also mention that three out of four of the offences committed by migrants concern violations of the Law for Aliens, i.e. illegal entry or stay in the country and illegal work, which have to do with their illegal status and are not of any real criminological interest. In this way, we end up with a percentage of criminality by the migrant community at under 1 per cent of the total. However, this would be a hasty conclusion, since migrants do not actually have the opportunity of committing some misdemeanours because of their way of life, such as traffic accidents, violations of labour and tax laws, etc. Also, they do not have any opportunity to commit certain 'white-collar' felonies, such as fraud, embezzlement, etc. because of their present position in the labour market. In this way, they are not represented in many categories of crime, which constitute a significant part of the overall reported criminality.

A better picture about the reported criminality of migrants is acquired by the

elaboration of criminal statistics concerning traditional criminal activity, such as robbery, homicide and rape. I selected these particular crimes because they are serious, characterized as felonies, involve the element of violence and also because two of them (homicide and robbery) are highly visible, thus reducing the impact of differential reporting. Rape is also significant – despite the extent of hidden criminality – because even if we accept that the victim is more likely to report a migrant offender than a Greek one, it is obvious that she will not be influenced in her decision by the particular nationality of the perpetrator. In this way, conclusions can be drawn about differences in the criminal activities of the different ethnic groups of migrants.

We notice that according to official statistics, irregular migrants are responsible for five to eleven per cent of these felonies. This percentage is actually lower if we consider the age variable and at most is the equivalent to the proportion of the

Table 22.1 Intentional homicide (murder)

| | *Offenders known to the police* | | | |
	1993		*1994*	
Total	254		264	
Alien offenders	23	9%	33	13%
Irregular migrants	19	7.5%	30	11%
Albanians	13	5%	21	8%

Table 22.2 Robbery

| | *Offenders known to the police* | | | |
	1993		*1994*	
Total	1505		1257	
Alien offenders	91	6%	78	6.2%
Irregular migrants	68	4.5%	60	4.7%
Albanians	51	3.5%	38	3%

Table 22.3 Rape

| | *Offenders known to the police* | | | |
	1993		*1994*	
Total	270		258	
Alien offenders	33	12%	29	11.6%
Irregular migrants	19	7%	21	8%
Albanians	16	6%	12	5%

migrant community to the economically active population, i.e. about nine per cent. Consequently, official statistics themselves belie the claims that the presence of the migrants has caused a serious wave of crime in the country and that illegal migration is a threat to public order.

On the other hand, we notice important differences between the different ethnic groups of migrants' involvement in criminal and deviant activities. Filippinos, Egyptians and Africans are almost absent from the criminal statistics. Polish people show very low rates compared to the size of their community. Albanians however are reported as having committed 70–80 per cent of the particular felonies attributed to migrants, while they comprise only half of the migrant population.

It is also noteworthy that despite the stereotype about the 'Albanian thief', Albanian nationals commit thefts at a percentage little over their proportion to the migrant population (56 per cent and 50 per cent respectively). However, Albanian adolescents make up almost the total of alien adolescents arrested for theft and loitering (Nova-Kaltsouni, 1993). The vast bulk of the property crime committed by migrants consists of petty thefts, motivated by poverty or even for survival. We will later refer to the important issue of the hidden incidence of crime within the migrant community and its significance.

These facts call for some explanation beyond the construction of false stereo-types, the consideration of economic and political interests and ideological expediency, which all exist but are not sufficient for explaining the phenomenon in the particular context and circumstances.

The impact of life conditions on crime

There is a significant body of literature in the field of criminology on immigration and crime, much of it in the field of environment and social-area analysis in relation to immigrant communities. But many of the more well known are not very helpful in understanding the particular reality of migration in Greece. For example, environmental criminology, stemming from the Chicago School, focuses on migrants living in poor, overcrowded conditions in the transitional zones in urban-centre neighbourhoods, but also making collective adaptations, for example, through colonization of particular areas and also by 'cultural transmission'. But the process of social disorganization described by the Chicago theorists (Shaw and McKay, 1942) is not verified in present circumstances in Greece. Cultural networks of different ethnic groups do not co-exist in the same areas, and the high mobility of the migrant population does not permit the setting up of the necessary mechanisms of cultural adaptation (Bottoms, 1994). Last but not least, environmental criminologists have discussed the lives of second-generation adolescents from migrant backgrounds who interact in a context of social disorganization. But this process is not observable at present in Greece. The same argument applies in my view to Merton's 'political economy of unequal opportunity' (Taylor, 1994: 478), with its vision of people trying to achieve the goals of material *prosperity* and social *ascent* by legal or, if necessary, by illegal means (Merton, 1938). The Mertonian scheme is simply not applicable to the situation facing the vast bulk of immigrants in Greece. Right now, a relatively affluent migrant would be one who has a decent place to sleep and a secure job, however underpaid. The aspirations of the great majority of migrants at the moment are to secure survival and maybe to save some money for the family back home. Some of Sutherland's theses, on the other hand, seem more pertinent (Sutherland, 1947). The illegal status of the majority of migrants forces them into the formation of very small intimate groups and close associations. They are rather less powerfully influenced by impersonal institutions such as school, church or social organizations. The perceptions of the legal order of the host society held by many migrants certainly result in them developing 'definitions favourable in principle to the violation of law'. Many illegal migrants live constantly under the fear of the police. Many have entered the country by bribery, forging documents or paying organized networks, and most of them have the feeling that their human rights are constantly violated. Sutherland also points to the fact of criminal behaviour being learnt in small groups and this is important for migrants in contemporary Greece, as we will see below.

Migrants commit crimes of poverty mainly within a background of the struggle for survival. A statement made by one migrant in interview is characteristic:

> Sometimes, when somebody has nothing to eat, one never knows what he can do. I realized that when we first came and the baby was hungry and crying and we did not have milk. If people did not help I am not sure what I could do.
>
> (Galanis, 1993: 52)

Bonger's thesis with respect to a class-determined deprivation affecting self-respect and human dignity as well as respect and consideration for other human beings among the poor (Bonger, 1969), better fits the reality of the migrant community in Greece, at least as far as property crime is concerned.

In general, the literature on subcultures focuses on adolescent gangs in ghetto-neighbourhoods of modern cities (Hood and Sparks, 1978: 80–109). However, this perspective is also unable to provide a satisfactory framework for the understanding of the migrant situation. I should mention however that there are indications for the existence of certain elements of a 'culture of violence' within the Albanian ethnic group. An Albanian migrant stated in some recent research:

> Murders of Albanians by Albanians are reported and you usually think that they are violent acts for insignificant things. For us however, most of the time this happens because of honor and for reasons of punishment
>
> (Psimmenos, 1995: 151).

There are frequent references in interviews to blood feuds, the classical vendetta for reasons of honour (Galanis, 1993; Psimmenos, 1995). But the suggestion must be not of a highly structured and consolidated 'subculture of violence' but rather a differential conception of the many particular situations which make sense in terms of the conditions of life of the Albanian migrant group. In Wolfgang's words :

> The significance of a jostle, a slightly derogatory remark, or the appearance of a weapon in the hands of an adversary are stimuli differentially perceived and interpreted by Negroes and whites, males and females. Social expectations of response in particular types of social interaction result in differential 'definitions of the situation'.
>
> (Wolfgang, 1958: 188)

The existence of these 'different definitions of the situation' is particularly encouraged by the illegal status of the overwhelming majority of the Albanian ethnic group. This insecurity of status results, as we have already suggested, in a reliance on small intimate groups in order to secure work and shelter, fear of the police and other authorities, and the feelings of exploitation, the non-existence of private space and life, and the loss of self-confidence and self-respect. Under these hostile circumstances, the search for identity strongly depends on acceptance by the intimate group, the interests and values of which must be protected. In addition, the members of such intimate groups have certain perceptions and expectations of what may be viewed as critical incidents (for example, threats to the honour of Albanians etc). In these circumstances, distrust becomes a dominant feeling. As a migrant stated in an interview:

> Most quarrels and homicides take place not for insignificant reasons. Me and my comrades protect each other and we trust nobody, not even the other Albanians.
>
> (Psimmenos, 1995: 151).

In other empirical research among migrants (80 per cent of the sample being Albanians), 30 per cent of the respondents said that they return home early, take many precautions, are very careful with their associations, and even that they keep a weapon (knife, screwdriver, etc) for defence. Twenty-five per cent of the sample (mostly Albanians) did not even trust their own compatriots because of their bad reputation, their involvement in criminal activities and the intra-group victimization. Indeed, in this research 15 respondents (out of 114) had been the victims of violence – five of them by Albanians, five by unknown offenders, two by their friends and only three by Greeks (Spinelli *et al.*, 1993). This brings us to the important issue of unreported intra-group criminality.

The hidden incidence of crime

The illegal status of the vast majority of the migrants seems to affect also the extent of the hidden incidence of crime within the migrant community. It is widely accepted in the criminological literature that ethnic minorities report traditional crimes against them much less than the general population – perhaps because the offender belongs to the same ethnic group, because they have no trust in law-enforcement agencies or they share a hostile attitude towards them (Smith, 1994). In the case of illegal migrants in Greece, another additional factor is present. That is, that if the victim turns to the police he/she is risking his/her own arrest and consequent repatriation, an outcome that may be worse than the crime itself, if that is not very serious. In this way, the migrant community becomes easy prey for criminals of their own and/or Greek nationality, who may expect impunity as a result of that fear. Preliminary research findings already point to a high incidence of unreported intra-group violence among Albanians, organized activity in the fields of prostitution, child sexual exploitation and even drug-trafficking (Psimmenos, 1995).

This situation could mean that a perfect hothouse has been created for organized crime, the roots of which will be fed and watered by the children who right now beg at the traffic lights or offer sexual services in street squares and cheap hotels, totally abandoned by a cruel social order and a myopic legislation – being a kind of 'people in parentheses', as more or less all illegal migrants now are. We should keep in mind that the construction of deviant subcultures needs both time and often very complicated ongoing interaction between social and psychological processes, a process nourished in the shadow of social indifference. Those who have nurtured this process will probably be the first to condemn the phenomenon when it appears and then propose more blind and repressive measures. At this level of analysis, the 'square of crime' proposed by the left realist Jock Young in Britain (Young, 1992) could be quite useful as a methodological tool for tackling the specific problems.

The necessary synthesis

I have attempted throughout this chapter to approach the issue of migration and crime from many sides. I have argued that the immigrant community suffers a collective victimization in successive concentric circles, from the outer circle of a myopic legal framework which does not face a changing social reality, down to the inner circle of unreported intra-group victimization, which is the prelude for organized criminal activities. I have also argued that the social construction of a criminal stereotype about the illegal immigrant reinforces the process of social exclusion and initiates a vicious circle of more deviance and more repression (Wilkins, 1971). At the same time, examining the ontology of crime, I have spelt out how there are big differences between migrant ethnic groups concerning their involvement with criminal activities. Consequently, the confrontation with and the demystification of – more or less – fictitious stereotypes about the 'dangerous Albanian criminal' must be set alongside the search for real causes of crime, as well as the shaping of a relevant policy towards a 'real crime' problem, generated in the specific social context and founded on the conditions of life of the migrant community, especially of the Albanian ethnic group.

Macro-political considerations concerning the phenomenon of crime and the concept of power are quite useful, but addressing specific problems of real living human beings is imperative, without abandoning theoretical insights (MacMahon, 1996). As Stan Cohen has put it: 'To travel the subways of New York I need more help than a deconstructed map of the category of "mugging"' (Cohen, 1990: 24). Adopting this stance, I submit the following concluding remarks.

- The reported criminality of migrants in Greece is quite normal, considering the indices of crime and the respective size of the migrant community, even more so if one considers the factors which negatively influence the official indices of crimes committed by migrants (for example, the disproportionate youthfulness of migrants). However, there are noticeable differences in the rates of criminality – at least for crimes against the person and property – between the Albanian ethnic group and other ethnic groups of migrants. This fact has mainly to do with the conditions of life of the Albanian community – newcomers to Greece on a massive scale – as well as with their illegal status and the negative interaction with Greek society, arising for a variety of cultural, historical and political reasons.

- The illegal status of the majority of migrants, mainly of the Albanian nationals, plays a decisive role in their marginalization and criminalization. This situation facilitates the creation of nuclei of organized crime within a socially vulnerable community and fertilizes the ground for the construction of criminal subcultures by deprived youngsters, who are today excluded from education and any social opportunities, stigmatized by the 'criminal stereotype', being a main target and easy prey of exploitation and victimization, losing their self-respect as well as respect for others' life and property.

- The dominant perspective on migration all over Europe has to do with crime, deviance, discrimination and distrust. The processes of European integration, the concern about the activities of international organized crime – linked to migration movements – worsen this situation. Political and ideological speculation complicates the matter even more. The situation becomes more complex in countries receiving large numbers of illegal migrants, like Greece and other Mediterranean countries.

- If the present situation remains the same, the processes of marginalization and criminalization which we notice will eventually produce an alienated 'underclass' consisting mainly of massively deprived migrants. Moreover, a possible view of themselves by a second generation of migrants as being personally or collectively deprived will facilitate their participation in deviant subcultures or even organized criminal networks, contrary to any anticipated improvement of their material conditions of life.

• It is essential that alternative strategies be promoted towards migrant communities at all levels of social exclusion. Social scientists should be involved in the formulation of such strategies conducting research, creating networks and submitting proposals. These include the imperative need for changes of the legal framework, more research into the victimization of and among migrants, propositions and initiatives at 'the middle level' for a preventive policy concerning education, housing and employment as well as for specific and co-ordinated interventions at the social micro-level where values and attitudes are generated and sustained in everyday existence and interaction.

Notes

1 This paper was submitted before the crisis in Albania in March 1997 with the encouragement given to further mass migration out of Albania.

2 The explanatory Government Report introducing the new Law to the Parliament declares that:

> There is imperative need for the state to obtain a new law harmonised with the legislation of the other member states of the U.C.

The Speaker for the major Opposition, Th. Kotsonis, explicitly stated that:
> Lastly – which is the most important – eight countries of the Community . . . signed the so-called Schengen Agreement . . . creating already the infrastructure for a common space of free movement of people.
> Minutes of Parliament, 10–10–1991

3 Compulsory administrative repatriation of Albanian migrants between 1991 and August 1995 totalled 948,956, according to the Ministry of Public Order, as reported in *Eleftherotypia*, 2 November 1995.

4 In the explanatory Government Report it is mentioned:

> Suddenly, Greece started to get flooded with aliens, who entering, staying and working illegally create enormous social problems to the state, while they inevitably try to solve their own problems engaging in criminality (drugs, robberies, thefts, etc).

The Speaker for the major Opposition said that:

> The presence of suspicious characters among the unfortunate illegal economic refugees and the commission of illegal acts by these elements created a psychology of defence in Greek society.
> Minutes of Parliament, 10–10–1991.

5 This has to do first of all with the fact that Albanians constitute half of the total migrant population. However, we will consider other reasons too, later in the text.

6 *E. Typos*, 24 May 1995.

7 S. Papathemelis, quoted in *Eleftherotypia*, 3 November 1993.

8 Quoted in *To Vema*, 12 March 1995. Another Minister of Public Order discovered dangers for the national purity and safety stating that migrants from Iraq and Pakistan 'are Muslims at a percentage of 80 per cent and settle mainly in the sensitive region of Thrace.'

   (S. Valyrakis, as quoted in *Eleftherotypia*, 2 November 1995)

9 According to Prof. E. K. Scheueh, German society discerns four different categories of foreigners. The 'noble aliens' (British, French, Americans and generally Northern Europeans) who are regarded positively. The 'aliens in general' (Spanish, Greeks, Yugoslavs) the opinion for whom is neutral. The 'peculiar aliens' (Portuguese, Italians, Vietnamese) who are treated neutrally, but often with some reservations. Lastly, aliens like Northern Africans, Negroes, Persians and Turks, who are collectively rejected by a significant part of the German population. Cited by Z. Papademetriou, 1995: 60.

10 Survey conducted by F. Tsalikoglou *et al.*, reported in *To Vema*, 12 March 1995.

References

Albrecht, H.-J. A. (1991), 'Ethnic Minorities. Crime and Criminal Justice in Europe', in F. Heidensohn and M. Farrell (eds), *Crime in Europe*, London and New York: Routledge.

Albrecht, H.-J. A. (1995), 'Ethnic Minorities and Crime. The Construction of Foreigners' Crime in the Federal Republic of Germany', unpublished paper, Dresden University.

Anderson, B. (1983), *Imagined Communities. Reflections on the Origin and Spread of Nationalism*, London–New York: Verso.

Bonger, W. (1969 [1916]), *Criminality and Economic Conditions*, Bloomington: Indiana University Press.

Bottoms, A. E. (1994), 'Environmental Criminology', in Maguire *et al.* 1994.

Chlepas, A. and Spyrakos, D. (1922), *O Nomos 1975/91 yia tous allodapous kai to Syntagma* (Law 1975/91 for the Aliens and the Constitution), Athens–Komotini: A. Sakkoulas.

Cohen, S. (1990), 'Intellectual Scepticism and Political Commitment: the Case of Radical Criminology', Inaugural Willem Bonger Memorial Lecture, University of Amsterdam.

Committee for the Prevention of Torture and Inhuman Treatment or Punishment, Preliminary Report, Council of Europe, cpt (93) 56/3–12–93.

Courakis, N. (1993), 'Crime in Modern-Day Greece. An Overview', *Chronicles* (8), Laboratory of Criminological Sciences, Democritus University of Thrace.

European Parliament (15–7–1993), Resolution on European Immigration Policy, PE, 174.419.

Galanis, G. (1993), *E gnomi ton katoikon ton Ioanninon yia tous Alvanous sten Ellada* (The Opinion of People of Ioannina about the Albanians in Greece), University of Ioannina.

Hood, R. and Sparks, R. (1978 [1970]), *Key Issues in Criminology*, London: Weidenfeld and Nicolson.

Hudson, B. (1993), 'Racism and Criminology: Concepts and Controversies', in D. Cook and B. Hudson (eds), *Racism and Criminology*, London: Sage Publications.

Karydis, V. (1993), 'Immigrants as a Political Enterprise. The Greek-Albanian Case', *Chronicles* (8),

Karydis, V. (1996a), *E eglematikoteta ton metanaston sten Ellada. Zetemata Theorias kai anteglematikes politikes* ('Criminality of Migrants in Greece. Issues of Theory and Preventive Policy'), Athens: Papazisis Publ.

Karydis, V. (1996b), 'Criminality of Migrants in Greece: Issues of Policy and Theory', in S. Palidda (ed.), *Délit d' immigration. La construction sociale de la déviance et la criminalite parmi les immigrés en Europe*, COST A2, Cariplo-Ismu, European Commission.

Katseli, L., Lianos, Th. and Sarris, A. (1996), *Oi synepeies tes paranomes metanastefses sten topike agora ergasias* ('The Consequences of Illegal Migration on the Local Labour Market'), unpublished research, Athens.

Kellens, G. and Lemaître, A. (1993), 'Victimization and the Fear of Crime', in S. P. S. Makkar and P. C. Friday (eds), *Global Perspective in Victimology*, India: ABS Publications.

Kitromilides, P. M. (1990), ' "Imagined Communities" and the Origins of the National Question in the Balkans', in M. Blinkhorn and Th. Veremis (eds), *Modern Greece: Nationalism and Nationality*, Athens: SAGE-ELIAMEP.

Linardos-Rylmon, P. (1993), *Allodapoi ergazomenoi kai agora ergasias sten Ellada* ('Alien Workers and Labour Market in Greece') Athens: General Confederation of Greek Workers.

MacMahon, M. (1996), 'Critical Criminology and the Problem of Power', *Chronicles* (10).

Maquire, M., Morgan, R. and Reiner R. (eds) (1994), *The Oxford Handbook of Criminology*, Oxford: Clarendon Press.

Mead, G. H. (1964), 'The Genesis of the Self and the Social Control', in *Selected Writings*, Indianapolis: Bobbs-Merrill.

Merton, R. K. (1938), 'Social Structure and Anomie', *American Sociological Review* (Oct.).

Nova-Kaltsouni, H. (1993), *Paravatekoteta Anelekon* (Deviance of Minors), Athens: Ministry of Public Order.

Palidda, S. (1996), 'Irregular Immigration in Italy', OECD, Working Party on Immigration.

Papademetriou, Z. (1995), 'Ratsismos kai Metanastefsi' (Racism and Immigration), *in Movement of Citizens against Racism* (ed.) *E Evropi antimetope me to phenomeno tou ratsismou* (Europe Facing the Phenomenon of Racism), Athens: Paraskinio.

Petrinioti, X. (1993), *E metanastefse pros ten Ellada* ('Immigration to Greece'), Athens: Ulisses Publications.

Psimmenos, I. (1995) *E metanastefse apo ta Valkania. Koinonikos apokleismos sten Athena* ('Immigration from the Balkans. Social Exclusion in Athens'), Athens: Glory Book–Papazisis Publ.

Said, E. W. (1996), *Orientalism*, Athens: Nefeli Publications, (trans. in Greek, F. Terzakis).

Shaw, C. R. and McKay, H. D. (1942), *Juvenile Delinquency and Urban Areas*, University of Chicago Press.

Smith, D. J. (1994) 'Race, Crime and Criminal Justice', in Maguire *et al*. 1994.

Spinelli, C. D., Vidali, S., Dermati, S. and Koulouris, N. (1993), '*Protection of Human Rights of Recent Migrant Groups in Greece with Emphasis on those deprived of their Freedom*', unpublished Report submitted to the Council of Europe. Summary in *Chronicles* (10).

Sutherland, E. H. (1947), *Principles of Criminology*, (4th ed.), Philadelphia: J. P. Lippincott and Co.

Taylor, I., (1994) 'The Political Economy of Crime', in Maguire *et al*. 1994.

Tontorova, M. (1996), *The Balkans: From their Discovery to their 'Construction'*, Athens: Themelio, (trans. in Greek).

Tsouderou,V. (1994), 'Oi scheses me ten Alvania kai i Ellenike meionotita' (The relations with Albania and the Greek minority), in D. K. Konstas and P. I. Tsakonas (eds) *Ellenike Exoterike Poleteke. Esoterikes kai diethneis parametroi* ('Greek external policy. Internal and international parameters'), Athens: Ulisses Publications

Ventoura, L. (1994), *Metanastefsi kai Ethnos* (Immigration and Nation), Athens: EMNE-MNIMON.

Voulgaris, G. *et al.* (1995), 'E proslepse kai e antemetopise tou "Allou" sten semerine Ellada. Porismata empeirikes ereunas' ('The Conception and the Treatment of the "Other" in Modern-Day Greece. Findings of an Empirical Research'), *Greek Review of Political Science (5)*.

Wilkins, L. T. (1971), 'The Deviance-Amplifying System', in W. G. Carson and P. N. Wiles (eds), *The Sociology of Crime and Delinquency in Britain. Sociological Readings*, London: Martin Robertson.

Wolfgang, M. E. (1958), *Patterns in Criminal Homicide*, University of Pennsylvania Press.

Young, J. (1992), 'Ten Points of Realism', in J. Young and R. Matthews (eds), *Rethinking Criminology: the Realist debate*, London: Sage Publications.

23

CRIME AND THE WELFARE STATE: THE CASE OF THE UNITED KINGDOM AND SWEDEN [1]

Henrik Tham

The issue

The welfare state has been seen as having a role both in the prevention and the production of crime. The first view has its roots in liberal and radical writings of the late nineteenth century. The vision was then clear: with improved universal education, ameliorated housing conditions, and reduced economic inequality, crime would sharply diminish. This tradition of thought has been carried through in the post-war era by, for example, the social democratic parties in Scandinavia.

That the promise of the welfare state in these respects was not fulfilled is by now quite clear. As Jock Young observed in the mid-1980s, commenting upon the situation in the United Kingdom after 1945:

> Real incomes became the highest in history, slums were demolished one by one, educational attainment rose, social services expanded in order to provide extensive welfare provisions and safety nets, and yet the crime rate continued to doggedly rise. All of the factors which should have led to a drop in delinquency if mainstream criminology were even half-correct were being ameliorated and yet precisely the opposite effect was occurring.
>
> (Young 1986: 5)

To say that the promise of the welfare state in terms of controlling or limiting the development of crime was not fulfilled is one thing. To argue that it actually *promotes* crime is, of course, to go much further. But this argument has been increasingly mobilized since the 1970s by conservative parties in both Europe and North America. The critique has run along different lines. The welfare state has been said to produce crime by exercising both too little and too much control.

368

The accusation of too little control can be summarized in the refrain that social democratic governments are 'soft on crime'. Too little control is also said to result from weakening the family and other traditional institutions which effectively could exercise control.

The argument of 'too much control resulting in crime' focuses, for example, on the alleged over-taxation and over-criminalization of different activities in private enterprise which the welfare state has undertaken in order to protect its redistributive policies. Too much control has also been said to contribute to crime in a psychological way. The welfare state is said to create a pressure towards conformity and an overly organized society which deprives the citizens of initiative, and boredom and feeling of being suffocated results in behaviour such as suicide, drunkenness and juvenile delinquency. Finally, the erratic or capricious control of the welfare state where the rewards and punishment do not seem to connect to good or bad behaviour has been said to lead to a version of the condition of 'learned helplessness' which can result in negative behaviour like destructiveness, aggressiveness and vandalism (Tham 1995).[2]

The conservative critique of crime in the welfare state aims at the very core commitment of the welfare state – equality. The political ambition of social democracy – to redistribute income, services and opportunities in an equalizing direction – leads, it is claimed, to increased state control, suppression of individual responsibility, weakening of moral discipline, high taxes, and to a soft criminal policy arising out of a concern for the underdog. It is in this connection that the issue of law and order also has become central in the welfare-state debate specifically in the new turn to discipline and punishment (Tham 1995).

Sweden was for a long time regarded as the welfare state *par excellence* in Europe. Even if this is less true today, the Social Democratic party has remained in power in Sweden during the post-war period with the exception of 1976–1982 and 1991–1994. From 1979–1997, one of the most ideologically committed conservative parties governed the United Kingdom. This Conservative government also put criminal policy high on its agenda, contrasting its firmness of resolve with the alleged failures of earlier Labour governments. The political critique has been formulated both as a general critique of welfare-state policies and as explicit accusations of opposition to law and order (Taylor 1981 c. 2, 1987; Windlesham 1993; Conservative Party News 1993; Jefferson and Shapland 1994).

If the conservative critique is correct, a development in the direction of 'market society' and away from the welfare state, together with a sharpening of criminal policy, should have positive effects on the development of crime. Could then any lesson be learnt about the welfare state and its impact upon crime and criminals from a comparison between the United Kingdom and Sweden? Obviously, a brief comparison could not answer such a complex question. A comparison of limited scope would have to use available indicators with all their shortcomings and on the whole disregard alternative explanations of the development of crime. But such a limited and somewhat shallow analysis also has its advantage. It accepts the simplified hypotheses prevalent in public political discussions and it makes use of state-produced official statistics on crime and inequality which are also the indicators available in public political discourse. So we will undertake such an analysis particularly with a view to comparing the two countries in respect of three questions. How has poverty and inequality developed? How has criminal policy developed? And how have crime and different categories of offenders developed?

Method

In this short article, then, we will be using only a limited number of summary indicators. The dependent variable – the development of crime and offenders – will be measured by indicators from official criminal statistics and national crime surveys.

The dangers in using official statistics for describing crime and offenders in general, and the use of such statistics in comparative research in particular, have been pointed out over and over again. Several of these warnings are quite reasonable. However, there does seem to be some agreement that comparisons can be undertaken for trends rather than levels and for secular trends rather than for yearly variations (von Hofer and Tham 1989; *European Sourcebook of Crime and Criminal Justice Statistics* 1995). An approach which concentrates on changes in trends between states does to some extent escape the problem of differences in legal definitions *as long as the definition stays the same within each country*.[3] An analysis of periods or secular trends also avoids the problem of chance variations which are difficult to interpret.

The objection that official crime statistics to a high degree reflect the activities of law enforcement agencies will depend on the type of crime measured and on the availability of alternative data sets. This analysis will mainly be limited to non-trivial crimes which tend to be reported regularly and faithfully by the public to the police and/or where the trends in police statistics can be supplemented by alternative indicators. And even if a more contextual analysis would be desirable (Vagg 1993), it may be possible to arrive at some persuasive conclusions if robust indicators point in the same direction. After all, the analysis is limited to a rather short period of time in two countries which are not *that* dissimilar in culture and structure.

The analysis of secular trends ideally requires long statistical series. For some of the indicators, the official statistics will here be of limited length. Our main interest will, however, be on the developments before and after 1980. The Conservative victory in Great Britain in 1979 and the return of the Swedish Social Democrats to power in 1982 could possibly be regarded as a natural (pseudo)experiment and will allow for some before-and-after analysis. The question posed was whether the claim that conservative politics would result in relatively less crime could be upheld.[4]

Poverty and inequality

Rhetoric is one thing, real politics another. It is not enough to document criticism of the welfare state by the British Conservative Party. The impact of changes in policy – for example on equality – should also be demonstrated. A few indicators available over time and for both countries will be analysed here.

Unemployment is central to the debate on equality and its curtailment has long had top priority in the welfare state. Figure 23.1 shows the development of unemployment since the 1970s in England and Wales and Sweden.

Compared to the mid-1970s, unemployment is much higher in both countries in the mid-1990s. There are, however, also clear differences. The Swedish level of unemployment throughout the period has been much lower and the increase did not start until the 1990s. This low level sets Sweden apart from other OECD countries during the period, and is a result of a pronounced policy to keep unemployment down. The figures for long-term (more than six months) unemployment develop in parallel with total unemployment in both countries (Halleröd, 1996: 145). Youth unemployment also follows the general unemployment trends. The British figures, though, reached their highest level in

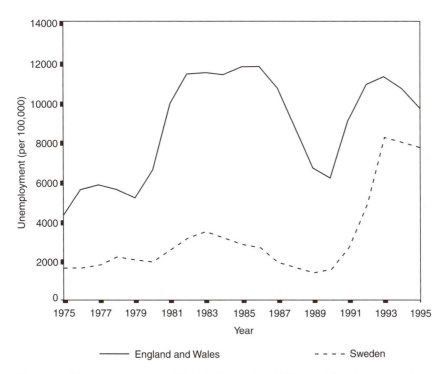

Figure 23.1 Unemployment per 100,000 in England and Wales and Sweden, 1975–1995
Source: OECD

the early 1980s while the Swedish unemployment rate for the young more than doubled in the 1990s compared to the earlier maximum at the beginning of the 1980s (Schröder 1996).

Another indicator of poverty and inequality is the number of households at below 50 per cent of average income. Time series exist for both countries. Swedish figures are available only since the mid-1970s. However, other indicators show that there was a continuing decrease in income inequality in Sweden from the early 1960s to the mid-1970s (Åberg *et al.* 1987).

Figure 23.2 shows key similarities and differences between the two countries. Inequality was decreasing in both the United Kingdom and Sweden up to the end of the 1970s and after that it increased. The trend towards increased inequality, however, was much more marked in the United Kingdom than in Sweden. The proportion of households below 50 per cent of average income in the United Kingdom has increased from around 8 per cent in the late 1970s up to 25 per cent in 1993 while the corresponding figures for Sweden are 4 per cent and 8 per cent.

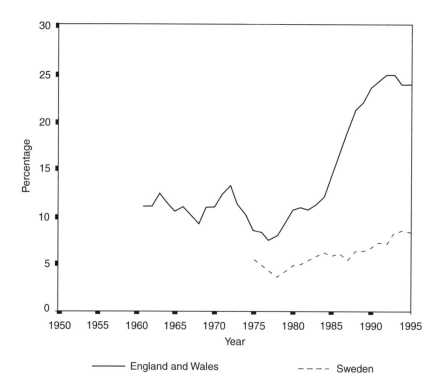

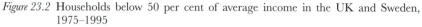

Figure 23.2 Households below 50 per cent of average income in the UK and Sweden, 1975–1995

Source: Goodman and Webb (1994): Households Below Average Income; Income distribution survey in 1994 plus tables from Statistics Sweden

An objection to this comparison is that while the available long-term time series for United Kingdom are based on *mean* income the Swedish are based on *median* income. The Swedish figures would therefore be less influenced by an increase in the numbers of high income-earners. It does, however, seem indisputable that the development towards larger income inequality is much more marked in the United Kingdom than in Sweden during the 1980s (Atkinson *et al.* 1995).[5] There also is little doubt that unemployment played an important part in this development. An analysis by Halleröd shows that the unemployed were clearly more deprived in Britain than in Sweden and also that means-tested benefits have been more generous and the situation for lone parents has been better in Sweden than in Britain during the 1980s (Halleröd 1996).

One further indicator of the development of poverty and inequality is that of homelessness. Data on homelessness in Great Britain showed a fivefold increase from the early 1980s to the early 1990s (Social Trends 26, 1996). Similar data do not exist for Sweden. However, data on evicted households show a clear increase during the same period but starting only in the 1990s. The numbers of evicted households then were 50 per cent higher than in the early 1980s (Kronofogdemyndigheten).[6] These different indicators on homelessness, on the whole, support the picture which emerged from the analysis of the development of unemployment and disposable income: poverty and inequality increased in both countries but the increases occurred earlier and were more marked in the United Kingdom than in Sweden.

Criminal policy

The criticism that has repeatedly been levelled by the Conservative Party against the Labour Party in the United Kingdom – that it was 'soft on crime' – can, of course, be compared to what has actually been done in the field of criminal policy by the Conservatives themselves when in power. The rhetoric itself, i.e. of 'penal severity', cannot be disregarded. It can 'be potent on its own' (Cavadino and Dignan 1997). Conservative law-and-order rhetoric in the 1979 election also had a general political purpose beyond criminal policy in trying to establish a moral society with a strong puritanical emphasis and a dichotomy between good and bad moral character (Taylor 1987). This strong ideological approach also characterized the Conservatives in power until their defeat in the 1997 General Election, even though a few years between 1987 and 1992 were marked by a more pragmatic approach (Downes and Morgan 1994; Cavadino and Dignan 1997).

The Conservatives have been quite active in the field of criminal policy since 1979. Five Criminal Justice Acts have been produced as well as some legislation on criminal procedure and public order; the notion of just deserts has been introduced as a legitimating ideology for punishment, 'short sharp shock' institutions and community service have been introduced (especially for juveniles), police manpower has been increased, and new prisons have been built and planned (Windlesham 1993; Taylor 1987; Cavadino and Dignan 1997, Conservative Party News 1993). During this long period of Conservative government, the number of young offenders sentenced to custody declined sharply, but the life-sentence prisoners have doubled and the prison population has reached its highest-ever level (Windlesham 1993; Home Office Statistical Bulletin 14/1996).

Sweden, by contrast, did not get a real 'law and order election' until 1991. This election was fought around the more fundamental question of the Swedish welfare-state model and the non-socialist parties were victorious. The conservative critique of the social democrats had been built up during the 1980s and continued during the non-socialist coalition government.[7]

The Social Democratic period in power, however, had hardly been marked by what we may call a liberal criminal policy. Compared with the preceding period in power during the first half of the 1970s, penal legislation expanded in the 1980s. This expansion was clearly influenced by an ambition to show toughness in fighting 'new' types of crime – drugs, economic crimes and crimes concerning sex and gender. As for sanctions, half-time parole, treatment contracts[8] and community service were introduced. Just deserts replaced rehabilitation, sanctions against recidivists were increased, and prison regime was sharpened.

In the 1991 election, the Social Democrats were clearly on the defensive in criminal policy. Being back in power in 1994, they have attempted to avoid making criminal policy a political issue, trying to find a compromise akin to the slogan of the British Labour Party: 'To be tough on crime – and tough on the causes of crime'.

The non-socialist government of 1991–94 was quite active in passing legislation, increasing prison sentences for some twenty crime categories, increasing police resources, restricting parole, and planning new prisons. Imprisonment also clearly increased during this government (Tham 1995).

A comparison between the United Kingdom and Sweden shows some clear similarities in the development of criminal policy from around 1980. In both countries 'just deserts' has been introduced as a sentencing principle, the questions of drugs and of crimes by ethnic minorities have been of great concern, alternatives to imprisonment have been expanded, the number of young offenders sentenced to custody has decreased, and prison populations have increased.

There are, however, also differences. A comparison between the developments of the prison populations in the two countries does, in a sense, reflect these differences. The development towards, on the whole, a tougher criminal policy is much more marked and occurred earlier in the United Kingdom than in Sweden. Up until the late 1960s, the size of the prison populations were very much the same in the two countries. The Swedish figures then decreased and the figures for the 1990s have still not surpassed those of the late 1960s. In comparison, the British prison population has continued to increase and is around forty per cent higher in 1995 than in the late 1960s (see Figure 23.3).

In summary, then, the Conservative period in power in the United Kingdom

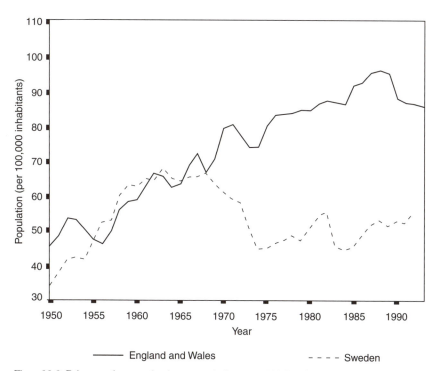

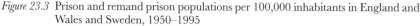

Figure 23.3 Prison and remand prison populations per 100,000 inhabitants in England and Wales and Sweden, 1950–1995

Source: Annual Abstract of Statistics; Home Office Statistical Bulletin 14/96; Yearbook of Judicial Statistics/Criminal Statistics (1950–64: prisoners at the end of the year; 1965–95: average prison population)

since 1979 in practice was a move towards greater inequality and a harsher criminal policy than in Sweden. The next question is how crime has developed in the two countries during the same period.

Crime

Figures for reported offences for both England and Wales and Sweden are available from 1950 (Figure 23.4). There was an increase in crime throughout the period in both countries. There was, however, also a clear difference in the rate of increase during different periods. The English trend accelerated both in terms of absolute numbers of crimes per year and also its relative rate of increase during the later part of the period. Sweden, which since the mid-1960s had had a somewhat sharper increase in crime than England and Wales, from the late 1970s showed a slowing down of the relative rate of increase. Since 1980, the yearly increase in reported crime is around five per cent for England and Wales compared to two per cent for Sweden.

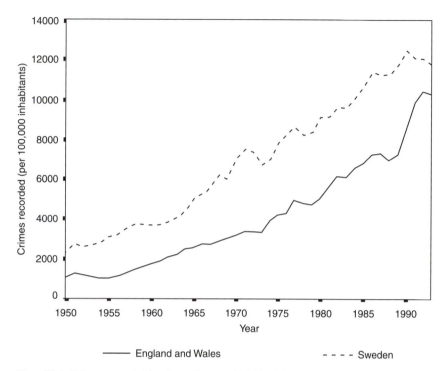

Figure 23.4 Crimes recorded by the police per 100,000 inhabitants in England and Wales
        and Sweden, 1950–1995 (index: 1980=100)
Source: Council of Europe 1985 (1950–83); Criminal Statistics, England and Wales; Yearbook of
        Judicial Statistics/Criminal Statistics

The crude comparisons of the overall crime rates can be supplemented by
analysis of trends in specific crime categories. For homicide there has been a clear
increase in both countries in the post-war period and both the level and the
development is on the whole similar. The police statistics here receive support
from the statistics on the causes of death (Figure 23.5).[9] Homicide in Sweden has
approximately doubled while England and Wales – starting on a somewhat lower
level – has shown a threefold increase. Since the mid-1970s, there is also a difference between the two countries in that there is a continuous increase in England
and Wales while the level of Swedish homicide rate is fairly stable.

Figures on wounding are notoriously difficult to compare both cross-nationally
and over time. The report rate is, of course, crucial for the police statistics. With
this reservation, the development for the two countries looks rather alike all
through the period since 1950 (Figure 23.6).

The national crime surveys provide us with an opportunity for checking the
police figures. In both England and Wales and Sweden, from the early 1980s, the
surveys show an increase in violence (Figures 23.7a and b). The increase shown

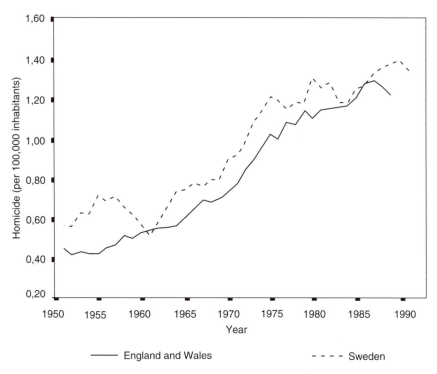

Figure 23.5 Homicide per 100,000 inhabitants in England and Wales and Sweden, 1951–
1994 (causes of death statistics; 3 years moving average)
Source: Mortality Statistics, serial tables; Causes of Death Statistics

in the surveys is, however, concentrated in the 1990s, especially for Sweden. For both countries there is also, according to the victim surveys, an increasing tendency to report crimes of violence to the police (Home Office Research Findings 14/1994, fig. 3; Statistics Sweden 1995: 88, p. 85).

There has been a clear increase in robbery in both countries since 1950, but the increase is markedly steeper in England and Wales from around 1980 (Figure 23.8). Robbery in the British Crime Survey has also shown a marked increase since 1981 but less sharply than in the police statistics. The Swedish survey does not include a question on robbery.

For the development of burglary in a dwelling there are clear differences between the two countries (Figure 23.9). After a marked increase in Sweden in the period up to the mid-1970s, the level is stable. For England and Wales the diagram suggests that burglary has more than doubled since 1979.

It could perhaps be argued that some of the increase in the English figures might be attributed to an increasing tendency to report burglaries to the police. This change could then be attributed to a long-term increase in household insurance (Home Office Research Findings 14/1994).[10] For Sweden, the risk of a

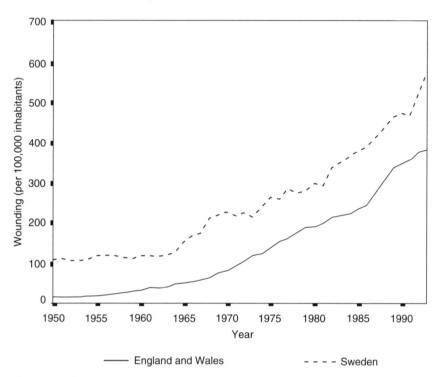

Figure 23.6 Wounding per 100,000 inhabitants in England and Wales and Sweden, 1950–
1995
Source: Criminal Statistics, England and Wales; Nordic Criminal Statistics (1991); Yearbook of Judicial
Statistics/Criminal Statistics

biased set of figures in this respect ought to be less. The number of insured
households increased from 91 per cent in 1978 to 95 per cent in 1984/85 and has
been constant since then (Statistics Sweden 1995: 169).

The impact of insurance has not been systematically analysed for the whole
period in England and Wales. However, since victim data for both countries
support the picture in police statistics, our reservations about insurance coverage
might be superfluous. The British Crime Survey reported a doubling of household burglaries between 1981 and 1995 (Home Office Statistical Bulletin 19/96)
while the Swedish victim data show no increase (Statistics Sweden 1995).

Finally, thefts of motor vehicles have increased sharply in both countries since
the 1950s (Figure 23.10). While the English figures started at a lower level than
the Swedish they surpassed the Swedish figures by the end of the period. The
faster increase for England and Wales started as early as the 1970s. Again,
increases from 1980 in both countries are supported by victim surveys (Home
Office Research Study 1993: 65; Statistics Sweden 1995: 133). Analysing the

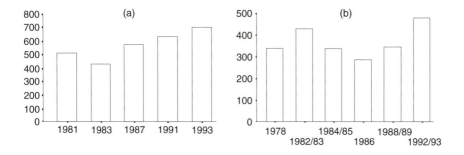

Figure 23.7a Victims of wounding, in England and Wales, 1981–1993
Source: The British Crime Survey

Figure 23.7b Victims of wounding, in Sweden, 1978–1993
Source: Statistics Sweden 1995

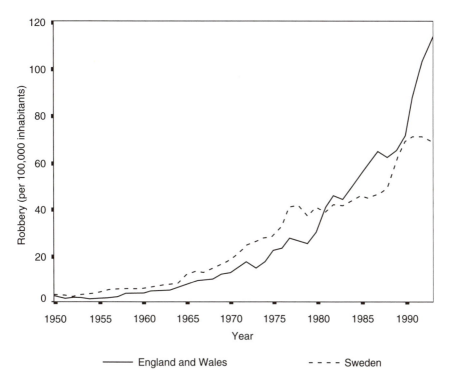

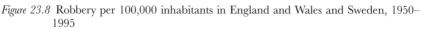

Figure 23.8 Robbery per 100,000 inhabitants in England and Wales and Sweden, 1950–
1995
Source: Criminal Statistics, England and Wales; Nordic Criminal Statistics (1991); Yearbook of Judicial
Statistics/Criminal Statistics

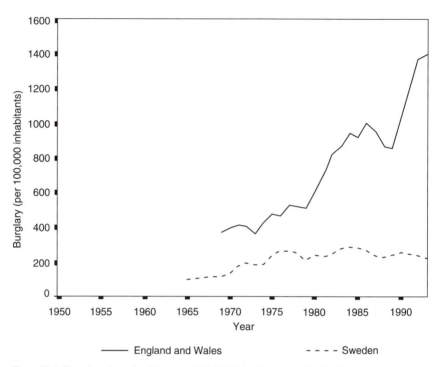

Figure 23.9 Burglary in a dwelling per 100,000 inhabitants in England and Wales, 1979–1995, and Sweden, 1975–1995

Source: Criminal Statistics, England and Wales; National Council for Crime Prevention 1994; Criminal Statistics

increases in thefts in relation to the number of registered cars since the late 1970s does not change the picture substantially.

In summary, there are both similarities and differences in the development of crime in the two countries. Crimes of violence, homicide and wounding showed on the whole a similar development. In respect of total crime and the key crimes of property, robbery and burglary in a dwelling, increases from around 1980 have been much more marked in England and Wales than in Sweden.

Offenders

An objection to using official statistics on offenders for describing the development of crime is, of course, that these statistics primarily reflect the activities of law enforcement. When crime increases, the clearance rate will fall because of limited police resources, and the number of convictions will bear no relation to the large number of crimes reported to the police.

While this objection might be true in many instances, the question remains whether the conviction statistics can be used for describing different categories of

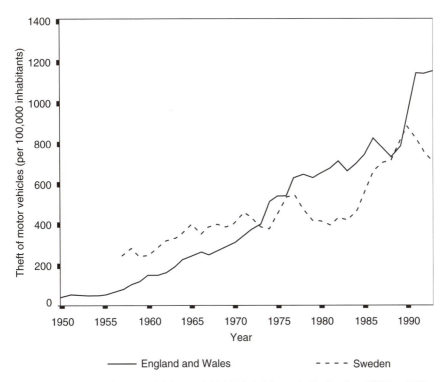

Figure 23.10 Theft of motor vehicles per 100,000 inhabitants in England and Wales, 1950–
1995, and Sweden, 1957–1995

Source: Council of Europe 1985 (1950–82); Criminal Statistics, England and Wales; Nordic Criminal
Statistics (1991); Yearbook of Judicial Statistics/Criminal Statistics

apprehended offenders *relative* to each other. If limited changes over shorter
periods of time in the handling of different categories are assumed, conviction
statistics can be used for analysing the development of crime.

The analysis of offender categories here will be limited to a few which are of
particular relevance for the development of crime and which have had high
priority in the public debate: crimes committed by ethnic minorities,[11] young
persons, and drug misusers. The concern with immigrants and ethnic minorities
relates to the public issue whether these segments of the population have substantially contributed to the development of crime in the United Kingdom and
Sweden. The number of young persons found guilty of crime is often thought to
be of relevance as an indicator of future adult crime. Narcotics have held a
central position in the discussion on crime and criminal policy since the late
1960s and dealing in drugs is in itself a crime, while the continued use of hard
drugs is in many cases clearly associated with repeated criminality.

Repeated criminality is also a category of interest. A relative increase of recidivists among those found guilty of crime might be an indicator of higher future

crime levels because of 'longer carriers'. Unfortunately, there are no figures for trends in recidivism from the United Kingdom which would allow a comparison. Existing cohort studies for England and Wales are based on court statistics. These statistics do not include cautions and this sanction has increased over time (Home Office Statistical Bulletin 14/95: 3 f.).

Finally, a differential development of female crime in the two countries could potentially have quite an impact upon crime. The logic of development does, however, seem similar. After a limited increase in the share of female offenders since the 1950s in the United Kingdom and Sweden, the female share of indictable offences has been relatively stable since 1980 in both countries (Heidensohn 1994; Legal Statistics for England and Wales; Criminal Statistics, Official Statistics of Sweden).

Crime among ethnic minorities

In the United Kingdom, it is primarily the black ethnic minority groups who show clear over-representation, for example in the prison population in England and Wales. The over-representation of these groups is also exaggerated by inclusion of a non-domiciled ethnic population which cannot be separated out in the official statistics (FitzGerald 1997). Between 1985 and 1992 there was no change in the share of males from ethnic minorities in the prison population (seventeen per cent each year). Among females there was an increase from twelve to twenty per cent, primarily among the non-domiciled (FitzGerald 1997 and private conversation). Given the small size of the total immigrant population, five per cent (Farrington 1992), however, and the fact that immigration has been very limited during recent decades, crime among minority groups can hardly explain the overall increase of crime in the United Kingdom.

Immigrants in Sweden – defined as persons who have at least one parent born abroad – account for approximately one fourth of all convictions. An additional four per cent involve non-domiciled foreign citizens. Immigrants are over-represented by a factor of 2. For homicide, rape and robbery, the over-representation is by a factor of 3.

This over-representation seems to have been fairly stable for at least a quarter of a century. With increasing immigration this could also mean increasing crime – unless a displacement of native Swedish offenders by immigrants is presumed.[12] Even though there has been an increasing immigration of political refugees since the 1980s, immigration primarily took place earlier. The conclusion must therefore be that the increase in the total crime rate since around 1980 has only to a limited extent been affected by immigrants (von Hofer *et al.* 1997).

One difference in crime among ethnic minorities in the two countries might be worthwhile noting. For example, there is evidence to suggest that crime among West Indians in the United Kingdom in the earlier post-war period was not very high but that the rates have increased since about 1970 (Smith 1995: 443). This suggests that the second- and third-generation West Indians are more over-represented in crime than the immigrant generations themselves. For Sweden, the situation is the other way around. The second-generation immigrants still have a higher risk of being convicted than those with Swedish-born parents but they have a lower risk than their parents (von Hofer *et al.* 1997). This is true also when the immigrant groups are analysed by country of origin (Ahlberg 1996, p. 84).

Young offenders

Comparing the numbers of young offenders since 1980 (figures from earlier periods have been difficult to obtain for England and Wales), the overall levels for both England and Wales and Sweden are fairly stable. The fact that there is no increase can, of course, at least partly be attributed to a falling clear-up rate. Correcting the figures for the young offenders by the changes in the overall clear-up rate results in a sharper increase for England and Wales in the 1990s (Figure 23.11).

Further analysis might give additional support to the picture of a slower development in youth crime in Sweden than in England and Wales. A separate study of youth crime in Sweden shows that since the 1970s, the development of convictions for theft was stable for the younger-age categories while increasing for the older (Estrada 1995). By limiting the study to theft and excluding shoplifting, this study was based on the major crime category for young people, which is also less susceptible to changes in reporting. The conclusion of an absence of increase among young offenders is also supported by cohort studies (von Hofer *et al.* 1987; Yearbook of Judicial Statistics 1993: p. 145). While there do not seem to be any such studies for the United Kingdom, there is some indication of an underestimate of young offenders in the United Kingdom, given that the admission of cautions by police is not routinely reported (Farrington 1992; Home Office Statistical Bulletin 16/96). The development of young offenders will be further analysed in the following section on drugs.

Drug misusers

The development of drug use in society can be described in terms of prevalence or incidence. Measures of prevalence show the number of drug users or abusers at a given time. Such a measure showing the development over time would for any year include both new arrivals and recidivists in drugs. An objection to such a time series for measuring the effects of policy would be that the series include a number of persons who entered drugs long before the period under study started. Therefore, incidence data, measuring new arrivals, will be used here.

Since initiation into hard-drug abuse is considered to be less likely after the mid-twenties (Skog 1993), the numbers of young drug abusers can be seen as a rough measure of the incidence. Two measures of the incidence of involvement with drugs will then be used in the comparison: new young drug abusers and

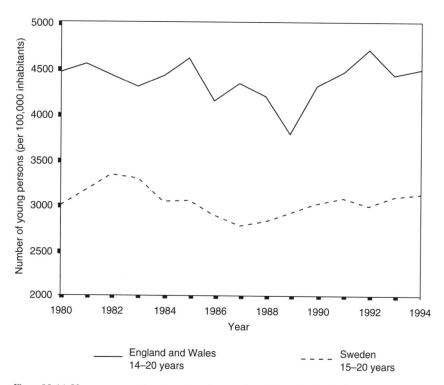

Figure 23.11 Young persons found guilty of or cautioned for criminal offences per 100,000 young inhabitants in England and Wales and Sweden, 1980–1994, (corrected for clear-up rate)

Source: Criminal Statistics, England and Wales; Yearbook of Judicial Statistics/Criminal Statistics

young persons found guilty of drug offences. Such measures exist over time for both countries.

For the United Kingdom, data exist on new drug addicts notified to the authorities each year. The series can be followed since 1981, sub-divided by age and by new and re-notified drug addicts. It is recognized that these data probably include only a small proportion of all regular misusers of opiates and cocaine and that there is considerable local variation in notifying. It has, however, been concluded that 'the statistics do give an indication of trends in the number dependent on notifiable drugs' (Home Office Statistical Bulletin 17/1995: 3).

For Sweden, there is no annual reporting to the authorities of the number of drug abusers. However, in 1979 and in 1992 national case-finding studies were undertaken in order to arrive at an estimate of the number of 'heavy' drug abusers. A heavy abuser was defined as one who injected drugs or who daily or almost daily used drugs, e.g. primarily cannabis.[13] The number of young abusers reported has been taken as an indicator of incidence and used as an evaluation of the Swedish drug policy (Olsson 1996; Swedish National Institute of Public Health 1993).

Figures for the age distribution of abusers around 1980 and in the early 1990s in the two countries are shown in Figures 23.12 and 23.13. For the situation around 1980, the age distribution of the drug abusers shows clear similarities between the two countries. This similarity has disappeared in the early 1990s. The age distribution for United Kingdom has an overall resemblance to the one in 1981. For Sweden, however, there is a clear relative (and absolute) decrease in the young ages and the population of abusers as a whole is aging.

The comparison can, of course, be called into question in different ways. The data from the United Kingdom show that half of the new addicts are above 25 years of age, challenging the view that first-time drug users are always young. A more accurate comparison should include the renotified young addicts since this group is included in the Swedish data. For this category figures exist only for the period from 1987 in the United Kingdom. An analysis of all notified drug addicts in 1987 and 1994 show that there is an increase in the average age of the population, but only of 1.4 years. It is therefore hardly probable that the different developments in terms of age distributions of the two populations would have

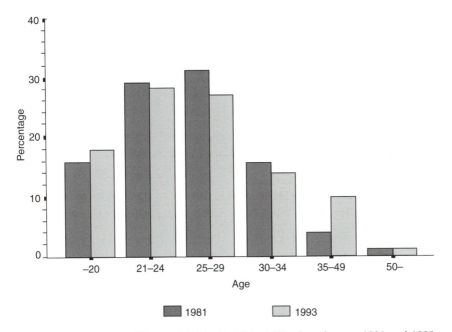

Figure 23.12 New drug addicts notified in the United Kingdom, by age, 1981 and 1993 (percentage)

Source: Home Office Statistical Bulletin 17/95

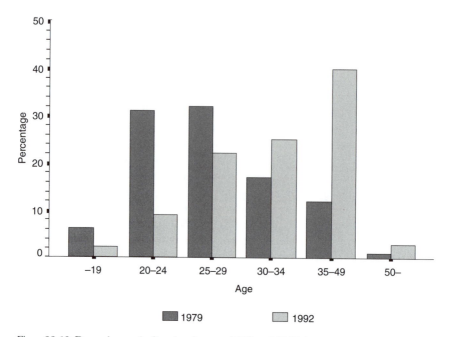

Figure 23.13 Drug abusers in Sweden, by age, 1979 and 1992 (percentage)
Source: Skog 1993.

disappeared if data for all notified drug addicts had been available for earlier years.

The validity of the changing age distribution could be checked against other data sources. For the United Kingdom data have existed since the early 1980s by age for 'persons found guilty, cautioned or dealt with by compounding for drug-related crimes'. For Sweden similar data are available from the late 1960s. Figures 23.14 and 23.15 show the numbers of persons found guilty of drug offences in the United Kingdom and in Sweden respectively. Neither the level nor the internal trajectory or logic of development can really be compared here since they might be influenced by different ways of dealing with drugs. Unless, how-ever, there is a change over time in ways of dealing with different age groups the statistics should be an indicator of the increase in drug-users.

For both countries there was an increase in the number of middle-aged abusers (30 years and older). However, while in the United Kingdom there was a sharp increase for the young (20 years and younger), the same age group showed a decrease in Sweden. This finding of a decline in the numbers of young abusers in Sweden which has gone on since the early 1970s is also supported by surveys among 15-year-old students and military conscripts who have tried drugs as well as by 'injection mark' research in Stockholm central jail (Alkohol- och narkotiakutvecklingen i Sverige, 1996; Kühlhorn 1996).[14]

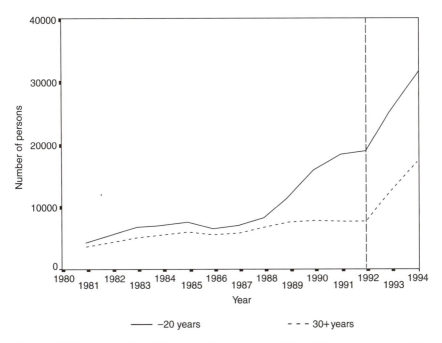

Figure 23.14 Persons dealt with for drug offences in the United Kingdom, by age, 1981–
1994
Source: Home Office Statistical Bulletin 24/95

In summary then, it seems as if there is a real difference in the development of officially recorded drug abuse in the United Kingdom and Sweden. Together with the findings from the analysis of young offenders, the data on drugs might indicate that there is a slower development of crime among young people in Sweden than in the United Kingdom.

Discussion

Summing up the results, a comparison of the development of crime and offenders in the United Kingdom and Sweden shows both similarities and differences. In the longer perspective, since 1950, crime has increased in both countries, and especially crimes of violence have developed in a fairly similar way. In the shorter perspective, since around 1980, there have been some clear differences between the two countries. For total crime and some central crimes against property the increase has clearly been much more marked in the United Kingdom. The homicide rate also remained stable in Sweden while it continued to increase in the United Kingdom. The most marked difference seems to be in the field of narcotic drugs where there was an increase in abuse and offending

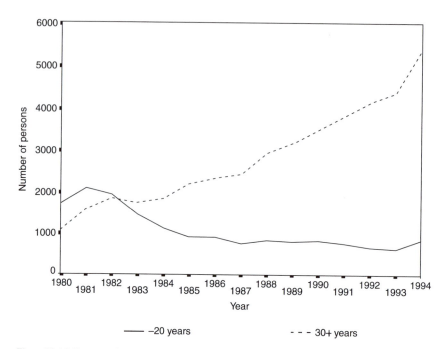

Figure 23.15 Persons dealt with for drug offences in Sweden, by age, 1981–1994
Source: Alkohol- och narkotikautvecklingen i Sverige, 1996

among the young in the United Kingdom while there was a decrease in Sweden. Second- and third-generation immigrants in some ethnic groups seem to have higher crime rates than the immigrants themselves in the United Kingdom while in Sweden the situation is the other way around. Finally, there are indicators that there is a slower increase in the total number of young offenders in Sweden than in the United Kingdom.

During the later part of this period there has been a sharpening of criminal policy in both countries. This sharpening has occurred earlier and has been more marked in the United Kingdom than in Sweden. A similar picture can be discerned in the development of poverty and inequality. Different indicators point towards increased inequality since the early 1980s in both countries. This trend is more clearly marked in the United Kingdom where it had already emerged in the early 1980s as compared to the early 1990s in Sweden.

The results of the comparison raise a number of issues. The first is that of the determinants of criminal policy and penal severity. The prison populations increased to very much the same extent in the two countries up till the late 1960s. Since then the increase has been markedly lower in Sweden. A not unreasonable explanation of this difference would be the higher British crime level. Pease has argued such a case for the United Kingdom, to mitigate criticism in a European context for its punitiveness (Pease 1994; see also Digest 3, 1995).

However, such an explanation makes no sense of the decline in the Swedish figures. In the early 1970s there was a clear political commitment in Sweden to reduce the prison population *in spite* of rising crime (Tham 1995). The perception of large and rising prison populations as problematic plays an important role in itself, certainly in Scandinavia. The USA and Finland have been taken to exemplify two opposite cases in this respect – while the first country in two decades trebled its prison population without political opposition, the second regarded the high figures as a source of embarrassment and actively tried to reduce them to a European level (Christie 1993).

The different developments of the prison populations in the first half of the 1970s is worth noting also in another respect – in that both countries at that time had Labour governments. This implies that other factors than just Labour versus Conservative governments were at work. Different histories and different party traditions seem to play a role. The drift towards a law-and-order politics in the United Kingdom is by some commentators said to have started well before the 1979 election (Norrie and Adelman 1989; Downes and Morgan 1994). It might also be the case that a 'realist' position stressing morale, discipline and family has been stronger in the British social-democratic tradition than in the Swedish one (Clarke 1976; Taylor 1981; Tham 1995).

A second issue is that of the connection between the development of inequality in the context of whether the country is ruled by a Labour or a Conservative Party. Clearly, there is no simple relationship. Income inequality continued to decrease in Sweden during the non-socialist government between 1976 and 1982 while it increased during the social-democratic rule between 1982 and 1991. There is also evidence that social exclusion is increasing in both countries in the 1990s – regardless of government. Neither is there any clear pattern between crime levels and the issue of what party was in power in the United Kingdom between the end of the Second World War and 1979. But since around 1980 inequality *has* developed much faster in the Conservative United Kingdom than in the social-democratic Sweden.

This leads to the third issue – that of the relationship between crime and inequality. The result of this comparison does not, of course, allow the conclusion that there is a causal relationship in the sense that welfare-state policies actually might have diminished crime. A number of objections could be raised to such a conclusion based on this analysis. Neither was the test of this hypothesis the object of this analysis. Rather, the question raised was whether there is any validity in the conservative hypothesis that welfare-state policies, including a less harsh criminal policy, actually *produce* crime. This proposition has been tested in this analysis and several objections considered. The analysis has been using crude state-produced statistics without much further interpretation. On the other hand, the indicators used do not seem to totally lack validity or meaning. The official statistics also provide the bulk of the systematic indicators which are available for public political discourse. We can therefore say with some force that this comparison of two Western European countries under different political regimes using central quantitative indicators from official statistics on crime and inequality showed no support for the conservative hypothesis.[15]

Notes

1 This chapter was largely prepared during a stay at the Department of Sociology, the University of Salford, in the spring of 1996. For material and spiritual support I would like to thank the department, Toni Makkai and, especially, Ian Taylor. Staff at the Home Office were also most helpful. For good work with the diagrams, thanks to Lars Westfeldt, Department of Criminology, Stockholm University.

2 The term 'learned helplessness' derived from an experiment in the USA where the pigeon which became frustrated and self-destructive when not rewarded for good job behaviour was labelled by the experimentor as 'welfare pigeon' (Seeligman 1976).

3 This does, of course, not minimize the importance of cross sectional analyses based on careful comparisons of legal definitions, reporting, and recoding. For such comparisons between Sweden and the United Kingdom, see McClintock and Wikström (1990), and Farrington and Wikström (1993) which also compares crime in England and Sweden 1981 and 1987.

4 The indicators will have to be limited to those where measures exist for both countries. For the United Kingdom, the indicators will sometimes be limited to England and Wales.

5 In a comparison of income distribution in OECD countries, the Gini coefficient changed between 1980 and 1990 from 19.6 to 21.9 for Sweden and from 28 to 36 in the United Kingdom (Atkinson *et al.* 1995).

6 An objection to using eviction data for showing increased poverty in Sweden could be that evictions rose sharply in the 1970s when there was a general decrease in income inequality. It has, however, been argued that the earlier rise in evictions was a result of giving apartments to poor people with mental problems or alcohol or drug abuse, thereby increasing the risk of evictions due to disturbing behaviour (Stenberg 1990).

7 A few examples could illustrate the conservative critique. In a motion to the Swedish Parliament, the Moderate Party (conservative) criticized the social democrats for 'a welfare state that undermines the morals, ethics and sense of community on which it is based (Motion till riksdagen 1985/86: So 206:9). In a report on criminal policy the party stated that 'the tendency towards softening penal sanctions for crimes against property is unacceptable. It is an expression of a socialist basic view where the individual is attached less importance than the collective (Rapport: Ökad rättstrygghet och rättssäkerhet, undated, p. 5). The conservative Swedish morning daily newspaper Svenska Dagbladet writes in one of many editorials: 'In the top-governed and centralized social democratic Sweden, traditional norms, social control, and other more self-regulating social mechansims have gradually been broken down' (Svenska Dagbladet 1987–07–24). In the same morning paper, the leader of the Moderate Party in Stockholm criticizes social democratic 'reversed welfare' for weakening the most important crime-preventing factor – the family – through high taxes, subsidies, and standardized solutions (Cederschiöld, Svesnak Dagbladet 1989–05–07). And the chairman of the

Moderate Party states that the Social Democratic Party is 'soft on crime' (Bildt 1991). For further references, see Tham 1995.

8 The court can choose probation instead of a prison sentence if the offender agrees to a contract of treatment of his substance abuse.

9 The series have been constructed as moving averages since the small absolute numbers in Sweden tend to produce large yearly variations which make the interpretations of trends more difficult.

10 There might, however, have been a decrease in areas harder-hit by crimes 1991 to 1993 (Home Office 14/94). Between 1993 and 1995, a drop in claims on insurance policies may lie behind the fall in burglaries reported to the police (Home Office 19/96).

11 Racist crimes and other crimes against minorities will not, although they also have had high priority in the public debate recently, be treated here.

12 It is not unlikely, either in the United Kingdom or in Sweden, that immigrant groups entering the new country at the bottom of society primarily have the same over-representation of crime as other poor groups have. Their crime rates should then not be analysed as crimes particular to ethnic minorities but as the effects of poverty and relative deprivation (Lea and Young 1984; von Hofer, et al. 1997).

13 Including daily or almost daily use of cannabis in the definition of heavy drug misuse would probably be disputed in many circles outside Sweden. However, this group constitutes only a small minority in the Swedish case finding studies. More than three out of four who are included in the definition in the 1992 study injected amphetamines (Olsson et al. 1993: 21–24).

14 During the 1990s there is, however, a marked increase in the number of military conscripts and also some increase in the number of 9 grade students who admit to having tried drugs (Alkohol- och narkotikautvecklingen i Sverige, 1996).

15 This paper was written in 1996, before the election in 1997 which brought Labour back to power. In the election campaign Labour presented a rather punitive profile in criminal policy. The Swedish Social Democrats have also clearly showed an ambition to follow the criminal policy message of British Labour. It might be that law and order politics in the future will be a characteristic of the left. These political developments, of course, further complicates the analysis presented here which might be regarded as having merely historic interest. The analysis should, however, be considered in the specific post-war context of strong welfare state ideologies upheld by the left but increasingly under attack from the right.

References

Åberg, R., Selén, J., and Tham, H. (1987), 'Economic Resources', in R. Erikson and R. Åberg (eds.), *Welfare in Transition. A Survey of Living Conditions in Sweden 1968–1981*. Oxford: Clarendon Press.

Ahlberg, J. (1996), *Invandrare och invandrares barns brottslighet* [Crime by immigrants and children of immigrants]. Stockholm: National Council for Crime Prevention.

Alkohol- och narkotikautvecklingen i Sverige. Rapport 96 [Trends in alcohol and other drugs in Sweden] (1996). Stockholm: Swedish National Institute of Public Health/Swedish Council for Information on Alcohol and Other Drugs.

Atkinson, A. B., Rainwater, L., and Smeeding, T. M. (1995), *Income Distribution in OECD Countries. Evidence from the Luxembourg Income Study*. OECD.

Bildt, C. (1991), *Svenska Dagbladet*, Brännpunkt 1991–05–05.

The British Crime Survey: The 1992 British Crime Survey (1993); Research Findings, No. 14 (September 1994); The 1996 British Crime Survey, England and Wales, Issue 19/96. London: Home Office.

The British Crime Survey: see under Home Office below.

Causes of Death Statistics, *Statistical Yearbook of Sweden*. Stockholm: Statistics Sweden.

Cavadino, M., and Dignan, J. (1997), *The Penal System: An Introduction*. 2nd ed. London: Sage.

Christie, N. (1993), *Crime Control as Industry. Towards GULAGs, Western Style?* London: Routledge.

Clarke, J. (1976), 'Social Democratic Delinquents and Fabian Families', in National Deviance Conference: *Permissiveness and Control*. London: Macmillan.

Conservative Party News. Speech by Michael Howard, Wednesday 6 October 1993. 400/93. London: Conservative Central Office.

Council of Europe (1985), *Economic Crises and Crime*. European Committee on Crime Problems. Strasbourg.

Criminal Statistics, England and Wales. London: Home Office.

Criminal Statistics [*Kriminalstatistik*]. Stockholm: National Council for Crime Prevention.

Digest 3. Information on the Criminal Justice System in England and Wales. London: Home Office, 1995.

Downes, D., and Morgan, R. (1994), ' "Hostages to Fortune"? The Politics of Law and Order in Post-War Britain', in M. Maguire, R. Morgan and R. Reiner (eds) *The Oxford Handbook of Criminology*. Oxford: Clarendon Press.

Estrada, F. (1995), *Ungdomsbrottslighetens utveckling 1975–1994* [Trends in youth crime in Sweden 1975–1994]. Department of Criminology, Stockholm University.

European Sourcebook of Crime and Criminal Justice Statistics (1995). Draft model. Strasbourg: Council of Europe.

Farrington, D. (1992), 'Trends in English Juvenile Delinquency and Their Explanation', *International Journal of Comparative and Applied Criminal Justice*, Vol. 16, No. 2.

Farrington, D., and Wikström, P.-O. (1993), 'Changes in Crime and Punishment in England and Sweden in the 1980s', *Studies on Crime and Crime Prevention*, Vol. 2.

FitzGerald, M. (1997), 'Minorities, Crime and Criminal Justice in Britain', in I. Haen Marshall (ed.), *Minorities and Crime: Diversity and Similarity Across Europe and the United States*. Thousand Oaks: Sage.

Goodman, A., and Webb, S. (1994), *For Richer, For Poorer. The Changing Distribution of Income in the United Kingdom, 1961–91*. London: Institute for Fiscal Studies.

Halleröd, B. (1996), 'Deprivation and Poverty: A Comparative Analysis of Sweden and Great Britain', *Acta Sociologica*, Vol. 39, No. 2.

Heidensohn, F. (1994), 'Gender and Crime', in M. Maguire, R. Morgan and R. Reiner (eds), *The Oxford Handbook of Criminology*. Oxford: Clarendon Press.

von Hofer, H., Lenke, L., and Thorsson, U. (1987), *Kriminalitetsutveckling och -belastning belyst genom födelsekohortstatistik. Födda 1951–1967*. [Crime trends and criminal loading illuminated through Swedish birth cohort statistics. Born 1951–1967]. RS-promemoria 1987:12. Stockholm: Statistics Sweden.

von Hofer, H. and Tham, H. (1989), 'General Deterrence in a Longitudinal Perspective. A Swedish Case: Theft, 1841–1985', *European Sociological Review*, Vol. 5, No. 1.

von Hofer, H., Sarnecki, J., and Tham, H. (1997), 'Ethnic minorities and Crime: An International Perspective. Sweden', in I. Haen Marshall (ed.), *Minorities and Crime: Diversity and Similarity Across Europe and the United States*. Thousand Oaks: Sage.

Home Office Research Findings, No. 14, Findings from the 1992 British Crime Survey, by P. Mayhew, N. Aye Maung and C. Mirrlees-Black. London: Home Office, 1993.

Home Office Research Study, No. 132, The 1992 British Crime Survey, by P. Mayhew, N. Aye Maung and C. Mirrlees-Black. London: Home Office, 1994.

Home Office Statistical Bulletin, Issue 14/1995, Criminal Careers of Those Born between 1953 and 1973. London: Home Office, 1995.

Home Office Statistical Bulletin, Issue 17/95, Statistics of Drug Addicts Notified to the Home Office, United Kingdom, 1994. London: Home Office, 1995.

Home Office Statistical Bulletin, Issue 24/95, Statistics of Drugs Seizures and Offenders Dealt with, United Kingdom, 1994. London: Home Office, 1995.

Home Office Statistical Bulletin, Issue 16/96, Cautions, Court Proceedings and Sentencing, England and Wales 1995. London: Home Office, 1996.

Home Office Statistical Bulletin, Issue 19/96, The 1996 British Crime Survey, England and Wales. London: Home Office, 1996.

Households Below Average Income. A Statistical analysis 1979–1992/93, A Publication of the Government Statistical Service. London: Department of Social Security.

Income distribution survey in 1994 [*Inkomstfördelningsundersökningen 1994*], Statistiska meddelanden, Be 21 SM 9601. Stockholm: Statistics Sweden.

Jefferson, T., and Shapland, J. (1994), 'Criminal Justice and the Production of Order and Control', *The British Journal of Criminology*, Vol. 34, No. 3.

Kronofogdemyndighetens verksamhetsberättelser [The Swedish enforcement service. Annual reports]. Stockholm: Riksskatteverket.

Kühlhorn, E. (1966), 'Går brottsligheten att minska?' [Can crime be reduced?], in *Minskad brottslighet – till vilket pris?* [Reduced crime – to what price?] En redovisning av rikskonferensen Polisen i samhället, Sunne 1995. Stockholm: Rikspolisstyrelsen.

Lea, J., and Young, J. (1984), *What is to be Done about Law and Order?* Harmondsworth: Penguin.

McClintock, F. H., and Wikström, P.-O. (1990), 'Violent Crime in Scotland and Sweden. Rate, Structure and Trends', *The British Journal of Criminology*, Vol. 30, No. 2.

Mortality Statistics, serial tables. London: Office of Population Census and Surveys.

National Council for Crime Prevention (1994), *Brottsutvecklingen 1992 och 1993* [Crime trends in Sweden 1992 and 1993], J. Ahlberg (ed.). Stockholm.

Nordic Criminal Statistics 1950–1989. Summary of a Report (1991). Copenhagen: Nordic Statistical Secretariat.

Norrie, A., and Adelman, S. (1989), ' "Consensual authoritarianism" and Criminal Justice in Thatcher's Britain', *Journal of Law and Society*, Vol. 16, No. 1.

OECD Employment Outlook; OECD Main Economic Indicators. Paris: OECD.

Olsson, O. (1996), *Liberalization of Drug Policies*. Stockholm: Swedish National Institute of Public Health/Swedish Council for Information on Alcohol and Other Drugs.

Olsson, O., Byqvist, S., and Gomér, G. (1993), *Det tunga narkotikamissbrukets omfattning i Sverige 1992* [The extent of hard drug use in Sweden 1992]. Stockholm: Swedish National Institute of Public Health/Swedish Council for Information on Alcohol and Other Drugs.

Pease, K. (1994), 'Cross-National Imprisonment Rates. Limitations of Methods and Possible Conclusions', *The British Journal of Criminolgy*, Vol. 34, special issue.

Schröder, L. (1996), *Patterns of Labour Market Entry and their Significance for Labour Market Policy*. Tema Nord 1996: 592. Nordic Council of Ministers.

Seeligman, M. (1976), *Hjälplöshet. Om depression, utveckling och död.* [Helplessness. On depression, development and death]. Stockholm: Aldus.

Skog, O.-J. (1993), 'Narkotikamisbrukets utvikling i Sverige 1979–1992' [The development of drug abuse in Sweden 1979–1992] in Olsson *et al.* 1993.

Smith, D. (1995), 'Youth Crime and Conduct Disorders', in M. Rutter and D. Smith (eds), *Psychosocial Disorders in Young People. Time Trends and Their Causes.* Chichester: John Wiley and Sons.

Statistics Sweden (1995), *Levnadsförhållanden,* [Living conditions], Rapport 88, Offer för vålds- och egendomsbrott 1978–1993 [Victims of violence and property crimes 1978–1993]. Stockholm: Statistics Sweden.

Stenberg, S.-Å. (1990), *Vräkt ur folkhemmet,* [Evicted from the 'People's home'], Stockholm: Carlssons.

Swedish National Institute of Public Health (1993). *A Restrictive Drug Policy. The Swedish Experience.* Stockholm.

Taylor, I. (1981), *Law and Order. Arguments for Socialism.* London: Macmillan.

Taylor, I. (1987), 'Law and Order, Moral Order: The Changing Rhetorics of the Thatcher Government', in R. Miliband, L. Panitch and J. Saville (eds), *Socialist Register 1987.* London: The Merlin Press.

Tham, H. (1995), 'From Treatment to Just Deserts in a Changing Welfare State', in A. Snare (ed.), *Beware of Punishment. On the Utility and Futility of Criminal Law.* Scandinavian Studies in Criminology, Vol. 14. Oslo: Pax.

Vagg, J. (1993), 'Context and Linkage. Reflections on a Comparative Research on "Internationalism" in Criminology', *The British Journal of Criminology*, Vol. 33, No. 4.

Windlesham, Lord (1993). *Responses to Crime. Penal Policy in the Making.* Vol. 2. Oxford: Clarendon Press.

Yearbook of Judicial Statistics [*Rättsstatistisk årsbok*]. Stockholm: Statistics Sweden.

Young, J. (1986), 'The Failure of Criminology: The Need for a Radical Realism', in R. Matthews and J. Young (eds): *Confronting Crime.* London: Sage.

24

RUNNING RISKS AND MANAGING DANGERS: STREET ROBBERY AS A MATTER OF TRUST

Willem de Haan

Abstract: Awareness of risks and dangers is for most people a source of anxiety. Therefore, a relatively secure environment of day-to-day life is of central importance in maintaining feelings of what Giddens (1991) has called "ontological security." Street robbery is a form of theft whereby unsuspecting people are attacked by strangers under threat of violence. When victims have been robbed as they go about in their immediate neighborhood, their ontological security is particularly jeopardized. Victims' moral indignation resides largely in the experience of a sudden breach of trust rather than in suffering from injuries or loss of money and valuables. For these victims, trust becomes an "inappropriate attitude for survival" and the resulting mistrust of fellow human beings a long-term mental burden. In this paper, I discuss my empirical research on the character, precipitation and development of street robbery in the city of Amsterdam. More generally, the consequences of street robbery for the social order will be explored.

Introduction

In this chapter I am going to explore some of the theoretical implications of street robbery. Street robbery – or "mugging" as it is often called – is a specific form of theft whereby innocent and usually vulnerable people are suddenly attacked or threatened by total strangers. As a criminologist, I became interested in the phenomenon of street robbery when I studied, more generally, the social and structural determinants of public safety in the city. I found that street robbery – together with certain types of sexual and physical assault – had an astonishing impact on public anxiety about crime. Even when these crimes occur in limited numbers, they can provoke disproportionate levels of public anxiety (Hall *et al.*, 1978). Unlike rape, street robbery had not been researched extensively and, therefore, I began to study this type of crime in my home town of Amsterdam in which almost half of all recorded cases of street robbery in The Netherlands are located.

In this introduction I will present a few of the results of this larger project which explored the nature, quantity, and increase of street robbery in The Netherlands, particularly in Amsterdam. The study was carried out between 1991–1994 and in order to assess the nature, quantity, and increase in street robbery, field work was done involving the observation of all the stages of the criminal justice process from police patrols to probation work.

I looked at police reports, court files and victimization surveys, interviewed dozens of victims and offenders and had also a number of group discussions with young offenders about various aspects of "doing stickup" (i.e. Street robbery). What I learned from them was, for example, that they did not have a preference for this kind of crime. On the contrary, they almost hated it. They would try to avoid it unless they had no alternative, for example in situations where – as they put it – "you gotta do what you gotta do."

Although my research did not attempt to evaluate police methods for combating street robbery, the results did raise some questions concerning the current crime-control policies and priorities. It should be mentioned first that the Amsterdam police have not been able to decrease the number of reported street robberies. Whereas the chief of police promised an annual decrease by 5–10 percent, a considerable increase in street robbery was reported in 1992, following the initial decrease from 1990 to 1991. Moreover, it appeared that foreign tourists received the primary benefit from police efforts, whereas the risk for residents of being "mugged" increased. Between 1990 and 1993, the risks for foreign tourists decreased by almost 5 percent, whereas the risks for residents increased by almost 25 percent.

Almost two thirds of the victimized residents had been robbed in their own neighborhood, street or apartment building. Therefore, their risk of victimization depends both on their own vulnerability and the relative safety of their neighborhood. My research showed that there are considerable differences in safety between boroughs and neighborhoods. Two-thirds of the residents of Amsterdam live in relatively safe neighborhoods with an average annual risk of less than two per thousand. Risks of victimization turned out to be unequally distributed with the elderly running a more-than-average risk and (migrant) residents of the projects in the South East a 10–20 times higher risk than the average for residents living in the rest of the city. Street robbery tended to concentrate in two areas: in the city center with its Red Light district the vast majority of victims are young male foreign tourists, whereas in a project called "The Bijlmer" in the South East of the city 90 percent of the victims are residents of the area (half of which are male and half female).[1] In this area which is characterized by high-rise apartment buildings, a high percentage of legal and illegal immigrants, high unemployment rates and welfare dependency, in 1993 the risk of becoming a victim of mugging in one's own neighborhood was fifteen times higher on the average for residents of the Bijlmer area than for the rest of Amsterdam.[2] Moreover, robberies in this area also tend to involve more violence and injury than in other parts of Amsterdam. In view of the number and nature of street robberies, it is not surprising that the percentage of residents who do not feel safe in the streets of their own communities is highest in this particular part of Amsterdam.

In the rest of this chapter I am going to explore some of the theoretical implications of street robbery. Its randomness and the feeling that one can do little to avoid or protect oneself against it, make street robbery one of the most frightening forms of criminal victimization. Like other forms of "stranger violence" (Reidel 1987), street robbery very much influences citizens' perceptions of public safety and the general quality of life. According to Michalowski high rates of robbery "have probably more than any other offense influenced the way people live" (Michalowski, 1985, 293). In the chapter, I want to address the question of how the astonishing impact of street robbery along with sexual and physical assault as forms of "stranger violence" can be explained. I will argue that trust is crucial to understand the dramatic effects that these violent crimes can have on people's lives, their social relationships and the social order which they reproduce.

Moral panic

Time and again, criminologists have explained the extraordinary anxiety evoked by street robbery in contrast to the relative infrequency of its occurrence as a "moral panic" (Cohen, 1972). The notion of a "moral panic" highlights the way the public becomes obsessed with a condition, episode, person or group defined as a threat to societal values and interests (ibid.: p. 28). Essential to the notion of a moral panic is that public anxiety is out of proportion in terms of the real threat posed by these phenomena. Hall *et al.* (1978), for example, have argued that the "mugging" scare in early-1970s England was a "moral panic" because the statistics did not offer a convincing explanation for such an anxiety. The public fear that a wave of muggings was washing over the country had, therefore, to be seen as an over-reaction, disproportionate to the real risk of becoming a victim of street robbery.

A key role in creating the mugging scare was assigned to the mass media. According to Hall *et al.*, the impression was given by the media of a sharp and unprecedented rise in the number of street robberies. Moreover, by drawing upon racist stereotypes and, in particular, creating the specific image of the "black mugger," the threat potential of the phenomenon was raised to the point that drastic action on the part of the state became imperative. In this way, a "silent majority" could be won over to support "more than usual" surveillance, particularly over young, black, unemployed males. Eventually, "law and order" emerged from a succession of "moral panics," coalescing in a growing general panic about rising crime and public safety in a "violent society."

Despite the attraction of Hall *et al.*'s version of a "moral panic" explanation for the social reaction to mugging, their focus on the media, ideology and the state apparatus also has its drawbacks. As Stanley Cohen put it in his Bonger Memorial Lecture given in 1990 in Amsterdam: "To travel the subways . . . you need more help than a deconstructed map of the category of 'mugging'" (Cohen 1990, 24). In their concern with deconstructing the "black mugger" as a fiction of the white racist imagination Hall and his colleagues leave the anxieties of ordinary citizens – both black and white – as they go about their daily routines, largely unaddressed and unexplored. As various critics have pointed out, they did not conduct interviews to find out what the public really thought or how the media discourse was actually being interpreted by the public (Sumner 1981: 283). In fact, little evidence was provided that there even was a moral panic about mugging. Explaining the anxiety caused by street robbery as a "moral panic" might have been taking the media just a little too seriously and the lived experiences of citizens not seriously enough.

In the rest of my paper, I will take a closer look at what street robbery means for victims and explore some of the consequences of the phenomenon of street robbery for interpersonal relationships and the social order at large.

Violence

Street robbery – that is, random violence perpetuated by a stranger – is anxiety-producing in the extreme. Victims of criminal violence live in constant fear that they will be attacked again. The world is no longer a safe place for them to live in. In addition to fear, street robbery significantly raises the victim's sense of vulnerability. But the most disorienting aspect of all is perhaps the senselessness of the experience itself. It shatters the victims' belief in the world as a rational, hence predictable, place over which they have at least some control. As their sense of self is bound up with their ability to control the personal space in which they live, victims of stranger violence might also experience a diminishment in their self-esteem. Male victims of street robbery may feel stripped of their masculinity (Silberman, 1978: 18). For women, stranger violence includes a latent threat of sexual violence and their fear is, therefore, even stronger than men's. In this respect, fear of street robbery is "gendered." Many victims not only feel powerless in their situations, but they also feel that they, too, are somehow to blame. In order to control their fear and provide some rationale for their random victimization, many look to fate and explain that they were simply "in the wrong place at the wrong time" (Ibid.: 86).

While people know that they have to be on guard in a strange neighborhood, especially at night, they expect to be safe in their own neighborhood. Therefore, mugging is particularly anxiety-producing when it is experienced on one's own turf (Lejeune and Alex, 1973: 9–10). It is also why for the elderly, who understandably fear more serious injury in case of an attack, street robbery has an even more dramatic impact on their daily lives. Contrary to what national crime surveys suggest, I found that the risk of women over 65 being robbed in Amsterdam was more than average, whereas their chances of being robbed in their own neighborhood and being injured were, in fact, higher than for any other group. As the elderly are most frequently attacked in their immediate environment – an environment on which they are heavily dependent – they are especially afraid of purse-snatching or "robbery's ugly stepchild" as it has also been called (Richardson, 1976).

Fear of crime is not exclusively nor predominantly precipitated by the media. Research shows that fear of crime is, in fact, more closely related to learning about crime from neighbors (Skogan and Maxfield, 1981). What they have to say is at least as important in creating anxiety. Unprovoked or senseless violence and suspicion of others are among the plot elements in the stories victims of crime have to tell about what is occurring – in the midst of ongoing urban activity – in public places like streets, parks, subways, apartment lobbies and elevators (Wachs, 1988: 61).

Trust

Awareness of risks and dangers is for most people a source of anxiety. Therefore, a relatively secure environment for day-to-day life is of central importance in maintaining feelings of what Giddens (1991) has called "ontological security." Ontological security refers to the confidence that most human beings have (and, indeed, need to have) in the constancy of their social environments. It is sustained primarily through daily routines. When these routines, for whatever reason, become radically disrupted, existential crises are likely to occur which involve the basic belief in the reliability of people. This is central to the notion of trust. Often, when people have been robbed, they suffer more from the sudden breach of trust than from injuries or loss of money. Trust suddenly seems an "inappropriate attitude for survival" for them. Although this feeling might subside somewhat with the passage of time, a heightened sense of vulnerability combined with a sense of distrust of fellow human beings, remains. When this distrust leads to an enduring transformation in the way the environment is perceived, it can become a long-term mental burden which impairs the quality of a person's life (Lejeune and Alex, 1973: 272–273).

As risks and dangers are implied by the very business of life and nobody can fully escape them, living in modern society is inherently unsettling. Every human being is likely to be overwhelmed by anxieties from time to time. In order to get on with the affairs of day-to-day life, people require what Giddens has called a "protective cocoon" (Giddens, 1991: p. 3). This protective cocoon is a sense of "invulnerability" which all normal individuals carry around with them. It is a means of getting on with the affairs of day-to-day life by bracketing possible events which could threaten the bodily or psychological integrity of the person (Ibid.: 40). Troubling thoughts are conveniently put out of mind. This fiction is necessary if people are to go about their lives with a sense of trust, hope, and confidence in their future (Lerner, 1980: 14). Unfortunate happenings like an accident or a criminal assault may pierce their protective cocoon, create a more or less temporary state of anxiety, and cause them to lose their trust in others.

Social order

In metropolitan areas, trust in anonymous others is indispensable to social existence. On city streets mutual trust is routinely displayed between strangers by
observing what Goffman has called a "civil indifference" (Goffman, 1971: 39). This
"civil indifference" serves to sustain attitudes of generalized trust on which
interaction in public settings depends. As the gearing mechanism of generalized
public trust, "civil indifference" represents an implicit contract of mutual
acknowledgement and protection drawn up by participants in the public settings
of modern social life (Giddens, 1991: 47). Ultimately, the whole fabric of urban
life is based on trust: trust that others will act predictably, in accordance with
generally accepted rules of behavior, and that they will not take advantage of
that trust. For life to go on in public places people must put themselves in other
people's hands (Silberman, 1978: 10).

As "a personal crime executed in an impersonal way," street robbery sets into
motion social psychological forces which contribute to an increasing *dis*order in
urban society (Lejeune and Alex, 1973: 260, 283). Apart from shattered trust and
insecurity about the future, victims respond with moral indignation about what
they perceive as a decline in the social order: a world where criminal violence is
both unpredictable, where the social order seems to be continually disrupted and
where they believe themselves to be without protection or recourse. For example,
it becomes almost axiomatic that one cannot ride the subway without fear, or feel
safe walking down a dimly lit street at night (Wachs, 1988: 82–83).

In their construction of a social order which is continually being disrupted by
crime, victims and potential victims of stranger violence draw on the experiences
of others to give meaning to their world and, paradoxically, create a sense of
order.

When the general level of trust in the urban community, not very high to begin
with, is further eroded by the emergent perceptions that the police are unable or
unwilling to protect the citizen and that fellow citizens (in part as a result of their
own lack of trust in others) are predictably unreliable as a source of assistance to
victims of crime, a more general transformation takes place: a Lockean sentiment
of man being rational and basically good gives way to the Hobbesian view of
human nature. The urban jungle is the metaphor to characterize the city as a
situation where others, particularly strangers, are not to be trusted (Lejeune and
Alex, 1973: 264, 284).

In this way, stranger violence does more than expose the weakness in social
relationships in urban society. It undermines the social order itself by destroying
the assumptions on which it is based. When people stay behind locked doors and
– to avoid contact with strangers – travel by taxi or car rather than public transportation or on foot, the general level of sociability in their environment will
decrease. Fear of crime breaks down neighborhood cohesion and undermines
neighborly sociability and concern for others. As a result, community solidarity
weakens, distrust and suspicion increase, informal social controls atrophy and

residents are less willing to help a stranger or intervene to stop a violent crime. The nototious Kitty Genovese case in New York where a woman was raped on the street in front of dozens of unresponsive observants, is a case in point. As there are fewer people on the streets, less surveillance of street life, and less chance of effective intervention, opportunities for committing violent street crimes increase. In this way, fear of crime can actually contribute to the incidence of crime (Merry, 1981). By restricting those with whom they will interact in public places, citizens not only diminish the quality of their life but also undermine the generalized trust which is essential for a civil society (Conklin, 1975; Reidel, 1987: 22).

Policy implications

Like many other forms of risk and danger, the possibility of becoming a victim of street robbery is part of the experience of urban society and cannot be completely eliminated. Therefore, we must recognize the existence of a risk (even when it is relatively small) and accept that, occasionally, things can go wrong.

In policy terms, an indiscriminate focus on a reduction of (reported) crimes is neither realistic nor effective. Instead, an approach to public safety should be adopted which assesses victimization risks within the city by taking into account the relative vulnerability of certain categories of victims, and the deficiencies in (formal and informal) social control in the communities to which they belong. Restoring trust would require much more realistic information and advice to the public than is currently given by the police.

Urban residents carry out their daily routines within certain spatial constraints as defined by their place of residence, work or school, and recreation. Their (objective) risks of becoming a victim of "stranger violence" are structured accordingly. As a result their real risks are merely a fraction of what they seem to be. Although victimization by certain forms of crime tends to be fairly infrequent and geographically and socially concentrated, the fear of them is much more diffuse. This discrepancy creates some serious problems for a fair and realistic approach to public safety.

A social policy for public safety needs to account for both the (in)frequency as well as the specific nature and seriousness of street robberies and other forms of stranger violence for various categories of victims. It needs to be guided by the principle that the risks and consequences of victimization – which are to some extent unavoidable – need to be equally or, rather, equitably distributed (Barr and Pease, 1990). Crime victimization should not exacerbate inequalities of other origin. An increasingly unequal distribution of crime, or violence, seems to have a kind of multiplier effect resulting in an overall rise of crime or violence and a disruption of social order. Therefore, it might be suggested that redistributing crime more equally or, rather, equitably, will help to reduce the overall level of crime, restore trust and bolster social order.

Notes

1 Obviously, there are different types of street robbery for which only certain categories of persons qualify as potential victims.
2 On the basis of robberies reported to the police, inhabitants of the Bijlmer ran a risk of 24 per thousand of being robbed in their own neighborhood in 1993. In absolute figures there are, on the average, about three reported robberies daily for a population of fifty thousand.

References

Barr, R. and Pease, K. "Crime Placement, Displacement, and Deflection" in Michael Tonry and Norval Morris (eds), *Crime and Justice: An Annual Review of Research*, Chicago, University Chicago Press, 1990: 277–318.

Cohen, S., *Folk Devils and Moral Panics*, Oxford, Martin Robertson, 1972 (2nd edition, 1980).

Cohen, S., *Intellectual Scepticism and Political Commitment: The Case of Radical Criminology* Amsterdam, Stichting W. A. Bonger Lezingen 1990.

Conklin, J., *The Impact of Crime*, New York, Macmillan, 1975.

Giddens, A., *Modernity and Self-Identity. Self and Society in the Late Modern Age*, Cambridge, Polity Press, 1991.

Goffman, E., *Relations in Public*, New York, 1971.

Hall, S., Critcher, C. Jefferson, T., Clarke, J. and Roberts, B., *Policing the Crisis. Mugging, the State, and Law and Order*, London, Macmillan, 1978.

Lejeune, R. and Alex, N. "On Being Mugged: The Event and its Aftermath," *Urban Life and Culture*, 2, 1973, 3, 259–287.

Lerner, M., *The Belief in a Just World: A Fundamental Delusion*, New York, Plenum Press, 1980.

Merry, S. *Urban Danger*, Philadelphia, Temple University Press.

Michalowski, R. *Order, Law, and Crime. An Introduction to Criminology*, New York, Random House, 1985.

Reidel, M., "Stranger Violence: Perspectives, Issues, and Problems", *The Journal of Criminal Law and Criminology*, 78, 1987, 2: 223–258.

Richardson, J., "Purse Snatch: Robbery's Ugly Stepchild," in J. Goldsmith and S. Goldsmith (eds) *Crime and the Elderly. Challenge and Response*, Lexington, Mass., Lexington Books D. C. Heath and Company 1976: 121–125.

Silberman, C., *Criminal Violence, Criminal Justice*, New York, Random House 1978.

Skogan, W. and Maxfield, M., *Coping with Crime: Individual and Neighborhood Reactions*, Beverly Hills, Sage, 1981.

Sumner, C., "Race, Crime and Hegemony: A Review Essay," *Contemporary Crises*, 5, 1981: 277–291.

Wachs, E., *Crime-Victim Stories. New York City's Urban Folklore*, Bloomington In., Indiana University Press, 1988.

Part V

HORIZONS

25

'IDEOLOGY WITH HUMAN VICTIMS'

The institution of 'crime and punishment'
between social control and social exclusion:
historical and theoretical issues[1]

Heinz Steinert

Introduction

In what follows I will present an analysis of the place of 'crime and punishment' in the present 'mode of domination'. My starting-point for this exercise was the recent shift towards an understanding of 'crime and punishment' as 'social exclusion' and the debates about this in German-speaking sociology. (See Sack 1993, Stehr 1994, Cremer-Schäfer, Funk, Scheerer, all 1995, as important and representative contributions.) My starting-point also involves a long-lasting astonishment (sometimes indignation) about how easily critical positions reached under the influence of labelling theory and abolitionism could be given up again, how we could fall back on a 'naturalistic' understanding of 'crime' on the one hand and an acceptance of state punishment up to the point of even demanding certain or stricter punishments on the other. A third aspect of the approach is that my aim is not a (critical or other) theory in criminology but a critique of criminology.

I will describe the function of 'crime and punishment' in the mode of domination by distinguishing three levels of analysis: an *interpersonal*, an *organizational* and a *societal* level, characterized by the height of abstraction of the units of analysis – people interacting, organized apparatuses (of regulation), (self-)identified cultures and subcultures, here and now often identical with states and state-analogues. All of this is given a frame by the mode of production, its basic institutions and its historical specifications.

The present and some-centuries-old *capitalist mode of production* as well as *mode of domination* can be described as a complicated web of four contradictory and mutually supporting forms: the defining form of capitalist domination is the *commodity form*, i.e. 'alienated' production and definition of everything according to its marketability. Inside the organizations of production and of reproduction, factory and family, relations cannot be all organized by the commodity form: here we have *discipline*[2] and *patriarchy*[3] instead and as prerequisites for it. As an additional aspect we find *subcultural solidarity*[4] in voluntary communities as a (non-commodity-form) basis of power that can be put to the service of the market, social discipline and patriarchy or can be turned against them. 'Crime and punishment' is just one (and certainly not the most important) institution in that mode of domination, determined by and using all those forms.

There are several important orientations that I take for granted and will not discuss:

- I talk about the *social institution* of 'crime and punishment' – a socially defined vocabulary of rule-breaking, responsibility, guilt, trial, judgment, punishment, and a concomitant organized praxis that can be and has historically been applied to changing situations, actions and persons. I certainly do *not* talk about any naturalistically conceived unpleasant actions or events about which something needs to be done, preferably by some authority.
- I am interested in tying this in with a social theory that has a notion of societies

  (a) being determined by a 'mode of production',
  (b) by contradictions that are the motor of development,
  (c) by different interests leading to conflicts over 'resolutions' of problems created,
  (d) by an apparatus of political regulation and
  (e) by a cultural apparatus, today a 'culture industry', that constitutes a mode of knowledge, today 'instrumental reason'.

- I am *not* interested in a middle-range theory of a socially defined field of something called 'crime'.
- I do feel bound and will certainly try to be true to a *reflexive* epistemology that takes the concepts, questions and answers of common-sense as well as common-science as starting-points, but as starting-points only. With this goes an awareness that research is a social practice that follows the same rules it is meant to analyse, that our material does not consist of 'facts', but presentations of self, stories and interactions of which we are part. And, perhaps most important: research and other intellectual work take place themselves as part of a 'culture industry'. Cultural products, among them the results of scientific work, are commodities. We cannot opt out of that or isolate public moves and remarks against such commodification. (We can, of course, remain 'private', but even then . . .) All we can do (and have to do) is reflexively take this state of affairs into our theorizing as one of its conditions.

This is all the same a materialist position in which hunger, lust and greed as well as misery, pain and destruction have their place as immediate impacts on and resistances against persons, including the researcher. It is exactly the knowledge of the vulnerability of human beings that makes 'crime and punishment' such a fascinating and depressing field of study.

As I said: all this will have to be taken for granted. Let me begin my deliberations with questions about the object of our inquiry and a reminder of what doubts we could (and should) have about criminology.

The subject-matter of criminology: 'crime and punishment' as a special case of what?

More than twenty years ago Nils Christie began a lecture celebrating the foundation of a Centre for Criminological Studies at the University of Sheffield with three remarkable sentences:

> Maybe we should not have any criminology. Maybe we should rather abolish institutes, not open them. Maybe the social consequences of criminology are more dubious than we like to think.
>
> (Christie 1977: 1)

The unfortunate effect of the very existence of a specialized and expert field of studies of 'crime', he continued, is one more contribution to the social process in which conflicts are 'taken away from the parties directly involved'. Calling certain conflicts 'crime' implies an equally certain way of managing them: by invoking state authority to decide the conflict and enforce the solution decided upon. Of course I expect the state's monopoly of force to take my side against the person I see as 'guilty' in and for the conflict. In the extreme case I expect the person to be taken away never to return again. As it is I am often in for a disappointment in respect of such expectations and will learn that the process, once initiated, is not fully under control. A reversal of roles – in which I come out as the 'guilty' party – is not impossible, in many cases not at all unlikely.

Nils Christie has pointed to a logical problem and to a practical one. The logical problem is that the 'explanation' of a phenomenon consists of stating the class of phenomena it belongs to and naming its specific difference. A science of 'crime and punishment' would, therefore, have the task of going *beyond* that category at all times and identifying the specific difference that makes some specimens of that larger category 'crimes'. Surprisingly criminology does not usually do that. It is very rarely that 'criminalized' conflicts are compared to others, that the different ways in which property changes hands are compared systematically to find out why some are seen as 'force majeure', some as 'fair', some as 'forced' – and some as 'fraud' or 'theft'.[5] Usually criminology just knows that a crime is a crime and only studies phenomena already so labelled. Little wonder the explanations given are so schematic, repetitive and uninformative as we have known them through the decades of criminological research. In fact these 'explanations' are descriptions of the population against which accusations of 'crime' can most successfully be laid. The *logical* problem is: inside the narrow scope of criminology – studying an object socially defined as 'crime' – there can be no proper explanation of 'crime'.

The *practical* problem behind this refusal to do the logical thing is the social refusal to treat some conflicts as conflicts. There is an interest in using them for a show of monopoly of force, there is an interest in occasions for punishment, there is an interest in dramatizing domination. We will come back to this.

'Crime and punishment' as 'trouble': the interpersonal level

The scientific problem, of course, is to properly identify the class into which 'crime' and different types of 'crime' belong as a special case.

Christie has suggested that crime is 'conflict'. There is a lot to this identification: mostly 'crimes' need someone to scandalize an event as 'crime', to charge a person with having done something 'criminal', with actually being 'a criminal'. This alone constitutes a conflict, even if there is not a longer story of conflicts between the persons involved that leads up to that charge.[6]

But then there are 'crimes' which are not even such secondary conflicts. When I call the police to the scene of a burglary or notify them of a theft I usually do not want to turn this into a conflict. I'd rather not see the person who did it but simply want my loss compensated. (We all know my chances are minimal unless I'm insured.) There is no interpersonal conflict when persons buy an illegal drug or have an abortion. In these cases it is the state only (and perhaps some moral entrepreneur backed by the state) that creates a problem.

There is a further complicating aspect of 'crime and punishment' on the interpersonal level: many, actually most of the relevant experiences are second-hand, are *stories* of experiences of other persons who are sometimes known, sometimes acquaintances of friends or relatives. The socially important thing here in the circulation of such stories, is communicating them to illustrate a moral point and engineer situational moral consensus. Thus, there are many more conflicts and their 'solutions' that we hear about than there are actually experienced ones. In fact these stories serve to identify places to avoid in order to avoid the possible experience. They are also 'morality tales' related to the stories collected and analysed as 'urban folklore' (Wachs 1988; Sasson 1995; Stehr 1996; Stangl 1996). There is no sharp border between them and the stories we read or see under the heading of 'crime reporting' (some of them more or less free fabrications) in diverse media, which we use in a similar way as 'morality tales' (Katz 1987). A greater part of our dealings with 'troubles' on the interpersonal level relates to *stories* of such troubles with a more or less personal background. They are the interpersonal equivalent of the ideologies represented on the next, the organizational level, and are an active remoulding or countering of them, and an autonomous participation in them.

'Conflict', thus, is a suitable category to include many, particularly everyday crimes, but it by no means covers all cases. One wider category that we found useful in our research even of everyday crimes would be 'troubles' or 'disruptions of routines', of which 'conflict' would be the special case of trouble arising in an interpersonal context. From this starting point it is obvious that to treat such an event as 'crime' is a rare and demanding strategy. More often we are after fast and pragmatic solutions of the problem and know our world well enough to be aware that the 'moral' response of treating the event as 'crime' is a luxury that usually hinders a pragmatic settlement. (Although sometimes calling the event 'crime' *is* a kind of non-moral pragmatic solution: for example, in the case of an insurance claim as mentioned above, when no conflict is involved.) But even this wider category does not cover all cases we are interested in: consuming illegal drugs or having homosexual relations may be totally 'routine' for all concerned. Also, conflicts are the stuff good stories are made of, a welcome opportunity for joint moral indignation and other entertainment.

'Crime and punishment' as 'representation of domination': the organizational level

There are theoretical reasons too, which make 'conflict' an unsatisfactory candidate for the superordinate class, in which 'crime' could be the special case. 'Conflict' casts the state and its monopoly of force – after they have 'taken away the conflict' – in a purely passive and service role: the state offers its good services should they be asked for. This is empirically true in a great number of cases, but not in all. Besides, the service offered is rather peculiar and often not what is demanded or really needed. The state metes out punishment which often does not help the person who made the charge. And there are many cases in which the relevant institutions, usually the police, act without being asked by the people immediately involved. The state is more often an apparatus of rule and domination and a service institution only to those who have the competence to use its resources. Even when it acts in the name of public service, the state does so on its own terms.

On this *organizational* level, then, 'conflict' does not describe the activities of which 'crime' is the special case. Rather the category is 'keeping order', 'avoiding possible disorder', 'representation of rule' (in a democracy 'rule of law'), 'representation of domination' (lawful and legitimate). This is what the state bureaucracies that administer the label of 'crime' are for and after. Historians have long taken for granted that the state is based on coercion, even if it 'civilizes' this violence and the potential for it.[7] The institution of 'crime and punishment' is only a small contribution to this 'protection racket' (even if the sums cashed in through traffic tickets alone seem quite remarkable) compared to other taxes even today. It also does not process a number of people big enough to be of real consequence for the labour market. But it is a 'show', a 'representation of domination', and of interest as such.[8]

Comparing these institutions concerned with keeping order and representing domination in different fields and on different levels there is one striking distinction in approach. There are 'individualizing' or 'personalizing' ways of keeping order on the one hand, 'structuralizing' ones on the other. Often it is the higher levels of administration and politics which regard 'structures' as their object of intervention, whereas the lower levels have to apply this to individual cases. But there are, of course, planning organizations that simply produce infrastructures like public transport, roads, schools, new towns, interest rates or labour-market regulations. This is very different from organizations responsible for traffic control, tax inspection or certificates of scholastic achievement. On the 'reactive' side, the individualizing modes of keeping order are the identification of those who are 'sick' or of those who are fully responsible for their actions and hence 'guilty'; and on the pro-active side, the process of 'disciplining' those who offend. The structuralizing modes are 'defining as a social problem' in the reactive case, and planning and providing of infrastructure in the pro-active case.[9]

There is a problem here. As an instrument of 'social control' punishment does not work very well.[10] Order is mostly kept by structures into which people are integrated, not by punishments. Even most deviance from established rules is managed by other means, mostly neglect or private (preferably on-the-spot) compensation. In the regulation of ecological, food and other merchandise quality, for example, the attempt to control by criminalization looks more like a deliberate manoeuvre *not* to do what would be efficient (because it would make life and production a little more costly for the industries concerned).

In the field of 'social control', we would argue, the institution of 'crime and punishment' is not so much organized for immediate material effects but falls into the category of an 'ideological state apparatus'.[11] Its effects of actually regulating social behaviour, i.e. as an instrument of administration and planning, are not very important, even though the consequences for the (under non-terrorist conditions few) individuals used for the demonstration are quite painful. But there certainly are ideological effects. This is the more so today when 'crime and punishment' is probably the single most popular theme of entertainment,[12] even more popular than the proverbial 'topic no. 1' and very often in combination with it. It has also become a major part of the type of entertainment that is still called 'political debate' or even 'information'. Law-and-order fantasies are fun and thrill. What is the thrill?

On the interpersonal level again we can easily know from research and introspection that one very satisfying aspect of such fantasies is that of 'protection': The foremost emotional element is the urge to protect the helpless, mainly kids and females, against the predator from outside, i.e. protect the familial sexual order; next comes the protection of other property,[13] then the protection of the work morale (the nexus of wage labour and consumption) and of the rules of 'fair' competition. The fantasy of 'crime and punishment' is patriarchal and privileges masculinity – not necessarily the masculinity of the (old and wise) patriarch himself, but that of the younger, still aspiring or already resigned, fighting, 'warrior' position.[14] And, as Connell (1987) has shown, there is the complementary and supporting (more or less 'emphasized') femininity that can tie in with this: the maternal urge to protect the kids, the contradictory female obligation and interest to moderate male aggressiveness and have morality enforced, if needs be by violent means – and to pair with a good provider and protector, as long as there still is the patriarchal pressure to pair heterosexually and permanently.

The 'crime and punishment' fantasy, then, is one in which we can enjoy fantasies of patriarchal masculinity *and* femininity, both of which are so notoriously hard to live in contemporary reality, particularly as the provider role is undermined from more than one side. But there are satisfactions for that provider role in the fantasy as well: on the one hand much of property crime is about having lots of money, being able to consume indiscriminately, to show off this capacity, to make friends and shame antagonists by this – to be a winner in the competition and to be a good and generous provider. At the same time censure is also satisfied: at the end of such stories and films mostly the stability of the wage-labour–consumption nexus and truly, unselfishly devoted friendship and love are affirmed. Usually the money made in one lucky and daring strike is lost similarly fast – or cannot buy what we really want, 'can't buy me love'.

The fantasy of 'crime and punishment' represents the dominant 'implicit contract'[15] regarding family, work and competition, plays out major themes in the complex of 'who should work, how and how much under what conditions for what rewards', appealing mainly to norms and relations of masculinity and femininity.

There is a more abstract level of cultural meaning of 'crime and punishment' in which the relation between rich and poor is redefined. This piece of ideology is independent of any damage the events categorized as 'crime' may cause, independent of the contents of prohibitions and sanctions threatening. This derives from the formal qualities of 'crime and punishment': being personalized and applying to the vast majority of actions typical of lower-class life and easier to police under lower-class conditions. According to these formal characteristics it is only *persons* who do harm and who have to be kept from continuing to do such harm; and it is mainly *lower-class* persons who produce these harmful actions – as can be read from any statistics of persons sentenced (if they contain information on social class) and seen in any prison-population. What 'we' have to be afraid of is young men, lower-class men, foreign men, most of all a combination of these. Accordingly there is no need to look for social structures that might harm us, no need to be suspicious of well-to-do and powerful persons, least of all a combination of the two, in the form of powerful organizations.[16]

It certainly does not all work out that way. There is in all societies a lot of distrust of those in power and often (particularly under conditions conducive to and used for 'populist' politics) this distrust is formulated in terms of 'crime and punishment'. Which is very useful for powerful organizations because they do not mind sacrificing the proverbial 'black sheep' and can this way go on doing business as usual. Ecological 'crime' is probably the most obvious case here: it is no secret that the world ecology is ruined by perfectly legal production the results of which we all enjoy.

This brings us back full circle to 'social control'. If the object of 'crime and punishment' really were 'social control' we would mostly know how to do it – and we would not choose a clumsy instrument like punishment with its complicated moral implications, but straightforward technical, economic and otherwise preventive control.[17]

Let me add as a historical remark that the idea of 'social control' by 'crime and punishment' is a quite young one. Up to the nineteenth century nobody thought of the criminal law as an instrument of control. Rather punishment was a demonstration and confirmation of domination – like the beating of a slave by the master or the rounding up of unruly members of the population by a detachment of an occupation army. It was only in the nineteenth century that 'general prevention' became a systematic part of thinking about criminal law and punishment. It was through this 'instrumental turn', that punishment came to be understood as an instrument of 'social control'. This idea became even more plausible when 're-socialization' was introduced as one or even the dominant function of punishment at the turn of the century.

From then on we can observe a struggle between 'soft technocrats', who try to turn state punishment into an opportunity for social integration, and 'hard technocrats', who opt for measures of social exclusion. It is the first who think about punishment in terms of 'social control'. Since punishment *is* degradation, *is* conferring of disadvantages, *is* at least partial and temporary social exclusion, their struggle is honourable but very uphill. On top of the lack of success there is the irony that their thinking has enforced *personalized* ascriptions of cause and agency and created a new category of people who cannot be 'reformed', the 'incorrigibles', and with that a powerful legitimation for social exclusion.

'Social control' is a fascinating field of study, but crime and crime control is only a small and marginal part of it. Its most interesting contribution may well be the avoidance of effective control. If we are not to assume that societies stick to a costly failure (like punishment under the aspect of social regulation is) for centuries, what, then, *is* the function that punishment *does* fulfil?

Methodological interlude: how do we identify the structure of a mode of domination?

We have again run into the problem we already had when we tried to pin down the function of 'crime and punishment' on the interpersonal level: we can identify a function, but the contribution of 'crime and punishment' is minimal. There are lots of 'functional equivalents'.

Let me pause for a moment at this point and retrace my steps: What have I been doing so far?

My starting-point was a critique of criminology, a (rudimentary) analysis of what this kind of knowledge, what the conceptualization of the object of this field of knowledge about 'crime and punishment', does to society and to the possible questions and answers posed and given in this discipline. In this way I have analysed the use of the concept of 'crime and punishment' as an instrument of expert rule. It was helpful to start with 'conflict' as the possible superordinate concept because this makes it very visible that punishment is *not* conflict-management, that there must be more to the concept of 'crime and punishment'. This 'more' could then, on a next level of domination, on the organizational level, be identified as 'keeping order' and 'representation of rule' as the more abstract prerequisites a functioning mode of domination will have to fulfil.

But here again punishment poses a problem. It is, on this level, treated as an instrument of social regulation and ordering. But we know as competent members of society and from a lot of research that as such a means of regulation punishment does not work very well, and certainly works worse than alternative instruments of control could work. It is exactly under this aspect of social control that punishment has a high degree of irrationality. This again forces us to ask more questions about the functions of 'crime and punishment' in a regime of domination. It also forces us to move higher again on the levels of analysis: what is the superordinate concept of which 'keeping order' and 'representation of rule' would be the special cases and which still includes 'crime and punishment'?

'Crime and punishment' as 'social exclusion': the societal level

Having arrived at this point it may be useful to look at an example again. This time I choose a text more than fifty years old, Georg Rusche's 'Labour Market and Punishment', published in 1933 as a kind of summary statement of his part of the text that was later turned into Rusche and Kirchheimer's 'Punishment and Social Structure', the first publication of the exiled Frankfurt 'Institut für Sozialforschung' in the USA in 1938. This will lead us into more historical considerations of punishment.

Georg Rusche summarizes:

> The history of punishment is more than the mere history of some institutions of law developing according to their own regularities. Rather it is the history of the relations between the 'two nations', as Disraeli called them, of which peoples consist: the rich and the poor.
>
> (Rusche 1933: 305; my translation)

In his theory Georg Rusche flatly assumed that the relevant part of these relations included punishment that had to be worse than the worst of living conditions the economy otherwise provides for the poor. And that can go as far as killing off 'superfluous' portions of the poor population. Rusche used that interpretation for the cruel punishments that spread in Europe in the late Middle Ages.

Only a short time after the publication of that article Rusche had to flee from Germany and had his intellectual career and in the end his life destroyed.

413

We would probably be a little hesitant to reduce what Rusche described and what he experienced to 'social control'.

What is obvious in these historical examples of the European experience since the state-building process of the Middle Ages, culminating in the Nazi attempt at a belated intra-European colonialism and in what has lately, after two short decades of 'integration' in the 1960/70s, become unavoidable contemporary reality again is the fact of 'social exclusion': societies draw limits as to who 'belongs', who fulfils the duties and who is entitled to the privileges of a bona-fide member. States have formally defined rules of citizenship and ways to acquire it. Foreigners allowed to stay often get the duties but not the benefits of membership. Bourgeois thinking has at times gone beyond this and has conceived of the improbable idea of *human* rights and of the possibility of belonging to an all-encompassing class of 'humanity'. This idea has, of course, not been realized (outside humanist drama on the 'classical' stage), but has since constituted a contradiction to the reality of the nation state, of class society, of patriarchy, of some – mainly educated men of property – being more equal than others. All others – females, young people, poor people, uneducated people, 'savages' – were simply neglected in constructions of 'mankind', were assumed to be represented by someone who qualified for full citizenship and/or had to wait and work for emancipation. At least the labour and the feminist movements were quite successful in the latter.

The twentieth century is full of reversals of bourgeois emancipation, full of examples of the 'dialectic of enlightenment', particularly on the grounds of a new political category: race. Biological thinking, an understanding of capitalism in terms of social Darwinism and thus 'degeneration' on the one, 'survival of the fittest' on the other hand, opened up 'scientific' ways of thinking about social exclusion: it became conceiveable to avoid 'degeneration' or even breed a super-race and to eliminate all persons who might not contribute to this or who might be detrimental to the process. What we get in this idea is a fatal combination of the personalizing and structuralizing modes of control into a legitimation for eliminating certain categories of persons. The new scientific criminology around 1900 was full of this type of thinking: a science of social exclusion. Criminology has from this beginning been a science of social exclusion and therefore connected to biologism, social Darwinism, racism, but with the rise of fascism in the 1930s it lost whatever weak ties it also had to a 'social problems'- or 'the social question'- (meaning: 'fear of the labour movement'-) approach. It has remained an at best technocratic field of knowledge, in which 'soft' and 'hard' technocrats still fight with changing gains and losses.

The functions of 'crime and punishment' in society are many and diverse, but among these one feature is obvious and cannot be disputed: punishment entails (graduated forms of) *social exclusion*. In the extremes of the death-penalty, transportation and exile it is total exclusion for ever or at least for a long time. The 'interior exile' of the prison and similar total institutions is similarly near-total exclusion, even if the person can be reached by visitors and counsel and even if it is temporary. Other punishments like bodily harm and pain (including hard labour to that effect) constitute at least temporary, if not permanent, exclusion due to honour lost, stigma and physical or psychic crippling. Fines can be seen as the mildest form of social exclusion: they take away (some of) the means of participation. Here we also have the most immediate and 'material' effects of punishment, while those we could identify on the lower levels tend to be immaterial and ideological.

Thus: Punishment *is* social exclusion.

Perhaps we can, for the time being, take this to be the societal function of punishment: to legitimate (partial and temporary) social exclusion. Next we have to turn this around and again ask what other forms of social exclusion we find. Again there are many forms of social exclusion and punishment is neither the most important nor the most frequent. But it has special and strategic importance: it incorporates and exemplifies the logic of social exclusion for a particularly legitimate case.

This logic is twofold: there is 'internalizing' social exclusion which produces a 'pariah population' which is useful in exactly this position, and there is 'externalizing' social exclusion of persons and populations that are 'redundant' and 'expendable'.

'Internalizing' social exclusion

In a capitalist social formation it is the 'alienation' of being typed according to commodity characteristics, the central commodity being labour-power, that forms the core dimension of 'social exclusion'. Capitalist development is a constant struggle for a supply of cheap and powerless labour on the one hand and coalitions to regulate competition for jobs on the other. Under conditions in which labour markets are being augmented by geographical widening and other measures to ensure the existence of a 'reserve army' the complicated coalitions of factions of labour and capital formed in attempts to regulate this labour market and positions in it have the consequence of excluding non-participants. The 'poor' and the 'redundant' fall out of all of these.[18] There has always been a 'shadow-economy' from and in which this part of the population has to live, part of which consists in providing cheap and otherwise unavailable labour and services (like drugs, prostitution, pornos, smuggling, but also cheap housework, bricklaying, electrical installations and other skilled jobs) for the 'legitimate' population. Some of this, conducted by small operators, is understood and treated as 'crime'.[19] The international organizers and supporters of this production and distribution of commodities and services are mostly members of 'legitimate' society, often from the very top of the economy and state, especially the state's armed and secret apparatuses.

It is poverty and the fact of being a recent immigrant (including internal migration) that easily positions people as having to offer their labour for 'dirty work' and at a sub-standard price. The important point is that the demand comes from the 'legitimate' part of society: clients, customers and employers can be found in all strata and positions. This is what 'organized crime' is about, which may be more or less ghettoized or integrated into the whole of the economy. It has been argued (Naylor 1996) that recently Western economies have increasingly blurred this distinction between legitimate and underground enterprise, not least helped by the enormous differences in living standards that have become exploitable in Europe.

Punishment helps just a little in recruiting people into this pariah sector of society and to reproduce it. But it is only auxiliary to ordinary poverty and lack of comparable legal opportunities. And it does not reach the customers, except 'black sheep' under exceptional conditions. The swelling discourse of 'organized crime' is interesting here in that it is about what constitutes 'legitimate business', what are opportunities that can be grasped by an 'honest businessman' and what are the limits to greed in a newly 'liberalized' economy. It is interesting that the representation of morality in the workplace, usually the domain of criminal law, is increasingly complemented by a discourse on morality in business enterprise. This points to a conflict between the state and the economy, that has just been unfettered by the state, over the spoils: will the gains all be privatized, or will some come back as taxes, or will it just be costs (in terms of unemployment and welfare expenditure) that will come back?

'Externalizing' social exclusion

The function of 'externalizing' social exclusion is routinely fulfilled by the institution of 'citizenship' and the legal as well as factual limits to immigration. It is also routinely fulfilled by differential living and working conditions: the poor not only pay more, they also die earlier.[20] It becomes conspicuous only when it is done by an (economic and political) administration. Punishment is the most explicit case of this.

From an administration and planning point of view people are useful or a problem through their number or through needed or problematic qualifications like 'labour power' or 'consumption power' or 'capacity to withhold needed contributions' (as in a strike), 'capacity to disrupt order' (as in riots), 'their status as voter', 'recruit', or their qualification for marriage, partnership or parenthood. Sometimes people are categorized as 'expendable', 'burdensome' or 'dangerous'. In a highly administered society many decisions depend on information about the distribution of these and similar characteristics and the assumed need for a certain amount of them (and accordingly number of their bearers). Thus, the categories according to which people are sorted and the depersonalized thinking about persons as 'bearers of a property' – indispensable pre-requisites for 'externalizing' social exclusion – are all there.

What is added by 'punishment' is the *legitimation* for the state and even the duty of the state to exclude the bearers of certain properties *for the common good*. Exclusion by 'crime and punishment' has the singular feature of being 'deserved' and therefore being morally justified. The pattern produced this way is a right to be here *on the condition* of proper conduct. Failure to meet this requirement makes the person liable to be excluded – by the proper authorities only, of course, but why not do the job for them if they are too slow or hindered by mere 'technicalities'?

'Externalizing' social exclusion by administrative means and on a numerically grand scale is never routine. It is always a political and social disaster of 'terror' or a 'terror regime'. Historical examples seem to show that it can only be upheld for any prolonged time when it is part of a war or can be coached in terms of 'war'. The 'enemy' and 'criminal' terms become interchangeable in war propaganda as well as law-and-order talk (Duster 1971; Keen 1986). This works both ways: routine social exclusion by 'crime and punishment' gains legitimacy by being declared to be a form of 'war' and the possibility of exceptional large-scale social exclusion is held alive by the model of 'deserved' social exclusion in punishment.

To make this connection between punishment and social exclusion more plausible without having to go into the detailed historical studies that this approach would call for, let me just mention two points:

- There is a lot of structural similarity between war propaganda and law-and-order talk.
- There is the undeniable fact that the instruments of punishment have also been applied in large-scale 'purges', even genocides.

Law-and-order talk does not often go to the same de-humanizing extremes as war-propaganda but it uses an analogous polarization into 'we' and 'them'. This has the required effect of forming a homogeneous whole to which 'we' belong. It is all the easier if a category for this does already exist – a national identification, a racial one like 'Aryan', or moral-political ones like 'honest worker' or 'solid citizen'. But it also works the other way around: a common enemy forms 'us' into a whole, even if there is nothing more in common.[21]

Law-and-order talk devalues and dehumanizes persons, not actions or structures, as does war propaganda. The enemy persons are dangerous and despicable 'by nature' (or by unchangeable cultural tradition). The definition of the 'enemy' as well as the 'criminal' has an affinity to 'natural' categories, as gender, age group or ethnic identification have under 'normal' circumstances. (Since we try to 'reform' criminals we have a new category: the 'persistent offender'.)

Law-and-order talk like war propaganda uses the patriarchal motive of 'protection of innocent children and women'. The 'enemy' as well as the 'criminal' are constructed as a threat to masculinity via children and women. The word 'innocent' that is routinely used in this context,[22] is quite an interesting indicator because it implies we would see things differently had these victims not been 'innocent', had they been 'guilty'. This, incidentally, is exactly the use to which this term was put in Antisemitism and by the Nazis: they were made 'guilty' and 'deserving' the treatment they got.

There is one element in war propaganda that has long been absent from the 'crime'-discourse: paranoia. War propaganda cannot be proved wrong: if the enemy cannot be seen that is just proof of how cunning they are. If a particular exemplar turns out to be fair and nice, he or she is an exception or is undermining our defences. War propaganda also knows of 'covert actions', 'subversives' and 'useful idiots' and wants us to be distrustful of everyone: evil is everywhere. To the author, it is just a little bit disquieting that very similar expressions of such thinking pop up again and again in law-and-order talk.

As to the second point we can just stay in the twentieth century to note the simple historical fact that the same instruments that were developed for state punishment – legal exclusion from citizen rights, confiscation of property, transportation, incarceration, forced labour, death penalty – were also used in outright and open social exclusion- and extermination-programmes in Nazi Germany and elsewhere. All this was done to categories of people who were defined in terms of race, 'incorrigibility' or (political or common) criminality (or more than one of these) – and the people so defined often met in the same concentration camps.

Fascinating fantasies – harsh realities

It seems we have to realize that in the institution of 'crime and punishment' the logic of 'deserved' administrative social exclusion is kept alive and so are the principal instruments that – under extraordinary conditions – can also be used in large-scale social exclusion programmes. There is also a strong connection between warfare / the military arm of the state's monopoly of force and punishment / the 'internalizing exclusion' arm of that monopoly.[23]

We can now comprehensively identify the functions 'crime and punishment' has in the mode of domination:

It legitimizes and executes social exclusion, it aspires to controlling morality, it is a specific form of regulating conflicts. But then, on all these levels, the contribution to actual social exclusion, social control and conflict management is minimal statistically compared to the basic mechanisms of the labour market, discipline and patriarchy in economic terms. These substantively effective social mechanisms go largely unnoticed in normal times, whereas the small and insignificant sector of 'crime and punishment' catches our attention and our fantasies, feeds a great part of the culture industry – and is in fact fascinating and satisfying for the consumer. Most 'crime and punishment' circulating in society does so as stories and action movies. Their genres can be correlated to our three levels again: there are stories of 'getting into trouble and out again'[24] at the interpersonal level, 'domination challenged and enforced' on the organizational level and 'belonging and dropping out' on the societal.

These fantasies are fascinating because they play on the basic motives of people acting in societies, not least on their masculinity / femininity, their rebellious as well as their authoritarian desires. Probably it is these 'harmless' fantasies by which the function of 'crime and punishment', which materially is not very important for the mode of domination, is kept intact and alive. What begins so harmlessly ends quite dangerously in keeping intact the logic and the instruments of social exclusion, which, under conditions that are not all that unlikely, are put to use in the historical disasters of large-scale social exclusion.

The expression 'crime and punishment' represents a significant coupling together of ideas, functions and institutions. This significance becomes frightening when we consider how easily they are mobilized toward warlike ends. In 'normal times', 'crime and punishment' may be largely ideologically constructed – but this remains ideology with human victims.

Notes

1 Enlarged manuscript of the lecture given in the opening session of the ESRC conference, Manchester, September, 1996. Thanks to Ian Taylor and Bill Chambliss for help with the revision.

   The paper is also a second part to my 1997 'Fin-de-siècle criminology' *Theoretical Criminology* 1(1): 111–129. As a third part I have since – in co-operation with Helga Cremer-Schäfer – developed further the approach presented here. The changing fates of state punishment and criminology (as the mostly all-too-willing ideological part of that apparatus) in this century can be described as integration and disintegration of two institutions: 'crime and punishment' and 'weakness and care'. This further paper will be published in *Kriminologisches Journal.*

2 Taking up Foucault's lead this means detailed regulation of co-ordinated actions and movements, invented and transported through the centuries in the monastery, later applied to other 'total institutions', including the factory settlement of early capitalism, eventually generalized to a self-monitored reliability in cycles of routines that does not need the corset of constant outside surveillance any more (Treiber and Steinert 1980; Steinert 1993).

3 The core of this is household production dominated by an older male who has to procreate, provide and protect, and for this uses and regulates the non-wage labour of the other household members. The positions, power relations and (self-)definitions so established certainly tranfers to other situations and have consequences for them.

4 Psychologically this has been constructed by Freud as 'brothers-horde', sociologically the 'commune', the 'subculture' as well as the 'interest group' are examples which have been widely studied (Schibel 1985). These are social organizations in which this type of solidarity becomes dominant, but it is also a *dimension* of other social forms.

5 Using materials of a contemporary and historical kind, mainly from everyday problem-solving I have myself done exercises of this kind in several research-projects and publications, among them Steinert (1979; 1985), Hanak *et al.* (1989).

6 Surprisingly the lead long ago provided by Garfinkel (1956) has not been followed up as it could have been. His description of public degradation can be generalized to the insight that the 'moral' reaction needs the successful scandalization of an event and a person, which again demands a relevant public (and the appointed state agency) to be pulled to one's side – which is an all-or-nothing, win-or-lose undertaking, and accordingly risky and time-consuming with doubtful pragmatic gains.

7 Charles Tilly (1990) has described European state-building as the outcome of warfare and the need to extort the means for that from the population. In his paper of 1985, based on the same material, he is even more explicit: he characterizes the state as

'organized crime' and 'protection racket'. For other not quite as comprehensive but more detailed recent studies see Bartlett (1994), Gay (1993). The Elias (1939) model of a 'process of civilization' does not seem to hold: 'dialectic of enlightenment' may be more appropriate. Interesting examples of a reformulation of what 'civilization' may mean in the light of the experience of the twentieth century are Breuer (1994) and Reemtsma (1994). My own reformulation is derived from military history: what Elias (mis)understands as a process of 'civilization of violence' was the simple shift from societies dominated by warriors and thus upper-class violence to societies in which the lower classes were made to do the dirty work of violence.

8 This position was developed in critical debates about Rusche and Kirchheimer (1938) and Foucault (1975). See Steinert (1981b, 1983, 1986, 1991), Steinert and Treiber (1978), Treiber and Steinert (1980), including further references.

9 For the distinction between reactive and pro-active social control see Hess (1983).

10 See Abel 1991; Schumann *et al.* 1987; Schumann 1989 amongst others. The assumption that under 'normal' conditions the number of people processed is not big enough to be of material consequence is just one, although an important, part of the argument. This has to be modified: the present development of criminal policy in the United States seems to suggest that it is possible to process enormous numbers through the apparatuses of punishment even under a fairly democratic regime. If this attack of control is sufficiently concentrated on a particular population, such as Afro-American young males, it will have some very real impact on this sub-culture. Cf. Christie (1993), Donziger (1996).

11 Althusser's (1970) concept with its distinction of a '(repressive) state apparatus' (government, administration, army, police, justice, punishment, etc.) and many 'ideological state apparatuses' is used here with the understanding that 'repression' and 'ideology' are two aspects of *any* institution, that some seemingly repressive apparatuses are in fact ideological – and that these two aspects cannot be easily separated anyway.

12 This is certainly not new, but goes from fairy tales through high literature to today's TV-series – and here in unprecedented numbers. See for instance Armstrong and Tennenhouse (1989), Lüderssen and Seibert (1978), Müller-Dietz (1990), Schönert (1983; 1991), Steinert (1978).

13 This 'other' is, of course, not a slip of the pen (or the keystroke), but acknowledges that these emotions are deeply patriarchal – which does not at all preclude that they are often shared by female or subordinate male members within this mode of domination.

14 For a detailed analysis of this position and the patriarchal mode of domination using the example of Clint Eastwood's five 'Dirty Harry'-movies see Steinert (1996). The 'classical' patriarchal genre in film, of course, is the Western with its central theme of community building by mutual acknowledgement of patriarchal (small) property-owners. As long as the genre was intact (as in 'Shane') they were the heroes, not the sheriff nor the lone rider, who were only instrumental in helping to put things right in the community, but then had to go. It is only in its late and critical forms, particularly in its European ('Spaghetti') variant, that the Western lost that motive of community building and put the lone rider into the foreground.

15 I have taken Barrington Moore's (1978) concept of an 'implicit social contract' and adapted it to describe changing requirements for labour qualifications in phases of the capitalist development with different 'strategies of capital reproduction'. See Steinert (1981a; 1984), Cremer-Schäfer and Steinert (1986).

16 For strong arguments to the contrary see Box (1983); Chambliss (1978).

17 This is not only true for the damages incurred through the 'peaceful operation' of hazardous production, but even for the classical field of 'steet crime' where efficient 'prevention' has to set in long before any questions of punishment arise and where the latter often is a cheap way out of doing what could be effective. See Steinert (1992, 1995a, b).

18 Jordan (1996) has constructed an interesting and sophisticated politico-economic theory of social exclusion from assumptions about the formation and effects of such 'clubs'.

19 Another advantage is that these people without social bonds and connections can be used for purposes of domination, partly for the 'dirty work' necessary, but also for positions that have to be 'trusted' (Coser 1974).

20 See Caplovitz (1963) on the first point, Wilkinson (1996) as a summary of findings as well as presentation of original comparative material on the second.

21 National stereotypes seem to be very dependent on images formed in wars and in war propaganda, even decades after the former enemies have become allies. One example is the Western image of Japan as analysed by Littlewood (1996) from literary and popular culture sources. It is quite obvious that the national stereotype of Germany is still heavily loaded by the Nazi past. Interestingly (and counter-factually) Austria has long managed to keep out of that shadow.

22 A recent example that I happened to come across is provided by the historian Hans Mommsen (1996) who, in the first paragraph of his essay, speaks of 'the systematic liquidation of millions of innocent human beings, primarily Jews' (my translation).

23 This, by the way, leads to the interesting conclusion that the third variety of the state monopoly of force – the police with its task of internal peace-keeping and disarmament – is actually the most 'civilized' of the three. It is not out to inflict pain like punishment and not aimed at the unregulated killing and destruction of warfare.

24 This is one of the descriptions of what classical Hollywood drama was about as well as the basic dimension of everyday stories about 'crime' and other troubles.

References

Abel, Richard L. (1991) 'The failure of punishment as social control', *Israel Law Review* 25 (3–4): 740–52.

Althusser, Louis (1970) 'Idéologie et appareils idéologiques d'Etat (Notes pour une recherche)', *La Pensée* no. 151; quoted from the German translation in: Althusser (1977) *Ideologie und ideologische Staatsapparate*: 108–53. Hamburg: VSA.

Armstrong, Nancy and Leonard Tennenhouse (1989) (eds) *The Violence of Representation: Literature and the History of Violence*. London: Routledge.

Bartlett, Robert (1994) *The Making of Europe: Conquest, Colonization and Cultural Change 950–1350*. Princeton: University Press.

Box, Steven (1983) *Power, Crime, and Mystification*. London: Tavistock.

Breuer, Stefan (1994) 'Erinnerungen an die Zivilisation', *Mittelweg 36* 3(6): 14–25.

Caplovitz, David (1963) *The Poor Pay More: Consumer Practices of Low-Income Families*. New York: Free Press.

Chambliss, William J. (1978) *On the Take: From Petty Crooks to Presidents*. Bloomington: Indiana University Press.

Christie, Nils (1977) 'Conflicts as property', *British Journal of Criminology* 17: 1–15.

Christie, Nils (1993) *Crime Control as Industry: Towards GULAGs, Western Style?* London: Routledge.

Connell, Robert W. (1987) *Gender and Power: Society, the Person and Sexual Politics.* Cambridge: Polity Press.

Coser, Lewis A. (1974) *Greedy Institutions: Patterns of Undivided Commitment.* New York: Free Press.

Cremer-Schäfer, Helga (1995) 'Einsortieren und Aussortieren: Zur Funktion der Strafe bei der Verwaltung der sozialen Ausschließung', *Kriminologisches Journal* 27: 89–119.

Cremer-Schäfer, Helga and Heinz Steinert (1986) 'Sozialstruktur und Kontrollpolitik: Einiges von dem, was wir glauben, seit Rusche und Kirchheimer dazugelernt zu haben', *Kriminologisches Journal* Beiheft 1 (Kritische Kriminologie heute): 77–118.

Donziger, Steven R. (1996) (ed.) *The Real War on Crime: The Report of the National Criminal Justice Commission.* New York: Harper.

Duster, Troy (1971) 'Conditions for guilt-free massacre', in Sanford N. Comstock *et al.* (eds) *Sanctions for Evil*: 25–36. San Francisco: Jossey-Bass.

Elias, Norbert (1939) *Über den Prozeß der Zivilisation: Soziogenetische und psychogenetische Untersuchungen.* Basel: Haus zum Falken. 2. Aufl. (1969) Frankfurt: Suhrkamp.

Foucault, Michel (1975) *Surveiller et punir: Naissance de la prison.* Paris: Gallimard.

Funk, Albrecht (1995) 'Ausgeschlossene und Bürger: Das ambivalente Verhältnis von Rechtsgleichheit und sozialem Ausschluß', *Kriminologisches Journal* 27: 243–56.

Garfinkel, Harold (1956) 'Conditions of successful degradation ceremonies', *American Journal of Sociology* 61: 420–24.

Gay, Peter (1993) *The Cultivation of Hatred.* New York: Norton.

Hanak, Gerhard, Johannes Stehr und Heinz Steinert (1989) *Ärgernisse und Lebenskatastrophen: Über den alltäglichen Umgang mit Kriminalität.* Bielefeld: AJZ-Verlag.

Hess, Henner (1983) 'Probleme der sozialen Kontrolle', in: H.-J. Kerner *et al.* (eds.) *Kriminologie – Psychiatrie – Strafrecht: Festschrift für Heinz Leferenz zum 70. Geburtstag.* pp. 3–24. Heidelberg: C.F.Müller.

Jordan, Bill (1996) *A Theory of Poverty and Social Exclusion.* Cambridge: Polity Press.

Katz, Jack (1987) 'What makes crime "news"?', *Media, Culture and Society* 9: 47–75.

Keen, Sam (1986) *Faces of the Enemy: Reflections of the Hostile Imagination.* San Francisco: Harper & Row.

Littlewood, Ian (1996) *The Idea of Japan: Western Images, Western Myths.* London: Secker & Warburg.

Lüderssen, Klaus and Thomas-Michael Seibert (1978) (ed.) *Autor und Täter.* Frankfurt: Suhrkamp.

Mommsen, Hans (1996) 'Die dünne Patina der Zivilisation', *Die Zeit* no. 36, Aug. 30: 14–15.

Moore, Barrington Jr. (1978) *Injustice: The Social Bases of Obedience and Revolt.* White Plains: Sharpe.

Müller-Dietz, Heinz (1990) *Grenzüberschreitungen: Beiträge zur Beziehung zwischen Literatur und Recht.* Baden-Baden: Nomos.

Naylor, R. T. (1996) 'From underworld to underground: Enterprise crime, "informal sector" business and the public policy response', *Crime, Law & Social Change* 24: 79–150.

Reemtsma, Jan Philipp (1994) 'Die Wiederkehr der Hobbesschen Frage. Dialektik der Zivilisation', *Mittelweg 36* 3(6): 47–56.

Rusche, Georg (1933) 'Arbeitsmarkt und Strafvollzug: Gedanken zur Soziologie der

Strafjustiz', *Zeitschrift für Sozialforschung* 2: 63–78. Quoted from the reprint in Rusche and Kirchheimer (1981): 298–313.

Rusche, Georg and Otto Kirchheimer (1938) *Punishment and Social Structure*. New York: Columbia University Press.

Rusche, Georg and Otto Kirchheimer (1981) *Sozialstruktur und Strafvollzug*. (Neuauflage) Frankfurt: Europäische Verlagsanstalt.

Sack, Fritz (1993) 'Strafrechtliche Kontrolle und Sozialdisziplinierung', in Frehsee *et al.* 1993: Strafrecht, soziale kontrolle, soziale disziplinierung. Jahrbuch für rechtssoziologie und rechtstheorie *XV*: 16–45. O pladen: Westdeutscher Verlag.

Sasson, Theodore (1995) *Crime Talk: How Citizens Construct a Social Problem*. New York: Aldine.

Scheerer, Sebastian (1995) 'Kleine Verteidigung der sozialen Kontrolle', *Kriminologisches Journal* 27: 120–33.

Schibel, Karl-Ludwig (1985) *Das alte Recht auf die neue Gesellschaft: Zur Sozialgeschichte der Kommune seit dem Mittelalter*. Frankfurt: Sendler.

Schönert, Jörg (1983) (ed.) *Literatur und Kriminalität: Die gesellschaftliche Erfahrung von Verbrechen und Strafverfolgung als Gegenstand des Erzählens*. Tübingen: Niemeyer.

Schönert, Jörg (1991) (ed.) *Erzählte Kriminalität: Zur Typologie und Funktion von narrativen Darstellungen in Strafrechtspflege, Publizistik und Literatur zwischen 1770 und 1920*. Tübingen: Niemeyer.

Schumann, Karl F. (1989), *Positive Generalprävention. Ergebnisse und Chancen der Forschung*, Heidelberg (C. F. Müller)

Schumann, Karl F., Claus Berlitz, Hans-Werner Guth and Reiner Kaulitzki (1987), *Jugendkriminalität und die Grenzen der Generalprävention*, Neuwied (Luchterhand)

Stangl, Wolfgang (1996) ' "Wien – Sichere Stadt": Ein bewohnerzentriertes Präventionsprojekt', *Kriminologisches Journal* 28: 48–68.

Stehr, Johannes (1994) 'Soziale Ausschließung als Abwehr von Herrschaft', *Kriminologisches Journal* 26: 273–95.

Stehr, Johannes (1996) *Sagenhafte Kriminalität: Über die private Aneignung von herrschender Moral*. Frankfurt: Ph.D. dissertation, FB 03, J. W. Goethe-Universität.

Steinert, Heinz (1978) 'Phantasiekriminalität und Alltagskriminalität', *Kriminologisches Journal* 10: 215–223.

Steinert, Heinz (1979) 'Etikettierung im Alltag', in: Annelise Heigl-Evers (ed.) *Lewin und die Folgen*. Die Psychologie des 20. Jahrhunderts Bd. VIII. pp. 388–404. Zürich: Kindler.

Steinert, Heinz (1981a) 'Widersprüche, Kapitalstrategien und Widerstand oder: Warum ich den Begriff "Soziale Probleme" nicht mehr hören kann. Versuch eines theoretischen Rahmens für die Analyse der politischen Ökonomie sozialer Bewegungen und "sozialer Probleme" ', *Kriminalsoziologische Bibliografie* 8(32/33): 56–88.

Steinert, Heinz (1981b) 'Dringliche Aufforderung, an der Studie von Rusche und Kirchheimer weiterzuarbeiten', Nachwort in Rusche and Kirchheimer (1981): 314–41.

Steinert, Heinz (1983) 'The development of "discipline" according to Michel Foucault: Discourse analysis vs. social history', *Crime and Social Justice* no. 20: 83–98.

Steinert, Heinz (1984) 'Morale del lavoro e indignazione morale: storia del controllo sociale, ovvero storia di strategie del capitale', *Dei Delitti E Delle Pene* 2(2): 213–40.

Steinert, Heinz (1985) 'Zur Aktualität der Etikettierungstheorie', *Kriminologisches Journal* 17: 29–43.

Steinert, Heinz (1986) 'Beyond crime and punishment', *Contemporary Crises* 10: 21–38.

Steinert, Heinz (1991) ' "Is there justice? No – just us!" "Justice" as an attempt to control domination and the problem of state-organized pain infliction', *Israel Law Review* 25(3–4): 710–28.

Steinert, Heinz (1992) 'Techno-prevention and conflict management versus moral-authoritarian control in criminal policy', in: Hans-Uwe Otto und Gaby Flösser (eds) *How to Organize Prevention: Political, Organizational, and Professional Challenges to Social Services*: 401–5. Berlin: de Gruyter.

Steinert, Heinz (1993) 'Die Widersprüche von Disziplin und Strafe', in: Frehsee et al. 1993: 238–56.

Steinert, Heinz (1995a) 'Prävention als kommunale Aufgabe: Jenseits von Polizei und Strafrecht', in: Rolf Gössner (ed.) *Mythos Sicherheit: Der hilflose Schrei nach dem starken Staat*: 403–14. Baden-Baden: Nomos.

Steinert, Heinz (1995b) 'The idea of prevention and the critique of instrumental reason', in: Günter Albrecht und Wolfgang Ludwig-Mayerhofer (eds) *Diversion and Informal Social Control*: 5–16. Berlin: de Gruyter.

Steinert, Heinz (1996) 'Schwache Patriarchen – gewalttätige Krieger: Über Männlichkeit und ihre Probleme zwischen Warenförmigkeit, Disziplin, Patriarchat und Brüderhorde: Zugleich eine Analyse von "Dirty Harry" und anderen Clint Eastwood Filmen', in: Joachim Kersten und Heinz Steinert (eds) *Starke Typen: Iron Mike, Dirty Harry, Crocodile Dundee und der Alltag von Männlichkeit. Jahrbuch für Rechts- und Kriminalsoziologie 1996*: 121–57. Baden-Baden: Nomos.

Steinert, Heinz, and Hubert Treiber (1978) 'Versuch, die These von der strafrechtlichen Ausrottungspolitik im Spätmittelalter "auszurotten": Eine Kritik an Rusche / Kirchheimer und dem Ökonomismus in der Theorie der Strafrechtsentwicklung', *Kriminologisches Journal* 10: 81–106.

Tilly, Charles (1985) 'War making and state making as organized crime', in: Peter B. Evans, Dietrich Rueschemeyer and Theda Skocpol (eds) *Bringing the State Back In*: 69–91. Cambridge: University Press.

Tilly, Charles (1990) *Coercion, Capital, and European States AD 990–1992*. Oxford: Blackwell.

Treiber, Hubert and Heinz Steinert (1980) *Die Fabrikation des zuverlässigen Menschen: Über die "Wahlverwandtschaft" von Kloster- und Fabriksdisziplin*. München: Heinz Moos Verlag.

Wilkinson, Richard G. (1996) *Unhealthy Societies*. London: Routledge.

Wachs, Eleanor (1988) *Crime Victim Stories*. Bloomington: Indiana University Press.

26

THE DELINQUENT AS A FADING CATEGORY OF KNOWLEDGE

Sebastian Scheerer

I Introduction

To the extent to which common sense perceives the social world as perfectly natural, it also takes the category of the delinquent (and the mentally ill, the patient, etc.) for granted. This "natural appearance" even extends to the institutions of confinement which are seen as the logical reaction to the existence of criminals, the mentally insane, etc. If Karl Marx's statement about the criminal who himself "produces the whole police and criminal justice, the catchpoles, judges, hangmen, jurors etc."[1] still had an ironic undertone (which nonetheless has all too often been overlooked by Marxist scholars), common sense would never hesitate to see the *raison d'être* of the prison as the "existence" of criminals. But it may be that the days of the criminal as a category of knowledge are counted. We are approaching a period in which it will make ever less sense to conceptualize a person as "delinquent" or "criminal." Sooner or later, and I think it might rather be sooner, even common sense will have to adapt to the fact that the dominant control forms are already starting to operate beyond and without both the habitual concept of the delinquent and the traditional institutions of confinement.[2]

In other words: the sub-universe of delinquency (as well as that of mental illness) has become so deeply entrenched in our sense of reality that we tend to treat "delinquency" and "mental illness" as parameters rather than products of our minds; while they are historical, we treat them as if they were anthropological; and while they are subject to social change, we treat them as if they were not. But times are a-changing, and there is a growing gap between our everyday conceptualization of the world and the changes that are happening within it.

II History

For the purposes of a short sketch, we can distinguish some distinct stages in the period from the sixteenth to the nineteenth century in the making of the category of "delinquent" as well as some recent stages which are currently leading to their dissolution. Examples given could refer to any part of Europe, but for practical purposes I will draw my historical illustrations from the German territories.

The first stage: pre-categorical internments (sixteenth – mid-eighteenth century)

Leper houses were the main segregating institutions of the Middle Ages. They obviously housed victims of leprosy or *Hanseniasis*, but as a metaphor at the level of popular anxieties they were seen as housing the incarnation of evil or the types of people who made rituals of purification a deeply felt necessity.

But leprosy disappeared rather suddenly, and the leper houses remained as empty vessels of fear, to be filled with whoever would inherit the stigma.

Foucault has demonstrated how, after the scourge of the Middle Ages had vanished, governments suddenly started to institutionalize more people than ever before (something like one in every hundred). And he showed how the leper houses were first used to house the syphilitic, but how in the end the leper stigma (and the right, or rather the obligation, to inhabit their institutions) was passed to the *mad*. In and around Hamburg the leper houses were turned into general hospitals as early as 1540; in some other countries even earlier, in France mostly later. At any rate it was the category of *madness* that inherited the central role as a threat to the self-image of society from the now departed scourge of leper. But it was to take centuries for madness to find its most mature, differentiated and systematically closed conceptual form.[3]

By the mid-eighteenth century, the Swedish scientist Carl Linnaeus invented his binary nomenclature for plants. The "Philosophia botanica" appeared in 1751. This was also the year, incidentally, when the first insane asylum was inaugurated in London. Those years witnessed the first climax of classification. Popular interest was almost getting out of hand. When Linnaeus published a complete list of all known animals, plants and minerals in 1766, his publisher had to release twelve "prints" within two years.

It seemed as if only the classification of the human animals was lagging a little behind, but if this was the case, then the situation was soon to be remedied. A century later, the diverse types of humans and their relation to power, morality and citizenship had been catalogued, mapped and internalized as self-concepts of Western societies. By the end of the nineteenth century, the universe of everyday knowledge allowed the framing of all situations and interactions with regard to their location on the general social map, the center of which was inhabited by responsible and law-abiding normal citizens, while the margins were distressed by groups of outsiders who were either unable to interact on the basis of equality (the mentally ill) or unworthy of such interaction (the criminals).

The second stage: categorical claims (1791–1826)

By the end of the seventeenth century, a look at the results of the Great Internment showed an unassorted mass of simple whores and debtors lumped together
with the most abominable murderers; men were locked away with women, old
people together with children, the sick with the healthy, and beggars and
vagabonds together with the lunatics. Outraged reformers like John Howard
in England (1777) and Balthasar Wagnitz in Germany (1791) revealed that the
classification of human individuals had come to a point where it wanted to
make itself manifest in the creation of institutions which corresponded to this
new way of perception.[4]

In the case of the prison, this process of typifying the prisoners and sealing the
institution off against the outside was duplicated by the rise of the solitary system. Indeed the rise and fall of this system can be used to determine the more
general course of development of prisons. Sealing off the prison from other
institutions – and sealing off each individual prisoner from all others – is the most
dramatic institutional expression of the era of the supposedly ontologically justified differentiations between (born) delinquents and (born) regular citizens. The
more impenetrable the walls of both prisons and insane asylums, the more
impenetrable became also the cognitive categories and their typifications and
reifications.[5]

At least by this standard, the categories of knowledge that concerned "delinquents" and "mentally ill" were on the rise through most of the nineteenth century, experienced a late (second) culmination during the Nazi era, and then went
into a fast decline. Today, it seems, we are experiencing a change of principle that
leads from internment to dissipated and generalized surveillance.

In Germany, the years between 1791 and 1826 see the growth of conscious
awareness of problems with the system of incarceration. An acute uneasiness
about prison and hospital conditions reigned. In 1803, the Prussian Minister of
Justice Albrecht Hermann von Arnim proposed a "progressive" system that
would start out with strict isolation, but lead to successive liberalizations during
the length of the prisoner's stay; in 1804, the Prussian government published a
reform plan for both criminal procedure and the prison system. This *Generalplan
zur allgemeinen Einführung einer besseren Kriminal-Gerichts-Verfassung und zur Verbesserung
der Gefängnis- und Strafanstalten* (General plan for the introduction of an improved
constitution for the criminal courts and for the improvement of prisons and
penitentiaries) was essentially a reformulation of von Arnim's memorandum.
But before it could be implemented, the Holy Roman Empire ceased to exist in
1806, and prison reform in Germany came to a standstill.[6]

The third stage: the rise of the solitary ideal (1827–45)

An energetic step towards the perfection of the prison as an instrument of
categorical isolation was initiated by Nikolaus Heinrich Julius (1783–1862), a

medical doctor from Hamburg with a keen interest in languages and social reform. In twelve public lectures on prisons (1827), Julius acquainted his listeners with John Howard in England and the philanthropic activities of the Quaker community in Pennsylvania. He also published the influential yearbooks on penitentiaries, translated Beaumont and Tocqueville's report on the American correctional system, and traveled extensively.[7] Luckily for him, one of the most enthusiastic students listening to his prison lectures had been the Prussian crown prince himself who, as King Friedrich Wilhelm IV (1840–61), was to make the introduction of solitary confinement in Prussia a political priority. When, for instance, the new Pentonville prison in England was inaugurated in 1842, both Julius and his King went there to study the model. In the very same year the state of Hesse adopted a new penal code that had been written by true believers in solitary confinement, stimulating Prussia to begin similar constructions in 1844. In 1845, the government of Baden decided to build a copy of the Pentonville prison at the town of Bruchsal and passed the first German law that formally introduced solitary confinement as the regular prison regime. The same year the Prussian King declared that the house rules of the prison at Rawicz were to go into effect for all Prussian prisons. As it happened the house rules of this prison (dating from 1835), were modeled after the "silent system" that had been operating in New York's Auburn prison since 1823, and prohibited any communication among inmates. In terms of isolation, they were as close to the solitary system as could be, given the non-existence of appropriate single cells. Planned by the King as a provisional step only, the *Rawiczer Regiment*[8] was to remain in effect until 1902.

The fourth stage: ideological domination (1846–68)

From 1846 onwards, one can speak of an undeniable ideological domination of the solitary system in Germany. This domination preceded its implementation in terms of laws, buildings, and prison regimes. In September of that year, the city of Frankfurt hosted the First International Prison Conference. The conference organizer was the medical doctor Georg Varrentrapp who, much like Julius, had traveled England, France, and Switzerland, and had been convinced of the advantages of the solitary system. The resolutions passed were a triumphant victory for the Pennsylvanian system. The rise of the solitary ideal was also reflected by the treatment of the correctional system in three subsequent editions of the *Staatslexikon*. While the first edition (1835) was hostile to it, the second (1846) added an article that can best be described as a hymn in praise of the solitary system, and the third (1858) defended it exclusively by leaving out the original article of 1835. In 1848, the Bruchsal prison was inaugurated. A year later, Moabit opened, with similar constructions following at Münster, Breslau, and Ratibor.

Still unsatisfied with the slow progress of his solitary confinement policy, the King appointed a staunchly conservative "child saver" and zealous supporter of the principles of solitary confinement, as his counsel in prison matters (1857).

Johann Hinrich Wichern (1808–1881), founder of a large Hamburg orphanage (*Das Rauhe Haus;* The Rough House), persuaded the King to introduce solitary confinement by decree instead of waiting for the *Diet* to vote the respective legislation.

This disrespect angered the Liberal Party, and from 1858 onwards, the relationship between the King and the *Abgeordnetenhaus* deteriorated noticeably, thus leading to a deep and bitter constitutional conflict between the Crown and Parliament as a result of which the introduction of solitary confinement came to a halt. The effect was that until 1869 there were no more than two prisons practicing solitary confinement as their regular regime.

By the time that a compromise put an end to the conflict between the King and the legislature in 1869, time had already passed over the solitary ideal. While it is true that, from 1880 onwards, practically all construction work in terms of prison buildings was undertaken with the one and only goal to supply more facilities for solitary confinement, intellectual support for this kind of punishment was waning. Experts in penology had begun to defect from the solitary ideal for some years, and ever more practitioners were leaning towards the social ideal of the Irish or "progressive" system. The solitary ideal still was the official government position, but every success of official politics only deepened the gap. The appointment of Karl Krohne as head of the Prussian prison department in 1894 was such a Pyrrhic victory. During his tenure, the single cell rate showed a steep increase and turned the Quakers' ideal into a bitter reality for a sizeable part of the prison population in the years before World War I. But by that time official prison politics had already lost touch with a different, mostly intellectual, but nevertheless strongly emerging reality.[9]

While it is generally assumed that the institutions as a whole only entered their phase of crisis and decline following World War II, our microscopic *pars pro toto* approach shows a different picture, in which the post-war crisis is only a continuation of a process that began during the late nineteenth century.

The first phase of decline: 1870–1945

Paradoxically, the guiding principles of and the philosophy behind the solitary system had already become obsolete at the peak of their realization. Solitary confinement started to look displaced amidst the processes of bureaucratization, rationalization, and massification that now characterized European societies.

The correctional ideal was not seen in the sinners' individual repentance, but in progressive social rehabilitation. The solitary ideal was giving way to the rehabilitative ideal.

While politicians were only starting to implement the system, the competing ideologies were gaining strength by the year. In the 1880s the government's policy, while now being implemented at increased speed, was rapidly losing the support of criminologists and penologists. One of the most influential advocates of the "progressive" system and the rehabilitative ideal was the founder of the *modern school* of penal theory, Franz von Liszt (1859–1919). With the enthusiastic reception of his *Marburger Programm* (1882) the defenders of the solitary ideal suddenly appeared to belong to a *Weltanschauung* of the distant past.[10]

From 1882 onwards, the solitary ideal was in visible decline. Its successor was to become the slowly emerging rehabilitative ideal. Seen in its light, of course, all newly built solitary prisons looked very old from the start. One of Liszt's pupils, Eberhard Schmidt, later was to denounce their anachronistic character by referring to them as petrified giant errors *(steingewordene Riesenirrtümer)*.[11]

Following World War I, the Quakers' principles of solitary confinement already looked like a thing from the distant past. Nazi Germany did not even consider returning to solitary confinement. Its concern was not the individual, but the management of masses, including the concentration and annihilation of segments of the population.[12]

The second phase of decline: 1946–77

After World War II, the use of solitary confinement declined drastically, in terms both of the absolute numbers so interned and the relative importance of this prison strategy. Imprisonment was increasingly modified, as well as justified, by psychotherapeutic and socially rehabilitative methods and goals. Solitary confinement was seen as counterproductive to these ends. The law of 1977 *(Strafvollzugsgesetz)* therefore introduced the most restrictive conditions for its use. From now on it could only be imposed when it was indispensable *("unerläßlich")*. If any prisoner was subjected to solitary confinement for (altogether) more than three months his case had to be reported to the state minister of justice. Prisons contracted psychologists, and for some time during the 1960s and 1970s, delinquents came to be seen as patients rather than criminals. More and more prisoners were being held in small collective living units *(Wohngruppenvollzug)* where they were subjected to all kinds of well-meaning psychological counseling, and something like a benevolent surveillance from the part of social workers, teachers and other professionals. There were serious efforts to transform prisons into therapeutic institutions *(sozialtherapeutische Anstalten)*. But public opinion remained skeptical, and the effectiveness of intramural treatment questionable.[13]

The third phase of decline: 1978–96

During the 1980s the decline of the rehabilitative ideal became impossible to ignore. Plans for *sozialtherapeutische Anstalten* were silently scrapped, and no effort was made to justify the boom in prison constructions with reference to a psychotherapeutical frame of reference. Disillusionment with any kind of intramural therapy of offenders – be it drug-related or crime-related – spread. The prison became increasingly seen as a simple instrument for selective incapacitation. A typical case in point was the strict solitary confinement imposed on members of the social-revolutionary Red Army Faction *(Rote Armee Fraktion, RAF)* during the early 1970s. But in the end "incapacitation," however selective, appears to be quite a thin layer of legitimation for an institution that once used to be able to mobilize much stronger moral arguments in its favor.[14]

Intramural segregation of the individual prisoner, once a venerated ideal, was now regarded an undesirable, albeit sometimes "indispensable" measure for security reasons, and while the future of confinement might be unclear, solitary confinement is likely to become ever more marginalized in the system of social control. As a matter of fact, today's era is characterized by a transition from the age of confinement (and discipline) into one of mere registration (and control by the management of desires).[15]

III Tendencies

Today, while some predict an uncontrollable growth of the prison system, others are observing a loss of functions that could soon lead to the abandonment of the institution as such, with its control functions taken over by electronic monitoring and other (post-)modern devices.

The following part of the chapter will sketch the general tendencies of social control and relate them to the modifications in the external prison system and internal prison regime.

The first tendency: socialization and the birth of the "dividual"

While the medieval person used to live with a low level of self-constraints and impulse controls, the fabrication of modern individuals at least since the sixteenth century has been marked by a steady increase in internalization and psychic integration of the originally divergent personality components.[16] The rise of the categories/institutions of both madness and crime accompanied this rise of the rational standard individual, who was imagined and positioned in simple hierarchical structures, from family via military to the firm, and whose life, opinions and styles reached a maximum of homogeneity and social discipline in the nineteenth century.

A reverse tendency was discovered by research in socialization since World War II. The emerging personality type is steered in his actions less by internalized norms and values than by the demands of the respective situations, interaction partners, and group commitments. The dominance of situational expectations and role requirements over conscience and convictions led David Riesman to speak of a "marketing character" ("outer-directed man"); others defined the new personality type of post-modern times as being "narcissistic."[17] This is a dramatic change that implies a whole array of highly ambivalent phenomena including, for example, the relation between adults and young persons – a battlefield of interests and morality that among other things might explain much of the present-day concerns over pedophilia.[18] However this may be, the common denominator of all the reviewed theory and research concerning personality-type changes seems to be the tendency of the person to experience a fracturing of their "single" identity and the increasing independence of their multiple roles from each other. As a result, her or his ability to construct and maintain a coherent self is seriously impaired. The once indivisible individual is slowly transforming itself into what French philosopher Gilles Deleuze called the forthcoming "dividual," i.e. a multiplicity of persons according to situational expectations and requirements.[19]

The second tendency: commodification as a medium of control

The new extroverted personality is subjected to a completely new kind of social control. After the decay of the medieval catholic church as a hegemonic force of social control, its functions are now being fulfilled by an intricate system of material and immaterial wants and what one may call "the politics of desires."

The new system is deeply rooted in both the capitalist production sphere as well as in a concomitant "consumerist ethos," an ethos which is itself closely, albeit contradictorily, related to the unbroken tendency towards ever more rationalization, routinization, and disenchantment with the world.[20]

Commodification itself requires the continual creation of new products and new markets, thus contributing to the desensitization of the individual and to the need for ever more stimulating experiences to produce excitement. And the more the capitalist system stresses cost-benefit rationality, purposive labor, etc., the stronger becomes the consumption ethic as its complementary component.

To attain self-realization and meaning in life, one must buy certain commodities that represent this meaning, for example security (life-insurance, home), experience of the inner self (courses in meditation, preferably in Tuscany), existential self-experience (free-climbing, bungee-jumping), complete relaxation (long and expensive vacations in the sun), etc. A prerequisite of all is, of course, conformity with the work ethic, but the harder one works the more one needs to compensate everyday alienation in leisure time. It was Herbert Marcuse who has provided us with the most profound analysis of this process, his main thesis being that Western societies are able to satisfy the basic needs and are at the same time solid enough to tolerate quite a lot of variations in behavior, thus producing a sense of freedom which, in a deeper sense, actually results in a submission to ever more processes of domination and manipulation. Post-modern societies evidently make especially great use of techniques that are able to neutralize potential revolt through what he called "repressive tolerance," that is, the harmless and sometimes only illusory satisfaction of real or artificially induced needs that pacify the working class and rob them of their revolutionary fervor.[21]

The third tendency: the commodification of security

Privatization is one of the common denominators of today's laboratories for the future of social systems, and hence one of the traits most likely to continue to shape them. But privatization has many faces and means many things. While it is an attractive idea for all those who see the state as the source of all evil, it may also represent uncontrolled vigilantism and infringements on civil rights. More than anything else, it is likely to lead to an ever more unequal distribution of security, because privatization is also a very euphemistic term for what would be more correctly termed "commodification" and "commercialization" of security. Its growth corresponds to significant changes in property ownership. In North America, for instance, many public activities which used to take place in public community-owned spaces, now take place within huge privately owned facilities, the so-called "mass private property," such as shopping centers with hundreds of individual retail establishments, enormous residential estates with hundreds, if not thousands, of housing units, equally large office, recreational, industrial, and manufacturing complexes, and university campuses.[22] The considerable demand for both services and goods from the security industry has already led to a reversal in the ratio of public and private police personnel in the United States (with private personnel outnumbering the public service by almost three to one, and where four to one is a current forecast for the year 2000). In the US, the private security industry's turnover was estimated at around 50 billion dollars in 1990, and in Germany, estimates rose from less than 11 billion Deutschmarks in 1990 to more than 14 billion in 1994.[23]

The fourth tendency: from control of individuals to control of situations

Foucault's disciplinary society still wanted the reliable individual, but Deleuze's control society wants to prevent (or monitor or analyze) situations. The individual as such is not interesting anymore – the idea of catching it, putting it in a cage and submitting it to psychological techniques in order to improve its character seems increasingly ridiculous. While treatment is *out*, surveillance, observation, registration of voices as well as the documentation of (real and genetic) finger-prints – and the creation of security/conformity standards (workplace drug test-ing, video registration, electronic admission systems) are *in*. Some sociologists even believe they can detect a tendency towards a shift from normative to cogni-tive control techniques – a belief that find some support in the trend towards *actuarial justice*.[24]

The fifth tendency: from overt, concentrated and reactive to covert, dissipated and proactive control

Nineteenth-century law enforcement reacted to a breach of law by individuals on whom it concentrated its efforts. Post-modern law-enforcement tendencies are rapidly moving in the opposite direction. Electronic surveillance is covert just like the use of informers and undercover agents. Instead of concentrating on single offenders, agencies of social control focus on structures and movements. The most popular pastime of police hierarchies is piling up data for possible future use in law-enforcement activities.

Beyond this, the increased emphasis on the architecture of defensible space and the inflation of preventive programmes indicate a trend towards prophylactic intervention that makes the focus on reacting to actually committed crimes look very old-fashioned indeed. Prevention, though, is necessarily less specific than reaction, since everyone is a potential offender and millions belong to "risk groups." Eavesdropping, computerized mass searches for life-style irregularities, etc. belong in this emerging picture of a generalized panopticon.

The mechanism of the "politics of wants" or "politics of desires" works best in artificial environments that preventively allow access only to those who are materially and ideologically prepared to participate in the consensual pursuit of commodified pleasures. Therefore, many analysts have come to believe that one only has to turn one's attention to the malls, the amusement parks, and the affluent suburbs of the metropolises in order to have a preview of things to come. The huge covered shopping areas just outside the metropolitan areas of North America and Europe look like laboratories for the construction of an artificially "cleansed" society. In the midst of a snowy Canadian winter, you will find palm trees and waterfalls, flowers and exotic birds, and when the seasons change you will find respite in the cool spring-like mall when everybody else is sweating their souls out. The malls are little cities or mini-countries of their own. They have border controls (private security with precise orders regarding who is and who is not to be granted entry) and internal policing (by private security firms), while the only real and ultimate sanction is expulsion from the artificial paradise. There are no beggars or loiterers, no (visibly) poor, nor will one find anyone who is not shopping (except, again, the omnipresent and helpful private security guard who makes a walk through the mall one of the safest experiences you can have).[25]

The malls are a good laboratory for a new system of social control that works not by nineteenth-century command structures, but via an unobtrusive politics of landscape (the malls are at a certain distance from the city, with practically non-existent public transport connections, thereby preventing access of undesired people from the very start), defensible and sterile architecture with pre-fabricated pleasure stimuli (unobtrusive techno-prevention), and a consensual atmosphere that makes it the unavoidable duty of every visitor to obey cheerfully all the rules of the game.

Similar to the malls, amusement parks are even more like simulated countries (or even the world: for example *Disney-World*). They are geared to please (and control) "the family," i.e. not the *individual*, but a good-humored, lovingly *harmonious entity* worth building a nation upon, and a worthy model for the structure of the "global village" (with the poor but happy countries in the role of the children). Everything must be safe, so everybody can have pleasure. Unlike the mall, the commodities that are for sale in the amusement parks are probably best described as highly standardized pleasurable experiences. To the extent that pleasure is the ultimate end of life activities in a secularized world, what you buy in amusement parks is as close to a sense of life as one can get in a commodified universe.

In there, safety control is to a large extent unobtrusive. Things have been constructed extremely cleverly so as to allow as little deviance and accident as possible. Amusement park employees are gentle, often costumed and entertaining, and always lend a helping hand when anyone shows any sign of behavior that is not perfectly in line with the expected routines. They act as unobtrusive engineers of consensus between the amusement park company, the parents, their children, and the other visitors. There is no quarrel, no command, nor need to obey.

There is an elective affinity between the very structures of the shopping mall and the amusement parks and the ever-growing number of affluent suburbs that begin to cover the globe like a pattern of "islands," or "fortresses" of the very rich. Maybe it is here that the results of the social laboratories are finding their way into a "real life" that, paradoxically enough, seems quite unable to shed the smell of the artificial in terms of social chemistry, social engineering, and a sad simulation of what the ancient philosophers used to refer to as the "Good Life." The pattern of islands or fortresses is really a community of communities, unrelated geographically, but structurally closer to each other than to their immediate environment where crimes of violence mingle with misery and desperation. On these paradise islands, there is no filth, no misery, no violence; the lawns are always well cut, the children happy and healthy, and people cheerful and positive in their thinking.

IV The future of the delinquent as a category of knowledge

We can now discover a relation between the decline of the prison (and the mental hospital) on one hand and the broader tendencies of social control on the other.

First, the neglect of internal determination of human actions and the emphasis on situational elements – "the birth of the dividual" – finds a reflection in the turn away from essentialist strategies that defined the *born criminal* and the new emphasis on human biographies as a *career* or rather a process of *drift*. People are seen as drifting into and out of phases of holding a job, of committing petty offenses, or even crimes. Instead of the eternal criminals (and mentally ill) confronting an equally stable core of normal citizens, we are accustomed to seeing relatives enter mental hospitals and leaving them, only to enter again after a few years during a more severe spell of psychosis. Fixed ontological concepts like the delinquent and the mentally ill do not fit this reality.

Maybe it is worthwhile to realize that *critical criminology* has both reflected this process and contributed to it. The idea of the ubiquity of criminal behavior – and the corresponding idea that the prison population differs from normal citizens not in terms of behavior, but only in terms of exposure to social control – dealt a severe blow to the very category of the delinquent.[26]

Second, the commodification of social control reaches deep into all institutions and puts them under an explosive pressure. The ambivalent preserve of commodities like television, stoves, telephones, etc. in prisoners' cells is clear: on the one hand these commodities serve as instruments that can be withheld for disciplinary purposes, on the other hand this system only works if these commodities are basically attainable. Thereby, the deprivation of liberty loses relevance. Most of the disciplinary mechanisms – like withholding money for the weekly purchase of extra food, cosmetics, cigarettes, etc. – would basically also work (or work even better) if the delinquent was on the other side of the walls, in a tight probation scheme. By substituting traditional repressive mechanisms of intramural control, these new kinds of control are undermining the very construction the prison rests upon.[27]

Third, the commodification of security implies not only the idea of privatizing prisons (and turning delinquents into quasi-customers), but also of using commodities (like electronic tags) instead of institutions, thus reducing the visibility of the delinquents as a class and blending everyday normal life with that of delinquents.

Fourth, the individual delinquent (and their "class") loses importance to the extent that he is seen as a normal person who spends a phase of his life breaking, but most of his life respecting, the law. To the extent that the control of situations becomes the paramount challenge for law enforcement, persons recede into the background, getting out of the focus of attention and losing the extreme attention of society that had coined their image for generations.

Fifth, the satellites that control phone, fax and e-mail communication are geared towards risky worlds, not dangerous individuals. Their covert, dissipated, and proactive control does not distinguish between electronic impulses sent from a prison yard and from an affluent suburb. The spatial concentration of deviants has no advantage over their spatial dissipation. Total institutions are outdated in the face of modern control techniques and priorities.[28]

V Contradictory evidence

There is contradictory evidence. While the aforementioned tendencies can be used as indicators in favor of a complete dissolution of both the total institutions and the corresponding concepts of "delinquents" and "mentally ill," there are quite a few data that seem to indicate the contrary.

While Gilles Deleuze did not look at prison figures and simply deduced from the overall technical development that prisons have become as anachronistic as any fixed categorization of people, Nils Christie proceeds from the empirical data he collected about prison populations and infers the emergence of a system of "GULAGs, Western Style."[29]

A look at the rates of imprisonment in the USA is indeed stunning. Numbers prove a steady and strong growth of the US prison population. The incarceration rate (per 100,000 resident population) went up from 102 in 1974 and 244 in 1988 to well over 500 in 1994. The US prison population rose from 200,000 in the early 1970s to 1,100,000 inmates in 1995 (*The Economist*, June 8, 1996: 24). This is an astonishing rate that leaves European countries trailing far behind (with between 50 and 120 per 100,000), but comes frighteningly close to that of Russia which also oscillates between 500 and 600. If the US development is any predictor for things to come in Europe, the message of these numbers is more than clear, and it spells "expansion of the prison system."

The qualitative shift in correctional philosophy evidently did not prevent any of this. The *new penology* is said to be markedly less concerned with responsibility, fault, moral sensibility, diagnosis, or treatment of the individual offender. But its concern with techniques to identify, classify and manage groupings sorted by dangerousness did not empty a single prison in the United States. Rather it has filled the USA with human warehouses. While earlier correctional discourses were concerned with clinical diagnosis or at least retributive judgement, guilt and responsibility, they are now increasingly being replaced by the language of probability and risk. In Germany the one-time *Behandlungsvollzug* of the 1970s (a treatment orientation within the correctional system) first turned into *Verwahrvollzug* (an orientation, primarily its safe-custody) and then into *Verwahrlosungsvollzug* (correction of "social derelicts").

The facts seem to be diametrically opposed to the perspective that has been developed by Herbert Marcuse, Michel Foucault, and Gilles Deleuze. Their prediction did not imply the exponential growth of incarceration, but much to the contrary a withering away of all kinds of camps, prisons, factories, school buildings, and other nineteenth-century means of spatial inclusion in large-scale buildings. Especially for Deleuze, all kinds of institutionalization and incarceration have already become obsolete in view of the system's growing ability to manipulate motivations and monitor citizens' movements at all times and on all occasions. Their analysis focuses on a shift having taken place from the cruel punishments of the past to medicalization, to admonition instead of infliction of pain, to decarceration and diversion instead of imprisonment, to normalization instead of exclusion, and to destructuring instead of centralization. To them, the construction of new therapeutic categories (diagnoses, syndromes, classifications) is more important than therapeutic systems that involve coercion (involuntary hospitalization, compulsory treatment of addicts, thought-control of political dissidents).

Why then do the data not comply? There are at least two aspects that could explain the dissonance and should cool down our expectations concerning the "withering away" of the categories of prisoners and mentally ill.

First, Horwitz[30] has stressed the fact that the therapeutic style of social control has "only a narrow range of effectiveness. It can promote positive change when clients voluntarily co-operate and share common value systems with controllers. This is usually only the case when people share the educational, class, and cultural orientations of their therapists." This holds true for many of the afore-mentioned trends. Diversion programs and house arrest, victim-offender recon-ciliation and compensation schemes, intensive parole and probation, but also ambulatory drug treatment programs and electronic surveillance all indicate a strong tendency towards non-custodial sentences. But at the same time, there is the rapidly increasing prison archipelago that applies to a different kind of clientele. This leads us to the second aspect.

Second, one just has to take a look at the deepening divide between the world's affluent and afflicted parts, between the growing number of both the very rich and the very poor, to come to think of the possibility that the introduc-tion of the new techniques of social control may find its limit right along the poverty line. While the new techniques will drive the old ones into oblivion at the top and maybe at the "core" of (post-)industrial societies, the old ones and even the very old ones will more probably than not be applied to those below and beyond the poverty line, that is, to the pauperized masses within and beyond the borders of the affluent world.

Those who live at the margins of society have little to expect from the gentle forms of medicalization, therapeutization, neutralization, and normalization. There, beyond the enclaves of commodified happiness, the coming of age of young persons is not the continuous learning game with electronically geared reinforcements, but an often violent struggle in an environment that comes as close to the Hobbesian state of nature as any. And as far as the reactions to deviance are concerned one will find all of them there – including the overt brutality of past stages of social formation which many theorists had long forgot-ten. Reactive social control still does rely on selective brutality that contains a peculiarly effective terrorizing element and which is regularly put in practice by powerful groups when they begin to define situations as critical for the survival of the(ir) system. On a grand historical scale, Mussolini, Hitler, and Franco repre-sent this method of controlling the working classes at a moment of dangerous social unrest. But one can also observe more restricted examples such as the virtually unconditional crack-down on leftist terrorists in Germany during the 1970s, or the extreme persecution of drug traffickers in the United States and other countries. Seemingly outdated and pre-modern as it is, this control method, which includes coercion of masses in camps, long-term imprisonment, the death sentence, extra-legal killings by death squads and/or corrupt police etc. will become ever more important to the extent that structural unemployment, inter-national mass migration, youth violence, and a restless lumpenproletariat will continue to grow, while social consensus is on the decline.

Internal polarizations of societies and the creation of an ever-deepening gap between the fortresses of the affluent and the migrating miserable masses are developments that are resulting in a marked bifurcation of control styles. The prospects are normalization and de-institutionalization for the "in-groups," and an increasing brutalization at the margins for the "out-groups." Each control style, in turn, generates its own dangers and panic-discourses. The amusement park scenario entails the risk of a totalized benevolent submergence of the individual in an ocean of techno-prevention and manipulated consensus, while the scenario at the margins justifies the vision of a complete breakdown of social order and entails the danger of brutal top-down control measures.

VI Discussion

Limiting ourselves to the most advanced countries and the most advanced sectors within them, we focus on the vanguard of social control. It is like looking at the Walnut Street Prison in Philadelphia, in 1796, where the first modern prison started to operate on a minute scale.

Visions of a new kind of society, including a new type of personality and social control, lurk on the horizon. It looks as if it could be very similar to Gilles Deleuze's diagnosis or prophecy. Had he not argued that prisons and other *milieux* of confinement (the mental hospital, the military barracks, the factory, the school, the family) had become anachronistic and were only waiting to be abolished? Just as the societies of sovereignty (which relied on corporal punishment) were followed by the societies of discipline (which relied on the prison as the *milieu* of confinement *par excellence*), the societies of discipline presently find their succession in the control societies of a Deleuzian variety. Control societies are independent from spatial segregation. Workers do not need to congregate in a factory, but simply switch on the electronic connection. Scientists do not need to go to a library, but study electronic journals on their own computer screen. The mentally ill are not segregated in mental hospitals, but given medication which intervenes directly and precisely into their disordered brain chemistry. To serve his sentence a convict does not have to enter a prison but will be assigned a tag that links him to an electronic monitoring system. In this system, the meaning of space changes, but that of incarceration is completely lost. The new methods of control are ambitious because they embrace the general population, but they are liberal insofar as they can leave freedom of movement to those who used to be confined in total institutions. At the same time public sensitivity to the suffering provoked by confinement is increasing. The less necessary confinement becomes from a purely technical point of view (that is, without loss of effectiveness), the more we seem to be ready to define its use as an offence to human dignity. The new techniques of control are ubiquitous and pervasive, but they are so radically different from such outdated devices as prisons, asylums, or any practice of solitary confinement that the present tendency of prison expansion may well reveal itself as a mere sham boom. To the extent that it is unlikely that confinement will play a significant role in the coming century, the very categories of "the delinquent" and "the mentally ill" will tend to dissolve.

Summary

This paper attempts to look at total institutions as correlates of systems of knowledge. Following the works of Michel Foucault, Gilles Deleuze and others, it stresses the historical emergence of the categories of the delinquent and, in some *obiter dicta*, the mentally ill, to lay some groundwork for an educated guess about what I consider the contemporary tendencies towards their dissolution. The main hypothesis of this chapter has been concerned with, and relates to, the process of decategorization in a fragmented society. My conclusion is that general changes in the nature of social control necessitate a fading away or withering away of the clear-cut categories of "delinquent" and "mentally ill."

Notes

1 K. Marx and F. Engels, *Marx-Engels-Werke*, vol. 26, pt.1: *Theorien über den Mehrwert (Das Kapital*: vol. 4: Abschweifung (Über produktive Arbeit) (East Berlin, 1976): 363–4.

2 Cf. S. Scheerer, "Beyond Confinement? Notes on the History and Possible Future of Solitary Confinement in Germany," in: N. Finzsch and R. Jütte, eds, *Institutions of Confinement. Hospitals, Asylums, and Prisons in Western Europe and North America, 1500–1950*. Cambridge University Press, Cambridge, New York, Melbourne 1996: 349–61.

3 Cf. Foucault, M. 1977, *Discipline and Punish: The Birth of the Prison*. Harmondsworth: Allen Lane (French ed. 1975); Bériac, F., *Histoire des lépreux au Moyen Age: une société d'exclus*. Paris 1980; Castel, R. 1976, *L'ordre psychiatrique. L'âge d'or de l'aliénisme*. Paris: Les éditions de minuit.

4 J. Howard, *The State of the Prisons*. London: Dent 1929 (orig. Warrington 1777); H. B. Wagnitz, *Historische Nachrichten und Bemerkungen über die merkwürdigsten Zuchthäuser in Deutschland*. Vol. 1, Halle 1791; Elisabeth Fry, *Observations on the Visiting, Superintendence, and Government of Female Prisoners*. London 1827.

5 Cf. G. Rusche and O. Kirchheimer, *Punishment and Social Structure*. New York 1939; also, with a focus on Italy, cf. D. Melossi and M. Pavarini, *The Prison and the Factory: Origins of the Penitentiary System*. London, 1981.

6 Cf. E. Schmidt, *Einführung in die Geschichte der deutschen Strafrechtspflege*. Göttingen, 1965: 186; G. Smaus, "The History of Ideas and Its Significance for the Prison System," in: Finzsch and Jütte, *Confinement* (note 2): 175–90.

7 N. H. Julius, *Jahrbücher der Straf- und Besserungsanstalten*, Frankfurt 1829–39; N. H. Julius, *Amerikas Besserungs-System und die Anwendung auf Europa*, Berlin 1833.

8 *Reglement für die Straf-Anstalt zu Rawicz. Genehmigt Berlin, den 4. November 1835. Ministerium des Innern und der Polizei.*

9 Cf. *Verhandlungen der ersten Versammlung für Gefängnisreform, zusammengetreten im September 1846 in Frankfurt am Main. Frankfurt am Main*, 1847; A. Streng, *Studien über Entwicklung, Ergebnisse und Gestaltung des Vollzugs der Freiheitsstrafe in Deutschland*. Stuttgart, 1886.

10 F. v. Liszt, "Der Zweckgedanke im Strafrecht" (1882), in: F. v. Liszt, *Strafrechtliche Aufsätze und Vorträge*, Vol. 1, Berlin 1905, pp 126–79.

11 Cf. E. Schmidt, *Zuchthäuser und Gefängnisse*. Göttingen, 1960.

12 Cf. R. Gellately, "The Prerogatives of Confinement in Germany, 1933–1945: 'Protective Custody' and Other Police Strategies," in: Finzsch/Jütte, *Confinement* (supra note 2): 191–211.

13 Cf. H. Jung, "Das Strafvollzugsgesetz und die Öffnung des Vollzugs,", in: *Zeitschrift für Strafvollzug und Straffälligenhilfe* 26.1977: 86–92.

14 Cf. Amnesty International *Arbeit zu den Haftbedingungen in der Bundesrepublik Deutschland für Personen, die politisch motivierter Verbrechen verdächtigt werden oder wegen solcher Verbrechen verurteilt sind: Isolation und Isolationshaft*. London, 1980.

15 As Pierre Bourdieu has argued, seduction takes over as the means of social control and integration. Cf. P. Bourdieu, *Distinction: A Social Critique of the Judgement of Taste*. London, New York, 1984; cf. also S. Scheerer and H. Hess, *Social Control: A Defence and Reformulation*, in: R. Bergalli and C. Sumner, eds, *Social Control and Political Order. European Perspectives at the End of the Century*. London, 1997: 96–130 (118–26).

16 Cf. N. Elias, *Über den Prozess der Zivilisation*, 2 vols. Bern and Munich, 1969 (N. Elias, *The Civilizing Process*. Oxford, 1978).

17 Cf. D. Riesman *et al.*, *Die einsame Masse*. Hamburg, 1958 (orig. *The Lonely Crowd*); Ch. Lasch, *Das Zeitalter des Narzissmus*. Munich 1980. At least the new type of personality represents less danger of being authoritarian than the type analyzed by Adorno, Th. W., E. Frenkel-Brunswik, D. J. Levinson, and R. J. Sanford in *The Authoritarian Personality*. New York, 1950.

18 Cf. R. Lautmann, *Die Lust am Kinde*. Hamburg, 1984.

19 Deleuze, G. "Das elektronische Halsband. Innenansicht der kontrollierten Gesellschaft". *Neue Rundschau* issue 4: 1990: 5–10 (also in: *Kriminologisches Journal* 24.1992: 181–6); cf. also Davis, M. *City of Quartz. Excavating the Future in Los Angeles*. London, New York, 1990: Verso Books.

20 Campbell, C. *The Romantic Ethic and the Spirit of Modern Consumerism*. Oxford, 1987: Basil Blackwell.

21 H. Marcuse, *One-Dimensional Man*. London, Boston, 1964.

22 Shearing, C. D., and Stenning, P. C. "Say 'Cheese!': The Disney Order That Is Not So Mickey Mouse," in: C. D. Shearing and P. C. Stenning, eds, *Private Policing*, Newbury Park, 1987: Sage; Shearing, C. D., Stenning, P. C. "Private Security: Implications for Social Control." *Social Problems* 30 No. 5 June 1983: 493–506.

23 Nogala, D. "Was ist eigentlich so 'privat' an der 'Privatisierung sozialer Kontrolle'? Anmerkungen zu Erscheinungen, Indikatoren und Politökonomie der zivilen Sicherheitsindustrie," in: F. Sack *et al.*, eds, *Privatisierung staatlicher Kontrolle: Befunde, Konzepte und Tendenzen*, Baden-Baden, 1995: Nomos.

24 Luhmann, N., *Rechtssoziologie*. Reinbek, 1972: Rowohlt; M. Feeley, J. Simon, "The New Penology: Notes on the emerging strategy of corrections and its applications." *Criminology* 4.1982: 449–74.

25 supra footnote 22.

26 Cf. R. Kreissl, "Soziologie und soziale Kontrolle. Mögliche Folgen einer Verwissenschaftlichung des Kriminaljustizsystems," in: U. Beck and W. Bonss, eds, *Weder Sozialtechnologie noch Aufklärung? Analysen zur Verwendung sozialwissenschaftlichen Wissens*. Frankfurt, 1989: 420–56.

27 Cf. Blomberg, T. G. "Criminal justice reform and social control: are we becoming a

minimum security society?," In: J. Lowman, R. J. Menzies, T. S. Palys, eds, *Transcarceration: Essays in the Sociology of Social Control*. Aldershot, 1987: Gower.

28 Cf. S. Scheerer, "Zwei Thesen zur Zukunft des Gefängnisses – und acht über die Zukunft der sozialen Kontrolle," in: T. v. Trotha, ed., Politischer Wandel, Gesellschaft und Kriminalitätsdiskurse. Baden-Baden, 1986: 321–334.

29 Christie, N. *Crime Control as Industry. Towards GULAGS, Western Style?* London, 1993: Routledge (2nd edition: *Crime Control as Industry. Towards GULAGS, Western Style*. London, 1995).

30 Horwitz, A. V. *The Logic of Social Control*. New York 1990: Plenum: 247.

27

CORPORATE AND STATE CRIMES AGAINST THE ENVIRONMENT

Foundations for a green perspective in European criminology

Nigel South

Risk-taking is said to be the motor of the capitalist economy; but someone has to pay the price of the inevitable failures.

(Nelken, 1994: 386)

Capitalism means progress, and progress can sometimes lead to inconvenience.

(Executive of the corporation responsible for the Seveso dioxin leak, quoted in Day, 1991: 220)

Introduction: why should European criminology 'think green'?

Think of western Europe in the 1940s and 1950s. Each nation was committed to a programme of reconstruction and reindustrialization. The aim was to build a better post-war world and indicators of economic growth suggested this was a possibility not a dream. However in major cities across Europe, centres of growing populations, expanding transport systems and new enterprises, as well as in regions of high industrial concentration, a new social problem was being produced. In itself, of course, this 'new' problem – pollution – was hardly unfamiliar to these cities and regions. The industries of the nineteenth century, mining, smelting, refining and so on, all changed the landscape and affected air quality, with health consequences for local populations. It was the scale and severity of pollution that were new. For example, in London in 1952, the number of deaths caused by the 'Killer Smog' (which sounds like a science-fiction fantasy but was actually dense atmospheric pollution), caused public alarm and calls for action, leading to the Clean Air Act of 1956. In parts of Eastern Europe, such problems were, we now realize, even greater (Carter and Turnock, 1993).

Historically, from the late eighteenth to the mid-twentieth centuries, this is clearly a story about the costs and consequences of industrialization, and about the development of public health responses (Howe, 1976). So what does it have to do with criminology? The argument here is that not only is this a story about public health, it is also a story about social controls.[1] In this sense, it introduces issues about regulation and law, about polluters and about who ultimately 'pays the price' of pollution. As Cohen (1996: 492) has observed, 'A major part of criminology is supposed to be the study of law making – criminalization – but we pay little attention to the driving force behind so many new laws: the demand for protection from "abuses of power".' Suggestively, Cohen (ibid.) argues that 'significant waves of moral enterprise and criminalization over the last decade are derived not from the old middle class morality, the Protestant ethic nor the interests of corporate capitalism, but from the feminist, ecological and human rights movements'.

The costs and consequences of post-war economic development

All of this is also a story about modernity, social change and consumption (Giddens, 1990). In the social concerns about public health noted above, societies were introduced to the beginnings of what are now popularly understood as 'green' issues. Of relevance to criminology, such concerns opened up whole new areas for study related to disputes and protests, deviance and criminality, and enforcement and control. To bring this story up to date, let us also consider the connection between the local and the global. For example, a power station in Wales starts to use a new fuel, and persists with this despite the change being identified as the cause of severe cases of asthma in the locality (BBC *Here and Now*, 27 March, 1996). This is a 'small scale' case but the *adding up* and *accumulation* of such localized examples provides a global picture of millions of other 'little' events which bring with them modest to devastating changes in people's experience of the environment and conditions of life. This chapter argues that negligence, violations and crimes for which corporations and states are responsible have led to great increases in pollution-related health harms as well as threats to the very sustainability of the planet (Porritt, 1990), and that criminology should take these issues more seriously. This argument applies to criminology generally, but the 'reunification' of Europe gives added weight to the proposition that green issues should have some prominence on the agenda of a pan-European criminology, for polluted air-currents know no borders and smugglers of toxic waste respect none.

Criminology and 'green fields' of study in other disciplines

If we examine the study of environmental issues across disciplines, it is striking that most other social and natural sciences, and even many of the humanities, have established clearly identifiable sub-fields concerned with green issues, yet criminology has not.[2] In our related discipline of sociology, environmental issues have stimulated a considerable amount of social-scientific work of both theoretical and empirical significance (e.g. Beck, 1992a, b; Benton, 1993; Hannigan, 1995; Lash, *et al.* 1996). Of course, this is not to say that criminology has paid no attention to green issues. There is a substantial (albeit scattered) literature on the environmental impacts of corporate and (to a lesser extent) state violations against the environment. I shall note some of these contributions shortly. However, these (often pathbreaking) contributions usually arise out of earlier debates and paradigms established within the traditional framework of a criminology of modernity.[3] In a late-modern society, anticipating the millennium, are there not new questions and issues for criminology (South, 1997)?

There is, (as yet) no clearly identifiable 'body', 'school', or 'field' of 'green' work in criminology. There are however, exceptional 'islands': contributions by individuals and groups which suggest such a critical 'land-mass' is building. Among these contributions we might note: Edwards *et al.* (1996) with their recent collection of essays on environmental crime and criminality; work on environment and law from HEUNI (Albrecht and Leppa, 1992); the section of four chapters on 'Crimes against the environment' in Pearce and Snider (1995); the work of Pearce and Tombs (1993), and see their debate (1990, 1991) with Hawkins (1990), also Hawkins' earlier work (e.g. 1984); on animals and criminology, see Beirne (1995), and Pocar (1992); and generally, see Beirne and South (1998). In this chapter I seek to draw further attention to some of the directions already pursued and also to suggest how a green perspective might be developed within European criminology.

Three foundations for a European 'green criminology'

In this section of the paper, I identify three possible Foundations for such a green perspective. First, studies of regulation, disasters and violations; second, legal and social censures; and third, social movements and environmental politics.

Foundations (1): studies of regulation, disasters and corporate and state violations

There is a huge literature on the varieties of corporate and state activity which may also be associated with crime. However, compared to other areas of such misconduct there are relatively few studies directly and principally concerned with what we may call 'crimes against the environment'. In general (but not exclusively or exhaustively), the themes of the relevant literature are concerns with (a) the study of *regulation*: for example the positive and negative features, and the consequences, of different regulatory models; (b) pollution, disasters and liabilities as *'single-event' case-studies*; and (c) *corporate and state misconduct or crimes* which have environmental consequences, with the focus bearing on the perpetrators, culpability and the nature of serial offending. This is, of course, a provisional 'typology' in the Weberian sense of representing 'ideal types'. In practice many studies cut across such 'types'. Let me briefly provide some empirical orientation here by noting *some* – I cannot review all – aspects of these three themes as part of 'Foundation 1'.

Studies in the sociology and criminology of environmental regulation and law

The focus of studies here is often on technical and legal issues and how these may translate into policy and the formulation of law (Albrecht and Leppa, 1992; Alvazzi del Frate and Norberry, 1993). Such work is important in several respects. First, it connects to the dyad of 'law and policy' (i.e. the process of criminalization, cf. Cohen, 1996: 492) in ways in which criminologists preoccupied by the dyads of 'crime and offender' or 'crime and enforcement' may find suggestive; second, it frequently (although not always) considers comparative or 'universal' questions, either out of necessity due to the applicability of international or European law (Winter, 1996) or out of intellectual inclination (Miller, 1995); and third, focused work on regulatory systems can often produce findings of a counter-intuitive nature. For example, when the water suppliers of England and Wales were privatized my assumption was that those responsible for water protection, initially the National Rivers Authority, now merged into the Environment Agency (Weale, 1996), would be weaker than former regulators. This has not necessarily proved the case, in large part for one reason. Previously the inspecting and regulation of water pollution was carried out by the water supply authorities themselves, yet these largely unaccountable bodies were often among the major polluting offenders! Such a conflict of interests within one organization reduced the efficacy and prosecuting power of inspectors, both of which increased dramatically after the separate NRA was created (Howarth, 1991). It would, of course, be extremely naive to suggest that this development or the more widely-empowered Environment Agency will prove to be a radical force for environmental policing. As investigative journalists have been documenting, some members of the Government-appointed executive management of the Environment Agency represent wholly inappropriate conflicting interests (Foote, 1996a, b). Nonetheless, whilst healthy political scepticism is therefore important, structurally, the creation of the Environment Agency remains significant and this position may be enhanced further if the European Environment Agency, established in Copenhagen in 1994, begins to press for European standards and targets for effective environmental policy performance (Weale, 1996: 42–3).

Studies of disasters, pollution, and liabilities as 'single-event' case-examples

Work by Pearce and Tombs (1993) on the Union Carbide explosion at Bhopal, India in December 1984 has done much to draw criminological attention to the scale of human and environmental disaster that may result from corporate negligence. Bhopal has generally been described as the world's worst industrial accident, although Chernobyl and its as yet unknown legacy, is a clear rival for this claim (Beck, 1987; Pope *et al.*, 1991: 52–6). Whilst western Europe has not (so far) experienced environmental disasters on quite the same scale as Bhopal or Chernobyl (though the latter certainly had a trans-continental impact: Pope *et al.*, ibid.), the rivers of Europe, most famously the Rhine, have long been polluted as the result of corporate negligence and illegal methods of waste disposal, permitted by lax regulation and domestic and cross-border jurisdictional confusions. However, it has principally been journalists who have documented this. Numerous cases have been reported in the western media, and now several eastern European media as well, in which European populations have suffered the consequences of the unsafe disposal of chemical and other industrial wastes. The difficulties of storing, processing and disposing of nuclear wastes present a particular challenge and have already been associated with problems such as leakage from containers and atmospheric pollution. Writers in the field of environmental law have addressed these offences and, writing on cross-border criminality, Ruggiero (1996) has recently drawn on some of this journalistic work. However, generally criminologists have been poor 'reporters' of such matters.

Corporate and state violations related to the environment

For the sake of brevity, I will merely note here that the examples above provide some indications of corporate contributions to environmental offending. But what of state violations? There are numerous minor and major examples of governments breaking their own regulations and contributing to environmental harms (Day, 1991). This is no surprise to any but the most innocent, so as a truly astonishing example of state violence in relation to green issues, let us consider the rather stranger picture of the state operating as anti-environment terrorist.

States condemn 'terrorism', but of course have always been perfectly capable of resorting to terrorist-type methods when in conflict with oppositional groups. A notorious example is the 1985 sinking of the Greenpeace flagship, Rainbow Warrior, in Auckland harbour, New Zealand. This was a crime of terrorist violence carried out by Commandos from the French Secret Service. In this operation, sanctioned at Cabinet level within the French government, 22 kilos of explosive were used to blow up the Greenpeace ship as an expression of French anger over its use in protest activities against French nuclear tests in the Pacific. Miraculously, of the 13 crew on board only one was killed in the blast (Day, 1991: 281–4).

In his book, *The Eco Wars*, Day (1991) charts a variety of state-sponsored acts of violence and intimidation against environmental activists or groups. His comments on these and the Rainbow Warrior affair are highly relevant to the idea of a criminology which takes environmental issues and politics seriously:

> The most unusual aspect of the Rainbow Warrior affair was that, to some degree at least, the murder mystery was solved. Although justice

was not done, the truth came out. There have been many other acts of state terrorism linked with the anti-nuclear war but it is seldom possible to prove that they are linked directly to government officials.

Indeed, if the agents had not been caught red-handed, there is no doubt that Greenpeace activists would have been scoffed at for pointing the finger at the French government. Their accusation would have been dismissed as just one more lunatic fringe conspiracy theory. Why after all, would the French government worry about the activities of a small-scale anti-nuclear protest group? Surely only a total paranoid would believe that violent action was necessary to stop such a group. . .

The answer is that when it comes to nuclear issues the French – and the governments of *all* nuclear powers – *are* paranoid. In every case where a government has committed itself to nuclear weapons or nuclear power, all those who oppose this policy are treated in some degree as enemies of the State.

(Day, 1991: 322)

Rowell (1996) has recently, painstakingly documented how state and corporate power has been mobilised against such new 'enemies':

. . . with the collapse of communism, environmentalists are now increasingly being identified as a global scapegoat for threatening the vested interest of power: the triple engines of unrestricted corporate capitalism, right-wing political ideology and the nation state's protection of the *status quo*.

The green backlash, born out of both the success of the environmental movement and its failure, is still to run its course. Many more activists will be intimidated, beaten up, vilified and killed for working on ecological issues.

(ibid.: 372)

Foundations (2): legal frameworks, criminalization and 'shaming'

The legal issues raised by environmentally damaging acts and how these should be classified (violations? crimes?) and responded to (by regulation? criminalization?. Inspectorates? police?) connect with many familiar, but also with some new, criminological problems. Today various populations may be exposed to hazardous waste and emissions but cases attempting to establish liability and responsibility for this, or legal claims concerning harms to human health or eco-systems resulting from such pollution, have often proved unresolvable in courts of law. Indeed, such cases may be difficult to prosecute in the first place: perhaps because of lack of evidence and proof; because of the blurring of the lines between the 'wilful criminal violator' and the 'legal risk-taking entrepreneur'; and/or because of the corrupt involvement of public officials. As Van Duyne (himself responsible for attempting to bring cases on behalf of the Netherlands Ministry of Justice), notes:

> The more crime-enterprises operate successfully on a legitimate market, the more one has to question the role of the upperworld, especially the authorities. This was the case with ... the waste-crime enterprises, which revealed [clear] evidence of an inexcusable profiting from the environmental violations of these crime-enterprises. Though plain corruption could only be proven for subordinate dumping site managers, the higher civil servants, responsible for the environmental interests of the towns or provinces, certainly did not act in good faith. However, I just could not *prove* that it was a matter of *criminal* negligence. (emphasis in original).
>
> (Van Duyne, 1993: 125–6)

The problem of how to respond to such offences in an effective legal manner through *criminalization* has recently been subjected to much debate. On the one hand, there are persuasive, if counter-intuitive, arguments against the criminalization strategy (Fisse and Braithwaite, 1993; Hawkins, 1992: 462; Di Mento, 1986: 73; Geis and Di Mento, 1995), while on the other hand, there are also powerful arguments in favour (Snider, 1990). Briefly summarizing the first position, it can be argued that (a) there are frequently legal problems in getting to the stage of bringing a prosecution, and (b) if this does happen, pollution cases are notoriously difficult to prove in terms of culpability and 'knowing intent'; (c) even if a prosecution is brought and is successful, penalties are usually modest relative to the damage done: if the corporation is fined it will absorb such costs and/or simply pass them onto consumers. Attempts to identify and sanction key, responsible individuals have had only rare success (Geis and Di Mento, 1995; Ridley and Dunford, 1994). Potentially more effective is Braithwaite's (1989) notion of 'shaming'. Adapted for present purposes, this is an argument based on the proposition that corporate image is a more vulnerable target for censure and sanctions than corporate assets. Bad publicity and the projection of a negative image about offending businesses can hurt public relations, profits and share prices. The argument would be that being a bad corporate citizen is bad news for a company, it hurts community relations and finds disfavour with government and other businesses in the same sector who desire a clean image. In some respects this view carries a degree of realism and sophistication in its strategy lacking in the 'get tough' enforcement, and 'let's cooperate' compliance models. However, this is also an argument with its own limitations, not least in that it may be naive about the extent to which corporate business really cares about 'image', or conversely it may well underestimate how hard business will fight to undermine critics (Rowell, 1996). It is also a view that may overestimate the extent to which the general public actually care about what corporations do, *especially* if their offences are committed in another country, and particularly if this is in the developing world. Clearly, while I believe there is much to recommend the reasoning of Braithwaite and others, it is equally important to acknowledge the force of the second position: that corporate misbehaviour and crime simply cannot be controlled by systems based on social pressure and voluntary compliance. The use of criminal and civil law, and of effective enforcement strategies, are essential. Otherwise, as Snider (1990) warns, the danger is that of 'capitulation through compromise'. In the end, this is a debate about *criminalization* as an effective tool for regulation. I cannot pursue this much further here and must instead suggest that perhaps in the present reality, the best we can do is seek the most powerful *combination* of 'shaming' and pressure-group, regulatory, and criminalization frameworks that we can. It is arguable that a critical criminology should be wary of adopting 'criminalization' as its *sole* and key policy proposal. Such a solution to offending invites capture by the discourse and logic of the new right, and the 'criminological imagination' (*pace* Mills, 1959) ought to be able to do better than this.

Foundations (3): social movements, 'green politics' and policy futures

Green politics, protest and conflict

Globally, there are numerous political and pressure groups working around environmental issues, albeit in both positive and negative ways, depending on one's standpoint. These include, of course, anti-environmentalist organizations powered by corporate and state interests (Rowell, 1996). Among pro-environment groups, diversity ranges from the extreme (with versions which embrace terrorism), and the controversial (a philosophy which puts animal life before human life), through the 'new social-movements' of New Age Travellers and eco-feminism, to middle-range political left, centre and right versions (Paehlke, 1995), as well as local, specific-interest groups ('save our wildlife' or NIMBY's – 'Not-in-my-backyard' – protesters; Szasz (1994)). The importance of the feminist critique of masculine violence against the environment (Collard and Contrucci, 1988), and, in the USA, the emergence of networks of black activists working against environmental damage to their communities (Bullard, 1990), are expressions of protest that a forward-looking criminology should take note of.

The 'terrorist' version of 'green politics' has particularly been associated with *some* extreme animal-rights campaigns. However, broader political critiques of the state and capitalism have also been directed toward environmental crimes which may symbolically be held to stand for much more. One of the most famous examples in Europe, described by Day (1991: 219–20) as being the 'first ecologically motivated assassination', was the 1980 murder by the far-left group Front Line of Enrico Paoletti. Paoletti was industrial director of a subsidiary of the Swiss Hoffman La Roche corporation which operated a chemical plant in

Seveso, northern Italy. In 1976 an explosion at the plant resulted in the release of a dioxin cloud that killed virtually all the town's domestic animals and caused severe skin-disease problems for many adults and children. The explosion was shown to be the result of negligence and Paoletti and several other executives were arrested. However defence lawyers produced various legal obstructions, causing delay, and all were released on bail. Paoletti's subsequent 'execution' was justified by Front Line as the exercise of punishment which the formal system of prosecution was unable to deliver.

Green politics, bureaucracy and political futures

We should also note the incorporation of green issues into mainstream political party agendas, into the work of the important bureaucracies charged with overseeing environmental issues, and into popular, (largely, but not exclusively) middle-class, eco-conscious frameworks: for example, in Britain, as membership of Trade Unions has declined, membership of green and animal welfare organizations has risen dramatically.

In this respect, according to one reading of the future (at least on the European stage), the politics of environmental issues have some significant popular appeal, and are not necessarily as closed as pessimists might assume. Although the 'backlash' against green concerns should certainly not be underestimated, Rowell (1996) rightly identifies the main source of such a movement as arising from corporate and political power in the USA. While we must acknowledge that such power is globalized, nonetheless it would be foolish to underestimate the specificities of European political and policy processes. Pressure groups and politicians concerned about pollution, the rights of communities, evasions of environmental law and so on, already work very successfully within the world of EU lobbying and legislation at Brussels, and in other parts of Europe (see e.g. Herrnkind, 1993). Furthermore, in his study of the construction of European environmental policy, Ruzza (1996: 216) encouragingly observes that:

> Because of their international background, [EU] bureaucrats are very sensitive to the climate of opinion in several countries, and far less isolated than some of their critics would argue. They are very aware of the Weberian metaphor of the iron cage and its shortcomings, and together with a strong pro-European ideology, often display apprehension on the way the [European] dream is actualised.

The implication of this analysis is that the ground on which to build policy-oriented criminological work is fertile rather than barren. Not least because the environment is treated as a pan-national responsibility, a 'public good' for which the EU may be more concerned than the individual member Governments who will often prioritize domestic interests (although they too must recognize that it is not in national interests to have a population suffering the consequences of a deteriorating environment). Hence, despite the complicity of the state in some cases of environmental damage and the power of corporate offenders, there is no desire here to present a 'conspiratorial' view or to assert or imply that 'nothing can be done'. The development of public health improvements, the massive pro-liferation of environmental legislation, and the resources put into regulation, inspection and prosecution, all affirm social commitment to environmental pro-tection. From the local activism of community groups through issue-prioritizing bureaucracies to the breadth of international law, there are powerful presures at work, and tools available, for environmental action. How long this may be the case is, however, a different question.

A criminology concerned about social justice on an equitable planet should take advantage of such current opportunities, for there are also less promising assessments of how environmental issues will fare *in the future*. As Paehlke (1995: 311) warns, an optimistic reading of the future for environmental politics may be mistaken. Instead, the future may belong to a demand for growth promoted by a coalition representing the combined interests of capital and labour, examples of which are not uncommon in times of 'external threats'. In this case the 'threats' are 'scarcity' and 'environmentalism'.

As Paehlke (ibid.) suggests:

> The politics of the future may belong to this growth coalition. As resource stocks decline and/or human population continues to grow, scarcity will occur more frequently. Conflicts will intensify over uncut forest lands, as-yet untapped (environmentally risky) energy supplies, and land use. In a context of high unemployment (a result of globalization and automation), the growth coalition and a politics of environmental denial may become strong.

This is a prediction shared by Rowell (1996: 372) as he considers the future of the global backlash against environmental concern:

> In all probability the backlash will get worse, as the resource wars of the coming decades intensify, as more people fight over less. We have already had the fish wars, but conflicts over water, wood, whales, metals, minerals, energy, cars and even consumerism will all happen and all inevitably create backlash.

Of all the disciplines that may be relevant here, a critical criminology in par-ticular should take note. For this is a future in which many of its core concerns are increasingly placed centre-stage among environmental issues: conflict and social order; theft and protection; relative deprivation and consumption; class, gender and ethnic inequality related to the new issues of access to energy and resources.

In this spirit, to help us move from these Foundations to a more concrete vision of what kind of work a green criminology might pursue, let me turn to an established issue: the illegal disposal of waste. As a policy challenge, crime enterprise and enforcement problem, this is a subject rapidly accelerating in significance.

A green issue for a green criminology: the illegal disposal of hazardous waste

The irony of prohibitions and regulations has always lain in the sophistication and enterprise then employed to avoid complying with them (Nadelmann, 1990). What even the limited tightening of regulations in advanced western industrial nations has done is create a highly profitable domestic and international trade in illegal disposal and dumping of hazardous toxic waste. This has manifested itself in new forms of corporate-organized crime symbiosis (Szasz, 1986; Scarpitti and Block, 1987; Van Duyne, 1993; Ruggiero, 1996), sometimes – perhaps even frequently – with tacit state acknowledgement. Some brief examples may illustrate the compass of such activity, from (a) the truly global operation, through (b) the regional (in this case involving European neighbours), to (c) the very local.

(a)   Toxic waste defined as unsuitable for landfill burial in western countries is being shipped to developing nations. Either these do not have tight regulatory requirements or they lack the inspectorate bureaucracies to enforce them. In some cases, toxic cargoes are welcomed because they bring with them profit and needed payments in foreign currency. The export of such waste would not normally be granted export licenses by Western European or North American regulators and proper procedures would involve re-processing to reduce toxicity before disposal. This is expensive, hence the attraction of moving and dumping waste illegally (Szasz, 1986). On a global scale, one example of such evasion of regulations and re-routing of waste is described by Block (1993). In this case, toxic waste was moved from the USA to northern Europe under false bills of lading and was then transhipped to the impoverished West-African nation of Benin. There the Government's soldiers unloaded the waste and drove it north, dumping it near Benin's border with the state of Niger (ibid.: 104).[4]

(b)   Van Duyne (1993: 124) notes another case of cross-border toxic-waste dumping, but one of a rather more localized variety, involving neighbouring Belgium and the Netherlands. In this case, Dutch entrepreneurs exploited various loopholes in Dutch environmental law and 'developed a network of (independent) crime-enterprises . . . . Of great importance' to their operation was 'the availability of a Belgian dumping site, whose corrupt executive manager allowed the daily dumping of substantial quantities of Dutch toxic waste'. In one case, a Dutch company employed a Dutch waste-collection firm and a Belgian transport company to dispose of clients' waste at the dump site of the accommodating manager. Some of this waste contained the dangerous chemical PCB. This was not declared and before crossing the border, the transporter simply covered it with a thin layer of earth. The dump site manager recorded the load delivered as 'loose earth from market gardening'. Van Duyne notes that some reports uncovered in the investigation of this operation suggest that not all the waste was transported to the dump site, 'some loads containing PCB's, simply disappeared somewhere in Belgium' (ibid.).

(c) If transnational shipping of waste lies at one end of the spectrum of sophistication in avoiding regulation of dumping, perhaps the Dutch–Belgian case of untruthful description and using false documentation lies somewhere along the mid-point of the spectrum. At the more 'local' end may be cases which simply rely on petty corruption and bribery. In my own earlier research on the less reputable areas of the private security sector, I interviewed a trade-union official who described (and held evidence of) how a land-fill site south of London which was designated for certain kinds of non-toxic waste only, nonetheless was being used for more dangerous waste. This occurred at night with the assistance of the bribed security guards.

Toxic and general waste-dumping is an increasingly significant crime. Ruggiero (1996: 139–40) cites recent cases involving criminal groups from Germany transporting hazardous waste into France, and an entrepreneur in northern England who ran a legal waste-disposal firm and alongside this a service providing illegal dumping of 'hard-to-dispose-of' waste. According to Ruggiero (ibid.), Italy has offered some particularly striking examples of this new area of criminal entrepreneuriality:

> In Italy, traditional organized crime based in the south has often offered waste-disposal services to entrepreneurs operating in the north. Among the firms serviced in 1990 was ACNA, which produced dioxane and operates in Lombardy. In describing this activity of organized crime in Naples, the Commissione Antimafia . . . commented: 'The seawater of large parts of Naples province is polluted mainly because of illegal waste dumping, authorized dumping constitutes only 10 per cent of the total waste actually disposed of in the bay of Naples.'

Ruggiero (ibid.) also notes that:

> The illegal disposal of hazardous waste has been thoroughly studied in the USA, where in some cases the involvement of organized crime reaches all aspects of the business, from the control of which companies are officially licensed to dispose of waste to those which earn contracts with public or private organizations and to the payment of bribes to dump-site owners, or the possession of such sites . . . . Paradoxically, the development of this illegal service runs parallel with an increase in

environmental awareness, the latter forcing governments to raise costs for industrial dumping, which indirectly encourages industrialists to opt for cheaper solutions.

As Van Duyne (1993: 123) comments:

> whether there exists a situation comparable with the US in Europe is most uncertain. However, several criminal cases [in the Netherlands and Northern Europe] involving toxic waste trafficking [have] revealed the existence of a number of crime-enterprises, which were specialised in illegal waste transports and 'processing' (throwing it into open water or dumping it on the land). The crime-enterprises appeared to be highly integrated in the upperworld of the legitimate industry and administration.

Conclusion: toward a green perspective for European criminology

A key question in this chapter is 'why has criminology so singularly failed to embrace green issues'? To respond to this question, let us consider the observations of other writers concerned with the project of bringing green issues into sociology and criminology, respectively.

Green criminology, the 'risk society' and 'social responsibility'

Why is there so little effective protest about environmental damage? Why is it so difficult to engage mass support for environmental concerns (Beck, 1995)? These questions find one answer in the perspective put forward by Beck in his celebrated book *Risk Society* (1992a). For Beck, the limited project outlined here – to suggest some foundations for a green criminology – would be *just one* aspect of the need to reformulate scientific and social thought *generally* in the direction of 'thinking green'. Beck argues that how pollution and other threats are interpreted is frequently limited and constrained by a hegemonic clutch of narrow ideas and viewpoints: environmental issues are 'generally viewed as matters of nature and technology, or of economics and medicine':

> what is astonishing . . . is that the industrial pollution of the environment and the destruction of nature, with their multifarious effects on the health and social life of people, which only arise in highly developed societies, are characterised by a *loss of social thinking*. This loss becomes caricature – this absence seems to strike no one, not even sociologists themselves. (emphasis in original)

> (*ibid.*: 25)

The argument here is that criminology similarly needs to be reminded of this absence of 'social thinking about the environment'. One source for criminological 'social thinking' about these issues is suggested in the recent work of Pitch (1995) who argues that 'The "natural environment" (non-human animals included) presents a . . . challenge' to traditional thinking about civil and social rights, insofar as they are considered to be beyond 'the horizon of the "social contract"', pose complex problems about equality, and confront 'the ways in which Western culture has understood and theorised its relation to "nature"' (ibid.: 73; on the latter point see also Snider, 1991: 226; Benton, 1993). Pitch argues that we must problematize and reconstruct the 'taken for granted' assumptions that prevail about the 'natural' order of things and that if this is done in relation to the social treatment of the environment and non-human animals then this new 'moral valuation' reveals 'injustice'. The theoretical and practical consequences of this revelation are that questions arise about 'the attribution of blame' for injustice and about fundamental issues of 'social responsibility'. Investigating such 'blame' and 'responsibility' provides a task for a green perspective within criminology. This is partly an argument for a *new* way of thinking but also an idea that embraces existing problems and questions in criminology.

Problems and questions for a green criminology

In virtually all advanced industrial societies, air quality is worsening, asthma and bronchial diseases are rising, meaning ill health for children and adults, and increased costs for health services and insurance companies. Yet states, businesses, and individuals, continue to break regulations and laws which should help reduce these problems. In various European and US cities, policy and policing are beginning to target such offenders (e.g. road users and factories which break rules on the emission of pollutants). Is this not an area of offending that should be taken at least as (or more) seriously than society takes some other forms of crime – think for example, of the huge criminal-justice efforts expended on trying to police recreational drug use?

Late-modern society is a consumption society but this also means it is a 'throwaway', 'discard-and-dispose' society: waste disposal is a major issue for the planet and the future. It will also be a major source of criminal revenue and stimulant to criminal organization. Green issues are also relevant to the emerging criminological study of other 'new' topics of international and global importance, notably crimes of war (Jamieson, this volume) and violations of human rights (Cohen, 1996). In mid-range areas of criminological research, between the global and the personal, considering the role of regulatory systems and agents involved in 'policing' environmental offending reveals further areas for study within the criminology of 'grey policing' (Hoogenboom, 1991). Green theory and green cultural politics also closely connect to recent criminological work exploring 'masculinities' and 'feminisms': consider, for example, science and corporate business and their talk of 'mastering nature' and 'conquering territories and hostile

CRIMINOLOGY AND THE ENVIRONMENT

environments'; while green issues connect with the impact of feminism in criminology via eco-feminism (Collard and Contrucci, 1988; Birke, 1994; Koser Wilson, 1996).

Criminologists should also consider the *future* potential for social damage generated by the irresponsible manipulation of environmental resources and of
human and animal populations by corporate interests and governments. Currently a clear case for criminological monitoring is the mass introduction of
genetically manipulated foodstuffs into supermarket products. Minimal attention
is being paid to consumer rights, regulatory issues and foodstuff labelling, or the
negative findings of past experiments, which include the 1989 Tryptophan case
linked to 37 deaths and over 1,500 people becoming paralysed (Uhlig, 1996).

International boundaries are becoming increasingly permeable. In this context
it may be that in the future, enforcement agencies and environmental groups will
be found in strange alliances. Van Altena (1987), a senior police investigator in the
Netherlands, has drawn attention to the significance of environmental crime for
law-enforcement agencies, and the need for cross-border monitoring, perhaps via
Interpol. In England, McKenna (1993), a police officer who compared the limited experience of responding to environmental crime in the UK with the more
extensive arrangements of other European nations and the US, suggested that:

> as society becomes increasingly concerned and informed of environ-
> mental issues, regulatory structures take on a more co-ordinated appear-
> ance and a civil tier of enforcement is often supported or reinforced by
> traditional police forces or agencies. . . . To believe that the environment
> will not continue to be a vital social and political issue, that will grow in
> importance as time goes on, could demonstrate an extraordinary lack of
> vision.
>
> (McKenna, 1993: 96,102)

In recent interviews with FBI and RCMP agents concerning cross-border
crime, the author asked each, independently, what they thought the key end-of-
the-century crime issues were going to be. Both identified toxic-waste dumping
(across borders or at sea) as a high priority issue.[5] Already, there is a large and
growing body of EU and global environmental law. As a case-study in itself, the
strength and diversity of EU law and policy in this area is testimony to the need
for European criminology to be aware of the developments occurring.[6] These
will have significant implications for the 'crime and criminalization' agendas of
the future.

The boundaries of the intellectual disciplines of late-modernity are also
changing (Ericson and Carriere, 1994) and the idea of a green criminological
perspective needs further suggestions from those involved in other related work;
particularly those concerned with environmental issues and gender and ethnicity,
as well as the socially-marginalized generally, population groups least able to
resist the impacts that environmental change and damage may have. We also

need to consult colleagues and research in other disciplinary areas – culture, law, economics, international studies, biological chemistry and the environmental sciences, and so on. A green perspective in criminology is not only essential to address and comprehend major issues for Europe and the planet into the twenty-first century, but will also offer criminology itself a new point of departure for stimulating and innovative work within the discipline and across disciplinary boundaries.

It seems to me (and evidently to others contributing to this volume), that 'end-of-the-century-criminology' (South, 1997) is in a position to engage with a new 'criminological imagination' (*pace* C. W. Mills) about its theoretical and practical concerns. I have touched on some of these possibilities here and elsewhere. As Ian Taylor has suggested (personal communication), criminology as a European (and transnational) enterprise could now pursue 'a call for a praxis (e.g. in respect of war crimes, firearms control, etc.) which might actually help to ground European criminology in a more exciting and imaginative fashion in the late 1990s, giving it a far wider public resonance'. The anxieties and insecurities of the public are too frequently responded to by hollow and cynical political promises and ploys. The momentum towards firearms control in Britain, largely carried forward by the Dunblane community pressure group, supported by other networks, shows what can be achieved when 'alternative' policy and practice proposals are forcefully pursued. There is a role for criminologists to play in such campaigns. This chapter has suggested that the environment will increasingly be an important issue and one which European criminologists should be engaging with.

Notes

1 Public-health medicine is itself a discipline of (generally) benign social controls, being concerned with the Foucauldian themes of epidemiology (surveillance), and control and change of dangerous or contagious behaviours.

2 Indeed, currently in criminology, the term 'environmental crime' is employed to describe criminal offending in relation to place and spatial patterns. Bottoms (1994: 586, n. 3) briefly acknowledges this limitation.

3 Here I am grateful to Fritz Sack for his comments as chair of the session at the ESRC 'European Criminology' conference at which this paper was first presented.

4 The rest of Block's *tour de force* of investigatory criminology is an excellent example of the kind of foundation stone upon which a green perspective could be built in criminology.

5 Given that these agencies may sometimes be involved in investigating the activities of environmental protest groups, the possibilities in the kinds of conversations that 'eco-conscious cops' and 'eco-warriors' may have are intriguing!

6 As Freestone (1991: 135) observes, current EU law is 'a monument to the pragmatic or flexible approach to the interpretation of the aims of the [original] EEC Treaty'. This is because the original Treaty of Rome made no mention of the need to develop an environmental protection policy, and nowhere in the main body of the original text is there provision for the development of Community legislation on the environment. This is not surprising, as the environment was not then seen as a major trade related issue. Today it certainly is!

References

Albrecht, H.-J. and Leppa, S. (1992) *Criminal Law and the Environment*, Helsinki: Helsinki Institute for Crime Prevention and Control, affiliated with the United Nations. Publication 22.

Alvazzi del Frate, A. and Norberry, J. (eds) (1993), *Environmental Crime, Sanctioning Strategies and Sustainable Development*, Rome: UNICRI and Canberra: Australian Institute of Criminology. Publication No. 50.

Beck, U. (1987) 'The anthropological shock: Chernobyl and the contours of the Risk Society', *Berkeley Journal of Sociology*, 32: 153–65.

Beck, U. (1992a) *Risk Society: Towards a New Modernity*, London: Sage.

Beck, U. (1992b) 'From industrial society to the risk society: questions of survival, social structure and ecological enlightenment', *Theory, Culture and Society*, 9: 97–123.

Beck, U. (1995) *Ecological Politics in an Age of Risk*, Cambridge: Polity.

Beirne, P. (1995) 'The use and abuse of animals in criminology: a brief history and current review', *Social Justice*, 22, 1: 5–31.

Beirne, P. and South, N. (eds) (1998) *For a Green Criminology*, special issue of *Theoretical Criminology* 2,2.

Benton, T. (1993) *Natural Relations*, London: Verso.

Birke, L. (1994) *Feminism, Animals and Science: the naming of the shrew*, Buckingham: Open University Press.

Block, Alan (1993) 'Defending the mountaintop: a campaign against environmental crime', in F. Pearce and M. Woodiwiss (eds) (1993): 91–140.

Bottoms, T. (1994) 'Environmental criminology', in M. Maguire, *et al.* (eds) (1994): 585–658

Braithwaite, J. (1989) *Crime, Shame and Reintegration*, Cambridge: Cambridge University Press.

Bullard, R. (1990) *Dumping in Dixie: Race, Class and Environmental Quality*, Boulder: Westview Press.

Carter, F. and Turnock, D. (1993) *Environmental Problems in Eastern Europe*, London: Routledge.

Cohen, S. (1996) 'Human rights and crimes of the state: the culture of denial' in J. Muncie, E. McLaughlin and M. Langan (eds) *Criminological Perspectives: A Reader*, London: Sage, (reprinted from *Australian and New Zealand Journal of Criminology*, 1993).

Collard, A. and Contrucci, J. (1988) *Rape of the Wild: Man's violence against animals and the earth*, London: Women's Press.

Day, D. (1991) *The Eco Wars*, London: Paladin.

Di Mento, J. (1986) *Environmental Law and American Business: Dilemmas of Compliance*, New York: Plenum Press.

Edwards, S. Edwards, T. and Fields, C. (eds) (1996) *Environmental Crime and Criminality: Theoretical and Practical Issues*, New York: Garland.

Ericson, R. and Carriere, K. (1994) 'The fragmentation of criminology' in D. Nelken (1994b).

Fisse, B. and Braithwaite, J. (1993) *Corporations, Crime and Accountability*, Cambridge: Cambridge University Press.

Foote, P. (1996a) 'High Pollutin'', *Private Eye*, 5th April: 27.

Foote, P. (1996b) 'Ready mixed contact', *Private Eye*, 24th September: 27.

Freestone, D. (1991) 'European Community environmental policy and law', *Journal of Law and Society*, (special issue), 18, 1: 135–54.

Geis, G. and Di Mento, J. (1995) 'Should we prosecute corporations and/or individuals?' in F. Pearce and L. Snider (eds) (1995): 72–86.

Giddens, A. (1990) *The Consequences of Modernity*, Cambridge: Polity.

Hannigan, J. (1995) *Environmental Sociology: A Social Constructionist Perspective*, London: Routledge.

Hawkins, K. (1984) *Environment and Enforcement: Regulation and the Social Definition of Pollution*, Oxford: Clarendon Press.

Hawkins, K. (1990) 'Compliance strategy, prosecution policy and Aunt Sally', *British Journal of Criminology*, 30, 4: 444–66.

Herrnkind, M. (1993) 'Grüne kriminalpolitik im Schweizer Kanton Zug', *Burgerrechte und Polizei*, 45, 2: 72–5.

Hoogenboom, B. (1991) 'Grey policing: a theoretical framework', *Policing and Society*, Spring, 2, 1: 17–30

Howarth, W. (1991) 'Crimes against the aquatic environment', *Journal of Law and Society*, (special issue), 18, 1: 95–109.

Howe, G. M. (1976) *Man, Environment and Disease in Britain: A Medical Geography through the Ages*, Harmondsworth: Penguin Pelican.

Koser Wilson, N. (1996) 'An ecofeminist critique of environmental criminal law', in S. Edwards, *et al.* (eds) (1996).

Lash, S. Szerszynski, B. and Wynne, B. (eds) (1996) *Risk, Environment and Modernity: Towards a New Ecology*, London: Sage / TCS.

Maguire M., Morgan R. and Reiner, R. (eds) (1994) *The Oxford Handbook of Criminology*, Oxford: Oxford University Press.

McKenna, S. (1993) 'The environment, crime and the police', *The Police Journal*, 66, 1: 95–103.

Miller, C. (1995) 'Environmental rights: European fact or English fiction?', *Journal of Law and Society*, 22, 3: 374–93.

Mills, C. W. (1959) *The Sociological Imagination*, New York: Oxford University Press.

Nadelmann, E. (1990) 'Global prohibition regimes: the evolution of norms in international society', *International Organization*, 44, 4: 479–526.

Nelken, D. (1994) 'White-collar crime' in M. Maguire *et al.* (eds) (1994).

Paehlke, R. (1995) 'Environmental harm and corporate crime' in F. Pearce and L. Snider (eds) (1995): 305–321.

Pearce, F. and Snider, L. (eds) (1995) *Corporate Crime: Contemporary Debates*, Toronto: University of Toronto Press.

Pearce, F. and Tombs, S. (1990) 'Ideology, hegemony and empiricism: compliance theories of regulation', *British Journal of Criminology*, 30, 4: 423–43.

Pearce, F. and Tombs, S. (1991) 'Policing corporate skid-rows: a reply to Keith Hawkins', *British Journal of Criminology*, 31, 4: 415–26.

Pearce, F. and Tombs, S. (1993) 'US Capital versus the Third World: Union Carbide and Bhopal' in F. Pearce and M. Woodiwiss (eds) (1993).

Pearce, F. and Woodiwiss, M. (eds) (1993) *Global Crime Connections: Dynamics and Control*, London: Macmillan.

Pitch, T. (1995) *Limited Responsibilities: Social Movements and Criminal Justice*, London: Routledge.

Pocar, V. (1992) 'Animal rights: a socio-legal perspective', *Journal of Law and Society*, vol. 19, 2, Summer, 1992: 214–230

Pope, S. Appleton, M. and Wheal, E.-A. (1991) *The Green Book*, London: Hodder and Stoughton.

Porritt, J. (1990) *Where On Earth Are We Going?*, London: BBC Books.

Ridley, A. and Dunford, L. (1994) 'Corporate liability for manslaughter: reform and the art of the possible', *International Journal of the Sociology of Law*, 22: 309–28.

Rowell, A. (1996) *Green Backlash: Global Subversion of the Environment Movement*, London: Routledge.

Ruggiero, V. (1996) *Organized and Corporate Crime in Europe: Offers That Can't Be Refused*, Aldershot: Dartmouth.

Ruzza, C. (1996) 'Inter-organisational negotiations in political decision-making: Brussels' EC bureaucrats and the environment' in C. Samson and N. South (eds) *The Social Construction of Social Policy*, London: Macmillan.

Scarpitti, A. and Block, A. (1987) 'America's toxic waste racket' in T. S. Bynum (ed.) *Organized Crime in America: Concepts and Controversies*, New York: Criminal Justice Publishers.

Snider, L. (1990) 'Cooperative models and corporate crime: panacea or cop-out?', *Crime and Delinquency*, 36, 3: 373–90.

Snider, L. (1991) 'The regulatory dance: understanding reform processes in corporate crime', *International Journal of the Sociology of Law*, 19: 209–36.

South, N. (1997) 'Late-modern criminology: 'late' as in 'dead', or 'modern' as in 'new'?', in D. Owen (ed.) *Sociology After Postmodernism*, London: Sage

Szasz, A. (1986) 'Corporations, organized crime, and the disposal of hazardous waste: an examination of the making of a criminogenic regulatory structure', *Criminology*, 24, 1: 1–27.

Szasz, A. (1994) *EcoPopulism: Toxic Waste and the Movement for Environmental Justice*, Minneapolis: University of Minnesota Press.

Uhlig, R. (1996) 'Gene-engineered foods are unsafe, says scientist', *Daily Telegraph*, September: 4.

Van Altena, M. J. (1987) 'Combating environmental crime: analogies with the fight against fraud', *International Criminal Police Review*, September–October, 26–9.

Van Duyne, P. (1993) 'Organised crime and business crime-enterprises in the Netherlands', *Crime, Law and Social Change*, 19: 103–142.

Weale, A. (1996) 'Grinding slow and grinding sure? The making of the Environment Agency', *Environmental Management and Health*, 7, 2: 40–43.

Winter, G. (ed.) (1996) *European Environmental Law: A Comparative Perspective*, Aldershot: Dartmouth.

28

WAR AND CRIME IN THE FORMER YUGOSLAVIA

Vesna Nikolić-Ristanović

Introduction

It may be a kind of "privilege" for a criminologist to have the opportunity to observe directly the perpetration of crimes. In order to make it more understandable for you, before I start speaking about war and crime in the former Yugoslavia, I want to describe my usual trip from my home to my office in Belgrade. I commute by bus for about 20 minutes. - People are anxious because buses are irregular and crowded, they swear and insult each other. Sometimes, a passenger is assaulted and beaten, sometimes he or she is the victim of pickpocketing. When I get out I am faced with one of the largest black markets in town where one can buy everything that is not accessible in stores: from sugar, milk and baby equipment to gasoline, cigarettes and foreign currency. Going further I usually meet armed men wearing military uniforms. Sometimes there are some arguments among them or between them and other people which not so rarely end up in violence and the use of firearms and bombs. Sometimes passers-by are exposed to police brutality. Fortunately, I survive and reach a small room which my colleagues and I now use as our office. In order to provide us with decent salaries and basic stationery, the head of our Institute had to rent our regular office rooms to a company which deals with smuggling of gasoline.

The text quoted above was part of my presentation on war and crime in the former Yugoslavia given on 17 September 1993 at a lunch seminar in the School of Criminology, University of Montreal. It illustrates the overall criminalization of Serbian society in the middle of the war in the former Yugoslavia and suggests the potential for direct observation in such a situation.

If we look at the literature on crime, we can see that the influence of war on crime has only rarely been the subject of criminological research and analysis. This is not so strange if we know that crime statistics in wartime are either unavailable or unreliable, and that empirical research is, for various reasons, impossible. Direct observation is also hardly possible since criminologists are, just like everybody else, overburdened by everyday fear and care for their own survival. Thus it seems that mainly secondary sources, including incomplete and unreliable statistical data and more or less biased press cuttings, may be used as a basis for analyses of crime causation during war. After the war, it becomes easier to follow crime trends since statistics become available and more reliable. This was the case in the former Yugoslavia as it has been in other countries affected by war. But the situation in the former Yugoslavia was in some ways specific as well.

The Federal Republic of Yugoslavia (Serbia and Montenegro) was not directly affected by the war but experienced many of its consequences. As can be seen from the quotation above, distance from the war, on the one hand, and a changed picture of crime as a consequence of war in neighboring areas, on the other, enabled us to observe the influence of war on crime. Distance from warfare also enabled us to interview refugees and learn more about crime in territories directly affected by the war. And, finally, crime statistics in the Federal Republic of Yugoslavia were constantly available during the war and were more reliable (if only relatively so) than statistics on crime in areas directly affected by war. Thus, official and other statistics for the Federal Republic of Yugoslavia reflect general trends in crime produced by the war and, at this moment (together with findings of a recent victimization survey for the capital, Belgrade) provide the most convenient bases for analysis of the influence of the war on crime.

Up-to-date research on war and crime

Studies of the influence of war on crime, usually considering total war waged by one nation against other nations (e.g. both world wars), have produced mainly similar findings. The very few authors who have dealt with war and crime, suggest that war, as a phenomenon of social disorganization followed by paralyzed or biased formal control, usually creates favorable conditions for the increase of the crime rate, weakens inhibitions, encourages primitive impulses and, in such a way, contributes to the temporary transformation of the rate, usual structure and phenomenology of crimes (Gassin 1988: 327). All available data for the First and Second World Wars shows that the crime rate increases during and after the war. As a consequence of war, the structure of crime changes as well. War leads to an increase of military, property and violent crimes, to an increase of juvenile and female crime while the rate of reported sexual crimes stagnates with an increase in the hidden incidence of crime. A war affects the regional distribution of crimes as well (Reckless 1940: 253; Exner quoted in Reckless 1940: 253; Kinberg 1960: 192; Archer and Gartner quoted in Gassin 1988: 327; Gassin 1988: 328; Schneider 1987: 243).

However, we still know almost nothing about the influence of civil wars on crime. Although some conclusions drawn from observations of crime in international wars may be applicable to civil wars as well, there are some particular attributes which result from the specific nature of civil wars. Having in mind the predominantly internal aspect of the war in the former Yugoslavia,[1] the main aim of this chapter is the observation and analysis of the phenomenology of crime as well as the causes of crime related to civil war. The causes of crime related to the external aspect of this war as a specificity of the civil war in the former Yugoslavia will be considered as well so that some of our conclusions are expected to be applicable to the impact of a war on crime in general, i.e. regardless of its nature. We will focus our analysis on the war in Bosnia-Herzegovina. As the sources for our analyses we use available official statistics, press cuttings, our own research findings (Nikolić-Ristanović *et al.*, 1995, 1996; Nikolić-Ristanović, 1996a), reports on human rights violations as well as data of the International Crime (Victim) Survey carried out in Belgrade during the months of April and May 1996.

How the war influenced crime in the former Yugoslavia: the impact on the extent, structure and main characteristics of crime

As we stated above, the war in Bosnia-Herzegovina was predominantly an internal armed conflict with external intervening factors. Another important characteristic of this war was its inter-ethnic nature: this was a war among people of different ethnic origins who had been living next to each other or in the same country for years before the conflict broke out. This fact, in addition to revived memories of ethnic conflicts and atrocities that took place during the Second World War, strongly shaped the extent, structure and seriousness of crimes committed during the war. National sentiments and resentments have been exploited by the media and politicians in Serbia, Croatia and Bosnia-Herzegovina. As British experts found out, the inter-ethnic nature of the war also impacted on the mental health of those who survived, and was interpreted by some as a potential source of influence on future criminal actions (quoted in *Vreme*, 1996).

The external intervening factors in this predominantly civil war affected crime significantly. The fact that Croatian and Serbian regular and irregular armies were involved is of crucial importance for understanding both the crimes committed in Bosnia-Herzegovina and the crimes in neighboring areas: Croatia and FR Yugoslavia.[2]

Areas directly affected by the war: Bosnia-Herzegovina

It is very difficult to find out even rough numbers of crimes committed during the war in Bosnia-Herzegovina. However, numerous reports on human-rights violations as well as our interviews with refugee women show that crimes were widespread, brutal and serious in their consequences. Civilians were not only targets of military action but were also the victims of deliberate and arbitrary murders, assaults, sexual violence and pillage. Available data suggests that during the war in Bosnia-Herzegovina violent and property-related crimes prevailed (Amnesty International Report, 1993; Final Report of UN experts, 1994; *Mazowietzki Report*, 1993 and 1994). Ethnic origin was the main victimization-risk factor and especially vulnerable were those people who were living in areas occupied by an enemy ethnic group.[3] The fact that formal control agencies were in the hands of the enemy ethnic group meant that they were biased. This not only means that crimes committed by members of their own ethnic group against people from different ethnic groups were condoned but also that their power was abused in cases of arbitrary arrests, torture, killings, rapes and pillage against members of different ethnic groups. There is no evidence that there were efforts made by political and military leaders to prevent such crimes against civilians (*Mazovietzki Report*, 1992, Annex II).

Arbitrary arrests, violent and property crimes were mainly committed by police and paramilitary forces (*Mazovietzki Report*, 1992, Annex II). The testimonies of refugees from Bosnia-Herzegovina suggest that the role of the police was often in the hands of people who were known as criminals before the war ("Kako su 'čišćeni' Šamac i Brčko," *Naša borba*, 1995; Bojič, 1995: 61–2; Nikolić-Ristanović *et al.* 1995: 51). Such police arrested people of other nationalities in the streets and put them in numerous unacknowledged places of detention (Amnesty International Report, 1992), which were also often under the control of criminals and where people were tortured, raped and killed. Police also entered apartments under the pretext of conducting a search, stole property and/or money, raped women, physically abused and arrested people of different ethnic origins. The choice of victims of different ethnic groups was not always accidental. For example, men eligible for mobilization as well as prominent people such as political activists, educated people and owners of businesses were targeted for detention and interrogation. Very often, former neighbors, colleagues or schoolmates were killed, raped or arrested in retaliation for some real or alleged wrong committed before the war, by the victim, victim's husband or other member of the family. Women and young girls were often sexually and/or physically abused[4] because their husbands, fathers or sons went into battle (Nikolić-Ristanović *et al.* 1995: 53–55).

The criminal behavior of members of the paramilitary forces from Bosnia-Herzegovina, Serbia and Croatia was almost the same as the criminal behavior of police forces. They were recruited from obsessed soccer fans,[5] criminals and alcoholics, and one in five volunteers had committed serious offenses, some going to battle directly after serving their time. According to unverified sources, some of the prisoners who were about to finish their sentence, were allowed to "reduce" it if they agreed to join the volunteers (Korać 1994: 510). Also, Croatian paramilitary forces, known by the acronym HOS, which was the military wing of a political party known as the Croatian Right Party whose ideology was openly fascist (Mazovietzki Report, 1992, Annex II), was one which committed the most serious crimes against Serbs in Croatia as well as against both Serbs and Moslems in Bosnia-Herzegovina. Refugees we spoke to also mentioned crimes committed by Moslem paramilitary forces such as *Zelene Beretke*.

Uniforms and weapons meant both power and a license for committing crimes. Even some of those who used to be law-abiding men started to kill, beat, rape and steal property from people of different nationalities since everything was allowed in the name of "national liberation" and "self-determination." As was well noted by Korać

> it was crucial for the male-ethnic leadership to create a "real warrior" who is capable of fighting "sacred" ethnic-national wars. It took time and a lot of manipulation and war propaganda to create "national enemies" and paranoia within ethnic-national communities, and consequently a "real man," a "patriot" who would fight back in "defence" from "the eternal enemy" of "our" ethnic-national communities.
>
> (Korać 1994: 510)

To be a national "hero" started to be the dream of many ordinary men who became unordinary by the simple fact that they had a uniform and weapons. For many of them the war was an opportunity to become rich overnight as well. We learned from testimonies of refugees that people who had wanted to leave towns under siege had to pay enormous amounts of foreign currency which was shared among soldiers of all ethnic groups involved in the conflict. There were also countless examples of pillaging of empty property (Ortakovski 1993: 254) with goods sold on the black markets, making the armed conflict profitable for some of its participants.

However, as in other wars (Liepmann, quoted in Reckless 1940: 253) some persons who had never been involved in crime before turned to it under the influence of dire necessity and the breaking down of inhibitions as well. Loss of a job and the impossibility of earning money, shortages and extremely high prices of essential goods, urged people to commit thefts and frauds in order to survive. For the same reasons, women turned to prostitution. War zones were also centers of organized crimes related to illicit trade of drugs, fuel, weapons and human organs ("Ljudski organi skuplji od oružja," *Politika*, 1996).

The status of complete social disorganization which led to overcriminalization, complete insecurity, fear and distrust associated with the formal control agencies, is best described by a man from Sarajevo: "Every day people were asked to show identity cards, they were taken away and did not come back, abducted in streets and put in trucks, police rushed into their apartments. ... Everyone was police or army and everyone had weapons" (Bojić 1995: 102).

Neighboring areas indirectly affected by the war: the Federal Republic of Yugoslavia

The Federal Republic of Yugoslavia, a part of the former Yugoslavia which now consists of two republics – Serbia and Montenegro, has borders with Bosnia-Herzegovina and Croatia, i.e. areas which were directly affected by war. The Federal Republic of Yugoslavia was not directly affected by the war. However, its position in relation to the war and its consequences was complex: on the one hand, the government never recognized that the Federal Republic of Yugoslavia was involved in the war while on the other, men from FRY went into battle and people suffered a lot of its (indirect) consequences. The main factors which contributed to the changes in the extent and structure of crimes in FR Yugoslavia committed during and after the war, include: the closeness of warfare, the fact that a lot of men from FR Yugoslavia went to battle in Bosnia-Herzegovina as well as a severe economic crisis as a consequence of the expenditure of a great part of the state budget on the war to help Serbs in Croatia and Bosnia-Herzegovina, an enormous influx of refugees, and UN sanctions.

If we look at the statistical data on reported crime in FR Yugoslavia for the period 1990–1994 (the last period for which we have available data, which includes the period of the war apart from the last war year – 1995) we can notice that crime showed trends that are very similar to the trends reported for both World Wars.

Data presented in Table 28.1 shows a constant increase in the total number of persons who reported crimes in FR Yugoslavia in the period 1990–1994. The crime trend in this period is completely different from the trend in the earlier period, 1984–1990, when crime had a stagnating tendency. Crime started to rise in 1991, or at the beginning of the war in the former Yugoslavia and culminated in the middle period of the war – 1993. In that year, there were reported 44 percent more offenders than in 1990. In the same year, the rise of reported juvenile delinquents was 38 percent in comparison with 1990. In 1994 the number of reported criminal offenders dropped but still remained high in comparison with 1990.

It is worth mentioning that in the same period, in spite of the increase of reported offenders, the number of persons convicted for crimes had a decreasing tendency. For example, in 1992 the number of convicted persons dropped by 27

Table 28.1 Reported crimes in FR Yugoslavia 1990–1994

Year	Total index (No/%)		Juvenile index (No/%)		Adults index (No/%)	
1990	120,442	100	5,368	100	115,074	100
1991	123,189	102	4,947	92	118,242	102
1992	135,105	112	5,798	108	129,307	112
1993	173,642	144	7,426	138	166,216	144
1994	159,016	132	5,781	107	153,235	133

percent in comparison with 1990. This discrepancy between the number of reported crimes and the number of convicted persons can be explained by the inefficiency of formal control agencies under the influence of the war and economic crisis. A good indicator of this is the great increase of the number of unsolved crimes, i.e. with unknown offenders. In 1993 the number of unknown offenders was 75,950 which was almost double the 1990 figure of 39,432.

The changes in crime during the war are more obvious when we consider the types of crime reported. The increase in crime was not equal for all crimes. The rate of property and economic crimes rose significantly. Property crimes increased by 59 percent, and economic crimes by 53 percent. The total number of offenders reported for crimes against life and limb had a decreasing tendency while the number of offenders reported for the most serious crimes, such as murders, attempted murders and serious bodily injuries, increased. Generally, the changes in crime structure are most obvious if we consider the most serious crimes.

As we can see from Table 28.2, illegal possession of weapons, robbery and burglary reached the highest rate of increase among the crimes under consideration. Illegal possession of weapons started to be reported during the war, i.e. 1992 and rose by 346 percent during 1994. In comparison with 1990 the number of reported robbery offenses increased by 344 percent, with far more frequent fatal consequences than previously. Burglaries also showed an enormous rise so that the number of persons reporting burglary increased by 115 percent (or more than double). At the beginning of the war, the number of reported assault and battery, robbery and burglary offenders dropped but in the middle period of the war they started to increase rapidly. With some minor oscillations, homicides had a tendency to increase and reached their highest point in 1993 with a 37 percent increase in comparison to 1990. The number of reported rape offenders had a tendency to decrease until 1994 when it started to go up slightly.

The most serious crimes committed by juveniles increased more than adult crimes. The rate of reported juvenile homicides and robberies doubled and burglaries almost tripled in 1994 in comparison with 1990. As with adult rape cases, reported rapes committed by juveniles had a tendency to decrease.

The increase of violent crimes is most striking in big cities such as Belgrade. More than half of all homicides reported in FRY were committed in Belgrade. In comparison with 1990, the number of homicides committed in Belgrade in 1995 increased more than three times. Both adult and juvenile homicides are very often committed as a result of conflicts between criminal gangs and, far more than previously, victims are killed by use of firearms which are most often in the illegal possession of offenders (Portret domaćeg ubice, *Vreme*, 1996). Firearms were often brought back from warfare by soldiers or purchased on the black market.[6] There are also refugees among both offenders and victims of violent and property crimes. People of ethnic origin other than Serbian, and also political opponents, were especially vulnerable to becoming victims of homicides and robberies.

Table 28.2 Adult offenders reported for selected crime 1990–1994

Year	Homicide		Assaults and batteries		Robbery		Burglary		Illegal possession of weapons		Rape	
	Total	Index	Total	Index	Total	Index	Total	Index	Total	Index	Total	Index
1990	503	100	1,860	100	477	100	22,626	100	—	—	364	100
1991	619	123	1,662	89	449	94	26,336	116	—	—	329	90
1992	570	113	1,373	73	482	101	31,629	139	2,111	100	311	85
1993	694	137	1,513	81	1,064	223	50,217	221	7,136	338	306	84
1994	619	123	1,648	88	2,118	444	48,869	215	9,432	446	341	93

Findings of an International Crime (Victim) Survey, conducted by Institute for Criminological and Sociological Research (in cooperation with UNICRI, Rome) in Belgrade during 1996, showed a high victimization rate in the previous five years as well. As many as 85.4 percent of 1,094 respondents reported they had been victims of crime during the past five years. 56.5 percent of the respondents reported theft, 16 percent assault or threat, 16 percent attempted burglary and burglary, and 4.3 percent reported being victimized by robbery. Theft from the car was reported by 45 percent, car vandalism by 29.3 percent, and theft of car by 8.2 percent of car owners. Among female respondents, 2 percent reported sexual incidents. The victimization rate was the highest in 1995: 40.9 percent of respondents reported being victimized in that year: 39 percent by attempted burglary, 32.7 percent by burglary, 35.7 percent by sexual violence, 34.9 percent by assault or threat, 33.6 percent by car vandalism and 31.1 percent by personal theft. Results related to victimization in 1995 could be evidence of rising rates of crime triggered by the approaching end of the war in the former Yugoslavia, i.e. by the economic crisis and state of anomie as a consequence of the war. These results may also be an indicator of a further rise of crime after the war (Nikolić-Ristanović, unpublished).

Although there is no systematic research on crime during the war, available data suggest that those who commit the most serious violent crimes are very often former soldiers. Some of these simply continue to do what they did in warfare but some become violent as the result of post-traumatic stress disorder resulting from their war experience. This latter phenomenon began to appear especially after the end of the war. Also, some criminals who had left the country and been "successful" elsewhere in their criminal activity before the war, returned to FRY when the war began, finding more favorable conditions for criminal activity and profit there. Some of these became symbolic carriers of certain messages about national politics and nationalism and as such were idolized in state media during the war ("Vreme prokriminalne kulture," *Naša borba*, 1995). Many young people found in them their idols and followed their example in engaging in crime. Juvenile and young adults' delinquency was strongly influenced by other adult criminals for whom the conditions created by the war were extremely profitable. The fact that crime is evidently more profitable than law-abiding behavior, i.e. that the nouveau riche in FRY are mainly criminals while law-abiding people hardly survive, led many young people to see the attractions of crime as a way to gain both social affirmation and profit. There are some indicators that a signifi-cant number of young people (about 30 years old but juveniles as well) are involved in organized crime. Older adult criminals hire them since they are cheap: they kill, steal cars, sell or grab narcotics for small amounts of money (Radovanović quoted in "Dažvni neprijatelj broj tri," *Vreme*, 1995; Ruggiero and South 1995: 199–200).

Organized crime appeared in FRY as well as in areas directly affected by the war because the war created various needs which could be satisfied by organized crime rather than by legal means. Apart from organized crime connected to the drugs and weapons trades which developed as a direct consequence of the war, UN sanctions imposed on FRY led to the creation of organizations for the trade of fuel, cigarettes and other scarce goods. The economic crisis which had resulted from both the war and UN sanctions led to the criminalization of society on an enormous scale. Although it was not reported officially, it is well known that during the war, almost every citizen in FRY was involved in some kind of illegal activity. Enormous inflation and the impossibility of earning a significant income legally, encouraged a large number of people to acquire and use foreign instead of national currency, smuggle and sell deficient goods on the black market or resort to other legally-questionable activities in order to survive. As Bolčić pointed out:

> hidden economy is also divided into two parts: a "black economy," where a small number of "criminalised businessmen" engaged in major import/export deals under the conditions of UN sanctions, and a small-scale, "flea market" or "street-corner economy" involving thousands of impoverished "ordinary" individuals who are trying to earn their elementary living ... this "flourishing" hidden economy has become indispensable for many individuals and "social" and private firms: it provided a "temporary alternative employment" for those nominally employed in regular enterprises and made possible all sorts of "businesses" which would not have been feasible under the existing regulations.
>
> (Bolčić 1995: 153)

In such social conditions, when crimes related to the hidden economy become useful and desirable, the state's interest in punishing offenders disappears. This further led to the creation of the state of complete anomie and generated a further rise of crime and other forms of deviant social behaviors (Ćirić 1993: 107).

Contrary to the incidence of male crimes, reported female crime had a decreasing tendency – from 9.5 percent of total reported crime in 1990 to 6.4 percent in 1994. The number of reported female offenders dropped by 60 percent from 1990 to 1994. In time of war women often turn toward the private, domestic sphere, spend a great deal of time taking care of their families' existential needs and are more ready than usual to sacrifice themselves for persons close to them rather than to respond to violence against them. Thus crimes women usually commit (theft, infraction, assault and battery and homicide against someone close to them) decreased. However, perhaps predictably, women did begin to commit more crimes connected to their worsened economic position and/or their new position as head of the family (in the absence of male members). It must be acknowledged that these are crimes for which statistics do not provide us with reliable data since they mainly remain unreported. However, it does seem to be the case that, as in earlier wars (Schneider 1987: 244), women become more involved in many illegal acts connected to smuggling and the black market economy which were generally under-reported. The available data does support the suggestion that, in spite of the decrease in the total number of women reported for offenses or crimes, the number of women reported for serious property crimes and some violent crimes (not including those against persons close to them or as a response to an attack) increased. For example, the number of women reported for burglary increased almost four times (224 in 1990 in comparison to 876 in 1994). Also, the number of women reported for robberies (including robberies with fatal consequences) more than doubled (13 in 1990 in comparison to 29 in 1994). However, as for male crimes, the most enormous rise is related to reported crimes of illegal possession of weapons – 43 in 1992 in comparison to 234 in 1994.

Nonetheless, during the war as in times of peace, women were victims more often than offenders in areas both directly and indirectly affected by the war. In the absence of research evidence, it is difficult to explain the decrease of reported rapes during the war. However, having in mind that rape was widespread in areas directly affected by war as well as the fact that a lot of men from FRY (many of them with a criminal past) were involved in the war, it may be that this decrease in rape was the temporary consequence of the absence of men who raped during the war. The slight increase in the number of reported rapes during 1994 may confirm this assumption if we bear in mind that at that time soldiers started to return home. In these circumstances their accumulated aggression and war experience made their crimes more brutal and more often led to fatal consequences. According to media coverage, which, with reliable statistics lacking, has become an important source of knowledge about crimes even for academics, it would seem that recently, sexual crimes are more often than previously, followed by inhuman cruelty and result in the death of the victims, with the offenders remaining unknown to the police even after a series of such cases.

A second explanation is that, the decrease in reported rapes in FRY during the war may in fact hide an increase in the number of unreported rape offenses, characteristic of rape in earlier wars as well (Schneider 1987: 245). During the war, women and men alike had less confidence in the police, who were regarded as more interested in protecting the political regime from its opponents than in resolving crimes. Thus the hidden incidence of rapes (which was always high) rose significantly during the war, reflecting both general distrust of the police and the particular distrust felt by women who may be afraid that the police, who were seen to prioritize more "important" duties, would be more sexist and uninterested toward them than ever. Young girls who became victims of trafficking in women as "commodities" for purposes of sexual exploitation were also afraid to turn to the police. Because of both a high unemployment rate (which has its most serious impact on women) and a low standard of living, young women who look for ways of earning money and improving their life, very easily become victims of internationally organized groups of criminals who take them abroad and keep them in bordellos where they become sex slaves.

472

Although – as was also the case earlier – domestic violence is under reported to the police, it became more widespread and serious during the war as well. One of the indicators of the large number of cases of victimization of women within the family is data on the cases reported to the SOS hotline in Belgrade. The number of women who called the SOS telephone increased from 499 in 1990 to 1,377 in 1995. Although the increase in the number of women who reported their victimization to the SOS hotline may be influenced by different factors, some of which may be related to the increase of women's awareness of the existence of SOS and its possible ability to advise or help them, these data obviously confirm our contention that domestic violence is widespread in society. Apart from the increase of calls from women who were molested by their husbands, the number of women who reported being beaten by their sons has also increased from 6.4 percent in 1991 to 11.4 percent in 1993. After 1993 the number of women who reported suffering violence from their sons started to decrease so that in 1995 9 percent of such calls were registered.

Findings of one recent research study (Nikolić-Ristanović 1994: 3) show that more than half of the women (112 or 58.3 percent) out of a sample of 192 women reported that they were victims of some kind of spouse abuse. 94 or 49 percent of women reported psychological violence while 36 or 18.7 percent of women reported that they were victims of wife battering. Also, 18.7 percent of women reported that they were raped by their husbands. Wife battering was usually followed by other kinds of violence. Women who were beaten by their husbands were at the same time victims of psychological (38.9 percent) or sexual violence (25 percent), or both of them (52.8 percent). The same research shows that most often women report that the reasons for their husband's violent behavior were quarrels over money matters (14.3 percent) or parents (10.4 percent). This is not surprising if we bear in mind the dire financial situation of the majority of families as well as the fact that very often married couples live with their parents and/or are dependent on them. While research findings show that a great majority of husbands have permanent (75.9 percent) or temporary (10.7 percent) jobs, this does not support a conclusion that violent husbands are simply those without financial problems. On the contrary, it seems that the findings of this particular study confirm earlier findings regarding the connection between financial problems and violence against women in marriage and the significance of frustration and stress as mediators (Straus, Gelles i Steinmetz, quoted by Smith 1989: 25). In fact, in the FR Yugoslavia, due to the conditions of economic crisis, having a permanent job does not mean having financial security. Even people with a high level of education and "permanent" jobs do not earn enough money to satisfy all their basic, let alone their existential, needs. It seems that this new situation in which even educated and employed men are not able to earn enough money to support their families (as is expected from husbands in a patriarchal society) produces frustration and aggression in husbands (Smith 1989: 25). And, as usual, wives are those who are seen as deficient when circumstances worsen (Klein 1981: 75).

One further recent analysis of the impact of the war on domestic violence (Nikolić-Ristanović 1996: 76–8) shows that a general package of characteristics in these cases is that the beginning or aggravation of violence is related to: soldiers' returning home, the ideology of nationalism, aggravation of social position and financial situation resulting from refugee status or from the economic constraints upon either the husband or wife as a consequence of economic crises or/and refugee status. All reported molesters regularly use weapons (pistols, bombs) in threatening their victims. Some of them have become more violent as a result of their experience of war. Some have started to increase alcohol consumption and beat their mothers and wives for the first time when they return home from warfare and some start to rape their wives. Differences arising from membership of different ethnic groups or differences in political opinions between spouses are also sources of conflict and violence in marriages. In some cases violence has become more severe because a wife belongs to a different ethnic group than that of her husband but in other cases it is nationalism that has provoked the violent behavior of the husband. Nationalism does not dominate discourse in politics and the media alone. Its reflection is obvious in all, even personal, relationships. As Smith has pointed out "everything that happens in global society is reflected in the family" (Smith 1989: 30). The phenomenon of abstract hatred directed against other nationalities has been smoothly transformed into a hatred against very close persons such as wives, children and relatives. In this respect, these persons may be seen as concrete symbols of "enemies" and/or as parts of their husbands' property which have become bad and worthless because of their ethnic origin as well as a source of shame for husbands and of problems arising in interactions with significant others outside of the family.

Conclusion: towards the explanation of the influence of the war in the former Yugoslavia on crime

In the light of the above analyses of crime in the former Yugoslavia, it is obvious that any general theory or explanation of the influence of the war on crime can be possible only if we place "micro-causal explanations in a wider socio-political context" (Lynch and Groves 1989: 55). What follows is our attempt to explain both "immediate" and "wider origins" (Taylor *et al.* quoted in Lynch and Groves 1989: 56) of crime during the war, starting from a radical perspective and using the main assumptions of theories of social disorganization, anomie and social-learning.

Social disorganization manifests itself in especially dramatic and pervasive forms in a war (Caldwell 1956: 221). War produces a breakdown of formal and informal control as well as the inability (or at least diminished ability) of groups or individuals in a community or neighborhood to solve problems collectively. As we can see from the above analyses of crime in war zones in Bosnia-Herzegovina, the breakdown of institutional control in war primarily creates favorable conditions for those who were criminals before the war. Selective and arbitrary arrests affect non-criminals rather than criminals, and force people to live in constant fear and legal insecurity since no one knows who should be considered as "a criminal," who are "the police" and who are "the army." Criminals become incorporated into formal control agencies, and criminal behavior is not only unpunished – it is even regarded as desirable as a strategy of inter-ethnic war. As we have observed above, during the war political leaders did not even try to do anything to prevent crimes against civilians. On the contrary, they perceived and pursued the benefits that may arise from these crimes in terms of the terror which served their aims: ethnic cleansing, demoralization of the enemy and so on. Another use of criminals by political leaders had played an especially import-ant role at the beginning of the war when law-abiding people still did not feel enough endangered to be ready to go into battle. Unsurprisingly, criminals were among the first who were ready to use weapons and join the war. The crimes they then committed were welcomed by political leaders as a pretext for a further call to arms, i.e. the creation of a sense of danger to the nation and call for law-abiding people to also join the battle. The lack of any wish to prevent or at least to control the participation of criminals in the war, either as a part of police or paramilitary forces, leads us to the assumption that war lords consciously used criminals in order to achieve their aims. This is confirmed by the fact that some criminals went directly from prisons to battle, as well as by the high social posi-tions and important roles in national politics given to some leading criminals involved in the war. While in "total wars" criminals have usually been involved as combatants because of added demand for all sources of manpower (Cavan 1956: 596), the civil war in the former Yugoslavia suggests a different central role. This is not surprising if we bear in mind the aforementioned suggestion that it was not so easy for leaders to convince previously law-abiding people, who had been living together for years, to kill each other. To succeed in this astonishing and terrible mission they had to rely on the services of criminals in both generating war propaganda and sustaining the war itself.[7]

However, the social disorganization generated by the war has not only encour-aged criminals to continue with criminal activity and to be more brutal and greedy, it has also promoted the criminal activity of those who, before the war, were conformists and law-abiding. As Shoemaker noticed, "the individuals who live in such situations of social disorganization are not necessarily themselves personally disoriented; instead, they are viewed as responding 'naturally' to dis-organized environmental conditions" (Shoemaker 1990: 81–2). This is how we can explain the enormous rise of crime in areas both directly and indirectly affected by the war, i.e. the fact that in wartime almost all the people were involved in some kind of criminal activity.

To explain the overcriminalization of society during the war, learning theories and the theory of anomie would also be useful. First of all, people learn criminal motives from general culture. Once violence is made legitimate by war, "people apparently believe that if their leaders can solve problems with violence, it is also a suitable means for them to resort to to resolve interpersonal differences" (Archer and Gartner quoted by Conklin 1992: 272). This kind of social learning of criminal behavior during the war is especially characteristic of young people and presents a good framework for the explanation of the rise in violent crimes committed by juveniles. In the process of learning criminal motives the media played an especially important role. Biased information and the presentation of scenes of war violence urged people to go to battle and commit crimes in order to retaliate. Apart from this, the media's idolization of criminals offered a model for the behavior of a large portion of young people and taught them that being criminal is far more profitable than conforming.

People who went to battle and who were not criminals before, learned to be criminal in association with others who were criminals or in response to an excess of attitudes favoring crime (Sutherland 1939: 4–9). The criminal behavior learned in the war has continued to be the way of life for many who have come back home. In a war, the prohibition against killing becomes relative which leads to the rationalization of other killings and rendering of human life as worthless (Killias 1991: 280). This is one possible explanation for the rise of homicides in FRY committed by former soldiers. The other, or supplementary explanation, which takes into consideration post-traumatic stress disorder (similar to post-Vietnam syndrome) as the individual's reaction to social disorganization, is also applicable. Although there is no systematic research, the problem is evident from both psychiatric and court experience in FRY and indicates that a lot of men who have come back from warfare tend to commit violent crimes under the influence of postwar stress disorder (Jelkić 1996: 84). Namely, many of those who were "normal" men before the war and who were manipulated by national politics are now angry or else have a sense of guilt and are accused of being participants in a politically wrong and "dirty" war. Their potential victims are all those who revive their sense of hopelessness, uselessness and guilt for killings in warfare, especially if they are of the same ethnic origin as the ethnic origin of the offender's wartime enemy (Jelkić 1996: 85). It is when soldiers return from war that the wider origins of the crimes they have committed are evident.

If, in addition to everything mentioned above, we add easy access to weapons during the war as well as the fact that the majority of those who came back from warfare brought back weapons with them, the rise of violent crimes both during and after the war should not be surprising.

The war has also produced economic crisis and the state of anomie and these further contribute to the enormous rise of property crimes. The war directly and indirectly (e.g. through economic sanctions) affected the economy and the distribution of work and economic rewards (Shoemaker 1990: 98), and encouraged the majority of people to turn to various illegal activities. A large number of people who found themselves at a disadvantage by pursuing legitimate economic activities therefore became motivated to engage in illegitimate, delinquent activities. These people are "willing to work or otherwise be productive members of society but, because of the unavailability of employment or an opportunity to develop job skills, they turn to criminality, perhaps out of frustration with their situation or perhaps because of economic necessity" (Shoemaker 1990: 98). As we saw above, the lack of paid jobs and essential goods during the war urged a large number of people to be involved in traditional property crimes and different illegal activities related to the hidden economy. In this way, anomie produced by the war has contributed to the criminalization of an enormous proportion of the population which threatens to be the generator of further increases in crime in the period after the war. Different forms of organized crime, which were useful for the state during the war, are prohibited after the war. But, once created, these organizations only change the field of their illegal activity, usually turning to more dangerous but less "useful" activities (Ćirić 1993: 106). Also, people learned to earn money through crime, so that the system of values has been completely disturbed and it is not so easy, especially in the conditions of a destroyed economy, to motivate people to conform again. As findings from the victimization survey for Belgrade show, crime continues to rise after the war since the majority of causes remain in place and, indeed, have become even more intensive than during the war.

Notes

1 Although there were and still are controversial opinions about the nature of the war in the former Yugoslavia, it is clear that it had all the features of civil war with intervening external factors. The internal aspect of the war in former Yugoslavia was predominant since it took place within the territorial boundaries of Croatia and Bosnia-Herzegovina, recognized by the international community and the UN as states within those boundaries. The fact that in the armed conflicts in Bosnia-Herzegovina, for instance, regular and irregular Croatian and Serbian armed groups were also involved, does not alter the basic premise that it was an internal armed conflict with intervening external factors. (See Ortakovski 1993: 247.)

2 We will try to highlight only the situation concerning crime in FR Yugoslavia, as being the neighboring area for which we have available data.

3 Although some data suggest that crimes were committed among members of the same ethnic groups as well, this is less clear. For example, a Moslem refugee woman spoke about Serbs killing each other during disputes related to dividing the property stolen from Moslems. She also spoke about fatal threats directed against Serbian women in order to prevent them from socializing with Moslem women.

4 For more details about sexual and physical abuse of women in former Yugoslavia see Nikolić-Ristanović, 1996a.

5 It is worth mentioning that, for example, Arkan, a well known leader of paramilitary forces in the wars in former Yugoslavia, was the leader of the famous Belgrade soccer team *Crvena Zvezda* (The Red Star), as well as a prominent European criminal. The first large-scale bloody clashes between ethnic-national groups occurred between supporters of the two famous soccer clubs from Zagreb (Croatia) *Dinamo* and from Belgrade (Serbia) *Crvena Zvezda*, during a match at Zagreb's Maksimir Stadium on 13 May, 1990 (Korać, 1994).

6 Every second citizen of Yugoslavia possesses firearms ("Vreme prokriminalne kulture," 1995).

477

7 How people (men) from former Yugoslavia were reluctant to engage in war is well illustrated by the picture given by Sherwell of the average soldier in what was the Yugoslav National Army at the time of the brief war in Slovenia which was the beginning of the disintegration of the former Yugoslavia: "Most are young conscripts who appear to have little idea what the fighting was about . . . Many of the captured soldiers are little older than the schoolchildren whose paintings still adorn the walls. Several said they had no idea why they were ordered to seize border crossings and many admitted they had given up without firing a shot . . . The general view among 12 prisoners interviewed was that Yugoslavia's problems have to be resolved without bloodshed" (Sherwell quoted by Korać, 1994).

References

Bolčić S. (1995) "Changing Features of the Work Force in the Early Nineties," *Sociološki pregled*, 2: 149–163.

Bojić, D. (ed.) (1995) *Suffering of the Serbs in Sarajevo (document book – records)*, Beograd: Komesarijat za izbeglice Srbije.

Caldwell, R. (1956) *Criminology*, New York: The Ronald Press Company.

Cavan, R. S. (1956) *Criminology*, New York: Thomas Y. Crowel Company.

Conklin, J. (1992) *Criminology*, New York: Macmillan Publishing Company.

Ćirić, J. (1993) "Hiper-inflacija – kriminološki i kriviěnopravni problemi" ("Hyperinflation – criminological and criminal law problems") *Zbornik Instituta za kriminološka i sociološka istraživanja*, 1: 104–117.

Gassin, R. (1988) *Criminologie*, Paris: Dalloz.

Jelkić, O. (1996) "Post-traumatski poremećaj i kriviěna odgovornost – sindrom ratnog stresa (vijetnamski sindrom)" (Post-traumatic disorder and criminal responsibility – war stress syndrome (Vietnam syndrome)" in *Teorijski i praktični problemi jugoslovenskog kaznenog zakonodavstva*, Beograd: Institut za kriminološka i sociološka istraživanja.

Kinberg, O. (1960) *Les problems fondamentaux de la criminologie*, Paris: Editions Cujas.

Korać, M. (1994) "Representation of Mass Rape in Ethnic-Conflicts in What Was Yugoslavia," *Sociologija*, 4: 496–512.

Klein, D. (1981) "Violence against women: some considerations regarding its causes and its eliminations," *Crime and delinquency*, 1: 64–81.

Killias, M. (1991) *Precis de criminologie*, Bern: Editions Staempfli and Cie SA.

Lynch, M. and Groves, W. B. (1989) *A Primer in Radical Criminology*, Albany: Harrow and Heston Publishers.

Nikolić-Ristanović, V. (1994) "Domestic Violence in Conditions of War and Economical Crises," 8th International symposium of victimology, Adelaide.

Nikolić-Ristanović, V., Mrvić-Petrović, N., Konstantinović-Vilić, S. and Stevanović, I. (1995) *Žene, nasilje i rat* (Women, Violence and War), Beograd: Institut za kriminološka i sociološka istraživanja.

Nikolić-Ristanović V., Mrvić-Petrović, N., Konstantinović-Vilić, S., Knežić, B. and Stevanović, I. (1996) *Žene Krajine: rat, egzodus i izbeglištvo* (Women of Krajina: War, Exodus and Exile), Beograd: Institut za kriminološka i sociološka istraživanja.

Nikolić-Ristanović, V. (1996) "Domestic Violence Against Women in the Conditions of War and Economical Crisis" in Sumner, C., Israel M., O'Connell, M. and Sarre, R. (eds) *International Victimology*, Canberra: Australian Institute of Criminology.

Nikolić-Ristanović, V. (1996a) " War and Violence against Women" in J. Turpin and L. Lorentzen (eds) *The Gendered New World Order: Militarism, Development and Environment*, New York: Routledge.

Nikolić-Ristanović, V. *The Report on International Crime Victim Survey in Belgrade*, Rome: UNICRI (unpublished).

Ortakovski, V. (1993) "Violation of International Humanitarian Law in the Armed Conflicts in Croatia and Bosnia-Herzegovina" in S. Biserko (ed.) *Yugoslavia: Collapse, War, Crimes*, Beograd: Center for Anti-war Action and Belgrade Circle.

Reckless, W. (1940) *Criminal Behavior*, New York and London: McGraw-Hill Book Company.

Ruggiero, V. and South, N. (1995) *Eurodrugs: Drug Use, Markets and Trafficking in Europe*, London: UCL Press.

Schneider, H. J. (1987) *Kriminologie*, Berlin: Walter de Gruyter.

Smith, L. (1989) *Domestic Violence: An Overview of the Literature*, London: Home Office research and planning unit report.

Shoemaker, D. (1990) *Theories of Delinquency*, New York-Oxford: Oxford University Press.

Sutherland, E. (1939) *Principles of criminology*, Philadelphia: Lippincott.

Reports and newspapers

Yugoslavia-Further Reports of Torture and Deliberate and Arbitrary Killings in War Zones, Amnesty International Report, 1992.

Bosnia-Herzegovina – Gross abuses of Basic Human Rights, Amnesty International Report, 1992.

Bosnia-Herzegovina – Rape and Sexual Abuse by Armed Forces, Amnesty International Report, 1993.

Final Report of UN experts, 1994.

Mazovietzki Report, 1992, Annex II.

Mazowietzki Report, 1993 and 1994.

"Portret domaćeg ubice," *Vreme*, 23.3.1996.

"Državni neprijatelj broj tri," *Vreme*, 15.10.1995.

"Kako su 'čišceni' Šamac i Brčko," Naša Borba, 29–30.7.1995.

"Ljudski organi skuplji od oružja," *Politika*, 30.5.1996.

"Vreme prokriminalne kulture," *Naša Borba*, 10.11.1995.

29

TOWARDS A CRIMINOLOGY OF WAR IN EUROPE

Ruth Jamieson

Introduction: why a criminology of war?

Despite recent and important discussions of the descent into 'barbarism' in twentieth century Europe (Anderson 1990; Hobsbawm 1994a, 1994b; Ignatieff 1994; Meštrović 1993, 1996) and the incidence and ferocity of wars and ethnic conflicts which show no sign of abating (Holsti 1996; Wallensteen and Sollenberg 1996), contemporary European criminology remains largely aloof and unmoved by these issues.[1] The disinclination of contemporary criminology to foreground war and armed conflict is all the more astonishing when one considers (a) that as an empirical area of study, war offers a dramatic example of massive violence and victimization *in extremis*; (b) that these acts of violence and violations of human rights are accomplished *inter alia* through state action – which some would treat, specifically, as an instance of *state crime* (Cohen 1993, 1995a), (c) that they often also involve concerted as well as individual (often gender-specific) human action and collusion – akin, in many ways to issues treated in 'subcultural' criminology (Stiglmayer 1994; African Rights 1995b, 1995c); (d) that war and states of emergency usher in massive increases in social regulation, punishment and ideological control (Bonger 1935;[2] Jamieson 1988, 1996; Müller 1991; Rusche and Kirchheimer 1939), new techniques of surveillance (Dandeker 1990; Giddens 1987) and, with that, a corresponding derogation of civil rights (Durkheim 1992: 56; Simpson 1992; Stammers 1983).

Despite the pressing historical and substantive reasons for doing so, contemporary criminology has not been attentive to the complex connections (conjunctural, material, moral, gendered, and emotional) which structure the relationship between war and crime. It is not sufficient to re-animate the existing criminological literature on war and crime. Recent transformations in the nature of war and the nation-state preclude this, as do theoretical advances on the issues of gender, violence and social exclusion.

Defining war and crime

In the conventional criminological literature 'war' is usually taken to mean conventional interstate war – as distinct from the protracted civil or internal armed conflicts waged by either state (regular) armies or paramilitary groups engaged in struggles of state formation or fragmentation. (Cohen (1993, 1995a, 1995b) is a notable exception.) Furthermore Holsti (1996) suggests that the wars of the late twentieth century are fundamentally different from the European and Cold War experience of war. He thinks some contemporary conflicts constitute 'wars of the third kind' wherein

> Attrition, terror, psychology, and actions against civilians highlight 'combat'. Rather than highly organized armed forces based on a strict command hierarchy, wars are fought by loosely knit groups of regulars, irregulars, cells, and not infrequently by locally-based warlords under little or no central authority.
>
> (Holsti 1996: 20)

This same criminological literature has also tended to treat 'crime' as an unchanging 'natural' category. Crimes in war (as distinct from 'war crimes') have been regarded largely as a continuation of ordinary crime in an altered social (demographic), legal and political context, with a few novel permutations in offence and enforcement needing to be factored into 'criminological' accounts or analyses (e.g., new offences against defence regulations, or the 'black-out', or the 'black market' itself (Durkheim 1992: 117; von Hentig 1947; Mannheim 1941, 1965; Reckless 1942; Smithies 1982)). War crimes – that is, violations of the Laws of War or international conventions on human rights – tend to be treated as exceptional occurrences which are somehow marginal to the proper concerns of social science (Bauman 1989) despite the blindingly obvious relevance of a well-developed literature on so-called 'crimes of obedience' particularly to criminology (Browning 1992; Kelman and Hamilton 1989; Lifton 1974; Milgram 1974; Taylor 1970). As Stanley Cohen has pointed out, what is at issue today is not so much the fact that ordinary people are capable of acts of exceptional cruelty in particular sets of circumstances, but the question of *how* this is achieved or denied both psychologically and rhetorically (see Cohen 1993, 1995a and 1995b). This work is, or ought to be, as theoretically consequential for a criminology of the 'normalcy' of late modernity as it is for a criminology of war.

However, before outlining the main conceptual elements of what should constitute a criminology of war, it will be useful to provide a brief overview of the main explanatory models which have underpinned commentaries made on the relationship between war and crime to date.[3] One of the most noticeable aspects of these commentaries on war and crime is the extent to which different and sometimes quite contradictory explanatory models are interwoven in the same accounts. The Dutch Marxist criminologist Willem Bonger is a striking example of this tendency. In his first text, *Criminality and Economic Conditions* (1916) written during the Great War, he emphasized the direct relationship between the logic of capitalist accumulation and the state's deployment of its monopoly of the means of violence against other states, notably in a struggle for new markets. He also argued that militaristic capitalist states were prone to use their monopoly of force against their own civil populations. However, by 1936 in *An Introduction to Criminology* Bonger had come to regard war as a kind of social 'experiment' which made possible some kind of clinical examination of the different etiologies of crime.

> Now, the war has driven up to the top almost all the factors which may lead to crime. Family life was torn asunder through the absence of the man and the outdoor labour of the married woman; large numbers of children were being neglected; sexual demoralization was another consequence; poverty and destitution played havoc with the population, chiefly in countries which were hit by the blockade, and the high value of certain articles increased the incentive to wrong doing; the urge to enjoyment and covetousness had humanity, which had groaned under so much accumulated suffering, in its grip; general demoralization prevailed throughout the war, with its killing and maiming, its terrible destruction, its requisitioning or whatever it is called; all of which was completely opposed to the morals of normal life . . . . The statistics show criminality to have swollen like an avalanche, but in reality it increased much more still. For a large part of the male population, at the most criminal age, was in military service, and thereby out of the jurisdiction of the ordinary courts . . . while owing to the weakening of the police and judiciary a considerably smaller number of offences was discovered and prosecuted.
>
> (Bonger 1936: 104–105)

Subsequent analyses of the relationship between war and crime by social thinkers have tended to turn on one or more of the causal relationships enumerated by Bonger (and Durkheim 1992). All take 'social disorganization' in wartime conditions to be axiomatic.

Explanatory models of the war/crime relationship

War as 'anomie'

Durkheim (1992) and Sorokin (1944) both insist that war (and revolution) inevitably usher in a state of social disorganization and normlessness. No doubt they would argue that the genocidal aspects of civil wars like those in Bosnia or Rwanda are explicable simply as extreme expressions of the anomic effects of war. It could be argued, however, that some wars – so far from producing a sense of 'normlessness' – may usher in a state of hyper-discipline (both military and civil) involving the enactment of thousands of new legal regulations (and therefore offences), ever more strident ideological exhortations to duty and sacrifice and corresponding accusations of treachery, betrayal, etc. It may also be argued that such forms of emergency regulation serve to *accelerate* the emergence and rate of social change. Here the war crisis is seen as 'hastening and reinforcing the current of social events' (Gotto 1918; Hamon 1918) – for example in the development of the welfare services (Skocpol 1992) or changes in the gendered division of labour (Braybon and Summerfield 1981). In some conventional wars (e.g. the 'total war' of 1939–1945) it is possible for highly regulated social relations and new forms of social discipline and surveillance to exist *alongside* conditions of social disorganization and anomie – the displacement of populations, homelessness, the black market, etc. Wars of the 'third kind', like that in Somalia, may occupy a space beyond anomie, in the Hobbesian realm of a war of all against all.

War as a 'temporary reversal' of moral progress

A second, and equally teleological explanation construes 'war' as a temporary *reversal* of the civilizing process (wherein it had been assumed that 'war and the social forms bound up with it' would recede and the 'organs of depredation [would] tend to disappear' (Durkheim 1992: 71, 117)). Such a reversal was thought to involve either a 'temporary moral revolution' [backwards] (von Hentig 1947: 330) or a more rapid descent into an earlier, more *barbaric* state (Hobsbawm 1994a). Both forms of reversal are characterized by the removal of painful restraints on 'deep-seated, unsubdued and thus unemployed urges' (Glover 1946; von Hentig 1947) for which warfare provides an outlet and expression (Durkheim 1992; Hamon 1918). The breakup of homes and the perpetual vision of death was seen to produce 'a state of moral vertigo' (Roux 1917 quoted in Abbott 1918: 40).

Apparently women are more prone to wartime moral reversals than men. Mannheim (1965: 597) remarks on the 'wholesale deterioration of female criminality' under these conditions, a wartime trend also noted by Bonger (1936: 104) and Ruiz-Funes (1959). Von Hentig (1947: 344) attributes the increased rates of violent crime among women in wartime to 'the heightened irritability of the female mind'. Mannheim cites women's loss of jobs in the early stages of war, 'hasty marriages concluded merely to get family allowances' and the increased shortages of consumer goods together with increased family responsibility as producing a flood of economic offending on the part of women, leading to sudden outbursts of female violence (Mannheim 1941: 118).

One corollary of the view that war involves a temporary reversal of moral progress is what Archer and Gartner (1984) call the 'catharsis' model. Here that violence which might otherwise find expression in private is provided with a public and legitimate object, thereby lessening the rate of violent crime among the civilian populations. Thus, Mannheim (1941: 127) argues that

483

If they ['human beings'] get their necessary quantum of violence by war, no further violence may be needed. To that extent war may act rather as an outlet for man's pugnacious instincts than as a stimulus to them.

Similarly, Hamon postulates that

Criminality diminishes during the war, not because men are more moral, but because men who have the instinct of murder, rapine, and parasitism – criminals, in short – find in the very feats of warfare an outlet and expression for these instincts. This is proved by the fact that feminine criminality does not diminish, while juvenile criminality increases.

(Hamon 1918: 63)

John Keegan makes a similar point, but in relation to the singularly bloody effects of contemporary internal wars which serve as

a vehicle through which the embittered, the dispossessed, the naked of the earth, and the hungry masses . . . express their anger, jealousy and pent-up urge to violence.

(Keegan 1993: 56)

Thus, on the one hand, these accounts are cast in terms of the removal of restraints on anti-social instincts, but on the other as a cathartic expression of violent instincts which would find expression regardless of war.

War as a 'temporary inversion of prevailing morality'

A third model regards war as entailing an *inversion* of prevailing moral precepts about the preservation of life and property (Hamon 1918; von Hentig 1947). This inversion legitimates the resort to violence *per se*, so promoting violent solutions to social problems even beyond the cessation of hostilities (Bonger 1916: 518; Hamon 1918; von Hentig 1947; Mannheim 1941). Bonger (1936: 63) suggests that this apparent inversion of morality might better be described as ethical dualism in which one set of moral standards applies to the community and another to its [excluded] enemies.

War as a 'school of crime'

A fourth model treats war as a 'school of crime' in general (Abbott 1918; Hamon 1918; von Hentig 1947: 33; Mannheim 1941, 1965; Wilkins 1960):

War thus becomes a school of crime, a university of hooliganism and worse, whose bitter fruit may well be tainted in the years after the war.

(Hamon 1918: 64)

484

Bonger (1936) also maintains that 'a spirit of violence' is *learned* in wartime. Some war-time and post-war (1945) work on juvenile delinquency is also articulated along these lines (Glueck 1942; Lunden, 1963; Mannheim 1941; Sellers 1918; Wilkins 1960) and is generally consistent with Bandura's social learning perspective (see Archer and Gartner 1976, 1984). Thus Mannheim (1941: 123) – surveying press coverage of juvenile delinquency in Britain between 1915 and 1918 – offers the example of male delinquents adopting the then current technologies of war:

> Boys of eighteen commit burglaries, wearing masks, carrying revolvers, life-preservers and bottles of ether.

A more contemporary instantiation of this is provided by Ignatieff:

> for some young European males, the chaos that resulted from the collapse of the state's monopoly [of the means of violence] offered the chance of entering an erotic paradise of the all-is-permitted. Hence the semi-sexual, semi-pornographic gun culture of the [Serbian and Croatian] checkpoints. For young men there was an irresistible erotic charge in holding lethal power in your hands and using it to terrorize the helpless.
>
> (Ignatieff 1994: 140–141)

This observation is echoed by Chazan (1994) in his discussion of the war-time recruitment of youths into the Serbian mafia.

Von Hentig (1947: 336) suggests that people may become habituated to violence in wartime and acquire the 'atrocity habit' and consequently require a period of withdrawal from violence in post-war conditions. This observation is most often made about the problems of readjustment experienced by veterans (Abbott 1918; Lifton 1974; Pilisuk 1995; Shay 1995) who, as early as the American civil war, were reported to be 'more or less incapacitated and demoralized by an apprenticeship to the trade of war' (Abbott 1918: 43).[4]

War as a 'continuance of economic relations'

A fifth explanatory model takes the relationship between war and crime to be inextricably linked to economic structures and imperatives. In his 1916 text, Bonger forcibly argued that militarism was closely linked to colonialism (the external struggle for the expansion of markets) and internal pacification. Sutherland (1983) and Sutherland and Cressey (1960) argued that profiteering, violations of wartime economic regulations – including violations of embargoes on the sale of arms – ought to be regarded as 'war crimes'. According to Sutherland (1983: 190) the executives of various American corporations regarded war as just another market opportunity. Thus for these executives 'Mr Hoover and his "cookie pushers" in the State Department' presented not 'the least occasion for alarm' while one of the Duponts advised the corporation to 'Deal with the Government and the rest of the squawkers the way you deal with a buyer in a seller's market' (Sutherland 1960: 190). In other words, the corporation should continue to extract the maximum profit without regard to non-market (ethical/ national) considerations. More recently Trepp (1993) has tried to trace the involvement of international banking in the laundering of the spoils of the Third Reich. Other damning disclosures of 'corporate war crimes' (largely unearthed in archives in the US and post-Soviet Russia) detailing the activities of German companies such as Degussa, Volkswagen, Deutsche Bank and Deutsche Bahn, on the one hand, and the receipt of looted Nazi gold by 'neutral' countries like Sweden, Spain, Portugal and Turkey, on the other are receiving considerable attention as this book goes to publication. (Traynor, 1997; Reuters 1997).

Von Hentig (1947: 339–341) and Mannheim (1941: 47) both tried to identify the importance of the economic boom conditions of wartime (full employment and high wages coupled with rationing) as contributing to wartime crime rates and the development of the black market. Karp (1994), Naylor (1995) and Ruggiero (1996) have all explored the relationship between war, war industries, the arms trade and organized transnational crime, suggesting relationships of complex interdependency. Wright (1996) describes how the trade in torture equipment ('repressive technologies') involves many of the same suppliers (e.g. especially from the UK and USA), and the same transshipment routes and customer regimes as the trade in lethal weapons.

War as an 'intensified expression of the gender order'

For over two decades feminist writers have argued that war crimes such as rape or mass rape are an expression of the gender order or of militarized masculinity (for example, Brownmiller 1975; Enloe 1983, 1990, 1993; Jeffords 1989; MacKinnon 1994; Nikolić-Ristanović 1996b). The intensification of violence against women and girls in the context of war (ranging from public denunciations to physical and sadistic sexual assaults or murder) has been widely noted (Amnesty International 1991, 1995). But this victimization literature has tended to foreclose discussion not only of the sexual victimization of men by other men, but also of the complicity or auxiliariness of women in acts of violence, repression and unwarranted intrusion – acts which range from the identification and rounding up of 'other' women as members of enemy groups and the control and (moral) regulation of other women (Koonz 1987, Jamieson 1988), to the commission of war crimes by women in Germany and Eastern Europe (for example, as documented by Ilsa Eschebach at the Free University, Berlin) and contemporary acts of genocide, for example, in the former Yugoslavia and post-colonial Rwanda (African Rights 1995c).

Both Bonger (1936: 104) and Mannheim (1941: 118) attribute attacks on women to their wider sphere of activity in wartime circumstances and specifically to the disruption of family life by war. What they fail to recognize is the possibility that the increase in violence on women may be 'domestic' in nature. (See Nikolić-Ristanović 1996a.) This idea of war as involving the routine (and, therefore, routinely gendered) 'order of things' also has an economic aspect: the higher wartime wages paid to women were thought to have 'demoralizing effects' because they disrupted the normal relations of female subordination.

In summing up this brief discussion of the criminological literature on war and crime, two points need to be stressed. First, when criminologists have shown an interest in war, it has tended to be from an 'artifacts' or war-as-a-social-'experiment' perspective (Bonger 1936; Exner 1927; Archer and Gartner 1976, 1984), where the intention is largely to determine the effects of war on crime *rates*, that is the effects of migration and displacement of populations, high wages, the absorption of large numbers of young men into the armed forces on *routinely* recorded crimes. My second, related observation is that, despite its yielding some very suggestive and thoughtful analyses of wartime and postwar criminal statistics (Tham 1990, 1992; Takala 1989; Archer and Gartner 1976, 1984), this empirical approach does not enable us to understand other equally important criminological consequences of war. For example, it has largely ignored the significance of the *new* offences and liabilities that are created through the enactment of emergency defence regulations (Allen 1956; Jamieson 1988) and of the discourses of 'necessity' in which they are conceived. Likewise, numerous other dimensions of the war/crime relationship are left unexplored and under-theorized. Among these are the cultural salience of militarized masculinities, ethnic and gendered violence, technologies of violence, etc. (Enloe 1990; Gibson 1994; Ignatieff 1994; Jeffords 1989; Philo 1995), or the social and psychological dynamics (shame, rage, fear, death, trauma, alienation) which animate the conduct of war and armed conflicts – namely death, depredation or the destruction of property (Braithwaite, 1989; Browning 1992; Gabriel 1987; Kelman 1973; Lifton 1974; Scheff 1994).

Moreover, this conventional approach to understanding 'war crimes' as such (torture, mass killings, etc.) also acknowledges the contingent nature of what constitutes 'crime' in wartime, recognizing that many moral and legal prohibitions against certain acts such as murder by or against specified categories of persons have been suspended during states of war.[5] Until recently, 'war crimes' have been understood within criminology, as in other spheres, as an exceptional historical occurrence, perpetrated by the mad and the bad on the hated or the hapless. But, as Bauman's (1989) work on the sociology of morality makes clear, criminology must now take on board the ethical implications of war crimes and 'crimes of obedience' (especially the truth that such acts are typically perpetrated by unexceptional, 'normal', ordinary people often acting under the authority of the state (Browning 1992; Christie 1972; Kelman and Hamilton 1989; Milgram 1971, 1974; Vietnam Veterans Against the War 1972).

I would argue that existing criminological paradigms are generally incapable of making much etiological (explanatory) sense of these kinds of war crimes. But, so also is the criminological project as currently constituted incapable of address-ing the wider ethical issues thrown up by war itself.[6] How could 'criminology' respond to the etiological and ethical challenge of war? It is clear that we do *not* need a criminology of war which works within and thereby reproduces the nar-row boundaries of existing 'administrative' criminology. But, by the same token, we need a criminology that can problematize the relationship between moral and immoral acts and social order in conditions of peace and war.

A 'criminology of war'

I want to suggest that a more systematic and comprehensive analysis of the relationship between war and crime should be articulated along five thematic axes. Theorizing the relationship between war and crime will involve (a) under-standing the *specificity* of the particular historical moment, (b) the nature of morality and the social conditions of a moral life, (c) the contingent nature of definitions of crime in war, (d) their relation to the prevailing gender order, and (e) the question of how the foregoing elements are underpinned and animated by human emotions.

Understanding the historical moment: 'barbarism in post-bloc Europe'

I do not think that it is possible to overstate the importance of getting beyond the narrow Keynesian, welfare state assumptions of disciplinary criminology to rec-ognize the profound changes we are currently experiencing in post-Cold War (or 'post-Bloc') Europe. There is an urgent need to think through the relations between these changes and the 'conceptual fields' of crime, violence and social dysfunction. Seeking to understand the material conditions for the existence [and continuation] of armed conflict is a prime example. One key feature of the cur-rent conjuncture is the changing patterns of war and armed conflict – that is, there are currently significantly fewer *inter[nation-]state* wars, but there is signifi-cantly more 'internal' or *intrastate* violence including genocide carried out along ethnic lines, either in civil wars (the former Yugoslavia or Rwanda) (Cigar 1995; African Rights 1996a) or in conflicts between different political, criminal and social interests (Albania, Algeria, Afghanistan, N. Ireland) (Wallensteen and Sol-lenberg 1996). Thus the Europe of late modernity is more marked by post-colonial and post-Bloc struggles, fragmentation, globalization, the crisis of the nation-state and the politics of exclusion than by interstate wars (like the Gulf War, Vietnam or even the Falklands/Malvinas war of 1982 fought between Britain and Argentina).

The 'barbarism' thesis

Explanations of post-Cold War and post-colonial patterns of war and armed conflict (and the rise of ethnic and internal conflicts in particular) have tended to be underpinned either by conceptions of 'nationalism', 'tribalism' or 'blood and belonging' politics (Anderson 1990; Ignatieff 1994), or by the notion of 'barbarism' (Hobsbawm 1994a, 1994b; Meštrović 1993, 1994, 1996). Both these notions presume a particular conception of the relationship between morality, social cohesion and 'progress'. Hobsbawm argues that the contemporary '*descent* into barbarism' involves a reversal of progress produced by two pernicious and mutually reinforcing historical processes. The first process (familiar to all students of Norbert Elias) involves

> the disruption and breakdown of the systems of rules and moral behaviour by which *all* societies regulate the relations among their members and, to a lesser extent, between their members and those of other societies.
>
> (Hobsbawm 1994a: 45)

The second (more specifically) represents

> the reversal of what we may call the project of the eighteenth-century Enlightenment, namely the establishment of a *universal* system of such rules and standards of moral behaviour, embodied in the institutions of states dedicated to the rational progress of humanity; to Life, Liberty and the Pursuit of Happiness, to Equality, Liberty and Fraternity or whatever.
>
> (Hobsbawm 1994a: 45)

This elision of morality and social cohesion with the 'etiological myth of moral progress', according to Zygmunt Bauman, 'long ago ossified into the commonsense of our era' (1989: 13). The effect of this uncritical acceptance of the myth of moral progress is that it limits our capacity to understand *all* of the moral consequences of the civilizing process.[7] Bauman observes that

> Although other sociological images of the civilizing process are available, the most common (and widely shared) is one that entails, as its two centre points, the suppression of irrational and essentially anti-social drives, and the gradual yet relentless elimination of violence from social life (more precisely: concentration of violence under control of the state, where it is used to guard the perimeter of national community and the conditions of social order).
>
> (Bauman 1989: 27)

What blends these two points together is the vision of the civilized society as a *moral force*, that is

> as a system of institutions that co-operate and complement each other in the imposition of a normative order and the rule of law, which in turn safeguard conditions of social peace and individual security poorly defended in pre-civilized societies.
>
> (Bauman 1989: 28)

However, an uncritical adoption of this one-sided vision of the civilizing process diverts attention from 'the *permanence* of the destructive potential of the civilizing process' (Bauman 1989: 28; my emphasis). So he argues, in particular, that the lesson of the Holocaust must be that the generalized mythology of ongoing social progress through rationality carries a 'tendency to demote, exprobate and delegitimize the ethical motivations of social action' (1989: 28). The Holocaust may be understood as a defining example of the outcome of the promotion of rationality to the exclusion of alternative criteria. Bauman postulates that because

> The Hobbesian world of the Holocaust did not surface from its too-shallow grave, resurrected by the tumult of irrational emotions. It arrived (in a formidable shape Hobbes would certainly disown) in a factory-produced vehicle wielding weapons only the most advanced science could supply, and following an itinerary designed by scientifically managed organization.
>
> (Bauman 1989: 13)

For this reason, he argues

> we need to take stock of the evidence that *the civilizing process is, among other things, a process of divesting the use and deployment of violence from moral calculus, and of emancipating the desiderata of rationality from interference of ethical norms or moral inhibitions.*
>
> (Bauman 1989: 28)

Thus Bauman insists that any rewriting of the theory of the civilizing process also must entail a transformation in sociology (I would add, in criminology) breaking its 'self-imposed moral silence of science'. The discipline [of sociology], says Bauman,

> has been engaged, since its birth in a mimetic relationship with its object – or rather, with the imagery of that object [rationality] – which it constructed and accepted as the frame for its discourse.
>
> (Bauman 1989: 29)

The amoral scientific rationality which is one of the moral consequences of the civilizing process has been a defining feature of criminology. As Steinert (1996) observes 'Criminology has from its beginning been a science of social exclusion and remains a technocratic field of knowledge, in which "soft" and "hard" technocrats fight with changing gains and losses'. It is also the case that the development of the technologies of destruction and repression provide the conditions of possibility of violence of a scale and efficiency unimaginable hitherto. Weapons such as the AK-47 or Kalashnikov rifle are now so cheap (ranging from the price of a chicken in Uganda [for an AK-47] or $4 for a rifle in Albania) and 'user-friendly' (light and easy to use) that they enable the active involvement of children in armed conflicts (Machel 1996: 17; Tihon 1997). The trade in such technologies takes place in the moral vacuum of the market (Forrest 1996; Boutwell *et al.* 1995; Karp 1994; Ruggiero 1996). I am not alone in arguing for a moral reflexivity in criminology (cf. Christie' arguments in respect of the 'Limits to Pain').[8] There are some vital issues here.

Theorizing morality

Another, no less telling lesson of Bauman's essay of 1989 for a criminology of war is the way it foregrounds the issue of the *social production of immorality* and the role of the modern [nation-]state and its agents in that process. This point is especially crucial for any analysis which purports to explain the nature of crime and punishment in contemporary war and internal conflicts, whether the impetus for these is territorial, genocidal, governmental (for example, the UN or the Organization for Security and Co-operation in Europe (OSCE) monitoring/ peace-keeping operations) or part of a project of state transformation (see African Rights 1995a, 1995b, 1995c; Cohen, 1993, 1995a, 1995b; Rusche and Kirchheimer 1939; Wallensteen and Sollenberg, 1996).

Society as a factory of morality

Just as Durkheim's conception of the relationship between morality and social discipline constitutes the core canon of sociological wisdom (Bauman 1989: 171), so it also serves as the dominant paradigm for mainstream criminology. Bauman suggests that

> The factory system has served as one of the most potent metaphors out of which the theoretical model of modern society is woven, and the vision of the *social production of morality* offers a most prominent example of its influence.
>
> (Bauman 1989: 174)

and expostulates further that

As long as morality is understood as a social product, and causally explained in reference to the mechanisms, which when they function properly ensure its 'constant supply' . . . events which . . . defy the common conception of good and evil . . . tend to be viewed as an outcome of failure or mismanagement of 'moral industry'.

(Bauman 1989: 174)

The embeddedness of this 'social factory' conception of morality is particularly marked in commentaries on military misconduct. So, for example, a feature in *The Guardian*, on scandals in the élite US Naval Academy in Annapolis, declared that 'the whiff of scandal has become a stench', and that 'this "leadership laboratory" stands charged with producing defective products' (Freedland 1996). In a similar vein, the explanations of the widespread corruption of the 1993 international peace-keeping force (UNPROFOR) in Bosnia and Croatia (primarily on the part of French and Ukrainian troops involved in the black-market trading of food, fuel, cars, cigarettes and alcohol in Sarajevo)[9] was widely attributed in the press to a lack of effective leadership on the part of the officers (Stone 1993). In other words, however systemic such corruption may be, it is seen as a management problem rather than a *social* product.

If the analogy of society as a 'factory of morality' is taken to its logical conclusion, *immoral* conduct becomes

the result of an inadequate supply of moral norms, or supply of faulty norms (i.e. norms with an insufficiently binding force); the latter in turn, is traced to the technical or managerial faults of the 'social factory of morality' – at best to the 'unanticipated consequences' of ineptly co-ordinated productive efforts, or to the interference of factors foreign to the productive system (i.e. incompleteness of control over the factors of production).

(Bauman 1989: 174)

And it is against this conception of the social production of morality that Bauman mounts his definitive critique. The logical loop represented by the equation, '*morality = social rules/social discipline/social cohesion = morality*', *precludes* the possibility of the social production of immorality. Furthermore this virtual identification of morality with social discipline works on a circular reasoning which serves to deny not just the possibility that immorality may be socially produced, but also, equally importantly, the potential existence or viability of any *independent* existential mode of moral norms (Bauman 1989: 170; Kappeler 1995).

But the social production of immorality is exactly what happens in the case of genocide or mass violations of human rights in situations of armed conflict. Such events clearly undermine positivistic criminology's commitment to the 'individuation' of criminality. Mass participation and group collusion in these events (the Holocaust, Srebrenica, Vukovar, etc.) also problematize the vocabularies of 'exceptionalism' within which much discussion of war crimes or human rights violations by social control agents during conditions of war are normally framed.[10] (See *Commission of Inquiry into the Deployment of Canadian Forces to Somalia* 1997; Vietnam Veterans Against the War 1972; Browning 1992; Lifton 1974; Helmer 1974; Kelman and Hamilton 1989.)

Bauman postulates a definition of immorality as 'behaviour which forsakes and abdicates responsibility for others' (1989: 183). He argues the case for a grounding of morality *outside* social discipline, but *within* an ethical relation of social proximity which entails a moral responsibility for others. I will return to this point in the discussion of contingent definitions of crime which follows.

As I have argued in my opening remarks, any investigation which is alive to the social production of immorality must become interested in the fact that such acts of violence and violations of human rights are unevenly accomplished *inter alia* through state action, as well as via concerted or individual human action and collusion. This raises the spectre of whether the criminological imagination can extend not only to the empirical reality of war, but also to the issue of how to discuss, analyse or make sense of socially obedient behaviour *in extremis* appearing outside the context of war.

Contingent definitions of war / crime

It is widely known that states of war, emergency and social transformation entail to varying degrees a rearticulation of concepts of 'crime' and morality at the levels of both law and ideology. Most recently, Heinz Steinert (1996) has alerted us to the highly contingent discursive relationship of the concepts of war and crime specifically as 'structures of domination'. I will briefly outline how this relationship is expressed in law, before turning to the question of its cultural expression.

The contingent nature of legal definitions of crime in war

Even if one assumes an essentialist definition of crime, acts which constitute serious crimes in peace – namely, murder, maiming, kidnapping, rape, pillaging and destruction of property – do not necessarily constitute crimes in war conditions. Indeed, these may be imposed as a *duty* and have the effect of criminalizing those who refuse to commit them. Alternatively, many of these ordinarily prohibited acts may not be regarded as crimes, so long as they are committed in compliance with the laws of war – for example, for so long as they observe the principle of non-combatant immunity and do not exceed the force and/or scale dictated by 'military necessity'.

Definitions of what constitutes 'crime' in the context of war are also potentially adjudicated in reference to international conventions on the conduct of war and internal conflicts. The laws of war (*jus in bello*) – or what is now often described as humanitarian law – are expressed in positive enactments like the

Geneva and the Hague Conventions or the 1948 Convention on Genocide as well as being governed by what Howard *et al.* (1994: 1) call the 'cultural regulation of violence'. Thus categories of crime in conditions of war are constituted according to both inward-looking (civil) and external (international community) referents. So the wartime redefinition of (civil) offences also may be accompanied by specific transformations of the citizen's relationship to the state (alongside social dimensions such as gender, class, ethnicity, civilian/military), typically involving, not just the imposition of new civil obligations, but also a derogation of civil rights. In addition, the accompanying exhortations to exemplary citizenship in the form of war propaganda entail very real penal consequences (Jamieson 1988; Mannheim, 1941; Rusche and Kirchheimer 1939). The nature of definitions of 'crime' in times of 'war' clearly depend on what conditions are being described as constituting 'war'. So, for example, in conventional, inter-state wars such as the 'world wars' of 1914–18 and 1939–45 the nation state could impose massively increased control on its citizens through its monopoly of the means of violence, whereas in internal or civil conflicts fought between armies, criminal or paramilitary groups, militia, mercenaries or warlords (Albania, Bosnia, Chechnya, Somalia) this particular form of governmentality clearly is not possible.

Cultural inscriptions of war, crime, law and order

As Steinert (1996) has observed, there is a structural similarity between war propaganda and law-and-order talk. War metaphors ('going ballistic', a Cold War reference – or 'getting a "bead"' [viewing through a gun sight] on a person or other object) continue to be re-worked both in fantasy and actual [gendered] social practice.[11] The idea of the 'enemy' is also constantly being reworked in political and social commentary. So, although the ambit of such war metaphors is most marked in law-and-order discourses like that of the 'war on crime', it certainly is not restricted to them. Neither do the discursive associations between war and crime work in one direction only. Crime-and-punishment metaphors (about 'what's right', 'justice' and 'deserts') have always been heavily thematized in 'war' narratives as animating the actions of warriors from Achilles to Rambo (Shay 1995). Steinert (1996) suggests that fantasies of crime and punishment privilege masculinity – specifically the masculinity of those occupying the 'warrior position'. This privileging of warrior masculinity is especially marked in moments of crisis and social transformation, for example in the reworking of warrior themes in post-Vietnam America and, more recently, in post-Soviet Russia. The elision of war/crime and masculinity is also explored by Gibson (1994), who suggests that the proliferation of warrior fantasies in post-Vietnam America draws its imagery and narratives from archaic warrior themes and depicts the (heavily armed) warrior as the epitome of masculine power, righteousness and self-development (Gibson 1994: 21). Significantly, these 'new warrior' narratives nearly always portray the hero as having been betrayed by leaders who sold them out [in foreign wars], or as having suffered 'self-imposed restraint' [in the war on crime] at home, when major social institutions – particularly the police and the court system – failed to combat the enemies of American [for which substitute Russian – RJ] society.

(Gibson 1994: 33)

Clearly there are parallels between the 'new warrior' masculinities (of the militia and war-games variety) described by Gibson, the 'Afghantsy' veterans movement in Russia, and the aping of ethnic-warrior (Afghani, Chechen, Cossak) style (replete with combat accessories) by young males in the former Soviet Union (Timoshenko 1996). Moreover, the privileged 'warrior position' is also claimed by paramilitary groups and organized criminal gangs operating, for example, in the former Yugoslavia, Serbia, Albania and Russia.

These narratives about moral crusaders and warriors in various guises (soldier/paramilitary/mercenary/police/criminal) are accompanied by prescriptions for exemplary citizenship which not only exhort new and exacting standards of behaviour, but also attempt to prescribe (constrain or manipulate) elements of the emotional life (for example, grief, anxiety, fear, rage, shame or attachment) of the exemplary citizen (worker, warrior, mother or wife) (Jamieson 1996). These prescriptions are underpinned by a system of (largely symbolic) rewards and (penal and material) punishments (Jamieson 1996; Rusche and Kirchheimer 1939: 174).[12] In this way the exemplars of virtue and criminality – especially in moments of social transformation, whether constituted by a state of 'crisis' (like war) or governmental 'project' of transformation (e.g. marketization) – bear a fairly direct relation to structures of regulation and punishment. One very consequential aspect of this relation is the way in which gender is written into exemplars of wartime or warrior citizenship which elaborate themes of fidelity, sacrifice, endurance, transcendence in class and gender specific terms.

Gender as a structure of domination

A criminology of war must be sensitive to what we have already said about the importance of the historical specificity of war, the social production of both morality and what Bauman (1989: 18) calls 'the social production of moral indifference', and the way in which these inscribe particular forms of citizenship and exclusion in peace and war. But it must also examine the critical social and emotional processes involved in the *re-ordering* of gender in the context of war. At a minimum, this must involve the description and analysis of the following relationships.

First there is a need to understand the nature of the relationship between the gender order and conceptions of necessity in specific social formations under different conditions of war. I have suggested elsewhere (Jamieson 1996) that one of the ways we can begin to understand the relationship between masculinity and wartime necessity is to locate the analysis in the context of what could be termed the 'politics of death' (Gabriel 1987; Moran 1945). In theory at least, it is the men who do the fighting and dying and the women who do the waiting and watching. Given this gendered division of labour in war, it then becomes a matter of 'public' necessity that certain men are persuaded to fight (and die) and that both women and men support this arrangement. In the context of total [inter-state] war fought between mass armies this gendered division of labour is invari-ably highly bureaucratized (for example in the welfare, medical/ psychiatric and disciplinary structures of [state] armies). But, in internal wars, especially those involving local warlords and loosely organized paramilitary groups, bureaucrat-izing the production of required masculinities (i.e. varieties of warriors) is not a possibility.

Second there is a need to examine how and in what ways a particular gender order is re-ordered in wartime to accommodate militarized masculinities such that certain women are made available to the military (for example, to French and Ukrainian UNPROFOR troops in Sarajevo), through the organization of prostitution (Enloe 1983, 1990; Sturdevant and Stoltfus 1992) or sexual slavery (Dolgopol 1995; Hicks 1995) while others are subjected to crisis forms of sexual regulation involving surveillance and intrusion by the state (e.g. through the implementation of army welfare policies) or via voluntary agencies led by assorted moral entrepreneurs (Jamieson 1988). We must understand (a) what animates the intensification of sexual regulation of women in wartime (often entailing the policing of women by women) and how this can be associated with militarized masculinities, and (b) how these complex and opaque processes are achieved both at the level of ideology and practice.

A third consideration is the need to identify the processes which produce the intensification of the sexual victimization of women in wartime (attacks by both combatant and non-combatant men on women). Feminists have tended to focus on the sexual victimization of women in wartime and its relation to pornography (Brownmiller 1975; Castel 1992; MacKinnon 1994; Seifert 1994). Much less is known about the sexual violation or torture of men, though some attempt has been made to theorize the relationship between war, sadism and pacifism (Glover 1946), or militarized masculinities and sadistic fantasy (Theweleit 1987).

Finally we must understand the persistence and continuing appeal in *peacetime* of forms of militarized masculinities expressed, for example, in the growing number of militia or paramilitary groups in the United States (Stern 1996; Gib-son 1994), the ethnic-warrior movements and youth-culture styles in post-Soviet Russia or the increasing appeal of guns clubs and weekend combat games (par-ticularly for middle-class men) in Britain. An important question is the intense desire on the part of particular groups (mainly men) to possess guns and wear military camouflage clothing (fondly known to the initiated as 'cammies') a ten-dency which seems especially marked among sections of the 'underclass'.[13] Hobsbawm observes that despite the fact that three quarters of Nazi Storm Troopers of 1933 were too young to have been in the First World War, nonetheless

War, quasi-uniforms (the notorious coloured shirts) and gun-carrying . . .
now provided a model for the dispossessed young.

(Hobsbawm 1994b: 48)

A more contemporary instantiation of paramilitarism is the American militia
movements with their deep distrust of the central state, their paranoid fear that
there is an elaborate conspiracy to install a 'new world order' in Post Cold-war
America and their embrace of firearms as well as computer technology, examined by Stern (1995) and Gibson (1994). Gibson (1994) suggests that a defining
feature of the contemporary 'new warriors' is their marginal relation to the
community – explicable in terms of their past loss (of a partner) or betrayal (by
leaders/the state). These narratives of trauma, loss and betrayal are consistent
with work on both American Vietnam veterans and the 'Afghantsy syndrome' of
veterans in Russia (for example by Lifton 1974; Shay 1995; Karsten 1978; *CJ-
Europe* 2(5):3), as well as finding a place in some contemporary anxious discussions
on the role of isolated single men, of different ages, in 'amok' or 'spree'-killings
(Dunblane and Port Arthur in 1996).

Emotion

There has been an increasing recognition recently of the significance of emotion in
social theory (Cohen 1995b; Connell 1987, 1995; Giddens 1991; Scheff 1994) and
in some criminological writing – for example on the issues of fear and anxiety
(Jefferson and Hollway 1996) and also about 'sensual pleasure' of transgression
(Katz 1988). There has also been an explosive growth of interest in masculinities and
particularly the question of men in groups. Many feminist accounts of extreme
violent (particularly sexually violent) behaviour on the part of men in war tend
to fall back on essentialist or reductionist conceptions of gender in which men are
seen as naturally or culturally produced as violent. But this ignores a significant
body of evidence which would suggest that it is actually more difficult to motivate
male soldiers to perform at the required level of combat aggressiveness than the
feminist perspective allows. Little (1964: 205) rejects the notion that men in combat behave in a certain way in order to 'live up to' being a man – acting
independently, aggressively and with great enthusiasm for the task of killing and
dying (Marshall 1947; Moran 1945; Gabriel 1987). Little's study suggests the
opposite, namely that such behaviour was feared and resented by the group
whose collective aim was the minimization of risk to the combat unit as a whole.
Gabriel (1987) argues that a primary cause of war neurosis is the conflict between
duty and fear of death and disablement. Even the most cursory examination of
Court Martial Sentencing Boards discloses an extensive discussion of men's *problems* (for example, of grief, fear and anxiety). Courts martial, like many other
aspects of the administrative bureaucracies of national armies, have the particular purpose of managing those men who are unable either to achieve or sustain
the level of performance required for being an effective soldier (Jamieson 1996).

In his most recent critical text on masculinities, Connell (1995: 10) follows Freud in suggesting that 'masculinity . . . never exists in a pure state'. He continues:

> Layers of emotion coexist and contradict each other. Each personality is a shade-filled, complex structure, not a transparent unit. Though his theoretical language changed, Freud remains convinced of the empirical complexity of gender and the ways in which femininity is always a part of man's character.
>
> (Connell, 1995: 11)

Connell also retrieves the psychoanalytical work of Karen Horney in order to highlight two key dimensions of masculinity, as so frequently revealed in clinical practice, namely:

> the extent to which adult masculinity is built on over-reactions to femininity and the connection of the making of masculinity with the subordination of women.
>
> (Connell 1995 : 11)

Students of the conventional criminological canon will be familiar with the emphasis placed on the struggle between 'masculinity' and 'femininity' in male adolescents in Walter Miller's analysis of the lower-class family in America in the 1950s – and notably the significance of 'delinquency' as an attempt by young men to escape the constraints of the matriarchally-dominated lower-class household (Miller, 1958). From my perspective, of course, following Connell, Miller's analysis is rather too one-dimensional and/or essentialist, in suggesting that the end result of the 'normal' transitions of adolescence is a fully-formed, autonomous and self-reliant masculine adult, impervious to anxiety and oblivious to care and affection. It is also an account of the role of gender in the production of crime which works within a modernist assumption of these relationships – namely, the assumption that these kinds of gender and class relations are likely, 'naturally' to be reproduced, in a more or less predictable fashion, from one historical moment (or generation) to the next.[14] Connell's own analysis of the gender order, however, alerts us to the contingent nature of such processes of social reproduction, and argues that there are now several 'crisis-tendencies' emerging in late twentieth-century masculinity, bound up with the crisis of modernist mass-manufacturing economies and with many other contradictory pressures on the system of gender relations of the earlier post-war period. As Connell observes, such crises in the assumed forms of 'hegemonic masculinity' (like the economic and other crises with which they are linked) are always going to produce a wide variety of responses, including what he calls ' "gun lobby" type of politics' (Connell 1995: 213) resonant of the 'new warrior masculinities discussed by Gibson (1994), Jeffords (1989) and Stern (1996), but also a whole new set of angry forms of personal and interpersonal behaviours, ranging from reactive misogyny entrenched in the individual psyche of men to the outright, and frequently expressed, angry violence of other men, openly and explicitly directed at the threatening feminine other. The refrain of Marc Lepine, machine-gunning down fourteen women engineering students at the École polytechnique in Montreal in 1989 was 'Death to feminists!'. It is impossible to ignore the extent to which many of the instances of mass killing, kidnapping and rape which have been the subject of headline press coverage in Europe in the 1990s are connected – both in the behaviours of the men who were implicated in them, and in the way which such incidents were reported – with the 'crisis of masculinity' to which Connell's psychoanalytically-sensitive but historically-framed sociology of gender directs us. It is also impossible to ignore the ways in which the analytical issues which such an approach recommends for the understanding of 'crime' (for example, the meaning of emotions (such as shame or rage) in social behaviour, grounded in an understanding of the social production of gendered identities, in which there is no guarantee of an untroubled final outcome, 'a Real Man') is illuminated by an understanding of the traumas of men at war. For it is in war that men confront, in an especially dramatic fashion, the socially-scripted responsibilities of being such 'a Man' – namely, the real possibility that such (warrior) masculinity involves a confrontation with mortality (Connell 1985; Jamieson 1996). The prospect of death is expressed rather bleakly in the Russian term 'zinky boys', used to describe the teenagers who were drafted into military service in Afghanistan and referring to the practice of shipping the casualties home to their mothers in zinc-lined coffins. The traumas associated with this recognition ('the politics of death' for men) at the level of the individual are frequently accentuated by a range of different 'shaming ceremonies', in which, in contrast to the recent writing of John Braithwaite (1989), the shaming is aimed at producing an involvement of men in the victimization or humiliation of others (which is reported to have been a feature of the mass rapes in Bosnia-Herzegovina). So also, of course, this can be true of men's behaviour in groups in particular sets of circumstances during 'peacetime'. In war, these traumas (of fear, guilt and shaming) are often 'resolved', as Mannheim observed without trying to ground it in any theoretical fashion, in various kinds of group catharsis – either in actions informed by men's often unfocussed, and uncontrolled, fear of death (My Lai) or, on occasion, more directly concerned with their 'fear of women' (the Taliban militia's aggressive, and fearful, desire to subordinate women in contemporary Afghanistan).

Conclusion

My concern in this chapter has been to explore the rationale for the construction of what I have called 'a criminology of war'. Following on from Eric Hobsbawm's observations, particularly with respect to the 'barbaric' condition of some parts of middle Europe and the old Soviet Union, we have also followed

Zygmunt Bauman in calling for a sociology of morality which does not see the issue of moral critique or moral responsibility resolved by (or collapsed into) the rise of the modern state in the late nineteenth and early twentieth century. The adoption of such a position in respect of the terrains both of war and of crime calls forth a distinctive programme of analytic strategies – touching on issues of the social production of the moral life as well as of immoral conditions of existence, the widely-discussed issue of 'masculinity' (but formulated here in a non-essentialist fashion), the cross-over between some key aspects of wartime contingencies and everyday life in 'peacetime' in the current period (especially for men in crisis), and a range of other issues that have been the subject of widespread discussion, for example, by scholars working in the fields of moral philosophy, psychoanalysis and the inter-disciplinary area of human rights violations. At the end of the 'short twentieth' century, as Eric Hobsbawm (1994b) has so powerfully proclaimed – especially in Europe (the epicentre of so many of these definitive and momentous developments) – criminologists should have the courage to make the theoretical, as well as the empirical, connections.

Notes

1 Notable [feminist] exceptions include Stiglmayer (1994) and Nikolić-Ristanović (1996 and this volume).

2 Reference here is to an English translation by Dr Ronnie Lippens, the University of Ghent.

3 Perhaps the most useful typology to date of attempts to explain the relationship between war and violent crime is that developed by Archer and Gartner (1976, 1984) who argue that most explanations of the war/crime relationship are based on (seven) causal models:

   1 war is viewed as altering statistical '*artifacts*' (e.g., demographics) or

   2 '*economic factors*' (scarcity, employment) relating to crime, or

   3 as producing increased '*social solidarity*' or

   4 increased '*social disorganization*', or

   5 as providing a public '*catharsis*' of violence otherwise expressed in private,

   6 as producing [proficient/ damaged] '*violent veterans*', or finally,

   7 war is seen as providing a climate for the '*legitimation* of violence'.

4 This literature does not address the issue of 'child soldiers', despite their presence in Vietnam. However, there is now a rapidly developing body on work on the subject done from a NGO perspective (for example the International Committee of the Red Cross) or from a specifically human-rights frame of analysis (Goodwin-Gill and Cohn 1994; Machel 1996).

5 However, this suspension of prohibition against particular acts is limited by the stipulations of Humanitarian Law or the Laws of War (on which see Best 1994; De Lupis 1987; Howard *et al.* 1994).

6 It is not mere inadvertence on the part of Garland (1995) that he characterizes [British] criminology as being constituted by two principal projects only, the one 'etiological' and the other 'governmental'. Garland's account of the development of discipline is

persuasive as far as it goes, but, in the end, it is more notable for what it fails to notice – namely, the *absence* of a *moral project* in criminology.

7 Moreover, he deplores what he calls the 'Eurocentric habit of accepting atrocities at the periphery' (e.g., Afghanistan, Rwanda, Sri Lanka, Somalia, Sudan, Turkey), but of experiencing/declaring a crisis of 'degeneracy' when 'barbaric' behaviour 'breaks out' in the West (e.g., in the former Yugoslavia).

8 And also in his work on concentration camp guards in Norway during the Second World War (Christie 1972).

9 See O'Kane 1993.

10 A contemporary instance of this is the way in which different national governments – Belgium, Italy and Canada – have responded to the disclosure of gross human rights violations (including *inter alia* torture, murder, beatings, mock executions of children, sexual abuse of women) committed against civilians by members of their forces serving in Somalia as part of the UN peacekeeping operation,'Restore Hope'. The publication of photographic evidence documenting these abuses ('trophy pictures' taken by the paratroops themselves) has forced the governments concerned to hold court-martial proceedings (Belgium in 1995 and 1997 and Canada in 1993) and/or official inquiries into the abuses allegedly committed by their troops (currently four in Italy, one in Canada 1995–97). At the time of writing the Italian paratroop regiment involved was serving in an international operation overseeing the 1997 elections in Albania ('Operation Alba'). Its Canadian counterpart was disbanded.

What these atrocious actions have in common is the resort to various forms of denial on the part of the relevant state officials (Cohen 1995b: 74–77). We are asked to accept that Belgian soldiers holding a Somali child over a fire was 'just a type of playing without violence' [a form of 'interpretive' denial] or that these were 'a series of problems with a very limited group in a limited zone' [what Cohen calls 're-framing as isolated incidents'] (Bates 1997).

11 One of the main sources of everyday talk's preoccupation with 'war' is the 'military-entertainments complex' – war toys, war dress and accessories, and war fictions (cinema, magazines) in which violence/gender are inscribed. See Patrick Regan (1994) on the relationship between war toys and war movies and popular support for war in the USA.

12 Otto Kirchheimer (1961) makes the observation that legal prescriptions and prohibitions are rarely intended to be universally enforced. Hence war regulations, like censorship, tend to be applied unevenly to different social groups and media, with the lower orders being thought to require the greatest degree of regulation and 'guidance'.

13 The unforgettable example of this Rambo-like presentation of self in Britain is that of Michael Ryan, killer of 16 people 'at random' in Hungerford in 1987.

14 Hilary Pilkington's (1996) analysis of the re-masculinization of youth culture post-Soviet Russia provides an excellent example of work on gender which avoids this trap.

References

Abbott, E. (1918) 'Crime and the War', *Journal of Criminal Law and Criminology*, 9: 32–45.

African Rights (1995a) *Rwanda: Death, Despair and Defiance*, London: African Rights.

—— (1995b) *Rwanda: Who is Killing? Who is Dying? What is to be Done?* (Discussion Paper No. 3), London: African Rights.

—— (1995c) *Not So Innocent: When Women Become Killers*, London: African Rights.

Allen, C. K. (1956) *Law and Orders*, London: Stevens & Sons Ltd.

Amnesty International (1991) *Women in the Front Line: Human Rights Violations Against Women*, London: Amnesty International.

—— (1995) *Human Rights Are Women's Rights*, New York: Amnesty International.

Anderson, B. (1990) *Imagined Communities*, London: Verso.

Archer, D. and Gartner, R. (1976) 'Violent Acts and Violent Times: A Comparative Approach to Postwar Homicide Rates', *American Sociological Review*, 41(6): 937–963.

—— (1984) 'Violent Acts and Violent Times: the Effects of Wars on Post-War Homicide Rates' in *Violence and Crime in Cross-National Perspective*, New Haven: Yale University Press.

Bates, S. (1997) 'Troops Cleared of Child Roasting', *Guardian* 1 July 1997.

Bauman, Z. (1989) *Modernity and the Holocaust*, Cambridge: Polity.

Best, G. (1994) *War and Law since 1945*, Oxford: Clarendon Press.

Bonger, W. [1916] (1967) *Criminality and Economic Conditions*, New York: Agathon Press.

—— (1935) 'The "new" criminal law', originally published in the journal *Rechsgeleerd Magazin*, 54: 236–266, English translation by Dr Ronnie Lippens, University of Ghent.

—— (1936) *An Introduction to Criminology*, London: Methuen & Sons.

Boutwell, J., Klare, M. T. and Reed, L. W. (eds) (1995) Lethal Commerce: *The Global Trade in Small Arms and Light Weapons*, Cambridge, Mass.: American Academy of Arts and Sciences.

Braithwaite, J. (1989) *Crime, Shame and Reintegration*, Cambridge: Cambridge University Press.

Braybon, G. and Summerfield, S. (1981) *Out of the Cage*, London: Pandora.

Browning, C. R. (1992) *Ordinary Men: Reserve Police Battalion 101 and the Final Solution in Poland*, New York: Harper Perennial.

Brownmiller, S. (1975) *Against Our Will*, New York: Simon and Schuster.

Castel, J. R. (1992) 'Rape, Sexual Assault and the Meaning of Persecution', *International Journal of Refugee Law*, 4(1): 39–56.

Chazan, Y. (1994) 'Youths Swell Serbian Mafia', *Guardian* 17 November 1994.

Christie, N. (1972) *Fangevoktere i Konsentrasjonsleire*, Oslo: Pax.

—— (1981) *Limits To Pain*, Oxford: Martin Robertson.

Cigar, N. (1995) *Genocide in Bosnia: The Policy of Ethnic Cleansing*, College Station, Texas: Texas A. & M. University Press.

CJ-Europe (Mar./Apr. 1992) 2(5):3.

Cohen, S. (1993) 'Human Rights and Crimes of the State: The Culture of Denial' *The Australian and New Zealand Journal of Criminology*, (26): 97–115.

—— (1995a) 'State Crimes of Previous Regimes: Knowledge, Accountability and the Policing of the Past', *Law and Social Inquiry*, 20(1): 7–50.

—— (1995b) 'Denial and Acknowledgement: The Impact of Information About Human Rights Violations', Jerusalem: Centre for Human Rights, The Hebrew University.

Connell, R. W. (1985) 'Masculinity, Violence and War', in Paul Patton and Ross Poole (eds) *War/Masculinity*, Sydney: Intervention Publications.

—— (1987) *Gender and Power*, Cambridge: Polity.

—— (1995) *Masculinities*, Cambridge: Polity.

Dandeker, C. (1990) *Surveillance, Power and Modernity*, Cambridge: Polity.

De Lupis, I. D. (1987) *The Law of War*, Cambridge: Cambridge University Press.

Dolgopol, U. (1995) 'Women's Voices, Women's Pain', *Human Rights Quarterly*, 17(1): 125–54.

Durkheim, E. (1992) *Professional Ethics and Civic Morals*, London: Routledge.

Enloe, C. (1983) *Does Khaki Become You? The Militarisation of Women's Lives*, London: Pluto.

—— (1990) *Bananas, Beaches and Bases: Making Feminist Sense of International Politics*, London: Pandora.

—— (1983; 1993) *The Morning After: Sexual Politics at the End of the Cold War*, Berkeley and London: University of California Press.

Exner, F. (1927) *Krieg und Kriminalitat Oesterreich*, Vienna: Holder-Pichler-Tempsky.

Forrest, D. (1996) (ed.) *A Glimpse of Hell*, London: Cassell.

Freedland, J. (1996) 'A high rank odour', *Guardian*, 2 May 1996.

Gabriel, R. A. (1987) *Madness and Psychiatry in War*, New York: Hill & Wang.

Garland, D. (1994) 'Of Crimes and Criminals: The Development of Criminology' in Maguire, M., Morgan, R. and Reiner, R. (eds) *The Oxford Handbook of Criminology*, Oxford: Clarenden Press.

Gibson, J. W. (1994) *Warrior Dreams: Violence and Manhood in Post-Vietnam America*, N.Y.: Hill & Wang.

Giddens, A. (1987) *The Nation State and Violence*, Cambridge: Polity.

—— (1991) *Modernity and Self-Identity: Self and Society in the Late-Modern Age*, Cambridge: Polity.

Goodwin-Gill, G. S. and Cohn, I. (1994) *Child Soldiers: The Role of Children in Armed Conflicts*, Oxford: Clarendon.

Gotto, S. (1918) 'The Changing Moral Standard', *The Nineteenth Century*, (Oct. 1918) vol. 84: 717–30.

Glover, E. (1946) *War, Sadism, and Pacifism*, London: George Allen & Unwin.

Glueck, E. T. (1942) 'Wartime Delinquency', *Journal of Criminal Law and Criminology*, 33: 119–35.

Hamon, A. (1918) *Lessons of the World War*, London: T. Fisher Unwin Ltd.

Helmer, J. (1974) *Bringing the War Home: The American Soldier in Vietnam and After*, London: The Free Press.

Hentig, H. von (1947) *Crime: Causes and Conditions*, New York and London: McGraw Hill.

Hicks, G. (1995) *The Comfort Women: Sex Slaves of the Japanese Imperial Forces*, London: Allen & Unwin.

Hobsbawm, E. (1994a) 'Barbarism: A User's Guide', *New Left Review*, (206): 44–54.

—— (1994b) *The Age of Extremes: The Short Twentieth Century, 1914–1989*, London: Michael Joseph.

Holsti, K. (1996) *The State, War, and the State of War*, Cambridge: Cambridge University Press.

Howard, M., Andreopoulous, G. J. and Shulman, M. R. (eds) (1994) *The Laws of War: Constraints on Warfare in the Western World*, New Haven: Yale University Press.

Ignatieff, M. (1994) *Blood and Belonging: Journeys Into the New Nationalism*, London: Vintage Books.

Jamieson, R. M. (1988) 'The Social Regulation of Women in Britain, 1939–1945', M.Phil. Dissertation, University of Cambridge (unpublished).

—— (1996) 'The Man of Hobbes: Masculinity and Wartime Necessity', *Journal of Historical Sociology*, 9(1): 19–42.

Jefferson, T. and Hollway, W. (1996) 'Anxiety, Fear of Crime, Risk and Difference: Exploring the Connections', paper presented at the Crime and Social Order in Europe Conference, Manchester, 7–10 September 1996.

Jeffords, S. (1989) *The Remasculinization of America: Gender and the Vietnam War*, Bloomington and Indianapolis: Indiana University Press.

Kappeler, S. (1995) *The Will to Violence: The Politics of Personal Behaviour*, Cambridge: Polity.

Karp, A. (1994) 'The Rise of Black and Grey Markets', *Annals of the American Academy of Political and Social Science*, 535: 175–89.

Karsten, P. (1978) *Law, Soldiers and Combat*, London: Greenwood Press.

Katz, J. (1988) *Seductions of Crime: Moral and Sensual Attractions of Doing Evil*, New York: Basic Books.

Keegan, J. (1993) *A History of Warfare*, New York: Alfred A. Knopf.

Kelman, H. C. (1973) 'Violence Without Moral Restraint: Reflections on the Dehumanization of Victims and Victimizers', *Journal of Social Issues*, 29(4): 25–61.

Kelman, H. and Hamilton, V. (1989) *Crimes of Obedience*, New Haven: Yale University Press.

Kirchheimer, O. (1961) *Political Justice*, Princeton, N.J.: Princeton University Press.

Koonz, C. (1987) *Mothers in the Fatherland: Women, the Family and Nazi Politics*, New York: St Martin's Press.

Lifton, R. J. (1974) *Home from the War, Vietnam Veterans: Neither Victims nor Executioners*, London: Wildwood House.

Little, R. W. (1964) 'Buddy Relations and Combat Performance', in Janowitz, M. *The New Military: Changing Patterns of Organization*, New York: Russell Sage Foundation.

Lunden, W. A. (1963) *War and Delinquency*, Ames, Iowa: The Art Press.

Machel, G. (1996) 'The Impact of Armed Conflict on Children', *Report of the Expert of the Secretary General, Ms. Graça Machel, submitted pursuant to General Assembly Resolution 48/157.* United Nations General Assembly, A/51/306, 26 August 1996.

MacKinnon, C. A. (1994) 'Rape, Genocide, and Women's Human Rights', in Stiglmayer, A. (ed.) *Mass Rape: The War Against Women in Bosnia-Herzegovina*, Lincoln: University of Nebraska Press.

Mannheim, H. (1941) *War and Crime*, London: Watts & Co.

—— (1965) *Comparative Criminology*, London: Routledge & Kegan Paul.

Marshall, S. L. A. (1947) *Men against Fire*, New York: William Morrow.

Meštrović, S. (1993) *The Barbarian Temperament*, London: Routledge.

—— (1994) *The Balkanization of the West*, London: Routledge.

—— (ed.) (1996) *Genocide After Emotion*, London: Routledge.

Milgram, S. (1971) *The Individual in a Social World*, Reading, Mass.: Addison & Wesley.

—— (1974) *Obedience to Authority: An Experimental View*, London: Tavistock.

Miller, W. (1958) 'Lower Class Culture as a Generating Milieu for Gang Delinquency', *Journal of Social Issues*, 14: 5–19.

Moran, Lord (1945) *Anatomy of Courage*, London: Constable.

Müller, I. (1991) *Hitler's Justice*, London: I. B. Tauris & Co. Ltd.

Naylor, R. T. (1995) 'The Structure and Operation of the Modern Arms Black Market', in Boutwell, J., Klare, M. T. and Reed, L. W. *Lethal Commerce: The Global Trade in Small Arms and Light Weapons*, Cambridge, Mass.: Committee on International Security Studies, American Academy of Arts and Sciences.

Nikolić-Ristanović, V. (1996a) 'War and Violence against Women', in Turpin, J. and Lorsentzen, L. (eds) *The Gendered New World Order: Militarism, Development and the Environment*, New York: Routledge.

—— (1996b) 'War and Crime in the former Yugoslavia', paper presented at the Crime and Social Order in Europe Conference, Manchester 7–10 September 1996, reproduced in this volume.

O'Kane, M. (1993) 'UN Troops in Corruption Inquiry', *Guardian*, 26 August 1993.

Philo, G. (ed.) (1995) *Industry, Economy, War and Politics*, Glasgow Media Group Reader, vol. 2, London: Routledge.

Pilisuk, M. (1995) 'The Legacy of the Vietnam Veteran', *Journal of Social Issues*, 3(4): 3–13.

Pilkington, H. (1996) 'Farewell to the *Tuscovka*: Masculinities and Femininities on the Moscow Youth Scene', in H. Pilkington (ed.) *Gender, Generation and Identity in Contemporary Russia*, London: Routledge.

Reckless, W. C. (1942) 'The Impact of War on Crime, Delinquency, and Prostitution', *American Journal of Sociology*, 48(3): 378–86.

Regan, P. (1994) 'War Toys, War Movies, and the Militarization of the United States, 1900–1985', *Journal of Peace Research*, 31(1): 45–58.

Reuters (1997) 'Swiss Bought Holocaust Victims' Gold U.S. Report Asserts', *International Herald Tribune* 3–4 May 1997.

Roux, J. A. (April 1917) 'Ce que sera la criminalité après la guerre?', *Revue politique et parlementaire*, 91: 27–42.

Ruggiero, V. (1996) 'War Markets: Corporate and Organized Criminals in Europe', *Social and Legal Studies*, 5 (1996): 5–20.

Ruiz-Funes, M. (1959) *Criminologia de la Guerra* Buenos Aires: Editorial Bibliografia Argentina.

Rusche, G. and Kirchheimer, O. (1939) *Punishment and Social Structure*, London: Russell & Russell.

Scheff, T. J. (1994) *Bloody Revenge: Emotions, Nationalism and War*, Boulder, Colorado: Westview Press.

Seifert, R. (1994) 'War and Rape: A Preliminary Analysis', in Stiglmayer A. (ed.) (1994) *Mass Rape: The War Against Women in Bosnia-Herzegovina*, Lincoln: University of Nebraska Press.

Sellers, E. (1918) 'Boy and Girl War Products', *The Nineteenth Century*, (Oct.) 1918: 702–16.

Shay, J. (1995) *Achilles in Vietnam: Combat Trauma and the Undoing of Character*, New York: Touchstone Books.

Simpson, A. W. B. (1992) *In the Highest Degree Odious: Detention Without Trial in Wartime Britain*, Oxford: Oxford University Press.

Skocpol, Theda (1992) *Protecting Soldiers and Mothers*, Harvard: Harvard University Press.

Smithies, E. (1982) *Crime in Wartime: A Social History of Crime in WW II*, London: Geo. Allen & Unwin.

Sorokin, P. (1944) 'The Conditions and Prospects for a World Without War', *American Journal of Sociology*, 49(5): 441–49.

Stammers, N. (1983) *Civil Liberties in Wartime: Britain During the 2nd World War, A Political Study*, London: Croom Helm.

Steinert, H. (1996) 'Ideologies With Victims', paper presented at the Crime and Social Order in Europe Conference, Manchester 7–10 September 1996, reproduced in this volume.

Stern, K. S. (1996) *A Force Upon The Plain: The American Militia Movement and the Politics of Hate*, New York: Simon and Schuster.

Stiglmayer, A. (ed.) (1994) *Mass Rape: The War Against Women in Bosnia-Herzegovina*, Lincoln: University of Nebraska Press.

Stone, N. (1993) 'The Soldiers of Misfortune', *Guardian* 27 August 1993.

Sturdevant, S. P. and Stoltzfus, B. (1992) *Let the Good Times Roll: Prostitution and the U.S. Military in Asia*, New York: The New Press.

Sutherland, E. (1983) *White Collar Crime: The Uncut Version*, New Haven and London: Yale University Press.

Sutherland, E. and Cressey, D. (1960) *Principles of Criminology*, Chicago: Lippencourt.

Takala, H. (1989) 'The War in Criminology', in Takala, H. and Tham, H. (eds) (1989) *Scandinavian Studies in Criminology*, 10, London: Norwegian University Press.

Taylor, T. (1970) *Nuremburg and Vietnam: an American Tragedy*, Chicago: Quadrangle Books.

Tham, H. (1990) 'Crime in Scandinavia during World War II', *Journal of Peace Research*, 27(4): 415–28.

Theweleit, K. (1987) *Male Fantasies*, Cambridge: Polity.

Tihon, F. (1997) 'What are we doing here, ask saviours of Albania', *European*, 19–25 June 1997.

Timoshenko, S. (1996) 'The Afghan Syndrome and Revivial of Warrior Culture', unpublished draft. Salford University.

Traynor, I. (1997) 'Nazi Shame of Germany's Boardrooms', *Guardian* 28 June 1997.

Trepp, G. (1993) *Bankgeschafte mit dem Feind: Die Bank fur Internationalen Zahlungsausgleich in Zweiten Weltkreig: von Hitlers Europabank zum Instrument des Marshallplans*, Zurich: Rotpunktverlag.

Vietnam Veterans Against the War (1972) *The Winter Soldier Investigation: An Enquiry Into War Crimes*, Boston: Beacon Press.

Wallensteen, P. and Sollenberg, M. (1996) 'The End of International War? Armed Conflict 1989–1995', *Journal of Peace Research*, 33(3): 353–70.

Wilkins, L. (1960) *Delinquent Generations*, London: HMSO.

Wright, S. (1996) 'The New Trade in Technologies of Restraint and Electroshock', in Duncan Forrest (ed.) *A Glimpse of Hell*, London: Cassell.

INDEX

NOTES

NOTES

NOTES

NOTES